THINGS TO COME

A Study in Biblical Eschatology

By

J. DWIGHT PENTECOST

INTRODUCTION

By

JOHN F. WALVOORD

Things to Come
Copyright © 1958 by Dunham Publishing Company

Academie Books is an imprint of Zondervan
Publishing House, 1415 Lake Drive, S.E.,
Grand Rapids, Michigan 49506

First Grand Rapids printing 1964

ISBN 0-310-30890-9

All rights reserved. No part of this publication may be reproduced, stored in a retrieval system, or transmitted in any form or by any means—electronic, mechanical, photocopy, recording, or any other—except for brief quotations in printed reviews, without the prior permission of the publisher.

Printed in the United States of America

91 92 93 94 / AF / 37 36 35 **34**

This edition is printed on acid-free paper and meets the American National Standards Institute Z39.48 standard.

To my beloved and devoted

WIFE,

faithful companion in the ministry of the Word,

this volume is affectionately dedicated.

PREFACE

The day in which we live has witnessed a surge of interest in Biblical Eschatology. Whereas a generation ago one theologian wrote: "Eschatology is usually loved in inverse proportion to the square of the mental diameter of those who do the loving,"[1] today another writes: "The problem of eschatology may shortly become, if it is not already, the framework of American theological discussion."[2] The theologian who, a short generation ago, could either ignore eschatological questions entirely, or treat them disdainfully, is outmoded in his thinking if he adopts such an attitude today. The easy optimism of the past generation has been shattered by two world wars, depression and inflation, with the accompanying social and moral evils. The humanistic emphasis that characterized that theological thinking has proved fallacious. Realism has taken the place of optimism, and men have been forced to turn to eschatological considerations as the source of hope for a sin-cursed world. The Bible and the revelation it contains proves to be the one source of hope and confidence for the future, and men are turning more and more to it for light in the present darkness.

God, the architect of the ages, has seen fit to take us into His confidence concerning His plan for the future and has revealed His purpose and program in detail in the Word. A greater body of Scripture is given to prophecy than any other one subject, for approximately one-fourth of the Bible was prophetic at the time it was written. That portion is devoted to the unfolding of God's program. Because of its prominence in Scripture it is only natural that much should have been written on the subject, and many excellent books have appeared dealing with prophetic subjects. However, the treatment of prophecy has gen-

---

1 Walter Rauschenbush, *A Theology for the Social Gospel*, p. 209.

2 Henry P. VanDusen, "A Preview of Evanston," *Union Seminary Quarterly Review*, IX:8, March, 1954.

erally been either apologetic or expository, and the themes have been developed individually apart from their relation to the whole revealed program so that much of our knowledge has been fragmentary and unrelated. There has been little attempt to synthesize the whole field of prophecy into a unified Biblical doctrine and there is a great need for a synthetic study and presentation of Biblical prophecy. In an effort to meet this need the author has attempted in this volume to synthesize the prophetic Scriptures into a systematic and complete Biblical Eschatology.

Grateful acknowledgment is given to the faculty of the Dallas Theological Seminary to whom these studies were first presented as a doctoral dissertation and by whose permission they are now presented in this form. Special appreciation is expressed to Dr. John F. Walvoord, President and Professor of Systematic Theology in that seminary, under whose personal guidance these studies were pursued, and to Dr. Charles C. Ryrie, Associate Professor of Systematic Theology, who read and corrected the manuscript. Deep appreciation is expressed to Miss Nancy Miller for her work, rendered as unto the Lord, in typing the manuscript, and to Mr. and Mrs. James H. Kelley for their material assistance in the publication of this volume.

In trying to cover a large field of study as succinctly as possible the author has made extensive use of summary material gleaned from others. Acknowledgment is therefore gratefully made to those authors and publishers whose works have contributed much to the thought of these pages.

May God the Father, who gave His Son, through whose first coming we were given salvation and through whose second coming we will be brought to glory, and who gave His Holy Spirit, through whom He "will shew you THINGS TO COME," be pleased to use this book to His glory as many are brought to a knowledge of His truth.

J. Dwight Pentecost,
Assistant Professor, New Testament Literature and Exegesis,
Dallas Theological Seminary
3909 Swiss Ave.,
Dallas, Texas

INTRODUCTION

Biblical Eschatology is the capstone of systematic theology. It is not only climactic, the terminus and consummation of theological study, but the presentation of eschatology is also the supreme demonstration of theological skill. Here as in no other field, except perhaps the doctrine of the person of Christ, are the important tools of exegesis, synthesis, hermeneutics, and theological system displayed. The fine judgment necessary to discern that which is to be literally interpreted in contrast to spiritual and allegorical interpretation is demanded. The consistency of the entire revelation of God contained in the Old and New Testament must be maintained. The intricate details of prophecy must be related without contradiction. A careful distinction must be observed between that which is certainly and plainly revealed and that which is still obscure. Major issues must be distinguished from minor points. The field of investigation must necessarily embrace both fulfilled and unfulfilled prophecy, the former providing an important guide to the character of prediction embraced in the latter.

Eschatology more than any other major field of theology has suffered much at the hands of its interpreters. Even among those whose confidence in the inspired Word of God is unquestioned there exist widely divergent schools of interpretation. For this reason, some theologians have contented themselves with presentation of the few major events of eschatology such as resurrection from the dead, the second advent, and the final judgment, to the neglect of vast portions of Scripture which deal with other prophetic matters.

Though many learned men have written in the field of eschatology to provide that which is usually lacking in standard theologies, few if any have attempted a detailed presentation of premillennial eschatology such as is provided in this volume. Dr. Pentecost has with rare skill dealt with many controversial issues, has met and solved many prophetic problems, and has provided in large measure the substance of the prophetic Word in systematic and theological form. He has condensed a mass of material often not contained in even larger prophetic libraries and has offered his own solution to many debatable points. In large measure, his conclusions are shared by the great body of premillenarians. The work as a whole merits classification as a standard and comprehensive text in Biblical Eschatology and should serve our generation in this capacity for many years to come.

John F. Walvoord.

Dallas, Texas.

TABLE OF CONTENTS

THINGS TO COME

SECTION ONE
THE INTERPRETATION OF PROPHECY

CHAPTER I

THE METHODS OF INTERPRETATION

INTRODUCTION

No question facing the student of Eschatology is more important than the question of the method to be employed in the interpretation of the prophetic Scriptures. The adoption of different methods of interpretation has produced the variant eschatological positions and accounts for the divergent views within a system that confront the student of prophecy. The basic differences between the premillennial and amillennial schools and between the pretribulation and posttribulation rapturists are hermeneutical, arising from the adoption of divergent and irreconcilable methods of interpretation.

The basic issue between premillennialists and amillennialists is clearly drawn by Allis, who writes:

> One of the most marked features of Premillennialism in all its forms is the emphasis which it places on the literal interpretation of Scripture. It is the insistent claim of its advocates that only when interpreted literally is the Bible interpreted truly; and they denounce as "spiritualizers" or "allegorizers" those who do not interpret the Bible with the same degree of literalness as they do. None have made this charge more pointedly than the Dispensationalists. *The question of literal versus figurative interpretation is, therefore, one which has to be faced at the very outset* [italics mine].[1]

When Allis acknowledges that "Literal interpretation has al-

[1] Oswald T. Allis, *Prophecy and the Church*, p. 17.

ways been a marked feature of Premillennialism"[2] he is in agreement with Feinberg, who writes:

> . . . it can be shown that the reason the early Church was premillennial was traceable to its interpretation of the Word in a literal manner, whereas the cause of the departure from this view in later centuries of the history of the Church is directly attributable to a change in method of interpretation beginning with Origen in particular.[3]

Hamilton says:

> Now we must frankly admit that a literal interpretation of the Old Testament prophecies gives us just such a picture of an earthly reign of the Messiah as the premillennialist pictures. That was the kind of a Messianic kingdom that the Jews of the time of Christ were looking for, on the basis of a literal interpretation of the Old Testament promises. That was the kind of a kingdom that the Sadducees were talking about when they ridiculed the idea of the resurrection of the body, drawing from our Lord the clearest statement of the characteristics of the future age that we have in the New Testament, when He told them that they erred "not knowing the Scriptures nor the power of God" (Matt. 22:29) . . . the Jews were looking for just such a kingdom as that expected by those premillennialists who speak of the Jews holding a preeminent place in an earthly Jewish kingdom to be set up by the Messiah in Jerusalem.[4]

He is thus acknowledging that the basic difference between himself, an amillennialist, and a premillennialist is not whether the Scriptures teach such an earthly kingdom as the premillennialist teaches, but how the Scriptures that teach just such an earthly kingdom are to be interpreted. Allis admits that "the Old Testament prophecies if literally interpreted cannot be regarded as having been yet fulfilled or as being capable of fulfillment in this present age."[5] Therefore, the antecedent to any discussion of the prophetic Scriptures and the doctrines of Eschatology is the establishment of the basic method of interpretation to be employed throughout. This is well observed by Pieters, who writes:

---

[2] *Ibid.*, p. 244. Cf. pp. 99, 116, 218, 227, 242, 256 where further reference is made to literal interpretation as the basis of premillennialism.

[3] Charles L. Feinberg, *Premillennialism or Amillennialism*, p. 51.

[4] Floyd E. Hamilton, *The Basis of Millennial Faith*, pp. 38-39.

[5] Allis, *op. cit.*, p. 238.

> The question whether the Old Testament prophecies concerning the people of God must be interpreted in their ordinary sense, as other Scriptures are interpreted, or can properly be applied to the Christian Church, is called the question of the spiritualization of prophecy. This is one of the major problems of biblical interpretation, and confronts everyone who makes a serious study of the Word of God. It is one of the chief keys to the difference of opinion between Premillenarians and the mass of Christian scholars. The former reject such spiritualization, the latter employ it; and *as long as there is no agreement on this point the debate is interminable and fruitless* [italics mine].[6]

A. *The problem.* If Rutgers be correct when he says of the premillennialist: "I regard their interpretation of Scripture as the fundamental error,"[7] and if the acknowledged difference between premillennialism and amillennialism rests on the basic proposition of the method to be used in interpreting Scriptures, the fundamental problem to be studied at the outset of any consideration of Eschatology is that of the hermeneutics of prophecy. It is the purpose of this study to examine the important methods currently advocated as the proper way to interpret Scripture so as to have a clear understanding of the difference in the methods, to study the history of the doctrine so as to be able to trace the divergent methods to their source, and to outline the rules to be employed in the interpretation so as to be able to apply correctly the established method of interpretation.

B. *The importance of the study.* "The primary need for a system of hermeneutics is to ascertain the meaning of the Word of God."[8] It is obvious that such widely divergent views as premillennialism and amillennialism and pretribulation and posttribulation rapturism cannot all be right. Since the interpreter is not handling a book of human origin, but the Word of God, he must be equipped with an accurate method of interpretation or error will be the necessary result of his study. The fact that the Word of God cannot be correctly interpreted apart from a correct method of and sound rules for interpretation gives the study its supreme importance.

---

[6] Albertus Pieters, *The Leader*, September 5, 1934, as cited by Gerrit H. Hospers, *The Principle of Spiritualization in Hermeneutics*, p. 5.

[7] William H. Rutgers, *Premillennialism in America*, p. 263.

[8] Bernard Ramm, *Protestant Biblical Interpretation*, p. 1.

While many diverse methods of interpreting the Scriptures have been propounded during the course of the history of interpretation,[9] today there are but two methods of interpretation which have a vital effect on Eschatology: the allegorical and the grammatical-historical methods. The literal method is generally held to be synonymous with the grammatical-historical method and will be so used throughout this discussion. These two methods will be considered in detail.

I. The Allegorical Method

An ancient method of interpreting which has had a current revival is the allegorical method.

A. *The definition of the allegorical method*. Angus-Green define an allegory as:

> Any statement of supposed facts which admits of a literal interpretation, and yet requires or justly admits a moral or figurative one, is called an *Allegory*. It is to narrative or story what trope is to single words, adding to the literal meaning of the terms employed a moral or spiritual one. Sometimes the allegory is *pure*, that is, contains no direct reference to the application of it, as in the history of the Prodigal Son. Sometimes it is mixed, as in Ps. 80, where it is plainly intimated (verse 17) that the Jews are the people whom the vine is intended to represent.[10]

Ramm defines the allegorical method thus: "Allegorism is the method of interpreting a literary text that regards the literal sense as the vehicle for a secondary, more spiritual and more profound sense."[11] In this method the historical import is either denied or ignored and the emphasis is placed entirely on a secondary sense so that the original words or events have little or no significance. Fritsch summarizes it thus:

> According to this method the literal and historical sense of Scripture is completely ignored, and every word and event is made an allegory of some kind either to escape theological difficulties or to maintain certain peculiar religious views. . . .[12]

---

[9] Cf. Milton S. Terry, *Biblical Hermeneutics*, pp. 163-74 where such methods as the Halachic, Hagadic, Allegorical, Mystical, Accommodation, Moral, Naturalistic, Mythical, Apologetic, Dogmatic, and Grammatico-historical are traced.

[10] Joseph Angus and Samuel G. Green, *The Bible Handbook*, p. 220.

[11] Ramm, *op. cit.*, p. 21.

[12] Charles T. Fritsch, "Biblical Typology," *Bibliotheca Sacra*, 104:216, April, 1947.

It would seem that the purpose of the allegorical method is not to interpret Scripture, but to pervert the true meaning of Scripture, albeit under the guise of seeking a deeper or more spiritual meaning.

B. *The dangers of the allegorical method.* The allegorical method is fraught with dangers which render it unacceptable to the interpreter of the Word.

1. The first great danger of the allegorical method is that it does not interpret Scripture. Terry says:

> . . . it will be noticed at once that its habit is to disregard the common signification of words and give wing to all manner of fanciful speculation. It does not draw out the legitimate meaning of an author's language, but foists into it whatever the whim or fancy of an interpreter may desire. As a system, therefore, it puts itself beyond all well-defined principles and laws.[13]

Angus-Green express the same danger when they write:

> There is . . . unlimited scope for fancy, if once the principle be admitted, and the only basis of the exposition is found in the mind of the expositor. The scheme can yield no *interpretation*, properly so called, although possibly some valuable truths may be illustrated.[14]

2. The above quotation suggests, also, a second great danger in the allegorical method: the basic authority in interpretation ceases to be the Scriptures, but the mind of the interpreter. The interpretation may then be twisted by the interpreter's doctrinal positions, the authority of the church to which the interpreter adheres, his social or educational background, or a host of other factors. Jerome

> . . . complains that the faultiest style of teaching is to corrupt the meaning of Scripture, and to drag its reluctant utterance to our own will, making Scriptural mysteries out of our own imaginations.[15]

Farrar adds:

> . . . When once the principle of allegory is admitted, when

---

13 Terry, *op. cit.*, p. 224.
14 Angus-Green, *loc. cit.*
15 Cited by F. W. Farrar, *History of Interpretation*, p. 232.

once we start with the rule that whole passages and books of Scripture say one thing when they mean another, the reader is delivered bound hand and foot to the caprice of the interpreter.[16]

3. A third great danger in the allegorical method is that one is left without any means by which the conclusions of the interpreter may be tested. The above author states:

> He can be sure of absolutely nothing except what is dictated to him by the Church, and in all ages the authority of "the Church" has been falsely claimed for the presumptuous tyranny of false prevalent opinions.[17]

Ramm adds:

> . . . to state that the principal meaning of the Bible is a second-sense meaning, and that the principal method of interpreting is "spiritualizing," is to open the door to almost uncontrolled speculation and imagination. For this reason we have insisted that the *control* in interpretation is the literal method.[18]

That these dangers exist and that the method of interpretation is used to pervert Scripture is admitted by Allis, who is himself an advocate of the allegorical method in the field of Eschatology, when he says:

> Whether the figurative or "spiritual" interpretation of a given passage is justified or not depends solely upon whether it gives the true meaning. If it is used to empty words of their plain and obvious meaning, to read out of them what is clearly intended by them, then allegorizing or spiritualizing is a term of reproach which is well merited.[19]

Thus, the great dangers inherent in this system are that it takes away the authority of Scripture, leaves us without any basis on which interpretations may be tested, reduced Scripture to what seems reasonable to the interpreter, and, as a result, makes true interpretation of Scripture impossible.

C. *The New Testament use of allegory.* In order to justify the use of the allegorical method it is often argued that the New Testament itself employs this method and thus it must be a justifiable method of interpretation.

---

16 *Ibid.*, p. 238.
17 *Ibid.*
18 Ramm, *op. cit.*, p. 65.
19 Allis, *op. cit.*, p. 18.

1. In the first place, reference is frequently made to Galatians 4:21-31, where Paul himself is said to use the allegorical method. On this usage of allegory Farrar observes:

> . . . of allegories which in any way resemble those of Philo or of the Fathers and the Schoolmen, I can find in the New Testament but one [Gal. 4:21-31]. It may be merely intended as an *argumentum ad hominem;* it is not at all essential to the general argument; it has not a particle of *demonstrative* force; in any case it leaves untouched the actual history. But whatever view we take of it, the occurrence of one such allegory in the Epistle of St. Paul no more sanctions the universal application of the method than a few New Testament allusions to the Haggada compel us to accept the accumulations of the Midrashim; or a few quotations from Greek poets prove the divine authority of all Pagan literature. . . .[20]

Gilbert, in the same vein, concludes:

> Since Paul explained one historical event of the Old Testament allegorically, it seems likely that he admitted the possibility of applying the principle of allegory elsewhere; but the fact that his letters show no other unmistakable illustration obviously suggests either that he did not feel himself competent to unfold the allegorical meaning of Scripture, or, what is more probable, that he was better satisfied on the whole to give his readers the plain primary sense of the text.[21]

Concerning the use of this method by other New Testament writers Farrar concludes:

> The better Jewish theory, purified in Christianity, takes the teachings of the Old Dispensation literally, but sees in them, as did St. Paul, the shadow and germ of future developments. Allegory, though once used by St. Paul by way of passing illustration, is unknown to the other Apostles, and is never sanctioned by Christ.[22]

It must be carefully observed that in Galatians 4:21-31 Paul is not using an allegorical method of interpreting the Old Testament, but was explaining an allegory. These are two entirely different things. Scripture abounds in allegories, whether types, symbols, or parables. These are accepted and legitimate media of communication of thought. They do not call for an allegorical

[20] Farrar, *op. cit.*, p. xxiii.
[21] George H. Gilbert, *The Interpretation of the Bible*, p. 82.
[22] Farrar, *op. cit.*, p. 217.

method of interpretation, which would deny the literal or historical antecedent and use the allegory simply as a springboard for the interpreter's imagination. They do call for a special type of hermeneutics, which will be considered later. But the use of allegories is not a justification for the allegorical method of interpretation. It would be concluded that the usage in Galatians of the Old Testament would be an example of interpretation of an allegory and would not justify the universal application of the allegorical method to all Scripture.

2. A second argument used to justify the allegorical method is the New Testament usage made of types. It is recognized that the New Testament makes typical application of the Old. On this basis it is argued that the New Testament uses the allegorical method of interpretation, contending that the interpretation and application of types is an allegorical method of interpretation. Allis argues:

> While Dispensationalists are extreme literalists, they are very inconsistent ones. They are literalists in interpreting prophecy. But in the interpreting of history, they carry the principle of typical interpretation to an extreme which has rarely been exceeded even by the most ardent of allegorizers.[23]

In reply to the accusation that because one interprets types he is using the allegorical method, it must be emphasized that the interpretation of types is not the same as allegorical interpretation. The efficacy of the type depends on the literal interpretation of the literal antecedent. In order to convey truth concerning the spiritual realm, with which realm we are not familiar, there must be instruction in a realm with which we are familiar, so that, by a transference of what is literally true in the one realm, we may learn what is true in the other realm. There must be a literal parallelism between the type and the antitype for the type to be of any value. The individual who allegorizes a type will never arrive at a true interpretation. The only way to discern the meaning of the type is through a transference of literal ideas from the natural to the spiritual realm. Chafer well writes:

> In the study of allegories of various kinds, namely, parables,

---

[23] Allis, *op. cit.*, p. 21.

> types and symbols, the interpreter must be careful not to treat plain statements of Scripture as is demanded of language couched in figurative expressions. A truth already expressed will bear repetition at this point: there is all the difference possible in interpreting a Scripture allegory, on the one hand, and the allegorizing of a plain Scripture on the other hand.[24]

It is concluded, then, that the Scriptural use of types does not give sanction to the allegorical method of interpretation.

II. The Literal Method

In direct opposition to the allegorical method of interpretation stands the literal or grammatical-historical method.

A. *The definition of the literal method.* The literal method of interpretation is that method that gives to each word the same exact basic meaning it would have in normal, ordinary, customary usage, whether employed in writing, speaking or thinking.[25] It is called the grammatical-historical method to emphasize the fact that the meaning is to be determined by both grammatical and historical considerations.[26] Ramm defines the method thus:

> *The customary, socially-acknowledged designation of a word is the literal meaning of that word.*
>
> The "literal" meaning of a word is the *basic, customary, social designation of that word.* The spiritual, or mystical meaning of a word or expression is one that arises after the literal designation and is dependent upon it for its existence.
>
> To interpret literally means nothing more or less than to interpret in terms of *normal, usual, designation.* When the manuscript alters its designation the interpreter immediately shifts his method of interpreting.[27]

B. *The evidence for the literal method.* Strong evidence can be presented to support the literal method of interpretation. Ramm gives a comprehensive summary. He says:

---

[24] Rollin T. Chafer, *The Science of Biblical Hermeneutics,* p. 80.
[25] Ramm, *op. cit.,* p. 53.
[26] Cf. Thomas Hartwell Horne, *An Introduction to the Critical Study and Knowledge of the Holy Scriptures,* I, 322.
[27] Ramm, *op. cit.,* p. 64.

In defence of the literal approach it may be argued:

(a) That the literal meaning of sentences is the normal approach in all languages. . . .

(b) That all secondary meanings of documents, parables, types, allegories, and symbols, depend for their very existence on the previous literal meaning of the terms. . . .

(c) That the greater part of the Bible makes adequate sense when interpreted literally.

(d) That the literalistic approach does not blindly rule out figures of speech, symbols, allegories, and types; but if the nature of the sentence so demands, it readily yields to the second sense.

(e) That this method is the only sane and safe check on the imaginations of man.

(f) That this method is the only one consonant with the nature of inspiration. The plenary inspiration of the Bible teaches that the Holy Spirit guided men into truth and away from error. In this process the Spirit of God used language, and the units of language (as meaning, not as sound) are words and thoughts. The thought is the thread that strings the words together. Therefore, our very exegesis must commence with a study of words and grammar, the two fundamentals of all meaningful speech.[28]

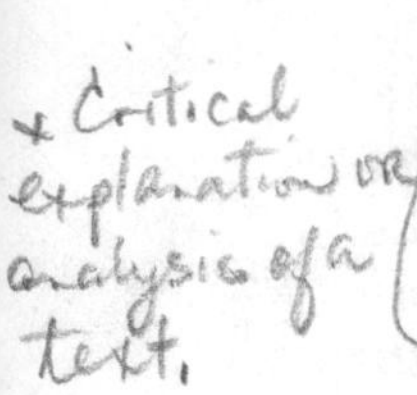

Inasmuch as God gave the Word of God as a revelation to men, it would be expected that His revelation would be given in such exact and specific terms that His thoughts would be accurately conveyed and understood when interpreted according to the laws of grammar and speech. Such presumptive evidence favors the literal interpretation, for an allegorical method of interpretation would cloud the meaning of the message delivered by God to men. The fact that the Scriptures continually point to literal interpretations of what was formerly written adds evidence as to the method to be employed in interpreting the Word. Perhaps one of the strongest evidences for the literal method is the use the New Testament makes of the Old Testament. When the Old Testament is used in the New it is used only in a literal sense. One need only study the prophecies which were fulfilled in the first coming of Christ, in His life, His ministry, and His death, to establish that fact. No prophecy which has been completely fulfilled has been fulfilled

[28] *Ibid.*, pp. 54 ff.

any way but literally.[29] Though a prophecy may be cited in the New Testament to show that a certain event is a partial fulfillment of that prophecy (as was done in Matthew 2:17-18), or to show that an event is in harmony with God's established program (as was done in Acts 15), it does not necessitate a non-literal fulfillment or deny a future complete fulfillment, for such applications of prophecy do not exhaust the fulfillment of it. Therefore such references to prophecy do not argue for a non-literal method.

From these considerations it may be concluded that there is evidence to support the validity of the literal method of interpretation. Further evidence for the literal method will be presented in the study of the history of interpretation which is to follow.

C. *The advantages of the literal method*. There are certain advantages to this method in preference to the allegorical method. Ramm summarizes some of these by saying:

> (a) It grounds interpretation in *fact*. It seeks to establish itself in objective data—grammar, logic, etymology, history, geography, archaeology, theology. . . .
>
> (b) It exercises a control over interpretation that experimentation does for the scientific method . . . *justification is the control on interpretations*. All that do not measure up to the canons of the literal-cultural-critical method are to be rejected or placed under suspect.
>
> In addition to this the method offers the only reliable check on the constant threat to place double-sense interpretation upon the Scripture. . . .
>
> (c) It has had the greatest success in opening up the Word of God. *Exegesis did not start in earnest till the church was a millennium and a half old.* With the literalism of Luther and Calvin the light of Scripture literally flamed up. . . . This method is the honored method of the highest scholastic tradition in conservative Protestantism. It is the method of Bruce, Lightfoot, Zahn, A. T. Robertson, Ellicott, Machen, Cremer, Terry, Farrar, Lange, Green, Oehler, Schaff, Sampey, Wilson, Moule, Perowne, Henderson Broadus, Stuart—to name but a few typical exegetes.[30]

In addition to the above advantages it may be added that (d) it gives us a basic authority by which interpretations may be

---

[29] Cf. Feinberg, *op. cit.*, p. 39.
[30] Ramm, *op. cit.*, pp. 62-63.

tested. The allegorical method, which depends on the rationalistic approach of the interpreter, or conformity to a predetermined theological system, leaves one without a basic authoritative test. In the literal method Scripture may be compared with Scripture, which, as the inspired Word of God, is authoritative and the standard by which all truth is to be tested. Related to this we may observe that (e) it delivers us from both reason and mysticism as the requisites to interpretation. One does not have to depend upon intellectual training or abilities, nor upon the development of mystical perception, but rather upon the understanding of what is written in its generally accepted sense. Only on such a basis can the average individual understand or interpret the Scriptures for himself.

D. *The literal method and figurative language*. It is recognized by all that the Bible abounds in figurative language. On this basis it is often argued that the use of figurative language demands a figurative interpretation. However, figures of speech are used as means of revealing literal truth. What is literally true in one realm, with which we are familiar, is brought over, literally, into another realm, with which we may not be familiar, in order to teach us truths in that unfamiliar realm. This relation between literal truth and the figurative language is well illustrated by Gigot:

> If the words are employed in their natural and primitive signification, the sense which they express is the *proper literal* sense; whereas, if they are used with a figurative and derived meaning, the sense, though still literal, is usually called the *metaphorical* or *figurative* sense. For example, when we read in St. John 1, 6, "There was a man whose name was John," it is plain that the terms employed here are taken properly and physically, for the writer speaks of a real man whose real name was John. On the contrary, when John the Baptist, pointing out Jesus, said, "Behold the Lamb of God" (John 1, 29), it is clear that he did not use the word "lamb" in that same proper literal sense which would have excluded every trope or figure, and which would have denoted some *real* lamb: what he wished proximately and directly to express, that is, the literal sense of his words, was that in the derived and figurative sense Jesus could be called "the Lamb of God." In the former case, the words are used in their proper literal sense; in the latter, in their tropical or figurative sense.
>
> That the books of Holy Writ have a literal sense (proper or

> metaphorical, as just explained), that is, a meaning proximately and directly intended by the inspired writers, is a truth so clear in itself, and at the same time so universally granted, that it would be idle to insist on it here. . . . Has any passage of Holy Writ more than one literal sense? . . . all admit that since the sacred books were composed by men, and for men, their writers naturally conformed to that most elementary law of human intercourse, which requires that only one precise sense shall be proximately and directly intended by the words of the speaker or writer. . . .[31]

Craven states the same relation between figurative language and literal truth:

> No terms could have been chosen more unfit to designate the two great schools of prophetical exegetes than *literal* and *spiritual*. These terms are not antithetical, nor are they in any proper sense significant of the peculiarities of the respective systems they are employed to characterize. They are positively misleading and confusing. *Literal* is opposed not to *spiritual* but to *figurative*; *spiritual* is in antithesis on the one hand to *material*, on the other to *carnal* (in a bad sense). The *Literalist* (so called) is not one who denies that *figurative* language, that *symbols*, are used in prophecy, nor does he deny that great *spiritual* truths are set forth therein; his position is, simply, that the prophecies are to be *normally* interpreted (i.e. according to the received laws of language) as any other utterances are interpreted—that which is manifestly figurative being so regarded. The position of the Spiritualists (so called) is not that which is properly indicated by the term. He is one who holds that whilst certain portions of the prophecies are to be *normally* interpreted, other portions are to be regarded as having a *mystical* (i.e. involving some secret meaning) sense. Thus, for instance, Spiritualists (so called) do not deny that when the Messiah is spoken of as "a man of sorrows and acquainted with grief," the prophecy is to be normally interpreted; they affirm, however, that when He is spoken of as coming "in the clouds of heaven" the language is to be "spiritually" (mystically) interpreted. . . . The terms properly expressive of the schools are *normal* and *mystical*.[32]

It will thus be observed that the literalist does not deny the existence of figurative language. The literalist does, however, deny that such figures must be interpreted so as to destroy the literal truth intended through the employment of the figures. Literal truth is to be learned through the symbols.

---

[31] Francis E. Gigot, *General Introduction to the Study of the Holy Scriptures*, pp. 386-87.

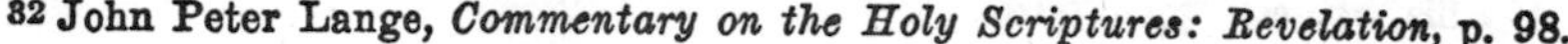

[32] John Peter Lange, *Commentary on the Holy Scriptures: Revelation*, p. 98.

E. *Some objections to the literal method.* Allis states three objections against the literal method of interpretation:

> (1) The language of the Bible often contains figures of speech. This is especially true of its poetry. . . . In the poetry of the Psalms, in the elevated style of prophecy, and even in simple historical narration, figures of speech appear which quite obviously are not meant to be and cannot be understood literally.
>
> (2) The great theme of the Bible is, God and His redemptive dealings with mankind. God is a Spirit; the most precious teachings of the Bible are spiritual; and these spiritual and heavenly realities are often set forth under the form of earthly objects and human relationships. . . .
>
> (3) The fact that the Old Testament is both preliminary and preparatory to the New Testament is too obvious to require proof. In referring the Corinthian Christians by way of warning and admonition to the events of the Exodus, the apostle Paul declared that these things were "ensamples" (types). That is, they prefigured things to come. This gives to much that is in the Old Testament a special significance and importance. . . . Such an interpretation recognizes, in the light of the New Testament fulfilment, a deeper and far more wonderful meaning in the words of many an Old Testament passage than, taken in their Old Testament context and connection, they seem to contain.[33]

In reply to the first of these arguments, one must recognize the use made of figures of speech. As has previously been emphasized, figures may be used to teach literal truth more forcefully than the bare words themselves and do not argue for allegorical interpretation. In regard to the second, while it is recognized that God is spiritual, the only way God could reveal truth in a realm into which we have not as yet entered is to draw a parallel from the realm in which we now live. Through the transference of what is literally true in the known realm into the unknown realm, that unknown realm will be revealed to us. The fact that God is spiritual does not demand allegorical interpretation. One must distinguish between what is spiritual and what is spiritualized. And, in respect to the third, while it is recognized that the Old Testament is anticipatory, and the New unfolds the Old, the fulness revealed in the New is not re-

---

[33] Allis, *op. cit.*, pp. 17-18.

vealed through the allegorization of what is typified in the Old, but rather through the literal fulfillment and the unfolding of the literal truth of the types. Types may teach literal truth and the use of types in the Old Testament is no support for the allegorical method of interpretation. Feinberg well observes:

> Spiritualizers seemed to think that because revelation came gradually that the later the prophecy or revealed matter is, the more valuable it is. The fact of a gradual revelation has no force in determining the method of interpretation. . . . Furthermore, a proper interpretation of 2 Cor. 3:6 does not detract in the slightest from our position. When Paul said: "the letter killeth, but the spirit giveth life," he was not authorizing the spiritualizing interpretation of Scripture. If the literal kills, then how is it that God gives His message in such a form? The meaning of the apostle evidently is that the mere acceptance of the letter without the work of the Holy Spirit related to it, leads to death.[34]

---

[34] Feinberg, *op. cit.*, p. 50

Chapter II

THE HISTORY OF INTERPRETATION

Inasmuch as the basic dispute between the premillennialist and the amillennialist is one of hermeneutics, it is necessary to trace the development of the two different hermeneutical methods on which these interpretations rest, namely, the literal and allegorical, in order that the authority of the literal method may be established.

I. The Beginning of Interpretation

It is generally agreed by all students of the history of hermeneutics that interpretation began at the time of the return of Israel from the Babylonian exile under Ezra as recorded in Nehemiah 8:1-8. Such interpretation was necessary, first of all, because of the long period in Israel's history in which the Mosaic law was forgotten and neglected. The discovery of the forgotten "book of the law" by Hilkiah in the reign of Josiah brought it back into a position of prominence for a brief season, only to have it forgotten again during the years of the exile.[1] It was necessary, further, because the Jews had replaced their native tongue with Aramaic while in exile. Upon their return the Scriptures were unintelligible to them.[2] It was necessary for Ezra to explain the forgotten and unintelligible Scriptures to the people. It can hardly be questioned but that Ezra's interpretation was a literal interpretation of what had been written.

II. Old Testament Jewish Interpretation

This same literal interpretation was a marked feature of Old Testament interpretation. Jerome, in rejecting the strict literal method of interpretation, "calls the literal interpretation

[1] Cf. F. W. Farrar, *History of Interpretation*, pp. 47-48.
[2] Cf. Bernard Ramm, *Protestant Biblical Interpretation*, p. 27.

'Jewish,' implies that it may easily become heretical, and repeatedly says it is inferior to the 'spiritual.'"[3] It would seem that the literal method and Jewish interpretation were synonymous in Jerome's mind.

Rabbinism came to have such a hold on the Jewish nation from the union of the authority of priest and king in one line. The method employed in Rabbinism by the scribes was not an allegorical method, but a literal method, which, in its literalism, circumvented all the spiritual requirements of the law.[4] Although they arrived at false conclusions, it was not the fault of the literal method, but the misapplication of the method by the exclusion of any more than the bare letter of what was written. Briggs, after summarizing the thirteen rules that governed Rabbinical interpretation, says:

> Some of the rules are excellent, and so far as the practical logic of the times went, cannot be disputed. *The fault of Rabbinical exegesis was less in the rules than in their application,* although latent fallacies are not difficult to discover in them, and they do not sufficiently guard against slips of argument [italics mine].[5]

It must be concluded, in spite of all the fallacies of the Rabbinism of the Jews, that they followed a literal method of interpretation.

III. Literalism in the Time of Christ

A. *Literalism among the Jews.* The prevailing method of interpretation among the Jews at the time of Christ was certainly the literal method of interpretation. Horne presents it thus:

> The allegorical interpretation of the sacred Scriptures cannot be historically proved to have prevailed among the Jews from the time of the captivity, or to have been common with the Jews of Palestine at the time of Christ and his apostles.
>
> Although the Sanhedrin and the hearers of Jesus often appealed to the Old Testament, yet they give no indication of the allegorical interpretation; even Josephus has nothing of it. The Platonic Jews of Egypt began in the first century, in imitation of the heathen Greeks, to interpret the Old Testament allegorically. Philo of Alexandria was distinguished among those Jews who

---

[3] Farrar, *op. cit.*, p. 232.
[4] Cf. *ibid.*, pp. 60-61.
[5] Charles Augustus Briggs, *General Introduction to the Study of Holy Scripture*, p. 431.

> practised this method; and he defends it as something new and before unheard of, and for that reason opposed by the other Jews. Jesus was not, therefore, in a situation in which he was compelled to comply with a prevailing custom of allegorical interpretation; for this method did not prevail at the time among the Jews, certainly not in Palestine, where Jesus taught.[6]

With this position present day amillennialists are in essential agreement.[7] Case, an ardent advocate of amillennialism, concedes:

> Undoubtedly the ancient Hebrew prophets announced the advent of a terrible day of Jehovah when the old order of things would suddenly pass away. Later prophets foretold a day of restoration for the exiles when all nature would be miraculously changed and an ideal kingdom of David established. The seers of subsequent times portrayed the coming of a truly heavenly rule of God when the faithful would participate in millennial blessings. Early Christians expected soon to behold Christ returning upon the clouds even as they had seen him in their visions literally ascending into heaven. . . . So far as the use of this type of imagery is concerned, millenarianism may quite properly claim to be biblical. Unquestionably certain biblical writers expected a catastrophic end of the world. They depicted the days of sore distress immediately to precede the final catastrophe, they proclaimed the visible return of the heavenly Christ, and they eagerly awaited the revelation of the New Jerusalem.
>
> Any attempt to evade these literalistic features of biblical imagery is futile. Ever since Origen's day certain interpreters of Scripture have sought to refute millennial expectations by affirming that even the most striking statements about Jesus' return are to be understood figuratively. It has also been said that Daniel and Revelation are highly mystical and allegorical works not intended to refer to actual events, whether past, present, or future, but have a purely spiritual significance like that of Milton's *Paradise Lost* or Bunyan's *Pilgrim's Progress*. These are evasive devices designed to bring these Scriptures into harmony with present conditions, while ignoring the vivid expectancy of the ancients. The afflicted Jews of Maccabean times were demanding, not a figurative, but a literal, end of their troubles, nor did Daniel promise them anything less than the actual establishment of a new heavenly regime. In a similarly realistic vein an early Christian wrote, "You shall see the Son of Man sitting at the right hand of power

---

[6] Thomas Hartwell Horne, *An Introduction to the Critical Study and Knowledge of the Holy Scriptures*, I, 324.

[7] Cf. Floyd Hamilton, *The Basis of Millennial Faith*, pp. 38-39; Oswald T. Allis, *Prophecy and the Church*, p. 258.

and coming with the clouds of heaven [Mark 14:62]," or again, "There are some here of them that stand by who shall in no wise taste of death till they see the kingdom of God come with power [Mark 9:1]." Imagine the shock to Mark had he been told that this expectation was already realized in the appearances of Jesus after the Resurrection, or in the ecstatic experiences of the disciples at Pentecost, or in the salvation of the individual Christians at death. And who can imagine Mark's feeling had he also been told, in certain modern fashion, that his prediction of Christ's return was to be fulfilled in the Lutheran Reformation, in the French Revolution, in the Wesleyan Revival, in the emancipation of the slaves, in the spread of foreign missions, in the democratization of Russia, or in the outcome of the present world-war? Premillennialists are thoroughly justified in their protest against those opponents who allegorize or spiritualize pertinent biblical passages, thus retaining scriptural phrases while utterly perverting their original significance.[8]

No one would argue that the literalism of the Jewish interpreters was identical with present day grammatical-historical interpretation. A decadent literalism had warped Scripture of all meaning. Ramm well observes:

> . . . the net result of a good movement started by Ezra was a degenerative hyper-literalistic interpretation that was current among the Jews in the days of Jesus and Paul. The Jewish literalistic school is literalism at its worst. It is the exaltation of the letter to the point that all true sense is lost. It grossly exaggerates the incidental and accidental and ignores and misses the essential.[9]

And yet it can not be denied that literalism was the accepted method. Misuse of the method does not militate against the method itself. It was not the method that was at fault, but rather the misapplication of it.

B. *Literalism among the apostles.* This literal method was the method of the apostles. Farrar says:

> The better Jewish theory, purified in Christianity, takes the teachings of the Old Dispensation literally, but sees in them, as did St. Paul, the shadow and germ of future developments. Allegory, though once used by St. Paul by way of passing illustration, is unknown to the other Apostles, and is never sanctioned by Christ.[10]

---

8 Shirley Jackson Case, *The Millennial Hope*, pp. 214-16.
9 Ramm, *op. cit.*, p. 28.
10 Farrar, *op. cit.*, p. 217.

As able a scholar as Girdlestone has written in confirmation:

> We are brought to the conclusion that there was one uniform method commonly adopted by all the New Testament writers in interpreting and applying the Hebrew Scriptures. It is as if they had all been to one school and had studied under one master. But was it the Rabbinical school to which they had been? Was it to Gamaliel, or to Hillel, or to any other Rabbinical leader that they were indebted? All attainable knowledge of the mode of teaching current in that time gives the negative to the suggestion. The Lord Jesus Christ, and no other, was the original source of the method. In this sense, as in many others, He had come a light into the world.[11]

Even as liberal as was Briggs, he recognized that Jesus did not use the methods of His day, nor follow the fallacies of His generation. He says:

> The apostles and their disciples in the New Testament use the methods of the Lord Jesus rather than those of the men of their time. The New Testament writers differed among themselves in the tendencies of their thought . . . in them all, the methods of the Lord Jesus prevail over the other methods and ennoble them.[12]

It was not necessary for the apostles to adopt another method to rightly understand the Old Testament, but rather to purify the existing method from its extremes.

Since the only citation of the allegorical use of the Old Testament by New Testament writers is Paul's explanation of the allegory in Galatians 4:24, and since it has previously been shown that there is a difference between explaining an allegory and the use of the allegorical method of interpretation, it must be concluded that the New Testament writers interpreted the Old literally.

IV. The Rise of Allegorism

A multitude of difficulties beset the writers of the first centuries. They were without an established canon of either the Old or New Testaments. They were dependent upon a faulty translation of the Scriptures. They had known only the rules of interpretation laid down by the Rabbinical schools and, thus,

---

[11] R. B. Girdlestone, *The Grammar of Prophecy*, p. 86.
[12] Briggs, *op. cit.*, p. 443.

had to free themselves from the erroneous application of the principle of interpretation. They were surrounded by paganism, Judaism, and heresy of every kind.[13] Out of this maze there arose three diverse exegetical schools in the late Patristic period. Farrar says:

> The Fathers of the third and later centuries may be divided into three exegetical schools. Those schools are the *Literal* and *Realistic* as represented predominantly by Tertullian; the *Allegorical,* of which Origen is the foremost exponent; and the *Historical* and *Grammatical,* which flourished chiefly in Antioch, and of which Theodore of Mopsuestia was the acknowledged chief.[14]

NB

In tracing the rise of the allegorical school, Farrar goes back to Aristobulus, of whom he writes that his

> . . . actual work was of very great importance for the History of Interpretation. He is one of the precursors whom Philo used though he did not name, and he is the first to enunciate two theses which were destined to find wide acceptance, and to lead to many false conclusions in the sphere of exegesis.
>
> The first of these is the statement that Greek philosophy is borrowed from the Old Testament, and especially from the Law of Moses; the other that all the tenets of the Greek philosophers, and especially of Aristotle, are to be found in Moses and the Prophets by those who use the right method of inquiry.[15]

Philo adopted this concept of Aristobulus and sought to reconcile Mosaic law and Greek philosophy so that the Mosaic law might become acceptable to the Greek mind. Gilbert says:

> [To Philo] Greek philosophy was the same as the philosophy of Moses. . . . And the aim of Philo was to set forth and illustrate this harmony between the Jewish religion and classic philosophy, or, ultimately, it was to commend the Jewish religion to the educated Greek world. This was the high mission to which he felt called, the purpose with which he expounded the Hebrew laws in the language of the world's culture and philosophy.[16]

In order to effect this harmonization it was necessary for Philo to adopt an allegorizing method of interpreting the Scriptures.

---

[13] Farrar, *op. cit.,* pp. 164-65.
[14] *Ibid.,* p. 177.
[15] *Ibid.,* p. 129.
[16] George Holley Gilbert, *The Interpretation of the Bible,* pp. 37 ff.

The influence of Philo was most keenly felt in the theological school of Alexandria. Farrar says:

> It was in the great catechetical school of Alexandria, founded, as tradition says, by St. Mark, that there sprang up the chief school of Christian Exegesis. Its object, like that of Philo, was to unite philosophy with revelation, and thus to use the borrowed jewels of Egypt to adorn the sanctuary of God. Hence, Clement of Alexandria and Origen furnished the direct antithesis of Tertullian and Irenaeus. . . .
>
> The first teacher of the school who rose to fame was the venerable Pantaenus, a converted Stoic, of whose writings only a few fragments remain. He was succeeded by *Clement of Alexandria,* who, believing in the divine origin of Greek philosophy, openly propounded the principle that all Scripture must be allegorically understood.[17]

It was in this school that Origen developed the allegorical method as it applied to the Scriptures. Schaff, an unbiased witness, summarizes Origen's influence by saying:

> Origen was the first to lay down, in connection with the allegorical method of the Jewish Platonist, Philo, a formal theory of interpretation, which he carried out in a long series of exegetical works remarkable for industry and ingenuity, but meagre in solid results. He considered the Bible a living organism, consisting of three elements which answer to the body, soul, and spirit of man, after the Platonic psychology. Accordingly, he attributed to the Scriptures a threefold sense: (1) a somatic, literal, or historical sense, furnished immediately by the meaning of the words, but only serving as a veil for a higher idea; (2) a psychic or moral sense, animating the first, and serving for general edification; (3) a pneumatic or mystic and ideal sense, for those who stand on the high ground of philosophical knowledge. In the application of this theory he shows the same tendency as Philo, to spiritualize away the letter of scripture . . . and instead of simply bringing out the sense of the Bible, he puts into it all sorts of foreign ideas and irrelevant fancies. But this allegorizing suited the taste of the age, and, with his fertile mind and imposing learning, Origen was the exegetical oracle of the early church, till his orthodoxy fell into disrepute.[18]

It was the rise of ecclesiasticism and the recognition of the authority of the church in all doctrinal matters that gave great

---

[17] Farrar, *op. cit.*, pp. 182-83.
[18] Philip Schaff, *History of the Christian Church,* II, 521.

impetus to the adoption of the allegorical method. Augustine, according to Farrar, was one of the first to make Scripture conform to to the interpretation of the church.

> The exegesis of St. Augustine is marked by the most glaring defects. . . . He laid down the rule that the Bible must be interpreted with reference to Church Orthodoxy, and that no Scriptural expression can be out of accordance with any other. . . .
>
> . . . Snatching up the Old Philonian and Rabbinic rule which had been repeated for so many generations, that everything in Scripture which appeared to be unorthodox or immoral must be interpreted mystically, he introduced confusion into his dogma of supernatural inspiration by admitting that there are many passages "written by the Holy Ghost," which are objectionable when taken in their obvious sense. He also opened the door to arbitrary fancy.[19]

And again:

> . . . When once the principle of allegory is admitted, when once we start with the rule that whole passages and books of Scripture say one thing when they mean another, the reader is delivered bound hand and foot to the caprice of the interpreter. He can be sure of absolutely nothing except what is dictated to him by the Church, and in all ages the authority of "the Church" has been falsely claimed for the presumptuous tyranny of false prevalent opinions. In the days of Justin Martyr and of Origen Christians had been driven to allegory by an imperious necessity. It was the only means known to them by which to meet the shock which wrenched the Gospel free from the fetters of Judaism. They used it to defeat the crude literalism of fanatical heresies; or to reconcile the teachings of philosophy with the truths of the Gospel. But in the days of Augustine the method had degenerated into an artistic method of displaying ingenuity and supporting ecclesiasticism. It had become the resource of a faithlessness which declined to admit, of an ignorance which failed to appreciate, and of an indolence which refused to solve the real difficulties in which the sacred book abounds. . . .
>
> Unhappily for the Church, unhappily for any real apprehension of Scripture, the allegorists, in spite of protest, were completely victorious.[20]

The previous study should make it obvious that the allegorical method was not born out of the study of the Scriptures, but

[19] Farrar, *op. cit.*, pp. 236-37.
[20] *Ibid.*, p. 238.

rather out of a desire to unite Greek philosophy and the Word of God. It did not come out of a desire to present the truths of the Word, but to pervert them. It was not the child of orthodoxy, but of heterodoxy.

Even though Augustine was successful in injecting a new method of interpretation into the blood stream of the church, based on Origen's method of perverting Scripture, there were those in this era who still held to the original literal method. In the School of Antioch there were those who did not follow the method introduced by the School of Alexandria. Gilbert notes:

> Theodore and John may be said to have gone far toward a scientific method of exegesis inasmuch as they saw clearly the necessity of determining the original sense of Scripture in order to make any profitable use of the same. To have kept this end steadily in view was a great achievement. It made their work stand out in strong contrast by the side of the Alexandrian school. Their interpretation was extremely plain and simple as compared with that of Origen. They utterly rejected the allegorical method.[21]

Of the value, significance, and influence of this school, Farrar says:

> . . . the *School of Antioch* possessed a deeper insight into the true method of exegesis than any which preceded or succeeded it during a thousand years . . . their system of Biblical interpretation approached more nearly than any other to that which is now adopted by the Reformed Churches throughout the world, and that if they had not been too uncharitably anathematised by the angry tongue, and crushed by the iron hand of a dominant orthodoxy, the study of their commentaries, and the adoption of their exegetic system, might have saved Church commentaries from centuries of futility and error. . . .
>
> . . . .
>
> *Diodorus of Tarsus* must be regarded as the true founder of the School of Antioch. He was a man of eminent learning and of undisputed piety. He was the teacher of Chrysostom and of Theodore of Mopsuestia. . . . His books were devoted to an exposition of Scripture in its literal sense, and he wrote a treatise, now unhappily lost, "on the difference between allegory and spiritual insight."
>
> But the ablest, the most decided, and the most logical representative of the School of Antioch was *Theodore of Mopsuestia*

21 Gilbert, *op. cit.*, p. 137.

> (428). That clear-minded and original thinker stands out like a "rock in the morass of ancient exegesis." . . .
>
> . . . He was a Voice not an Echo; a Voice amid thousands of echoes which repeated only the emptiest sounds. He rejected the theories of Origen, but he had learnt from him the indispensable importance of attention to linguistic details especially in commenting on the New Testament. He pays close attention to particles, moods, prepositions, and to terminology in general. He points out the idiosyncrasies . . . of St. Paul's style. . . . He is almost the earliest writer who gives much attention to Hermeneutic matter, as for instance in his Introductions to the Epistles to Ephesus and Colossae. . . . His highest merit is his constant endeavor to study each passage as a whole and not as "an isolated congeries of separate texts." He first considers the sequence of thought, then examines the phraseology and the separate clauses, and finally furnishes us with an exegesis which is often brilliantly characteristic and profoundly suggestive.[22]

We would have a different history of interpretation had the method of the Antioch School prevailed. Unfortunately for sound interpretation, the ecclesiasticism of the established church, which depended for its position on the allegorical method, prevailed, and the views of the Antioch School were condemned as heretical.

V. The Dark Ages

As one might expect from the general tenor of the period, there was no effort made to interpret the Scriptures accurately. The inherited principles of interpretation were unchanged. Berkhof observes:

> In this period, the fourfold sense of Scripture (literal, tropological, allegorical, and analogical) was generally accepted, and it became an established principle that the interpretation of the Bible had to adapt itself to tradition and to the doctrine of the Church.[23]

The seeds of ecclesiasticism sown by Augustine have borne fruit and the principle of conformity to the church has become firmly entrenched. Farrar summarizes the whole period by saying:

> . . . we are compelled to say that during the Dark Ages, from the seventh to the twelfth century, and during the scholastic epoch, from the twelfth to the sixteenth, there are but a few of

---

[22] Farrar, *op. cit.*, pp. 213-15.
[23] Louis Berkhof, *Principles of Biblical Interpretation*, p. 23.

the many who toiled in this field who add a single essential principle, or furnished a single original contribution to the explanation of the Word of God. During these nine centuries we find very little except the "glimmerings and decays" of patristic exposition. Much of the learning which still continued to exist was devoted to something which was meant for exegesis yet not one writer in hundreds showed any true conception of what exegesis really implies.[24]

VI. The Reformation Period

It is not until the Reformation era that one can find again any sound exegesis being produced. The whole Reformation movement may be said to have been activated by a return to the literal method of interpretation of the Scriptures. This movement began with certain precursors whose influence turned men back to the original literal method. According to Farrar:

Valla, a Canon of St. John Lateran . . . is one chief link between the Renaissance and the Reformation. He had . . . learnt from the revival of letters that Scripture must be interpreted by the laws of grammar and the laws of language.[25]

Erasmus is viewed as another link in that he emphasized the study of the original texts of Scripture and laid the foundation for the grammatical interpretation of the Word of God. He, according to Farrar, "may be regarded as the chief founder of modern textual and Biblical criticism. He must always hold an honoured place among the interpreters of Scripture."[26]

The translators, who did so much to stir up the flame of Reformation, were motivated by the desire to understand the Bible literally. Of these early translators Farrar writes:

Wiclif, indeed made the important remark that "the whole error in the knowledge of Scripture, and the source of its debasement and falsification by incompetent persons, was the ignorance of grammar and logic."[27]

And of Tyndale, he says:

"We may borrow similitudes or allegories from the Scrip-

[24] Farrar, *op. cit.*, p. 245.
[25] *Ibid.*, pp. 312-13.
[26] *Ibid.*, p. 320.
[27] *Ibid.*, pp. 278-79.

tures," says the great translator Tyndale, "and apply them to our purposes, which allegories are not sense of the Scriptures, but free things besides the Scriptures altogether in the liberty of the Spirit. Such allegory proveth nothing, it is a mere simile. God is a Spirit and all his words are spiritual, and *His literal sense is spiritual.*" "As to those three spiritual senses," says Whitaker, the opponent of Bellarmine, "it is surely foolish to say there are as many senses in Scripture as the words themselves may be transferred and accommodated to bear. For although the words may be applied and accommodated tropologically, anagogically, allegorically, *or any other way, yet there are not therefore various senses, various interpretations, and explications of Scripture, but there is but one sense and that the literal,* which may be variously accommodated, and from which various things may be collected."[28]

Briggs, certainly no friend to the literal interpretation of the Word, quotes Tyndale himself, who says:

> Thou shalt understand, therefore, that the Scripture hath but one sense, which is the literal sense. And that literal sense is the root and ground of all, and the anchor that never faileth, whereunto if thou cleave, thou canst never err or go out of the way. And if thou leave the literal sense, thou canst not but go out of the way. Nevertheláter, the Scripture useth proverbs, similitudes, riddles, or allegories, as all other speeches do; but that which the proverb, similitude, riddle, or allegory signifieth, is over the literal sense, which thou must seek out diligently. . . .[29]

The foundations of the Reformation were laid in the return to the literal method of interpretation.

In the Reformation period itself two great names stand out as exponents of the truths of Scripture: Luther and Calvin. Both of these are marked by their strong insistences on the literal method of interpretation.

> Luther says: "Every word should be allowed to stand in its natural meaning and that should not be abandoned unless faith forces us to it. . . . It is the attribute of Holy Scripture that it interprets itself by passages and places which belong together, and can only be understood by the rule of faith."[30]

That Luther advocated a position that today would be called the grammatical-historical method is observed from his own writing.

[28] *Ibid.*, p. 300.
[29] Briggs, *op. cit.*, pp. 456-57.
[30] *Ibid.*

> . . . Luther, in his preface to Isaiah (1528) and in other parts of his writings, lays down what he conceives to be the true rules of Scripture interpretation. He insists (1) on the necessity for grammatical knowledge; (2) on the importance of taking into consideration times, circumstances, and conditions; (3) on the observance of the context; (4) on the need of faith and spiritual illumination; (5) on keeping what he called "the proportion of faith"; and (6) on the reference of all Scripture to Christ.[31]

So great was Luther's desire, not only to give the people the Word of God, but to teach them to interpret it, that he laid down the following rules of interpretation:

> i. First among them was the supreme and final authority of Scripture itself, apart from all ecclesiastical authority or interference. . . .
>
> ii. Secondly, he asserted not only the supreme authority but the *sufficiency* of Scripture. . . .
>
> iii. Like all the other reformers he set aside the dreary fiction of the fourfold sense. . . . "The literal sense of Scripture alone," said Luther, "is the whole essence of faith and of Christian theology." " I have observed this, that all heresies and errors have originated, not from the simple words of Scripture, as is so universally asserted, but from *neglecting* the simple words of Scripture, and from the affectation of purely subjective . . . tropes and inferences." "In the schools of theologians it is a well-known rule that Scripture is to be understood in four ways, literal, allegoric, moral, anagogic. But if we wish to handle Scripture aright, our one effort will be to obtain *unum, simplicem, germanum, et certum sensum literalem.*" "Each passage has one clear, definite, and true sense of its own. All others are but doubtful and uncertain opinions."
>
> iv. It need hardly he said, therefore, that Luther, like most of the Reformers, rejected the validity of allegory. He totally denied its claim to be regarded as a *spiritual* interpretation.
>
> v. Luther also maintained the *perspicuity* of Scripture. . . . He sometimes came near to the modern remark that, "the Bible is to be interpreted like any other book."
>
> vi. Luther maintained with all his force, and almost for the first time in history, the absolute indefeasible *right of private judgment,* which, with the doctrine of the spiritual priesthood of all Christians, lies at the base of all Protestantism.[32]

Calvin holds a unique place in the history of interpretation. Of him Gilbert writes:

---

[31] Farrar, *op. cit.,* pp. 331-32.
[32] *Ibid.,* pp. 325-30.

> . . . For the first time in a thousand years he gave a conspicuous example of *non-allegorical* exposition. One must go back to the best work of the school of Antioch to find so complete a rejection of the method of Philo as is furnished by Calvin. Allegorical interpretations which had been put forth in the early Church and indorsed by illustrious expositors in all the subsequent centuries, like the interpretation of Noah's ark and the seamless garment of Christ, are cast aside as rubbish. This fact alone gives an abiding and distinguished honor to Calvin's exegetical work. What led him to reject allegorical interpretation as something peculiarly satanic, whether it was his legal training at Orleans and Bourges or his native judgment, is not possible to say, but the fact is clear and is the most striking feature of his interpretation.[33]

Calvin states his own position very clearly. In the commentary to Galatians he writes: "Let us know then, that the true meaning of Scripture is the natural and obvious meaning, and let us embrace and abide by it resolutely."[34] In the Preface to *Romans* Calvin says: "It is the first business of an interpreter to let his author say what he does say, instead of attributing to him what we think he ought to say."[35] Concerning Calvin's contribution Schaff writes:

> Calvin is the founder of the grammatico-historical exegesis. He affirmed and carried out the sound hermeneutical principle that the Biblical authors, like all sensible writers, wished to convey to their readers one definite thought in words which they could understand. A passage may have a literal or a figurative sense; but cannot have two senses at once. The Word of God is inexhaustible and applicable to all times, but there is a difference between explanation and application, and application must be consistent with explanation.[36]

Concerning this entire period Farrar writes:

> . . . the Reformers gave a mighty impulse to the science of Scriptural interpretation. They made the Bible accessible to all; they tore away and scattered to the winds the dense cobwebs of arbitrary tradition which had been spun for so many centuries over every book, and every text of it; they put the Apocrypha on

---

[33] Gilbert, *op. cit.*, p. 209.

[34] John Calvin, *Commentary on Galatians*, p. 136, cited by Gerrit H. Hospers, *The Principle of Spiritualization in Hermeneutics*, p. 11.

[35] Cited by Farrar, *op. cit.*, p. 347.

[36] Philip Schaff, cited by Hospers, *op. cit.*, p. 12.

> an altogether lower level than the sacred books; they carefully studied the original languages; they developed the plain, literal sense; they used it for the strengthening and refreshing of the spiritual life.[37]

And Gilbert summarizes:

> . . . It is to be said to the credit of the period under consideration that its normal type of exegesis regards the literal sense of the text. The words of Richard Hooker (1553-1600) have a wide application throughout the period. "I hold it," he says, "for a most infallible rule in exposition of Sacred Scriptures that when a literal construction will stand, the farthest from the letter is commonly the worst. There is nothing more dangerous than this deluding art which changeth the meaning of words as alchymy doth or would do the substance of metals, making of anything what it listeth, and bringing in the end of all truth to nothing." In general, the example of Calvin in rejecting allegorical interpretation was followed by the leading divines and scholars of the next two centuries.[38]

If one is to return to the Reformers for his theology, he must accept the method of interpretation on which their theology rests.

VII. The Post-Reformation Period

The post-Reformation period was marked by the rise of men who followed closely in the footsteps of the Reformers themselves in the application of the literal or grammatical-historical method of interpretation. Farrar writes:

> . . . If Luther was the prophet of the Reformation *Melanchthon* was the teacher. . . . *Zwingli,* with absolute independence, had arrived at opinions on this subject which in all essential particulars coincided with those of Luther. . . . A host of Reformation expositors endeavoured to spread the truths to which they had been led by the German and Swiss Reformers. It will be sufficient here merely to mention the names of Oecolampadius (1581), Bucer (1551), Brenz (1570), Bugenhagen (1558). Musculus (1563), Camerarius (1574), Bullinger (1575), Chemnitz (1586), and Beza (1605). Among all of these there was a general agreement in principles, a rejection of scholastic methods, a refusal to acknowledge the exclusive dominance of patristic authority and church tradition; a repudiation of the hitherto dominant fourfold meaning; an avoid-

[37] Farrar, *op. cit.,* p. 357.
[38] Gilbert, *op. cit.,* pp. 229-30.

> ance of allegory; a study of the original languages; a close attention to the literal sense; a belief in the perspecuity and sufficiency of Scripture; the study of Scripture as a whole and the reference of its total contents to Christ. . . .[39]

It might be expected, since the foundation has been laid for the literal method of interpretation, that we would witness a full growth of Scriptural exegesis based on this foundation. However, the history of interpretation reveals such an adherence to creeds and church interpretations that there is little progress in sound Scriptural interpretation in this period.[40] Yet, out of this period did come such exegetes and scholars as John Koch, Professor at Leyden (1669), John James Wetstein, Professor at Basle (1754), who advocated that the same principles of interpretation apply to Scripture as to other books, John Albert Bengel (1752), and others who were renowned for their contribution to criticism and exposition and who laid the foundation for such modern exegetes as Lightfoot, Westcott, Ellicott, and others.

One man of great influence in the systematization of the literal method of interpretation was John Augustus Ernesti, of whom Terry writes:

> Probably the most distinguished name in the history of exegesis in the eighteenth century is that of John Augustus Ernesti, whose Institutio Interpretis Nove Testamenti (Lipz. 1761), or Principles of New Testament Interpretation, has been accepted as a standard textbook on hermeneutics by four generations of Biblical Scholars. "He is regarded," says Hagenbach, "as the founder of a new exegetical school, whose principle simply was that the Bible must be rigidly explained according to its own language, and in this explanation, it must neither be bribed by any external authority of the Church, nor by our own feeling, nor by a sportive and allegorizing fancy—which had frequently been the case with the mystics—nor, finally, by any philosophical system whatever.[41]

The statement of Horatius Bonar is taken to be a summary of the principle of exegesis that came to be the foundation of all real Scriptural interpretation. He says:

---

[39] Farrar, *op. cit.*, p. 342.
[40] Cf. *ibid.*, pp. 358-59.
[41] Milton S. Terry, *Biblical Hermeneutics*, p. 707.

> . . . I feel a greater certainty as to the literal interpretation of that whole Word of God—historical, doctrinal, prophetical. "Literal, if possible," is, I believe, the only maxim that will carry you right through the Word of God from Genesis to Revelation.[42]

In spite of the shackles which dogmatism and creedalism sought to impose on interpretation, there did emerge from this period certain sound principles of interpretation, which became the basis for the great exegetical works of following centuries. These principles are summarized by Berkhof:

> . . . it became an established principle that the Bible must be interpreted like every other book. The special divine element of the Bible was generally disparaged, and the interpreter usually limited himself to the discussion of the historical and critical questions. The abiding fruit of this period is the clear consciousness of the necessity of the *Grammatico-Historical* interpretation of the Bible. . . .
>
> The Grammatical School. This school was founded by *Ernesti*, who wrote an important work on the interpretation of the New Testament, in which he laid down four principles. (a) The manifold sense of Scripture must be rejected, and only the literal sense retained. (b) Allegorical and typological interpretations must be disapproved, except in cases which the author indicates that he meant to combine another sense with the literal. (c) Since the Bible has the grammatical sense in common with other books, this should be ascertained similarly in both cases. (d) The literal sense may not be determined by a supposed dogmatical sense.
>
> The Grammatical School was essentially supernaturalistic, binding itself to "the very words of the text as the legitimate source of authentic interpretation and of religious truth" (Elliott).[43]

As this history of interpretation is summarized, it is to be noted that all interpretation began with the literal interpretation of Ezra. This literal method became the basic method of Rabbinism. It was the accepted method used by the New Testament in the interpretation of the Old and was so employed by the Lord and His apostles. This literal method was the method of the Church Fathers until the time of Origen when the allegorical method, which had been devised to harmonize Platonic philosophy and Scripture, was adopted. Augustine's influence brought this allegorizing method into the established

---

[42] Cited by Girdlestone, *op. cit.*, p. 179.
[43] Berkhof, *op. cit.*, pp. 32-33.

church and brought an end to all true exegesis. This system continued until the Reformation. At the Reformation the literal method of interpretation was solidly established and, in spite of the attempts of the church to bring all interpretation into conformity to an adopted creed, literal interpretation continued and became the basis on which all true exegesis rests.

It would be concluded, then, from the study of the history of interpretation that the original and accepted method of interpretation was the literal method, which was used by the Lord, the greatest interpreter, and any other method was introduced to promote heterodoxy. Therefore, the literal method must be accepted as the basic method for right interpretation in any field of doctrine today.

Chapter III

GENERAL CONSIDERATIONS IN INTERPRETATION

The history of interpretation has shown us that the adoption of the correct method of interpretation does not necessarily guarantee correct conclusions by those who hold this method. Rabbinism, which used the literal method, produced a host of erroneous views and interpretations through the misuse of the method. It is therefore necessary to lay down some principles of interpretation, even after establishing the right method, so that the method be not misapplied so as to produce false conclusions.

I. The Interpretation of Words

It is recognized without question that words form the medium of communication of thought. All sound exegesis must of necessity, then, begin with an interpretation of the words themselves. Horne, in his invaluable *Introduction to the Critical Study and Knowledge of the Holy Scriptures,* has given an excellent summary of the principles to be employed in the interpretation of words.

1. Ascertain the *usus loquendi,* or notion affixed to a word by the persons in general, by whom the language either is now or formerly was spoken, and especially in the particular connection in which such notion is affixed.

2. The received signification of a word is to be retained unless weighty and necessary reasons require that it should be abandoned or neglected.

3. Where a word has several significations in common use, that must be selected which best suits the passage in question, and which is consistent with an author's known character, sentiments, and situation, and the known circumstances under which he wrote.

4. Although the force of particular words can only be derived from etymology, yet too much confidence must not be placed in

that frequently uncertain science; because the primary signification of a word is frequently very different from its common meaning.

5. The distinctions between words, which are apparently synonymous, should be carefully examined and considered.

6. The epithets introduced by the sacred writers are also to be carefully weighed and considered, as all of them have either a declarative or explanatory force, or serve to distinguish one thing from another, or unite these two characters together.

7. General terms are used sometimes in their whole extent, and sometimes in a restricted sense, and whether they are to be understood in the one way or in the other must depend upon the scope, subject-matter, context, and parallel passages.

8. Of any particular passage the most simple sense—or that which most readily suggests itself to an attentive and intelligent reader, possessing competent knowledge—is in all probability the genuine sense or meaning.

9. Since it is the design of interpretation to render in our own language the same discourse which the sacred authors originally wrote in Hebrew or Greek, it is evident that our interpretation or version, to be correct, ought not to affirm or deny more than the inspired penmen affirmed or denied at the time they wrote; consequently we should be more willing to take a sense from Scripture than to bring one of it.

10. Before we conclude upon the sense of a text, so as to prove anything by it, we must be sure that such sense is not repugnant to natural reason.[1]

Angus-Green supplement Horne by saying:

The words of Scripture must be taken in their common meaning, unless such meaning is shown to be inconsistent with other words in the sentence, with the argument or context, or with other parts of Scripture. Of two meanings, that one is generally to be preferred which was most obvious to the comprehension of the hearers or original readers of the inspired passage, allowing for the modes of thought prevalent in their own day, as well as for those figurative expressions which were so familiar as to be no exception to the general rule.

The true meaning of any passage of Scripture, then, is not every sense which the words will bear, nor is it every sense which is true in itself, but that which is intended by the inspired writers, or even by the Holy Spirit, though imperfectly understood by the writers themselves. . . .[2]

---

[1] Thomas Hartwell Horne, *Introduction to the Critical Study and Knowledge of the Holy Scriptures*, I, 325-26.

[2] Joseph Angus and Samuel G. Green, *The Bible Hand-Book*, p. 180.

Words must be interpreted, then, in the usual, natural, literal sense.

II. The Interpretation of the Context

The second great subject of consideration must be the context in which any passage appears. There are certain rules which will guide in the contextual interpretation. These are summarized by Horne:

> 1. . . . a careful consideration of the preceding and subsequent parts will enable us to determine that signification, whether literal or figurative, which is best adapted to the passage in question.
>
> 2. The context of a discourse or book in the Scriptures, may comprise either one verse, a few verses, entire periods or sections, entire chapters, or whole books.
>
> 3. Sometimes a book of Scripture comprises only one subject or argument, in which case the whole of it must be referred to precedents and subsequents, and ought to be considered together.
>
> . . . .
>
> In examining the context of a passage, it will be desirable,
>
> 1. To investigate each word of every passage: and as the connection is formed by *particles,* these should always receive that signification which the subject-matter and context require.
>
> 2. Examine the entire passage with minute attention.
>
> 3. A verse or passage must not be connected with a remote context, unless the latter agree better with it than a nearer context.
>
> 4. Examine whether the writer continues his discourse, lest we suppose him to make a transition to another argument, when, in fact, he is prosecuting the same topic.
>
> 5. The parentheses which occur in the sacred writings should be particularly regarded: but no parenthesis should be interposed without sufficient reason.
>
> 6. No explanation must be admitted, but that which suits the context.
>
> 7. Where no connection is to be found with the preceding and subsequent part of a book, none should be sought.[3]

III. The Historical Interpretation

The third consideration in any interpretation must be the historical interpretation, in which the immediate historical set-

---

[3] Horne, *op. cit.,* I, 336 ff.

ting and influence is carefully weighed. Berkhof gives us an excellent summary of considerations in this phase of interpretation.

1. Basic Assumptions for Historical Interpretation.

a. The Word of God originated in a historical way, and therefore, can be understood only in the light of history.

b. A word is never fully understood until it is apprehended as a living word, i.e., as it originated in the soul of the author.

c. It is impossible to understand an author and to interpret his words correctly unless he is seen against the proper historical background.

d. The place, the time, the circumstances, and the prevailing view of the world and of life in general, will naturally color the writings that are produced under those conditions of time, place, and circumstances.

2. Demands on the Exegete. In view of these presuppositions, historical interpretation makes the following demands on the exegete:

a. He must seek to know the author whose work he would explain: his parentage, his character and temperament, his intellectual, moral, and religious characteristics, as well as the external circumstances of his life. . . .

b. It will be incumbent on him to reconstruct, as far as possible, from the historical data at hand, and with the aid of historical hypotheses, the environment in which the particular writings under consideration originated; in other words, the author's world. He will have to inform himself respecting the physical features of the land where the books were written, and regarding the character and history, the customs, morals and religion of the people among whom or for whom they were composed.

c. He will find it to be of the utmost importance that he consider the various influences which determined more directly the character of the writings under consideration, such as: the original readers, the purpose which the author had in mind, the author's age, his frame of mind, and the special circumstances under which he composed his book.

d. Moreover, he will have to transfer himself mentally into the first century A. D., and into Oriental conditions. He must place himself on the standpoint of the author, and seek to enter into his very soul, until he, as it were, lives his life and thinks his thoughts. This means that he will have to guard carefully against the rather common mistake of transferring the author to the present day and making him speak the language of the twentieth century. . . .[4]

---

[4] Louis Berkhof, *Principles of Interpretation*, pp. 113 ff.

IV. The Grammatical Interpretation

The fourth consideration in any interpretation must be the interpretation of the grammar of the language in which the passage was originally given. This of course can not be done apart from a knowledge of the original languages. Elliott and Harsha, translating Cellerier, state the basic rule:

> The interpreter should begin his work by studying the grammatical sense of the text, with the aid of Sacred Philology. As in all other writings, the *grammatical* sense must be made the starting-point. The meaning of the words must be determined according to the linguistic usage and the connection.[5]

Terry adds:

> "Grammatical and historical interpretation, when rightly understood," says Davidson, "are synonymous. The special laws of grammar, agreeably to which the sacred writers employed language, were the result of their peculiar circumstances; and history alone throws us back into these circumstances. A new language was not made for the authors of Scripture; they conformed to the current language of the country and time. Their compositions would not have been otherwise intelligible. They took up the *usus loquendi* as they found it, modifying it, as is quite natural, by the relations internal and external amid which they thought and wrote." The same writer also observes: "The grammatico-historical sense is made out by the application of grammatical and historical considerations. The great object to be ascertained is the *usus loquendi,* embracing the law or principles of universal grammar which form the basis of every language. . . . It is the *usus loquendi* of the inspired authors which forms the subject of the grammatical principles recognized and followed by the expositor. . . . we attain to a knowledge of the peculiar *usus loquendi* in the way of historical investigation. . . ."[6]

Terry well describes the methodology and intent of the grammatical-historical method. He says:

> . . . we may name the Grammatico-Historical as the method which most fully commends itself to the judgment and conscience of Christian scholars. Its fundamental principle is to gather from the Scriptures themselves the precise meaning which the writers intended to convey. It applies to the sacred books the same principles, the same grammatical process and exercise of common

---

[5] Charles Elliott and W. J. Harsha, *Biblical Hermeneutics,* p. 73.
[6] Milton S. Terry, *Biblical Hermeneutics,* pp. 203-4.

sense and reason, which we apply to other books. The grammatico-historical exegete, furnished with suitable qualifications, intellectual, educational, and moral, will accept the claims of the Bible without prejudice or adverse prepossession, and, with no ambition to prove them true or false, will investigate the language and import of each book with fearless independence. He will master the language of the writer, the particular dialect which he used, and his peculiar style and manner of expression. He will inquire into the circumstances under which he wrote, the manners and customs of his age, and the purpose or object which he had in view. He has a right to assume that no sensible author will be knowingly inconsistent with himself, or seek to bewilder and mislead his readers.[7]

V. The Interpretation of Figurative Language

One major problem facing the interpreter is the problem of interpreting figurative language. Since the prophetic Scriptures frequently make use of figurative language this form of communication must be studied in detail.

A. *The use of figurative language.* It is generally recognized that figurative language is used both to embellish a language by way of adornment and to convey abstract ideas by way of transfer.

> It is a necessity of the human intellect that facts connected with the mind, or with spiritual truth, must be clothed in language borrowed from material things. To words exclusively spiritual or abstract we can attach no definite conception.
>
> And God is pleased to condescend to our necessity. He leads us to new knowledge by means of what is already known. He reveals Himself in terms previously familiar.[8]

B. *When is language literal or figurative?* The first problem facing the interpreter is that of determining when the language is literal and when it is figurative. The implications of this problem are stated by Horne:

> In order, then, to understand fully the figurative language of the Scriptures, it is requisite, *first,* to ascertain and determine what is really figurative, lest we take that to be literal which is figurative, as the disciples of our Lord and the Jews frequently did, or lest we pervert the literal meaning of words by a figurative in-

[7] *Ibid.,* p. 173.
[8] Angus-Green, *op. cit.,* p. 215.

terpretation; and, *secondly,* when we have ascertained what is really figurative, to interpret it correctly, and deliver its true sense.[9]

A simple rule to follow in determining what is literal and figurative is given by Lockhart, who says:

> If the literal meaning of any word or expression makes good sense in its connections, it is literal; but if the literal meaning does not make good sense, it is figurative.[10]

Later the same author adds:

> Since the literal is the most usual signification of a word, and therefore occurs much more frequently than the figurative, any term will be regarded as literal until there is good reason for a different understanding. . . . The literal or most usual meaning of a word, if consistent, should be preferred to a figurative or less usual signification.[11]

Thus, the interpreter will proceed on the presupposition that the word is literal unless there is a good reason for deciding otherwise. Hamilton, who advocates the use of allegorical interpretation in prophecy, states this very supposition.

> . . . a good working rule to follow is that the literal interpretation of the prophecy is to be accepted unless (a) the passages contain obviously figurative language, or (b) unless the New Testament gives authority for interpreting them in other than a literal sense, or (c) unless a literal interpretation would produce a contradiction with truths, principles or factual statements contained in non-symbolic books of the New Testament. Another obvious rule to be followed is that the clearest New Testament passages in non-symbolic books are to be the norm for the interpretation of prophecy, rather than obscure or partial revelations contained in the Old Testament. In other words, we should accept the clear and plain parts of Scripture as a basis for getting the true meaning of the more difficult parts of Scripture.[12]

It will usually be quite obvious if the language is figurative. Fairbairn says:

> . . . it may be noted that in a large number of cases, by much the larger number of cases where the language is tropical, the fact that it is so appears from the very nature of the language or

---

[9] Horne, *op. cit.*, I, 356.
[10] Clinton Lockhart, *Principles of Interpretation*, p. 49.
[11] *Ibid.*, p. 156.
[12] Floyd Hamilton, *The Basis of Millennial Faith*, pp. 53-54.

> from the connexion in which it stands. Another class of passages in which the figure is also, for the most part, quite easy of detection are those in which what is called *synechdoche* prevails.[13]

The same author goes on to give us some principles by which one may determine whether a passage is literal or figurative. He says:

> The first of these is that, when anything is said which if taken according to the letter would be at variance with the essential nature of the subject spoken of, the language must be tropical. A second principle applicable to such cases is that, if the language taken literally would involve something incongruous or morally improper, the figurative and not the literal sense must be the right one. A third direction may be added, viz., that where we have still reason to doubt whether the language is literal or figurative we should endeavor to have the doubt resolved by referring to parallel passages (if there be any such) which treat of the same subject in more explicit terms or at greater length.[14]

On settling this problem Cellerier writes:

> This investigation cannot be successfully accomplished by intellectual science alone. Judgment and good faith, critical tact and impartiality are also necessary. A few general indications are all that can be given in this connection. (a) *A priori*. The probability that the language is figurative is strong in the poetical or sententious writings and also in the oratorical and popular discourses. Generally this probability is augmented when it is a fair supposition that the writer has been induced by his situation, his subject, or his object to make use of such language. There is a probability of the same kind, but much stronger, when the passage under examination is animated and highly wrought and seems to make allusion to objects of another nature. (b) *A posteriori*. There is a probability still greater when the literal sense would be absurd. . . . All these probabilities, however, are still insufficient. It is further necessary to examine the passage in all its details, critically, exegetically, and faithfully. The figurative sense must be sustained by all these processes before it can be relied upon as the true interpretation.[15]

This whole problem of when language is figurative and when literal has been well summarized by Terry, who comments:

---

[13] Patrick Fairbairn, *Hermeneutical Manual*, p. 138.
[14] *Ibid.*
[15] Elliott and Harsha, *op. cit.*, pp. 144-45.

> It is scarcely necessary, and, indeed, quite impracticable, to lay down specific rules for determining when language is used figuratively and when literal. It is an old and oft-repeated hermeneutical principle that words should be understood in their literal sense unless such literal interpretation involves a manifest contradiction or absurdity. It should be observed, however, that this principle, when reduced to practice, becomes simply an appeal to every man's rational judgment. And what to one seems very absurd and improbable may be to another altogether simple and self-consistent. . . . Reference must be had to the general character and style of the particular book, to the plan and purpose of the author, and to the context and scope of the particular passage in question. Especially should strict regard be had to the usage of the sacred writers, as determined by a thorough collation and comparison of all parallel passages. The same general principles, by which we ascertain the grammatico-historical sense, apply also to the interpretation of figurative language, and it should never be forgotten that the figurative portions of the Bible are as certain and truthful as the most prosaic chapters. Metaphors, allegories, parables, and symbols are divinely chosen forms of setting forth the oracles of God, and we must not suppose their meaning to be so vague and uncertain as to be past finding out. In the main, we believe the figurative parts of the Scriptures are not so difficult to understand as many have imagined. By a careful and judicious discrimination the interpreter should aim to determine the character and purport of each particular trope, and explain it in harmony with the common laws of language, and the author's context, scope, and plan.[16]

A rule to guide us as to when to interpret literally and when figuratively has been carefully stated by Cooper. He says:

> When the plain sense of Scripture makes common sense, seek no other sense; therefore, take every word at its primary, ordinary, usual, literal meaning unless the facts of the immediate context, studied in the light of related passages and axiomatic and fundamental truths, indicate clearly otherwise.[17]

This might well become the axiom of the interpreter.

C. *The interpretation of figurative language.* The second problem rising out of the use of figurative language is the method to be used in interpreting that which is figurative.

It should be observed at the very outset that the purpose

---

16 Terry, *op. cit.*, pp. 159-60.
17 David L. Cooper, *The God of Israel*, p. iii.

of figurative language is to impart some literal truth, which may more clearly be conveyed by the use of figures than in any other way. The literal meaning is of greater importance than the literal words. Chafer states it:

> The literal sense of the words employed in a figure of speech is not to be taken as the meaning of the figure, but rather the sense intended by the use of the figure. In all such instances, therefore, there is but one meaning. In such cases the literal is not the sense. In this connection Cellerier says: "Revelation . . . has been clothed with popular forms strongly impressed with the habits of the East, that is to say, with metaphorical, poetical, and parabolical forms, which convey a meaning different from that of the literal sense of the words. But even then there are not two senses, the literal and metaphorical. The metaphorical is alone the real sense; the literal does not exist as a sense; it is only the vehicle of the former; it contains in itself no result, no truth. There is therefore only one true sense [Ma. d'Hermen., p. 41]."[18]

Horne has given an extensive set of rules in order to determine properly the sense implied in any figure:

> 1. The literal meaning of words must be retained, more in the historical books of Scripture than in those which are poetical.
>
> 2. The literal meaning of words is to be given up, if it be either improper, or involve an impossibility, or where words, properly taken, contain anything contrary to the doctrinal or moral precepts delivered in other parts of Scripture.
>
> 3. That we inquire in what respects the thing compared, and that with which it is compared, respectively agree, and also in what respects they have any affinity or resemblance.
>
> (1.) The sense of a figurative passage will be known, if the resemblance between the things or objects compared be so clear as to be immediately perceived.
>
> (2.) As, in the sacred metaphors, one particular is generally the principal thing thereby exhibited, the sense of a metaphor will be illustrated by considering the context of a passage in which it occurs.
>
> (3.) The sense of a figurative expression is often known from the sacred writer's own explanation of it.
>
> (4.) The sense of a figurative expression may also be ascertained by consulting parallel passages; in which the same thing is

[18] Rollin T. Chafer, *The Science of Biblical Hermeneutics*, pp. 80-81.

expressed properly and literally, or in which the same word occurs, so that the sense may be readily apprehended.

(5.) Consider history.

(6.) Consider the connection of doctrine, as well as the context of the figurative passage.

(7.) In fixing the sense exhibited by a metaphor, the comparison ought never to be extended too far, or into anything which cannot be properly applied to the person or thing represented.

(8.) In the interpretation of figurative expressions generally, and those which particularly occur in the moral parts of Scripture, the meaning of such expressions ought to be regulated by those which are plain and clear.

4. Lastly, in explaining the figurative language of Scripture, care must be taken that we do not judge of the application of characters from modern usage; because the inhabitants of the East have very frequently attached a character to the idea expressed widely different from that which usually presents itself to our views.[19]

It will be observed from these rules that the same fundamental principles apply to the interpretation of figurative language that apply to any other language. The use of figurative language does not necessitate a non-literal interpretation. The same sound exegesis required elsewhere is required in this field.

[19] Horne, *op. cit.*, I, 356-58.

CHAPTER IV

THE INTERPRETATION OF PROPHECY

I. GENERAL OBSERVATION CONCERNING PROPHECY

The problem that is of particular concern to the student of Eschatology is the problem of interpreting the prophetic portions of Scripture. Before considering the specific rules governing the interpretation of prophecy, it would be well to draw certain general observations concerning the nature of prophetic language.

A. *The characteristic of prophecy.* Some of the general characteristics which are marked features of the prophetic Scriptures are given to us by Oehler, who summarizes:

> The characteristics of Old Testament prophecy are: (1). The matter of revelation being given to the prophet in the form of intuition, the future was made to appear to them as either immediately present, complete, or all events in progress. (2). The fact that the matter of prophecy is given in the form of intuition also furnishes the reason why it always sees the realization of that matter in particular events which are complete in themselves; i.e., a prophecy may appear as just one event, but in reality there may be a two-, three-, or four-fold fulfillment. (3). Since the matter of prophecy presents itself to view as a multitude of individual facts, it may sometimes appear as though single predictions contradict each other when they are, in fact, only those parts into which the ideas revealed have been separated, mutually completing each other, e.g., contrasting pictures of the Messiah in states of suffering and states of glory. (4). The matter of prophecy is in the form of intuition which further means that as far as its form is concerned, it is on the plane of the beholder himself, i.e., the prophet spoke of future glory in terms of his own society and experience.[1]

Von Orelli adds to these basic observations the following:

> (1). Prophecy may be fulfilled shortly after its delivery or at

[1] Gustav Friedrich Oehler, *Theology of the Old Testament*, pp. 488 ff.

a much later date. (2). Prophecy is ethically conditioned, that is, some of it is conditioned as to fulfillment on the behaviour of the recipients. It may even be recalled. (3). Prophecy may be fulfilled successively. (4). We must not pedantically demand that the prophecy be fulfilled exactly as given. Orelli means by this that we must separate the kernel of prediction from the husk of the contemporary garb. (5). Many prophecies, especially those about Christ, are literally fulfilled. (6). The form and character of prophecy are conditioned by the age and location of the writer. (7). Prophecies frequently form parts of a whole and, therefore, must be compared with other prophecy. (8). The prophet sees things together which are widely separated in fulfillment.[2]

B. *The time element in prophecy.* It is to be observed that the time element holds a relatively small place in prophecy. Angus-Green summarize the relationships thus:

> In regard to the language of prophecy, especially in its bearing upon the future, the following points should also be noted:—
>
> 1. The prophets often speak of things that belong to the future as if present to their view. (Isa. 9:6)
>
> 2. They speak of things future as past. (Isa. 53)
>
> 3. When the precise time of individual events was not revealed, the prophets describe them as continuous. They saw the future rather in space than in time; the whole, therefore, appears foreshortened; and perspective, rather than actual distance, is regarded. They seem often to speak of future things as a common observer would describe the stars, grouping them as they appear, and not according to their true positions.[3]

C. *The law of double reference.* Few laws are more important to observe in the interpretation of prophetic Scriptures than the law of double reference. Two events, widely separated as to the time of their fulfillment, may be brought together into the scope of one prophecy. This was done because the prophet had a message for his own day as well as for a future time. By bringing two widely separated events into the scope of the prophecy both purposes could be fulfilled. Horne says:

> The same prophecies frequently have a double meaning, and refer to different events, the one near, the other remote; the one temporal, the other spiritual or perhaps eternal. The prophets thus

---

[2] C. Von Orelli, "Prophecy, Prophets," *International Standard Bible Encyclopaedia,* IV, 2459-66, summarized by Ramm, op. cit., p. 158.

[3] Joseph Angus and Samuel G. Green, *The Bible Hand Book,* p. 245.

> having several events in view, their expressions may be partly applicable to one, and partly to another, and it is not always easy to make the transitions. What has not been fulfilled in the first, we must apply to the second; and what has already been fulfilled, may often be considered as typical of what remains to be accomplished.[4]

It was the purpose of God to give the near and far view so that the fulfillment of the one should be the assurance of the fulfillment of the other. Girdlestone emphasizes this when he says:

> Yet another provision was made to confirm men's faith in utterances which had regard to the far future. It frequently happened that prophets who had to speak of such things were also commissioned to predict other things which would shortly come to pass; and the verification of these latter predictions in their own day and generation justified men in believing the other utterances which pointed to a more distant time. The one was practically a "sign" of the other, and if the one proved true the other might be trusted. Thus the birth of Isaac under the most unlikely circumstances would help Abraham to believe that in his seed all the families of the earth should be blessed.[5]

D. *Conditional prophecies.* It has been stated by Allis that ". . . a condition may be involved in a command or promise without its being specifically stated. This is illustrated by the career of Jonah."[6] On the basis of Jonah's message it is often implied that there are hidden conditions connected with every prophecy which may be the basis for the withdrawal of the fulfillment. In reply to such a contention Horne says:

> Predictions, denouncing judgments to come, do not in themselves speak the absolute futurity of the event, but only declare what is to be expected by the persons to whom they are made, and what will certainly come to pass, unless God in his mercy interpose between the threatening and the event.[7]

Girdlestone deals with the problem of conditioned prophecies at length. He says:

---

[4] Thomas Hartwell Horne, *Introduction to the Critical Study and Knowledge of the Holy Scriptures*, I, 390.

[5] R. B. Girdlestone, *The Grammar of Prophecy*, p. 21.

[6] Oswald T. Allis, *Prophecy and the Church*, p. 32.

[7] Horne, *op. cit.*, I, 391.

Among the points bearing on the nature and fulfilment of prophecy, few call for more special attention than this,—that some predictions are conditional, whilst others are absolute. Many of the utterances of Scripture (*e.g.* Lev. 26) present alternative prospects. . . .

But the conditional nature of a prediction is not always plainly stated in Scripture. Thus, Jonah is said to have preached that within forty days Nineveh should be destroyed; the people repented at his preaching, and Nineveh was not destroyed; yet so far as we know, the people were not told that if they repented the judgment should not fall on them.

Predictions of this class are so numerous that we conclude that there must have been some unexpressed but underlying condition in all such cases which justified God in departing from the literal fulfilment of the prophetic utterance. What that condition is we may gather from such chapters as Jer. 18 and Ezek. 33. After Jeremiah had watched the potter at his work and had learned the great lesson of the Sovereignty of God, a further message was presented to him: "At what instant I shall speak concerning a nation, and concerning a kingdom, to pluck up, and to pull down, and to destroy it; If that nation, against whom I have pronounced, turn from their evil, I will repent of the evil that I thought to do unto them. And at what instant I shall speak concerning a nation, and concerning a kingdom, to build and to plant it; If it do evil in my sight, that it obey not my voice, then I will repent of the good, wherewith I said I would benefit them" [Jer. 18:7-10]. Acting on this principle, Jeremiah speaks thus to the princes when the priests and prophets wanted to have him slain: "Then spake Jeremiah unto all the princes and to all the people, saying, The Lord sent me to prophesy against this house and against this city all the words that ye have heard. Therefore now amend your ways and your doings, and obey the voice of the Lord your God; and the Lord will repent him of the evil that he hath pronounced against you [Jer. 26:12-13]." If the people would repent, in one sense, the Lord would repent, in another. And on what ground? On the ground of the original, essential and eternal attributes of the Divine nature, and on the ground of the old promises and covenants which God had made with the fathers as a result of these attributes.[8]

Even though Girdlestone recognizes that prophecies of judgment may be conditioned on repentance and, according to God's universal dealing with sin and the sinner, judgment might be averted if the sinner turns to God, he does not mean that one can

[8] Girdlestone, *op. cit.*, pp. 25 *ff.*

imply conditions where none are stated in other areas of prophecy. He safeguards against this false conclusion by adding:

> Shall it be said that all prophetic utterances are conditional? By no means. There are some things concerning which "the Lord hath sworn and will not repent" (Ps. 110:4)....
>
> These irreversible promises do not depend on man's goodness, but on God's. They are absolute in their fulfilment, even though they may be conditional as to the time and place of their fulfilment. . . .
>
> Times and seasons may be modified, days may be shortened, events may be accelerated or delayed, individuals and nations may come within the scope of the promises or may stand outside; but the events themselves are ordered and sure, sealed with God's oath, and guaranteed by His very life.[9]

The relationship between the conditional and unconditional aspects of prophecy has been observed by Peters, who comments:

> The prophecies relating to the establishment of the Kingdom of God are both conditioned and unconditioned.
>
> By this paradox is simply meant that they are conditioned in their fulfilment by the antecedent gathering of the elect, and hence susceptible of postponement . . . and that they are unconditioned so far as their ultimate fulfilment is concerned, which the conduct or action of man cannot turn aside. . . . The kingdom itself pertains to the Divine Purpose, is the subject of sacred covenants, is confirmed by solemn oath, is to be the result or end designed in the redemptive process, and therefore cannot, will not, fail. The inheritors of the kingdom, however, are conditioned—a certain number known only to God—and the kingdom itself, although predetermined . . . is dependent . . . as to its manifestation upon their being obtained. . . .[10]

It may then be concluded that although a prophecy which depends on human agency may be conditional yet that which depends on God can not be conditional unless conditions are clearly stated. Prophecies based on unchanging covenants cannot admit the addition of any condition. Thus there is no warrant for assuming any conditions to the fulfillment of prophecy.

---

[9] *Ibid.*, pp. 28 *ff.*
[10] George N. H. Peters, *The Theocratic Kingdom*, I, 176.

II. Methods of Prophetic Revelation

In addition to the straightforward prophetic utterance, future events are revealed through types, symbols, parables, dreams, and prophetic ecstasy. Since there are attendant problems concerning the interpretation of such prophetic revelations, consideration must be given to each of these before considering the problem of the interpretation of prophecy as a whole, for there will be no understanding of prophecy apart from understanding its channels. The student must therefore familiarize himself with the language of prophecy—its figures and symbols as well as its method of communication. Terry says:

> A thorough interpretation of the prophetic portions of the holy Scripture is largely dependent upon a mastery of the principles and laws of figurative language, and of types and symbols. It requires also some acquaintance with the nature of vision-seeing ecstasy and dreams.[11]

A. *Prophetic revelation through types.* Terry has given us a good brief definition of a type, when he says: "In the science of theology it properly signifies the preordained representative relation which certain persons, events and institutions of the Old Testament bear to corresponding persons, events and institutions in the New."[12] This basic concept is enlarged by Angus-Green, as they point out that the following points must be especially noted:

> 1. That which is symbolized—the "antitype"—is the ideal or spiritual reality, at once corresponding to the type and transcending it.
>
> 2. The type may have its own place and meaning, independently of that which it prefigures. Thus the brazen serpent brought healing to the Israelites, even apart from the greater deliverance which it was to symbolize.
>
> 3. Hence it follows that the type may at the time have been unapprehended in its highest character.
>
> 4. As with regard to symbols generally, the essence of a type must be distinguished from its accessories.
>
> 5. The only secure authority for the application of a type is to be found in Scripture. The mere perception of analogy will not

---

[11] Milton R. Terry, *Biblical Hermeneutics*, p. 405.
[12] *Ibid.*, p. 336.

> suffice. Expositors have often imagined correspondence where none in fact exists, and where, even if it did, there is nothing to prove a special Divine intent. . . .
>
> In the words of Bishop Marsh: "To constitute one thing the type of another, as the term is generally understood in reference to Scripture, something more is wanted than mere resemblance. The former must not only resemble the latter, but must have been *designed* to resemble the latter. It must have been so designed *in its original institution.* It must have been designed as *preparatory* to the latter. The type, as well as the antitype, must have been preordained, and they must have been preordained as constituent parts of the same general scheme of Divine Providence. It is this *previous design* and this *preordained* connexion which constitute the relation of type and antitype."[13]

Fritsch not only defines a type carefully, but goes on to give a helpful distinction between a type and an allegory, which it is well to observe. He writes:

> The definition which I propose for the word "type" in its theological sense is as follows: A type is an institution, historical event or person, ordained by God, which effectively prefigures some truth connected with Christianity. . . .
>
> Firstly, by defining the type as an institution, historical event or person we are emphasizing the fact that the type must be meaningful and real in its own right. . . .
>
> In this respect a type differs from an allegory. . . . For an allegory is a fictitious narrative, or to put it less bluntly, in an allegory the historical truth of the narrative dealt with may or may not be accepted, whereas in typology, the fulfillment of an antitype can only be understood in the light of the reality of the original type.
>
> Secondly, there must be a divinely intended connection between the type and the antitype. As Bishop Westcott says, "A type presupposes a purpose in history wrought out from age to age. An allegory rests finally in the imagination. . . ."
>
> Thirdly, the type is not only real and valid in its own right, but it is efficacious in its own immediate milieu. It can only effectively prefigure the antitype because it has inherent in it already at least some of the effectiveness which is to be fully realized in the antitype.
>
> . . . .
>
> Fourthly, the most important characteristic of the type, as has come out in the preceding point, is the fact that it is predictive of

[13] Angus-Green, *op. cit.,* pp. 225-26.

some truth connected with Christianity, or of Christ Himself. . . . Typology differs from prophecy in the strict sense of the term only in the means of prediction. Prophecy predicts mainly by means of the word, whereas typology predicts by institution, act or person.

. . . .

It is most important to make the distinction . . . between type and allegory, for in the early church the allegorical method of interpretation had blurred the true meaning of the Old Testament to such an extent that it was impossible for a legitimate typology to exist. According to this method the literal and historical sense of Scripture is completely ignored, and every word and event is made an allegory of some kind either to escape theological difficulties or to maintain certain peculiar religious views. . . .[14]

Without question, it has been the failure to observe this last distinction which has led some to feel that the Scriptural use of types warrants the allegorical method of interpretation. Fairbairn makes the same observation, which must be heeded, when he writes:

. . . When we interpret a prophecy, to which a double meaning is ascribed, the one relating to the Jewish, the other to the Christian, dispensation, we are in either case concerned with an interpretation of *words*. For the same words which, according to one interpretation, are applied to one event, are, according to another interpretation, applied to another event. But in the interpretation of an allegory, we are concerned only in the *first* instance with in interpretation of words; the *second* sense, which is usually called the allegorical, being an interpretation of *things*. The interpretation of the words gives nothing more than the plain and simple narratives themselves (the allegory generally assuming the form of a narrative); whereas the *moral* of the allegory is learnt by an application of the things signified by those words to other things which resemble them, and which the former were intended to suggest. There is a fundamental difference, therefore, between the interpretation of an allegory, and the interpretation of a prophecy with a double sense.[15]

By its very nature a type is essentially prophetic in character. This has been observed by Fairbairn, who points out:

A type, as already explained and understood, necessarily

---

[14] Charles T. Fritsch, "Biblical Typology," *Bibliotheca Sacra*, 104:214, April, 1947.

[15] Patrick Fairbairn, *The Typology of Scripture*, pp. 131-32.

possesses something of a prophetical character, and differs in form rather than in nature from what is usually designated prophecy. The one images or prefigures, while the other foretells, coming realities. In the one case representative acts or symbols, in the other verbal delineations, serve the purpose of indicating beforehand what God has designed to accomplish for His people in the approaching future. The difference is not such as to affect the essential nature of the two subjects. . . .[16]

In interpreting the prophecies revealed through types, it is important to observe that the same sound hermeneutical maxims that have been previously established apply here as well. Angus-Green give an adequate summary, by saying:

> In the interpretation of all these types, and of history in its secondary or spiritual allusions, we use the same rules as in interpreting parables and allegories properly so called; compare the history or type with the general truth, which both the type and the antitype embody; expect agreement in several particulars, but not in all; and let the interpretation of each part harmonize with the design of the whole, and with the clear revelation of Divine doctrine given in other parts of the sacred volume.
>
> Cautions.—In applying these rules, it is important to remember that the inspired writers never destroyed the historical sense of Scripture to establish the spiritual; nor did they find a hidden meaning in the words, but only in the facts of each passage; which meaning is easy, natural, and Scriptural; and that they confined themselves to expositions illustrating some truth of practical or spiritual importance.[17]

B. *Prophetic revelation through symbols.* The second method of prophetic revelation is through the use of symbols. Ramm, following a generally accepted pattern, says that there may be six kinds of symbols that are prophetic in character: (1) persons, (2) institutions, (3) offices, (4) events, (5) actions, and (6) things.[18]

Bahr gives the following rules to guide in the interpretation of such symbols:

> (1) The meaning of a symbol is to be determined first of all by an accurate knowledge of its nature. (2) The symbols of the Mosaic cultus can have, in general, only such meaning as accords

---

16 *Ibid.*, p. 106.
17 Angus-Green, *op. cit.*, p. 227.
18 Bernard Ramm, *Protestant Biblical Interpretation*, p. 147.

> with the religious ideas and truths of Mosaism, and with its clearly expressed and acknowledged principles. (3) The import of each separate symbol is to be sought, in the first place, from its name. (4) Each individual symbol has, in general, but one signification. (5) However different the connexion in which it may occur, each individual symbol has always the same fundamental meaning. (6) In every symbol, whether it be object or action, the main idea to be symbolized must be carefully distinguished from that which necessarily serves only for its appropriate exhibition, and has, therefore, only a secondary purpose.[19]

Terry presents three fundamental principles in dealing with symbols. He writes:

> . . . we accept the following as three fundamental principles of symbolism: (1) The names of symbols are to be understood literally; (2) the symbols always denote something essentially different from themselves; and (3) some resemblance, more or less minute, is traceable between the symbol and the thing symbolized.
>
> The great question with the interpreter of symbols should, therefore, be, What are the probable points of resemblance between this sign and the thing which it is intended to represent? And one would suppose it to be obvious to every thoughtful mind that in answering this question no minute and rigid set of rules, as supposably applicable to all symbols, can be expected. . . . In general it may be said that in answering the above question the interpreter must have strict regard (1) to the historical standpoint of the writer or prophet, (2) to the scope and context, and (3) to the analogy and import of similar symbols and figures elsewhere used. That is, doubtless, the true interpretation of every symbol which most fully satisfies these several conditions, and which attempts to press no point of supposable resemblance beyond what is clearly warranted by fact, reason, and analogy.[20]

Certainly what has been said by the above writers on the subject of the interpretation of symbols in general will apply to the interpretation of the prophetic symbolism. Terry, however, has added a particular word concerning this specialized field of symbolism:

> In the exposition, therefore, of this class of prophecies it is of the first importance to apply with judgment and skill the hermeneutical principles of biblical symbolism. This process requires,

---

[19] Cited by Terry, *op. cit.*, pp. 357-58.
[20] Terry, *op. cit.*, pp. 356-57.

especially, three things: (1) that we be able clearly to discriminate and determine what are symbols and what are not; (2) that the symbols be contemplated in their broad and striking aspects rather than in their incidental points of resemblance; and (3) that they be amply compared as to their general import and usage, so that a uniform and self consistent method be followed in their interpretation. A failure to observe the first of these will lead to endless confusion of the symbolical and the literal. A failure in the second tends to magnify minute and unimportant points to the obscuring of the greater lessons, and to the misapprehension, ofttimes, of the scope and import of the whole. . . . A care to observe the third rule will enable one to note the differences as well as the likeness of similar symbols. . . .[21]

There is one observation which seems to have been overlooked by many students of the interpretation of prophecy and that is the fact that Scripture interprets its own symbols. Feinberg says:

. . . some prophecy is conveyed to us by means of symbolic language. But whenever such is the case, the symbols are explained in the immediate context, in the book in which they occur, or elsewhere in the Word, no room being left to the imaginations of man to devise explanations.[22]

This same fact is evidenced by Girdlestone, who writes:

Taking the Apocalypse as a whole, there is hardly a figure or vision in it which is not contained in germ in Isaiah, Ezekiel, Daniel, or Zechariah. Probably the study of these Books in his old age had prepared the seer for the visions which had to do with the near or the far future.[23]

Since this is true, diligence in searching the Word is the price of accurate exegesis in symbolic portions.

C. *Prophetic revelation through parables.* A third method of revealing future events is through the use of the parabolic method of instruction. A parable, according to Angus-Green "denotes a narrative constructed for the sake of conveying important truth. . . ."[24] The Lord makes frequent use of this method as the

---

21 *Ibid.*, p. 415.
22 Charles L. Feinberg, *Premillennialism or Amillennialism*, p. 37.
23 Girdlestone, *op. cit.*, p. 87.
24 Angus-Green, *op. cit.*, p. 228.

channel of prophetic revelation. Thus the interpretation of parables is of utmost importance.

Ramm has succinctly stated the rules to guide in interpretation of parables.

> (1). Determine the exact nature and details of the customs, practices, and elements that form the material or natural part of the parable. . . .
>
> (2). Determine the one central truth the parable is attempting to teach.
>
> (3). Determine how much of the parable is interpreted by the Lord Himself. . . .
>
> (4). Determine if there are any clues in the context as to the parable's meaning.
>
> (5). Don't make a parable walk on all fours. . . .
>
> (6). Be careful of the doctrinal use of parables. . . .
>
> (7). A clear understanding of the time-period that many of the parables are intended for is necessary for their full interpretation.[25]

Consistency seems to be the major emphasis in the rules given to us by Angus-Green. They write:

> The first rule of interpretation is: Ascertain what is the scope, either by reference to the context, or to parallel passages; and seize the one truth which the parable is intended to set forth, distinguishing it from all the other truths which border upon it, and let the parts of the parable that are explained be explained in harmony with this one truth. . . .
>
> Any interpretation of a parable or allegory that is inconsistent with the great truth, which it is thus seen to involve, must be rejected.
>
> . . . From the inspired interpretation of parables given us in Scripture, we may gather that we are to avoid both the extreme of supposing that only the design of the whole should be regarded, and the extreme of insisting upon every clause as having a double meaning.
>
> Second rule of interpretation.—Even of doctrines consistent with the design of the parable or type, no conclusion must be gathered from any part of either of them which is inconsistent with other clear revelations of Divine truth. . . .

---

[25] Ramm, *op. cit.*, pp. 179 ff.

Third rule of interpretation.—It is important that parables should not be made the first or sole source of Scripture doctrine. Doctrines otherwise proved may be further illustrated or confirmed by them, but we are not to gather doctrine exclusively or primarily from their representations. . . .[26]

It is of extreme importance when dealing with parables to separate that which is essential from that which is only attendant to the theme. If this is not done false emphasis may be placed on the parable and wrong conclusions drawn.

Horne has given a careful and thorough system of rules to guide in the interpretation of parables. He writes:

1. The first excellence of a parable is, that it turns upon an image well known and applicable to the subject, the meaning of which is clear and definite; for this circumstance will give it that perspicuity which is essential to every species of allegory.

2. The image, however, must not only be apt and familiar, but must also be elegant and beautiful in itself, and all its parts must be perspicuous and pertinent; since it is the purpose of a parable, and especially of a poetic parable, not only to explain more perfectly some proposition, but frequently to give it animation and splendour.

3. Every parable is composed of three parts: 1. The *sensible similitude* . . . the bark. . . . 2. The *explanation* or *mystical sense* . . . the sap or fruit. . . . 3. The *root* or *scope* to which it tends.

4. For the right explanation and application of parables, their general *scope* and design must be ascertained.

5. Wherever the words of Jesus seem to be capable of different senses, we may with certainty conclude that to be the true one which lies most level to the apprehension of his auditors.

6. As every parable has two senses, the *literal* or external, and the *mystical* or internal sense, the literal sense must be first explained, in order that the correspondence between it and the mystical sense may be the more readily perceived.

7. It is not necessary, in the interpretation of parables, that we should anxiously insist upon every single word; nor ought we to expect too curious an adaptation or accommodation of it in every part to the spiritual meaning inculcated by it; for many circumstances are introduced into parables which are merely ornamental, and designed to make the similitude more pleasing and interesting.

[26] Angus-Green, *op. cit.*, pp. 230-33.

8. Attention to *Historical Circumstances,* as well as an acquaintance with the nature and properties of the things whence the similitudes are taken, will essentially contribute to the interpretation of the parables.

9. Lastly, although in many of his parables Jesus Christ has delineated the future state of the church, yet he intended that they should convey some important moral precepts, of which we should never lose sight in interpreting parables.[27]

D. *Prophetic revelation through dreams and ecstasies.* In the earlier periods of prophetic revelation the revelation was frequently made through dreams and ecstatic trances. Terry, on this phase of prophetic revelation, writes:

> Dreams, night visions, and states of spiritual ecstasy are mentioned as forms and conditions under which men receive such revelations. In Num. xii, 6, it is written: "And he said, Hear now my words: if there be a prophet among you, I the Lord will make myself known unto him in a vision, and will speak unto him in a dream."
>
> . . . .
>
> The dream is noticeably prominent among the earlier forms of receiving divine revelations, but becomes less frequent at a later period. The most remarkable instances of dreams recorded in the Scriptures are those of Abimelech (Gen. xx, 3-7), Jacob at Bethel (xxviii, 12), Laban in Mt. Gilead (xxxi, 24), Joseph respecting the sheaves and the luminaries (xxxvii, 5-10), the Midianite (Judg. vii, 13-15). Solomon (1 Kings iii, 5; ix, 2), Nebuchadnezzar (Dan. ii and iv), Daniel (Dan. vii, 1), Joseph (Matt. i, 20; ii, 13, 19), and the Magi from the East (Matt. ii, 12). The "night vision" appears to have been essentially the same nature as the dream (comp. Dan. ii, 19; vii, 1; Acts xvi, 9; xviii, 9; xxvii, 23).
>
> . . . .
>
> But dreams, we observed, were rather the earlier and lower forms of divine revelation. A higher form was that of prophetic ecstasy, in which the spirit of the seer became possessed of the Spirit of God, and, while yet retaining its human consciousness, and susceptible of human emotion, was rapt away into visions of the Almighty and made cognizant of words and things which no mortal could naturally perceive.
>
> . . . .
>
> The prophetic ecstasy . . . was evidently a spiritual sight seeing, a supernatural illumination, in which the natural eye was either closed . . . or suspended from its ordinary functions, and the inner

[27] Horne, *op. cit.,* I, 366-68.

senses vividly grasped the scene that was presented, or the divine word which was revealed.[28]

The interpretation of the prophecies given through dreams or prophetic ecstasy will present no special problems of interpretation. Although the method of giving the prophecy may have been unique that which was given did not differ from a prophecy stated in clear language. In such a revelation the method differed, not the words, and so they may be interpreted without added problems.

III. Rules for the Interpretation of Prophecy

The last section has dealt with the problems relative to the interpretation of prophecies that arise because of the nature of the language involved. Attention is now directed to a discussion of the general principles involved in the interpretation of the prophecies when once that which is prophesied is clearly understood.

The interpretation of prophecy requires attention to the same considerations in regard to words, context, grammar, and historical situations that are the accepted principles in respect to any field of interpretation. Terry states this thus:

> . . . it will be seen that, while duly appreciating the peculiarities of prophecy, we nevertheless must employ in its interpretation essentially the same great principles as in the interpretation of other ancient writings. First, we should ascertain the historical position of the prophet; next the scope and plan of his book; then the usage and import of his words and symbols; and, finally, ample and discriminating comparison of the parallel Scriptures should be made.[29]

There is no lack of lists of rules to guide us in the interpretation of prophecy.[30] Perhaps those suggested by Ramm are the most helpful:

> (1) Determine the historical background of the prophet and the prophecy. (2) Determine the full meaning and significance of all proper names, events, geographical references, references to cus-

---

28 Terry, *op. cit.*, pp. 396-97.

29 *Ibid.*, p. 418.

30 Cf. Ramm, *op. cit.*, pp. 157-162 for a summary of the rules by various writers on hermeneutics.

toms or material culture, and references to flora and fauna. (3) Determine if the passage is predictive or didactic. (4) If predictive determine if fulfilled, unfulfilled, or conditional. (5) Determine if the same theme or concept is also treated elsewhere. (6) As a reminder, keep vividly in mind the flow of the passage, i.e., pay attention to context. (7) Notice that element of the prophecy that is purely local or temporal. (8) Take the literal interpretation of prophecy as the limiting guide in prophetic interpretation.[31]

A. *Interpret literally.* Perhaps the primary consideration in relation to the interpretation of prophecy is that, like all other areas of Biblical interpretation, it must be interpreted literally. Regardless of the form through which the prophetic revelation is made, through that form some literal truth is revealed. It is the problem of the interpreter to discover that truth. Davidson affirms:

> This I consider the first principle in prophetic interpretation —to read the prophet literally—to assume that the literal meaning is *his* meaning—that he is moving among realities, not symbols, among concrete things like peoples, not among abstractions like *our* Church, world, etc.[32]

The reason a non-literal method of interpretation is adopted is, almost without exception, because of a desire to avoid the obvious interpretation of the passage. The desire to bring the teaching of Scripture into harmony with some predetermined system of doctrine instead of bringing doctrine into harmony with the Scriptures has kept the method alive.[33]

Without doubt the greatest confirmation of the literal method of interpreting prophecies comes from an observation of the method God has employed to fulfill the prophecies that have already been fulfilled, Masselink says:

> We can therefore derive our method of interpretation for the unfulfilled prophecy from the fulfilled, because we may safely deduce the guiding principles for the unfulfilled prophecy from the fulfilled predictions which are recorded in the New Testament.[34]

From our vantage point in time prophecy is divided into that which has been fulfilled and that which is unfulfilled. From

---

[31] Ramm, *op. cit.*, pp. 163-73.
[32] A. B. Davidson, *Old Testament Prophecy*, p. 167.
[33] Cf. Angus-Green, *op. cit.*, pp. 247-48.
[34] William Masselink, *Why Thousand Years?*, p. 36.

God's viewpoint prophecy is a unit, indivisible on the time basis. Since it is a unit, and therefore indivisible, that method used in those prophecies that are now fulfilled will also be the method used to fulfill those prophecies that await future fulfillment. In the field of fulfilled prophecy it is not possible to point to any prophecy that has been fulfilled in any way other than literally. The New Testament knows of no other method of fulfilling the Old. God has thus established His divine principle. Feinberg says:

> . . . in the interpretation of prophecy that has not yet been fulfilled, those prophecies which have been fulfilled are to form the pattern. The only way to know how God will fulfill prophecy in the future is to ascertain how He has done it in the past. All the prophecies of the suffering Messiah were literally fulfilled in the first advent of Christ. We have no reason to believe that the predictions of a glorified and reigning Messiah will be brought to pass in any other manner.[35]

The conclusion must be that the New Testament literal method of fulfillment establishes the literal method as God's method in regard to unfilled prophecy.

B. *Interpret according to the harmony of prophecy.* The second rule is laid down in 2 Peter 1:20-21, where the author affirms that no prophecy is of "private interpretation." Prophecy must be interpreted in harmony with the whole prophetic program. Feinberg says:

> There are several well-defined laws for the interpretation of prophecy. The Scripture itself lays down the first and most essential of all. Peter tells us in his second letter that "no prophecy of the scripture is of any private interpretation." By this it is not meant that no private individual can interpret prophecy. The idea intended by the apostle is that no prophecy of the Word is to be interpreted solely with reference to itself . . . but all other portions of the prophetic revelation are to be taken into account and considered. Every prophecy is part of a wonderful scheme of revelation; for the true significance of any prophecy the whole prophetic scheme must be kept in mind and the interrelationship between the parts in the plan as well.[36]

This will call for a careful study, not only of the general

---

35 Feinberg, *op. cit.*, p. 39.
36 *Ibid.*, p. 37.

themes of prophecy, but also of all passages related to any given theme so a harmonized view be gained, for one prediction will often throw light upon another.

C. *Observe the perspective of prophecy.* Events which bear some relationship to one another and are parts of one program, or an event typical of another so that there is a double reference, may be brought together into one prophecy even though separated widely in fulfillment. Feinberg states:

> . . . in the interpretation of prophecy . . . due attention must be paid to perspective. Certain events of the future are seen grouped together in one circumscribed area of vision, although they are really at different distances. This is particularly true of the predictions of the so-called major prophets where many times prophecies concerning the Babylonian captivity, the events of the day of the Lord, the return from Babylon, the world wide dispersion of Israel, and their future regathering from all the corners of the earth, are grouped together seemingly almost indiscriminately.[37]

Failure to observe this principle will result in confusion.

D. *Observe the time relationships.* As has previously been pointed out, events that are widely separated as to the time of their fulfillment may be treated within one prophecy. This is particularly true in the prophecies concerning Christ, where events of the first and second advents are spoken of together as though taking place at the same time. In like manner the second and third dispersions of the Jews are viewed in prophecy as taking place without interruption. Feinberg refers to this principle by saying:

> Another rule of prophetic interpretation is what is known as foreshortening which, according to Dr. Arthur T. Pierson, may assume any one of several forms. Two or more events of a like character may be described by a common profile. . . . Furthermore, a common and important example of foreshortening is evident where future events are placed side by side whereas in the fulfillment there is a great gap. . . .[38]

It is important to observe that the prophet may view widely separated events as continuous, or future things as either past or present.

---

[37] *Ibid.*, p. 38.
[38] *Ibid.*

E. *Interpret prophecy Christologically.* The central theme of all prophecy is the Lord Jesus Christ. His person and His work is the grand theme of the prophetic story. Peter writes:

> Of which salvation the prophets have inquired and searched diligently, who prophesied of the grace that should come unto you; Searching what, or what manner of time the Spirit of Christ which was in them did signify, when it testified beforehand the sufferings of Christ, and the glory that should follow [1 Pet. 1:10-11].

John writes: "... the testimony of Jesus is the spirit of prophecy" (Rev. 19:10). Both are emphasizing this very fact.

F. *Interpret historically.* It hardly need be pointed out that before one can interpret he must know the historical background of the prophet and the prophecy. Ramm says; ". . . a study of history is the *absolute first* starting point in any study of prophecy, whether the prophecy be didactic or predictive."[39] This historical background will include ". . . the full meaning and significance of all proper names, events, geographical references, references to customs or material culture, and references to flora and fauna."[40]

G. *Interpret grammatically.* Sufficient has been said earlier on this point to make it necessary to do no more here than remind the interpreter of prophecy that the strict rules that govern grammatical interpretation must be applied to this field of study with no less care.

H. *Interpret according to the law of double reference.* This has likewise been dealt with previously. It is sufficient to be reminded that oftentimes in a prophecy there may be a near view and far view. Of these the near view may have been fulfilled and the far view await fulfillment, or both may be in the realm of fulfilled prophecy. Again there may have been a double reference to two events of similar character, both of which were in the distant future. The fact that part of the prophecy has been fulfilled without the fulfillment of the rest of it does not argue for a figurative or non-literal method of fulfillment

[39] Ramm, *op. cit.*, p. 163.
[40] *Ibid.*, p. 164.

of that unfulfilled portion, but such a partial fulfillment does promise a complete, literal, future fulfillment of the whole.

I. *Interpret consistently.* It is impossible to mix the methods of interpretation in the field of prophecy. One method must be adopted and used consistently throughout. It may safely be stated that the problem in the interpretation of prophecy is this problem of consistency. To the degree we have been inconsistent in the application of sound hermeneutical principles we have been in error in our conclusions and interpretations. The observance of these sound rules of prophetic interpretation will lead one into a correct interpretation of the Scriptures.

SECTION TWO

THE BIBLICAL COVENANTS AND ESCHATOLOGY

CHAPTER V

THE ABRAHAMIC COVENANT

INTRODUCTION

The covenants contained in the Scriptures are of primary importance to the interpreter of the Word and to the student of Eschatology. God's eschatological program is determined and prescribed by these covenants and one's eschatological system is determined and limited by the interpretation of them. These covenants must be studied diligently as the basis of Biblical Eschatology.

It must be observed at the very outset of this study that the Biblical covenants are quite different from the theological covenants posited by the Covenant theologian. He sees the ages of history as the development of a covenant made between God and sinners, by which God would save, through the value of the death of Christ, all who come to Him by faith. The covenants of the Covenant theologian may be summarized as follows:

> *The Covenant of Redemption* (Titus 1:2; Heb. 13:20) into which, it is usually thought by theologians, the Persons of the Godhead entered before all time and in which each assumed that part in the great plan of redemption which is their present portion as disclosed in the Word of God. In this covenant the Father gives the Son, the Son offers Himself without spot to the Father as an efficacious sacrifice, and the Spirit administers and empowers unto the execution of this covenant in all its parts. This covenant rests upon but slight revelation. It is rather sustained largely by the fact that it seems both reasonable and inevitable.
>
> *The Covenant of Works,* which is the theologian's designation

> for those blessings God has offered men and conditioned on human merit. Before the fall, Adam was related to God by a covenant of works. Until he is saved, man is under an inherent obligation to be in character like his Creator and to do His will.
>
> *The Covenant of Grace,* which is the term used by theologians to indicate all aspects of divine grace toward man in all ages. The exercise of divine grace is rendered righteously possible by the satisfaction to divine judgments which is provided in the death of Christ.[1]

While there is much in the position of the Covenant theologian that is in agreement with Scripture, Covenant theology is woefully inadequate to explain the Scriptures eschatologically, for it ignores the great field of the Biblical covenants which determine the whole eschatological program. The above author says:

> The theological terms, *Covenant of Works* and *Covenant of Grace,* do not occur in the Sacred Text. If they are to be sustained it must be wholly apart from Biblical authority. . . . Upon this human invention of two covenants Reformed Theology has largely been constructed. It sees the empirical truth that God can forgive sinners only by the freedom which is secured by the sacrifice of His Son—anticipated in the old order and realized in the new—but that theology utterly fails to discern the purposes of the ages; the varying relationships to God of the Jews, the Gentiles, and the Church, with the distinctive, consistent human obligations which arise directly and unavoidably from the nature of each specific relationship to God. A theology which penetrates no further into Scripture than to discover that in all ages God is immutable in His grace toward penitent sinners, and constructs the idea of a universal church, continuing through the ages, on the one truth of immutable grace, is not only disregarding vast spheres of revelation but is reaping the unavoidable confusion and misdirection which part-truth engenders.[2]

This study, then, is not occupied with the covenants contained in Reformed theology, but rather with the determinative covenants set forth in the Scriptures.

A. *The Scriptural use of the word* covenant. If one consults a concordance it will be seen that the word *covenant* is one which occurs with frequency in both the Old and New Testaments. It is used of relationships between God and man, man and man,

---

[1] Lewis Sperry Chafer, *Systematic Theology,* I, 42.
[2] *Ibid.,* IV, 156.

nation and nation. It is used in things temporal and things eternal. There are references to minor and temporal covenants in Scripture. Covenants are made by individuals with other individuals (Gen. 21:32; 1 Sam. 18:3). Covenants may be made between an individual and a group of individuals (Gen. 26:28; 1 Sam. 11:1-2). Covenants may be made by one nation with another nation (Ex. 23:32; 34:12, 15; Hos. 12:1). There were covenants in the social realm (Prov. 2:17; Mal. 2:14). Certain natural laws were viewed as covenants (Jer. 33:20, 25). With the exception of these last, which were established by God, all of the uses above govern the relationships made between men.

The Scriptures also contain references to five major covenants, all of which were made by God with men. Lincoln summarizes these:

> The four unconditional covenants, with the formula "I WILL," are found in (1) Genesis 12:1-3, where the formula is found, either expressed or understood, seven times; (2) Deuteronomy 30:1-10, where it is found, either expressed or understood, twelve times; (3) II Samuel 7:10-16, where it is found seven times; and (4) Jeremiah 31:31-40, where it is found seven times. The conditional covenant, with the formula "IF YE WILL," is found (5) besides in Exodus 19:5 ff., also in Deuteronomy 28:1-68; verses 1-14, "If thou shalt hearken diligently . . . blessings"; verses 15-68, "If thou wilt not hearken . . . cursing."[3]

It will be quite obvious that eschatological studies are not concerned with the minor covenants made by man with man, nor with the Mosaic covenant made by God with man, inasmuch as all these are temporary and non-determinative in respect to future things, but only with the four eternal covenants given by God, by which He has obligated Himself in relation to the prophetic program.

B. *The definition of a covenant.* A covenant may be defined as follows:

> A divine covenant is (1) a sovereign disposition of God, whereby he establishes an unconditional or declarative compact with man, obligating himself, in grace, by the untrammelled formula, "I WILL," to bring to pass of himself definite blessings for the covenanted ones, or (2) a proposal of God, wherein he promises,

[3] Charles Fred Lincoln, "The Covenants," p. 26.

> in a conditional or mutual compact with man, by the contingent formula "IF YE WILL," to grant special blessings to man provided he fulfills perfectly certain conditions, and to execute definite punishment in case of his failure.[4]

It is to be observed that this definition does not depart from the customary definition and usage of the word as a legal contract into which one enters and by which his course of action is bound.

C. *The kinds of covenants.* There are two kinds of covenants into which God entered with Israel: conditional and unconditional. In a conditional covenant that which was covenanted depends for its fulfillment upon the recipient of the covenant, not upon the one making the covenant. Certain obligations or conditions must be fulfilled by the receiver of the covenant before the giver of the covenant is obligated to fulfill that which was promised. It is a covenant with an "if" attached to it. The Mosaic covenant made by God with Israel is such a covenant. In an unconditional covenant that which was covenanted depends upon the one making the covenant alone for its fulfillment. That which was promised is sovereignly given to the recipient of the covenant on the authority and integrity of the one making the covenant apart from the merit or response of the receiver. It is a covenant with no "if" attached to it whatsoever.

To safeguard thinking on this point, it should be observed that an unconditional covenant, which binds the one making the covenant to a certain course of action, may have blessings attached to that covenant that are conditioned upon the response of the recipient of the covenant, which blessings grow out of the original covenant, but these conditioned blessings do not change the unconditional character of that covenant. The failure to observe that an unconditional covenant may have certain conditioned blessings attached to it had led many to the position that conditioned blessings necessitate a conditional covenant, thus perverting the essential nature of Israel's determinative covenants.

D. *The nature of the covenants.* There are certain facts which are to be observed concerning the covenants into which God has entered.

---

[4] *Ibid.*, pp. 25-26.

1. First of all, these covenants are *literal* covenants and are to be interpreted literally. Peters has well stated the proposition:

> In all earthly transactions, when a promise, agreement, or contract is entered into by which one party gives a promise of value to another, it is *universally* the custom to explain such a relationship and its promises *by the well-known laws of language* contained in our grammars or in common usage. It would be regarded absurd and trifling to view them in any other light.
>
> . . . .
>
> . . . the very nature of a covenant demands, that it should be so worded, so plainly expressed, that it conveys *a decisive meaning*, and not a hidden or mystical one that requires many centuries to revolve in order to develop.[5]

Such an interpretation would be in harmony with the established literal method of interpretation.

2. In the second place, these covenants, according to the Scriptures, are *eternal*. Lincoln points out:

> All of Israel's covenants are called eternal except the Mosaic covenant which is declared to be temporal, i.e., it was to continue only until the coming of the Promised Seed. For this detail see as follows: (1) The Abrahamic Covenant is called "eternal" in Genesis 17:7, 13, 19; I Chronicles 16:17; Psalm 105:10; (2) The Palestinian Covenant is called "eternal" in Ezekiel 16:60; (3) The Davidic Covenant is called "eternal" in II Samuel 23:5; Isaiah 55:3; and Ezekiel 37:25; and (4) The New Covenant is called "eternal" in Isaiah 24:5; 61:8; Jeremiah 32:40; 50:5; and Hebrews 13:20.[6]

3. In the third place, inasmuch as these covenants are literal, eternal, and depend solely upon the integrity of God for their fulfillment they must be considered to be *unconditional* in character. This question will be considered in detail later.

4. Finally, these covenants were *made with a covenant people*, Israel. In Romans 9:4 Paul states that the nation Israel had received covenants from the Lord. In Ephesians 2:11-12 he states, conversely, that the Gentiles have not received any such covenants and consequently do not enjoy covenant relationships with God. These two passages show us, negatively, that the Gentiles were without covenant relationships and, positively, that God had entered into covenant relationships with Israel.[7]

---

[5] G. N. H. Peters, *The Theocratic Kingdom*, I, 290-91.
[6] Lincoln, *op. cit.*, p. 181.
[7] Cf. *ibid.*, pp. 174-76.

I. The Importance of the Abrahamic Covenant

The first of the four great determinative covenants made by God with the nation Israel was the Abrahamic covenant, which must be considered as the basis of the entire covenant program.

The Scriptures abound in references to the covenant into which God entered with Abraham and its application is seen in many different realms. This covenant has an important bearing on the doctrines of Soteriology. Paul, in writing to the Galatians, shows that believers enter into the blessings promised to Abraham.[8] The argument of Paul in Romans is based upon this same covenant promise made with Abraham.[9] Immediately after the fall of man God revealed His purpose to provide salvation for sinners. This program was gradually unfolded by God to man. The promise made to Abraham represents a progressive step in this revelation.

> In him the Divine Purpose becomes more specific, detailed, contracted, definite, and certain. *Specific,* in distinguishing and separating him from others of the race; *detailed,* in indicating more of the particulars connected with the purpose of salvation; *contracted,* in making the Messiah to come directly in his line, to be his "seed"; *definite,* in entering into covenant relation with him, as his God; and *certain,* in confirming his covenant relationship by an oath.[10]

Again, this covenant has an important bearing on the doctrine of resurrection. The promise entailed in the covenant is the basis of the Lord's refutation of the unbelief of the Sadducees in the fact of resurrection.[11] To those who denied the possibility of resurrection the Lord affirmed that resurrection was not only possible but necessary. Since God had revealed Himself as the God of Abraham, Isaac, and Jacob (Ex. 3:15), with whom He had entered into covenant relationships, and since these men had died without receiving the fulfillment of the promises (Heb. 11:13), inasmuch as the covenants could not be broken it was necessary for God to raise these men from the dead in order

---

[8] Galatians 3:14, 29; 4:22-31.
[9] Romans 4:1-25.
[10] Peters, *op. cit.*, I, 293.
[11] Matthew 22:23-32.

to fulfill His word. Paul, before Agrippa (Acts 26:6-8), unites "the promise to the fathers" with the resurrection of the dead in his defense of the doctrine. Thus the fact of physical resurrection is proved by the Lord and Paul from the necessity laid upon God to fulfill His covenant, even though it entails physical resurrection to do so. Consequently the fact of the believer's resurrection is united to the question of the kind of covenant made with Abraham.[12]

Further, this covenant has a most important bearing on the doctrines of Eschatology. The eternal aspects of this covenant, which guarantee Israel a permanent national existence, perpetual title to the land of promise, and the certainty of material and spiritual blessing through Christ, and guarantee Gentile nations a share in these blessings, determine the whole eschatological program of the Word of God. This covenant becomes the seed from which are brought forth the later covenants made with Israel. The essential areas of the Abrahamic covenant, the land, the seed, and the blessing, are enlarged in the subsequent covenants made with Israel. Lincoln has drawn the comparison thus:

> The inter-relationship of the eternal, gracious covenants of God with Israel might be graphically set forth in the following manner:

(The general, basic covenant with Abraham)	(The other covenants)
1. The promise of a national land. Genesis 12:1 13:14-15, 17	1. The Palestinian Covenant gave Israel particular assurance of final, permanent restoration to the *land.* Deuteronomy 30:3-5 Ezekiel 20:33-37, 42-44
2. The promise of *redemption,* national and universal. Genesis 12:3 22:18 Galatians 3:16	2. The New Covenant has particularly to do with Israel's spiritual blessing and *redemption.* Jeremiah 31:31-40 Hebrews 8:6-13, etc.

[12] Cf. Peters, *op. cit.*, I, 295-97.

3. The promise of numerous descendents to form a great nation.
   Genesis 12:2
   13:16
   17:2-6, etc.

3. The Davidic Covenant has to do with promises of ***dynasty, nation,*** and ***throne.***
   II Samuel 7:11, 13, 16
   Jeremiah 33:20, 21
   31:35-37, etc.[13]

Thus it may be said that the land promises of the Abrahamic covenant are developed in the Palestinian covenant, the seed promises are developed in the Davidic covenant, and the blessing promises are developed in the new covenant. This covenant, then, determines the whole future program for the nation Israel and is a major factor in Biblical Eschatology.

II. The Provisions of the Abrahamic Covenant

The covenant made with Abraham in Genesis 12:1-3, and confirmed and enlarged to him in Genesis 12:6-7; 13:14-17; 15:1-21; 17:1-14; 22:15-18, entitled certain basic promises. These have been summarized:

> The things promised by God are the following: 1. That Abraham's name shall be great. 2. That a great nation should come from him. 3. He should be a blessing so great that in him shall all families of the earth be blessed. 4. To him personally ("to thee") and to his seed should be given Palestine forever to inherit. 5. The multitude of his seed should be as the dust of the earth. 6. That whoever blessed him should be blessed, and whosoever cursed him should be cursed. 7. He should be the father of many nations. 8. Kings should proceed from him. 9. The covenant shall be perpetual, "an everlasting covenant." 10. The land of Canaan shall be "an everlasting possession." 11. God will be a God to him and to his seed. 12. His seed shall possess the gate of his enemies. 13. In his seed shall all the nations of the earth be blessed.[14]

When these particulars are analyzed it will be seen that certain *individual* promises were given to Abraham, certain *national* promises respecting the nation Israel, of which he was the father, were given to him, and certain *universal* blessings that encompassed all nations were given to him. These have been stated by Walvoord:

---

[13] Lincoln, *op. cit.*, pp. 206-7.
[14] Peters, *op. cit.*, I, 293-94.

> The language of the Abrahamic Covenant is plain and to the point. The original covenant is given in Genesis 12:1-3, and there are three confirmations and amplifications as recorded in Genesis 13:14-17; 15:1-7; and 17:1-18. Some of the promises are given to Abraham personally, some to Abraham's seed, and some to Gentiles, or "all families of the earth" (Gen. 12:3).
>
> *The promise to Abraham.* Abraham himself is promised that he would be the father of a great nation (Gen. 12:2), . . . including kings and nations other than the "seed itself" (Gen. 17:6). God promises His personal blessing on Abraham. His name shall be great and he himself shall be a blessing. . . .
>
> *The promise of Abraham's seed.* . . . The nation itself should be great (Gen. 12:2) and innumerable (Gen. 13:16; 15:5). The nation is promised possession of the land . . . the Abrahamic Covenant itself is expressly called "everlasting" (Gen. 17:7) and the possession of the land is defined as "an everlasting possession" (Gen. 17:8).
>
> . . . .
>
> *The promise to Gentiles.* . . . "all families of the earth" are promised blessing (Gen. 12:3). It is not specified what this blessing shall be. As a general promise it is probably intended to have a general fulfillment.[15]

In the development of this covenant it is of utmost importance to keep the different areas in which promise was made clearly in mind, for if the things covenanted in one area are transferred to another area only confusion will result in the subsequent interpretation. Personal promises may not be transferred to the nation and promises to Israel may not be transferred to the Gentiles.

III. The Character of the Abrahamic Covenant

Since the Abrahamic covenant deals with Israel's title deed to the land of Palestine, her continuation as a nation to possess that land, and her redemption so that she may enjoy the blessings in the land under her King, it is of utmost importance to determine the method of the fulfillment of this covenant. If it is a literal covenant to be fulfilled literally, then Israel must be preserved, converted and restored. If it is an unconditional covenant, these events in Israel's national life are inevitable. The

[15] John F. Walvoord, "Millennial Series," *Bibliotheca Sacra*, 108:415-17, October, 1951.

answer to these questions determines one's whole eschatological position.

A. *The conditional element in the covenant program with Abraham.* While Abraham was living in the home of Terah, an idolator (Josh. 24:2), God spoke to him and commanded him to leave the land of Ur, even though it entailed a journey to a strange land he did not know (Heb. 11:8), and made certain specific promises to him that depended on this act of obedience. Abraham, in partial obedience inasmuch as he did not separate himself from his kindred, journeyed to Haran (Gen. 11:31). He did not realize any of the promises there. It was not until after the death of his father (Gen. 11:32) that Abraham begins to realize anything of the promise God had given to him, for only after his father's death does God take him into the land (Gen. 12:4) and there reaffirm the original promise to him (Gen. 12:7). It is important to observe the relation of obedience to this covenant program. Whether God would institute a covenant program with Abraham or not depended upon Abraham's act of obedience in leaving the land. When once this act was accomplished, and Abraham did obey God, God instituted an irrevocable, unconditional program. This obedience, which became the basis of the institution of the program, is referred to in Genesis 22:18, where the offering of Isaac is just one more evidence of Abraham's attitude toward God. Walvoord clearly states this fact when he writes:

> As given in the Scriptures, the Abrahamic Covenant is hinged upon only one condition. This is given in Genesis 12:1. . . . The original covenant was based upon Abraham's obedience in leaving his homeland and going to the land of promise. No further revelation is given him until he was obedient to this command after the death of his father. Upon entering Canaan, the Lord immediately gave Abraham the promise of ultimate possession of the land (Gen. 12:7), and subsequently enlarged and reiterated the original promises.
>
> The one condition having been met, no further conditions are laid upon Abraham; the covenant having been solemnly established is now dependent upon divine veracity for its fulfillment.[16]

---

[16] Walvoord, *op. cit.*, 109:37.

Whether there would be a covenant program with Abraham depended upon Abraham's act of obedience. When once he obeyed, the covenant that was instituted depended, not upon Abraham's continued obedience, but upon the promise of the One who instituted it. The *fact* of the covenant depended upon obedience; the *kind* of covenant inaugurated was totally unrelated to the continuing obedience of either Abraham or his seed.

B. *Arguments to support the unconditional character of the covenant.* The question as to whether the Abrahamic covenant is conditional or unconditional is recognized as the crux of the whole discussion of the problem relating to the fulfillment of the Abrahamic covenant. Extensive argument has been presented to support the contention of the premillennialist as to the unconditional character of this covenant. Walvoord presents ten reasons for believing that this covenant is unconditional. He argues:

> (1) All Israel's covenants are unconditional except the Mosaic. The Abrahamic Covenant is expressly declared to be eternal and therefore unconditional in numerous passages (Gen. 17:7, 13, 19; 1 Chron. 16:17; Ps. 105:10). The Palestinian Covenant is likewise declared to be everlasting (Ezek. 16:60). The Davidic Covenant is described in the same terms (2 Sam. 7:13, 16, 19; 1 Chron. 17:12; 22:10; Isa. 55:3; Ezek. 37:25). The new covenant with Israel is also eternal (Isa. 61:8; Jer. 32:40; 50:5; Heb. 13:20).
>
> (2) Except for the original condition of leaving his homeland and going to the promised land, the covenant is made with no conditions whatever. . . .
>
> (3) The Abrahamic Covenant is confirmed repeatedly by reiteration and enlargement. In none of these instances are any of the added promises conditioned upon the faithfulness of Abraham's seed or of Abraham himself . . . nothing is said about it being conditioned upon the future faithfulness of either Abraham or his seed.
>
> (4) The Abrahamic Covenant was solemnized by a divinely ordered ritual symbolizing the shedding of blood and passing between the parts of the sacrifice (Gen. 15:7-21; Jer. 34:18). This ceremony was given to Abraham as an assurance that his seed would inherit the land in the exact boundaries given to him in Genesis 15:18-21. No conditions whatever are attached to this promise in this context.
>
> (5) To distinguish those who would inherit the promises as individuals from those who were only physical seed of

Abraham, the visible sign of circumcision was given (Gen. 17:9-14). One not circumcised was considered outside the promised blessing. The ultimate fulfillment of the Abrahamic Covenant and possession of the land by the seed is not hinged, however, upon faithfulness in the matter of circumcision. In fact the promises of the land were given before the rite was introduced.

(6) The Abrahamic Covenant was confirmed by the birth of Isaac and Jacob to both of whom the promises are repeated in their original form (Gen. 17:19; 28:12-13). . . .

(7) Notable is the fact that the reiterations of the covenant and the partial early fulfillment of the covenant are in spite of acts of disobedience. It is clear that on several instances Abraham strayed from the will of God. . . . In the very act . . . the promises are repeated to him.

(8) The later confirmations of the covenant are given in the midst of apostasy. Important is the promise given through Jeremiah that Israel as a nation will continue forever (Jer. 31:36). . . .

(9) The New Testament declares the Abrahamic Covenant immutable (Heb 6:13-18; cf. Gen. 15:8-21). It was not only promised but solemnly confirmed by the oath of God.

(10) The entire Scriptural revelation concerning Israel and its future as contained in both the Old and New Testaments, if interpreted literally, confirms and sustains the unconditional character of the promises given to Abraham.[17]

From these considerations it must be acknowledged that the premillennial position rests upon many varied and weighty arguments.[18]

A word of explanation is necessary concerning the event recorded in Genesis 15 because of its bearing on the question of the unconditional character of this covenant. In Genesis 14 Abraham, because he was trusting God, refused to take riches from the king of Sodom. Lest a question should arise in Abraham's mind as to whether he had made a mistake in thus trusting God, Abraham is given an assurance from God that He is Abraham's protection (shield) and provision (reward) (Gen. 15:1). In response to Abraham's question about the promised heir, God affirms that he will have a son, and "Abraham believed God" (Gen. 15:6). In response to Abraham's faith, as substantiating evidence that he has not trusted God in vain, a sign is given to Him that

[17] *Ibid.*, 109:38-40.
[18] Cf. Charles C. Ryrie, *The Basis of the Premillennial Faith*, pp. 53-61.

that promise will be fulfilled (Gen. 15:9-17). In order to reaffirm the covenant to Abraham concerning the *seed* and the *land* (Gen. 15:18) Abraham is told by God to prepare animals of sacrifice that together they might enter into a blood covenant. Concerning this ritual Keil and Delitzsch say:

> The proceeding corresponding rather to the custom, prevalent in many ancient nations, of slaughtering animals when concluding a covenant, and after dividing them into pieces, of laying the pieces opposite to one another, that the persons making the covenant might pass between them. Thus . . . God condescended to follow the custom of the Chaldeans, that He might in the most solemn manner confirm His oath to Abram the Chaldean. . . . it is evident from Jer. xxxiv. 18, that this was still customary among the Israelites of later times.[19]

Abraham would be familiar with this manner of entering into a binding agreement. Without doubt the large number of animals prescribed by God would impress Abraham with the importance of that which was being enacted, since one animal would have been sufficient for the enactment of the covenant. When the sacrifice was prepared Abraham must have expected to walk with God through the divided animals, for custom demanded that the two who entered into a blood covenant should walk together between the parts of the sacrifice. He would recognize the solemnity of the occasion, for the ritual meant that the two who were entering into the covenant were bound by blood to fulfill that covenanted or the one breaking the covenant would be required to pour out his blood in forfeit, as the blood of the animals that bound them had been poured out. However, when the covenant was to be entered into, Abraham was put to sleep so that he could not be a participant in the covenant, but could only be a recipient of a covenant to which he brought nothing in the way of obligations. Keil and Delitzsch explain the passage thus:

> From the nature of this covenant, it followed, however, that God alone went through the pieces in a symbolical representation of Himself, and not Abram also. For although a covenant always establishes a reciprocal relation between two individuals, yet in that covenant which God concluded with a man, the man did not stand on an equality with God, but God established the rela-

[19] C. F. Keil and Franz Delitzsch, *The Pentateuch*, I. 214.

> tion of fellowship by His promise and His gracious condescension to the man.[20]

God is thus binding Himself by a most solemn blood covenant to fulfill to Abraham, unconditionally, the promises concerning the seed and the land which were given to him. It is scarcely possible for God to make it any clearer that what was promised to Abraham was given to him without any conditions, to be fulfilled by the integrity of God alone.

C. *The amillennial arguments against the unconditional character of the covenant.* Allis, one of the leading exponents of the amillennial position, systematizes the thinking of that school of interpretation. He presents a number of arguments against the unconditional character of the covenant.

> (1) First of all it is to be observed that a condition may be involved in a command or promise without its being specifically stated. This is illustrated by the career of Jonah. Jonah was commanded to preach judgment, unconditioned, unqualified: "Yet forty days, and Nineveh shall be overthrown." . . . The unstated condition was presupposed in the very character of God as a God of mercy and compassion. . . . The judgment on Eli's house (I Sam. ii: 30) is a very striking illustration of this principle. . . .[21]

Allis thus argues that conditions may be implied that are not stated.

In reply to this argument it will readily be observed that Allis begins with a most damaging admission—there are no stated conditions in Scripture to which the amillennialist may turn for confirmation of his position. His whole case rests on silence, on implied and unstated conditions. In the case of Eli, there is no parallel whatsoever, for Eli was living under the Mosaic economy, which was conditional in character, and the Mosaic economy was unrelated to the Abrahamic covenant. Because the Mosaic covenant was conditional it does not follow that the Abrahamic must be also. And again, in reference to Jonah, it must be seen that there is no parallel there either. Jonah's preached word was not a covenant, and in no way parallels the Abrahamic covenant. It was a well-established Scriptural principle (Jer.

---

[20] *Ibid.*, I, 216.
[21] Oswald T. Allis, *Prophecy and the Church*, p. 32.

18:7-10; 26:12-13; Ezek. 33:14-19) that repentance would remove judgment. The people repented and judgment was removed. But the preaching of Jonah, of which only a summary statement is given, in no way alters the character of the Abrahamic covenant.

> (2) It is true that, in the express terms of the covenant with Abraham, obedience is not stated as a condition. But that obedience was presupposed is clearly indicated by two facts. The one is that obedience is the precondition of blessing under all circumstances. . . . The second fact is that in the case of Abraham the duty of obedience is particularly stressed. In Gen. xviii. 17f it is plainly stated that, through His choice of Abraham, God proposed to bring into being, by pious nurture, a righteous seed which would "keep the way of the Lord," in order that as a result and reward of such obedience "the Lord may bring upon Abraham that which he hath spoken of him."[22]

Once again Allis admits that the Scriptures nowhere contain any statement of a stipulated condition. While this ought to be sufficient in itself, there are other considerations concerning this argument. First of all, it is wrong to state that obedience is always a condition of blessing. If this were true, how could a sinner ever be saved? Walvoord writes:

> It is not true that obedience is always the condition of blessing. The seed of Abraham have been disobedient in every moral category. Yet in spite of that disobedience they have fulfilled many of the promises of the covenant. The very principle of grace is that God blesses the unworthy. . . . The security of the believer . . . is quite independent of human worth or faithfulness. . . . As a Calvinist, where is Allis' doctrine of unconditional election?[23]

Again, it is important to observe that an unconditional covenant, which renders a covenanted program certain, may have conditional blessings attached. The program will be carried to fulfillment, but the individual receives the blessings of that program only by conforming to the conditions on which the blessings depend. Such is true with the Abrahamic covenant. And further, it has already been pointed out that whether God instituted a covenant program with Abraham depended on his act of obedience in leaving his home, but when once the covenant

---

[22] *Ibid.*, p. 33.
[23] Walvoord, *op. cit.*, 109:40-41.

was inaugurated it was without any conditions whatsoever. And finally, the covenant is reaffirmed and enlarged to Abraham after definite acts of disobedience (Gen. 12:10-20, 16:1-16).

> (3) That obedience was vitally connected with the Abrahamic covenant is shown with especial clearness by the fact that there was connected with it a sign, the rite of circumcision, to the observance of which the utmost importance was attached. Cutting off from the covenant people was the penalty for failure to observe it. . . . The rite was in itself an act of obedience (1 Cor. vii. 19).[24]

In reply to this allegation it is sufficient to point out that the rite of circumcision, given in Genesis 17:9-14, comes many years after the institution of the covenant, and after repeated reaffirmations of that covenant to Abraham (Gen. 12:7; 13:14-17; 15:1-21). What point is there in requiring a sign to continue the covenant when the covenant is clearly operative before the institution of the sign? Then, again, it is seen from a study of the rite that circumcision is related to the enjoyment of the blessings of the covenant rather than to the institution or continuance of that covenant. Walvoord observes:

> All agree that the individual enjoyment of blessing under the covenant is to a large degree dependent upon the individual's faith and obedience. This is quite different than stating that the fulfillment of the covenant as a whole is conditioned upon obedience of the nation as a whole.[25]

Related to the same general line of thinking, Allis continues:

> (4) That those who insist that the Abrahamic covenant was wholly unconditional, do not really so regard it is shown also by the great importance which Dispensationalists attach to Israel's being "in the land" as the precondition of blessing under this covenant.[26]
>
> (5) That Dispensationalists do not regard the Abrahamic covenant as wholly unconditional is indicated also by the fact that we never hear them speak of the restoration of Esau to the land of Canaan and to full blessing under the Abrahamic covenant. . . . But if the Abrahamic covenant was unconditional why is Esau excluded from the blessings of the covenant?[27]

---

24 Allis, *op. cit.*, p. 34.
25 Walvoord, *op. cit.*, 109:42.
26 Allis, *loc. cit.*
27 *Ibid.*, p. 35.

These two arguments may be answered together. It will be observed, in each case, that it is relationship to the blessings which is in view, not relationship to the continuation of the covenant. As stated previously, the blessings were conditioned upon obedience, upon remaining in the place of blessing. But the covenant itself was operative whether they were in the land or the recipients of blessing or not. Contrariwise, if the disobedience and removal from the land annulled the covenant, it would not matter whether Esau remained in the land or not. But since blessings would come on the covenant people, Esau was excluded because he was not eligible to receive the blessings since he was in unbelief. It will be observed that the birthright (Gen. 25:27-34) which Esau despised was the promise to which he was heir under the Abrahamic covenant. Since it rested on the integrity of God, Esau must be seen to be a man who did not believe God could or would fulfill His word. In like manner the blessing forfeited (Gen. 27) was that blessing due him under the covenant, which must be forfeited because of his unbelief manifested in surrendering the birthright. The rejection of Esau illustrates the fact that the covenant was selective, and to be fulfilled through God's own chosen line.

> (6) . . . the certainty of the fulfillment of the covenant is not due to the fact that it is unconditional, or is its fulfillment dependent upon the imperfect obedience of sinful men. The certainty of the fulfillment of the covenant and the security of the believer under it, ultimately depends wholly on the obedience of Christ.[28]

One can not help but notice the complete change in the line of reasoning at this point. Heretofore it has been argued that the covenant will not be fulfilled because it is a conditional covenant. Now it is argued that the covenant will be fulfilled on the basis of the obedience of Christ. Because our spiritual blessings are the outgrowth of this covenant (Gal. 3), the amillennialist is forced to concede some fulfillment of it. If it were abrogated Christ would never have come. If the security offered under it were conditional there would be no assurance of salvation. While it is freely agreed that all the fulfillment rests on the

[28] *Ibid.*, p. 36.

obedience of Christ, that fact does not alter the essential character of the covenant that made the coming of Christ necessary. If Christ came as a partial fulfillment of the covenant, His coming promises a complete fulfillment.

Allis follows another line of argument when he writes concerning the fulfillment of this covenant:

> (1) As to the *seed,* it is to be observed that the very words which appear in the covenant . . . are used of the nation of Israel in the time of Solomon. . . . This would indicate that the promise was regarded as fulfilled in this respect in the golden age of the Monarchy. . . .
>
> (2) As to the *land,* the dominion of David and of Solomon extended from the Euphrates to the River of Egypt . . . Israel did come into possession of the land promised to the patriarchs. She possessed it, but not "for ever." Her possession of the land was forfeited by disobedience . . . it can be regarded as having been fulfilled centuries before the first advent. . . .[29]

He argues now that the covenant will not have a future fulfillment because it has already been fulfilled historically.

The question of the historical fulfillment of the covenant will be considered later. Suffice it to say at the present that Israel's history, even under the glories of the Davidic and Solomonic reigns, never fulfilled that promised originally to Abraham. Therefore that historical experience cited can not be construed to be the fulfillment of the covenant. Further, if the covenant were conditional, since Israel was in disobedience many times between the institution of the covenant and the establishment of the Davidic throne, how can any fulfillment at all be explained? The unbelief following the Davidic era did not differ in kind from the unbelief that preceded it. If the subsequent unbelief abrogated the covenant, the preceding unbelief would have prevented any fulfillment of it at all.

D. *The partial fulfillment of the covenants supports the premillennial view.* Any examination of the portions of the Abrahamic covenant that have had either a partial or complete fulfillment supports the contention that the covenant was to be interpreted as a literal and unconditional covenant. Ryrie says:

---

[29] *Ibid.,* pp. 57-58.

> . . . God's method in fulfilling parts of the Abrahamic covenant has been *literal.*
>
> (1) In fulfillment of the personal promises, Abraham was specially blessed of God. Lincoln has pointed out:
>
> "a. Abraham was blessed personally in temporal things: (1) he had land (Gen. 13:14, 15, 17); (2) He had servants (Gen. 15:7, etc.); (3) He had much cattle, silver, and gold (Gen. 13:2, 24:34, 35).
>
> "b. Abraham was blessed personally in spiritual matters: (1) He had a happy life of separation unto God, (Gen. 13:8; 14:22, 23); (2) He enjoyed a precious life of communion with God, (Gen. 13:18); (3) He had a consistent life of prayer, (Gen. 28:23-33); (4) He was sustained of God constantly, (Gen. 21:22); (5) He possessed the peace and confidence that comes from an obedient life, (Gen. 22:5, 8, 10, 12, 16-18)."
>
> (2) He had a great name. . . .
>
> (3) He was a channel of divine blessing to others, for he not only blessed his household, his posterity, but the world at large through the Bible, the Saviour, and the gospel.
>
> (4) History has borne out the fact that nations which have persecuted Israel, even when that very persecution was in fulfillment of God's discipline, have been punished for dealing with Abraham's seed. This has been true in both blessings and cursing in the case of the slaughter of the kings (Gen. 14:12-16); in the case of Melchizedek (Gen. 14:18-20); in the case of Abimelech (Gen. 20:2-18; 21:22-34); in the case of Heth (Gen. 23:1-20); and in other experiences in Israel's history (Deut. 30:7; Isa. 14:1-2; Joel 3: 1-8; Matt. 25:40-45).
>
> (5) Abraham did have an heir by Sarah (Gen. 21:2). . . .
>
> Denial that these aforementioned promises have been fulfilled is puerile.[30]

This point is well illustrated from Psalm 69. All of the predictions concerning the humiliation and affliction of Christ were literally fulfilled. That which follows His death is seen to be the fulfillment of the covenants, for the Psalmist says:

> For God will save Zion, and will build the cities of Judah, that they may dwell there and have it in possession. The seed also of His servants shall inherit it; and they that love His name shall dwell therein [Ps. 69:35-36].

As the picture of Messiah's death was literally fulfilled it can

---

[30] Ryrie, *op. cit.*, pp. 50-52.

only be concluded that that which flows from Messiah's death in fulfillment of the covenants will be literally fulfilled also.[31] It should be obvious that the method used by God to fulfill prophecies that have been fulfilled historically will be His method in the fulfillment of all prophecies. Inasmuch as all prophecies that have been fulfilled have been fulfilled literally, consistency demands that this method must be adopted for those portions of the prophetic Scriptures that, as yet, may be unfulfilled. Since the portions of the Abrahamic covenant that have been fulfilled were fulfilled literally, it would be concluded that the unfulfilled portions will be fulfilled in like manner.

It seems quite evident that the patriarchs themselves understood the covenant to be eternal, unconditional, unequivocable, and therefore certain as to its fulfillment.[32] The statement of Isaac to Jacob when Jacob went away bears this out:

> God Almighty bless thee, and make thee fruitful, and multiply thee, that thou mayest be a multitude of people; and give thee the blessing of Abraham, *to thee and to thy seed with thee,* that *thou* mayest inherit the land, wherein *thou* art a stranger, which God gave unto Abraham [Gen. 28:3-4. Italics mine.]

IV. The Eschatological Implications of the Abrahamic Covenant

When it has been determined that the Abrahamic covenant is an unconditional covenant made with Israel, and therefore cannot be either abrogated or fulfilled by people other than the nation Israel, it is seen that Israel has promises regarding a *land* and a *seed,* which determine the future program of God. These words *land* and *seed,* together with the word *blessing,* summarize the essential features of the eschatological portion of the covenant. An examination of the promises of God to Abraham will show this twofold emphasis in the promise.

> Unto thy *seed* will I give this *land* [Gen. 12:7].
>
> For all the *land* which thou seest, to thee will I give it, and to thy *seed* forever. And I will make thy *seed* as the dust of the earth: so that if a man can number the dust of the earth, then shall their *seed* also be numbered [Gen. 13:15-16].

---

31 Cf. Peters, *op. cit.*, I, 303-4.
32 Cf. *ibid.*, I, 294.

> In the same day the Lord made a covenant with Abram, saying, Unto thy *seed* have I given this *land* [Gen. 15:18].
>
> And I will establish my covenant between me and thee and thy *seed* after thee in their generations for an everlasting covenant, to be a God unto thee, and to thy *seed* after thee. And I will give unto thee, the *land* wherein thou art a stranger, all the *land* of Canaan, for everlasting possession [Gen. 17:7-8. Italics mine.]

It is impossible to escape the conclusion that the promise included features related to the physical seed of Abraham and features related to the land given that seed. It is necessary, then, to examine the areas of the *seed* and the *land* to determine their effect on future events.

Ryrie outlines the implications of the covenant. He says:

> All agree that the Abrahamic covenant is one of the outstanding covenants in the Word of God. Its crucial issues in relation to premillennialism are two: (1) Does the Abrahamic covenant promise Israel a permanent existence as a nation? If it does, then the Church is not fulfilling Israel's promises, but rather Israel as a nation has a future yet in prospect; and (2) does the Abrahamic covenant promise Israel permanent possession of the promised land? If it does, then Israel must yet come into possession of the land, for she has never fully possessed it in her history.[33]

A. *Who is the seed of Abraham?* It would seem obvious to all who are not deliberately trying to pervert the plain teaching of Scripture that the seed of Abraham, of necessity, is the term applied to the physical descendants of Abraham. Walvoord writes:

> An examination of the whole context of the Abrahamic Covenant shows that first of all it was vitally connected with Abraham's physical seed, Isaac. God said of Isaac before he was born, "I will establish my covenant with him for an everlasting covenant and with his seed after him" (Gen. 17:19). How did Abraham understand the term *seed* here? Obviously, it had reference to the physical seed, Isaac, and his physical descendants. God did not say that no spiritual blessing would come to those outside the physical seed, but the physical line of Isaac would inherit the promises given to the "seed of Abraham."
>
> . . . Nothing should be plainer than that Abraham, Isaac, and Jacob understood the term *seed* as referring to their physical lineage.[34]

---

[33] Ryrie, *op. cit.*, pp. 48-49.
[34] Walvoord, *op. cit.*, 109:137-38.

And again:

> The term "Israel." . . . As a title given to Jacob, meaning *prince of God,* it has commonly been used to designate the physical descendants of Jacob.[35]

This seems so obvious one is no little surprised to read the statement of a leading amillennialist, who says:

> Carrying to an almost unprecedented extreme that literalism which is characteristic of Millenarianism, they insist that Israel must mean Israel, and that the kingdom promises in the Old Testament concern Israel and are to be fulfilled to Israel literally.[36]

It may be pointed out that the view advocated by the premillennialist can hardly be called an "unprecedented extreme" of literalism, for others beside premillennialists, forced to do so because of consistency in interpretation, have held that Israel means just what the word implies. Hodge,[37] a postmillennialist, as well as Hendricksen,[38] an amillennialist, have so held. It is important to observe that one must distinguish between the personal promises to Abraham himself, the national promises to Abraham's seed, and the universal promises to "all families of the earth." It is not denied that the Abrahamic covenant offers universal blessings to those who are not the physical seed of Abraham, but it is affirmed that the national promises can only be fulfilled by the nation itself. Thus, the word Israel is taken in its usual, literal, sense to mean the physical descendants of Abraham.

B. *The amillennial view of the seed of Abraham.* Pieters, a leading exponent of the amillennial system, defines the seed:

> The expression "Seed of Abraham," in biblical usage, denotes that visible community, the members of which stand in relation to God through the Abrahamic Covenant, and thus are heirs to the Abrahamic promise.[39]

He enlarges this by saying:

> Whenever we meet with the argument that God made certain promises to the Jewish race . . . [certain] facts are pertinent.

---

[35] *Ibid.,* 109:139.
[36] Allis, *op. cit.,* p. 218.
[37] Charles Hodge, *Commentary on Romans,* p. 589.
[38] William Hendriksen, *And So All Israel Shall Be Saved,* p. 33.
[39] Albertus Pieters, *The Seed of Abraham,* pp. 19-20.

> God never made any promises to any race at all, as a race. All the promises were to the continuing covenanted community, without regard to its racial constituents or to the personal ancestry of the individuals in it. Hence no proof that those whom the world now calls "the Jews" are descended from Abraham, if it could be supplied (which it can not), would be of any avail to prove that they are entitled to the fulfillment of any divine promise whatsoever. These promises were made to the covenanted group called "The Seed of Abraham," and to that community they must be fulfilled. What is needed is that one shall bring forward proof of his membership in that group.[40]

Walvoord succinctly summarizes this view by saying:

> The amillennial viewpoint as represented by Pieters holds then, to the following position: (1) God never made any promises to the physical seed of Abraham as a race; (2) the Abrahamic promises are given only to the spiritual seed of Abraham or the "continuing covenanted community"; (3) Jews today have no claim on the promise to Abraham because (a) they are not the spiritual seed; (b) they could not prove that they are the physical seed anyway.[41]

According to the amillennial view the seed would be the whole "household of faith," or all believers of all ages. The determining factor, then, in this whole discussion is the method of interpretation. If the Scriptures are to be interpreted figuratively then the amillennial view is logical, but if they are to be interpreted literally the premillennial view is necessary.

C. *The kinds of seeds mentioned in Scripture.* The whole issue may be clarified if one observes that the Scripture does not present just one kind of seed that is born to Abraham. The failure to observe this differentiation of Scripture has led to confusion. Walvoord writes:

> There are, then, three different senses in which one can be a child of Abraham. First, there is the natural lineage, or natural seed. This is limited largely to the descendants of Jacob in the twelve tribes. To them God promises to be their God. To them was given the law. To them was given the land of Israel in the Old Testament. With them God dealt in a special way. Second, there is the spiritual lineage within the natural. These are the Israelites who believed in God, who kept the law, and who met the conditions for present enjoyment of the blessings of the covenant.

---

40 *Ibid.*
41 Walvoord, *op. cit.*, 109:137.

> Those who ultimately possess the land in the future millennium will also be of spiritual Israel. Third, there is the spiritual seed of Abraham who are not natural Israelites. Here is where the promise to "all the families of the earth" comes in. This is the express application of this phrase in Galatians 3:6-9. . . . in other words, the children of Abraham (spiritually) who come from the heathen or Gentiles fulfill that aspect of the Abrahamic Covenant which dealt with Gentiles in the first place, not the promises pertaining to Israel. The only sense in which Gentiles can be Abraham's seed in the Galatians context is to be "in Christ Jesus" (Gal. 3:28). It follows: "And if ye be Christ's, then are ye Abraham's seed, and heirs according to the promise" (Gal. 3:29). They are Abraham's seed in the spiritual sense only and heirs of the promise given "to all the families of the earth."
>
> While premillenarians can agree with amillenarians concerning the fact of a spiritual seed for Abraham which includes Gentiles, they deny that this fulfills the promises given to the natural seed or that the promises to the "seed of Abraham" are fulfilled by Gentile believers. To make the blessings promised all the nations the same as the blessings promised the seed of Abraham is an unwarranted conclusion.[42]

This distinction will explain how the church may be related to the promises of the covenant without being the covenant people in whom the national promises will be fulfilled. Because we are the seed of Abraham spiritually by the new birth, it does not mean we are the physical seed of the patriarch.

D. *The church is not Israel.* The only logical conclusion that can grow out of this discussion is that the Gentile believers of the present day, while reckoned as *a* seed to Abraham, are not *the* seed in which national promises are to be fulfilled. This is well proved by observing certain facts in the New Testament usage of the words. (1) Natural Israel and the Gentiles are contrasted in the New Testament (Acts 3:12; 4:8; 21:28; Rom. 10:1). The fact that Israel is addressed as a nation after the establishment of the church and that the term *Jew* continues to be used as distinct from the church (1 Cor. 10:32) shows that the Gentiles do not supplant Israel in God's covenant program. (2) Natural Israel and the church are contrasted in the New Testament (Rom. 11:1-25; 1 Cor. 10:32). In Romans 11 it is shown that God has taken the nation Israel out of the place of blessing tem-

---

[42] *Ibid.*, 108:420.

porarily, but will restore them to that place of blessing when His program with the church is terminated. This consideration shows that the church does not supplant Israel in God's covenant program. (3) Jewish Christians, who would be a part of spiritual Israel, and Gentile Christians are contrasted in the New Testament (Rom. 9:6, where Paul contrasts these promises which belong to Israel according to the flesh and those which belong to Israel who enter into them by faith; Gal. 6:15-16, where Paul specifically mentions believing Jews in the benediction pronounced on the whole body of Christ).[43] The point seems to be well established, then, that the church today is not Israel in whom these covenants are fulfilled. It is strange that the amillennialist, who argues that the covenants need not be fulfilled because they were conditional and the conditions were not met by Israel, and who argues further that they will not be fulfilled because they have been historically fulfilled in the Solomonic kingdom, now argues that they are being fulfilled by the church. If they were conditional or already fulfilled why not ignore the covenant promises entirely? Why make such an issue of it? The only answer is that the covenants form such a foundation for the whole expectation of the Word of God that they can not be ignored, even by those who deny their existence or their relevancy to the eschatological program.

E. *The relation of the church to the covenant.* Since the church is not the seed in whom the covenants will be finally and literally fulfilled, it is well to consider the question of her relation to the whole covenant program. Any relationship which the church sustains to the promises is based, not on physical birth, but on a new birth, and is hers because the individuals are "in Christ." Peters well points this out:

> It is said that "the Seed" shall inherit the land; and we are told by many that this was fulfilled in the history of the Jews under Joshua, the Judges, and the Kings. What, however, are *the facts as given by the Holy Spirit?* Certainly, in the interpretation of covenant promise, Holy Writ should be allowed to be *its own interpreter,* that we may ascertain the meaning intended by God. Let God, then, and not man, explain: "Now (Gal. 3:16) to Abraham and his seed were the promises made. He saith not, 'And

[43] Cf. Ryrie, *op. cit.,* pp. 63-70.

> to seeds' as of many, but as of one, 'And to thy seed,' which is Christ." If language has any definite meaning, then, without doubt we have here the simple declaration that when God promised "Unto thy seed will I give this land," He meant that the land of Canaan should *be inherited by a single Person—pre-eminently the Seed—descended from Abraham, even Jesus Christ.*[44]

The church receives of the promises solely because of relationship to the One in whom the promises find fulfillment. She participates with Him in all He does to bring the covenant to completion. In citing the Abrahamic covenant, Peter, in Acts 3:25, applies only the universal aspects of the covenant to those to whom he speaks. The national aspects must await future fulfillment by the nation Israel.

F. *Will the seed possess the land?* It is evident from the previous discussion of the covenant that the physical seed of Abraham was promised the eternal possession of the land. Walvoord says:

> The promise of possession of the land by the seed of Abraham is a prominent feature of the covenant, and the way the promise is given enhances its significance. The promise as given emphasizes that (1) it is gracious in its principle; (2) the land is an inheritance of the seed; (3) its title is given forever; (4) the land is to be possessed forever; (5) the land promised includes specific territory defined by boundaries.[45]

This promise is the basis of the expectation of the Old Testament, and the substance of the prophets' message.[46] If Israel has been rejected as a nation because of its unbelief, this great line of Old Testament prophecy would be without the possibility of fulfillment. Ryrie well answers the argument that Israel has been set aside. He writes:

> . . . Since some insist that the nation has been completely rejected of God, two passages of Scripture must be carefully examined.
>
> The first one is Matthew 21:43: "Therefore say I unto you,

[44] Peters, *op. cit.*, I, 302.

[45] Walvoord, *op. cit.*, 109:218.

[46] Cf. Isa. 11:1-11; 14:1-3; 27:12-13; 43:1-8; 49:8-16; 66:20-22; Jeremiah 16:14-16; 30:10-11; 31:8, 31-37; Ezekiel 11:17-21; 20:33-38; 34:11-16; 39:25-29; Hosea 1:10-11; Joel 3:17-21; Amos 9:11-15; Micah 4:4-7; Zeph. 3:14-20; Zech. 8:4-8.

The kingdom of God shall be taken from you, and given to a nation bringing forth the fruits thereof." . . . an accurate interpretation of this verse must answer these questions: what will be taken away, from whom is it taken, and to whom is it given?

It is the kingdom of God that is taken from them . . . the kingdom of God is the sphere of true faith in God. . . . The Lord is saying to these Jews that, because they had rejected Him, they could not enter the kingdom of God, for "except a man be born again, he cannot see the kingdom of God" (John 3:3).

From whom was the kingdom of God taken? It seems clear the *you* refers to the generation to whom the Lord was speaking. . . .

To whom would the kingdom be given? By application, the "nation bringing forth the fruits thereof" may mean any generation which will turn to Christ; but in its strict *interpretation* it refers to the nation Israel when she shall turn to the Lord and be saved before entering the millennial kingdom. . . .

The second passage which shows conclusively that Israel will be restored is the passage which deals with her future salvation, Romans 11:26-27.

And so all Israel shall be saved: as it is written. There shall come out of Sion the Deliverer, and shall turn away ungodliness from Jacob; For this is my covenant unto them, when I shall take away their sins.

. . . careful exegetes agree that Israel means Israel in this passage. . . . This passage teaches, then, that all Israel, in contrast to the remnant being saved today, will be saved at the Second Coming of Christ. From these two passages it is clear that Israel has not been cast off but will be restored to the place of blessing in the future. Israel, because she has not been disinherited, will be in a position to fulfill the Abrahamic covenant.[47]

G. *Has the Abrahamic covenant been fulfilled?* There are those who contend that this covenant will not be fulfilled in the future because it has been fulfilled already in the past. Murray is representative when he says:

There is ample proof to be adduced from the Word that God fulfilled to Abraham and to Abraham's seed the promise that they should possess Canaan. Today, the ashes of Abraham, Isaac and Jacob mingle with the soil of the "Cave of the field of Machpelah before Mamre . . . in the land of Canaan," which Abraham bought "for a possession of a burying place." He possessed Canaan during his earthly life, and his ashes rest in Canaan until the resur-

[47] Ryrie, *op. cit.*, pp. 70-73.

> rection. The same can be said of his seed, Isaac and Jacob, "The heirs with him of the same promise." Surely God has fulfilled his promise to Abraham to give him and his seed a permanent place in the land.
>
> [After quoting Gen. 15:13-14, he says:] This covenant does not include the word "forever" although it is contended by some that its full terms are yet to be fulfilled, and that the Israelites have never possessed the land to the extent described here. Happily, the Word of God gives the true and final answer here, too. We invite our readers to turn to I Kings 4:21, 24 where we read: "And Solomon reigned over all kingdoms from the river (the Euphrates) unto the land of the Philistines, and unto the border of Egypt. . . . For he had dominion over all the region on this side the river, from Tiphsah even to Assah, over all the kings on this side the river; and he had peace on all sides round about him."[48]

In order to hold to an historical fulfillment it is necessary to deny that this covenant was eternal in character. It is interesting to see what the amillennialist does with this word *eternal*. The same author writes:

> The literalist reminds us of the word "forever" which to him is the all important word here. We are frequently reminded that the "forever" must mean "FOR EVER." This is not without difficulty even for the literalist. Man's tenure of any part of the earth is not permanent. "It is appointed unto man once to die and after that the judgment." His leases and contracts in material possessions must come to an end. What, then, does God mean? What would Abraham understand by the word "forever"? If a man is threatened with eviction from his home and a friend of proven ability, to implement his promises, will give him a promise that he shall possess that home forever, how shall he interpret those words? He will not expect to live there eternally. The most he could expect from the promise would be that he should spend his natural life there and that his dust should rest there after death. This was what God plainly promised and fulfilled to Abraham. He possessed the land of Canaan in every sense in which a man can possess a land.[49]

How empty to contend that the covenanted possession of the land is fulfilled in that the ashes of Abraham rest in its soil!

The argument for historical fulfillment is met by Peters, who writes:

---

[48] George Murray, *Millennial Studies*, pp. 26-27.
[49] *Ibid.*, p. 26.

> To say that all this was fulfilled in the occupation of Palestine, by the preparatory or initiatory possession of it by the descendants of Abraham, is not only contradicted by Scripture, but is a virtual limiting of the promise. Kurtz . . . observes, what history attests, that the descendants never possessed the land promised to Abraham from the Nile to the Euphrates. . . .[50]

And additional weight is added as he argues:

> Whatever may be said respecting the temporary possession of Canaan . . . or whatever may be asserted respecting the descendants being meant "as yet in his loins," etc., one thing is most positively stated in the Bible, viz.: that this promise was not fulfilled in the Patriarchs, in any of the forms alleged by unbelief. The Spirit, foreseeing this very objection, provided against it, lest our faith should stumble. Thus Stephen, full of the Holy Ghost, tells us (Acts 7:5) that "He (God) gave him (Abraham) none inheritance in it, no, not so much as to set his foot on, yet He promised that He would give it to him for a possession and to his seed after him. This . . . should be decisive, especially when confirmed by Paul (Heb. 9:8, 9, and 11:13-40), who expressly informs us that the Patriarchs sojourned in "the land of promise," which they were to receive as "an inheritance," "pilgrims and strangers," and that "they died in faith, not having received the promises, but having seen them afar off, and were persuaded of them, and embraced them, and confessed that they were pilgrims and strangers on the earth." How, with such evidence before us, can we attribute to only their posterity what is directly asserted of themselves personally?[51]

This Abrahamic covenant, which contained individual promises to Abraham, promises of the preservation of a nation, and the possession of a land by that nation, was given to a specific covenant people. Since it was unconditional and eternal, and has never yet been fulfilled, it must await a future fulfillment, Israel must be preserved as a nation, must inherit her land, and be blessed with spiritual blessings to make this inheritance possible. Walvoord aptly concludes:

> The restoration of Israel is the capstone of the grand structure of doctrine relating to the Abrahamic Covenant. In bringing to a close consideration of this covenant as it pertains to premillennialism, attention should be directed again to the strategic importance of this revelation to Scriptural truth. It has been seen that the

[50] Peters, *op. cit.*, I, 297.
[51] *Ibid.*, I, 294-95.

covenant included provisions not only to Abraham but to Abraham's physical seed, Israel, and to Abraham's spiritual seed, i.e., all who follow the faith of Abraham whether Jew or Gentile in this age. It has been shown that Abraham interpreted the covenant literally as pertaining primarily to his physical seed. The unconditional character of the covenant has been demonstrated—a covenant resting upon God's promise and faithfulness alone. The partial fulfillment recorded to the present has confirmed the intent of God to give literal fulfillment to the promises. It has been shown that Israel's promise of perpetual possession of the land is an inevitable part and conclusion of the general promises given to Abraham and confirmed to his seed. Israel's continuance as a nation, implied in these promises, has been sustained by the continued confirmation of both Testaments. It was shown that the New Testament church in no wise fulfills these promises given to Israel. Finally, Israel's restoration as the natural outcome of these promises has been presented as the express teaching of the entire Bible. If these conclusions reached after careful examination of the Scriptural revelation are sound and reasonable, it follows that premillennialism is the only satisfactory system of doctrine that harmonizes with the Abrahamic Covenant.[52]

---

52 Walvoord, *op cit.*, 109:302-3.

CHAPTER VI

THE PALESTINIAN COVENANT

In the closing chapters of the book of Deuteronomy the children of Israel, the physical seed of Abraham, are facing a crisis in their national existence. They are about to pass from the proved leadership of Moses into the unproven leadership of Joshua. They are standing at the entrance to the land that was promised to them by God in such terms as:

> Unto thy seed will I give this land [Gen. 12:7].
>
> For all the land which thou seest, to thee will I give it, and to thy seed for ever [Gen. 13:15].
>
> And I will establish my covenant between me and thee and thy seed after thee in their generations for an everlasting covenant, to be a God unto thee, and to thy seed after thee. And I will give unto thee, and to thy seed after thee, the land wherein thou art a stranger, all the land of Canaan, for an everlasting possession; and I will be their God [Gen. 17:7-8].

But this land is possessed by Israel's enemies, who have shown they will resist any attempt by Israel to enter the land promised them. It is impossible for them to return to their former status as a slave nation and the land to which they were journeying as "strangers and pilgrims" seemed shut before them. As a result, certain important considerations must be faced by the nation. Is the land of Palestine still their possession? Did the inauguration of the Mosaic covenant, which all agree was conditional, set aside the unconditional Abrahamic covenant? Could Israel hope to enter into permanent possession of their land in the face of such opposition? To answer these important questions God stated again His covenant promise concerning Israel's possession of and inheritance in the land in Deuteronomy 30:1-10, which statement we call the Palestinian covenant, because it answers the question of Israel's relation to the land promises of the Abrahamic covenant.

I. The Importance of the Palestinian Covenant

Great importance is attached to this covenant (1) in that it reaffirms to Israel, in no uncertain terms, their title deed to the land of promise. In spite of unfaithfulness and unbelief, as manifested so frequently in Israel's history from the time of the promise to Abraham until that time, the covenant was not abrogated. The land was still theirs by promise. (2) Further, the introduction of a conditional covenant, under which Israel was then living, could and did not set aside the original gracious promise concerning the purpose of God. This fact is the basis of Paul's argument when he writes: "The covenant, that was confirmed before of God in Christ, the law, which was four hundred and thirty years after, cannot disannul, that it should make the promise of none effect" (Gal. 3:17). (3) This covenant is a confirmation and enlargement of the original Abrahamic covenant. This Palestinian covenant amplifies the *land* features of the Abrahamic covenant. The amplification, coming after wilful unbelief and disobedience in the life of the nation, supports the contention that the original promise was given to be fulfilled in spite of disobedience.

II. The Provisions of the Palestinian Covenant

The Palestinian covenant is stated in Deuteronomy 30:1-10, where we read:

> And it shall come to pass, when all these things are come upon thee, the blessing and the curse, which I have set before thee, and thou shalt call them to mind among all the nations, whither the Lord thy God hath driven thee, And shalt return unto the Lord thy God, and shalt obey his voice according to all that I command thee this day, thou and thy children, with all thine heart, and with all thy soul; That the Lord thy God will turn thy captivity, and have compassion upon thee, and will return and gather thee from all the nations, whither the Lord thy God hath scattered thee. . . . And the Lord thy God will bring thee into the land which thy fathers possessed, and thou shalt possess it; . . . And the Lord thy God will circumcise thine heart, and the heart of thy seed, to love the Lord thy God with all thine heart, and with all thy soul, that thou mayest live. And the Lord thy God will put all these curses upon thine enemies. . . . And thou shalt return and obey the voice of the Lord, and do all his commandments which I command thee

> this day. And the Lord thy God will make thee plenteous . . . for the Lord will again rejoice over thee for good. . . .

An analysis of this passage will show that there are seven main features in the program there unfolded: (1) The nation will be plucked off the land for its unfaithfulness (Deut. 28:63-68; 30:1-3); (2) there will be a future repentance of Israel (Deut. 28:63-68; 30:1-3); (3) their Messiah will return (Deut. 30:3-6); (4) Israel will be restored to the land (Deut. 30:5); (5) Israel will be converted as a nation (Deut. 30:4-8; cf. Rom. 11:26-27); (6) Israel's enemies will be judged (Deut. 30:7); (7) the nation will then receive her full blessing (Deut. 30:9).[1]

As one surveys the wide areas included in this one passage, which sets forth this covenant program, one is compelled to feel that God takes Israel's relation to the land as a matter of extreme importance. God not only guarantees its possession to them, but obligates Himself to judge and remove all Israel's enemies, give the nation a new heart, a conversion, prior to placing them in the land.

This same covenant is confirmed at a later time in Israel's history. It becomes a subject of Ezekiel's prophecy. God affirms His love for Israel in the time of her infancy (Ezek. 16:1-7); He reminds her that she was chosen and related to Jehovah by marriage (vv. 8-14); but she played the harlot (vv. 15-34); therefore, the punishment of dispersion was meted out to her (vv. 35-52); but this is not a final setting aside of Israel, for there will be a restoration (vv. 53-63). This restoration is based on the promise:

> Nevertheless I will remember my covenant with thee in the days of thy youth, and I will establish unto thee an everlasting covenant. Then thou shalt remember thy ways, and be ashamed, when thou shalt receive thy sisters, thine elder and thy younger; and I will give them unto thee for daughters, but not by thy covenant. And I will establish my covenant with thee; and thou shalt know that I am the Lord [Ezek. 16:60-62].

Thus the Lord reaffirms the Palestinian covenant and calls it an eternal covenant by which He is bound.

---

[1] Lewis Sperry Chafer, *Systematic Theology*, IV, 317-23.

III. The Character of the Palestinian Covenant

This covenant made by God with Israel in regard to their relation to the land must be seen to be an unconditional covenant. There are several reasons to support this. First, it is called by God an eternal covenant in Ezekiel 16:60. It could be eternal only if its fulfillment were divorced from human responsibility and brought to rest on the Word of the Eternal one. Second, it is only an amplification and enlargement of parts of the Abrahamic covenant, which itself is an unconditional covenant, and, therefore, this amplification must be eternal and unconditional also. Third, this covenant has the guarantee of God that He will effect the necessary conversion which is essential to its fulfillment. Romans 11:26-27; Hosea 2:14-23; Deuteronomy 30:6; Ezekiel 11:16-21 all make this clear. This conversion is viewed in Scripture as a sovereign act of God and must be acknowledged to be certain because of His integrity. Fourth, portions of this covenant have already been fulfilled literally. Israel has experienced the dispersions as judgments for unfaithfulness. Israel has experienced restorations to the land and awaits the final restoration. Israel's history abounds in examples of her enemies who have been judged. These partial fulfillments, which were literal fulfillments, all indicate a future literal fulfillment of the unfulfilled portions in like manner.

It may be argued by some that this covenant is conditional because of the statements of Deuteronomy 30:1-3: "when . . . then." It should be observed that the only conditional element here is the time element. The program is certain; the time when this program will be fulfilled depends upon the conversion of the nation. Conditional time elements do not make the whole program conditional, however.

IV. The Eschatological Implications of the Palestinian Covenant

From the original statement of the provisions of this covenant, it is easy to see that, on the basis of a literal fulfillment, Israel must be converted as a nation, must be regathered from her world-wide dispersion, must be installed in her land, which she is made to possess, must witness the judgment of her enemies, and must receive the material blessings vouchsafed to her. This covenant, then, is seen to have a wide influence on our eschatological expectation. Since these things have never been fulfilled, and an eternal and unconditional covenant demands a fulfillment, we must provide for just such a program in our outline of future events. Such is the expectation of the prophets who write to Israel: Isaiah 11:11-12; 14:1-3; 27:12-13; 43:1-8; 49:8-16; 66:20-22; Jeremiah 16:14-16; 23:3-8; 30:10-11; 31:8, 31-37; Ezekiel 11:17-21; 20:33-38; 34:11-16; 39:25-29; Hosea 1:10-11; Joel 3:17-21; Amos 9:11-15; Micah 4:4-7; Zephaniah 3:14-20; Zechariah 8:4-8. Such was the promise offered to those saints. Whether they should live to see the Messiah confirm these promises, or whether they reached the land through resurrection, peace was theirs as they awaited that which God promised.

CHAPTER VII

THE DAVIDIC COVENANT

The eschatological implications of the Abrahamic covenant lie in the words *land* and *seed*. The land promises are enlarged and confirmed through the Palestinian covenant. In the next of Israel's great covenants, that made with David, God is enlarging and confirming the seed promises. This will be noted in the passages dealing with the formulation of the Davidic covenant.

> And when thy days be fulfilled, and thou shalt sleep with thy fathers, I will set up thy *seed* after thee, which shall proceed out of thy bowels, and I will establish his kingdom [2 Sam. 7:12].
>
> I have made a covenant with my chosen, I have sworn unto David my servant, Thy *seed* will I establish forever, and build up thy throne to all generations [Ps. 89:3-4].
>
> As the host of heaven cannot be numbered, neither the sand of the sea measured; so will I multiply the *seed* of David my servant, and the Levites that minister unto me.
>
> Thus saith the Lord; If my covenant be not with day and night, and if I have not appointed the ordinances of heaven and earth; then will I cast away the *seed* of Jacob, and David my servant . . . . [Jer. 33:22, 25-26. Italics mine.]

The seed promise contained in the Abrahamic covenant is now made the center of the Davidic promise. The seed promises in general and the seed line of David, with his kingdom, house, and throne, are amplified.

I. THE IMPORTANCE OF THE DAVIDIC COVENANT

Inherent in the Davidic covenant are many of the crucial issues facing the student of Eschatology. Will there be a literal millennium? Is the church the kingdom? What is God's kingdom? What is Christ's kingdom? Will the nation Israel be regathered and restored under her Messiah? Is the kingdom present or future? These and many more crucial issues can be decided only by a correct interpretation of that which was covenanted to David. Berkhof is representative of amillenarians when he says: "The only Scriptural basis for this theory [the premillennial view of a literal thousand year kingdom] is Rev. 20:1-6, after an Old Testament content has been poured into it."[1] Such a view will be refuted only by enlarging on that which forms so large a determining place in the Scriptures—the Davidic covenant—with its promises of a kingdom and king.

II. The Provisions of the Davidic Covenant

The promise made by God to David is given in 2 Samuel 7:12-16, where we read:

> And when thy days be fulfilled, and thou shalt sleep with thy fathers, I will set up thy seed after thee, which shall proceed out of thy bowels, and I will establish his kingdom. He shall build an house for my name, and I will establish the throne of his kingdom for ever. I will be his father, and he shall be my son. If he commit iniquity, I will chasten him with the rod of men, and with the stripes of the children of men: But my mercy shall not depart away from him, as I took it from Saul, whom I put away before thee. And thine house and thy kingdom shall be established forever before thee: thy throne shall be established forever.

The historical background of the Davidic covenant is well known. Inasmuch as David had come to power and authority in the kingdom and now dwelt in a house of cedar, it seemed incongruous that the One from whom he derived his authority and government should still dwell in a house of skins. It was David's purpose to build a suitable dwelling place for God. Because he had been a man of war, David was not permitted to build this house. That responsibility was left to Solomon, the prince of peace. However, God does make certain promises to David concerning the perpetuity of his house.

> The provisions of the Davidic covenant include, then, the following items: (1) David is to have a child, yet to be born, who shall succeed him and establish his kingdom. (2) This son (Solomon) shall build the temple instead of David. (3) The throne of his kingdom shall be established forever. (4) The throne will not be taken away from him (Solomon) even though his sins justify

---

[1] Louis Berkhof, *Systematic Theology,* p. 715.

chastisement. (5) David's house, throne, and kingdom shall be established forever.[2]

The essential features, eschatologically, of this covenant are implicit in three words found in 2 Samuel 7:16: *house, kingdom, throne.* Walvoord well defines these terms as used in this covenant. He writes:

> What do the major terms of the covenant mean? By David's "house" it can hardly be doubted that reference is made to David's posterity, his physical descendants. It is assured that they will never be slain *in toto,* nor displaced by another family entirely. The line of David will always be the royal line. By the term "throne" it is clear that no reference is made to a material throne, but rather to the dignity and power which was sovereign and supreme in David as king. The right to rule always belonged to David's seed. By the term "kingdom" there is reference to David's political kingdom over Israel. By the expression "for ever" it is signified that the Davidic authority and Davidic kingdom or rule over Israel shall never be taken from David's posterity. The right to rule will never be transferred to another family, and its arrangement is designed for eternal perpetuity. Whatever its changing form, temporary interruptions, or chastisements, the line of David will always have the right to rule over Israel and will, in fact, exercise this privilege.[3]

As in other of Israel's covenants, we find that this covenant is restated and confirmed in later Scriptures. In Psalm 89 the Psalmist is extolling God for His mercies. In verse 3 these mercies are seen to come because:

> I have made a covenant with my chosen. I have sworn unto David my servant, Thy *seed* will I establish for ever and build up thy *throne* to all generations [Ps. 89:3-4. Italics mine.]

These promises are sure because:

> My covenant will I not break, nor alter the thing that is gone out of my lips. Once have I sworn by my holiness that I will not lie unto David. His *seed* shall endure for ever, and his *throne* as the sun before me [Ps. 89:34-36].

It is confirmed again in such passages as Isaiah 9:6-7; Jeremiah 23:5-6; 30:8-9; 33:14-17, 20-21; Ezekiel 37:24-25; Daniel 7:13-14;

---

[2] John F. Walvoord, "Millennial Series," *Bibliotheca Sacra,* 110:98-99, April, 1953.
[3] *Ibid.*

Hosea 3:4-5; Amos 9:11; Zechariah 14:4, 9. This promise to David is established by God as a formal covenant and then thereafter is referred to as the basis on which God is operating in regard to the kingdom, the house, and the throne.

III. The Character of the Davidic Covenant

As in the preceding covenants, the determinative factor is the character of the covenant itself. Is it conditional and temporary, or unconditional and eternal? The amillennialist is bound to argue for a conditional covenant and a spiritualized fulfillment, so that the throne on which Christ is now seated at the right hand of the Father becomes the "throne" of the covenant, the household of faith becomes the "house" of the covenant, and the church becomes the "kingdom" of the covenant. Murray gives the accepted amillennial view when he writes:

> The Davidic covenant, of which much has been said, was to the effect that his seed would sit upon his throne and had its natural fulfillment in the reign of King Solomon. Its eternal aspects include the Lord Jesus Christ of the seed of David; and in the book of Acts, Peter insists that Christ's resurrection and Ascension fulfilled God's promise to David that his seed should sit upon his throne. (See Acts 2:30.) Why insist, then, on a literal fulfillment of a promise which the Scriptures certify to have had a spiritual fulfillment?[4]

It will be noted that all the temporal aspects of the covenant are said to have been fulfilled by Solomon and the eternal aspects fulfilled by the present reign of Christ over the church. This makes the church the "seed" and the "kingdom" promised in the covenant. The kingdom becomes heavenly, not earthly. The Davidic rule becomes but a type of the reign of Christ. Only by extensive allegorization can such a view be held.[5]

A. *The Davidic covenant is unconditional in its character.* The only conditional element in the covenant was whether the descendents of David would continually occupy the throne or not. Disobedience might bring about chastening, but never abrogate the covenant. Peters says:

---

[4] George Murray, *Millennial Studies*, p. 44.
[5] G. N. H. Peters *Theocratic Kingdom*, I, 344-45.

> Some . . . wrongfully infer that the entire promise is conditional over against the most express declarations to the contrary as to the distinguished One, the pre-eminent Seed. It was, indeed, conditional as to the ordinary seed of David (comp. Ps. 89:30-34, and see force of "nevertheless," etc.), and if his seed would have yielded obedience, David's throne would *never* have been vacated until the Seed, par excellence, came; but being disobedient, the throne was overthrown, and will remain thus "a tabernacle fallen down," "a house desolate," until rebuilt and restored by the Seed. The reader will not fail to observe that if fulfilled in Solomon, and not having respect unto the Seed, how incongruous and irrelevant would be the prophecies given afterward, as e.g. Jer. 33:17-26, etc.[6]

David anticipated that there would not be an unbroken succession of kings in his line, but nevertheless he affirms the eternal character of the covenant. In Psalm 89 David foretold the overthrow of his kingdom (vv. 38-45) before the realization of that which had been promised (vv. 20-29). Yet he anticipates the fulfillment of the promise (vv. 46-52) and blesses the Lord.[7] Such was the faith of David.

Several reasons support the position that the covenant is unconditional. (1) First of all, like the other of Israel's covenants, it is called eternal in 2 Samuel 7:13, 16; 23:5; Isaiah 55:3; and Ezekiel 37:25. The only way it can be called eternal is that it is unconditional and rests upon the faithfulness of God for its execution. (2) Again, this covenant only amplifies the "seed" promises of the original Abrahamic covenant, which has been shown to be unconditional, and will therefore partake of the character of the original covenant. (3) Further, this covenant was reaffirmed after repeated acts of disobedience on the part of the nation. Christ, the Son of David, came to offer the Davidic kingdom after generations of apostasy. These reaffirmations would and could not have been made if the covenant were conditioned upon any response on the part of the nation.

B. *The Davidic covenant is to be interpreted literally.* Peters goes into the question of literal fulfillment more throughly, perhaps, than any other author. He argues for the literal interpretation of the covenant as follows:

---

[6] *Ibid.*, I, 343.
[7] Cf. *ibid.*, I, 319

> Before censuring the Jews . . . for believing that Jesus would literally restore the Davidic throne and Kingdom, we must consider in fairness, that they were justified in so doing by the very language of the covenant. It is incredible that God should in the most important matters, affecting the interests and the happiness of man and nearly touching His own veracity, clothe them in words, which, if not true in their obvious and common sense, would deceive the pious and God-fearing of many ages. . . .
>
> (1) The words and sentences in their plain grammatical acceptation, do expressly teach their belief. This is denied by no one, not even by those who then proceed to spiritualize the language. . . .
>
> (2) The covenant is distinctively associated with the Jewish nation and none other. . . .
>
> (3) It is called a perpetual covenant, i.e. one that shall endure forever. It may, indeed, require time before its fulfillment; it may even for a time be held, so far as the nation is concerned, in the background, but it must be ultimately realized.
>
> (4) It was confirmed by oath (Ps. 132:11, and 89:3, 4, 33), thus giving the strongest possible assurance of its ample fulfilment. . . .
>
> (5) To leave no doubt whatever, and to render unbelief utterly inexcusable, God concisely and most forcibly presents His determination (Ps. 89:34): "My covenant will I not break, nor alter the thing that is gone out of my lips." It would have been sheer presumption and blindness in the Jews to have altered (under the plea—modern—of spirituality) the covenant, and to have refused to accept of the obvious sense covered by the words; and there is a heavy responsibility resting upon those, who, even under the most pious intentions, deliberately alter the covenant words and attach to them a foreign meaning.[8]

He then proceeds to give a list of some twenty-one reasons for believing that the whole concept of the Davidic throne and kingdom is to be understood literally. He writes:

> If the Davidic throne and Kingdom is to be understood literally, then all other promises necessarily follow; and as the reception of this literal fulfilment forms the main difficulty in the minds of many, a brief statement of reasons why it must be received, is in place. 1. It is solemnly covenanted, confirmed by oath, and hence cannot be altered or broken. 2. The grammatical sense alone is becoming a covenant. 3. The impression made on David, if erroneous, is disparaging to his prophetical office. 4. The conviction of Solomon (2 Chron. 6:14-16) was that it referred to the

[8] *Ibid.*, I, 315-16.

literal throne and Kingdom. 5. Solomon claims that the covenant was fulfilled in himself, but only in so far that he too as David's son sat on David's throne. . . . 6. The language is that ordinarily used to denote the literal throne and Kingdom of David, as illustrated in Jer. 17:25 and 22:4. 7. The prophets adopt the same language, and its constant reiteration under Divine guidance is evidence that the plain grammatical sense is the one intended. 8. The prevailing belief of centuries, a national faith, engendered by the language, under the teaching of inspired men, indicates how the language is to be understood. 9. This throne and Kingdom is one of promise and inheritance and hence refers not to the Divinity but to the Humanity of Jesus. 10. The same is distinctively promised to David's son "according to the flesh" to be actually realized, and, therefore, He must appear the Theocratic King as promised. 11. We have not the slightest hint given that it is to be interpreted in any other way than a literal one; any other is the result of pure inference. . . . 12. Any other view than that of a literal interpretation involves the grossest self contradiction. 13. The denial of a literal reception of the covenant robs the heir of His covenanted inheritance. . . . 14. No grammatical rule can be laid down which will make David's throne to be the Father's throne in the third heaven. 15. That if the latter is attempted under the notion of "symbolical" or "typical," then the credibility and meaning of the covenants are left to the interpretations of men, and David himself becomes "the symbol" or "type" (creature as he is) of the Creator. 16. That if David's throne is the Father's throne in heaven (the usual interpretation), then it must have existed forever. 17. If such covenanted promises are to be received figuratively, it is inconceivable that they should be given in their present form without some direct affirmation, in some place, of their figurative nature, God foreseeing (if not literal) that for centuries they would be preeminently calculated to excite and foster false expectations, e.g. even from David to Christ. 18. God is faithful in His promises, and deceives no one in the language of His covenants. 19. No necessity existed why, if this throne promised to David's Son meant something else, the throne should be so definitely promised in the form given. 20. The identical throne and Kingdom overthrown are the ones restored. 21. But the main, direct reasons for receiving the literal covenanted language [is that] . . . David's throne and Kingdom [are made] a requisite for the display of that Theocratic ordering which God has already instituted (but now holds in abeyance until the preparations are completed) for the restoration and exaltation of the Jewish nation (which is preserved for this purpose), for the salvation of the human race (which comes under the Theocratic blessing), and for the dominion of a renewed curse-delivered world. . . . Such a

> throne and Kingdom are necessary to preserve the Divine Unity of Purpose in the already proposed Theocratic line.[9]

This whole proposition is supported by certain additional evidence.

1. The portions of the covenant that have been fulfilled have been fulfilled literally. As has been seen before, the partial fulfillment determines the method to be used in the unfulfilled portions. Ryrie says:

> It is only necessary to mention briefly that David had a son, that David's throne was established, that David's kingdom was established, that Solomon built the temple, that his throne was established, and that he was punished for disobedience.[10]

2. Evidence is added from the way in which David was led to understand it. It is seen that he had no thought but that it was a literal covenant, to be fulfilled literally. Peters says:

> How did David himself understand this covenant? This is best stated in his own language. Read e.g. Ps. 72, which describes a Son infinitely superior to Solomon; reflect over Ps. 132, and after noticing that "the Lord hath sworn in truth unto David, He will not turn from it; of the fruit of thy body will I set upon thy throne" (which Peter, Acts 2:30, 31, expressly refers to Jesus); consider the numerous Messianic allusions in this and other Psalms (89th, 110th, 72nd, 48th, 45th, 21st, 2d, etc.), so regarded and explicitly quoted in the New Test. by inspired men; ponder the fact that David calls Him "my Lord," "higher than the kings of the earth," and gives Him a position, power, dominion, immortality, and perpetuity, that no mortal King can possibly attain to, and most certainly we are not wrong in believing that David himself, according to the tenor of the covenant "thy Kingdom shall be established forever before thee," expected to be in this Kingdom of His Son and Lord both to witness and experience its blessedness. . . .[11]

And again:

> David himself, in his last words (2 Sam. 23:5), emphatically says: "He hath made with me an everlasting covenant, ordered in all things and sure; for this is all my salvation and all my desire." The prophet Isaiah reiterates (55:3), pronouncing it "an everlasting covenant, even the sure mercies of David." Surely no one can

9 *Ibid.*, I, 343-44.
10 Charles C. Ryrie, *The Basis of the Premillennial Faith*, p. 78.
11 Peters, *op. cit.*, I, 314.

> fail to see that this denotes, as Barnes (Com. loci), "an unchanging and unwavering covenant,—a covenant which was not to be revoked,"—one which was not to be abrogated, but which was to be perpetual,—and that "God would ratify this covenant."[12]

And yet again:

> That David himself expected a literal fulfilment of the promise is evident from his language which follows the giving of the covenant; and in this literal anticipation of the promise he returns thanks to God and praises Him for thus selecting his house for honor and in thus establishing it for the ages, even forever (2 Sam. 7:8, etc., 1 Chron. 17:16, etc.). It is presumption to suppose that David returned thanks, and thus prayer under a mistaken idea of the nature of the covenant.[13]

It is therefore evident that David was led by God to interpret the covenant literally.

3. There is evidence for the literal interpretation of the covenant from the interpretation of the covenant by the nation Israel. Reference has been made to the literal aspects emphasized in all the Old Testament prophetic books. This literal emphasis continued throughout Jewish history. Ryrie says:

> The concept which the Jews had of this kingdom at this time may be summed up under these five characteristics: earthly, national, Messianic, moral, and future.
>
> The hope was for an earthly kingdom. When Israel saw Palestine under the rule of a foreign power, her hope was the more intensified, because the kingdom she expected was one that would be set up on the earth and one that would naturally carry with it release from foreign domination. . . .
>
> The kingdom was to be national; that is, the expected kingdom had a specific relationship to Israel, being promised to that nation alone. . . .
>
> The kingdom was to be a moral kingdom, for Israel was to be cleansed as a nation. . . .
>
> Obviously the kingdom was not yet in existence and was therefore future at the time of the first coming of the Lord Jesus Christ. Even all the glory under David and Solomon was not comparable to the expected kingdom. Consequently, all of Israel's beliefs concerning this kingdom were of the nature of unrealized hopes. Israel looked to the future.[14]

---

12 *Ibid.*, I, 316.
13 *Ibid.*, I, 342.
14 Ryrie, *op. cit.*, pp. 89-91.

4. There is evidence for the literal interpretation from the New Testament references to the covenant made with David. Walvoord speaks of the New Testament as a whole, when he writes:

> The New Testament has in all fifty-nine references to David. It also has many references to the present session of Christ. A search of the New Testament reveals that there is not one reference connecting the present session of Christ with the Davidic throne. . . . it is almost incredible that in so many references to David and in so frequent reference to the present session of Christ on the Father's throne there should be not one reference connecting the two in any authoritative way. The New Testament is totally lacking in positive teaching that the throne of the Father in heaven is to be identified with the Davidic throne. The inference is plain that Christ is seated on the Father's throne, but that this is not at all the same as being seated on the throne of David.[15]

It can be shown that in all the preaching concerning the kingdom by John (Matt. 3:2), by Christ (Matt. 4:17), by the twelve (Matt. 10:5-7), by the seventy (Lk. 10:1-12), not once is the kingdom offered to Israel anything but an earthly literal kingdom. Even after the rejection of that offer by Israel and the announcement of the mystery of the kingdom (Matt. 13) Christ anticipates such a literal earthly kingdom (Matt. 25:1-13, 31-46).[16] The New Testament never relates the kingdom promised to David to Christ's present session.

It is interesting to observe that the angel, who did not originate his own message, but announced that which was delivered to him by God, says to Mary:

> And, behold, thou shalt conceive in thy womb, and bring forth a son, and shalt call his name JESUS. He shall be great, and shall be called the Son of the Highest: and the Lord God shall give unto him the *throne* of his father David: And he shall reign over the *house* of Jacob forever; and of his *kingdom* there shall be no end [Luke 1:31-33. Italics mine.]

The angelic message centers around the three key words of the original Davidic covenant, the throne, the house, and the kingdom, all of which are here promised a fulfillment.

The Davidic covenant holds an important place in the dis-

---

[15] Walvoord, *op. cit.*, 109:110.
[16] Cf. Ryrie, *op. cit.*, pp. 91-102.

cussion at the first church council. Walvoord comments on Acts 15:14-17, where this covenant is discussed, as follows:

> The problem of this passage resolves into these questions: (1) What is meant by the "tabernacle of David"? (2) When is the "tabernacle of David" to be rebuilt? The first question is settled by an examination of its source, Amos 9:11, and its context. The preceding chapters and the first part of chapter nine deal with God's judgment upon Israel. It is summed up in two verses which immediately precede the quotation: "For, lo, I will command, and I will sift the house of Israel among all the nations, like as grain is sifted in a sieve, yet shall not the least kernel fall upon the earth. All the sinners of my people shall die by the sword who say, The evil shall not overtake nor meet us" (Amos 9:9-10.)
>
> Immediately following this passage of judgment is the promise of blessing *after* the judgment, of which the verse quoted in Acts fifteen is the first. . . .
>
> The context of the passage deals, then, with Israel's judgment. . . . The entire passage confirms that the "tabernacle of David" is an expression referring to the whole nation of Israel, and that in contrast to the Gentile nations. . . .
>
> What then is the meaning of the quotation of James? . . .
>
> He states, in effect, that it was God's purpose to bless the Gentiles as well as Israel, but in their order. God was to visit the Gentiles *first,* "to take out of them a people for his name." James goes on to say that this is entirely in keeping with the prophets, for they had stated that the period of Jewish blessing and triumph should be *after* the Gentile period. . . . Instead of identifying the period of Gentile conversion with the rebuilding of the tabernacle of David, it is carefully distinguished by the *first* (referring to Gentile blessing), and *after this* (referring to Israel's coming glory.) The passage, instead of identifying God's purpose for the church and for the nation Israel, established a specific time order. Israel's blessing will not come until "I return," . . . God will first conclude His work for the Gentiles in the period of Israel's dispersion; then He will return to bring in the promised blessings for Israel. It is needless to say that this confirms the interpretation that Christ is not now on the throne of David, bringing blessing to Israel as the prophets predicted, but He is rather on His Father's throne waiting for the coming earthly kingdom and interceding for His own who form the church.[17]

Ryrie, dealing with the same passage, comments:

> [In regard to] the Amos quotation in Acts 15:14-17. . . . Gaebelein gives a good analysis of James' words citing four points in

[17] Walvoord, *op. cit.*, 109:110.

> the progression of thought. First, God visits the Gentiles, taking from them a people for His name. In other words, God has promised to bless the Gentiles as well as Israel, but each in his own order. The Gentile blessing is first. Secondly, Christ will return. This is *after* the outcalling of the people for His name. Thirdly, as a result of the Coming of the Lord, the tabernacle of David will be built again; that is, the kingdom will be established as promised in the Davidic covenant. Amos clearly declares that this rebuilding will be done "as in the days of old" (9:11); that is, the blessings will be earthly and national and will have nothing to do with the Church. Fourthly, the residue of men will seek the Lord, that is, all the Gentiles will be brought to a knowledge of the Lord after the kingdom is established. Isaiah 2:2; 11:10; 40:5; 66:23 teach the same truth.[18]

Thus, throughout the New Testament, as well as in the Old, the Davidic covenant is everywhere treated as literal.

C. *The problems of literal fulfillment.* The position that the Davidic covenant is to be interpreted literally is not without its problems. Attention is given to several of these now.

1. There is the problem as to the relation of Christ to the covenant. Two contradictory answers are given.

> The problem of fulfillment does not consist in the question of whether Christ is the one who fulfills the promises, but rather on the issue of *how* Christ fulfills the covenant and *when* He fulfills it. Concerning this question, there have been two principal answers: (1) Christ fulfills the promise by His present session at the right hand of the Father in heaven; (2) Christ fulfills the promise of His return and righteous reign on earth during the millennium.[19]

In reply to the first of these interpretations Peters writes:

> No sophistry in spiritualizing, symbolizing, or typicalizing can transmute the promise of the Davidic throne and kingdom into something else, as e.g. into the Father's throne, the Divine Sovereignty, the Kingdom of Grace, Gospel Dispensation, etc., for the simple reason that the identical throne and Kingdom, now overturned, is the one that is promised to the Messiah to be reestablished by Himself, as e.g. Amos 9:11, Acts 15:16, Zech. 2:12, Zech. 1:16, 17, etc. The Theocratic crown cast down, the Theocratic throne overturned, the Theocratic Kingdom overthrown, is the crown,

---

[18] Ryrie, *op. cit.*, pp. 102-3.
[19] Walvoord, *op. cit.*, 109:110.

> throne, the Kingdom that the Christ is to restore. These belong to Christ by "right" (Ezek. 31:25-27), and will be "given to Him." These, too, are linked with a restoration of the Jewish nation, Jer. 33:14, Micah 4:6, 8, etc. These facts—the existence of the throne at one time, its non-existence for a period, its restoration again, its connection at the restoration with the ancient people and land that formed the original Kingdom—these facts, as well as many others that will be brought forward, indicate as fully as language can possibly express it, that the ancient faith in covenanted language must not be discarded. . . .[20]

According to the established principles of interpretation the Davidic covenant demands a literal fulfillment. This means that Christ must reign on David's throne on the earth over David's people forever.

2. The second problem is in relation to the history of Israel since David's and Solomon's day. Ryrie deals with this problem when he writes:

> The question which must be answered is this: does the historic *partial* fulfillment . . . disallow a future literal fulfillment? The chief difficulties which history brings up are three: (1) there has been no continuous development or continued authority of the political kingdom of David, (2) Israel's captivity and the downfall of the kingdom would seem to argue against a literal interpretation for a future fulfillment, and (3) the centuries which have passed since the first advent of Christ would seem to indicate that a literal fulfillment should not be expected. . . . the premillennial position holds that the partial historic fulfillment in no way mitigates against the future fulfillment for these four reasons. First, the Old Testament prophets expected a literal fulfillment even during Israel's periods of great apostasy. Secondly, the covenant demands a literal interpretation which also means a future fulfillment. Thirdly, the New Testament teaches that the present mystery form of the kingdom no way abrogates the future literal fulfillment. Fourthly, the very words of the covenant teach that, although Solomon be disobedient, the covenant would nevertheless remain in force, and that Solomon's seed was not promised perpetuity. The only necessary feature is that the lineage cannot be lost, *not that the throne be occupied continuously.*[21]

The interruption of the kingdom did not mean the whole pro-

---

[20] Peters, *op. cit.*, I, 347.
[21] Ryrie, *op., cit.*, p. 80.

gram was set aside. As long as the prerogatives of the throne were intact the kingdom might be re-established. Walvoord says:

> . . . the line which was to fulfill the promise of the eternal throne and eternal kingdom over Israel was preserved by God through a lineage which in fact did not sit on the throne at all, from Nathan down to Christ. It is, then, not necessary for the line to be unbroken as to actual conduct of the kingdom, but it is rather that the lineage, royal prerogative, and right to the throne be preserved and *never lost,* even in sin, captivity, and dispersion. It is not necessary, then, for continuous political government to be in effect, but *it is necessary that the line be not lost.*[22]

Reference has already been made to many New Testament passages to show that the expectation there was for a literal fulfillment. The interruption in the Davidic kingdom did not militate against the expectancy of a literal restoration of that same kingdom as far as the New Testament writers were concerned.

D. *Has this covenant been fulfilled historically?* The argument is presented by the amillennialist that this covenant has been fulfilled historically in the Solomonic empire. Their contention is that the land ruled over by Solomon according to 1 Kings 4:21 fulfills the covenant so that no future fulfillment is to be expected. To this it may be replied:

> In the very fact of using this text the amillennialist is admitting that the covenant was *literally* fulfilled! Why, then, does he look for a spiritual fulfillment by the Church? However, we can point out four things which were not fulfilled by Solomon. There was no permanent possession of the land as promised to Abraham. All the land was not possessed. "From the river of Egypt" (Gen. 15:18) and "from the border of Egypt" (1 Kings 4:21) are not equivalent terms geographically. Solomon did not occupy all this land; he merely collected tribute. Temporary overlordship is not everlasting possession. Finally, hundreds of years after Solomon's time the Scriptures still abound in promises concerning future possession of the land. This must prove that God and His prophets realized, whether the amillennialist does or not, that Solomon had not fulfilled the Abrahamic covenant.[23]

---

[22] John F. Walvoord, "The Fulfillment of the Davidic Covenant," *Bibliotheca Sacra* 102:161, April, 1945.

[23] Ryrie, *op. cit.*, pp. 60-61.

Inasmuch as this covenant has not been fulfilled literally in Israel's history, there must be a future literal fulfillment of the covenant because of its unconditional character.

IV. The Eschatological Implications of the Davidic Covenant

Because of an anticipated future literal fulfillment, certain facts present themselves concerning Israel's future. (1) First of all, Israel must be preserved as a nation. Peters writes:

> The covenanted Davidic throne and Kingdom, allied as it is with the Jewish nation . . . necessarily requires . . . a *preservation* of the nation. This has been done; and today we see that nation wonderfully continued down to the present, although enemies, including the strongest nations and most powerful empires, have perished. This is not chance work; for, if our position is correct, this is demanded, seeing that without a restoration of the nation *it is impossible* to restore the Davidic Kingdom. The covenant language, the oath of God, the confirmation of promise by the blood of Jesus, the prophetic utterances—all, notwithstanding the nations' unbelief, requires its perpetuation, that through it finally God's promises and faithfulness may be vindicated. God so provides that *His Word* may be fulfilled. Every Jew, if we will but ponder the matter, that we meet on our streets is a living evidence that the Messiah will yet some day reign gloriously on David's throne and over His Kingdom, from which to extend a world-wide dominion.[24]

(2) Israel must have a national existence, and be brought back into the land of her inheritance. Since David's kingdom had definite geographical boundaries and those boundaries were made a feature of the promise to David concerning his son's reign, the land must be given to this nation as the site of their national homeland. (3) David's Son, the Lord Jesus Christ, must return to the earth, bodily and literally, in order to reign over David's covenanted kingdom. The allegation that Christ is seated on the Father's throne reigning over a spiritual kingdom, the church, simply does not fulfill the promises of the covenant. (4) A literal earthly kingdom must be constituted over which the returned Messiah reigns. Peters states:

---

24 Peters, *op. cit.*, I, 351.

> The fulfilment of the covenant promises implies, in view of this restored Davidic throne and Kingdom, that the Messianic Kingdom is a *visible, external* Kingdom, not merely spiritual, although embracing spiritual and divine things. Its visibility, and a corresponding acknowledgement of the same, is a feature *inseparable* from the language of promise. . . .[25]

(5) This kingdom must become an eternal kingdom. Since the "throne," "house," and "kingdom" were all promised to David in perpetuity, there must be no end to Messiah's reign over David's kingdom from David's throne.

It thus becomes evident that the Davidic covenant is of vital importance to the understanding of future events.

---

25 *Ibid.*

Chapter VIII

THE NEW COVENANT

The last of the four great determinative covenants into which God entered with Israel is the new covenant.

I. The Importance of the New Covenant

The new covenant guarantees Israel a converted heart as the foundation of all her blessings. According to the Old Testament principle that such a conversion can not be effected permanently without the shedding of blood, this covenant necessitates a sacrifice, acceptable to God, as the foundation on which it is instituted. Inasmuch as the offering up of the Son of God is the center of the age-long plan of redemption, and since this covenant entails that offering, great importance is to be attached to it. The whole covenant takes on importance, in addition, for amillennialism attempts to show that the church is fulfilling Israel's covenants because the church today is redeemed by blood. If the church fulfills this covenant, she may also fulfill the other covenants made with Israel and there is no need for an earthly millennium. Because of these considerations the covenant must be examined.

II. The Provisions of the New Covenant

The new covenant promised to Israel was stated in Jeremiah 31:31-34, where we read:

> Behold, the days come, saith the Lord, that I will make a new covenant with the house of Israel, and with the house of Judah: Not according to the covenant that I made with their fathers in the day that I took them by the hand to bring them out of the land of Egypt; which my covenant they brake, although I was an husband unto them, saith the Lord: But this shall be the covenant that I will make with the house of Israel; after those days, saith the Lord, I will put my law in their inward parts, and write it in

their hearts; and will be their God, and they shall be my people. And they shall teach no more every man his neighbour, and every man his brother, saying, Know the Lord: for they shall all know me, from the least of them unto the greatest of them, saith the Lord: for I will forgive their iniquity, and I will remember their sin no more.

Ryrie well summarizes the provisions of this covenant when he says:

The following provisions for Israel, the people of the new covenant, to be fulfilled in the millennium, the period of the new covenant, are found in the Old Testament.

(1) The new covenant is an unconditional, grace covenant resting on the "I will" of God. The frequency of the use of the phrase in Jeremiah 31:31-34 is striking. *Cf.* Ezekiel 16:60-62.

(2) The new covenant is an everlasting covenant. This is closely related to the fact that it is unconditional and made in grace. . . . (Isa. 61:2, *cf.* Ezek. 37:26; Jer. 31:35-37).

(3) The new covenant also promises the impartation of a renewed mind and heart which we may call regeneration. . . . (Jer. 31:33, *cf.* Isa. 59:21).

(4) The new covenant provides for restoration to the favor and blessing of God. . . . (Hos. 2:19-20, *cf.* Isa. 61:9).

(5) Forgiveness of sin is also included in the covenant, "for I will remove their iniquity, and I will remember their sin no more" (Jer. 31:34b).

(6) The indwelling of the Holy Spirit is also included. This is seen by comparing Jeremiah 31:33 with Ezekiel 36:27.

(7) The teaching ministry of the Holy Spirit will be manifested, and the will of God will be known by obedient hearts. . . . (Jer. 31:34).

(8) As is always the case when Israel is in the land, she will be blessed materially in accordance with the provisions of the new covenant. . . . Jeremiah 32:41; . . . Isaiah 61:8 . . . Ezekiel 34:25-27.

(9) The sanctuary will be rebuilt in Jerusalem, for it is written "I . . . will set my sanctuary in the midst of them for evermore. My tabernacle also shall be with them" (Ezek. 37:26-27a).

(10) War shall cease and peace shall reign according to Hosea 2:18. The fact that this is also a definite characteristic of the millennium (Isa. 2:4) further supports the fact that the new covenant is millennial in its fulfillment.

(11) The blood of the Lord Jesus Christ is the foundation of

> all the blessings of the new covenant, for "by the blood of thy covenant I have sent forth thy prisoners out of the pit wherein is no water" (Zech. 9:11).
>
> By way of summary, it may be said that as far as the Old Testament teaching on the new covenant is concerned, the covenant was made with the Jewish people. Its period of fulfillment is yet future beginning when the Deliverer shall come and continuing throughout all eternity. Its provisions for the nation Israel are glorious, and they all rest and depend on the very Word of God.[1]

Confirmation of this covenant is given in the statement in Isaiah 61:8-9, where it is called everlasting, and again in Ezekiel 37:21-28. There the following points are to be observed:

> (1) Israel to be regathered: (2) Israel to be one nation, ruled by one king; (3) Israel no longer to be idolatrous, to be cleansed, forgiven; (4) Israel to dwell "forever" in the land after regathering; (5) the covenant of peace with them to be everlasting; (6) God's tabernacle to be with them, i.e., He will be present with them in a visible way; (7) Israel to be known among Gentiles as a nation blessed of God. All of these promises are implicit in the basic passage of Jeremiah, but they confirm, enrich, and enlarge the covenant.[2]

This covenant, then, has to do with the regeneration, forgiveness, and justification of Israel, the outpouring of the Holy Spirit with His subsequent ministries, Israel's regathering and restoration to the place of blessing, all founded on the blood of Jesus Christ.

III. The Character of the New Covenant

Once again the principle is observed that, like all Israel's covenants, this covenant is a literal and unconditional covenant. (1) It is called eternal in Isaiah 24:5; 61:8; Jeremiah 31:36, 40; 32:40; 50:5. (2) This covenant is a gracious covenant that depends entirely upon the "I will" of God for its fulfillment, Jeremiah 31:33. It does not depend upon man. (3) This covenant amplifies the third great area of the original Abrahamic covenant, the area of "blessing." Inasmuch as this is only an amplification of the original Abrahamic covenant, which has been shown

---

1 Charles C. Ryrie, *The Basis of the Premillennial Faith*, pp. 112-14.

2 John F. Walvoord, "Millennial Series," *Bibliotheca Sacra*, 110:197, July, 1953.

to be unconditional and literal, this covenant must be also. (4) This covenant is largely occupied with the question of salvation from sin and the impartation of a new heart. Salvation is solely the work of God. Thus the covenant that guarantees salvation to the nation Israel must be apart from all human agency and therefore unconditional.

IV. The Fulfillment of the New Covenant

Amillenarians use the New Testament references to the new covenant to prove that the church is fulfilling the Old Testament promises to Israel. Thus there would be no need for a future earthly millennium inasmuch as the church is the kingdom. Allis is representative when he discusses Hebrews 8:8-12; and says:

> The passage speaks of the new covenant. It declares that this new covenant has been already introduced and that by virtue of the fact that it is called "new" it has made the one which it is replacing "old," and that the old is about to vanish away. It would be hard to find a clearer reference to the gospel age in the Old Testament than in these verses in Jeremiah. . . .[8]

In reply to such allegations, it is necessary to observe certain essential facts about the new covenant.

A. *The nation with whom the covenant is made.* It should be clear from a survey of the passages already cited that this covenant was made with Israel, the physical seed of Abraham according to the flesh, and with them alone. This is made clear for three reasons:

> First, it is seen by the fact of the words of establishment of the covenant . . . Jeremiah 31:31. . . . Other passages which support this fact are: Isaiah 59:20-21; 61:8-9; Jeremiah 32:37-40; 50:4-5; Ezekiel 16:60-63; 34:25-26; 37:21-28.
>
> Secondly, that the Old Testament teaches that the new covenant is for Israel is also seen by the fact of its very name. . . . contrasted with the Mosaic covenant . . . the new covenant is made with the same people as the Mosaic . . . the Scripture clearly teaches that the Mosaic covenant of the law was made with the nation Israel only. Romans 2:14 . . . Romans 6:14 and Galatians 3:24-25 . . . 2 Corinthians 3:7-11 . . . Leviticus 26:46 . . . Deuteronomy 4:8.

---

[8] Oswald T. Allis, *Prophecy and the Church*, p. 154.

There can be no question as to whom pertains the law. It is for Israel alone, and since this old covenant was made with Israel, the new covenant is made with the same peonle. no other group or nation being in view.

Thirdly, that the Old Testament teaches that the new covenant is for Israel is also seen by the fact that in its establishment the perpetuity of the nation Israel and her restoration to the land is vitally linked with it (Jer. 31:35-40). . . .

Thus we conclude that for these three incontrovertible reasons, the very words of the text, the name itself, and the linking with the perpetuity of the nation, the new covenant according to the teaching of the Old Testament is for the people of Israel.[4]

B. *The time of the fulfillment of the New Covenant.* It has been agreed that the time of the new covenant was *future.* It was always viewed as future when reference is made to it in the Old Testament prophecies. Hosea (2:18-20), Isaiah (55:3), Ezekiel (16:60, 62; 20:37; 34:25-26) all spoke of it as future. It must be viewed as yet future, for this covenant can not be realized by Israel until God has effected her salvation and restoration to the land. Ryrie says:

The sequence of events set up by the prophet [Jer. 32:37, 40-41] is that Israel will first be regathered and restored to the land and then will experience the blessings of the new covenant *in the land.* History records no such sequence. God cannot fulfill the covenant until Israel is regathered as a nation. Her complete restoration is demanded by the new covenant, and this has not yet taken place in the history of the world. . . . Fulfillment of the prophecies requires the regathering of all Israel, their spiritual rebirth, and the return of Christ.[5]

This covenant *must follow the return of Christ* at the second advent. The blessings anticipated in the covenant will not be realized until Israel's salvation, and this salvation follows the return of the Deliverer.

And so all Israel shall be saved: as it is written. There shall come out of Sion the Deliverer, and shall turn away ungodliness from Jacob: for this is my covenant unto them, when I shall take away their sins [Rom. 11:26-27].

The covenant referred to here must of necessity be the new

[4] Ryrie, *op. cit.*, pp. 108-10.
[5] *Ibid.*, p. 111.

covenant, for that is the only covenant expressly dealing with the removal of sins. And it is said to be actual after the coming of the Deliverer.

This covenant will be *realized in the millennial age.* Passages such as Jeremiah 31:34; Ezekiel 34:25; and Isaiah 11:6-9, which give descriptions of the blessings to be experienced in the time of the fulfillment of the new covenant, show that the new covenant will be realized by Israel in the millennial age.[6]

The conclusion, therefore, would be that this covenant, which was future in the time of the prophets, and was future in the New Testament, can only be realized following the second advent of Christ in the millennial age.

C. *The relation of the church to the new covenant.* There are five clear references to the new covenant in the New Testament: Luke 22:20; 1 Corinthians 11:25; 2 Corinthians 3:6; Hebrews 8:8; 9:15. In addition to these there are six other references to it: Matthew 26:28; Mark 14:24; Romans 11:27; Hebrews 8:10-13, and 12:24. The question arises as to the relationship of the believers of this present age to the new covenant of Jeremiah 31:31-34. This question is important, for, as has been seen previously, the contention of the amillennialist is that the church is now fulfilling these Old Testament prophecies and therefore there need be no earthly millennium.

1. There are three premillennial views as to the relation of the church to the new covenant made with Israel.

a. The first view is that of Darby. He presented the view that there was one and only one new covenant in Scripture, made with the houses of Israel and Judah and to be realized at a future time, to which the church bears no relationship whatsoever. He writes:

> This covenant of the letter is made with Israel, not with us; but we get the benefit of it. . . . Israel not accepting the blessing, God brought out the church, and the Mediator of the covenant went on high. We are associated with the Mediator. It will be made good to Israel by-and-by.[7]

---

[6] Cf. *ibid.*, p. 110-12.

[7] William Kelly, editor, *The Collected Writings of J. N. Darby*, XXVII, 565-66.

And again:

> The gospel is not a covenant, but the revelation of the salvation of God. It proclaims the great salvation. We enjoy indeed all the essential privileges of the new covenant, its foundation being laid on God's part in the blood of Christ, but we do so in spirit, not according to the letter.
>
> The new covenant will be established formally with Israel in the millennium.[8]

Further:

> . . . the foundation of the new has been laid in the blood of the mediator. It is not to us that the terms of the covenant, quoted from Jeremiah by the apostle, have been fulfilled, or that we are Israel and Judah; but that while the covenant is founded, not upon the obedience of a living people, to whom the blessing thereupon was to come, and the blood of a victim shed by a living mediator, but upon the obedience unto death of the Mediator Himself, on which (as its secure, unalterable foundation of grace) the covenant is founded.[9]

And finally:

> It is, then, the annexed circumstances of the covenant with which we have to do, not the formal blessings which in terms have taken place of the conditions of the old, though some of them may, in a sense, be accomplished in us.[10]

It would thus seem to be Darby's view that, in all its New Testament references, the new covenant is to be equated with the covenant of Jeremiah 31. In the New Testament it has no reference whatever to the church in this age, although the blessing of that covenant comes to others beside Israel now, since the blood was "shed for many." It will, however, be fulfilled literally in the millennium.

There are certain propositions in the view presented by Darby with which there is full agreement. (1) The new covenant of Jeremiah 31 necessitated the work of a Mediator and the death of Christ is that which makes a new covenant possible. (2) The new covenant was originally made with the houses of Israel and Judah and will be fulfilled in them literally in the

---

[8] J. N. Darby, *Synopsis of the Books of the Bible,* V, 286.
[9] Kelly, *op. cit.,* III, 79.
[10] *Ibid.,* p. 82.

millennium. The covenant can only be fulfilled literally by those with whom it was made and, since the church is not Israel, the church can not fulfill that covenant. (3) All the blessings which come to the church today are based upon the blood of Christ, which was necessarily shed to make possible the new covenant.

b. The second view is that of Scofield. This view, more generally held than Darby's view, says: "The New Covenant . . . secures the perpetuity, future conversion, and blessing of Israel . . ."[11] and it ". . . secures the eternal blessedness . . . of all who believe."[12] Thus, according to this view, there is one new covenant with a two-fold application; one to Israel in the future and one to the church now. Lincoln says:

> The blood of the New Covenant shed upon the cross of Calvary is the basis of all of the blessings of the believer in the present age. The believer, therefore, participates in the worth to the sinner of the New Covenant, so that he partakes of the Lord's supper in remembrance of the blood of the New Covenant, (I Cor. 11:25), and he is also a minister of the New Covenant, (II Cor. 3:6). It is also said of the believer that he is a child of Abraham because he is of faith (Gal. 3:7), and of Christ, (Gal. 3:29). He is also said to partake of the root and fatness of the olive tree, which is Abraham and Israel, (Rom. 11:17). So too, though as an unbelieving Gentile he is an "alien" and a "stranger," (Eph. 2:12), he is no longer such, (Eph. 2:19), because he has been made nigh by the blood of Christ, (Eph. 2:13). He benefits in the New Covenant as a fellow-citizen of the saints and of the household of God, (Eph. 2:19), and not as a member of the commonwealth of Israel, (Eph. 2:12).[13]

Grant says:

> . . . we must remember that God is speaking here explicitly of His earthly people, and not of any heavenly one. . . . the people with whom this covenant will be made will be a people in that day entirely according to His mind.
>
> It will be asked how, according to this, the new covenant applies at all to us. Other scriptures answer this clearly by assuring us that if we have not the covenant *made* with us, it can yet, in all the blessings of which it speaks, be *ministered* to us.[14]

---

[11] C. I. Scofield, editor, *The Scofield Reference Bible*, p. 1297.
[12] *Ibid.*, p. 1298.
[13] C. Fred Lincoln, "The Covenants," pp. 202-3.
[14] F. W. Grant, *The Numerical Bible*, VII, 48.

This view places the church under the new covenant, and views the relationship as a partial fulfillment of the covenant.

There can be agreement with Scofield that the blood of Christ is the basis for the new covenant with Israel and any covenant relation which the church may sustain to Christ, for it was not necessary for Christ to die once for Israel and then again for the church. The church, however, can not be placed under Israel's covenant. Scofield agrees with Darby fully that the covenant was primarily for Israel and will be fulfilled by them. Any application of it to the church, as the Scofield position holds, does not nullify the primary application to Israel.

c. The third view is the two-covenant view.[15] This view holds that there are two new covenants presented in the New Testament; the first with Israel in reaffirmation of the covenant promised in Jeremiah 31 and the second made with the church in this age. This view, essentially, would divide the references to the new covenant in the New Testament into two groups. The references in the gospels and in Hebrews 8:6; 9:15; 10:29; and 13:20 would refer to the new covenant with the church, Hebrews 8:7-13 and 10:16 would refer to the new covenant with Israel, and Hebrews 12:24 would refer, perhaps, to both, emphasizing the fact of the mediation accomplished and the covenant program established without designating the recipients. This view would accept the Darbyist concept that Israel's new covenant is to be fulfilled by Israel alone. In addition it would see the church as brought into relation to God by a new covenant that was established with them.

It is not in the scope of this treatment to attempt to settle the difference of opinion among premillennialists on this question of the relation of the church to the new covenant. It is sufficient here to establish but one point. Regardless of the relationship of the church to the new covenant as explained in these three views, there is one general point of agreement: the new covenant of Jeremiah 31:31-34 must and can be fulfilled only by the nation Israel and not by the church. Since this was a

---

15 Lewis Sperry Chafer, *Systematic Theology,* IV, 325; Walvoord, *op. cit.,* 110: 193-205; Ryrie, *op. cit.,* pp. 105-25.

literal covenant made with the physical seed of Abraham, any relationship of the church to the blood required by that covenant can not change the essential promises of God in the covenant itself. Apart from any relationship of the church to this blood, the covenant stands as yet unfulfilled and awaits a future literal fulfillment.

2. The question may arise as to why reference is made to Jeremiah 31 in Hebrews 8 if the church is not fulfilling that covenant. In spite of the contention of Allis that Hebrews 8 "declares that this new covenant has been already introduced,"[16] no such statement or intimation is made in the passage. On the contrary, the quotation from Jeremiah is used to show that the old covenant itself was recognized as ineffectual and temporary and was ultimately to be superseded by an effectual covenant, so that the Hebrews should not be surprised that a new and better covenant should be preached, nor should they place further trust in that which had been done away. Walvoord says:

> The argument of Hebrews 8 reveals the truth that Christ is the Mediator of a better covenant than Moses, established upon better promises (Heb. 8:6). The argument hangs on the point that the Mosaic covenant was not faultless—was never intended to be an everlasting covenant (Heb. 8:7). In confirmation of this point, the new covenant of Jeremiah is cited at length, proving that the Old Testament itself anticipated the end of the Mosaic law in that a new covenant is predicted to supplant it. The writer of Hebrews singles out of the entire quotation the one word *new* and argues that this would automatically make the Mosaic covenant old (Heb. 8:12). A further statement is made that the old covenant is "becoming old" and "is nigh unto vanishing away." It should be noted that nowhere in this passage is the new covenant with Israel declared to be in force. The only argument is that which was always true—the prediction of a new covenant automatically declares the Mosaic covenant as a temporary, not an everlasting covenant.[17]

Thus, in Hebrews 8 the promise of Jeremiah is quoted only to prove that the old covenant, that is the Mosaic, was temporary from its inception, and Israel never could trust in that which

---

[16] Allis, *op. cit.*, p. 154.
[17] Walvoord, *op. cit.*, 110:201.

was temporary, but had to look forward to that which was eternal. Here, as in Hebrews 10:16, the passage from Jeremiah is quoted, not to state that what is promised there is now operative or effectual, but rather that the old covenant was temporary and ineffectual and anticipatory of a new covenant that would be permanent and effectual in its working. It is a misrepresentation of the thinking of the writer to the Hebrews to affirm that he teaches that Israel's new covenant is now operative with the church.

3. In its historical setting, the disciples who heard the Lord refer to the new covenant in the upper room the night before His death would certainly have understood Him to be referring to the new covenant of Jeremiah 31. Several things are to be observed concerning the record of this reference on that occasion. In Matthew 26:28 and Mark 14:24 the statement is recorded: "This is *my blood* of the new covenant . . ." [italics mine]. In this statement emphasis would be placed upon the soteriological aspects of that covenant. The blood that was being offered was that required by the promised new covenant and was for the purpose of giving remission of sins. In Luke 22:20 and 1 Corinthians 11:25 the statement is recorded: "This is the *new covenant* in my blood . . ." [italics mine]. This statement would emphasize the eschatological aspects of the new covenant, stating that the new covenant is instituted with His death. This would be according to the principle of Hebrews 9:16-17:

> For where a testament is, there must also of necessity be the death of the testator. For a testament is of force after men are dead: otherwise it is of no strength at all while the testator liveth.

Since the disciples would certainly have understood any reference to the new covenant on that occasion as reference to Israel's anticipated covenant of Jeremiah, it seems that the Lord must have been stating that that very covenant was being instituted with His death, and they were ministers of the blood (the soteriological aspects) of that covenant (2 Cor. 3:6), but these to whom it was primarily and originally made will not receive its fulfillment nor its blessings until it is confirmed and made actual to them at the second advent of Christ, when "all Israel shall be saved . . . for this is my covenant unto them, when I shall take away their sins" (Rom. 11:26-27). There certainly is a difference between the institution of the covenant and the realization of the benefits of it. Christ, by His death, laid the foundation for Israel's covenant, but its benefits will not be received by Israel until the second advent (Rom. 11:26-27).

4. There are several considerations which support the view that the church is not now fulfilling Israel's new covenant. (1) The term *Israel* is nowhere used in the Scriptures for any but the physical descendents of Abraham. Since the church today is composed of both Jews and Gentiles without national distinctions, it would be impossible for that church to fulfill these promises made to the nation. (2) Within the new covenant, as its provisions have previously been outlined, there were promises of spiritual blessings and promises of earthly blessing. While the church, like Israel, is promised salvation, the forgiveness of sin, the ministry of the Holy Spirit, yet the church is never promised inheritance in a land, material blessings on the earth, and rest from oppression, which were parts of the promise to Israel. The new covenant not only promised Israel salvation, but a new life on the millennial earth as all her covenants are realized. The church certainly is not fulfilling the material portions of this covenant. (3) Since the church receives blessings of the Abrahamic covenant (Gal. 3:14; 4:22-31) by faith without being under or fulfilling that covenant, so the church may receive blessings from the new covenant without being under or fulfilling that new covenant. (4) The time element contained within the covenant itself, both in its original statement and in its restatement in Hebrews, precludes the church from being the agent in which it is fulfilled. The covenant can not be fulfilled and realized by Israel until after the period of Israel's tribulation and her deliverance by the advent of Messiah. While the church has had periods of persecution and tribulation it never has passed through the great tribulation of prophecy. Certainly the church is not now in the millennial age. Romans 11:26-27 clearly indicates that this covenant can only be realized after the second advent of the Messiah. Since the tribulation, second advent, and millennial age are yet future, the fulfillment of this promise must be yet future, and therefore the church can not now be fulfilling this covenant.

V. The Eschatological Implications of the New Covenant

A reference to the provisions of this covenant, stated earlier, which have never been fulfilled to the nation Israel, but which must yet be fulfilled, will show how extensive an eschatological program awaits fulfillment. Israel, according to this covenant, must be restored to the land of Palestine, which they will possess as their own. This also entails the preservation of the nation. Israel must experience a national conversion, be regenerated, receive the forgiveness of sins and the implantation of a new heart. This takes place following the return of Messiah to the earth. Israel must experience the outpouring of the Holy Spirit so that He may produce righteousness in the individual and teach the individual so that there will be the fulness of knowledge. Israel must receive material blessings from the hand of the King into whose kingdom they have come. Palestine must be reclaimed, rebuilt, and made the glorious center of a new glorious earth in which dwelleth righteousness and peace. The Messiah who came and shed His blood as the foundation of this covenant must personally come back to the earth to effect the salvation, restoration, and blessing of the national Israel. All of these important areas of eschatological study are made necessary by this covenant.

Conclusion

Four of the five covenants with the nation Israel have been surveyed to show that they are unconditional and eternal covenants, made with a covenant people, and to be fulfilled because of the faithfulness of the One making the covenants with those to whom they are given. These covenants not only had a relation to the nation at the time of their inception and gave a basis on which God dealt with Israel, but they bind God to a course of action in relation to future events, which determine the course of Eschatology. When the covenants are studied analytically we find seven great features which are determinative: (1) a nation forever, (2) a land forever, (3) a King forever, (4) a throne forever, (5) a kingdom forever, (6) a new covenant, and (7) abiding blessings.[18] These seven features will be developed later in the course of these studies.

---

[18] Chafer, *op. cit.*, IV, 315.

SECTION THREE

PROPHECIES OF THE PRESENT AGE

Chapter IX

THE COURSE OF THE PRESENT AGE

I. The Divine Program of the Ages

Any individual who refers to the Scriptures as the Old and New Testaments bears witness to the fact that God has divided His program into time segments. The history of revelation evidences the progress of divine revelation through successive ages. Chafer sets forth this program as he writes:

> The dispensational study of the Bible consists in the identification of certain well-defined time-periods which are divinely indicated, together with the revealed purpose of God relative to each. . . .
>
> The unrestrained, sovereign purpose of God is seen in the ordering of the succession of the ages. That God has a program of the ages is disclosed in many passages (cf. Deut. 30:1-10; Dan. 2:31-45; 7:1-28; 9:24-27; Hos. 3:4, 5; Matt. 23:37—25:46; Acts 15:13-18; Rom. 11:13-29; 2 Thess. 3:1-12; Rev. 2:1—22:31). Likewise, there are well-defined periods of time related to the divine purpose. The Apostle Paul writes of the period between Adam and Moses (Rom. 5:14); John speaks of the law as given by Moses, but of grace and truth as coming by Christ (John 1:17). Christ also speaks of the "times of the Gentiles" (Luke 21:24), which are evidently to be distinguished from Jewish "times and seasons" (Acts 1:7; 1 Thess. 5:1). Likewise, He spoke of a hitherto unannounced period between His two advents and indicated its distinctive features (Matt. 13: 1-51), and predicted a yet future time of "great tribulation" and defined its character (Matt. 24:9-31). There are "last days" for Israel (Isa. 2:1-5) as well as "last days" for the Church (2 Tim. 3:1-5). The Apostle John anticipates a period of one thousand years and relates this to the reign of Christ, at which time the Church, His bride, will reign with Him (Rev. 20:1-6). That Christ will

> sit on the throne of David and reign over the house of Jacob forever is declared by the angel Gabriel (Luke 1:31-33), and that there will be an ever abiding new heaven and new earth is as clearly revealed (Isa. 65:17; 66:22; 2 Pet. 3:13; Rev. 21:1). In Hebrews 1:1, 2 sharp contrast is drawn between "time past" when God spoke to the fathers by the prophets and "these last days" when He is speaking unto us by His son. Similarly, it is clearly disclosed that there are *ages past* (Eph. 3:5; Col. 1:26), the *present age* (Rom. 12:2; Gal. 1:4) and the *age, or ages, to come* (Eph. 2:7; Heb. 6:5; note Eph. 1:10, where the future age is termed *the dispensation* . . . of the fullness . . . of times . . .[1]

As one turns, then, to this present age, he is examining only one portion of the eternal program of God.

A. *The relation of Christ to the ages.* An examination of passages in the New Testament that make reference to the program of the ages will show us that Christ is the very center of that program. In Hebrews 1:2 He is said to be the one on whose account the ages were ordered.[2] In 1 Timothy 1:17 Christ is related to the program of the ages, where He is called the "king of the ages." In Hebrews 9:26 and 1 Corinthians 10:11 the ages are seen to center in His cross work for the sins of the world. This very work was planned before the ages began, 1 Corinthians 2:7; 2 Timothy 1:9; Titus 1:2, and in past ages that which is now known was not revealed, Romans 16:25. Thus the ages are the time periods[3] within which God is revealing His divine purpose and program as it centers in the Lord Jesus Christ.

B. *The use of age in the New Testament.* The word *aiōn* (age), frequently translated *world,* is essentially a time word. Abbott-Smith defines it thus:

> 1. . . . *a space of time,* as, a life, a generation, period of history, an indefinitely long period; in NT of an indefinitely long period, *an age, eternity.* 2. . . . the sum of the periods of time, including all that is manifested in them. . . .[4]

While *kosmos* (world) refers to the ordered universe, the scheme of material things, and *oikoumenē* (world) refers to the inhabited

---

[1] Lewis Sperry Chafer, *Systematic Theology,* I, xi-xii.
[2] Cf. B. F. Westcott, *The Epistle to the Hebrews,* p. 8.
[3] Cf. Chafer, *op. cit.,* I, 254-55.
[4] G. Abbott-Smith, *Manual Greek Lexicon of the New Testament,* p. 15.

earth, this word *aiōn* (world) views the world under the aspect of time. There are occasions when it seems to be synonymous with *oikoumenē,* and to be used of the inhabited earth, as in Titus 2:12. Again, on occasion, it seems to be used synonymously with *kosmos,* to refer to the organized system under the domination of Satan, as in 2 Corinthians 4:4; Ephesians 6:12 and 2 Timothy 4:10. When it is so used it has the same ethical connotation as *kosmos,* which Abbott-Smith says is used "in ethical sense, of the ungodly, the world as apart from God and thus evil in its tendency: Jo 7:7, 14:17, 27, 1 Co 1:21, Ja 1:27, 1 Jo 4:4. . . ."[5]

Aiōn is frequently used in the sense of eternity, the sum total of all the ages (Matt. 6:13; Luke 1:33, 55; John 6:51, 58; 8:35; 12:34; Rom. 9:5; 11:36; 2 Cor. 9:9; Phil. 4:20; Heb. 7:17, 21; 1 Pet. 1:25; Rev. 15:7 are but a few). It is also used frequently in regard to the separate ages of God's dealing with men. When so used it may refer to a past age, the present age, or a coming age. There is reference to a present age for Israel in Matthew 12:32 and Mark 4:19, and also to a future age for Israel in Matthew 12:32; 13:39-40; 24:3; Mark 10:30; and Luke 18:30; 20:35. In regard to the program for the church there is also a reference to this present age in 1 Corinthians 1:20; Galatians 1:4, and to a future age in Ephesians 1:21. In the use of these terms *present age* and *future age* it should be borne in mind that their connotation may not always be the same. The present age for the church, spoken of by Paul, is not the same as the present age for Israel, spoken of by Christ. Nor is the expectation in the future age for the church the same as that for Israel. In order to determine the usages of these terms one must clearly define the scope of the passage and those to whom it is addressed. Confusion has resulted from a failure to see this distinction.

As it is used in the New Testament, according to the normal usage of the words, *this present age* refers to that period of time in which the speaker or writer then lived. As used in reference to Israel in the Gospels *this present age* referred to the period of time in which Israel was anticipating the coming of the Messiah to fulfill all her covenant promises. The coming age was the age to be inaugurated by the Messiah at His advent. In

[5] *Ibid.,* p. 255.

reference to the church the term *this present age* refers to the inter-advent period, that period from the rejection of the Messiah by Israel to the coming reception of the Messiah by Israel at His second coming. The phrase *the coming age* could be used in its earthly aspect, to which the church will be related (as in Eph. 1:21), or in its eternal aspect (as in Eph. 2:7).

According to the New Testament this present age has an unwholesome designation. It is called "an evil age" (Gal. 1:4). It is so called because it is under the dominion of Satan, who is its "God" (2 Cor. 4:4). This age is marked by spiritual "darkness" (Eph. 6:12). This darkness produces its own wisdom, in which there is no light (1 Cor. 2:6-7). As a result it is marked by "ungodliness" and "lusts" (Titus 2:12), from which the believer is to turn away (Rom. 12:2), even though formerly he walked in conformity to its wisdom and standards (Eph. 2:2).

C. *The distinction between this present age and the preceding ages.* There are a number of ways in which this present age differs from all the ages that preceded. (1) In all previous ages Christ was anticipated, but in this present age He has not only come, but has died, been resurrected and is looked to now in His position at the right hand of the Father. (2) The Holy Spirit, who in previous ages came upon certain men to empower them to a given task, has taken up His residence in every believer. (3) In previous ages the good news announced was anticipatory, but in this present age the declaration of the good news announces an accomplished salvation through Christ. (4) The revelation in previous ages was incomplete, but in this present age, since Christ came to reveal the Father, revelation is completed. (5) Since this present age is marked by antagonism to God and His anointed, it bears a distinct characterization as an evil age, which was not applied to any previous age. (6) This age is, consequently, under the domination of Satan, its god, in a unique and unprecedented way. (7) The nation Israel has been set aside as the particular object of God's dealing and can not expect the fulfillment of her promises during this age.[6] These seven distinctions establish the fact that this present age is distinct from all preceding ages.

---

[6] Cf. A. C. Gaebelein, *Studies in Prophecy*, pp. 7-14.

II. The Divine Purpose in the Present Age

The Old Testament age, in which the purpose of God for Israel is stated in the covenants into which God entered and by which He is bound, closes with those purposes unrealized. After the death of Christ, God instituted a new divine program, not to replace the program for Israel, but to interrupt that divinely covenanted program. This new program is anticipated by the Lord in His upper room discourse in John thirteen to sixteen and becomes actual after the advent of the Holy Spirit at Pentecost. The Jerusalem council (Acts 15:14) announced that "God at the first did visit the Gentiles, to take out of them a people for his name." The "taking out of a people" thus constitutes God's present-age program. This people constitutes the church, the body of which He is the head (Eph. 1:22-23), the bride of which He is the bridegroom (Eph. 5:25-27, 32), the branch of which He is the supporting vine (John 15:1), the flock of which He is the Shepherd (John 10:7-27), the temple of which He is the cornerstone (Eph. 2:19-22; 1 Pet. 2:5), the ministering priests of which He is the high priest (1 Pet. 2:5-9), the new creation of which He is the head and the first fruits (1 Cor. 15:45). The reason for this calling out is stated in Ephesians 2:7, "That in the ages to come he might shew the exceeding riches of his grace in his kindness toward us through Jesus Christ." The divine purpose in the outcalling of the church is to display the infinity of His grace. Chafer writes:

> There was that in God which no created being had ever seen. They had seen His glory, His majesty, His wisdom, and His power; but no angel or man had ever seen His grace. Other attributes might be subject to a variety of demonstrations; but the manifestation of grace is restricted to what God may do for those among men who, in spite of the fact that they deserve His judgments, are objects of His grace. As every other attribute or capacity of God must have its perfect exercise and exhibition—even for His own satisfaction—in like manner His grace must also have its infinitely perfect revealing within the restricted undertaking by which He saves the lost. To say that a sinner is saved by grace is to declare that, on the ground of a Substitute's death and in response to faith in that Savior, God has wrought a work so perfect in its entirety and so free from the cooperation of other beings that it is a complete all-satisfying-to-God demonstration of His grace. A statement of this kind may be made as easily as words form a sentence; but

> who on earth or in heaven is able to comprehend the infinity of such a salvation? This demonstration, it should be added, will, by the very nature of the case, have its outshining in the life of each individual thus saved. It may be assumed that, had but one of all the human family been selected for the supreme honor of exhibiting eternally before all created beings the infinity of sovereign grace, the salvation of that one would be no different than the salvation of any one of the unnumbered throng from every kindred, tribe, and people who are saved by grace.[7]

It would seem, then, that God, in this present age, is pursuing a program through which His infinite grace shall be perfectly displayed throughout all eternity.

III. The Character of This Present Age

This present age, dating from the rejection of the Messiah by Israel unto the coming reception of the Messiah by Israel at His second advent, is viewed in Scripture as a mystery. Paul makes this clear, when he writes:

> Who now rejoice in my sufferings for you, and fill up that which is behind of the afflictions of Christ in my flesh for his body's sake, which is the church: Whereof I am made a minister, according to the dispensation of God which is given to me for you, to fulfil the word of God: Even the mystery which hath been hid from ages and from generations, but now is made manifest to his saints: To whom God would make known what is the riches of the glory of this mystery among the Gentiles; which is Christ in you, the hope of glory [Col. 1:24-27].

In this passage the apostle Paul very clearly calls the divine program developed in the church a *mystery,* something which was not formerly revealed, and therefore unknown, but now is made known by God. With this teaching other Scripture is in agreement (Rom. 16:25-26; 1 Cor. 2:7; Eph. 3:5-9).

While the modern usage of the word relates a mystery to that which is mysterious or unknown, Scripture uses the word for that divine purpose or program of God, known to Him from eternity, but which could not and would not have been known unless it was revealed by God; unknown in other ages, but now known by revelation. Mysteries are sacred secrets, hitherto un-

[7] Chafer, *op. cit.,* III, 228-29.

known, but now known by revelation. In the twenty-seven New Testament usages of the word *mystery* (excluding 1 Corinthians 2:7, where the marginal reading is preferred), it will be observed that the body of truth referred to as a mystery is particular truth related to this present age. These mysteries comprise the added revelation given concerning this present age, which supplements the Old Testament revelation. Chafer, commenting on Ephesians 3:5, writes:

> No better definition of a New Testament mystery will be found than that set forth in this context. A New Testament mystery is a truth hitherto withheld, or "hid in God" (vs. 9), but now revealed. The sum total of all the mysteries in the New Testament represents that entire body of added truth found in the New Testament which is unrevealed in the Old Testament. On the other hand, the New Testament mystery is to be distinguished from the mystery of the cults of Babylon and Rome, whose secrets were sealed and held on penalty of death; for the New Testament mystery, when it is revealed, is to be declared to the ends of the earth (vs. 9), and is restricted only to the extent of the limitation of the natural man (I Cor. 2:14).[8]

The existence of this present age, which was to interrupt God's established program with Israel, was a mystery (Matt. 13:11). That Israel was to be blinded so that Gentiles might be brought into relation to God was a mystery (Rom. 11:25). The formulation of the church, made up of Jews and Gentiles to form a body, was a mystery (Eph. 3:3-9; Col. 1:26-27; Eph. 1:9; Rom. 16:25). This whole program of God that results in salvation was called a mystery (1 Cor. 2:7). The relation of Christ to men in redemption was called a mystery (Col. 2:2; 4:3). The incarnation itself is called a mystery (1 Tim. 3:16), not as to fact but as to its accomplishment. The development of evil unto its culmination in the man of sin (2 Thess. 2:7) and the development of the great apostate religious system (Rev. 17:5, 7) both constitute that which was called a mystery. That there should be a new method by which God received men into His presence apart from death was a mystery (1 Cor. 15:51). These, then, constitute a major portion of God's program for the present age, which was not revealed in other ages, but is now known by revelation from God.

---

[8] *Ibid.*, IV, 75-76

The existence of an entirely new age, which only interrupts temporarily God's program for Israel, is one of our strongest arguments for the premillennial position. It is necessary for one who rejects that interpretation to prove that the church itself is the consummation of God's program. To do so he must prove that there is no new revealed program of God in this present age. Allis, defending amillennialism, writes concerning the mysteries thus:

> . . . to describe a person or subject as a mystery, does not necessarily imply that he or it was entirely unknown. It might be known, yet be a mystery because not fully known. . . . Consequently, according to Paul, a mystery may be a truth which can only be understood by believers or a truth only partly known to them, but not necessarily something entirely new or utterly unknown.[9]

Commenting on the mystery of the oneness of the body comprised of both Jew and Gentile, he continues:

> He describes it first of all as something which "in other generations was not made known to the sons of men." This declaration taken by itself would seem to imply that it was absolutely new. So we must note that it is at once qualified by three supplementary and limiting statements: (1) "as it hath now been revealed," (2) "unto his holy apostles and prophets in the Spirit," (3) "that the Gentiles are fellow-heirs, and fellow-members of the body, and fellow-partakers of the promise in Christ Jesus through the gospel." . . . we would do well to examine these three limiting clauses very carefully. . . .[10]

Allis admits that what is stated here seems to be an entirely new revelation of truth. He rejects the obvious implication that this truth is absolutely new by making the "as" clause in Ephesians 3:5 a limiting or restrictive clause. In reply to this Walvoord writes:

> Just what is the significance of the clause "as it hath now been revealed"? . . .
>
> Any student of the New Testament Greek will find it rather amazing that a scholarly writer would in this way ignore the other possibilities in this grammatical construction. Allis is assuming that the only possible interpretation is a restrictive clause. The Greek word . . . [*hōs*], here translated "as," is subject to many in-

---

[9] Oswald T. Allis, *Prophecy and the Church*, pp. 90-91.
[10] *Ibid.*

> terpretations. It is used principally as a relative adverb of manner and as a conjunction in the New Testament. A. T. Robertson in one of many discussions of this word lists its various uses as "exclamatory," "declarative," "temporal," and used with superlatives, comparatives, and correlatives. He notes further that basically most clauses of this kind are "adjectival." While used in an adverbial clause in this passage, the force grammatically is relative. Robertson says significantly in this connection, "The relative clause may indeed have the resultant effect of cause, condition, purpose or result, but in itself it expresses none of these things. It is like the participle in this respect. One must not read into it more than is there . . ." [Allis] has assumed that a clause which is normally an adjectival idea, i.e., merely giving additional information, is a restrictive—qualifying absolutely the preceding statement. In support of his arbitrary classification of this clause, he supplies no grammatical argument whatever, and gives the impression that his interpretation is the only possible one.[11]

Paul then is explaining, not limiting, the mystery there set forth. The concept must stand that this whole age with its program was not revealed in the Old Testament, but constitutes a new program and new line of revelation in this present age.

It has been illustrated how this whole age existed in the mind of God without having been revealed in the Old Testament.

> There are many places in Scripture in which this passing over of the present Dispensation is very plainly evident; and where, in our reading, we have, like our Lord, to "close the book." If we fail to do this, and if we refuse to notice these so-called "gaps," we cannot possibly understand the Scriptures which we read.
>
> We give a few by way of example, placing this mark (—) to indicate the parenthesis of this present Dispensation, which comes between the previous Dispensation of Law, and the next Dispensation of Judgment which is to follow this Present Dispensation of Grace.
>
> Ps. cxviii. 22, "The stone which the builders refused (—) is become the head-stone of the corner."
>
> Isa. ix. 6, "For unto us a child is born, unto us a son is given: (—) and the government shall be upon his shoulder: and his name shall be called Wonderful, Counsellor, The mighty God, The everlasting Father, The Prince of Peace." (Compare Luke 1, 31, 32.)
>
> Isa. liii. 10, 11, "It pleased the Lord to bruise him; he hath put him to grief; when thou shalt make his soul an offering for

[11] John F. Walvoord, "Millennial Series," *Bibliotheca Sacra*, III:4-5, January, 1954.

sin (—) he shall see his seed, he shall prolong his days, and the pleasure of the Lord shall prosper in his hands. He shall see of the travail of his soul and be satisfied."

Zech. ix. 9, 10, "Rejoice greatly, O daughter of Zion; shout, O daughter of Jerusalem; behold, thy King cometh unto thee: he is just, and having salvation: lowly, and riding upon an ass, and upon a colt the foal of an ass. (—) And I will cut off the chariot from Ephraim, and the horse from Jerusalem, and the battle bow shall be cut off: and he shall speak peace unto the heathen: and his dominion shall be from sea even to sea, and from the river even to the ends of the earth."

Luke i. 31, 32, "And, behold, thou shalt conceive in thy womb, and bring forth a son, and shalt call his name Jesus. (—) He shall be great, and shall be called the Son of the Highest: and the Lord God shall give unto him the throne of his father David:[12]

Allowance was thus made for this present age, without its actual existence ever having been specifically revealed in the Old Testament. Pember well states the relationship thus:

> . . . the times of the Church are not properly a part of the fifth dispensation, but a parenthesis fixed in it on account of the perversity of the Jews; an inserted period, unknown to Old Testament prophecy, and set apart for the preparation of a heavenly, and not an earthly people.[13]

IV. The Course of This Present Age

The age from the rejection of the Messiah by Israel unto His reception by Israel at His second advent is outlined in two portions of the Word: Matthew thirteen and Revelation two and three; the former from the viewpoint of God's kingdom program, and the latter from the viewpoint of the church program. The course of this present age will be traced from these two passages.

A. Matthew Thirteen

Matthew 13:11 reveals that our Lord is speaking in order that He may give the course of the "mysteries of the kingdom of heaven." This instruction comes through the proper interpretation of the parables which are recorded here. There are three different basic approaches to this chapter. There are, first of all, those who divorce any prophetic significance from this passage

12 E. W. Bullinger, *How to Enjoy the Bible*, pp. 103-4.
13 G. H. Pember, *The Great Prophecies*, p. 231.

and study it only for its spiritual or moral lessons as it affects believers today. Since they emphasize the unity of God's purpose from the fall of man until the eternal state, they fail to make any distinction between God's program for Israel and that for the church and, as a consequence, they see only church truth in this portion. In spite of the contradictions that such a method entails, they persist in it. Such is the non-dispensational approach of postmillennialism and amillennialism.

There are those, in the second place, who, recognizing the distinction between Israel and the church, hold that this portion is totally limited to God's program for Israel and relegate it to a revelation concerning Israel in the tribulation period when God is preparing them for the coming King. This is the ultra-dispensational approach.

Then there are those, in the third place, who believe that this portion of Scripture gives a picture of conditions on the earth in respect to the development of the kingdom program during the time of the King's absence from the earth. These parables describe the events of the entire inter-advent period. Such is the approach to the passage adopted in this study.

1. *The use of the parabolic method.* There seems to be a note of surprise and amazement in the question "Why speakest thou unto them in parables?" (Matt. 13:10). A variation in emphasis in the reading of this question will indicate several possible causes for this surprise. If it is read, "Why speakest thou unto *them* in parables?" the question would raise the problem as to why the Lord would speak to the multitude, as He is in Matthew 13:1-3, when, in the previous chapter, after the manifest rejection of the testimony of the Holy Spirit to the person of Christ by the nation Israel, He has characterized them as "an evil and adulterous generation" (v. 39). The problem thus would be: Why do you continue to teach a nation that has publicly announced their decision that you are a son of Satan?

The nature of the Lord's reply in the verses that follow would indicate that the question ought to be understood, "Why speakest thou unto them *in parables?*" There was nothing new in the use of parables themselves, for the Lord had used such with frequency before, both to instruct and to illustrate the truths

He desired to convey. The disciples must have recognized a new emphasis in our Lord's teaching method.

In reply to the disciples' question the Lord gives three purposes in the use of this parabolic method of instruction. (1) It was a means of substantiating His claim to Messiahship (Matt. 13:34-35). In addition to the other signs to prove His claim there was the sign in relation to Isaiah's prophecy. (2) It was a method of imparting truth to the believing hearer (Matt. 13:11). (3) It was a method of hiding truth from the unbelieving hearer (Matt. 13:13-15). The reason why it was necessary to hide truth will be seen in the following consideration.

2. *The setting of the chapter in the Gospel.* The Gospel of Matthew is the Gospel which presents the Lord Jesus Christ as Jehovah's King and Israel's Messiah. It unfolds the presentation of the Messiah to Israel. Scroggie says:

> More than any other of the Gospels, Matthew's is allied with the Hebrew Scriptures in theme and tone; their subjects are its subjects, the Messiah, Israel, the Law, the Kingdom, the Prophecy. Jewish ideas and terms characterize the whole record. Its witness would not have impressed either the Roman, for whom Mark wrote, or the Greek, for whom Luke wrote, but to Jews its significance would be inescapable.[14]

This fact is borne out by the numerous references to the Son of David (1:1, 20; 9:27; 12:23; 15:22; 20:30-31; 21:9, 15; 22:42, 45), to the fulfillment of prophecy (1:22; 2:5, 15, 17, 23; 4:14; 8:17; 12:17; 13:35; 21:4, 42; 26:31, 54, 56; 27:9-10), to Jewish customs (15:1-2; 27:62), to the Mosaic Law (5:17-19, 21, 27, 31, 33, 38, 43; 7:12; 11:13; 12:5; 15:6; 22:36, 40; 23:23), to the Sabbath (12:1-2, 5, 8, 10, 11, 12; 24:20; 28:1), and to the holy city and the holy place (4:5; 24:15; 27:53). Christ is related to prophecy throughout. This will have important bearing on the meaning of the term "kingdom of heaven."

This thirteenth chapter holds a unique place in the development of the theme of the Gospel. Throughout the book Christ is seen in His presentation as Messiah. In chapters one and two His legal right to the throne is presented; in chapter three is depicted

---

[14] Graham Scroggie, *A Guide to the Gospels*, p. 248.

the dedication of the King; in chapter four the moral right of the King is demonstrated; in five through seven the judicial right of the King is shown; in eight through ten is presented the authority of the King, as his prophetical right is demonstrated by His ministry to Israel; and in chapters eleven and twelve we see the opposition to the King. The great question before Israel is: "Is not this the son of David?" (Matt. 12:23). It is evident that Israel is answering in the negative. Christ shows that both He and His forerunner have been rejected (11:1-9), and this rejection will result in judgment (11:20-24). Because of the ultimate rejection of the cross Christ can give a new invitation (11:28-30), an invitation to all. In chapter twelve the rejection comes to a climax. The populace was debating the person of Christ (12:23). The answer given by the Pharisees was: " This fellow doth not cast out devils, but by Beelzebub the prince of the devils (12:24.) The Holy Spirit had borne His witnesses to the Person of Christ through His words and His works, and the leaders who examined the evidence have decided that His credentials are the credentials of hell, not those of heaven. The great warning of judicial blindness and judgment is given by the Lord to the nation (12:31-32). As the chapter closes (12:46-50) the Lord indicates that He is setting aside all natural relationships, such as Israel sustained to Him and to the covenant promises by a physical birth, and establishes a new relationship, based on faith. Kelly states it:

> He renounced all earthly connection for the present time. The only tie *He acknowledges* now is relationship to a heavenly Father, formed through the word of God received into the soul.
>
> Thus we have in this chapter the Lord closing with Israel, as far as testimony is concerned. In the next chapter we shall find what comes dispensationally of those new relations that the Lord was about to unfold.[15]

Now that Israel has rejected the offered kingdom, the question naturally arises, "What will happen to God's kingdom program now that the kingdom has been rejected and the King is to be absent?" Since this kingdom was the subject of an irrevocable covenant it was unthinkable that it could be abandoned. The chapter gives the events in the development of the kingdom pro-

---

[15] Wm. Kelly, *Lectures on the Gospel of Matthew,* P. 262.

gram from the time of its rejection until it is received when the nation welcomes the King at His second advent.

3. *The use of the term* kingdom of heaven. In the Scriptures the term *kingdom* is used in seven different ways: (1) the Gentile kingdoms, (2) the kingdoms of Israel and Judah, (3) the kingdom of Satan, (4) God's universal kingdom, (5) a spiritual kingdom, (6) the millennial Davidic kingdom, and (7) the mystery form of the kingdom. It is noted that there is general agreement among theologians concerning the first four of these classifications. The last three are concerned with the realm of Eschatology and are the subject of debate. It is necessary to make some observations concerning these.

a. The spiritual kingdom, which is closely related with God's universal kingdom, is composed of the elect of all the ages, who have experienced a new birth by the power of the Holy Spirit. This kingdom can not be entered apart from such a new birth. It is referred to in Matthew 6:33; 19:16, 23, 24; John 3:3-5; Acts 8:12; 14:22; 19:8; 20:25; 28:23; Romans 14:17; 1 Corinthians 4:20; 6:9-10; 15:50; Galatians 5:21; Ephesians 5:5; Colossians 4:11; 1 Thessalonians 2:12; 2 Thessalonians 1:5.

b. The millennial kingdom is declared to be a literal, earthly kingdom over which Christ rules from David's throne in fulfillment of the Davidic covenant (2 Sam. 7:8-17; Matt. 1:1; Luke 1:32). This kingdom is the subject of Old Testament prophecy (2 Sam. 7:8-17; Isa. 9:6-7; 11:1-16; Jer. 23:5; 33:14-17; Ezek. 34:23; 37:24; Hosea 3:4-5; Micah 4:6-8; 5:2; Zech. 2:10-12; 8:20-23; Psalm 2:6, 8-10; 72:11, 17; Mal. 3:1-4). This kingdom was proclaimed as being "at hand" at Christ's first advent (Matt. 3:2; 4:17; 10:5-7); but was rejected by Israel and therefore postponed (Matt. 23:37-39). It will again be announced to Israel in the tribulation period (Matt. 24:14). It will be received by Israel and set up at the second advent of Christ (Isa. 24:23; Rev. 19:11-16; 20:1-6).

c. The mystery form of the kingdom brings us a concept entirely distinct from the preceding two. That God was going to establish a kingdom on the earth was no mystery. Since the first sin in heaven, when God's sovereignty was challenged, it was His purpose to manifest His sovereignty by the establishment of a kingdom over which He ruled. When Adam was created dominion was given to him (Gen. 1:26) so he might manifest the sovereignty that belonged to God, which was Adam's by appointment. But Adam sinned and there was no such manifestation of God's authority. The reign of conscience was intended to bear evidence to the individual as to his responsibility to the sovereignty of God, but man failed under this test. Human government was ordained that men might recognize that government as a manifestation of God's sovereignty, but man rebelled against that. God appointed judges so that these might manifest God's authority, but man rejected this display of sovereignty. God instituted a theocracy, in which God was recognized as sovereign, but the nation chosen to manifest this display of sovereignty rebelled (1 Sam. 8:7). God then revealed His purpose to manifest His sovereignty through David's seed who would reign (2 Sam. 7:16). And when Christ came even this manifestation of God's purpose to re-establish sovereignty was rejected. Sinful man has consistently rejected each manifestation of the authority of God. Within this program of God it was not the fact that God was going to establish a kingdom that was an unrevealed secret. The mystery was the fact that when the One in whom this program was to be realized was publically presented He would be rejected and an age would fall between His rejection and the fulfillment of God's purpose of sovereignty at His second advent. The mystery form of the kingdom, then, has reference to the age between the two advents of Christ. The mysteries of the kingdom of heaven describe the conditions that prevail on the earth in that interim while the king is absent. These mysteries thus relate this present age to the eternal purposes of God in regard to His kingdom.

Concerning this mystery form of the kingdom, it is observed, in the first place, that it can not be equated with the millennial kingdom, for that kingdom was no mystery but was clearly predicted in the Old Testament. In the second place, it can not refer to the spiritual kingdom, for that kingdom is constituted only of saved individuals, who enter it by the new birth, but this mystery form of the kingdom is composed of saved and unsaved alike (wheat and tares, good and bad fish). It cannot refer, thirdly, to the eternal kingdom for these mysteries are limited in time to the inter-advent period. It can not be limited, fourthly, to the church, for this mystery form of the kingdom includes more than the church. On the other hand, it must be observed, this mystery form of the kingdom has reference to things that were hitherto unrevealed, is definitely limited as to time, and represents the entire sphere of profession in the present age. It is most important, eschatologically, to keep these three usages of the term *kingdom* separate and distinct.

d. In regard to the terms *kingdom of God* and *the kingdom of the heavens* it is to be observed that, while not synonymous, they are used interchangeably. What distinctions there are are not inherent in the words themselves, but in their usage in the context. Both of these terms are used to designate the millennial kingdom, the spiritual kingdom, and the mystery form of the kingdom. While we recognize the distinctions between the earthly and the eternal aspects of the kingdom program,[16] we must guard against making the terms *kingdom of God* and the *kingdom of the heavens* absolute. Only the context can determine the meaning intended to be conveyed by the terms.

4. *The time element in Matthew thirteen.* Ryrie writes to show that these parables are limited to the inter-advent period. He says:

> "The kingdom of the heavens has become like unto." This sets the time limit for the *beginning* of the subject matter involved. In other words, the kingdom of heaven was assuming the form described in the parables at that time when Christ was personally ministering on the earth. The end of the time period covered by these parables is indicated by the phrase "end of the world" or more literally "the consummation of the age" (verses 39-49). This is the time of the Second Advent of Christ when He shall come in power and great glory. Therefore, it is clear that these parables are concerned only with that time between the days when Christ spoke them on earth and the end of this age. This gives a clue to the meaning of the phrase "the mysteries of the kingdom of heaven."[17]

5. *The interpretation of the chapter.* There are several keys to be used in the interpretation of this passage which will keep

---

[16] Cf. Chafer, *op. cit.*, VII, 223-24.
[17] Charles C. Ryrie, *The Basis of the Premillennial Faith*, pp. 94-95.

one from error. (1) First of all, some of the parables are interpreted by the Lord Himself. There can be no uncertainty as to their meaning, nor the method by which the rest of the parables are to be interpreted. Any interpretation of the whole must, of necessity, be in harmony with that which has been interpreted by the Lord. (2) A second important key is to observe that, while many of the parables are in figurative language, these figures are familiar ones throughout the Word and, therefore, will have the same usage here as used consistently elsewhere. The fact that these are not isolated figures makes interpretation easier.

Scroggie has given us what he considers the key to interpretation when he writes:

> It appears to me that the key to the interpretation of these parables is in ver. 52 of this chapter: "Every scribe which is instructed unto the kingdom of heaven is like unto a man that is an householder, which bringeth forth out of his treasure *things new and old.*" These words are spoken of the things which precede, and surely speak of the parables as some *new* and some *old.* But which are old and which are new? In ver. 1, we read that our Lord "went out of the house, and sat by the seaside" and taught; and in ver. 36 "then Jesus sent the multitude away, and went into the house" and taught. Thus the parables are divided into four spoken in public, and three spoken in private; and the evidence goes to show (if ver. 52 is the key) that the first four are the *new* treasures of truth, and the last three are the *old*—that is, truths revealed before. Assuming this, the present Age is presented to our view in a series of seven progressive pictures, describing the course of the kingdom in mystery.
>
> THE NEW THINGS
>
> 1. *The Seed and the Soils:* The *Proclamation* of the Kingdom.
> 2. *The Wheat and the Darnel:* false *Imitation* in the Kingdom.
> 3. *The Mustard Tree:* Wide, visible *Extension* of the Kingdom.
> 4. *The Leaven in the Meal:* insidious *Corruption* of the Kingdom.
>
> THE OLD THINGS
>
> 5. *The Treasure:* The Israelitish Nation.
> 6. *The Pearl:* The Jewish Remnant during the Tribulation.[18]
> 7. *The Drag-net:* The Judgment of the Nations at the end of the Tribulation.[19]

[18] Many see this as a reference to the church rather than to Israel.
[19] Graham Scroggie, *Prophecy and History*, pp. 123-25.

6. *The interpretation of the parables.* It is not possible nor necessary to give a detailed exposition of these parables at this point. To trace the Lord's revelation concerning the course of this present age will suffice in this eschatological consideration.

a. The Sower and the Soils (Matt. 13:3-9; 18-23). From the interpretation given by the Lord several important facts are to be learned concerning this present age. (1) This age is one that is characterized by the sowing of seed, which, in the parallel portion in Mark 4:14, is shown to be the Word, but here is seen to be men who are sons of the kingdom. (2) Within the age there is a marked difference in the preparation of the soils for the reception of the seed sown. (3) The age is marked by opposition to the word from the world, the flesh, and the devil. (4) During the course of the age there will be a decreasing response to the sowing of the seed, from "a hundredfold" to "sixty" to "thirty." Such is the course of the age. Mark 4:13 reveals that this parable, with the revelation of the program which it makes, is basic to the understanding of the other parables in the discourse. The remaining parables deal with the development of the seed-sowing program.

b. The Wheat and the Tares (Matt. 13:24-30; 36-43). This second parable is likewise interpreted by the Lord. Several important facts are revealed through it concerning the course of the age. (1) The true sowing, mentioned in the first parable, is to be imitated by a false sowing. (2) There is to be a side-by-side development of that which is good with that which is evil as the result of these two sowings. (3) There will be a judgment at the end of the age to separate the good from the evil. The good will be received into the millennial kingdom and the evil excluded. (4) The essential character of each sowing can be determined only by the fruitfulness or fruitlessness of that which was sown, not by outward observation.

Many feel that this second parable is to be related particularly to the tribulation period and is to be distinguished from the sowing of the first parable.[20] In the first parable the emphasis was on the "Word," and in the second on the "children of the

---

[20] J. F. Strombeck, *First the Rapture*, pp. 162-67.

kingdom" (Matt. 13:38). In the first parable the seed is sown in the hearts of men and in the second in the world. In the first parable there is no mention of judgment and in the second the age ends in judgment. This would seem to indicate that two sowings are indicated; the first that throughout the age, principally by the church, and the second in the tribulation period just prior to the end of the age when God is again dealing with Israel. There are indications in the second parable that this is related to Israel, rather than to the church: (1) the term *children of the kingdom* is used in Matthew to refer to Israel (Matt. 8:11-12); (2) the judgment outlined relates to the time when God will again be dealing with Israel as a nation, that is at the end of the age; (3) the wheat and tares grow together until the judgment, but the church will be raptured before the tribulation begins; (4) the judgment that falls upon the wicked comes through the angels before the righteous are rewarded, so that the chronology here depicts the removal of the wicked so that only righteous are left; (5) the millennial kingdom is set up immediately after this judgment; (6) the church is never judged to determine who will enter into glory and who will be excluded. This seems to indicate that this parable has primary reference to Israel during the tribulation period. Yet it is true that the entire age is to be characterized by a false sowing in competition with the true.

c. The Mustard Seed (Matt. 13:31-32). In Jewish idiom a mustard seed was used to weigh what was considered the smallest measurable amount. Thus the insignificant beginning of the new form of the kingdom is being stressed. The mustard is a plant that grows in one year from seed to a height of twenty to thirty feet. This part of the parable stresses the great growth of the kingdom when once it is introduced. The kingdom will grow from an insignificant beginning to great proportions. Historically the new form of the kingdom had its beginning with only a few to propogate it, but in spite of that it will reach to great size. In Daniel's prophecy (4:1-37) the tree represented Nebuchadnezzar's kingdom (vs. 20-22). The birds in the tree represented the peoples that received benefit from Nebuchadnezzar's kingdom (v. 12). Here the mustard reveals that the kingdom in its new form will have an insignificant beginning, but will grow to great size and multitudes will benefit from it.

d. The Leaven Hidden in the Meal (Matt. 13:33). When leaven is used in Scripture it frequently connotes evil (Ex. 12:15; Lev. 2:11; 6:17; 10:12; Matt. 16:6; Mark 8:15; 1 Cor. 5:6, 8; Gal. 5:9). Its use in the sacrifices that represent the perfection of the person and work of Christ (Lev. 2:1-3) shows it is not always so used. Here the emphasis is not on leaven itself as though to emphasize its character, but rather on the fact that the leaven has been hidden in meal, thus stressing the way leaven works when once introduced into the meal. When leaven is introduced into the meal an irreversible process has begun that will continue until it has completed its leavening action. This is intended to stress the way the new form of the kingdom will develop. The power in the kingdom will not be external but internal. By its internal working it will effect an external transformation. All previous kingdoms had been introduced by military might; Babylon came to power by defeating Assyria, Medo-Persia ruled by defeating Babylon, Greece came to ascendancy by conquering Medo-Persia, and Rome dominated by overwhelming Greece. But this new kingdom will flourish, not by military might, but by a new principle—the power within.

The parable of the mustard and the leaven hidden in meal, then, stress the growth of the new form of the kingdom.

e. The Hid Treasure (Matt. 13:44). The purpose of this parable is to depict the relationship of Israel to this present age. Although set aside by God until this age is completed, yet Israel is not forgotten and this age does have reference to that program. We observe (1) that an individual, who is the Lord Jesus Christ, is purchasing a treasure. This purchase was effected at the cross. (2) This treasure is hidden away in a field, unseen by men, but known to the purchaser. (3) During the age the purchaser does not come into the possession of His purchased treasure, but only into the possession of the place in which the treasure resides. The parable is showing that Christ has laid the foundation for Israel's acceptance in this age, even though the age ends without His having appropriated His treasure. The treasure will be unearthed when He comes to establish His kingdom. Israel is now in blindness, but possessed.

f. The Pearl (Matt. 13:45-46). While some relate the pearl to the believing remnant saved at the end of the age, most interpreters relate the pearl to the church. Thus the Lord is showing that within this present age, in addition to acquiring the treasure, Israel, He will also acquire for His personal possession that which was born through injury, the church. We observe (1) that the church, like the pearl, becomes the possession of the "merchantman," Christ, by purchase; (2) the church, like the pearl, is to be formulated by gradual accretion; (3) the church, like the pearl, can only become His adornment by being lifted out of the place in which it was formed. This is to be related to the present age purpose, previously considered.

g. The Dragnet (Matt. 13:47-50). This parable indicates that the age is to end in a judgment, principally upon Gentile nations, since the net is to be cast into the sea (Matt. 13:47). This is in contrast to the judgment on Israel depicted in the second parable. The unsaved will be excluded from the kingdom that is to be established, as previously taught in the parables, and the righteous taken into it.

It is to be observed that there is a parallel between the "mysteries of the kingdom of heaven" of Matthew 13 and the mysteries referred to by Paul. The mystery of the sower closely parallels the mystery of godliness of 1 Timothy 3:16. The parable of the wheat and tares and the parable of the mustard seed parallel the mystery of lawlessness of 2 Thessalonians 2:7, which depicts the individual who is the head of a system. The parable of the leaven parallels the mystery Babylon of Revelation 17:1-7. The parable of the hid treasure parallels the mystery of Israel's blindness of Romans 11:25. The parable of the pearl parallels the mystery applicable to the church mentioned in Ephesians 3:3-9; Colossians 1:26-27; Romans 16:25.

B. The Letters to the Seven Churches in Revelation Two and Three

The course of this present age is presented in a second major passage found in Revelation two and three. Whereas Matthew thirteen surveyed this present age in its relation to the kingdom program Revelation two and three outline the present age in reference to the program in the church.

1. *The time period of Revelation two and three.* John, in the book of Revelation, is writing concerning things that were past, things that are present, and things that are future (Rev. 1:19). Scott writes:

> The great divisions of the book are here written for the instruction of the Church of God. "What thou hast seen" refers to the vision of Christ just beheld (verses 12-16). "The things that are" refer to the several successive, broadly-defined features of the professing Church and of Christ's relation thereto, till its final rejection, not yet accomplished (chaps. 2 and 3). "The things that are about to be after these things." In this third division, the world and the Jews, and, we may add, the corrupt and apostate Church, *i.e.*, that which is to be "spued out," are embraced in this strictly prophetic part of the Apocalypse (4—22:5).
>
> Nothing has more contributed to throw discredit on prophetic studies, than the erroneous principle on which it has been sought to interpret this book. Here is the key for its interpretation hanging at the door; take it down, use it, and enter in. There is simplicity and consistency in apportioning the main contents of the book to a *past*, a *present*, and a *future*.[21]

It would seem evident, then, that John, in writing to the seven churches, is depicting this present age from the inception of the church to the judgment of the apostate church prior to the second advent. Thus the period of time covered by these chapters would essentially parallel the period covered by Matthew thirteen.

2. *The purpose of the seven letters.* A threefold purpose in the writing of the seven letters may be suggested.

a. John is writing to seven local congregations in order to meet the needs of these individual assemblies. Pember says: "There can be no doubt that these letters were primarily intended for the communities to which they are inscribed, and deal with actual circumstances of the time."[22] There would be, then, a direct historical application of what is here recorded to each of the seven churches.

---

21 Walter Scott, *Exposition of the Revelation*, p. 50.
22 Pember, *op. cit.*, p. 278.

b. These letters would reveal the various kinds of individuals and assemblies throughout the age. Seiss states it thus:

> . . . the seven Churches represent seven varieties of Christians, both true and false. Every professer of Christianity is either an Ephesian in his religious qualities, a Smyrnaote, a Pergamite, a Thyatiran, a Sardian, a Philadelphian, or a Laodicean. It is of these seven sorts that the whole church is made up. . . .
>
> . . . every community of Christian professors has some of all the varied classes which make up Christendom at large . . . there are Protestant Papists, and Papistical Protestants; sectarian anti-sectarians, and partyists who are not schismatics; holy ones in the midst of abounding defection and apostasy, and unholy ones in the midst of the most earnest and active faith; light in dark places, and darkness in the midst of light.
>
> I thus find the seven Churches in every Church, giving to those Epistles a directness of application to ourselves, and to professing Christians of every age, of the utmost solemnity and importance.[23]

Pember says:

> . . . when taken together, they exhibit every phase of Christian society which would ever be found in the various parts of Christendom, and so enabled the Lord to give comfort, advice, exhortation, warning, and threatening, from which something could be found to suit any possible circumstance of His people till the end of the age.[24]

Thus, there would be a spiritual application, in addition to the historical interpretation.

c. There is a prophetic revelation as to the course of the age in the letters. Pember states: "In the order in which they were given, they foreshadowed the successive predominant phases through which the nominal Church was to pass, from the time when John saw the vision until the Lord came."[25] The seven churches, which were only seven of many which John could have chosen to address, seem to have been specifically chosen because of the significance of their names. Ephesus means "beloved" or perhaps "relaxation." Smyrna means "myrrh" or "bitter-

---

[23] Joseph Seiss, *Lectures on the Apocalypse*, I, 144-45.
[24] Pember, *op. cit.*, p. 289.
[25] *Ibid.*

ness." Pergamos means "high tower" or "thoroughly married." Thyatira means "pereptual sacrifice" or "continual offering." Sardis means "those escaping" or "renovation." Philadelphia means "brotherly love." Laodicea means "the people ruling or speaking" or "the judgment of the people."[26] The names themselves suggest the succession of the development of the periods within the age. Concerning this development Scott writes:

> Ecclesiastical pretension and departure from first love characterized the close of the apostolic-period—*Ephesus* (2:1-7). Next succeeded the martyr-period, which brings us down to the close of the tenth and last persecution, under Diocletian—*Smyrna* (2:8-11). Decreasing spirituality and increasing worldliness went hand in hand from the accession of Constantine and his public patronage of Christianity on to the seventh century—*Pergamos* (2:12-17). The papal church, which is Satan's masterpiece on earth, is witnessed in the assumption of universal authority and cruel persecution of the saints of God. Its evil reign covers "the middle ages," the moral characteristics of which have been well termed "dark." Popery blights everything it touches—*Thyatira* (2:18-29). The Reformation was God's intervention in grace and power to cripple papal authority and introduce into Europe the light which for 300 years has been burning with more or less brilliancy. Protestantism with its divisions and deadness shows clearly enough how far short it comes of God's ideal of the Church and Christianity—*Sardis* (3:1-6). Another Reformation, equally the work of God characterized the beginning of last century—*Philadelphia* (3:7-13). The present general state of the professing Church which is one of lukewarmness is the most hateful and nauseous of any yet described. We may well term the last phase of church-history on the eve of judgment, the christless period—*Laodicea* (3:14-22).
>
> Note that the history of the first three churches is consecutive; whereas the history of the remaining four overlaps, and then practically runs concurrently to the end—the Coming of the Lord.[27]

While these seven epochs are seen to be successive, it is important to observe that the succeeding epoch does not terminate the preceding one. Pember well observes:

> The number of parables [in Matthew 13] and of epistles is seven, that number being significant of dispensational completeness; and, in each of the two prophecies, we apparently have set before us seven successive phases or characteristic epochs . . . which embrace the whole. . . . These epochs commence in the order

[26] Cf. *ibid.*, p. 279.
[27] Scott, *op. cit.*, pp. 55-56.

in which they are given; but any of them may overlap that which succeeds it, or even extend its influence, in a greater or less degree, to the end of the age.[28]

3. *The parallelism between Matthew thirteen and Revelation two and three.* While the mystery form of the kingdom is not synonymous with the visible church, yet, since the time period is essentially the same in the two passages, we may reasonably expect that there would be a parallelism of development. The following chart will illustrate this general parallelism.

Matt. 13	*Rev. 2-3*	*Meaning of the name*	*Approximate dates*	*Characteristic*
Sower	Ephesus	Desired	Pentecost to 100 A.D.	Time of sowing, organization, and evangelism
Wheat and Tares	Smyrna	Myrrh	Nero to 300 A.D.	Persecution. Enemy revealed
Mustard Seed	Pergamos	Thoroughly Married	300 to 800 A.D.	Worldly alliance. Great external growth
Leaven	Thyatira	Continual sacrifice	800 to 1517	Papal domination. Doctrinal corruption
Treasure Hid	Sardis	Those escaping	Reformation	Empty profession. Rise of the state church
Pearl	Philadelphia	Brotherly love	The last days	True church of the last days
Dragnet	Laodicea	People ruling	Last days	Apostasy

It is not intended to infer that there is an identity in the revelation in the two passages, rather, that there is a similarity in the progress of the course of the age as revealed in the two portions.

---

[28] Pember, *op. cit.*, p. 233.

C. The Close of the Present Age

Within this present age between the two advents of Christ, God is bringing to fulfillment two distinct programs: that with the church, which will be completed at the rapture of the church, and that with Israel, which will be completed after the rapture at the second advent of Christ. Both of these have descriptive passages concerning the end times of their respective programs. There is a reference to the "last times" for the church (1Pet. 1:20 and Jude 18) and to the "last time" for the church (1 Pet. 1:5 and 1 John 2:18). There is reference to the "latter days" for Israel (Dan. 10:14; Deut. 4:30) and for the church (1 Tim. 4:1). Scripture refers to the "last days" for Israel (Isa. 2:2; Micah 4:1; Acts 2:17) and also for the church (2 Tim. 3:1; Heb. 1:2). There is also a reference to the "last day" for Israel (John 6:39, 40, 44, 54), although this usage of "day" may refer to a program rather than to a time period. In these observations it is important to observe that the references to any given time period must be related to the program of which it is a part. When used in reference to Israel's program it can not refer to the program for the church. Chafer writes:

> . . . distinction must be made the "last days" for Israel—the days of her kingdom glory in the earth (cf. Isa. 2:1-5)—and the "last days" for the Church, which are days of evil and apostasy (cf. 2 Tim. 3:1-5). Likewise, discrimination is called for between the "last days" for Israel and for the church and "the last day," which, as related to the Church, is the day of the resurrection of those who have died in Christ (cf. John 6:39-40, 44, 54).[29]

Careful distinction must be made, or one will relegate to the church that which constitutes closing events for Israel or vice-versa.

In this present consideration attention is not directed to the events concerning the close of the age in reference to Israel. This will be considered later and will include all those prophecies which take place after the translation of the church preceding the second advent of Christ. Attention is directed to the events connected with the close of the age in relation to God's program for the church.

---

[29] Chafer, *op. cit.*, IV, 374-75.

Concerning the last days for the church Chafer writes:

> A very extensive body of Scripture bears on the last days for the Church. Reference is to a restricted time at the very end of, and yet wholly within, the present age. Though this brief period immediately precedes the great tribulation and in some measure is a preparation for it, these two times of apostasy and confusion—though incomparable in history—are wholly separate the one from the other. Those Scriptures which set forth the last days for the Church give no consideration to political or world conditions but are confined to the Church itself. These Scriptures picture men as departing from the faith (1 Tim. 4:1-2). There will be a manifestation of characteristics which belong to unregenerate men, though it is under the profession of "a form of godliness" (cf. 2 Tim. 3:1-5). The indication is that, having denied the power of the blood of Christ (cf. 2 Tim 3:5 with Rom. 1:16; 1 Cor. 1:23-24; 2 Tim. 4:2-4), the leaders in these forms of righteousness will be unregenerate men from whom nothing more spiritual than this could proceed (Cf. 1 Cor. 2:14). The following is a partial list of the passages which present the truth respecting the last days of the Church: 1 Timothy 4:1-3; 2 Timothy 3:1-5; 4:3-4; James 5:1-8; 2 Peter 2:1-22; 3:3-6; Jude 1:1-25.[30]

Since the church is given the hope of an imminent return of Christ there can be no signs given to her as to when this event will take place. Therefore we pass by the subject of "the signs of the times" in reference to the closing days for the church. However, from the Scriptures cited above, there are certain revelations concerning the condition within the professing church at the end of the age. These conditions center around a system of denials. There is a denial of God (Luke 17:26; 2 Tim. 3:4-5), a denial of Christ (1 John 2:18; 1 John 4:3; 2 Pet. 2:6), a denial of Christ's return (2 Pet. 3:3-4), a denial of the faith (1 Tim. 4:1-2; Jude 3), a denial of sound doctrine (2 Tim. 4:3-4), a denial of the separated life (2 Tim. 3:1-7), a denial of Christian liberty (1 Tim. 4:3-4); a denial of morals (2 Tim. 3:1-8, 13; Jude 18), a denial of authority (2 Tim. 3:4).[31] This condition at the close of the age is seen to coincide with the state within the Laodicean Church, before which Christ must stand to seek admission. In view of its close it is not surprising that the age is called an "evil age" in Scripture.

---

30 *Ibid.*
31 D. H. Prichard, "The Last Days," pp. 51-58.

CHAPTER X

THE PARTIAL RAPTURE POSITION

The present age, in respect to the true church, terminates with the translation of the church into the Lord's presence. The doctrine of the translation of the church is one of the major considerations of the Eschatology of the New Testament (John 14:1-3; 2 Thess. 2:1; 1 Thess. 4:13-18; 1 Cor. 1:8; 15:51-52; Phil. 3:20-21; 2 Cor. 5:1-9). It is one of the questions on which Bible students are most in disagreement at the present time. Interpreters of the premillennial school are divided into such camps as the partial rapturist, who raises the issue of the subjects of the rapture, and the pretribulationist, midtribulationist and posttribulationist, who raise the issue of the time of the rapture in relation to the tribulation period.

I. DEFINITION OF TERMS

It would be well, at this point, to set forth the various words used in the New Testament in relation to the second advent of Christ: *parousia, apokalupsis,* and *epiphaneia.* Even though these are frequently held to be technical terms, with specific designations, Walvoord writes:

> It is the viewpoint of the writer that all three terms are used in a general and not a technical sense and that they are descriptive of both the rapture and the glorious return of Christ to the earth. . . .
>
> I. PAROUSIA
>
> The word most frequently used in the Scriptures to describe the return of Christ is [parousia] . . . it occurs twenty-four times in the New Testament in a variety of connections. As its etymology indicates the word means *to be near* or *alongside.* . . . It involves all that the English word *presence* connotes. . . . It has come to mean not simply *presence* but the act by which the presence is brought about, i.e., by the *coming* of the individual.

A brief survey of its usage in the New Testament includes . . . 1 Corinthians 16:17 . . . 2 Corinthians 7:6, 7 . . . Philippians 1:26 . . . 2 Thessalonians 2:9 . . . 2 Peter 3:12. All must concede that these instances are general and not technical.

. . . That it is used frequently of the rapture of the church is clear in the following references (1 Cor. 15:23; 1 Thess. 2:19; 4:15; 5:23; 2 Thess. 2:1 (?); James 5:7, 8; 2 Pet. 3:4 (?); 1 John 2:29). . . .

The word is also used, however, of the return of Christ to the earth with the church in a number of passages (Mt. 24:3, 27, 37, 39; 1 Thess. 3:13; 2 Thess. 2:8; 2 Pet. 1:16). . . .

The conclusion is inevitable that the same word is used in all these passages in a general and not specific sense. Its contribution to the doctrine is to emphasize the bodily presence of Christ. . . .

II. APOKALUPSIS

The second important word for the coming of Christ, . . . [apokalupsis] occurs . . . eighteen times in noun form, twenty-six times in the verb form. It is obviously derived from . . . [apo] and . . . [kaluptō], the latter meaning *to cover,* or *to veil,* and with the prefix, *to uncover* or *to unveil,* and hence *to reveal.* . . .

A survey of those passages in which the word is used in relation to Christ demonstrates that in a number of instances it is used of the second coming of Christ (1 Pet. 4:13; 2 Thess. 1:7; Lk. 17:30). . . .

In other passages, however, it is clearly used in reference to the coming of Christ in the air for His church (1 Cor. 1:7; Col. 3:4; 1 Pet. 1:7, 13). . . .

The doctrine that is involved in the use of the word in relation to Christ is an emphasis on the future manifestation of the glory of Christ. . . .

III. EPIPHANEIA

The third word used of the return of Christ is, . . . [epiphaneia] . . . [epi] and, [phanēs]. The root meaning of *to bring forth into the light, cause to shine, to show* is found from Homer down (Thayer). The addition of the preposition gives it an intensive meaning. . . . it is used of the first coming of Christ to the earth in His incarnation (Lk. 1:79; 2 Tim. 1:10). . . .

As used of the return of the Lord, two instances are found where it refers to the rapture of the church and two instances seem to refer to the second coming of Christ. . . . it would seem sound exegesis to classify 1 Timothy 6:14 and 2 Timothy 4:8 as referring to the rapture. . . .

In 2 Timothy 4:1 and Titus 2:13, however, there seems to be reference to His second coming. . . .

> The emphasis given to the truth in the use of . . . [epiphaneia] is to reassure us that Christ will actually appear, that He will be seen and will be manifested in a visible way.[1]

These words, then, emphasize three great facts in relation to the second advent: Christ will be visibly present, His glory consequently will be fully revealed, and He Himself will be fully manifested.

II. The Partial Rapture Theory

The first theory associated with the translation of the church is not concerned with the time of the translation in relation to the tribulation period, but rather with the subjects to be translated. It is contended that not all believers will be taken at the translation of the church, but rather only those who are "watching" and "waiting" for that event, who have reached some degree of spiritual attainment that makes them worthy to be included. This view has been held by such men as R. Govett, G. H. Lang, D. M. Panton, G. H. Pember, J. A. Seiss, and Austin Sparks to mention but a few. The view is stated by Waugh, who says:

> But there are not a few—some of them deep and prayerful students of the Scriptures—who believe that only a prepared and expectant section of believers will be then translated. They believe that a clear inference from Luke 21:36 is that those Christians who do *not* "watch" will *not* "escape all these things that shall come to pass," and will *not* be accounted worthy "to stand before the Son of Man." They gather from such passages as Phil. 3:20, Titus 2:13, II Tim. 4:8, Hebrews 9:28, that those only will be taken who "wait," "look for," and "have loved His appearing."[2]

A. *The doctrinal difficulties of the partial rapture theory.* The partial rapture position rests on certain misunderstandings of the doctrines of the Word.

1. The partial rapturist position is based on a misunderstanding of the value of the death of Christ as it frees the sinner from condemnation and renders him acceptable to God.

---

[1] John F. Walvoord, "New Testament Words for the Lord's Coming." *Bibliotheca Sacra,* 101:284-89, July, 1944.

[2] Thomas Waugh, *When Jesus Comes,* p. 108.

This doctrine is bound up in three New Testament words: propitiation, reconciliation, and redemption. In regard to propitiation Chafer writes:

> Christ by having His own blood sprinkled, as it were, over His body at Golgotha, becomes the Mercy Seat in reality. He is the Propitiator and has made propitiation by so answering the just demands of God's holiness against sin that heaven is rendered propitious. This fact of propitiation existing is to be believed. . . .
>
> Propitiation is the Godward side of the work of Christ on the cross. The death of Christ for the sin of the world changed the whole position of mankind in its relation to God, for He recognizes what Christ did in behalf of the world whether man enters into it or not. God is never said to be reconciled, but His attitude toward the world is altered when the world's relation to Him becomes radically changed through the death of Christ.[3]

In regard to reconciliation the same author says:

> Reconciliation means that someone or something is thoroughly changed and adjusted to something which is a standard, as a watch may be adjusted to a chronometer. . . . By the death of Christ on its behalf, the whole world is thoroughly changed in its relation to God. . . . The world is so altered in its position respecting the holy judgments of God through the cross of Christ that God is not now imputing their sin unto them. The world is thus rendered savable. . . .
>
> Since the position of the world before God is completely changed through the death of Christ, God's own attitude toward man cannot longer be the same. He is prepared to deal with souls now in the light of what Christ has accomplished. . . . God . . . believes completely in the thing which Christ has done and accepts it, so as to continue being just although able thereby to justify any sinner who accepts the Savior as his reconciliation.[4]

Concerning redemption, he writes:

> Redemption is an act of God by which He Himself pays as a ransom the price of human sin which the outraged holiness and government of God requires. Redemption undertakes the solution of the problem of sin, as reconciliation undertakes the solution of the problem of the sinner, and propitiation undertakes the problem of an offended God. . . .
>
> The redemption provided for and offered to the sinner is a re-

---

[3] Lewis Sperry Chafer, *Systematic Theology,* VII, 259.
[4] *Ibid.,* VII, 262-63.

> demption from sin. . . . Divine redemption is by blood—the ransom price—and by power.[5]

The result of this threefold work is a perfect salvation, by which the sinner is justified, made acceptable to God, placed in Christ positionally, to be received by God as though he were the Son Himself. The individual who has this perfect standing of Christ can never be less than completely acceptable to God. The partial rapturist, who insists that only those who are "waiting" and "watching" will be translated, minimizes the perfect standing of the child of God in Christ and presents him before the Father in his own experimental righteousness. The sinner, then, must be less than justified, less than perfect in Christ.

2. The partial rapturist must deny the New Testament teaching on the unity of the body of Christ. According to 1 Corinthians 12:12-13, all believers are united to the body of which Christ is the Head (Eph. 5:30). This baptizing experience is true of every regenerated individual. If the rapture includes only a portion of those redeemed, then the body, of which Christ is the head, will be a dismembered and disfigured body when it is taken to Him. The building, of which He is the chief cornerstone, will be incomplete. The priesthood, of which He is the High Priest, will be without a portion of its complement. The bride, in relation to whom He is the Bridegroom, will be disfigured. The new creation, of which He is the Head, will be incomplete. Such is impossible to imagine.

3. The partial rapturist must deny the completeness of the resurrection of the believers at the translation. Since not all the living saints could be raptured, logically, not all the dead in Christ could be resurrected, inasmuch as many of them died in spiritual immaturity. But since Paul teaches that "we shall all be changed," and that all those that "sleep in Jesus" will God bring (1 Cor. 15:51-52; 1 Thess. 4:14), it is impossible to admit a partial resurrection.

4. The partial rapturist confuses the Scriptural teaching on rewards. The rewards are gratuitously given by God as the recompense for faithful service. The New Testament is very

---

[5] *Ibid.*, III, 88.

clear in its teaching about rewards (Rev. 2:10; James 1:12; 1 Thess. 2:19; Phil. 4:1; 1 Cor. 9:25; 1 Peter 5:4; 2 Tim. 4:8). Nowhere in its teaching about rewards is the rapture included as the reward for watching. Such a teaching would make rewards a legal obligation on the part of God, rather than a gracious gift.

5. The partial rapturist confuses the distinction between law and grace. If his view is correct, the believer's position before God, eternally, would depend on his works, for what he did and what attitudes he developed would then be the basis of his acceptance. It scarcely needs be said that acceptance by God will be solely on the basis of the individual's position in Christ, not his own preparation of himself for the translation.

6. The partial rapturist must deny the distinction between Israel and the church. It will be observed in the discussion of problem passages to follow that he uses Scriptures that are applicable to God's program for Israel and applies them to the church.

7. The partial rapturist must place a portion of the believing church in the tribulation period. This is impossible. One of the purposes of the tribulation period is to judge the world in preparation for the kingdom to follow. The church needs not such a purging judgment unless the death of Christ be ineffective. From these considerations then, it is believed that the partial rapture position is untenable.

B. *Problem passages.* There are certain passages which the partial rapturist uses to support his position, which, at first glance, seem to support this view.

1. Luke 21:36, "Watch ye therefore and pray always, that ye may be accounted worthy to escape all those things that shall come to pass, and to stand before the Son of man."[6] It will be observed that the primary reference in this chapter is to the nation Israel, who is already in the tribulation period, and therefore this is not applicable to the church. The things to be escaped are the judgments associated with "that day" (vs. 34), that is, the Day of the Lord. Watchfulness is enjoined upon

[6] Cf. G. H. Lang, *Revelation*, pp. 88-89.

the church (1 Thess. 5:6; Titus 2:13) apart from being found worthy to participate in the translation.

2. Matthew 24:41-42, "Two women shall be grinding at the mill; the one shall be taken and the other left. Watch therefore: for ye know not what hour your Lord doth come."[7] Again, this passage is in that discourse in which the Lord outlines His program for Israel, who is already in the tribulation period. The one taken is taken to judgment and the one left is left for the millennial blessing. Such is not the prospect for the church.

3. Hebrews 9:28, "...unto them that look for him shall he appear the second time without sin unto salvation." The phrase "unto them that look for him" is used here as synonymous with "believers" or "the church" since this attitude constitutes the normal attitude of God's redeemed. Believers are those that "look for the Saviour" (Phil. 3:20) or anticipate the "blessed hope" (Titus 2:13). These who look for him are not contrasted with those who do not look for him in this passage. It simply teaches that as he appeared once to put away sin (vs. 26) and now appears in heaven for us (vs. 24), to that same group He will again appear (vs. 28) to complete the work of redemption. The inference is that the same group to whom He appeared, and for whom He now appears, will be the one to whom He will appear.

4. Philippians 3:11, "If by any means I might attain unto the resurrection of the dead."[8] Some hold that Paul was in doubt about his own rapture. The context does not support this view. Verse 11 looks back to verse 8 where Paul reveals that, because of the superior value of the knowledge of Christ Jesus, he gave up all in which he had trusted that he "might win Christ," and, having found Christ, "attain unto the resurrection of the dead." The resurrection, thus, is seen to be the result of "winning Christ," not the result of preparing himself for the translation. He has revealed the innermost secret of His service, a complete devotion to Christ since He met Him on the Damascus road.

---

[7] Cf. R. Govett, "One Taken and One Left," *The Dawn*, 22:515-18, February 15, 1936.

[8] Cf. R. Govett, *Entrance into The Kingdom*, p. 35.

5. 1 Corinthians 15:23, "... every man in his own order." This is made by the partial rapturist to teach a division in the ranks of the believer in the resurrection of the church. However, it must be noted, Paul is not giving instruction on the order of the resurrection for the church, but rather the divisions or "marching bands" within the whole resurrection program, which will include not only church saints, but also Old Testament saints and tribulation saints as well.

6. 2 Timothy 4:8, "... unto all them also that love his appearing." This is used by the adherents of this position to show that the rapture must be a partial one. However, it is to be noticed that the subject of translation is not in view in this passage, but rather the question of reward. The second advent was intended by God to be a purifying hope (1 John 3:3). Because of such purifying a new life is produced because of the expectancy of the Lord's return. Therefore those that truly "love his appearing" will experience a new kind of life which will bring a reward.

7. 1 Thessalonians 1:10, "And to wait for his son from heaven ... which delivered us from the wrath to come," and 1 Thessalonians 4:13-18 together with 1 Corinthians 15:51-52 are used by the partial rapturist to teach that the church that was unprepared for the rapture will meet the Lord in the clouds on His way to the earth at the second advent.[9] Such a view coincides with the interpretation of the posttribulationist and will be shown to be contrary to the teaching of Scripture.

An examination of the Scriptures used by the partial rapturists to support their position shows that their interpretation is not consistent with true exegesis. Since this view is out of harmony with true doctrine and true exegesis, it must be rejected.

---

[9] Cf. G. H. Lang, *op. cit.*, pp. 236-37.

CHAPTER XI

THE POSTTRIBULATION RAPTURE THEORY

A theory coming into greater prevalence at the present time to explain the time of the translation of the church in relation to the tribulation period is the posttribulation rapture theory. This theory holds that the church will continue on the earth until the second advent at the end of this present age, at which time the church will be caught up into the clouds to meet the Lord who has come into the air on His way from heaven to earth for the second advent, to return immediately with Him. Reese, a leading exponent of this theory, states his proposition thus:

> The Church of Christ will not be removed from the earth until the Advent of Christ at the very end of the present Age: the Rapture and the Appearing take place at the same crisis; hence Christians of that generation will be exposed to the final affliction under Antichrist.[1]

I. THE ESSENTIAL BASES OF POSTTRIBULATION RAPTURISM

Before considering the arguments used by the advocates of this position, one should observe the essential bases on which posttribulationism rests. (1) Posttribulationism must be based on a denial of dispensationalism and all dispensational distinctions. It is only thus that they can place the church in that period which is particularly called "the time of Jacob's trouble" (Jer. 30:7). (2) Consequently, the position rests on a denial of the distinctions between Israel and the church. (3) The position must rest on a denial of the Scriptural teaching concerning the nature and purpose of the tribulation period. Whereas Scripture uses such terms as wrath, judgment, indignation, trial, trouble, and destruction to describe this period, and states

[1] Alexander Reese, *The Approaching Advent of Christ*, p. 18.

that the divine purpose in the period is to pour out judgment on sin, the advocate of this position must deny this essential teaching of the Word. (4) The posttribulationist must deny all the distinctions observed from the Scriptures between the rapture and the second advent, making them one and the same event. (5) The posttribulationist must deny the doctrine of imminence, which says that the Lord may come at any time, and substitute the teaching that a multitude of signs must be fulfilled before the Lord can possibly come. (6) The posttribulationist denies any future fulfillment to the prophecy of Daniel 9:24-27, claiming for it an historical fulfillment. (7) The posttribulationist must apply major passages of Scripture that outline God's program for Israel (Matt. 13; Matt. 24-25; Rev. 4-19) to the church in order to support his views. It will thus be observed that the position rests essentially on a system of denials of the interpretations held by the pretribulation rapturist, rather than on a positive exposition of Scripture.

II. The Essential Arguments of the Posttribulation Rapturist

A. *The historical argument.* There are several major arguments on which the posttribulationist rests his case. The first of these is the historical argument. His position is that pretribulationism is a new doctrine, arising in the last hundred years, and therefore to be rejected because it is not apostolic. Reese states:

> About 1830 . . . a new school arose within the fold of Premillennialism that sought to overthrow what, since the Apostolic Age, have been considered by all pre-millennialists as established results, and to institute in their place a series of doctrines that had never been heard of before. The school I refer to is that of "The Brethren" or "Plymouth Brethren," founded by J. N. Darby.[2]

Cameron speaks in the same line:

> Now, be it remembered, that prior to that date, no hint of any approach to such belief can be found in any Christian literature from Polycarp down. . . . Surely, a doctrine that finds no exponent or advocate in the whole history and literature of Christendom, for eighteen hundred years after the founding of the Church—a doc-

---

[2] *Ibid.*, p. 19.

> trine that was never taught by a Father or Doctor of the Church in the past—that has no standard Commentator or Professor of the Greek language in any Theological School until the middle of the Nineteenth century, to give it approval, and that is without a friend, even to mention its name amongst the orthodox teachers or the heretical sects of Christendom—such a fatherless and motherless doctrine, when it rises to the front, demanding universal acceptance, ought to undergo careful scrutiny before it is admitted and tabulated as part of "the faith once for all delivered unto the saints."[3]

In reply to the argument several things are to be noted. (1) Such an argument is an argument from silence. If the same line of reasoning were followed one would not accept the doctrine of justification by faith, for it was not clearly taught until the Reformation. The failure to discern the teaching of the Scripture does not nullify that teaching. (2) The early church lived in the light of the belief in the imminent return of Christ.[4] Their expectation was that Christ might return at any time. Pretribulationism is the only position consistent with this doctrine of imminence. If an argument from silence be followed, the weight of evidence favors the pretribulation view. (3) It should be observed that each era of church history has been occupied with a particular doctrinal controversy, which has become the object of discussion, revision, and formulation, until there was general acceptation of what Scripture taught. The entire field of theology was thus formulated through the age. It was not until the last century that the field of Eschatology became a matter to which the mind of the church was turned. This has well been developed by Orr, who writes:

> Has it ever struck you . . . what a singular *parallel* there is between the historical course of dogma, in the one hand, and the scientific order of the text-books on a systematic theology on the other? The history of dogma, as you speedily discover is simply the system of theology spread out through the centuries . . . and this not only as regards its general subject-matter, but even as respects the definite succession of its parts. . . . One thing, I think it shows unmistakably, viz., that neither arrangement is arbitrary—that there is law and reason underlying it; and another thing which

---

[3] Robert Cameron, *Scriptural Truth About The Lord's Return*, pp. 72-73.
[4] Cf. G. H. N. Peters, *Theocratic Kingdom*, I, 494-96.

forces itself upon us is, that the law of these two developments—the logical and the historical—is the same.

. . . the second century in the history of the Church—what was that? The age of *Apologetics* and of the vindication of *the fundamental ideas of all religion*—of the *Christian* especially—in conflict with Paganism and with the Gnostics.

We pass to the next stage in the development, and what do we find there? Just what comes next in the theological system—*Theology Proper*—the Christian doctrine of God, and specially the doctrine of the Trinity. This period is covered by the *Monarchian, Arian,* and *Macedonian* controversies of the third and fourth centuries.

. . . What comes next? As in the logical system theology is succeeded by *Anthropology,* so in the history of dogma the controversies I have named are followed in the beginning of the fifth century by the *Augustinian* and *Pelagian* controversies, in which . . . the centre of interest shifts from God to man.

. . . From the time of Augustine's death we see the Church entering on that long and distracting series of controversies known as Christological— *Nestorian, Eutychian, Monophysite, Monothelite* —which kept it in continual ferment, and rent it with the most unchristlike passions during the fifth and sixth, on even till near the end of the seventh, centuries.

. . . Theology, Anthropology, Christology have each had its day—in the order of the theological system, which the history still carefully follows, [but] it was not the turn of *Soteriology* . . . [until] the next step, that taken by the Reformers in the development of the doctrine of the *Application of Redemption.* This . . . is the next great division of the theological system.

What now shall I say of the remaining branch of the theological system, the Eschatological? An Eschatology, indeed, there was in the early Church, but it was not theologically conceived; and a Mythical Eschatology there was in the Mediaeval Church—an Eschatology of Heaven, Hell, and Purgatory . . . but the Reformation swept this away, and, with its sharply contrasted states of bliss and woe, can hardly be said to have put anything in its place, or even to have faced very distinctly the difficulties of the problem. . . . Probably I am not mistaken in thinking that, besides the necessary revision of the theological system as a whole, which could not properly be undertaken till the historical development I have sketched had run its course, the modern mind has given itself with special earnestness to eschatological questions, moved thereto, perhaps, by the solemn impression that on it the

> ends of the world have come, and that some great crisis in the history of human affairs is approaching.[5]

This whole concept of the progress of dogma would be our strongest argument against the posttribulation rapturist who argues that the doctrine must be rejected because it was not clearly taught in the early church.

B. *The argument against imminency.* A second major argument of the posttribulation rapturist is the argument against imminency.[6] It is evident that if belief in the imminent return of Christ is the Scriptural doctrine then the church must be raptured before the signs of the tribulation period unfold. The adherent of that position discounts all the Scriptural admonitions to the church to watch for Christ and bids us watch for signs. His position rests on the argument that the announcements of events such as the destruction of Jerusalem, the death of Peter, the imprisonment of Paul, and the announced program for the age as set forth in Matthew 28:19-20, together with the outlined course of the age. with its development of apostasy, all make an imminent return impossible; therefore the Lord could not come until these events had taken place. Such argument fails to see that the very men who received such announcements themselves believed that what would be the natural course of history could be interrupted by the translation of the believers out of the sphere in which history unfolds and held to the imminent return.

The doctrine of imminency is taught in Scripture in such passages as John 14:2-3; 1 Corinthians 1:7; Philippians 3:20-21; 1 Thessalonians 1:9-10; 4:16-17; 5:5-9; Titus 2:13; James 5:8-9; Revelation 3:10; 22:17-22. While the views of the early church will be studied later, several citations may be made at this point to show that the early church held to the doctrine of imminency. Clement wrote in the *First Epistle to the Corinthians*:

> Ye see how in a little while the fruit of the trees come to maturity. Of a truth, soon and suddenly shall His will be accomplished, as the Scriptures also bear witness, saying "Speedily

[5] James Orr, *The Progress of Dogma*, pp. 21-31.
[6] Cf. Reese, *op. cit.*, pp. 108-19.

will He come, and will not tarry"; and "The Lord shall suddenly come to His temple, even the Holy One, for whom ye look."[7]

Again, Clement writes:

> If therefore we shall do what is just in the sight of God, we shall enter into His kingdom, and shall receive the promises, which neither eye hath seen, nor ear heard, nor have entered into the heart of man. Wherefore, let us every hour expect the kingdom of God in love and righteousness, because we know not the day of the Lord's appearing.[8]

In the *Didache* we read:

> Watch for your life's sake. Let not your lamps be quenched, nor your loins unloosed; but be ye ready, for ye know not the hour in which our Lord cometh.[9]

Cyprian says: "It were a self-contradictory and incompatible thing for us, who pray that the kingdom of God may quickly come, to be looking for a long life here below...."[10] These give evidence that the exhortation to watchfulness addressed to the church became the hope of the early church and that they lived in the light of the expectation of the imminent return of Christ. The testimony of the Scriptures and the evidence of the early church cannot be denied.

C. *The promise of tribulation.* A third major argument of the posttribulation rapturist is the argument based on the promise of tribulation given to the church.[11] Passages such as Luke 23:27-31; Matthew 24:9-11; Mark 13:9-13, which are addressed to Israel and promise them tribulation, are used to prove that the church will go through the tribulation period. In addition, passages such as John 15:18-19; and John 16:1-2, 33, which are addressed to the church, are also so used. Their argument is that in the light of such specific promises it is impossible to say that the church will be raptured prior to the tribulation period. Their argument is substantiated by citing the persecutions recorded in Acts into which the church came (Acts 8:1-3;

---

7 Alexander Roberts and James Donaldson, *The Ante-Nicene Fathers*, I, 11.
8 Cited by J. F. Silver, *The Lord's Return*, p. 59.
9 Roberts and Donaldson, *op. cit.*, VII, 382.
10 Cited by Silver, *op. cit.*, p. 67.
11 Cf. George Rose, *Tribulation Till Translation*, pp. 67-77.

11:19; 14:22; Rom. 12:12) as being a partial fulfillment of those warnings.

1. In reply to this argument it is necessary to notice, first of all, that Scripture abounds in promises that Israel will be brought into a time of purging to prepare them as a nation for the millennium to follow the advent of Messiah. However, since Israel is to be distinguished from the church in the economy of God, those scriptures which promise tribulation to Israel can not be made to teach that the church is to experience the tribulation period. Israel and the church are two distinct entities in the plan of God and must be so regarded.

2. Further, it must be noticed that the term *tribulation* is used in several different ways in Scripture. It is used in a non-technical, non-eschatological sense in reference to any time of suffering or testing into which one goes. It is so used in Matthew 13:21; Mark 4:17; John 16:33; Romans 5:3; 12:12; 2 Corinthians 1:4; 2 Thessalonians 1:4; Revelation 1:9. It is used in its technical or eschatological sense in reference to the whole period of the seven years of tribulation, as in Revelation 2:22 or Matthew 24:29. It is also used in reference to the last half of this seven year period, as in Matthew 24:21. When the word *tribulation* is used in reference to the church, as in John 16:33, it is used in a non-technical sense, in which the church is promised an age-long opposition from the god of this age, but it is not teaching that the church will be brought into the period technically known as the tribulation. Otherwise one would have to teach that the tribulation has already existed for over nineteen hundred years.

Since the posttribulation rapturist insists that the church is not only promised tribulation, but is even now experiencing that tribulation, as has the church down through the ages, he must give that period a different character from that set forth in the Scriptures. It will be shown in detail at a later time that the characterization of that period, according to the Scripture, is described by such words as wrath, judgment, indignation, trial, trouble, destruction. This essential characterization must be denied by the adherent to this position.

D. *The historical fulfillment of Daniel 9:24-27.* A fourth

major argument of the posttribulation rapturist is the historical fulfillment of the prophecy of Daniel.[12] It is held that the prophecy, particularly that of Daniel 9:24-27, has been historically fulfilled in its entirety. Rose writes:

> All the evidence of the New Testament, and of Christian experience agree with the greatest teachers of the Christian church that, the seventieth week of Daniel's prophecy has all been fulfilled more than 1900 years ago. This leaves no future seventieth week yet to be fulfilled in "the great tribulation after the rapture."[13]

He holds that there is no gap between the 69th and 70th week of the prophecy, saying:

> If there were "gaps" and "intermissions" the prophecy would be vague, misleading, and deceptive. . . . The "62 weeks" joined immediately unto the "7 weeks," and their combined "69 weeks" reached "UNTO MESSIAH." Beyond His birth, but not to his "triumphal entry"; only "UNTO" His public anointing. There was no "gap" between the "69th, and the 70th weeks." . . . The "one week" of prophetic "seventy weeks" began with John the Baptist; from his first public preaching the kingdom of God, the gospel dispensation commenced. These seven years, added to the 483 years, completes the 490 years . . . so that the whole of the prophecy from the times and corresponding events, has been fulfilled to the very letter.[14]

He holds, further, that:

> John began His ministry as the "seventieth week" was ushered in, and Christ was baptized, tempted, and began to preach a few months later.
>
> The first half of the week was used in preaching the gospel of the kingdom . . . The middle of the week was reached at Passover time. . . .
>
> . . . .
>
> The Passover . . . was exactly in "the middle of the seventieth week," or 486½ years after "the commandment to RESTORE, and to build Jerusalem."[15]

Christ, according to this theory, becomes the one who confirms

---

12 Cf. *Ibid.*, pp. 24-66.
13 *Ibid.*, p. 62.
14 *Ibid.*, pp. 46-47.
15 *Ibid.*, pp. 64-66.

the Covenant and in the period of His ministry the six great promises of Daniel 9:24 have already been fulfilled.

1. In reply to this interpretation it can be noted that the six great areas of promise in Daniel 9:24 are related to Daniel's people and Daniel's holy city, that is, related to the nation Israel. These promises are the logical outgrowth of God's covenants with that nation. Israel as a nation has not yet experienced her national salvation. The church can not be now fulfilling these promises. Thus we must conclude that these six areas are awaiting a future fulfillment.

2. Again, the "he" of Daniel 9:27 must have as its antecedent "the prince that shall come" of the preceding verse. Because this one is related to the people who destroyed the city and the sanctuary, that is the Romans, this one confirming the covenant can not be Christ, but must be the man of sin, spoken of by Christ (Matt. 24:15), by Paul (2 Thess. 2), and John (Rev. 13), who will make a false covenant with Israel. The fact that sacrifices and oblation continued after the death of Christ until the year 70 A.D. would point out the fact that it was not Christ who caused these sacrifices to terminate. It is interesting to note that the Lord, in that great eschatological passage dealing with the future of Israel (Matt. 24-25), speaks of a yet future fulfillment of Daniel's prophecy (Matt. 24:15) after His death.

3. It is of importance to note that the prophecies of the first sixty-nine weeks were fulfilled literally. Thus a literal fulfillment of the seventieth week, both as to time and events, is made necessary. Walvoord writes:

> The important point . . . is that the first sixty-nine weeks had a *literal* fulfillment, both as to details and as to chronology. In approaching the task of interpreting the prophecy concerning the seventieth week, we must in all fairness to the principles approved by the fulfillment of the sixty-nine weeks, expect a literal fulfillment of the seventieth week both in its detail and in its chronology.[16]

Since the posttribulation rapture interpretation is out of harmony with the principle of literal interpretation, for the prophe-

[16] John F. Walvoord, "Is the Seventieth Week of Daniel Future?" *Bibliotheca Sacra,* 101:35, January, 1944.

cies must be spiritually interpreted to have them fulfilled historically, it must be denied.

E. *The argument from resurrection.* The fifth argument, on which the posttribulation rapturist most strongly depends, is the argument from resurrection.[17] The argument, based on Reese, is summarized by McPherson, who says:

> Clearly the resurrection of the holy dead takes place at the rapture of the Church (I Thess. 4:16). Therefore, "wheresoever the resurrection is, there will the Rapture be also." Upon examining passages that speak of the resurrection of the holy dead, which is the first resurrection (Rev. 20:5-6), we find that this first resurrection is associated with the coming of the Lord (Isa. 26:19), the conversion of Israel (Rom. 11:15), the inauguration of the Kingdom (Luke 14:14-15; Rev. 20:4-6), the giving of rewards (Rev. 11:15-18), the Great Tribulation coming before it (Dan. 12:1-3).[18]

Stanton states the thinking of Reese clearly when he writes:

> Reese's argument takes on the form of a syllogism, the major premises being (1) the Old Testament Scriptures prove that the resurrection of the Old Testament saint is at the revelation of Christ, just prior to the millennial kingdom; the minor premise being (2) all Darbyists agree that the resurrection of the church synchronizes with the resurrection of Israel; hence, the conclusion is drawn (3) therefore the resurrection of the church sets the time of the rapture as posttribulational.[19]

1. In reply to the conclusion of Reese it need only be pointed out that many present day pretribulation rapturists do not agree with the position of Darby that the resurrection at the time of the rapture includes the Old Testament saints. It seems better to place the resurrection of these Old Testament saints at the time of the second advent. This position will be examined later in detail. But, if one separates the resurrection of the church from the resurrection of Israel, there is no strength left in Reese's argument. Stanton's corrected syllogism makes the point clear:

> (1) The Old Testament saints are raised after the tribulation; (2) Darby says that Israel's resurrection occurs before the tribu-

---

[17] Cf. Reese, *op. cit.*, pp. 34-94.

[18] Norman S. McPherson, *Triumph Through Tribulation*, p. 41.

[19] Gerald Stanton, *Kept From the Hour*, p. 320.

lation with that of the church; (3) therefore, Darby was wrong in respect to the time of Israel's resurrection.[20]

It does seem strange that Reese, who argues that Darby is wrong so frequently, insists that he is infallible on this point as to the relation of Israel's resurrection to that of the church.

2. A second line of argument followed by Reese is to insist that the whole resurrection program takes place within one day. This he does on the basis of such passages as John 5:28-29; 11:24. He argues:

> . . . we were able to locate with relative exactness the time of that resurrection. It is to take place at the Day of the Lord, when Antichrist is destroyed, Israel converted, and the Messianic Age introduced by the Coming of the Lord. . . . The "resurrection of the just" . . . in every case . . . takes place "at the last day." Here is a very definite point of time. . . . there can be no doubt that "the last day" is the closing day of the Age that precedes the Messianic Kingdom of glory.[21]

3. In reply to this contention it is sufficient to point out that the term *Day of the Lord,* or *that day,* is not a term which applies to a twenty-four hour period, but rather the whole program of events, including the tribulation period, the second advent program, and the entire millenial age. It may be said to be that whole period beginning with the judgments of the seventieth week and extending through the millennial age. Chafer says:

> This period extends from Christ's coming "as a thief in the night" (Matt. 24:43; Luke 12:39-40; 1 Thess. 5:2; 2 Pet. 3:10; Rev. 16:15) to the passing of the heavens and the earth that now are and the melting of the elements with fervent heat. . . . It may then be seen that this day includes the judgments of God upon the nations and upon Israel and that these judgments occur at Christ's return. It includes both Christ's return and the kingdom of a thousand years which follows. It extends indeed to the final dissolution with which the kingdom ends. . . .[22]

Reese, himself, is forced to agree, for he says:

> Something might be said in favour of this, for Peter has a saying that one day with the Lord is as a thousand years; and the Day of the Lord in the O. and N. Testaments sometimes refers, not

---

20 *Ibid.*, p. 321.
21 Reese, *op. cit.*, 52-54.
22 Lewis Sperry Chafer, *Systematic Theology*, VII, 110.

> only to the day when Messiah comes in glory, but also the period of His Reign.[23]

Thus it is wrong to conclude that "that day" or "the last day" must teach that all saints will be resurrected at the same moment of time. It must be observed, also, that the passages Reese uses from the Gospels (John 6:39-54; Luke 20:34-36; Matt. 13:43; Luke 14:14-15) all apply to God's program for Israel. If it be shown that this resurrection does take place at the second advent, it does not prove posttribulation rapturism, unless the church must be resurrected at the same point of time. This is a false premise.

4. In dealing with the resurrection in the Epistles (Rom. 11:15; 1 Cor. 15:50-54; 1 Thess. 4:13-18; 1 Cor. 15:21-26) Reese argues the time of the resurrection from 1 Corinthians 15:54: "So when this corruptible shall have put on incorruption, and this mortal shall have put on immortality, then shall be brought to pass the saying that is written, Death is swallowed up in victory." His argument is:

> The resurrection and transfiguration of the faithful dead will take place in fulfillment of an O. T. prophecy. This occurs in Isaiah xxv. 8. . . . The resurrection of the saints, and the victory over death, *synchronise with the inauguration of the Theocratic Kingdom, the Coming of Jehovah, and the conversion of living Israel.*[24]

5. In reply to this contention we would point out that Paul is not quoting the passage from Isaiah to establish the time of the resurrection. The institution of the millennial age necessitates the abolition of death for those in it. Israel will experience resurrection at the time of the inception of the millennium, but the church will have been resurrected previously. Reese's error is in supposing all the righteous dead must be raised at the same time.

6. Concerning the resurrection mentioned in Revelation 20:4-6, Reese argues that since it is called first resurrection it must necessarily be the first numerically. He writes:

---

23 Reese, *op. cit.*, p. 55.
24 *Ibid.*, p. 63.

> Not a word is said by John in the whole of the Revelation of any such resurrection. Nothing can be found of an earlier one, either here or in any other part of the Word of God. If such a prior resurrection was known to John—as the theory presupposes—then how is it conceivable that he would call this resurrection the *first?* . . . But that he wrote *first* resurrection will be proof to all candid readers that he knew of none before it.[25]

It will be observed that Reese is arguing from silence here. John could hardly be expected to mention the resurrection of the dead in Christ, which had taken place earlier, in connection with the events at the close of the tribulation period related only to the tribulation saints.

One essential fact that Reese seems to have overlooked in all his discussion of resurrection is the teaching of 1 Corinthians 15:23, "every man in his own order." The first resurrection is composed of different groups: church saints, Old Testament saints, tribulation saints. Even though these groups are raised at different times, they are a part of the first resurrection program and are "orders" in that program. Therefore the resurrection of tribulation saints at the time of the second advent (Rev. 20:4-6) does not prove that all who are resurrected unto life are raised at this time. This whole doctrine of resurrection will be considered at a later time, but sufficient has been said to show that the doctrine of resurrection does not support posttribulationism.

F. *The argument from the wheat and tares.* A sixth argument used by the posttribulationist is the argument based on the parable of the wheat and the tares in Matthew 13. Reese sets forth what he believes to be the pretribulation rapture interpretation of this parable. Quoting Kelly, he outlines the position:

> . . . the phrase " 'time of the harvest' implies a certain period occupied with the various processes of ingathering." At the beginning of this period the angels are sent forth in a purely providential way, immediately before the Lord's Coming 'for the Church.' In some mysterious way, secret and providential, the angels gather professors into bundles *in readiness* for judgment. But no judgment whatever really takes place yet. The Lord then comes for the true Church, symbolized by the wheat, and gathers

---

[25] *Ibid.*, p. 81.

> it to Himself. The ungodly professors, however, who had previously been bundled by the angels, are still left in the world for a number of years, until the Lord comes forth in judgment.[26]

Thus the pretribulation interpretation is said to be that angels will bind the tares at the end of the age, prior to the rapture, but will translate the church, represented by the wheat out of the field, and leave the tares, bound unto judgment, in their place until the second advent. Reese observes that this explanation seems to violate the Lord's words: "Let both grow together until the harvest: and in the time of harvest I will say to the reapers, Gather ye together first the tares, and bind them in bundles to burn them, but gather the wheat into my barn" (Matt. 13:30). It would seem that Reese has a justifiable complaint against this interpretation.

It must be borne in mind that the purpose of Matthew 13 is not to divulge the history of the church, but the history of the kingdom in its mystery form. The time is not that of the church—from Pentecost to the rapture—but the entire age from the rejection of Christ to His coming reception. Therefore it seems to have been a mistake, into which many writers fell, to say that the wheat of the parable represents the church, which will be raptured. If such be the case the posttribulation rapture position seems to fit the literal normal interpretation of the parable more consistently. Rather, the Lord is indicating that during the age there is to be a sowing of the seed (the parable of the sower) and also a counter-sowing (the parable of the tares), and that this condition will continue throughout the age. At the end of the age there will be a separation of those who were the children of the kingdom and those who were the children of the evil one. Since the rapture question is not in view in the parable, it can not be used to support posttribulation rapturism. The tribulation period ends with judgment on all enemies of the King. Thus every unbeliever is removed. Following these judgments the kingdom is instituted into which the righteous are taken. This is perfectly consistent with the teaching of the parable.

From the above considerations of the arguments presented

[26] *Ibid.*, pp. 96-97.

by the posttribulation rapturist it can be seen that his arguments are far from being "well-nigh unanswerable."[27] Though many of the arguments may sound weighty, they can be met through a consistent interpretation of the text.

---

[27] Cf. McPherson, *loc. cit.*

CHAPTER XII

THE MIDTRIBULATION RAPTURE POSITION

A view less prevalent than the posttribulation rapture theory to explain the time of the rapture in relation to the tribulation period is the midtribulation theory. According to this interpretation the church will be raptured at the end of the first three and one-half years of the seventieth week of Daniel. The church will endure the events of the first half of the tribulation, which, according to the mid-tribulation rapturist, are not manifestations of divine wrath, but will be translated before the last half of the week begins, which, according to this theory, contains all the outpouring of the wrath of God. The rapture is said to occur in connection with the sounding of the seventh trumpet and the catching up of the two witnesses in Revelation 11. The midtribulation rapture view is essentially a compromise between the posttribulation and pretribulation positions. It concurs with the pretribulation view in holding that the church will be raptured as an event distinct from the second advent, that the restrainer of 2 Thessalonians 2 is the Holy Spirit, that the church is promised deliverance from wrath. In common with posttribulationism it holds that the church is promised tribulation on the earth and is in need of purging, that Scripture does not teach the doctrine of imminence, and that the church is seen on the earth after Revelation 4:1.

I. THE ESSENTIAL BASES OF MIDTRIBULATION RAPTURISM

In studying the midtribulation position it is well to observe that many of its essential bases are those of the posttribulation position. (1) Midtribulationism must either deny or at least weaken the dispensational interpretation of the Scriptures, and, (2) deny the strict distinctions between Israel and the church. This is observed in that this position places the church in the first half of the last seven years of the period determined upon

Daniel's people and city. (3) The position must rest on a view of the tribulation that divides the period into two separate and unrelated halves, so that the church can go through the first half, even though it has no part in the last half. (4) The position must deny the doctrine of imminence, for all the signs of the first half of the week apply to the church. (5) The position must deny the concept of the church as a mystery, so that the church age may overlap God's program with Israel. (6) The position must depend, to a certain extent, on the spiritualizing method of interpretation. This is particularly evident in the explanation of the portions of Scripture dealing with the first half of the tribulation period.

II. The Essential Arguments of the Midtribulation Rapturist

A study of the arguments used by midtribulation rapturists to support their view reveals that they use many of the same arguments of the posttribulation rapturist.

A. *The denial of imminence.* First, the midtribulation rapturist denies the doctrine of imminence. Harrison writes:

> There are those who object to the Rapture being placed at the last Trumpet on the ground that it militates against our hopes in the imminent return of Christ. . . .
>
> To be consistently Scriptural in the matter we should take into account the following:
>
> 1. *For Peter* there was no possibility of such an experience, our Lord having told him that he would live to old age and die a martyr's death . . . John 21:18, 19. . . . *And yet,* Peter became the Apostle of Hope and exhorts believers of his day; "Wherefore gird up the loins of your mind, be sober, and hope to the end for the grace that is to be brought unto you at the revelation of Jesus Christ" (1 Pet. 1:13).
>
> 2. *For Paul* his Lord's commission . . . Acts 22:21 left him facing a long preaching career that precluded, for much of his lifetime, any momentary return of Christ. He warns that the apostasy must come first (2 Thess. 2:3) and "that in the last days perilous times shall come" (2 Tim. 3:1). *And yet,* Paul constantly envisions the Coming of Christ as an incentive to holy living for

> the Christians of his day . . . Titus 2:11-13; . . . 1 Corinthians 15:51; Philippians 3:20 . . . 1 Thessalonians 4:17.
>
> 3. *For the Apostles* was a far-flung program contained in the Great Commission to carry the gospel "into all the world" (Mark 16:15). . . . *And yet,* whenever any of these apostles wrote to the believers of their day, they failed not to exhort them concerning their Lord's return.
>
> 4. *For the Early Church,* our Lord from heaven revealed a seven-fold historical development of the Church (Revelation 2 and 3), evidently requiring an extended period of time. *And yet,* to that early Church were given the reiterated words of assurance, "Behold I come quickly" (Rev. 22:7, 12, 20). . . .
>
> . . . We see from the Scriptures that Christ could not have returned in the lifetime of Peter; nor yet in the days of the Apostles; nor yet before the Reformation; nor yet before the missionary program is completed; nor yet before the apostasy has overtaken us; nor yet before the last days in which we seem to be living.[1]

While Harrison is seeking to disprove the doctrine of imminence by the Scripture quotations he cites, it is evident that the New Testament writers themselves believed in an imminent return. There is a distinction between the *soon* coming of Christ and the *imminent* coming. Scripture nowhere taught that the coming would be soon, but it consistently taught that the coming could be expected at any time. The prophecy concerning the natural course of history, which would come to pass unless interrupted by the termination of history by the coming of Christ, did not rob the writers, as Harrison's very quotations show, of an imminent hope. Since the belief that the church must look for all the signs of the first half of the tribulation period would destroy the doctrine of imminency, the midtribulation view must be rejected.

B. *The promise of tribulation.* A second argument of the midtribulationist is the argument that the church was promised tribulation and, therefore, can expect to experience the first half of the tribulation period. Since this question has been dealt with previously reference need only be made to the fact that tribulation may be used in either a technical sense, referring to the seven years of Daniel's prophecy, or in a nontechnical sense,

[1] Norman B. Harrison, *The End,* pp. 231-33.

referring to any time of trial or distress. The tribulation promised to the church is of this nontechnical kind.

C. *The denial of the church as a mystery.* A third argument of the midtribulationist is an argument that essentially denies the mystery concept of the church. It has been shown previously that this present age is a mystery and the church program in this present age is itself a mystery. It has been demonstrated that the mystery program must be brought to termination before God can and will deal with Israel to complete the covenant program. Harrison argues:

> To think of the Ages as abruptly abutting each other is fatal. To carry that conception over into the series that make up the endtime is equally fatal. In actuality they overlap, which may lead to an ultimate blending.
>
> Speaking of the two ages, Church and Jewish: at its inception, 30 A.D., the Church parallelled for 40 years the Jewish age, till the latter closed with the destruction of Jerusalem in 70 A.D. This argues for a similar overlapping at the close of the Church Age. If, for the moment, we think of the Church continuing up to the Tribulation, the time from which our Lord has promised to keep her, realizing that Israel will have been restored as a nation for three and one-half years prior to the Tribulation's setting in . . . we again have the same overlapping.[2]

The fallacy of this argument lies in the fact that although God was extending an invitation to the "Jew first" after the Day of Pentecost, even until the destruction of Jerusalem in 70 A.D., it was an invitation which, when received, brought the believer into the body of Christ, the church. God was not carrying on two programs, but one. There was no overlapping of the covenant program with the mystery church program. When the program with the church began that with Israel had already been interrupted. In this line of reasoning the inconsistent dispensational application inherent in the view is seen.

D. *The nature of the seals and trumpets.* A fourth argument of the midtribulation rapturist is the interpretation which holds that the seals and trumpets are not manifestations of divine wrath. This view is stated by Harrison, who writes:

---

[2] *Ibid.*, p. 50.

> The breaking of the seals is the point to be kept in mind. . . . It is the removal of restraints. The Seals have graciously operated for the protection and preservation of society all these centuries. The forces of evil, making for total war and destruction have been held in providential check. . . .
>
> The amazing thing is that expositors persistently speak of the Seal Judgments. The Bible never calls them judgments. It is a name that is reserved for a later and more awful series. . . .
>
> Why blame God with what Man has brought upon himself? Man has been dancing to the music of a godless civilization; it has been a war dance in worship of Force. Now that he has to pay the fiddler, why blame God? . . . He has withdrawn these restraints, and what is man experiencing? Merely the operation of the law of sowing and reaping![3]

Speaking of the trumpets, the same author states:

> These experiences. though so very severe, are not judgments. Commentators invariably call them Trumpet Judgments. God never does, and He ought to Know. . . . It is utter confusion to call these things—Seals and Trumpets—by a name which God has purposely reserved for His own peculiar work.
>
> These surely appear to be judgments. But, let Job's experience instruct us. . . . Satan was given permission of God to afflict him by way of testing and discipline; but he could go only so far. . . . This is what happens in the Trumpets; Satan working; God permitting.[4]

The midtribulation view, as presented by one of its chief advocates, is that the seals represent the outworking of the program of man, and the trumpets the outworking of the program of Satan, in which God is only a permissive agent.

The very contention of the above author concerning the so-called "parentheses" in each series seems to be a sufficient refutation of his view. He holds:

> The Reach in any series is always explained after the sixth in the series. It is a part of the structural plan of The Revelation to give this explanation in each series that the reader may know what is being effected.[5]

According to this observation John announced (Rev. 6:16-17)

---

[3] *Ibid.*, pp. 87-88.
[4] *Ibid.*, pp. 104-5.
[5] *Ibid.*, p. 91.

that the program there being unfolded is related to the "wrath of the Lamb." The aorist tense in verse 17, *ēlthen* (has come), signifies, not something that is about to happen, but that which has taken place. Thus, in unfolding the program of the seals, John announces that these represent "the wrath" that has already come. In the same connection, with the sounding of the seven trumpets, John again relates these trumpets to the program of the outpouring of the wrath of God, for in Revelation 11:18 it is set forth that these events are connected with the wrath that "has come" (aorist tense again).[6] Thus, neither the seals nor the trumpets can be divorced from the divine program associated with the pouring out of wrath upon the earth.

E. *The duration of the tribulation period.* A fifth argument used by the advocates of this position is the argument that the tribulation period is only three and one-half years in length. The same writer, after showing how Daniel's seventieth week is to be divided into two parts, says:

> This should moreover save us from the common mistake of speaking of the Tribulation as a seven-year period. The Bible never so refers to it; rather, it begins in the middle of the seven. It is the latter three and a half years. All that leads up to it Jesus refers to as merely "the beginning of sorrows."[7]

Or again:

> The first half of the week, or period of seven years, was a "sweet" anticipation to John, as it is to them; under treaty protection, they will be "sitting pretty," as we say. But the second half—"bitter" indeed: the treaty is broken; the storm breaks; they experience the wrath of the Antichrist on the one hand and of God on the other. This is their "day of trouble." It is the Great Tribulation.[8]

1. While it is recognized that Daniel gave notice that the seventieth week was to be broken into two parts (Dan. 9:27) and while the Lord, speaking of this same period, spoke of the latter half of it as "great tribulation" (Matt. 24:21), yet nowhere in the Scriptures is this period divided into two unrelated parts,

[6] Harrison's view that the verb may be translated "has only now come" (p. 119) is not borne out by the aorist tense.
[7] *Ibid.*, p. 229.
[8] *Ibid.*, p. 111.

each with a different characterization. The midtribulation view essentially divides the seventieth week into two disassociated parts, while still calling it the "seventieth week," holding that the church may go through the first half because it has a different characterization than the last half. This, it is impossible to do. When this period is anticipated in the Scriptures it is always dealt with as a unit, as far as its character is concerned, even though divided as to the time elements and the degree of the intensity of the wrath poured out. The unity of the seventieth week of Daniel in the program for Israel prevents us from dividing it into two separate parts. It is hard to understand how a writer can hold that all the events poured out under the seals and trumpets will be viewed as "sweet" to anyone undergoing those rigorous judgments. Only by spiritualization can this view be held.

2. Further, it is necessary to observe, if the church goes into the first three and a half years of the tribulation, the 144,000 would be saved into the church, since the church is still on the earth. Yet these are seen to be Jewish witnesses during the entire period. If they were saved while God is still adding to the body of Christ, and if, when the translation took place, they were left behind, the body would be dismembered and incomplete. The necessity of terminating the mystery program before undertaking the covenant program shows us that the tribulation can not be confined to just half of the week.

3. Again, if the tribulation period is to be dated from the making of the false covenant (Daniel 9:27), the church would know the time of the translation. While signs were given to Israel preceding the advent of the Messiah, no such signs were given to the church. The time of His coming for the church is a divine secret and men will not be able to determine the time by any such sign.

4. Revelation 7:14 seems to give final evidence. In the parenthesis between the sixth and seventh seal, where the scope of the whole vision is given, those saved in that time are said to have come out of "great tribulation." This seems to indicate clearly that the time covered by the seals is considered a part of the tribulation period.

F. *The argument from Revelation 11.* A sixth argument presented in defense of this position is the argument that the rapture is described in Revelation 11. To support this view Harrison argues that the two witnesses are symbolic of a "larger company of witnesses"; that they represent two groups: the dead and the living at the rapture; that the cloud represents the *parousia*—the Lord's presence; that the great voice is the shout of 1 Thessalonians 4:16; the trumpet is the trumpet of the same verse.[9]

1. It will be observed that this is entirely argument by analogy, not by exegesis. Such argument is always weak. It is to be observed that these two witnesses are treated as two individuals in the passage, not as symbolic representatives of the church. The fact that as "two olive trees" they are related to Israel (Zech. 4:2-3) would prevent them from representing the church. The claim that these two are Moses and Elijah and therefore represent the dead and the translated at the rapture is not certain. The cloud was so universally used in Scripture for God's presence that it does not need to be associated with the *parousia* at this point, particularly since this is in a portion dealing with Israel, where the cloud would not signify the rapture to a Jew. The voice of authority is referred to a number of times in the Revelation and it can not be substantiated that it is the same "shout" of which Paul spoke. It must be observed that this interpretation is not based on a strictly literal interpretation, but rather the spiritualizing method.

2. Perhaps the strongest evidence that the rapture does not take place in Revelation 11 is to observe carefully the result of the blowing of the seventh trumpet. The scene depicted is not that of the rapture, but of the revelation of Christ to the earth. With this event is associated the subjugation of the world kingdoms to the authority of Christ, the assumption of the Messianic reign, the judgment on the nations, the rewarding of those who shall share the reign of the Messiah, the judgment on the beasts who "destroy the earth." This chronology of events is never associated with the rapture, but rather with the second advent. The result of the blowing of the seventh trumpet is not transla-

[9] *Ibid.*, p. 117.

tion for the church but triumph for Christ over all his enemies in the institution of His kingdom at the second advent.

3. A necessary corollary of this argument is the interpretation of the midtribulationist that the mystery of God that is finished (Rev. 10:7) is the mystery program of the church.[10] The explanation of Ironside provides a better interpretation. He says:

> This is the theme of the seven-sealed roll; the vindication of God's holiness in having so long tolerated evil in His universe. What greater mystery confronts and confuses the human mind than the question, Why does God allow unrighteousness so often to triumph? . . . This is His secret. He will disclose it in due time, and all shall be clear as the day. . . . His final triumph over all evil is what is so vividly presented in the rapidly-shifting tableau of the Revelation. . . .[11]

God is now terminating the program with evil.

G. *The chronology of the book of Revelation.* A seventh argument depends on their interpretation of the chronology of the book of Revelation. According to this view, as has already been observed, the seven seals and the seven trumpets bring us through the events of the first three and one-half years of the seventieth week, which period terminates in the rapture taking place in chapter eleven. The seven bowls describe the outpouring of the wrath of God in the last three and one-half years of the tribulation, developed in chapters twelve through nineteen. Thus chapters four through eleven describe the first half of the week and chapters twelve through nineteen the last half of the week. This chronology we believe to be faulty. John has outlined the events of the first half of the tribulation period under the seals (4:1-7:17), the last half of the tribulation under the trumpets (8:1-11:14), and closes the period with the return of the Lord to reign (11:15-18). Between the sixth and seventh trumpets John is told (10:11) that "It is necessary for you to prophesy again concerning many peoples and nations and tongues and kings [lit.]." Concerning the word "again" (*palin*) Thayer says that "it denotes renewal or repetition of the action."[12] This would seem to be a divine notice that, since John has taken

---

[10] *Ibid.*, pp. 107-8.
[11] H. A. Ironside, *The Mysteries of God*, pp. 95-96.
[12] Joseph Henry Thayer, *Greek-English Lexicon of the New Testament*, p. 475.

us through the entire period once, it is God's intention to have him retrace his way through the period again. Therefore, beginning in chapter twelve, John surveys the period a second time, placing emphasis on the individuals who play so important a part in the events of the seventieth week. The bowls (Rev. 16:1-17) evidently come at the close of the period and occupy only a brief span of time and can not be spread over the last three and one-half years of the period. This second survey, like the first, terminates the period by the return of Christ and the consequent judgment of His enemies (Rev. 19).

Thus, the observation that Revelation 11:15-18 describes the revelation, not the rapture, paralleling Revelation 19:11-16, and the notification of repetition in Revelation 10:11 would make the midtribulation interpretation of the chronology of Revelation untenable. It must be observed that this position depends on the allegorical method of interpretation, particularly in making Revelation 11 describe the rapture.

H. *The identity of the last trump.* An eighth argument of the midtribulation rapturist is the argument that the seventh trumpet of Revelation 11:15 and the last trump of 1 Corinthians 15:52 and 1 Thessalonians 4:16 are identical. Harrison states the midtribulation view thus:

> St. Paul, by inspiration of the Spirit, definitely places the Resurrection and the Rapture of the saints through the coming of Christ *"at the last trumpet"* (I Cor. 15:5, 52). This is a specific locating of the event. Unquestionably the Holy Spirit revealed the fact and inspired the recording of it. How dare any one locate it otherwise? . . . Can we postulate the Rapture at any other place than that given by and through the Apostle Paul and claim to maintain the integrity of God's Word?
>
> . . . .
>
> Turn to Matthew 24:29-31. Here Jesus pictures the Tribulation as follows by "a great sound of the trumpet." This is the last recorded in time.
>
> When, however, we reach the last Trumpet in The Revelation, last in the series, we shall find much satisfying evidence that the event is actually taking place.[18]

---

[18] Harrison, *op. cit.*, p. 75.

His whole argument depends on making the last of the seven trumpets identical with the last trump mentioned by Paul in connection with the rapture in 1 Corinthians 15:52. The argument rests on the use of the word *last* in connection with both events.

Harrison himself admits that "'Last' can mean one of two things: last in point of time, or last in point of sequence."[14] By so stating he is admitting that last in point of sequence may not necessarily be the same as last in point of time. The word *last* may signify that which concludes a program, but is not necessarily the last that will ever exist. Inasmuch as the program for the church differs from that for Israel, each may be terminated by the blowing of a trumpet, properly called the last trumpet, without making the two last trumpets identical and synchronous as to time. On this identification of the last trumpet with the seventh trump, Thiessen has written:

> . . . with Ellicott we say: "There are no sufficient grounds for supposing that there is here any reference to the seventh Apocalyptic trumpet (Rev. 11:15). . . . This *salpigx* (trumpet) the Apostle here terms *eschate* (last), not with reference to any preceding series . . . but as connected with the close of this *aion* (age) and the last scene of this world's history." With this we agree, except that when Christ comes only the history of this age will come to a close. Ellicott was a premillennialist, and this is, no doubt, what he means by the statement. Meyer takes the same view, on the ground that in 1 Thess. 4:16, "only one trumpet is mentioned, and that one taken for granted as well known." The same conclusion may be drawn from the fact that Paul follows the reference to the "last trump" with the impersonal statement, "for the trumpet shall sound" (see the Greek). If he had thought of this trumpet as one of seven, he would undoubtedly have said something like the following: "For when the trumpets will be sounded and the time comes for the last one to sound, the dead in Christ shall be raised." At any rate, there is no ground for identifying the "trump" in 1 Cor. 15:52 with the seventh trumpet in Rev. 11:15.[15]

There seem to be a number of observations which make it impossible for one to identify these two trumps. (1) The trumpet of I Corinthians 15:52, even the midtribulationist agrees, sounds

---

[14] *Ibid.*
[15] Henry C. Thiessen, *Will the Church Pass through the Tribulation?* pp. 55-56.

before the wrath of God descends, while, as it has been shown, the chronology of Revelation indicates that the trumpet in Revelation 11:15 sounds at the end of the time of wrath, just prior to the second advent. (2) The trumpet that summons the church is called the *trump of God,* while the seventh trump is an angel's trumpet. Strombeck well observes:

> In the search for "the last trump" one must, then, be guided by the fact that it is God's own trumpet, sounded by the Lord himself. In view of this one would hardly be willing to contend that the last trumpet of God is the last of a series of trumpets blown by the priests of the Aaronic priesthood. These were not in a class with the trumpet of God. Remembering that the angels are only a little higher than man, it is just as contrary to the laws of logic to say that "the last trump," which is God's own trumpet, is the last of a series of trumpets blown by angels. Both men and angels are creatures of God. They cannot sound the trumpet of the Creator.[16]

(3) The trumpet for the church is singular. No trumpets have preceded it so that it can not be said to be the last of a series. The trumpet that closes the tribulation period is clearly the last of a series of seven. (4) In 1 Thessalonians 4 the voice associated with the sounding of the trumpet summons the dead and the living and consequently is heard before the resurrection. In the Revelation, while a resurrection is mentioned (11:12), the trumpet does not sound until after the resurrection, showing us that two different events must be in view. (5) The trumpet in 1 Thessalonians issues in blessing, in life, in glory, while the trumpet in Revelation issues in judgment upon the enemies of God. (6) In the Thessalonian passage the trumpet sounds "in a moment, in the twinkling of an eye." In Revelation 10:7 the indication is that the seventh trumpet shall sound over a continued period of time, probably for the duration of the judgments that fall under it, for John speaks of the angel that shall "begin to sound." The duration gives evidence of the distinction in these two. (7) The trumpet in 1 Thessalonians is distinctly for the church. Since God is dealing with Israel in particular, and Gentiles in general, in the tribulation, this seventh trumpet, which falls in the period of the tribulation, could not have reference to the church with-

---

[16] J. F. Strombeck, *First the Rapture,* p. 109.

out losing the distinctions between the church and Israel. (8) The passage in Revelation depicts a great earthquake in which thousands are slain, and the believing remnant that worships God is stricken with fear. In the Thessalonian passage there is no earthquake mentioned. There will be no believing remnant left behind at the rapture to experience the fear of Revelation 11:13. Such a view would only be consistent with a partial rapture position. (9) While the church will be rewarded at the time of the rapture, yet the reward given to "thy servants the prophets, and to the saints" can not be that event. The rewarding mentioned in Revelation 11:18 is seen to take place on the earth after the second advent of Christ, following the judgment on His enemies. Since the church is rewarded in the air, following the rapture, these must be two distinct events.

In the light of Matthew 24:31 it is difficult to see how the midtribulation rapturist can hold his interpretation that Revelation 11:15 is the last trumpet in the chronological sense. The trumpets of Revelation are completed before the second advent of the Messiah. Matthew records the Lord's own words, in which He teaches that Israel will be regathered by the sounding of a trumpet after the second advent. If *last* must mean *last chronologically,* why should not it be argued that both the trumpets of Revelation and 1 Thessalonians coincide with that of Matthew 24?

Concerning the use of the phrase *last trump* in 1 Corinthians 15:52, English writes:

> The significance of the term, "the last trump," in 1 Corinthians 15:52, inasmuch as this sounding is not one of a series of trumpetings, may possibly be that of a rallying call, or an alarm. In Numbers 10 we read of the sounding of trumpets for calling an assembly of the people and for their journeyings. There were specific calls for each of the camps of the Israelites and special calls for the whole congregation. In connection with this Dr. Carl Armerding has an interesting comment: "The *last trump* would signify that the whole congregation was finally on the move. In a way this may illustrate what we find in 1 Corinthians 15:23, 'Every man in his own order [or rank—tagmati]: Christ the firstfruits; afterward they that are Christ's at His coming.' These last are certainly divided into at least two groups: those who have 'fallen asleep,' and those 'who are alive and remain.' . . ."

> "'In a moment' and 'in the twinkling of an eye' are expressions," continues Dr. Armerding, "which are used the world around to indicate suddenness and rapidity. The fact that the third phrase 'at the last trump,' is so closely associated with them would lead us to believe that it should be understood in the same way. If so, it will be in the nature of an *alarm*, which is the very word used in Numbers 10:5, 6 in connection with the 'journeying of the camps.' The quickening and assembling already accomplished [the former by the voice of the Lord, and the latter by the voice of the archangel—I Thess. 4:16] . . . there is only one more thing necessary to set all in motion. It is 'the last trump.' That will be the final note struck on that momentous occasion."[17]

Examination of the midtribulation rapture position has shown us that the essential arguments of the view will not stand the examination of true interpretation of Scripture and must be rejected as false.

---

[17] Schuyler English, *Rethinking the Rapture*, p. 109.

CHAPTER XIII

THE PRETRIBULATION RAPTURE THEORY

The third prevalent interpretation of the question of the time of the rapture in relation to the tribulation period is the pretribulation interpretation, which holds that the church, the body of Christ, in its entirety, will, by resurrection and translation, be removed from the earth before any part of the seventieth week of Daniel begins.

I. THE ESSENTIAL BASIS OF THE PRETRIBULATION RAPTURE POSITION

Pretribulation rapturism rests essentially on one major premise—the literal method of interpretation of the Scriptures. As a necessary adjunct to this, the pretribulationist believes in a dispensational interpretation of the Word of God. The church and Israel are two distinct groups with whom God has a divine plan. The church is a mystery, unrevealed in the Old Testament. This present mystery age intervenes within the program of God for Israel because of Israel's rejection of the Messiah at His first advent. This mystery program must be completed before God can resume His program with Israel and bring it to completion. These considerations all arise from the literal method of interpretation.

II. THE ESSENTIAL ARGUMENTS OF THE PRETRIBULATION RAPTURIST

A number of arguments may be presented in support of the pretribulation rapture position. While not all of them are of equal weight, the cumulative evidence is strong.

A. *The literal method of interpretation.* It is frankly and freely admitted by amillennialists that the basic issue in the controversy between premillennialists and themselves is the issue of the method of interpretation to be employed in the interpretation of prophecy. Allis says, "The question of literal versus figurative interpretation is, therefore, one which has to be faced at the very outset."[1] He admits that if the literal method of interpretation of the Scriptures be the right method premillennialism is the correct interpretation. Thus we can see that our doctrine of the premillennial return of Christ to institute a literal kingdom is the outcome of the literal method of interpretation of the Old Testament promises and prophecies. It is only natural, therefore, that the same basic method of interpretation must be employed in our interpretation of the rapture question. It would be most illogical to build a premillennial system on a literal method and then depart from that method in consideration of the related questions. It can easily be seen that the literal method of interpretation demands a pretribulation rapture of the church. The posttribulationist must either interpret the book of Revelation historically, which is basically a spiritualizing method, or else treat it as yet future, but spiritualize away the literalness of the events in an attempt to harmonize these events with other Scriptures in the light of his interpretation. Either explanation violates the principle of literal interpretation. The midtribulation rapturists will apply the literal method of interpretation to the last half of the seventieth week, but spiritualize the events of the first half of the week to permit the church to encounter those. This, again, is a basic inconsistency. There can not be one method employed to establish premillennialism and another method employed in the interpretation of the rapture promises. The literal method of interpretation, consistently employed, can lead to no other conclusion than that the church will be raptured before the seventieth week.

It should be noted in passing that this method does not lead one on into ultradispensationalism, for that system is not the outgrowth of the use of greater literalness, but rather is based on exegetical considerations.

B. *The nature of the seventieth week.* There are a number of words used in both the Old and New Testaments to describe the seventieth week period, which, when considered together, give us the essential nature or character of this period: (1) wrath (Rev. 6:16-17; 11:18; 14:19; 15:1, 7; 16:1, 19; 1 Thess. 1:9-10;

[1] Oswald T. Allis, *Prophecy and the Church*, p. 17.

5:9; Zeph. 1:15, 18); (2) judgment (Rev. 14:7; 15:4; 16:5-7; 19:2); (3) indignation (Isa. 26:20-21; 34:1-3); (4) punishment (Isa. 24:20-21); (5) hour of trial (Rev. 3:10); (6) hour of trouble (Jer. 30:7); (7) destruction (Joel 1:15); (8) darkness (Joel 2:2; Zeph. 1:14-18; Amos 5:18). It must be noted that these references describe the period in its entirety, not just a portion of it, so that the whole period bears this characterization. As to the nature of the tribulation (although limiting it to the last half of the week) Harrison says:

> Let us get clearly in mind the *nature of the Tribulation*, that it is divine "wrath" (11:18; 14:8, 10, 19; 15:1, 7; 16:1, 19 [observe he omits 6:16, 17] and divine "judgment" (14:7; 15:4; 16:7; 17:1; 18:10; 19:2). We know that our blessed Lord bore for us the wrath of God and His judgment; therefore we who are in Him "shall not come into judgment." The antithesis of I Thess. 5:9 is conclusive evidence: "For God appointed us not unto wrath, but unto the obtaining of salvation through our Lord Jesus Christ." Wrath for others, but salvation for us at the Rapture, "whether we wake or sleep" (vs. 10).[2]

C. *The scope of the seventieth week.* There can be no question that this period will see the wrath of God poured out upon the whole earth. Revelation 3:10; Isaiah 34:2; 24:1, 4-5, 16-17, 18-21, and many other passages make this very clear. And yet, while the whole earth is in view, this period is particularly in relation to Israel. Jeremiah 30:7, which calls this period "the time of Jacob's trouble," makes this certain. The events of the seventieth week are events of the "Day of the Lord" or "Day of Jehovah." This use of the name of deity emphasizes God's peculiar relationship to that nation. When this period is being anticipated in Daniel 9, God says to the prophet, "Seventy weeks are determined upon thy people and upon thy holy city" (v. 24). This whole period then has special reference to Daniel's people, Israel, and Daniel's holy city, Jerusalem.

Inasmuch as many passages in the New Testament such as Ephesians 3:1-6; Colossians 1:25-27 make it clear that the church is a mystery and its nature as a body composed of Jew and Gentile alike was unrevealed in the Old Testament, the church could not have been in view in this or any other Old Testament proph-

---

[2] Norman B. Harrison, *The End*, p. 120.

ecy. Since the church did not have its existence until after the death of Christ (Eph. 5:25-26), until after the resurrection of Christ (Rom. 4:25; Col.3:1-3), until after the ascension (Eph. 1:19-20), and until after the descent of the Holy Spirit at Pentecost with the inception of all His ministries to the believer (Acts 2), the church could not have been in the first sixty-nine weeks of this prophecy. Since it had no part in the first sixty-nine weeks, which are related only to God's program for Israel, it can have no part in the seventieth week, which is again related to God's program for Israel after the mystery program for the church has been concluded.

In an extended treatment of each major passage in the Word on the subject of the tribulation,[3] in which he deals with passages such as Matthew 24, Daniel 12, Luke 21, Mark 13, Jeremiah 30, Revelation 7, Kelly concludes:

> . . . the view here maintained follows on a close investigation of every distinct passage that Scripture affords upon the subject of the great tribulation. I should be obliged to any one who will produce me other passages that refer to it; but I am not aware of them. I demand of those . . . whether they can point out one word which supposes a Christian or the Church on the earth when the great tribulation arrives? Have we not seen that the doctrine of Old and New Testament—of Jeremiah, of Daniel, of the Lord Jesus, and of the apostle John—is this, that, just before the Lord appears in glory, will come the last and unequalled trouble of Israel, though Jacob shall be delivered from it; that there will be . . . "the great tribulation," out of which a multitude of Gentiles emerge; but that both Jacob and the Gentiles are totally distinct from the Christians or the Church. As regards the Christian, the positive promise of the Lord is, that such as have kept the word of His patience He will keep out of the hour of trial, which is about to come upon the whole habitable world, to try them that dwell upon the earth.[4]

It must be concluded with the above author, since every passage dealing with the tribulation relates it to God's program for Israel, that the scope of the tribulation prevents the church from participating in it.

---

[3] Wm. Kelly, *Lectures on the Second Coming of the Lord Jesus Christ*, pp. 186-237.

[4] *Ibid.*, p. 235.

D. *The purpose of the seventieth week.* The Scriptures indicate that there are two major purposes to be accomplished in the seventieth week.

1. The first purpose is stated in Revelation 3:10, "I also will keep thee from the hour of temptation, which shall come upon all the world, to try them that dwell upon the earth." Apart from the question involved as to who will be in this time of testing there are several other important considerations in this verse. (1) First of all we see that this period has in view "them that dwell on the earth" and not the church. This same expression occurs in Revelation 6:10; 11:10; 13:8, 12, 14; 14:6 and 17:8. In its usage it is not giving us a geographical description but rather a moral classification. Thiessen writes:

> Now the word "dwell" used here (*katoikeo*) is a strong word. It is used to describe the fulness of the Godhead that dwelt in Christ (Col. 2:9); it is used of Christ's taking up a permanent abode in the believer's heart (Eph. 3:17), and of demons returning to take absolute possession of a man (Matt. 12:45; Luke 11:26). It is to be distinguished from the word *oikeo,* which is the general term for "dwell," and *paroikeo,* which has the idea of transitoriness, "to sojourn." Thayer remarks that the term *katoikeo* has the idea of permanence in it. Thus the judgment referred to in Rev. 3:10 is directed against the earth-dwellers of that day, against those who have settled down in the earth as their real home, who have identified themselves with the earth's commerce and religion.[5]

Since this period is related to "earth dwellers," those that have settled down to permanent occupancy, it can have no reference to the church, which would be subjected to the same experiences if it were here. (2) The second consideration to be noted here is the use of the infinitive *peirasai* (to try) to express purpose. Thayer defines this word, when God is its subject, "to inflict evils upon one in order to prove his character and the steadfastness of his faith."[6] Since the Father never sees the church except in Christ, perfected in Him, this period can have no reference to the church, for the true church does not need to be tested to see if her faith is genuine.

2. The second major purpose of the seventieth week is in relation to Israel. In Malachi 4:5-6 it is stated:

---

[5] Henry C. Thiessen, *Will the Church Pass Through the Tribulation?* pp. 28-29.
[6] Joseph Henry Thayer, *Greek-English Lexicon of the New Testament,* p. 498.

> Behold, I will send you Elijah the prophet before the coming of the great and terrible day of the Lord: And he shall turn the heart of the fathers to the children, and the heart of the children to their fathers, lest I come and smite the earth with a curse.

The prophet states that the ministry of this Elijah was a ministry to prepare the people for the King who was shortly to come. In Luke 1:17 it is promised that the son born to Zacharias would "go before him in the spirit and power of Elias" to perform this very ministry and "to make ready a people prepared for the Lord." Concerning the coming of Elijah which was to have been a sign to Israel, the Lord states:

> Elias verily cometh first, and restoreth all things; and how it is written of the Son of man, that he must suffer many things, and be set at naught. But I say unto you, that Elias is indeed come, and they have done unto him whatsoever they listed, as it is written of him [Mk. 9:12-13].

The Lord was showing the disciples that John the Baptist had this ministry of preparing a people for Him. And to remove all doubt, the word in Matthew 11:14 is conclusive, "if ye will receive it, this is Elias, which was for to come." John's ministry was a ministry to prepare the nation Israel for the coming of the King. It can only be concluded then that Elijah, who is to come before the great and terrible day of the Lord, can have only one ministry: that of preparing a remnant in Israel for the advent of the Lord. It is evident that no such ministry is needed by the church since she by nature is without spot or wrinkle or any such thing, but is holy and without blemish.

These two purposes, the testing of earth dwellers, and the preparation of Israel for the King, have no relation to the church whatsoever. This is supporting evidence that the church will not be in the seventieth week.

E. *The unity of the seventieth week.* It should be observed from the three preceding considerations that the entire seventieth week is in view when it is described and predicted in prophecy. While all would agree, on the basis of Daniel 9:27; Matthew 24:15; and Revelation 13, that the week is divided into two parts of three and one-half years each, yet the nature and character of the week is one, permeating both parts in their entirety. It becomes impossible to permit the existence of the church in the week as a unit and it becomes equally impossible to adopt the position that the church, although exempt from a portion of the seventieth week, may be in the first half of it, for its nature is the same throughout. The impossibility of including the church in the last half makes it equally impossible to include it in the first half, for while Scripture divides the time of the week, it does not make any distinction as to the nature and character of the two parts of it.

F. *The nature of the church.* One must carefully observe certain distinctions between the church and Israel which are clearly set forth in the Scripture, but often neglected in the consideration at hand. (1) There is a distinction between the professing church and national Israel. It should be observed that the professing church is composed of those who make a profession of faith in Christ. To some this profession is based on reality and to some on no reality at all. This latter group will go into the tribulation period, for Revelation 2:22 indicates clearly that the unsaved professing church will experience this visitation of wrath. Membership in the group called national Israel is based on a physical birth, and all in this group who are not saved and removed by rapture and who are alive at the time of the rapture will, with the professing church, be subjected to the wrath of the tribulation. (2) There is a distinction between the true church and the professing church. The true church is composed of all those in this age who have received Christ as Saviour. Over against this we have the professing church composed of those who make a profession of receiving Christ without actually receiving Him. Only the true church will be raptured. (3) There is a distinction between the true church and true or spiritual Israel. Prior to Pentecost there were saved individuals, but there was no church, and they were a part of spiritual Israel, not the church. After the day of Pentecost and until the rapture we find the church which is His body, but no spiritual Israel. After the rapture we find no church, but a true or spiritual Israel again. These distinctions must be kept clearly in mind.

The rapture will remove, not all who make a profession of faith in Christ, but only those who have been born again and have received His life. The unbelieving portion of the visible church, together with unbelievers in the nation Israel, will go into the tribulation period.

1. Since the church is the body, of which Christ is the Head (Eph. 1:22; 5:23; Col. 1:18), the bride, of which He is the Bridegroom (1 Cor. 11:2; Eph. 5:23), the object of His love (Eph. 5:25), the branch of which He is the Root and Stem (John 15:5), the building, of which He is the Foundation and Cornerstone (1 Cor. 3:9; Eph. 2:19-22), there exists between the believer and the Lord a union and a unity. The believer is no longer separated from Him, but brought into the closest oneness with Him. If the church is in the seventieth week, she is subjected to the wrath, judgment, and indignation which characterizes the period, and because of her oneness with Christ, He, likewise, would be subjected to that same visitation. This is impossible according to 1 John 4:17, for He can not be brought into judgment again. Inasmuch as the church has been perfected and delivered from all judgment (Rom. 8:1; John 5:24; 1 John 4:17), if she is subjected to judgment again the promises of God would be of none effect and the death of Christ would be ineffectual. Who would dare to assert that the death of Christ could fail to accomplish its purpose? While the members may be experimentally imperfect and need experimental cleansing, yet the church, which is His body, has a perfect standing in Christ and could not need such cleansing. The nature of the testing in the seventieth week, as stated in Revelation 3:10, is not to bring the individual to cleansing, but to reveal the degradation and need of the unregenerate heart. The nature of the church prevents such a testing.

2. Again, Revelation 13:7 makes it clear that all who are in the seventieth week are brought into subjection to the Beast and through him to Satan, who gives the Beast His power. If the church were in this period she would be subjected to Satan, and Christ would either lose His place as Head, or He, Himself, because of His union with the Church, would be likewise subjected to Satan's authority. Such a thing is unthinkable. Thus it is concluded that the nature of the church and the completeness of her salvation prevent her from being in the seventieth week.

G. *The concept of the church as a mystery.* Closely related to the previous consideration is the concept given to us in the

New Testament that the church is a mystery. It was no mystery that God was going to provide salvation for the Jews, nor that Gentiles would be blessed in salvation. The fact that God was going to form Jews and Gentiles alike into one body was never revealed in the Old Testament and forms the mystery of which Paul speaks in Ephesians 3:1-7; Romans 16:25-27; Colossians 1:26-29. This whole mystery program was not revealed until after the rejection of Christ by Israel. It was after the rejection of Matthew 12:23-24 that the Lord first makes a prophecy of the coming church in Matthew 16:18. It is after the rejection of the Cross that the church had its inception in Acts 2. It was after the final rejection by Israel that God called out Paul to be the Apostle of the Gentiles through whom this mystery of the nature of the church is revealed. The church is manifestly an interruption of God's program for Israel, which was not brought into being until Israel's rejection of the offer of the Kingdom. It must logically follow that this mystery program must itself be brought to a conclusion before God can resume His dealing with the nation Israel, as has been shown previously He will do. The mystery program, which was so distinct in its inception, will certainly be separate at its conclusion. This program must be concluded before God resumes and culminates His program for Israel. This mystery concept of the church makes a pretribulation rapture a necessity.

H. *The distinctions between Israel and the church.* Chafer has set forth twenty-four contrasts between Israel and the church which show us conclusively that these two groups can not be united into one, but that they must be distinguished as two separate entities with whom God is dealing in a special program.[7] These contrasts may be outlined as follows: (1) The extent of Biblical revelation: Israel—nearly four-fifths of the Bible; Church—about one-fifth. (2) The Divine purpose: Israel—the earthly promises in the covenants; Church—the heavenly promises in the gospel. (3) The seed of Abraham: Israel—the physical seed, of whom some become a spiritual seed; Church—a spiritual seed. (4) Birth: Israel—physical birth that produces a relationship; Church—spiritual birth that brings relationship. (5) Headship: Israel—Abraham; Church—Christ. (6) Covenants: Israel—

[7] Lewis Sperry Chafer, *Systematic Theology*, IV, 47-53.

Abrahamic and all the following covenants; Church—indirectly related to the Abrahamic and new covenants; (7) Nationality: Israel—one nation; Church—from all nations. (8) Divine dealing: Israel—national and individual; Church—individual only. (9) Dispensations: Israel—seen in all ages from Abraham; Church—seen only in this present age. (10) Ministry: Israel—no missionary activity and no gospel to preach; Church—a commission to fulfill. (11) The death of Christ: Israel—guilty nationally, to be saved by it; Church—perfectly saved by it now. (12) The Father: Israel—by a peculiar relationship God was Father to the nation; Church—we are related individually to God as Father. (13) Christ: Israel—Messiah, Immanuel, King; Church—Saviour, Lord, Bridegroom, Head. (14) The Holy Spirit: Israel—came upon some temporarily; Church—indwells all. (15) Governing principle: Israel—Mosaic law system; Church—grace system. (16) Divine enablement: Israel—none; Church—the indwelling Holy Spirit. (17) Two farewell discourses: Israel—Olivet discourse; Church—upper room discourse. (18) The promise of Christ's return: Israel—in power and glory for judgment; Church—to receive us to Himself. (19) Position: Israel—a servant; Church—members of the family. (20) Christ's earthly reign: Israel—subjects; Church—co-reigners. (21) Priesthood: Israel—had a priesthood; Church—is a priesthood. (22) Marriage: Israel—unfaithful wife; Church—bride. (23) Judgments: Israel—must face judgment; Church—delivered from all judgments. (24) Positions in eternity: Israel—spirits of just men made perfect in the new earth; Church—church of the firstborn in the new heavens.

These clear contrasts, which show the distinction between Israel and the church, make it impossible to identify the two in one program, which it is necessary to do if the church goes through the seventieth week. These distinctions give further support to the pretribulation rapture position.

I. *The doctrine of imminence.* Many signs were given to the nation Israel, which would precede the second advent, so that the nation might be living in expectancy when the time of His coming should draw nigh. Although Israel could not know the day nor the hour when the Lord will come, yet they can know that their redemption draweth nigh through the fulfillment of these signs. To the church no such signs were ever given. The church was told to live in the light of the imminent coming of the Lord to translate them in His presence (John 14:2-3; Acts 1:11; 1 Cor. 15:51-52; Phil. 3:20; Col. 3:4; 1 Thess. 1:10; 1 Tim. 6:14; Jas. 5:8; 1 Pet. 3:3-4). Such passages as 1 Thessalonians 5:6; Titus 2:13; Revelation 3:3 all warn the believer to be watching for the Lord Himself, not for signs that would precede His coming. It is true that the events of the seventieth week will cast an adumbration before the rapture, but the object of the believer's attention is always directed to Christ, never to these portents.

This doctrine of imminence, or "at any moment coming," is not a new doctrine with Darby, as is sometimes charged, although he did clarify, systematize, and popularize it. Such a belief in imminency marked the premillennialism of the early church fathers as well as the writers of the New Testament. In this connection Thiessen writes:

> . . . they held not only the premillennial view of Christ's coming, but also regarded that coming as imminent. The Lord had taught them to expect His return at any moment, and so they looked for Him to come in their day. Not only so, but they also taught His personal return as being immediately. Only the Alexandrians opposed this truth; but these Fathers also rejected other fundamental doctrines. We may say, therefore, that the early Church lived in the constant expectation of their Lord, and hence was not interested in the possibility of a Tribulation period in the future.[8]

Although the Eschatology of the early church may not be altogether clear on all points, for that subject was not the subject of serious consideration, yet the evidence is clear that they believed in the imminent return of Christ. This same view of imminence is clearly seen in the writings of the Reformers, even though they have had different views on eschatological questions. Chafer quotes some of the reformers to show that they believed in the imminency of the return of Christ.

> . . . Luther wrote, "I believe that all the signs which are to precede the last days have already appeared. Let us not think that the Coming of Christ is far off; let us look up with heads lifted

[8] Thiessen, *op. cit.*, p. 15.

up; let us expect our Redeemer's coming with longing and cheerful mind" . . . Calvin also declares . . . "Scripture uniformly enjoins us to look with expectation for the advent of Christ." To this may be added the testimony of John Knox: "The Lord Jesus shall return, and that with expedition. What were this else but to reform the face of the whole earth, which never was nor yet shall be, till that righteous King and Judge appear for the restoration of all things." Similarly, the words of Latimer: "All those excellent and learned men whom, without doubt, God has sent into the world in these latter days to give the world warning, do gather out of the Scriptures that the last days can not be far off. Peradventure it may come in my day, old as I am, or in my children's days." . . .[9]

The doctrine of imminence forbids the participation of the church in any part of the seventieth week. The multitude of signs given to Israel to stir them to expectancy would then also be for the church, and the church could not be looking for Christ until these signs had been fulfilled. The fact that no signs are given to the church, but she, rather, is commanded to watch for Christ, precludes her participation in the seventieth week.

J. *The work of the Restrainer in 2 Thessalonians 2.* The Thessalonian Christians were concerned for fear that the rapture had already taken place and they were in the day of the Lord. The persecutions which they were enduring, as referred to in the first chapter, had given them a basis for this erroneous consideration. Paul writes to show them that such a thing was impossible. First, he shows them in verse 3 that the day of the Lord could not take place until there was a departure. Whether this departure be a departure from the faith or a departure of the saints from the earth, as already mentioned in verse 1, is beside the point here. Second, he reveals there was to be the manifestation of the man of sin, or the lawless one, further described in Revelation 13. Paul's argument in verse 7 is that although the mystery of iniquity was operative in his day, that is, the lawless system that was to culminate in the person of the lawless one was manifesting itself, yet this lawless one could not be manifested until the Restrainer was taken out of the way. In other words, some One is preventing the purpose of Satan from coming to culmination and He will keep on performing this min-

[9] Chafer, *op. cit.*, IV, 278-79.

istry until He is removed (vv. 7-8). Explanations as to the person of this Restrainer such as human government, law, the visible church will not suffice, for they will all continue in a measure after the manifestation of this lawless one. While this is essentially an exegetical problem, it would seem that the only One who could do such a restraining ministry would be the Holy Spirit. This problem will be considered in detail later. However, the indication here is that as long as the Holy Spirit is resident within the church, which is His temple, this restraining work will continue and the man of sin cannot be revealed. It is only when the church, the temple, is removed that this restraining ministry ceases and lawlessness can produce the lawless one. It should be noted that the Holy Spirit does not cease His ministries with the removal of the church, nor does He cease to be omnipresent, with her removal, but the restraining ministry does cease.

Thus, this ministry of the Restrainer, which will continue as long as His temple is on the earth and which must cease before the lawless one can be revealed, requires the pretribulation rapture of the church, for Daniel 9:27 reveals that that lawless one will be manifested at the beginning of the week.

K. *The necessity of an interval.* The word *apantēsis* (to meet) is used in Acts 28:15 with the idea of "to meet to return with." It is often argued that that same word used in 1 Thessalonians 4:17 has the same idea and therefore the church must be raptured to return instantly and immediately with the Lord to the earth, denying and making impossible any interval between the rapture and the return. Not only does the Greek word not require such an interpretation, but certain events predicted for the church after her translation make such an interpretation impossible. These events are: (1) the judgment seat of Christ, (2) the presentation of the church to Christ, and (3) the marriage of the Lamb.

1. Passages such as 2 Corinthians 5:9; 1 Corinthians 3:11-16; Revelation 4:4; 19:8, 14 show that the church has been examined as to her stewardship and has received her reward at the time of the second advent of Christ. It is impossible to conceive of

this event as taking place without the expiration of some period of time.

2. The church is to be presented as a gift from the Father to the Son. Scofield writes:

> This is the moment of our Lord's supreme joy—the consummation of all his redemptive work.
>
> "Husbands, love your wives, even as Christ also loved the church, and gave himself for it; that he might sanctify and cleanse it by the washing of water by the word, THAT HE MIGHT PRESENT IT UNTO HIMSELF a glorious church, not having spot or wrinkle, or any such thing; but that it should be holy and without blemish" (Eph. 5:25-27).
>
> "Now unto him that is able to keep you from falling, and to present you faultless BEFORE THE PRESENCE OF HIS GLORY with exceeding joy" (Jude 24).[10]

3. In Revelation 19:7-9 it is revealed that the consummation of the union between Christ and the church precedes the second advent. In many passages, such as Matthew 25:1-13; 22:1-14; and Luke 12:35-41, the King is seen in the role of Bridegroom at His coming, indicating that the marriage has taken place. This event, likewise, requires the expiration of a period of time and makes the view that the rapture and revelation are simultaneous events impossible. While the length of time is not indicated in this consideration, yet an interval between the rapture and the revelation is required.

L. *Distinction between the rapture and the second advent.* There are a number of contrasts to be drawn between the rapture and the second advent which will show that they are not viewed as synonymous in Scripture. The fact of two separate programs is best seen by a number of contrasts drawn in Scripture between the two events. (1) The translation entails the removal of all believers, while the second advent entails the appearing or manifestation of the Son. (2) The translation sees the saints caught up into the air, and in the second advent He returns to the earth. (3) In the translation Christ comes to claim a bride, but in the second advent He returns with the bride. (4) The translation results in the removal of the church and the inception of the tribulation, and the second advent results in

[10] C. I. Scofield, *Will the Church Pass Through the Great Tribulation?* p. 13.

the establishment of the millennial kingdom. (5) The translation is imminent, while the second advent is preceded by a multitude of signs. (6) The translation brings a message of comfort, while the second advent is accompanied by a message of judgment. (7) The translation is related to the program for the church, while the second advent is related to the program for Israel and the world. (8) The translation is a mystery, while the second advent is predicted in both Testaments. (9) At the translation believers are judged, but at the second advent the Gentiles and Israel are judged. (10) The translation leaves creation unchanged, while the second advent entails the change in creation. (11) At the translation Gentiles are unaffected, while at the second advent Gentiles are judged. (12) At the translation Israel's covenants are unfulfilled, but at the second advent all her covenants are fulfilled. (13) The translation has no particular relation to the program of God in relation to evil, while at the second advent evil is judged. (14) The translation is said to take place before the day of wrath, but the second advent follows it. (15) The translation is for believers only, but the second advent has its effect on all men. (16) The expectation of the church in regard to the translation is "the Lord is at hand" (Phil. 4:5), while the expectation of Israel in regard to the second advent is "the kingdom is at hand" (Matt. 24:14). (17) The expectation of the church at the translation is to be taken into the Lord's presence, while the expectation of Israel at the second advent is to be taken into the kingdom.[11] These, and other contrasts which might be presented, support the contention that these are two different programs and can not be unified into one event.

M. *The twenty-four elders.* In Revelation 4:4 John is given a vision of twenty-four elders who are seated on thrones, clothed in white raiment, crowned with golden crowns, and in heaven in the presence of God. Several answers are given as to the question of the identity of these twenty-four. Some, because they are associated with the four living creatures in this book, insist that they are angels. This seems an attempt to evade the implication of taking the literal identification because it is contrary to

---

[11] W. E. Blackstone, *Jesus Is Coming,* pp. 75-80

their system. What is said of the twenty-four elders could not be true of angelic beings, for angels are not crowned with victors' crowns (*stephanos*) received as rewards, nor are they seated on thrones (*thronos*), which throne speaks of royal dignity and prerogative, nor are angels robed in white as a result of judgment. The impossibility of this view argues for the second view which sees them as resurrected redeemed men, who are clothed, crowned, and seated on thrones in connection with royalty in heaven. Scofield presents evidence to support the view that these are the representatives of the church. He writes:

> Five inerrant marks identify the elders as representing the church. These are: (1) Their *position*. They are enthroned "round about" the rainbow encircled central throne. To the church and to the church only of all groups of the redeemed is co-enthronement promised (Rev. 3:21). Not yet is Christ seated upon his own throne on earth, but these kingly ones having been presented faultless, with the exceeding joy of the Lord, must be with him (Jno. 17:24; 1 Thess. 4:17). (2) The *number* of these representative elders, in the book where numbers are so great a part of the symbolism, is significant. For twenty-four is the number of the choruses into which the Levitical priesthood was divided (1 Chron. 24:1-19), and of all the groups of the redeemed only the church is a priesthood (1 Pet. 2:5-9; Rev. 1:6). (3) The *testimony* of the enthroned elders marks them as representing the church: "And they sing a new song, saying, "worthy art thou to take the book, and to open the seals thereof: for thou wast slain, and didst purchase unto God with thy blood men of every kindred, and tongue, and people, and nation, and madest them to be unto our God a kingdom and priests; and they reign upon the earth" (Rev. 5:9, 10, R.V.). The church, and the church only, can thus testify. (4) Eldership is a *representative* office (Acts 15:2; 20:17). (5) The *spiritual intelligence* of the elders points them out as sharers of the most intimate divine counsels (e.g., Rev. 5:5; 7:13). And to whom amongst the redeemed should those counsels be made known if not to those to whom our Lord said: "Henceforth I call you not servants; . . . but I have called you friends. . . ." (Jno. 15:15). The elders are, symbolically, the church, and they are seen in heaven in the place which the Scriptures assign to the church before a seal is opened or a woe uttered, and before a vial of the wrath of God is poured out. And in all that follows, to the twentieth chapter, the church is never once referred to as on earth.[12]

---

[12] Scofield, *op. cit.*, pp. 23-24.

Since, according to Revelation 5:8, these twenty-four are associated in a priestly act, which is never said of angels, they must be believer-priests associated with the Great High Priest. Inasmuch as Israel is not resurrected until the end of the seventieth week, nor judged nor rewarded until the coming of the Lord according to Isaiah 26:19-21 and Daniel 12:1-2, these must be representatives of the saints of this present age. Since they are seen to be resurrected, in heaven, judged, rewarded, enthroned at the beginning of the seventieth week, it is concluded that the church must have been raptured before the seventieth week begins. If the church is not resurrected and translated here, as some insist, and not until Revelation 20:4, how could the church be in heaven in Revelation 19:7-11? Further study will be devoted to this question, but such considerations give further support to the pretribulation position.

N. *The problem behind 1 Thessalonians 4:13-18.* The Thessalonian Christians were not ignorant of the fact of resurrection. This was too well established to need presentation or defense. That which elicited this revelation from Paul to them was their misunderstanding of the relation between the resurrection and the saints who were asleep in Christ to the rapture. Paul writes then, not to teach the fact of resurrection, but rather the fact that at the rapture the living would not have an advantage over the dead in Christ. If the Thessalonians had believed that the church would be going through the seventieth week they would have rejoiced that some of their brethren had missed this period of suffering and were with the Lord without experiencing the outpouring of wrath. If the church were going through the tribulation it would be better to be with the Lord than to have to await the events of the seventieth week. They would be praising the Lord that their brethren were spared these events instead of feeling that those had missed some of the Lord's blessings. These Christians evidently believed that the church would not go through the seventieth week and in their anticipation of the return of Christ mourned for their brethren, whom they thought had missed the blessing of this event.

O. *The announcement of peace and safety.* In 1 Thessalonians 5:3 Paul tells the Thessalonian church that the Day of the

Lord will come after the announcement of "peace and safety." This false security will lull many into a state of lethargy in relation to the Day of the Lord so that that day comes as a thief. This announcement that has produced this lethargy precedes the Day of the Lord. If the church were in the seventieth week there would be no possibility that, during the period when believers are being persecuted by the beast to an unprecedented degree, such a message could be preached and find acceptation so that men would be lulled into complacency. All the signs would point to the fact that they were not in a time of "peace and safety." The fact that the visitation of wrath, judgment and darkness is preceded by the announcement of such a message indicates that the church must be raptured before that period can begin.

P. *The relation of the church to governments.* In the New Testament the church is instructed to pray for governmental authorities, since they are God-appointed, so that those in authority may be saved and the saints live in peace as a result. Such is the instruction in 1 Timothy 2:1-4. The church is further instructed to be in subjection to such powers according to 1 Peter 2:13-16; Titus 3:1; Romans 13:1-7, because these governments are God's representatives to carry out His will. According to Revelation 13:4 the government during the seventieth week is controlled by Satan and is carrying out his will and his purpose in the manifestation of lawlessness. Because of the relationship of the church to governments in this age and because of the Satanic control of government in the seventieth week, the church must be delivered before this Satanic government manifests itself. The church could not subject herself to such a government. Israel during the seventieth week will rightly call down the judgment of God upon such godless men, and cry for God to vindicate Himself, as is seen in the imprecatory Psalms. Such is not the ministry nor the relationship of the church to governments in this age.

Q. *The silence concerning the tribulation in the Epistles.* The Epistles of James, 1 Peter and, in a measure, 2 Thessalonians were specifically written because of the impending persecution of the church. Many passages, such as John 15:18-25; 16:1-4; 1 Peter 2:19-25; 4:12; James 1:2-4; 5:10-11; 2 Thessalonians

1:4-10; 2 Timothy 3:10-14; 4:5, were written to give a revelation concerning the persecution, give the reasons for it, and give help and assistance so the believer might endure it. Evidently the writers of the epistles had no knowledge that the church would endure the seventieth week, for they certainly would have given help and guidance to meet the most severe persecution men will ever have known, since they were concerned with giving help for the persecutions of a past day. They would not prepare for the persecutions common to all and neglect the outpouring of wrath in which the believer would need special help and assistance if he were to be in it. In this connection Scofield writes:

> Not only is there no syllable of Scripture which affirms that the church will enter the great tribulation, but neither the upper-chamber discourse, the new promise, nor the Epistles which explain that promise, *so much as mention the great tribulation.*
>
> Not once in that great body of inspired writing, written expressly for the church, is the expression found.[13]

Inasmuch as the persecutions of this age and the wrath of the seventieth week vary in kind and character, not just in intensity, it is not sufficient to say that if one is prepared for the lesser he will be also for the greater. The silence in the Epistles which would leave the church unprepared for the tribulation argues for her absence from that period altogether.

R. *The message of the two witnesses.* In Revelation 11:3 two special emissaries are sent to Israel. Their ministry is accompanied by signs to substantiate the divine origin of their message according to the Old Testament prophetic use of signs. The substance of their preaching is not revealed, but its content may be seen as suggested by the clothing of those messengers. They are said to be clothed with sackcloth (*sakkos*), which is defined by Thayer as:

> *a coarse cloth, a dark coarse stuff made especially of the hair of animals*: a garment of the like material, and clinging to the person like a sack, which was wont to be worn by mourners, penitents, suppliants . . . and also by those, who, like the Hebrew prophets, led an austere life.[14]

---

[13] *Ibid.*, p. 11.
[14] Thayer, *op. cit.*, p. 566.

When we compare the ministry of Elijah in 2 Kings 1:8 and that of John the Baptist in Matthew 3:4, whose ministries were parallel in that they were sent to Israel in a time of apostasy to call the nation to repentance, with the ministry of the two witnesses, we see that the sign of their message in each case is the same, the garment of hair cloth, which was the sign of the national mourning and repentance. It may be concluded, from their distinctive dress, that the two witnesses are announcing the same message as John did, that of repentance because the King is coming. Their good news is "the gospel of the kingdom" of Matthew 24:14. They do not neglect the preaching of the cross, for Revelation 7:14 and Zechariah 13:8-9 indicate that the preaching of the gospel of the kingdom in the seventieth week is accompanied by the preaching of the cross. The message committed to the church is the message of grace. The church has no other message. The fact that the message announced is one of judgment, repentance, and preparation in view of the coming of the King indicates that the church must no longer be present, for no such message is committed to her.

S. *The destiny of the church.* No one will deny that the destiny of the church is a heavenly destiny. All her promises and expectations are heavenly in character. When we study the destiny of the saved in the seventieth week we find that their expectation and promise is not heavenly but earthly. Matthew 25:34 makes this very plain. If the church is on earth during the seventieth week all who are saved during that period would be saved to a place in the body. If the rapture did not take place till the end of the seventieth week, and part of the saved went into an earthly blessing and part into a heavenly destiny, the body of Christ would be dismembered and the unity destroyed. Such dismemberment is impossible. This can only indicate that those saved during this seventieth week to go into the millennium must have been saved after the termination of the program for the church.

T. *The message to Laodicea.* In Revelation 3:14-22 John gives a message to the church in Laodicea. This church represents the final form of the professing church, which is rejected by the Lord and vomited out of His mouth because of the unreality of its profession. If the church goes into the seventieth week in its entirety and not just the professing portion of it, it would have to be concluded that this Laodicean Church is the picture of the true church. Several things are obvious then. The true church could not go through the persecutions of the seventieth week and still be lukewarm to her Lord. The persecution would fan the fire and turn the lukewarmness into an intense heat, or else it would extinguish the fire altogether. Such has always been the ministry of persecutions in the past. What is even more obvious, if this represents the true church, is that this church is vomited out from before the Lord, completely rejected of Him. This could only teach that one could be a part of the true church and then finally be cast out altogether. Such is an impossibility. The only alternative is to see that the true church terminates with the Philadelphia church, which is removed from the earth according to the promise of Revelation 3:10 before the tribulation begins, and the false professing church, from which the true has been separated by rapture, is left behind, rejected by the Lord, and vomited out into the seventieth week to reveal the true nature of her profession so that such may be rejected justly by the Lord.

U. *The times of the Gentiles.* In Luke 21:24 the Lord indicates that Jerusalem will continue in Gentile dominion "until the times of the Gentiles be fulfilled." Zechariah 12:2; 14:2-3 indicate that this will not be until the second advent, when the armies of the Beast are destroyed by the Lord, as He is seen to do in Revelation 19:17-19. In Revelation 11:2, in the parenthesis between the sixth and seventh trumpets, there is a reference to the times of the Gentiles. John indicates that Jerusalem is still in Gentile power and that from the beginning of the series of judgments, which this parenthesis interrupts, until the end of the Gentile dominion is three and one-half years. This is important to observe, for, according to the midtribulation view, the trumpets are events of the first three and one-half years of that seventieth week. If their view be correct the times of the Gentiles would have to end at the middle of the week, or at least before the termination of the seventieth week, and Jerusalem would then have to be delivered by some other event or person than the returning Lord. This time element indicated in Revelation 11:2 makes that view untenable.

V. *The waiting remnant at the second advent.* Passages such as Malachi 3:16; Ezekiel 20:33-38; 37:11-28; Zechariah 13:8-9; Revelation 7:1-8, and many others, indicate clearly that when the Lord returns to earth there will be a believing remnant in Israel awaiting His return. Along with these are passages such as Matthew 25:31-40 and such parables as Matthew 22:1-13 and Luke 14:16-24 that show that there will be a multitude of believers among the Gentiles who will believe and await His return. In order for the Lord to fulfill the promises made in the Abrahamic, Davidic, Palestinic, and new covenants at His second advent, it is necessary that there be a believing remnant over whom He can reign and to whom the covenants can be fulfilled. There must also be a group of believing Gentiles who can receive, through faith, the benefits of the covenants in His reign. These groups go into the millennium in their natural bodies, saved, but not having experienced death and resurrection. If the church were on earth until the time of the second advent, these saved individuals would have been saved to a position in the church, would have been raptured at that time, and consequently there would not be one saved person left on the earth. Who then would be waiting to meet Christ at His return? With whom could Christ literally fulfill the covenants made with Israel? These considerations make necessary the pretribulation rapture of the church, so that God may call out and preserve a remnant during the tribulation in and through whom the promises may be fulfilled.

W. *The sealed 144,000 from Israel.* As long as the church is on the earth there are none saved to a special Jewish relationship. All who are saved are saved to a position in the body of Christ as indicated in Colossians 1:26-29; 3:11; Ephesians 2:14-22; 3:1-7. During the seventieth week the church must be absent, for out of the saved remnant in Israel God seals 144,000 Jews, 12,000 from each tribe, according to Revelation 7:14. The fact that God is again dealing with Israel on this national relationship, setting them apart to national identities, and sending them as special representatives to the nations in place of the witness of the church, indicates that the church must no longer be on earth.

X. *The chronology of the book of Revelation.* In dealing

with both the midtribulation and posttribulation rapture positions the chronology of the Revelation has been examined. It is mentioned in this place only as further evidence. Chapters 1—3 present the development of the church in this present age. Chapters 4—11 cover the events of the entire seventieth week period and conclude with the return of Christ to the earth to reign in 11:15-18. Thus the seals are the events of the first three and one-half years and the trumpets events of the last three and one-half years. According to the instructions given John in 10:11, chapters 12—19 survey the seventieth week a second time, this time with a view to revealing the actors on the stage of the drama. This chronology makes a midtribulation view of the rapture impossible, for the so-called midtribulation rapture of 11:15-18 is seen to be the posttribulation return to the earth, not the rapture at all. This gives further supporting evidence for the pretribulation rapture position.

Y. *The great object of satanic attack.* According to Revelation 12, the object of satanic attack during the tribulation period is "the woman" who produced the child. Since this child is born "to rule all nations with a rod of iron" (Rev. 12:5), it can only refer to Christ, the one whose right it is to rule. The Psalmist confirms this interpretation in Psalm 2:9, which is admittedly Messianic. The one from whom Christ came can only be Israel. At the time Satan is cast out of heaven (Rev. 12:9) he goes forth with "great wrath because he knoweth that he hath but a short time" (Rev. 12:12). The church must not be here, for, since it is the "body of Christ" and the "bride of Christ" and consequently precious to Christ, it would be the object of satanic attack then as it has been all through the age (Eph. 6:12) if it were present. The reason Satan turns against Israel can only be explained by the absence of the church from that scene.

Z. *The apostasy of the period.* The complete apostasy of the period on the part of the professing church prevents the church from being in the world. The only organized church ever mentioned in the tribulation period is the Jezebel system (Rev. 2:22) and the harlot system (Rev. 17 and 18). If the true church were on earth, since it is not mentioned as separate from the apostate system, it must be a part of that apostasy. Such a conclusion is impossible. The believing witnesses, converted during the period, are specifically said to have kept themselves from defilement by this apostate system (Rev. 14:4). Since the church is not mentioned as also having kept herself from this system it must be concluded that the church is not there.

AA. *The promises to the true church.* There are certain passages of Scripture which definitely promise the church a removal before the seventieth week.

1. Revelation 3:10. "I will keep thee from the hour of temptation." John uses the word *tēreō.* Thayer says that when this verb is used with *en* it means "to cause one to persevere or stand firm in a thing"; while when used with *ek* it means "by guarding to cause one to escape in safety out of."[15] Since *ek* is used here it would indicate that John is promising a removal from the sphere of testing, not a preservation through it. This is further substantiated by the use of the words "the hour." God is not only guarding from the trials but from the very hour itself when these trials will come on those earth dwellers. Thiessen comments on this passage:

> . . . we want to know what is the meaning of the verb "will keep" (*tereso*) and of the preposition "from" (*ek*). Alford says on the preposition *ek,* that it means "out of the midst of: but whether by immunity from, or by being brought safe through, the preposition does not clearly define." . . . Thus he points out that grammatically the two terms can have the same meaning, so that Rev. 3:10 may mean, not "passing unscathed through the evil," but "perfect immunity from it." . . . the grammar permits the interpretation of absolute immunity from the period. Other scholars say the same thing as to the preposition *ek* (*out of, from*). Buttmann-Thayer says that *ek* and *apo* "often serve to denote one and the same relation," referring to John 17:15; Acts 15:29; Rev. 3:10 as examples of this usage. Abbott doubts "if in the LXX and John, *ek* always implies previous existence in the evils from which one is delivered when used with *sozo* and *tereso*" (i.e. with the verbs *to save* and *to keep*). Westcott says regarding *ek sozo* (to save from) that it "does not necessarily imply that that is actually realized out of which deliverance is granted (*cf.* 2 Cor. 1:10), though it does so commonly (John 12:27). Similarly we read in 1 Thess. 1:10 that Jesus delivers us "from (ek) the wrath to

[15] *Ibid.,* p. 622.

come." This can hardly mean protection *in* it; it must mean exemption *from* it. It would seem, then, to be perfectly clear that the preposition "from" may be taken to mean complete exemption from that which is predicted. It is clear that the context and other statements in Scriptures require that this be the interpretation. As for the context, note that the promise is not merely to be kept from the temptation, but from the *hour* of temptation, *i.e.* from the period of trial as such, not only from the trial during the period. And, again, why should the Apostle write *ek tes horas* (*from the hour*), as he did, when he might easily have written *en te hora* (*in the hour*), if that is what he meant to say? Surely the Spirit of God guided him in the very language he employed.[16]

2. 1 Thessalonians 5:9. "God hath not appointed us to wrath, but to obtain salvation by our Lord Jesus Christ." The contrast in this passage is between light and darkness, between wrath and salvation from that wrath. 1 Thessalonians 5:2 indicates that this wrath and darkness is that of the Day of the Lord. A comparison of this passage with Joel 2:2; Zephaniah 1:14-18; Amos 5:18 will describe the darkness mentioned here as the darkness of the seventieth week. A comparison with Revelation 6:17; 11:18; 14:10, 19; 15:1, 7; 16:1, 19 will describe the wrath of the Day of the Lord. Paul clearly teaches in verse 9 that our expectation and appointment is not to wrath and darkness, but rather to salvation, and verse 10 indicates the method of that salvation, namely, to "live together with him."

3. 1 Thessalonians 1:9-10. Again Paul clearly indicates that our expectation is not wrath, but the revelation of "his son from heaven." This could not be unless the Son were revealed before the wrath of the seventieth week falls on the earth.

BB. *The agreement of typology.* While argument from analogy is a weak argument in itself, yet if a teaching is contrary to all typology it can not be a true interpretation. Scripture abounds in types which teach that those who walked by faith were delivered from the visitations of judgment which overtook the unbelieving. Such types are seen in the experience of Noah and Rahab, but perhaps the clearest illustration is that of Lot. In 2 Peter 2:6-9 Lot is called a righteous man. This divine commentary will shed light on Genesis 19:22, where the angel sought

[16] Thiessen, *op. cit.*, pp. 22-24.

to hasten the departure of Lot with the words "Haste thee, escape thither; for I cannot do anything till thou be come thither." If the presence of one righteous man prevented the outpouring of deserved judgment on the city of Sodom, how much more will the presence of the church on earth prevent the outpouring of divine wrath until after her removal.

A number of reasons for belief in the pretribulation rapture position have been presented. Some of them are particularly applicable to the midtribulation rapture position and others applicable to the posttribulation rapture position. It should be borne in mind that it is not claimed that all the arguments have the same importance or weight. The pretribulation doctrine is not based on these arguments singly, but rather they are considered as cumulative evidence that the church will be delivered by rapture before the inception of Daniel's seventieth week.

Chapter XIV

THE EVENTS FOR THE CHURCH FOLLOWING THE RAPTURE

There are two events portrayed in Scripture into which the church will be brought following the rapture which have special eschatological significance: the judgment seat of Christ and the marriage of the Lamb.

I. The Judgment Seat of Christ

In 2 Corinthians 5:10 and Romans 14:10, although in the latter passage the corrected reading is "judgment seat of God," it is stated that believers are to be brought into an examination before the Son of God. This event is explained in more detail in 1 Corinthians 3:9-15. A matter of such seriousness demands careful attention.

A. *The meaning of judgment seat.* There are two different words translated "judgment seat" in the New Testament. The first is the word *critērion* as used in James 2:6; 1 Corinthians 6:2, 4. This word, according to Thayer, means "the instrument or means of trying or judging anything; the rule by which one judges" or "the place where judgment is given; the tribunal of a judge; a bench of judges."[1] Hence the word would refer to the standard or criterion by which judgment is meted out or the place where such judgment is meted. The second word is the word *bēma*, about which Thayer says:

> . . . a raised place mounted by steps; a platform, tribune; used of the official seat of a judge, Acts xviii. 12, 16 . . . of the judgment seat of Christ, Rom. xiv. 10 . . . of the structure, resembling a throne, which Herod built in the theatre at Caesarea,

[1] Joseph Henry Thayer, *Greek-English Lexicon of the New Testament*, p. 362.

> and from which he used to view the games and make speeches to the people. . . .[2]

Concerning its meaning and usage Plummer writes:

> The . . . [*bēma*] is the *tribunal,* whether in a basilica for the praetor in a court of justice, or in a camp for the commander to administer discipline and address the troops. In either case the tribunal was a platform on which the seat (*sella*) of the presiding officer was placed. In LXX . . . [*bēma*] commonly means a platform or scaffold rather than a seat. (Neh. viii. 4 . . .) In N.T. it seems generally to mean the seat. . . . But in some of the passages it may mean the platform on which the seat was placed. On the Areopagus the . . . [*bēma*] was a stone platform . . . Fond as St. Paul is of military metaphors, and of comparing the Christian life to warfare, he is not likely to be thinking of a military tribunal here.[3]

According to Sale-Harrison:

> In Grecian games in Athens, the old arena contained a raised platform on which the president or umpire of the arena sat. From here he rewarded all the contestants; and here he rewarded all winners. It was called the "*bema*" or "*reward seat.*" It was never used of a judicial bench.[4]

Thus, associated with this word are the ideas of prominence, dignity, authority, honor, and reward rather than the idea of justice and judgment. The word that Paul chose to describe the place before which this event takes place suggests its character.

B. *The time of the bema of Christ.* The event herein described takes place immediately following the translation of the church out of this earth's sphere. There are several considerations that support this. (1) In the first place, according to Luke 14:14 reward is associated with the resurrection. Since, according to 1 Thessalonians 4:13-17, the resurrection is an integral part of the translation, reward must be a part of that program. (2) When the Lord returns to the earth with His bride to reign, the bride is seen to be already rewarded. This is observed in Revelation 19:8, where it must be observed that the "right-

---

[2] *Ibid.*, p. 101.

[3] Alfred Plummer, *A Critical and Exegetical Commentary on the Second Epistle to the Corinthians*, p. 156.

[4] L. Sale-Harrison, *Judgment Seat of Christ*, p. 8.

eousness of the saints" is plural and can not refer to the imparted righteousness of Christ, which is the believer's portion, but the righteousnesses which have survived examination and have become the basis of reward. (3) In 1 Corinthians 4:5; 2 Timothy 4:8; and Revelation 22:12 the reward is associated with "that day," that is, the day in which He comes for His own. Thus it must be observed that the rewarding of the church must take place between the rapture and the revelation of Christ to the earth.

C. *The place of the bema of Christ.* It is scarcely necessary to point out that this examination must take place in the sphere of the heavenlies. It is said in 1 Thessalonians 4:17 that we shall be caught up . . . in the clouds, to meet the Lord in the air." Since the bema follows this translation, the "air" must be the scene of it. This is further supported by 2 Corinthians 5:1-8, where Paul is describing events that take place when the believer is "absent from the body, and . . . present with the Lord." Thus this event must take place in the Lord's presence in the sphere of the "heavenlies."

D. *The Judge at the bema of Christ.* 2 Corinthians 5:10 makes it clear that this examination is conducted before the presence of the Son of God. John 5:22 states that all judgment has been committed into the hand of the Son. The fact that this same event is referred to in Romans 14:10 as "the judgment seat of God" would indicate that God has committed this judgment into the hand of the Son also. A part of the exaltation of Christ is the right to manifest divine authority in judgment.

E. *The subjects of the bema of Christ.* There can be little doubt that the bema of Christ is concerned only with believers. The first personal pronoun occurs with too great frequency in 2 Corinthians 5:1-19 to miss this point. Only the believer could have "an house not made with hands, eternal in the heavens." Only the believer could experience "mortality . . . swallowed up of life." Only the believer could experience the working of God, "who also hath given unto us the earnest of the Spirit." Only the believer could have the confidence that "whilst we are at home in the body, we are absent from the Lord." Only the believer could "walk by faith, not by sight."

F. *The basis of the examination at the bema of Christ.* It is to be observed carefully that the issue here is not to determine whether the one judged is a believer or not. The question of salvation is not being considered. The salvation given the believer in Christ has perfectly delivered him from all judgment (Rom. 8:1; John 5:24; 1 John 4:17). To bring the believer into judgment concerning the sin question, whether his sins before his new birth, his sins since his new birth, or even his unconfessed sins since the new birth, is to deny the efficacy of the death of Christ and nullify the promise of God that "their sins and iniquities will I remember no more" (Heb. 10:17). Pridham writes:

> A saint will never again come into judgment on account of his natural or inherited iniquity, for he is already dead judicially with Christ, and is no longer known or dealt with on the footing of his natural responsibility. As a man he has been weighed and found wanting. He was born under condemnation, to a natural heritage of wrath, and nothing good has been discovered in his flesh; but his guilt has been obliterated by the blood of his Redeemer, and he is freely and justly pardoned for His Saviour's sake. Because Christ is risen from the dead, he is no longer in his sins. He is *justified* by faith, and is presented in the name and on the merits of the Just One before God; and of this new and ever-blessed title to acceptance the Holy Spirit is the living seal and witness. Into judgment, therefore, on his own account he cannot come. . . .[5]

This whole program is related to the glorification of God through the manifestation of His righteousness in the believer. Kelly commenting on 2 Corinthians 5:10, says:

> So again it is not a question of rewarding service as in 1 Corinthians iii, 8, 14, but of retribution in the righteous government of God according to what each did whether good or bad. This covers all, just or unjust. It is for the divine glory that every work done by man should appear as it really is before Him who is ordained by God Judge of living and dead.[6]

The word translated "appear" in 2 Corinthians 5:10 might better be rendered "to be made manifest," so that the verse reads, "For

---

[5] Arthur Pridham, *Notes and Reflections on the Second Epistle to the Corinthians*, p. 141.
[6] William Kelly, *Notes on the Second Epistle of Paul the Apostle to the Corinthians*, p. 95.

it is necessary for all of us to be made manifest." This suggests that the purpose of the bema is to make a public manifestation, demonstration or revelation of the essential character and motives of the individual. Plummer's remark: "We shall not be judged *en masse,* or in classes, but one by one, in accordance with individual merit,"[7] substantiates the fact that this is an individual judgment of each believer before the Lord.

The believer's works are brought into judgment, called "the things done in his body" (2 Cor. 5:10), in order that it may be determined whether they are good or bad. Concerning the word *bad* (*phaulos*), it is to be observed that Paul did not use the usual word for bad (*kakos* or *ponēras*), either of which would signify that which is ethically or morally evil, but rather the word, which, according to Trench, means:

> ". . . evil under another aspect, not so much that either of active or passive malignity, but that rather of its good-for-nothingness, the impossibility of any true gain ever coming forth from it. . . . This notion of worthlessness is the central notion. . . .[8]

Thus the judgment is not to determine what is ethically good or evil, but rather that which is acceptable and that which is worthless. It is not the Lord's purpose here to chasten His child for his sins, but to reward his service for those things done in the name of the Lord.

G. *The result of the examination at the bema of Christ.* In 1 Corinthians 3:14-15 it is declared that there will be a twofold result of this examination: a reward received or a reward lost.

That which determines whether one receives or loses a reward is the trial by fire, for Paul writes "Every man's work shall be made manifest [the same word used in 2 Cor. 5:10]: for the day shall declare it, because it shall be revealed by fire; and the fire shall try every man's work of what sort it is" (1 Cor. 3:13). From this statement it is evident, first of all, that it is the realm of the believer's works that is undergoing examination. Further, it is seen that the examination is not an external judgment, based on outward observation, but rather on a test that determines the inner character and motivation. The

---

7 Plummer, *op. cit.,* p. 157.
8 Richard C. Trench, *New Testament Synonyms,* pp. 296-97.

entire purpose of the trial by fire is to determine that which is destructible and that which is indestructible.

The apostle has affirmed that there are two classes of building materials which the "labourers together with God" may use in building the edifice upon the foundation already laid. The gold, silver, costly stones are indestructible materials. These are the work of God, which man only appropriates and uses. On the other hand, the wood, hay, and stubble are destructible materials. These are the work of men which man has produced by his own effort. The apostle is revealing the fact that the examination at the bema of Christ is to determine that which was done by God through the individual and that which the individual did in his own strength; that which was done for the glory of God and that which was done for the glory of the flesh. It can not be determined by outward observation into which class any "work" falls, so that work must be put into the crucible in order that its true character may be proved.

1. On the basis of this test there will be two decisions. There will be *loss of reward* for that which is proven by the fire to be destructible. Things done in the strength and for the glory of the flesh, regardless of what the act might be, will be disapproved. Paul expresses his fear of depending on the energy of the flesh rather than the empowerment of the Spirit in the light of this fact when he writes: "I keep under my body, and bring it into subjection; lest that by any means, when I have preached to others, I myself should be a castaway (1 Cor. 9:27)."

When Paul uses the word *castaway* (*adokimos*) he is not expressing fear that he will lose his salvation, but rather that which he has done shall be found to be "good-for-nothing." On this word Trench writes:

> In classical Greek it is the technical word for putting money to the... [*dokimē*] or proof, by aid of the... [*dokimion*] or test ... that which endures this proof being... [*dokimos* approved], that which fails... [*adokimos*, disapproved or rejected]...[9]

To safeguard against the possible interpretation that to suffer

[9] *Ibid.*, p. 260.

loss means the loss of salvation, Paul adds "he himself shall be saved; yet so as by fire" (1 Cor. 3:15).

2. There will be *a reward* bestowed for that work that is proved to be indestructible by the fire test. In the New Testament there are five areas in which specific mention is made of a reward: (1) an incorruptible crown for those who get mastery over the old man (1 Cor. 9:25); (2) a crown of rejoicing for the soul winners (1 Thess. 2:19); (3) a crown of life for those enduring trials (Jas. 1:12); (4) a crown of righteousness for loving his appearing (2 Tim. 4:8); and (5) a crown of glory for being willing to feed the flock of God (1 Pet. 5:4). These seem to suggest the areas in which rewards will be bestowed.

Something of the nature of the crowns or rewards is suggested in the word used for crown (*stephanos*). Mayor says of it that it is used:

> (1) For the wreath of victory in the games (1 Corinthians 9:25; 2 Timothy 2:5): (2) as a festal ornament (Proverbs 1:9; 4:9; Cant. 3:11; Isa. 28:1); (3) as a public honour granted for a distinguished service or private worth, as a golden crown was granted to Demosthenes. . . .[10]

In contrasting this word with *diadema* Trench writes:

> We must not confound these words because our English "crown" stands for them both. I greatly doubt whether anywhere in classical literature . . . [*stephanos*] is used of the kingly or imperial crown. . . . In the New Testament it is plain that the . . . [*stephanos*] whereof St. Paul speaks is always the conqueror's and not the king's (1 Cor. 9:24-26; 2 Tim. 2:5). . . . The only occasion on which . . . [*stephanos*] might seem to be used of a kingly crown is Matthew 27:29; cf. Mark 15:17; John 19:2.[11]

Thus the very word Paul chooses to describe the rewards is that associated with honor and dignity bestowed on the overcomer. Although we will reign with Christ, the kingly crown is His alone. The victor's crowns are ours.

In Revelation 4:10, where the elders are seen to be casting their crowns before the throne in an act of worship and adoration, it is made clear that the crowns will not be for the eternal

---

[10] J. B. Mayor, *The Epistle of James*, p .46.
[11] Trench, *op. cit.*, p. 79.

glory of the recipient, but for the glory of the Giver. Since these crowns are not viewed as a permanent possession, the question of the nature of the rewards themselves arises. From the Scriptures it is learned that the believer was redeemed in order that he might bring glory to God (1 Cor. 6:20). This becomes his eternal destiny. The act of placing the material sign of a reward at the feet of the One who sits on the throne (Rev. 4:10) is one act in that glorification. But the believer will not then have completed his destiny to glorify God. This will continue throughout eternity. Inasmuch as reward is associated with brightness and shining in many passages of Scripture (Dan. 12:3, Matt. 13:43; 1 Cor. 15:40-41, 49), it may be that the reward given to the believer is a capacity to manifest the glory of Christ throughout eternity. The greater the reward, the greater the bestowed capacity to bring glory to God. Thus in the exercise of the reward of the believer, it will be Christ and not the believer that is glorified by the reward. Capacities to radiate the glory will differ, but there will be no personal sense of lack in that each believer will be filled to the limit of his capacity to "show forth the praises of him who hath called you out of darkness into His marvelous light" (1 Pet. 2:9).

II. The Marriage of the Lamb

In many New Testament passages the relation between Christ and the church is revealed by the use of the figures of the bridegroom and the bride (John 3:29; Rom. 7:4; 2 Cor. 11:2; Eph. 5:25-33; Rev. 19:7-8; 21:1-22:7). At the translation of the church Christ is appearing as a bridegroom to take His bride unto Himself, so that the relationship that was pledged might be consummated and that the two might become one.

A. *The time of the marriage* is revealed in Scripture as falling between the translation of the church and the second advent. Prior to the rapture the church is still anticipating this union. According to Revelation 19:7 this marriage has taken place at the time of the second advent, for the declaration is: "the marriage of the Lamb is come." The aorist tense, *ēlthen,* translated "is come," signifies a completed act, showing us that the marriage has been consummated. This marriage is seen to follow the events of the bema of Christ, inasmuch as when the wife appears she appears in the "righteousness of the saints" (Rev. 19:8), which can only refer to those things that have been accepted at the judgment seat of Christ. Thus the marriage itself must be placed between the judgment seat of Christ and the second advent.

B. *The place of the marriage* can only be in heaven. Inasmuch as this follows the judgment seat of Christ, which has been shown to be in the heavenlies, and it is from the air the church comes when the Lord returns (Rev. 19:14), the marriage must take place in heaven. No other location would fit a heavenly people (Phil. 3:20).

C. *The participants in the marriage.* The marriage of the Lamb is an event which evidently involves only Christ and the church. It will be shown later, according to Daniel 12:1-3 and Isaiah 26:19-21, that the resurrection of Israel and the Old Testament saints will not take place until the second advent of Christ. Revelation 20:4-6 makes it equally clear that tribulation saints will not be resurrected until that time also. While it would be impossible to eliminate these groups from the place of observers, they can not be in the position of participants in the event itself.

In this connection it seems necessary to distinguish between the marriage of the Lamb and the marriage supper. The marriage of the Lamb is an event that has particular reference to the church and takes place in heaven. The marriage supper is an event that involves Israel and takes place on the earth. In Matthew 22:1-14; Luke 14:16-24; and Matthew 25:1-13, where Israel is awaiting the return of the bridegroom and the bride, the wedding feast or supper is located on the earth and has particular reference to Israel. The wedding supper, then, becomes the parabolic picture of the entire millennial age, to which Israel will be invited during the tribulation period, which invitation many will reject and so they will be cast out, and many will accept and they will be received in. Because of the rejection the invitation will likewise go to the Gentiles so that many of them will be included. Israel, at the second advent, will be waiting for the Bridegroom to come from the wedding ceremony and invite them to that supper, at which the Bridegroom will introduce His bride to His friends (Matt. 25:1-13).

In reference to the announcement in Revelation 19:9: "Blessed are they which are called unto the marriage supper of the Lamb" two interpretations are possible. Chafer says: "Distinction is called for at this point between the marriage supper which is in heaven and celebrated before Christ returns, and the marriage feast (Matthew 25:10, R.V.; Luke 12:37) which is on earth *after* His return."[12] This view anticipates two suppers, one in heaven preceding the second advent, and the one following the second advent on earth. A second interpretation views the announcement as anticipatory of the wedding supper that will be held on earth following the marriage and the second advent, about which an announcement is being made in heaven prior to the return to earth for that event. Inasmuch as the Greek text does not distinguish between marriage supper and marriage feast, but uses the same word for both, and since the marriage supper consistently is used in reference to Israel on the earth, it may be best to take the latter view and view the marriage of the Lamb as that event in the heavens in which the church is eternally united to Christ and the marriage feast or supper as the millennium, to which Jews and Gentiles will be invited, which takes place on the earth, during which time the bridegroom is honored through the display of the bride to all His friends who are assembled there.

The church, which was God's program for the present age, is now seen to have been translated, resurrected, presented to the Son by the Father, and has become the object through which the eternal glory of God is forever manifested. The present age will thus witness the inception, development, and completion of God's purpose in "taking out . . . a people for His name" (Acts 15:14).

---

12 Lewis Sperry Chafer, *Systematic Theology*, IV, 396.

SECTION FOUR

PROPHECIES OF THE TRIBULATION PERIOD

CHAPTER XV

THE SCRIPTURAL DOCTRINE OF THE TRIBULATION

I. THE DAY OF THE LORD

One of the major lines of prophecy running throughout the Old Testament and continuing through the New Testament is the prophetic truth related to the Day of the Lord.

A. *The time areas within the Day of the Lord.* The scope of the Day of the Lord has been a matter of debate among interpreters of the Scriptures. Some refer the Day of the Lord to the years of the tribulation period only. Others relate this to the second coming of Christ to the earth and the judgments immediately connected with that event. There are, however, two major interpretations of this question. The one is the view of Scofield who says:

> The day of Jehovah (called, also, "that day," and "the great day") is that lengthened period of time beginning with the return of the Lord in glory, and ending with the purgation of the heavens and the earth by fire preparatory to the new heavens and new earth (Isa. 65:17-19; 66:22; 2 Pet. 3:13; Rev. 21:1).[1]

Thus the day of the Lord would cover that time period from the return of Christ to the earth to the new heaven and earth after the millennium. The other view is that expressed by Ironside who says:

> . . . when at last the day of grace is ended the day of the Lord will succeed it. . . . The day of the Lord follows [the rapture].

[1] C. I. Scofield, *Reference Bible*, p. 1349.

> It will be the time when the judgments of God are poured out upon the earth. It includes the descent of the Lord with all His saints to execute judgment on His foes and to take possession of the kingdom . . . and to reign in righteousness for a thousand glorious years.[2]

This second view coincides with the previous one as to the terminus, but begins the Day of the Lord with the tribulation period so that the events of the tribulation, the second advent, and the millennium are all included within the scope of the Day of the Lord.

The term *Day of the Lord* occurs in the following passages: Isaiah 2:12; 13:6, 9; Ezekiel 13:5; 30:3; Joel 1:15; 2:1, 11, 31; 3:14; Amos 5:18 (twice), 20; Obadiah 15; Zephaniah 1:7, 14 (twice); Zechariah 14:1; Malachi 4:5; Acts 2:20; 1 Thessalonians 5:2; 2 Thessalonians 2:2; 2 Peter 3:10. In addition, the phrase *that day* or *the day* or *the great day* occurs more than seventy-five times in the Old Testament. The frequency with which it occurs will evidence its importance in the prophetic Scriptures. These passages reveal that the idea of judgment is paramount in all of them. This is so clearly brought out in Zephaniah 1:14-18. This judgment includes not only the specific judgments upon Israel and the nations at the end of the tribulation that are associated with the second advent, but, from a consideration of the passages themselves, includes judgments that extend over a period of time prior to the second advent. Thus, it is concluded that the Day of the Lord will include the time of the tribulation. Zechariah 14:1-4 makes it clear that the events of the second advent are included in the program of the Day of the Lord. 2 Peter 3:10 gives authority for including the entire millennial age within this period. If the Day of the Lord did not begin until the second advent, since that event is preceded by signs, the Day of the Lord could not come as a "thief in the night," unexpected, and unheralded, as it is said it will come in 1 Thessalonians 5:2. The only way this day could break unexpectedly upon the world is to have it begin immediately after the rapture of the church. It is thus concluded that the Day of the Lord is that extended period of time beginning with God's

[2] Harry A. Ironside, *James and Peter,* pp. 98-99.

dealing with Israel after the rapture at the beginning of the tribulation period and extending through the second advent and the millennial age unto the creation of the new heavens and new earth after the millennium.

B. *The events of the Day of the Lord.* It will be evident that the events within the Day of the Lord are indeed momentous, and a study of this period must include a study of a great part of the prophetic Scriptures. It will include the prophesied events of the tribulation period, such as: the federation of states into a Roman Empire (Dan. 2 and 7); the rise of the political ruler of this empire, who makes a covenant with Israel (Dan. 9:27; Rev. 13:1-10); the formulation of a false religious system under the false prophet (Rev. 13:11-18); the pouring out of the judgments under the seals (Rev. 6); the separation of the 144,000 witnesses (Rev. 7); the trumpet judgments (Rev. 8-11); the rise of God's witnesses (Rev. 11); the persecution of Israel (Rev. 12); the pouring out of the bowl judgments (Rev. 16); the overthrow of the false professing church (Rev. 17 and 18); the events of the campaign of Armageddon (Ezek. 38 and 39; Rev. 16:16; 19:17-21); the proclamation of the gospel of the kingdom (Matt. 24:14). It will also include the prophesied events connected with the second advent, such as: the return of the Lord (Matt. 24:29-30); the resurrection of Old Testament and tribulation saints (John 6:39-40; Rev. 20:4); the destruction of the Beast and all his armies and the False Prophet and his followers in the Beast worship (Rev. 19:11-21); the judgment on the nations (Matthew 25:31-46); the regathering of Israel (Ezek. 37:1-14); the judgment on living Israel (Ezek. 20:33-38); the restoration of Israel to the land (Amos 9:15); the binding of Satan (Rev. 20:2-3). Further it will include all the events of the millennial age, with the final revolt of Satan (Rev. 20:7-10); the great white throne judgment (Rev. 20:11-15); and the purging of earth (2 Pet. 3:10-13). These, and many related subjects, must then be studied.

C. *The Day of Christ.* A closely related term, which has brought confusion into the minds of some, is the term *Day of Christ.* Scofield says:

> The expression "day of Christ," occurs in the following passages: 1 Cor. 1:8; 5:5; 2 Cor. 1:14; Phil. 1:6, 10; 2:16. A.V. has "day

of Christ," 2 Thes. 2:2, incorrectly, for "day of the Lord" (Isa. 2:12; Rev. 19:11-21). The "day of Christ" relates wholly to the reward and blessing of saints at His coming, as "day of the Lord" is connected with judgment.[3]

Scroggie writes:

> It would appear that this event, which is frequently referred to as the "day of Christ," must be distinguished from the "Day of the Lord" of 1 Thes. 5:2; 2 Thes. 2:2 R.V. The latter expression comes from the Old Testament, and relates to Christ's universal kingdom; but the former expression is found in the New Testament only, and relates to His advent for the church.[4]

It thus appears that two separate programs are in view when these two expressions are used although not two separate time areas. They can not be made to refer to the same event. In each case in which Day of Christ is used it is used specifically in reference to the expectation of the Church, her translation, glorification, and examination for reward.

The word *day* as used in Scripture is not necessarily a time word, but may be used for the events which fall within any period. Paul so uses it in 2 Corinthians 6:2, when he speaks of the "day of salvation." Some, failing to see this, have felt that because Scripture mentions "the Day of the Lord" and the "Day of Christ" these two must come at two different periods of time, usually saying that the "Day of Christ" refers to events of the tribulation period and the "Day of the Lord" refers to events related to the second advent and the millennium to follow. Certainly two different programs are in view in these two days, but they may fall within the same time area. Thus the two days may have the same beginning, even though two different programs are in view. It may be that in 1 Corinthians 1:8 reference is made to "the day of the Lord Jesus Christ" to show that He is related to both of these days, being both "Lord and Christ" (Acts 2:36).

II. The Tribulation Period in Scripture

Although this subject has been touched on briefly in a

---

[3] Scofield, *op. cit.*, p. 1212.
[4] Graham Scroggie, *The Lord's Return*, pp. 53-54.

previous connection, it is necessary to set forth the teaching of the Scriptures on this important eschatological doctrine.

A. The Nature of the Tribulation

There is no better way to come to an understanding of the Scriptural concept of the tribulation than to let Scripture speak for itself. It is impossible to set forth all the declarations of the Word on this subject. A few will suffice. The line of revelation begins early in the Old Testament and continues through the New.

> When thou art in tribulation, and all these things are come upon thee, even in the latter days, if thou turn to the Lord thy God, and shall be obedient unto his voice;...he will not forsake thee, neither destroy thee, nor forget the covenant of thy fathers which he sware unto them [Deut. 4:30,31].
>
> And they shall go into the holes of the rocks, and into the caves of the earth, for fear of the Lord, and for the glory of his majesty, when he ariseth to *shake terribly* the earth [Isa. 2:19].
>
> Behold, the Lord *maketh the earth empty,* and maketh it *waste,* and turneth it upside down, and scattereth abroad the inhabitants thereof.
>
> The land shall be utterly *emptied,* and utterly *spoiled;* for the Lord hath spoken this word.
>
> Therefore hath the curse *devoured* the earth, and they that dwell therein are *desolate*: therefore the inhabitants of the earth are *burned,* and few men left [Isa. 24:1, 3, 6].
>
> The earth is utterly *broken down,* the earth is clean *dissolved,* the earth is moved exceedingly. The earth shall *reel* to and fro like a drunkard, and shall be removed like a cottage; and the transgression thereof shall be heavy upon it; and it shall fall, and not rise again. And it shall come to pass in that day, that the Lord shall *punish* the host of the high ones that are on high, and the kings of the earth upon the earth [Isa. 24:19-21].
>
> Come, my people, enter thou into thy chambers, and shut thy doors about thee: hide thyself as it were for a little moment, until the *indignation* be overpast. For, behold, the Lord cometh out of his place to *punish* the inhabitants of the earth for their iniquity: the earth also shall disclose her blood, and shall no more cover her slain [Isa. 26:20, 21].
>
> Alas! for that day is great, so that none is like it: it is even the time of Jacob's *trouble,* but he shall be saved out of it [Jer. 30:7. Italics mine.]

And he shall confirm the covenant with many for one week: and in the midst of the week he shall cause the sacrifice and the oblation to cease, and for the overspreading of abominations he shall make it desolate, even until the consummation, and that determined shall be poured upon the desolate [Dan. 9:27].

And at that time shall Michael stand up, the great prince which standeth for the children of thy people: and there shall be a time of *trouble,* such as never was since there was a nation even to that same time... [Dan. 12:1].

Alas for the day! for the day of the Lord is at hand, and as a *destruction from the Almighty* shall it come [Joel 1:15].

...the day of the Lord cometh, for it is nigh at hand; a day of *darkness* and of *gloominess,* a day of *clouds* and of *thick darkness* . . . there hath not been ever the like, neither shall be any more after it, even to the years of many generations [Joel 2:1-2].

Woe unto you that desire the day of the Lord! to what end is it for you? the day of the Lord is *darkness,* and not light. Shall not the day of the Lord be *darkness,* and not light? even *very dark,* and *no brightness* in it [Amos 5:18, 20]?

The great day of the Lord is near, it is near, and hasteth greatly . . . That day is a day of *wrath,* a day of *trouble* and *distress,* a day of *wasteness* and *desolation,* a day of *darkness* and *gloominess,* a day of *clouds* and *thick darkness.*

Neither their silver nor their gold shall be able to deliver them in the day of the Lord's wrath; but the whole land shall be devoured by the *fire of his jealosy* . . . [Zeph. 1:14-15, 18].

For then shall be *great tribulation,* such as was not since the beginning of the world to this time, no, nor ever shall be. And except those days should be shortened, there should no flesh be saved: but for the elect's sake those days shall be shortened [Matt. 24:21-22].

And there shall be signs in the sun, and in the moon, and in the stars; and upon the earth *distress of nations,* with perplexity; the sea and the waves roaring; Men's hearts failing them for fear, and for looking after those things which are coming on the earth; for the powers of heaven shall be shaken [Luke 21:25-26].

For when they shall say, Peace and safety; then sudden *destruction* cometh upon them, as travail upon a woman with child; and they shall not escape [1 Thess. 5:3].

. . . I also will keep thee from the hour of temptation, which shall come upon all the world, *to try* them that dwell upon the earth [Rev. 3:10].

> And the kings of the earth and the great men, and the rich men, and the chief captains, and the mighty men, and every bondman, and every free man, hid themselves in the dens and in the rocks of the mountains; And said to the mountains and rocks, Fall on us, and hide us from the face of him that sitteth on the throne, and from the *wrath* of the Lamb: For the *great day of his wrath* is come; and who shall be able to stand [Rev. 6:15-17]?

From these Scriptures it is inescapable that the nature or character of this period is that of *wrath* (Zeph. 1:15, 18; 1 Thess. 1:10; 5:9; Rev. 6:16-17; 11:18; 14:10, 19; 15:1, 7; 16:1, 19), *judgment* (Rev. 14:7; 15:4; 16:5, 7; 19:2), *indignation* (Isa. 26:20-21; 34:1-3), *trial* (Rev. 3:10), *trouble* (Jer. 30:7; Zeph. 1:14-15; Dan. 12:1), *destruction* (Joel 1:15; 1 Thess. 5:3), *darkness* (Joel 2:2; Amos 5:18; Zeph. 1:14-18), *desolation* (Dan. 9:27; Zeph. 1;14-15), *overturning* (Isa. 24:1-4, 19-21), *punishment* (Isa. 24:20-21). No passage can be found to alleviate to any degree whatsoever the severity of this time that shall come upon the earth.

B. The Source of the Tribulation

Because the posttribulation rapturist refuses to distinguish between the tribulations of this age, which the church will endure, and the unique and unprecedented period of tribulation which shall come on the earth, they insist that the rigors of the tribulation come only through the agency of man or of Satan, but disassociate God from the period entirely. Reese writes:

> According to Darby and his followers, the Great Tribulation is the wrath of *God* against the Jewish people for their rejection of *Christ.* According to Scripture, it is the *Devil's* wrath against the saints for their rejection of Antichrist, and adherence to Christ.
>
> Let the reader once see the Scripture truth on this point, and the whole Darbyist case will be exposed as a campaign of assumptions, mis-statements, and sentiment.[5]

The tribulation period will witness the wrath of Satan in his animosity against Israel (Rev. 12:12-17) and of Satan's puppet, the Beast, in his animosity against the saints (Rev. 13:7). Yet even this manifestation of wrath does not begin to exhaust the outpouring of wrath of that day.

Scripture abounds in assertions that this period is not

[5] Alexander Reese, *The Approaching Advent of Christ*, p. 284.

the wrath of men, nor even the wrath of Satan, but the time of the wrath of God.

> ... *the Lord* maketh the earth empty ... [Isa. 24:1].
>
> . . . *the Lord* cometh out of his place to punish the inhabitants of the earth for their iniquity ... [Isa. 26:21].
>
> ... as a destruction from the *Almighty* shall it come [Joel 1:15].
>
> Neither their silver nor their gold shall be able to deliver them in the day of *the Lord's* wrath ... [Zeph. 1:18].
>
> And said to the mountains and rocks, Fall on us, and hide us from the face of *him that sitteth on the throne,* and from the *wrath of the Lamb:* For the great day of *his wrath is come;* and who shall be able to stand [Rev. 6:16-17]?
>
> And the nations were angry, and *thy wrath* is come ... [Rev. 11:18].
>
> . . . Fear God, and give glory to him; for the hour of *his judgment* is come: and worship him ... [Rev. 14:7].
>
> The same shall drink of the wine of the *wrath of God* . . . [Rev. 14:10].
>
> And the angel thrust in his sickle into the earth, and gathered the vine of the earth, and cast it into the great winepress of the *wrath of God* [Rev. 14:19].
>
> Who shall not fear thee, O Lord, and glorify thy name? . . . for *thy judgments* are made manifest [Rev. 15:4].
>
> And one of the four beasts gave unto the seven angels seven golden vials full of the *wrath of God,* who liveth for ever and ever [Rev. 15:7].
>
> . . . Go your way and pour out the vials of the *wrath of God* upon the earth [Rev. 16:1].
>
> . . . Even so, Lord God Almighty, true and righteous are *thy judgments* [Rev. 16:7].
>
> . . . give unto her the cup of the wine of the fierceness of *his wrath* [Rev. 16:19].
>
> Salvation, and glory, and honour, and power, unto the Lord our God: For true and righteous are *his judgments*: for he hath judged ... [Rev. 19:1-2].

From these Scriptures it cannot be denied that this period is peculiarly the time when God's wrath and judgment fall upon the earth. This is not wrath from men, nor from Satan, except as God may use these agencies as channels for the execution of His will; it is tribulation from God. This period differs from all preceding tribulation, not only in intensity but also in the kind of tribulation, since it comes from God Himself.

C. The Purpose of the Tribulation

1. The first great purpose of the tribulation is to prepare the nation Israel for her Messiah. The prophecy of Jeremiah (30:7) makes it clear that this time that is coming has particular reference to Israel, for it is "the time of Jacob's trouble." Stanton shows the Jewish character of the period by saying:

> The tribulation is primarily Jewish. This fact is borne out by Old Testament Scriptures (Deut. 4:30; Jer. 30:7; Ezek. 20:37; Dan. 12:1; Zech. 13:8-9), by the Olivet Discourse of Christ (Matt. 24:9-26), and by the book of Revelation itself (Rev. 7:4-8; 12:1-2; 17, etc.). It concerns "Daniel's people," the coming of "false Messiah," the preaching of the "gospel of the kingdom," flight on the "sabbath," the temple and the "holy place," the land of Judea, the city of Jerusalem, the twelve "tribes of the children of Israel," the "son of Moses," "signs" in the heavens, the "covenant" with the Beast, the "sanctuary," the "sacrifice and the oblation" of the temple ritual—these all speak of Israel and prove that the tribulation is largely a time when God deals with His ancient people prior to their entrance into the promised kingdom. The many Old Testament prophecies yet to be fulfilled for Israel further indicate a future time when God will deal with this nation (Deut. 30:1-6; Jer. 30:8-10, etc.)[6]

God's purpose for Israel in the Tribulation is to bring about the conversion of a multitude of Jews, who will enter into the blessings of the kingdom and experience the fulfillment of all Israel's covenants. The good news that the King is about to return will be preached (Matt. 24:14) so that Israel may be turned to their deliverer. As John the Baptist preached such a message to prepare Israel for the first coming, Elijah will preach to prepare Israel for the second advent.

> Behold, I will send you Elijah the prophet before the coming of the great and terrible day of the Lord: And he shall turn the heart of the fathers to the children, and the heart of the children to their fathers, lest I come and smite the earth with a curse [Mal. 4:5-6].

This witness is seen to be effective in that multitudes of Jews

---

[6] Gerald Stanton, "Kept From the Hour," pp. 30-31.

are converted during the tribulation period and are waiting for the Messiah (Rev. 7:1-8 and the wise virgins of Matt. 25:1-13). It is also God's purpose to populate the millennium with a multitude of saved Gentiles, who are redeemed through the preaching of the believing remnant. This is accomplished in the multitude from "all nations, and kindreds, and people, and tongues" (Rev. 7:9) and in the "sheep" (Matt. 25:31-46) that enter the millennial age. God's purpose, then, is to populate the millennial kingdom by bringing a host from among Israel and the Gentile nations to Himself.

2. The second great purpose of the tribulation is to pour out judgment on unbelieving man and nations. It is stated in Revelation 3:10 "I also will keep thee from the hour of temptation, which shall come upon all the world, to try them that dwell upon the earth." This passage has been considered earlier. That this period will reach out to all nations is clearly taught in other Scriptures as well:

> Thus saith the Lord of hosts, Behold, evil shall go forth from nation to nation, and a great whirlwind shall be raised up from the coasts of the earth. And the slain of the Lord shall be at that day from one end of the earth even unto the other end of the earth: they shall not be lamented, neither gathered, nor buried . . . [Jer. 25:32-33].
>
> For, behold, the Lord cometh out of his place to punish the inhabitants of the earth for their iniquity... [Isa. 26:21].
>
> And for this cause God shall send them strong delusion, that they should believe a lie: That they all might be damned who believe not the truth, but had pleasure in unrighteousness [2 Thess. 2:12]

From these Scriptures it will be seen that God is judging the nations of the earth because of their godlessness. The nations of the earth have been deceived by the false teaching of the harlot system (Rev. 14:8) and have partaken of the "wine of the wrath of her fornication." They have followed the false prophet in the worship of the beast (Rev. 13:11-18). For this godlessness the nations must be judged. This judgment comes on "...the kings of the earth, and the great men, and the rich men, and the chief captains, and the mighty men, and every bondman, and every freeman . . ." (Rev. 6:15), all of whom "blasphemed the name of God... and they repented not to give him glory" Rev. 16:9). Since the kingdom to follow is a reign of righteousness, this judgment must be viewed as another step in the progress of God's program in dealing with sin so that the Messiah may reign. This program of judgment on sinners constitutes the second great purpose of the tribulation period.

D. The Time of the Tribulation

In order to understand the time elements in the tribulation period it is necessary to go back to the prophecy of Daniel where the chronology of Israel's future history is outlined in the great prophecy of the seventy weeks (Dan. 9:24-27).

1. *The importance of Daniel's prophecy of the seventy weeks.* Many importances may be attached to this prophecy. *a.* It establishes the literal method of interpretation of prophecy. Walvoord writes:

> Properly interpreted, the prophecy of Daniel furnishes an excellent example of the principle that prophecy is subject to literal interpretation. Practically all expositors, however opposed to prophecy *per se,* agree that at least part of the seventy weeks of Daniel is to be interpreted literally. . . . if the first sixty-nine weeks of Daniel were subject to literal fulfillment, it is a powerful argument that the final seventieth week will have a similar fulfillment.[7]

b. It demonstrates the truth of Scripture. McClain observes:

> . . . the prophecy of the Seventy Weeks has an immense evidential value as a witness to the truth of Scripture. That part of the prophecy relating to the first sixty-nine weeks has already been accurately fulfilled . . . only an omniscient God could have foretold over five hundred years in advance the very day on which the Messiah would ride into Jerusalem and present Himself as the "Prince" of Israel.[8]

c. The prophecy supports the view that the church is a mystery that was not revealed in the Old Testament. Walvoord says:

---

[7] John F. Walvoord, "Is Daniel's Seventieth Week Future?" *Bibliotheca Sacra,* 101:30, January, 1944.

[8] Alva J. McClain, *Daniel's Prophecy of the Seventy Weeks,* p. 5.

> The seventy weeks of Daniel, properly interpreted, demonstrate the distinct place of the Christian church and Israel in the purposes of God. The seventy weeks of Daniel are totally in reference to Israel and her relation to Gentile powers and the rejection of Israel's Messiah. The peculiar purpose of God in calling out a people from every nation to form the church and the program of the present age are nowhere in view in this prophecy.[9]

This gives supporting evidence that the church is not in Revelation four through nineteen, but must have been raptured before Israel's program began again.

d. The prophecy gives us the divine chronology of prophecy. McClain comments:

> In the predictions of the Seventy Weeks, we have the indispensable chronological key to all New Testament prophecy. Our Lord's great prophetical discourse recorded in Matthew and Mark fixes the time of Israel's final and greatest trouble definitely within the days of the Seventieth Week of Daniel's prophecy (Dan. 9:27; Matt. 24:15-22; Mark 13:14-20). And the greater part of the Book of Revelation is simply an expansion of Daniel's prophecy within the chronological framework as outlined by the same Seventieth Week, which is divided into two equal periods, each extending for 1260 days, or 42 months, or 3½ years (Rev. 11:2-3; 12:6, 14; 13:5). Therefore, apart from an understanding of the details of the Seventy Weeks of Daniel, all attempts to interpret New Testament prophecy, must fail in large measure.[10]

2. *The important factors in Daniel's prophecy.* It is necessary to observe the major emphases in the prophecy given through Daniel. McClain summarizes these as follows:[11]

> 1. The entire prophecy has to do with Daniel's "people" and Daniel's "city," that is, the Nation of *Israel* and the city of *Jerusalem* (24).
>
> 2. Two different princes are mentioned, who should not be confused: the first is named Messiah the Prince (25); and the second is described as *the Prince that shall come* (26).
>
> 3. The entire time-period involved is exactly specified as *Seventy Weeks* (24); and these Seventy Weeks are further divided into three lesser periods: first, a period of *seven weeks;* after

---

[9] Walvoord, *loc. cit.*
[10] McClain, *op. cit.*, pp. 6-7.
[11] *Ibid.*, pp. 9-10.

that a period of *three-score and two weeks;* and finally, a period of *one week* (25, 27).

4. The beginning of the whole period of the Seventy Weeks is definitely fixed at *"the going forth of the commandment to restore and to build Jerusalem"* (25).

5. The end of the *seven weeks and threescore and two weeks* (69 weeks) will be marked by the *appearance of Messiah as the "Prince" of Israel* (25).

6. At a later time, "after the threescore and two weeks" which follows the first seven weeks (that is, after 69 weeks), *Messiah the Prince will be "cut off,"* and *Jerusalem will again be destroyed* by the people of another "prince" who is yet to come (26).

7. After these two important events, we come to the last, or Seventieth Week, the beginning of which will be marked by the establishment of a *firm covenant* or treaty between the Coming Prince and the Jewish nation for a period of "one week" (27).

8. In the "midst" of this Seventieth Week, evidently breaking his treaty, the coming prince will suddenly *cause the Jewish* sacrifice to cease and precipitate upon this people a time of wrath and desolation lasting to the "full end" of the Week (27).

9. With the full completion of the whole period of the Seventy Weeks, there will be ushered in *a time of great and unparallelled blessings for the nation of Israel* (24).

These blessings are: (1) finish up the transgression, (2) make an end of sins, (3) make reconciliation for iniquity, (4) bring in everlasting righteousness, (5) seal up the vision and prophecy, and (6) anoint the most holy.[12]

The six promised blessings are related to the two works of the Messiah: His death and His reign. The first three have special reference to the sacrifice of the Messiah, which anticipate the removal of sin from the nation. The second three have special reference to the sovereignty of the Messiah, which anticipate the establishment of His reign. The "everlasting righteousness" can only refer to the millennial kingdom promised Israel. This was the goal and expectation of all the covenants and promises given to Israel and in its institution prophecy will be fulfilled. This kingdom can only be established when the Holy One or the Holy Place in the millennial temple is anointed. The millennium will witness the reception of the Messiah by

[12] Dan. 9:24.

Israel and will also witness the return of the Shekinah to the Holy of Holies. Thus we see the prophecy anticipates the whole work of the Messiah for Israel: He will redeem and He will reign at the expiration of time stipulated in the prophecy.

3. *The meaning of weeks.* Before one can determine the chronology of this prophecy it is first necessary to understand Daniel's use of the term *weeks* as it is here employed. On this McClain has written:

> The Hebrew word is *shabua,* which means literally a "seven," and it would be well to read the passage thus. . . . Thus the twenty-fourth verse of Daniel's ninth chapter simply asserts that "seventy *sevens* are determined" . . . and what these "sevens" are must be determined from the context and from other Scriptures. The evidence is quite clear and sufficient as follows:
>
> . . . the Jews had a "seven" of *years* as well as a "seven" of *days.* And this Biblical "week" of years was just as familiar to the Jew as the "week" of days. It was, in certain respects, even more important. *Six years* the Jew was free to till and sow his land, but the *seventh year* was to be a solemn "Sabbath of rest unto the land" (Lev. 25:3-4). Upon a multiple of this important week of years—"seven Sabbaths of years"—there was based the great jubilee year. . . .
>
> Now there are several reasons for believing that the "Seventy Sevens" of Daniel's prophecy refer to this well known "seven" of years. In the first place, the prophet Daniel had been thinking not only in terms of years rather than days, but also in a definite multiple of "sevens" (10 x 7) of years (Dan. 9:1-2). Second, Daniel also knew that the very length of Babylonian captivity had been based on Jewish violation of the divine law of the Sabbatic year. Since according to II Chron. 36:21 the Jews had been removed from off the land in order that it might rest for *seventy* years, it should be evident that the Sabbatic year had been violated for 490 years, or exactly seventy "sevens" of years. How appropriate, therefore, that now at the end of the judgment for these violations the angel should be sent to reveal the start of a *new era* of God's dealing with the Jew which would extend for the same number of years covered by his violations of the Sabbatic year, namely, a cycle of 490 years, or "Seventy Sevens" of years (Dan. 9:24).
>
> Furthermore, the context of the prophecy demands that the "Seventy Sevens" be understood in terms of years. For if we make them "sevens" of days, the entire period would extend for merely 490 days or a little over one year. Considering now that within

> this brief space of time the city is to be rebuilt and once more destroyed (to say nothing of the tremendous events of verse 24), it becomes clear that such an interpretation is altogether improbable and untenable. Finally . . . the Hebrew word *shabua* is found only in one other passage of the book (10:2-3), where the prophet states that he mourned and fasted "three full weeks." Now, here it is perfectly obvious that the context demands "weeks" of days. . . . And significantly, the Hebrew here reads literally "three sevens of *days.*" Now, if in the ninth chapter, the writer intended us to understand that the "seventy sevens" are composed of days, why did he not use the same form of expression adopted in chapter ten? The quite obvious answer is that Daniel used the Hebrew *shabua* alone when referring to the well known "week" of years . . . but in chapter ten, when he speaks of the "three weeks" of fasting, he definitely specifies them as "weeks of *days*" in order to distinguish them from the "weeks" of *years* in chapter nine.[13]

Interesting substantiating evidence is found in Genesis 29:27 where it is said, "Fulfill her week, and we will give thee this also for the service which thou serve with me yet seven other years." Here the "week" is specified to be a week of years or seven years.

It is also necessary, in this consideration, to observe that the year in prophetic Scriptures is a year composed of 360 days. The same author states:

> . . . there is conclusive evidence to show that the prophetic year of Scripture is composed of 360 days, or twelve months of 30 days.
>
> The first argument is *historical.* According to the Genesis record, the Flood began on the seventeenth day of the second month (7:11), and came to an end on the seventeenth day of the seventh month (8:4). Now, this is a period of exactly five months, and fortunately the length of the same period is given in terms of days—"an hundred and fifty days" (7:24; 8:3). Thus the earliest known month used in Biblical history was evidently thirty days in length, and twelve such months would give us a 360-day year.
>
> The second argument is *prophetical* . . . Dan. 9:27 mentions a period of Jewish persecution. . . . Since this persecution begins in the "midst" of the Seventieth Week and continues to the "end" of the Week, the period is obviously three and one-half years. Dan. 7:24-25 speaks of the same Roman Prince and the same persecution

[13] McClain, *op. cit.*, pp. 12-15.

fixing the duration as "a time and times and the dividing of time" —in the Aramaic, three and a half times. Rev. 13:4-7 speaks of the same great political Ruler and his persecution of the Jewish "saints" lasting "forty and two months." Rev. 12:13-14 refers to the same persecution, stating the duration in the exact terms of Dan. 7:25 as "a time and times and half a time"; and this period is further defined in Rev. 12:6 as "a thousand two hundred and three score days." Thus we have the same period of time variously stated as 3½ years, 42 months, or 1260 days. Therefore, it is clear that the length of the year in the Seventy Weeks prophecy is fixed by Scripture itself as exactly 360 days.[14]

4. *The beginning of the sixty-nine weeks.* Daniel was told that this 490 year period would begin "from the going forth of the commandment to restore and to build Jerusalem" (Dan. 9:24). In the Scriptures are contained several decrees that have to do with the restoration of the Jews from the Babylonian captivity. There was the decree of Cyrus in 2 Chronicles 36:22-23; Ezra 1:1-3; the decree of Darius in Ezra 6:3-8; and the decree of Artaxerxes in Ezra 7:7. However, in all these permission was granted for the rebuilding of the temple and nothing was said about the rebuilding of the city. In Ezra 4:1-4 the rebuilding of the temple was stopped because the Jews were rebuilding the city without authorization. In none of these decrees was the condition of Daniel 9:25 met. When we turn to the decree of Artaxerxes, made in his twentieth year, recorded in Nehemiah 2:1-8, for the first time is permission granted to rebuild the city of Jerusalem. This then becomes the beginning of the prophetic time appointed by God in this prophecy.

It, then, becomes necessary to establish the date of the decree of Artaxerxes. On this point Anderson writes:

> The date of Artaxerxes's reign can be definitely ascertained—not from elaborate disquisitions by biblical commentators and prophetic writers, but by the united voice of secular historians and chronologers.
>
> . . . .
>
> The Persian edict which restored the autonomy of Judah was issued in the Jewish month of Nisan. It may in fact have been dated from the 1st of Nisan. . . . The seventy weeks are therefore to be computed from the 1st of Nisan B.C. 445.

[14] *Ibid.*, pp. 16-17.

Now the great characteristic of the Jewish sacred year has remained unchanged ever since the memorable night when the equinoctial moon beamed down upon the huts of Israel in Egypt, bloodstained by the Paschal sacrifice; and there is neither doubt nor difficulty in fixing within narrow limits the Julian date of the 1st of Nisan in any year whatever. In B.C. 445 the new moon by which the Passover was regulated was on the 13th of March at 7h. 9m. A.M. And accordingly the 1st Nisan may be assigned to the 14th March.[15]

5. *The fulfillment of the sixty-nine weeks.* No more careful study has been made of the problem of the seventy weeks of Daniel than that of Sir Robert Anderson in *The Coming Prince.* Anderson reckons the chronology of the sixty-nine weeks thus:

"From the going forth of the commandment to restore and to build Jerusalem *unto Messiah the Prince* shall be seven weeks and threescore and two weeks." An era therefore of sixty-nine "weeks," or 483 prophetic years reckoned from the 14th March, B.C. 445, should close with some event to satisfy the words, "unto the Messiah the Prince."

. . . .

No student of the Gospel narrative can fail to see that the Lord's last visit to Jerusalem was not only in fact, but in the purpose of it, the crisis of His ministry . . . now the twofold testimony of His words and His works had been fully rendered, and His entry into the Holy City was to proclaim His Messiahship and to receive His doom. . . .

. . . .

And the date of it can be ascertained. In accordance with the Jewish custom, the Lord went up to Jerusalem upon the 8th Nisan, "six days before the Passover." But as the 14th, on which the Paschal Supper was eaten, fell that year upon a Thursday, the 8th was the preceding Friday. He must have spent the Sabbath, therefore, at Bethany; and on the evening of the 9th, after the Sabbath had ended, the Supper took place in Martha's house. Upon the following day, the 10th Nisan, He entered Jerusalem as recorded in the Gospels.

The Julian date of that 10th Nisan was Sunday the 6th April, A.D. 32. What then was the length of the period intervening between the issuing of the decree to rebuild Jerusalem and the public advent of "Messiah the Prince,"—between the 14th March, B.C. 445, and the 6th April, A.D. 32? THE INTERVAL CONTAINED EXACTLY AND TO THE VERY DAY 173,880 DAYS, OR SEVEN

---

[15] Robert Anderson, *The Coming Prince*, pp. 121-23.

TIMES SIXTY-NINE PROPHETIC YEARS OF 360 DAYS, the first sixty-nine weeks of Gabriel's prophecy.[16]

Anderson arrives at his figures as follows:

> The 1st Nisan in the twentieth year of Artaxerxes (the edict to rebuild Jerusalem) was 14th March, B.C. 445.
>
> The 10th Nisan in Passion Week (Christ's entry into Jerusalem) was 6th April, A.D. 32.
>
> The intervening period was 476 years and 24 days (the days being reckoned inclusively, as required by the language of the prophecy, and in accordance with the Jewish practice).
>
> | | |
> |---|---|
> | But 476 x 365 = | 173,740 days |
> | Add (14 March to 6th April, *both* inclusive | 24 days |
> | Add for leap years | 116 days |
> | | 173,880 days |
>
> And 69 weeks of prophetic years of 360 days (or 69 x 7 x 360) = 173,880 days.[17]

Thus Anderson shows us that the sixty-nine weeks began with the decree to rebuild Jerusalem and terminated at the triumphal entry into Jerusalem on the Sunday of the week of the Lord's death. The corrected reading of Luke 19:42, spoken as our Lord came into Jerusalem on that day is most significant: "If thou also hadst known, even *on this day,* the things which belong to thy peace; but now they are hid from thine eyes!"[18] The accuracy of Daniel's prophecy is observed in that he states *"after* threescore and two weeks shall Messiah be cut off" (Dan. 9:26).

6. *Is there a gap between the sixty-ninth and seventieth week?* The posttribulation rapturist joins with the amillennialist in asserting, *a.* that the seventieth week of Daniel's prophecy was fulfilled historically in the years immediately following the death of Christ. Some hold that Christ was cut off at the end of the sixty-ninth week and that the seventieth week followed immediately after His death. Others hold that Christ was cut off in the middle of the seventieth week so that the last half of the week followed His death.[19] Some go so far as to assert that the

---

16 *Ibid.*, pp. 124-28.
17 *Ibid.*, p. 128.
18 *Ibid.*, p. 126.
19 Cf. Philip Mauro, *The Seventy Weeks and the Great Tribulation*, pp. 55ff.

entire present age is the seventieth week.[20] The fallacy of this consecutive view is seen in the fact that only by spiritualizing the prophecy can the results of Messiah's work, as outlined in Daniel 9:24, be said to have been fulfilled. The nation Israel, to whom the prophecy was addressed, simply has not experienced a single one of the prophesied benefits of Messiah's coming as yet. Since this interpretation depends on a method of interpretation that is unacceptable, the view must be rejected.

b. Opposed to the view that the seventieth week is to be viewed as chronologically consecutive is the view that that period is separated from the other sixty-nine by an indefinite period of time. There are several considerations to support this view. (1) Such a gap is seen in many passages of Scripture. Walvoord writes:

> Dr. Ironside shows a number of instances of parentheses in God's program: (1) The interval between the "acceptable year of the Lord" and the "day of vengeance of our God" (Isa. 61:2—a parenthesis already extending more than nineteen hundred years). (2) The interval between the Roman empire as symbolized by the legs of iron of the great image of Daniel 2 and the feet of ten toes. *Confer* also Daniel 7:23-27; 8:24, 25. (3) The same interval is found between Daniel 11:35 and Daniel 11:36. (4) A great parenthesis occurs between Hosea 3:4 and verse 5, and again between Hosea 5:15 and 6:1. (5) A great parenthesis occurs also between Psalm 22:22 and 22:23 and between Psalm 110:1 and 110:2. (6) Peter in quoting Psalm 34:12-16 stops in the middle of a verse to distinguish God's present work and His future dealing with sin (1 Pet. 3:10-12).
>
> (7) The great prophecy of Matthew 24 becomes intelligible only if the present age be considered a parenthesis between Daniel 9:26 and 9:27. (8) Acts 15:13-21 indicates that the apostles fully understood that during the present age the Old Testament prophecies would not be fulfilled, but would have fulfillment "after this" when God "will build again the tabernacle of David" (Acts 15:13). (9) Israel's yearly schedule of feasts showed a wide separation between the feasts prefiguring the death and resurrection of Christ and Pentecost, and the feasts speaking of Israel's regathering and blessing. (10) Romans 9-11 definitely provide for the parenthesis, particularly the future of the olive tree in chapter 11. (11) The revelation of the Church as one body requires a parenthesis between God's past dealings and His future dealings

---

[20] George L. Rose, *Tribulation Till Translation*, pp. 68-69.

> with the nation Israel. (12) The consummation of the present parenthesis is of such a nature that it resumes the interrupted events of Daniel's last week.[21]

If there can be no parenthesis in any revealed prophetic program, prophecy can not have a literal fulfillment, for in many major prophecies the events were not consecutive. The gap in Daniel's prophecy is in accord with an established principle in the Word of God.

(2) In the second place, the events of Daniel 9:26 require a gap. Two major events are said to take place *after* the sixty-ninth week and before the seventieth week: the cutting off of the Messiah and the destruction of the city and the temple in Jerusalem. These two events did not take place in the seventieth week, for that is not introduced to us until verse twenty-seven, but in an interval between the sixty-ninth and seventieth week. It will be observed that the cutting off of the Messiah took place only a few days after the sixty-ninth week terminated, but the destruction of the city and temple did not take place until 70 A.D., or about forty years after the termination of the sixty-ninth week. If a few days gap be admitted, it is not difficult to concede the possibility of a gap of forty years. If one of forty years is admitted, it is not difficult to see that the gap may extend over the present age.

(3) In the third place, the New Testament teaching that Israel has been set aside (Matt. 23:37-39) until the restitution of God's dealing with them demands a gap between the last two weeks. If the seventieth week has been fulfilled, the six promised blessings must likewise have been fulfilled to Israel. None of these have been experienced by the nation. Since the church is not Israel, the church can not now be fulfilling them. Inasmuch as God will fulfill that which He promised literally, He must fulfill those things with the nation. It is seen, then, that there must be a gap between their rejection and the consummation of these promises.

(4) In the fourth place, since all the promised blessings are associated with the second coming of Christ (Rom. 11:26-27), if there were no gap, the Lord would have returned three and a

---

21 Walvoord, *op. cit.*, 101:47-48.

half or seven years after His death to fulfill the promises. Since His coming is still anticipated there must be a gap between the last two weeks of the prophecy.

(5) Finally, the Lord, in dealing with the prophecy, anticipates a gap. In Matthew 24:15 reference is made to the coming of the "abomination of desolation" and this is a sign to Israel that the great tribulation is approaching (Matt. 24:21). But even in this time there is hope, for "immediately after the tribulation of those days . . . they shall see the Son of man coming in the clouds of heaven with power and great glory" (Matt. 24: 29-30). Thus the Lord is placing the seventieth week of Daniel at the end of the age immediately before His second advent to the earth. Coupling this with Acts 1:6-8, we see that a whole age of undetermined duration is to intervene between the sixty-ninth and seventieth weeks of the prophecy. The only conclusion must be that the events of the seventieth week are as yet unfulfilled and await a future literal fulfillment.

7. *The beginning of the seventieth week.* It is evident from Daniel 9:27 that the seventieth week begins with a covenant that is made with "many" for one week, or for seven years. This "one week," following the method of interpretation established for the sixty-nine weeks, demonstrates the fact that the period in question will be of seven years duration. The question that must be faced is the identity of the one who makes the covenant that marks the inception of this seven year period. Daniel identifies him as "he" in 9:27. This must refer back to the "prince that shall come" in the previous verse. McClain, identifying this individual, writes:

> . . . there are two different princes mentioned: first, *"Messiah the Prince"*; and second, *"the prince that shall come."* The expression "prince that shall come" cannot possibly refer to "Messiah, the Prince" for the simple reason that it is "the *people* of the prince that shall come" who are to destroy Jerusalem after the death of Messiah. And since it is now a matter of history that Jerusalem was destroyed in A.D. 70 by the *Roman* people, not by the Jewish people, it follows that "the prince that shall come" cannot be the Jewish Messiah but is some great prince who will arise out of the Roman Empire.[22]

[22] McClain, *op. cit.*, p. 42.

Concerning this individual Gaebelein says: "Out of the Roman empire there shall arise in the future a prince. This prince or chief of the fourth empire is identical with the little horn of Daniel vii."[23] He is further to be identified with the "king of fierce countenance" of Daniel 8:23, with the "wilful king" of Daniel 11:36, with the "man of sin" of 2 Thessalonians 2, and with the "beast out of the sea" of Revelation 13:1-10. Inasmuch as all the covenants made by Messiah with Israel are eternal covenants, Messiah can not be the one making the covenant, inasmuch as it will be temporary. This covenant, which will guarantee Israel the possession of their land and the restoration of their religious and political autonomy, is to be viewed as a false fulfillment of the Abrahamic covenant. This covenant deceives many in Israel into believing that this "man of sin" is God (2 Thess. 2:3). It is the proclamation of this false covenant that marks the beginning of the seventieth week.

8. *The program of the seventieth week.* McClain has stated six features of this program that well summarize its relation to the prophetic picture.

> 1. This Seventieth Week is a period of seven years which lies prophetically between the translation of the church and the return of Christ in glory.
>
> 2. This Seventieth Week also provides the exact chronological framework for the great events recorded in chapters six to nineteen of the Book of Revelation.
>
> 3. The Seventieth Week will begin with the making of a "firm covenant" between the coming Roman prince and the Jewish people.
>
> 4. In the middle of the Seventieth Week, the Roman prince will suddenly reverse his friendly attitude toward the Jews and "cause the sacrifice and the oblation to cease."
>
> 5. The breaking of the "firm covenant" between the Jews and the Roman prince will make the beginning of a period of unparalleled "desolations" for the Jewish people.
>
> 6. The end of this final seven-year period will bring to its close the entire series of the Seventy Weeks, and therefore usher in the great blessings promised to Israel in Dan. 9:24.[24]

---

[23] Arno C. Gaebelein, *The Prophet Daniel*, p. 142.
[24] McClain, *op. cit.*, pp. 45ff.

CHAPTER XVI

THE RELATION OF THE CHURCH TO THE TRIBULATION

It has been demonstrated previously that the church will not be in the tribulation period. The peculiar relationship of the church to this period is seen in the position and activity of the twenty-four elders who appear in Revelation. John indicates that the Book of Revelation falls into three parts (Rev. 1:19): "the things which thou hast seen" constitutes the first division and embodies the vision of Christ of chapter one; "the things which are" constitutes the second division and includes the letters to the seven churches, contained in chapters two and three, which outlines the entire present church age; and "the things which shall be hereafter" (*meta tauta*) constitutes the third division and includes all revealed in chapters four through twenty-two. As John begins to write of the things which shall be hereafter, he shows us by his introductory words in 4:1 that he is beginning his third major division, for the chapter begins with "hereafter" (*meta tauta*). John, as he is caught up into the heavens, sees a throne and One occupying the throne. Then he sees twenty-four throne sitters, who are associated with the One on the throne, called the four and twenty elders.

> And round about the throne were four and twenty seats [thrones]: and upon the seats I saw four and twenty elders sitting, clothed in white raiment; and they had on their heads crowns of gold [Rev. 4:4].

The relation of the church to the events of the tribulation period is revealed by the identification of these individuals.

I. The Ministry of Elders

Concerning the term *elder,* Ottman writes:

> Elders in Israel were not only representatives of the people,

> but judges of them, and therefore God's representatives in passing judgment upon the people. They were identified with God in the exercise of judgment. The four and twenty elders now before us in connection with God's throne are also enthroned, and identified with Him in the judgment about to be executed upon the earth.[1]

In the New Testament the basic concept of elder is that of a representative of the people, one who rules or judges on behalf of God over the people (Acts 15:2; 20:17). Concerning these representatives in the Book of Revelation, Scott writes:

> "Elders" as a term occurs twelve times. The varied actions and services in which they take part show clearly enough that they are the representatives of the redeemed and risen saints. They are enthroned, fall down and worship; one of them comforts the weeping Seer and interprets the mind of heaven; they have harps, and vials of incense; they sing (never said of angels); are the nearest company to the throne and to the Lamb; intelligently explain as to the redeemed on earth; celebrate the millennial and eternal triumph of God; and add their "amen" and "hallelujah" to the judgment of the whore—the corruptress of the earth. The passages where the word is found are as follows: chapters 4:4, 10; 5:5, 6, 8, 11, 14; 7:11, 13; 11:16; 14:3; 19:4.[2]

An examination of the passages in which their activities are mentioned will emphasize the fact that the elders give worship and glory to God as each new step in the plan of God to establish His kingdom and overthrow the kingdom of the evil one is unfolded before them.

The number of these elders is not without its significance. Scott comments:

> But why *"twenty-four"*? The significance of the numeral must be sought for in the first book of Chronicles 24, 25. David divided the priesthood into twenty-four orders or courses, each course serving in turn (Luke 1:5, 8, 9). The respective elders or chiefs of these courses would represent the whole of the Levitical priesthood. There would thus be twenty-four chief priests and one high priest. Their varied service corresponded to that of the elders in heaven, for the temple (no less than the tabernacle), in structure, vessels, and services, was framed according to things in the heavens. God's people are termed "an *holy*" priesthood (1 Pet. 2:

---

[1] Ford C. Ottman, *The Unfolding of the Ages*, p. 108.
[2] Walter Scott, *Exposition of the Revelation*, p. 122.

> 5) and "a *royal*" priesthood (v. 9), and in both characters they are here seen in action.[3]

Thus they seem to be representatives of the entire heavenly priesthood, associated with Christ, the Great High Priest, in the unfolding of the consummation of the age.

II. The Identity of the Twenty-four Elders

Interpreters have been divided into three classes over the identity of these elders.

A. *Angelic beings.* The first interpretation is that they are angelic beings. This view is stated by Reese:

> (i) They are glorious heavenly beings taking the lead in the praise and worship of God.
>
> (ii) They celebrate with joy each crisis in the onward march of events to the consummation of the Kingdom.
>
> (iii) They seem never to have known the experience of conflict, sin, pardon and victory; yet they rejoice over the blessedness of those who have, and give glory to God for His grace in the victory of those who overcome.
>
> (iv) They distinctly dissociate themselves from the prophets, saints, and godly of ages past who rise in the resurrection at the Last Trumpet, and are rewarded. This passage indicates that *they* disappear from the scene when the new assessors—the great multitude of the heavenly redeemed—sit down on thrones and exercise judgment with the Lord Jesus at His coming. See xx. 4; I Cor. vi. 2; Matt. xix. 28.[4]

There is no disagreement with the first two propositions, but observe that such occupation does not require them to be angels. Such activity is more befitting the redeemed of this age who have been translated. Concerning the third proposition, one needs only to observe that the elders are seen to be crowned with *stephanos,* victor's crowns, to see that they must have known conflict, sin, pardon, and victory. Concerning the fourth proposition, if these are the church saints it would be natural for them to dissociate themselves from the tribulation saints, who are the ones being resurrected and rewarded in Revelation 11:16-18,

---

[3] *Ibid.*, p. 123.
[4] Alexander Reese, *The Approaching Advent of Christ,* pp. 92-93.

for the tribulation saints are not a part of the body of Christ, although redeemed by the blood of Christ. And in reply to the fifth proposition, it is not necessary to say that the elders must vacate their thrones in Revelation 20:4, as Reese insists, so that the resurrected of the tribulation period may occupy them. There is no basis for saying the thrones into which the resurrected enter are the same as these thrones. In Matthew 19:28 it was promised to the disciples that there would be thrones set up from which to manifest millennial authority and rule. Revelation 20:4 associates the tribulation saints with this millennial authority, but does not necessitate the dethroning of the elders.

Scott demonstrates that these elders can not be angels. He writes:

> The elders are a distinct company from the beasts or living creatures, and from the angels. In chapter v. the action of the elders as distinguished from that of angels makes it impossible to regard them as one and the same; verse 11 distinguishes by title the three companies. The elders *sing* (v. 9), the angels *say* (v. 12). The angels are never numbered (Heb. 12:22); the elders are; six times the representative number "twenty-four" occurs. Angels are not said to be crowned, the elders are. The choral praise of heaven—both harp and song—seems the peculiar function of the elders. Heavenly intelligence, especially in themes and subjects connected with redemption, is ascribed to the elders and not to angels. By the elders we understand, therefore, the innumerable company of the redeemed saints—raised and changed, and caught up to meet Christ in the air (1 Thess. 4:17). Their crown and thrones betoken their royal dignity; the harp and song their joy in worship; while their robes and vials point to priestly character and action.[5]

B. *Old Testament and New Testament saints.* The second view is that these elders represent the Old Testament and New Testament saints. Ironside summarizes this view when he writes:

> The elders in heaven represent the whole heavenly priesthood—that is, all the redeemed who have died in the past, or who shall be living at the Lord's return. . . . The church of the present age and Old Testament saints alike are included. All are

[5] Scott, *loc. cit.*

> priests. All worship. There were twelve patriarchs in Israel, and twelve apostles introducing the new dispensation. The two together would give the complete four and twenty.[6]

This view unites Israel and the church into one company, without distinction, at the time of the rapture.

While this view is less objectionable than the first view, there seem to be reasons for rejecting the interpretation that Israel is a part of the scene here. In the first place, this view is based on the assumption that Israel and the church are both resurrected at the time of the rapture and translated together into the heavenlies. The problem of Israel's resurrection will be considered later, but certain Scriptures (Dan. 12:1-2; Isa. 26:19; John 11:24) indicate that Israel's resurrection is to be connected with the second advent of Messiah to the earth. Thus Israel could not be translated. In the second place, the rapture is the program for the church that brings the church into her eternal blessing. The program with Israel is entirely distinct, taking place with different subjects at a different time. Israel could not be resurrected and rewarded until the close of her age. Since these twenty-four elders are resurrected, rewarded, and glorified, and the church is the only body that has experienced these things as yet in the program of God, the saints of the Old Testament could not be included in the group.

C. *Saints of this age.* The third view is the view that the twenty-four elders represent the saints of this age, the church, resurrected and translated into the heavenlies. There are several important considerations to support this view.

1. The *number twenty-four,* which represents the entire priesthood (1 Chron. 24:1-4, 19), as it was divided for purposes of representation by David, suggests that this is the church. While Israel was called to a priestly function (Ex. 19:6), that nation never entered into this chief function because of their sin. To the tribulation saints the promise is given that they shall minister as priests in the millennium (Rev. 20:6). However, at the beginning of the tribulation period Israel has not been

[6] Harry A. Ironside, *Lectures on the Revelation,* p. 82.

restored to the place of a priestly nation, for they must await the millennial age for the realization of that privilege. The tribulation saints, likewise, must wait the millennial age for their realization of it. The church is the only body definitely constituted a priesthood that could fulfill the function of priests ministering under the High Priest (1 Pet. 2:5, 9).

2. Their *position* suggests that they represent the church. In Revelation 4 the elders are seated on thrones, surrounding the throne of God, intimately associated with the One seated on His throne. The church has been promised this very position (Rev. 3:21; Matt. 19:28). Such a position could not be true of angels, who surround the throne, but do not occupy positions on the throne, nor could it be true of Israel, for Israel will be subjected to the authority of the throne, not associated with its authority. Lincoln ably comments:

> They sit down before God—aye, and covered or crowned before Him. Surely never before did creature the most exalted sit down in the presence of God! From Job i. it would appear as if not always were the angels in the immediate presence of God, but only on certain occasions. And Gabriel evidently of high rank in the heavenly hierarchy, in his address to Zechariah, says, "I am Gabriel, that *stand* in 'the presence of God,'" (Luke 1. 19). Also in 1 Kings xxii., Micaiah states that he saw the Lord sitting on His Throne and all the host of heaven *standing* by Him (Dan. vii.). But here we have quite a new order of things, indeed; viz., the redeemed saints of the present dispensation seen in their heavenly Home, and in their representative character, seated and covered, as to their heads, before God.[7]

3. Their *white raiment* suggests that they represent the church. It is made clear in Isaiah 61:10 that the white raiment represents righteousness that has been imputed to the believer. It was promised to those in Sardis (Rev. 3:4-5) that they would be robed in white. This white raiment was first seen at the transfiguration (Mark 9:3) and suggests that that which was Christ's inherently has become the possession of these elders by imputation.

4. Their *crowns* suggest that they represent the church. These twenty-four are not wearing monarch's crowns (*diadēma*)

---

[7] William Lincoln, *Lectures on the Book of Revelation*, pp. 76-77.

but victor's crowns (*stephanos*), which had been won in a conflict. They therefore have been both resurrected, for a spirit would not be wearing a crown, and judged, for they could not receive a crown as a reward apart from judgment. Further, the judgment must have only recently taken place, for they are seen in the act of casting their crowns at Christ's feet (Rev. 4:10).[8]

5. Their *worship* suggests that they represent the church. Worship is given to God from the elders because of His acts of creation (Rev. 4:11), redemption (Rev. 5:9), judgment (Rev. 19:2) and reigning (Rev. 11:17). Some have sought to dissociate the elders from the redemption of which they sing (Rev. 5:9) by deleting the word "us" from the text, affirming on that basis that these could not be the representatives of the church. On this point several things are to be observed. First, there is good manuscript evidence to include the word in the text.[9] The word need not be deleted on textual grounds. In the second place, even if it were to be deleted it does not mean that the elders were not singing of their own redemption. In Exodus 15:13, 17, where Moses and the people of Israel are praising God for His judgment, which they manifestly experienced themselves, they sing in the third person. Scripture gives precedent, therefore, for dealing with that which is subjective as an objective fact. And in the third place, if the word were omitted and it could be proved that they were singing about a redemption which they did not experience themselves, it need not prove that the elders are not the church, for as these elders are brought into a knowledge of judgments of God being poured out on the earth they anticipate the victory of the saints who are on the earth through these experiences and they can praise God for the redemption of these from "every kindred, and tongue, and people, and nation" (Rev. 5:9) who have experienced the tribulation, been saved in it, and who will be made "kings and priests, and shall reign on the earth," (Rev. 5:10; 20:6). As they praise God for the judgment He exercises during the tribulation period (Rev. 19:2), so they may praise God for the redemption He accomplishes during it.

---

[8] Cf. Gerald Stanton, "Kept from the Hour," p. 290.

[9] Joseph Seiss, *The Apocalypse*, I, 249.

6. Their *intimate knowledge of the program of God* suggests that the elders represent the church. In passages such as Revelation 5:5; 7:13-14 it is seen that they have been taken into the confidence of God concerning His program as it is being unfolded. Such intimacy is the ultimate fulfillment of that promised by our Lord to the disciples in John 15:15. The very use of the word "elder" suggests this maturity in spiritual understanding, for the Scriptural concept of an elder was one mature either in years or experience. The promise of such maturity, as indicated in 1 Corinthians 13:12, is now actual.

7. Their *association with Christ in a priestly ministry* suggests that they represent the church. In Revelation 5:8 they are seen "having harps and golden vials full of odours, which are the prayers of the saints." Of this ministry Scott writes:

> . . . the elders neither act as mediators nor intercessors. They do not present these supplications to God, nor add by mediation to their value. The elders in heaven are the brethren of those holy sufferers on earth. Strange, therefore, that they should not be interested in the struggles and conflicts here in which they formerly had their part! But theirs, while deeply sympathetic, is a passive attitude. The angel-priest who adds incense to the prayers of the saints is no created being (8:3-4); Christ, and He alone, is competent to do this.[10]

The close association into which these elders have been brought in this priestly ministry suggests that the church, which has been constituted as a ministering priest, is here represented.

The conclusion formed by Armerding will form a suitable conclusion to the examination of these elders. He writes:

> . . . the last thing that is said of them is that they fall down, in company with the four living creatures, and worship Him Who sits on the throne, saying, "Amen, Alleluia" (Rev. 19:4). This last act of theirs is characteristic of them. Indeed, there are three things which seem to characterize them all through: (1) their intimate knowledge of Christ, (2) their nearness to Him, and (3) the worship they give Him. And we recall that our Lord, when praying for His own, asked that they might know Him, that they might be with Him, and that they might behold His glory (John 17:3, 25). And they were none other than the men which the Father had given Him out of the world.[11]

---

[10] Scott, *op, cit.*, pp. 138-39.
[11] Carl Armerding, *The Four and Twenty Elders*, p. 10.

CHAPTER XVII

THE RELATION OF THE HOLY SPIRIT TO THE TRIBULATION

One of the important considerations accompanying a study of the tribulation period is the relation sustained by the Holy Spirit to that period and the work He will accomplish in it.

I. THE IDENTITY OF "THE RESTRAINER"

Much of the question of the Spirit's relation to the tribulation is determined by the interpretation of 2 Thessalonians 2:7-8. It had been erroneously reported that the Thessalonians were already in the Day of the Lord. To correct this misinterpretation Paul states that they could not be in the Day of the Lord for that day could not come until the man of sin had been revealed. His manifestation was being prevented by a restraining work of one whose ministry was to remain. Only after the removal of this restrainer could the man of sin be revealed and the Day of the Lord begin. Chafer writes:

> The central truth of the passage under discussion is that, though Satan would long ago have consummated his evil program for his *cosmos* world, and have brought forward its last human ruler, there is a Restrainer who restrains to the end that Satan's program shall be developed and completed only at God's appointed time.[1]

John bears testimony that this program of introducing the man of sin had already begun to operate in his day (1 John 4:3). That Satanic program has continued through the age, but has been kept in check by the restrainer.

A. *Who is the Restrainer?* A number of answers have been given as to the identity of this restraining agency. 1. Some have

[1] Lewis Sperry Chafer, *Systematic Theology*, IV, 372.

held that the restrainer was *the Roman Empire* under which Paul lived. Reese says:

> The oldest and best interpretation is that Paul hesitated to set down in words what he meant, because he had in mind the Roman Empire. The impersonal influence was the magnificent system of law and justice throughout the Roman world; this held lawlessness and the Man of Lawlessness in check. Then the line of emperors, in spite of wicked individuals, had the same influence.[2]

2. A second view, closely associated with this, is the view of Hogg and Vine that the restrainer was *human government and law*. They write:

> In due time the Babylonian Empire, to whose king the words were spoken, was succeeded by the Persian, that by the Grecian, and that again by the Roman, which flourished in the Apostle's day. . . . The laws under which these states maintain their existence were inherited from Rome as Rome inherited them from the Empires that preceded her. Thus the existing authorities are ordained of God . . . constituted authority is intended to act in restraint of lawlessness.[3]

It is clearly seen that "the powers that be are ordained by God" (Rom. 13:1). Yet human power does not seem to be a satisfactory answer to the identity of the restrainer. Walvoord writes:

> Human government, however, continues during the period of the tribulation in which the man of sin is revealed. While all forces of law and order tend to restrain sin, they are not such in their own character, but rather as they are used and empowered to accomplish this end by God. It would seem a preferable interpretation to view all restraint of sin, regardless of means, as proceeding from God as a ministry of the Holy Spirit. As Thiessen writes: "But who is the one that restraineth? Denney, Findlay, Alford, Moffatt, hold this refers to law and order, especially as embodied in the Roman Empire. But while human governments may be agencies in the restraining work of the Spirit, we believe that they in turn are influenced by the Church. And again, back of human government is God Who instituted it (Gen. 9:5, 6; Rom. 13:1-7) and controls it (Ps. 75:5-7). So it is God by His Spirit that restrains the development of lawlessness."[4]

---

[2] Alexander Reese, *The Approaching Advent of Christ*, p. 246.

[3] C. F. Hogg and W. E. Vine, *The Epistles of Paul the Apostle to the Thessalonians*, pp. 259-60.

[4] John F. Walvoord, *The Holy Spirit*, p. 115.

3. A third view is the view that *Satan* is the restrainer. One advocate of this view writes:

> Why should every one conclude that this hinderer must be some good thing? May not this restraining power be Satan himself? Has he not a plan for the manifesting of the Son of Perdition, as truly as God had a time appointed for the incarnation of His divine Son?[5]

The obvious answer to this allegation would be the reply of the Lord to those who accuse Him of working His signs by Satanic power: "If a house be divided against itself, that house cannot stand" (Mark 3:25). Further, the removal of this restrainer does not free the world from Satanic activity, as would be the case if Satan were the restrainer, but thrusts him into the world with unleashed fury (Rev. 12:12). Walvoord says:

> This idea is hardly compatible with the revelation of Satan in the Scriptures. Satan is nowhere given universal power over the world, though his influence is inestimable. A study of 2 Thessalonians 2:3-10 indicates that the one who restrains is removed from the scene before the man of sin is revealed. This could hardly be said of Satan. The period of tribulation on the contrary is one in which Satan's work is most evident. The Scriptures represent him as being cast into the earth and venting his fury during those tragic days (Rev. 12:9). The theory that Satan is the great restrainer of lawlessness is, accordingly, untenable.[6]

4. A fourth interpretation is the view that the restrainer is *the church.* It is recognized that believers were likened to salt, which is a preservative, and to light, which is a purifying agent, a dispeller of darkness. It would be agreed that the church could be one of the means through which restraint is felt but that which is the channel could not at the same time be the agent. Stanton writes:

> . . . the church is at best an imperfect organism, perfect in standing before God, to be sure, but experimentally before men, not always blameless or above reproach. Like human government, the church is used of God to hinder the full manifestation of the Evil One in this present age, but He who effectively restrains is not the believer, but the One who empowers the believer, the

---

[5] Mrs. George C. Needham, *The Anti-Christ*, p. 94.
[6] Walvoord, *op. cit.*, p. 116.

indwelling Holy Spirit (John 16:7; 1 Cor. 6:19). Apart from His presence, neither church nor government would have ability to hinder the program and power of Satan.[7]

5. The fifth interpretation is the interpretation that holds the restrainer is *the Holy Spirit.* The above author gives reasons to support this conclusion.

> (1) By mere elimination, the Holy Spirit must be the restrainer. All other suggestions fall far short of meeting the requirements. . . .
>
> (2) The Wicked One is a personality, and his operations include the realm of the spiritual. The restrainer must likewise be a personality and a spiritual being . . . to hold Antichrist in check until the time for his revealing. Mere agencies or impersonal spiritual forces would be inadequate.
>
> (3) To achieve all that is to be accomplished, the restrainer must be a member of the Godhead. He must be stronger than the Man of Sin and stronger than Satan who energizes him. In order to restrain evil down through the course of the age, the restrainer must be eternal. . . . The theater of sin is the entire world: therefore, it is imperative that the restrainer be one who is not limited by time or space. . . .
>
> (4) This age is in a particular sense the "dispensation of the Spirit," for He works in a way uncommon to other ages as an abiding Presence within the children of God. . . . The church age commenced with the advent of the Spirit at Pentecost, and will close with a reversal of Pentecost, the removal of the Spirit. This does not mean that He will not be operative—only that He will no longer be resident.
>
> (5) The work of the Spirit since His advent has included the restraint of evil . . . John 16:7-11 . . . 1 John 4:4. How different it will be in the tribulation. . . .
>
> (6) . . . although the Spirit was not resident on earth during Old Testament days, yet he exerted a restraining influence. . . . Isaiah 59:19b . . . .

B. *The work of the Holy Spirit to believers in the tribulation.* The fact that the Holy Spirit is the restrainer, to be removed from the earth before the tribulation period begins, must not be interpreted to mean that the Holy Spirit is no longer omnipresent, nor operative in the age. The Spirit will

[7] Gerald Stanton, "Kept from the Hour," p. 110.
[8] *Ibid.*, pp. 111-15.

work in and through men. It is only insisted that the particular ministries of the Holy Spirit to the believer in this present age (baptism, 1 Cor. 12:12-13; indwelling, 1 Cor. 6:19, 20; sealing, Eph. 1:13; 4:30; and filling, Eph. 5:18) do terminate. On this question Walvoord writes:

> There is little evidence that believers will be indwelt by the Spirit during the tribulation. . . . The tribulation period . . . seems to revert back to Old Testament conditions in several ways; and in the Old Testament period, saints were never permanently indwelt except in isolated instances, though a number of instances of the filling of the Spirit and of empowering for service are found. Taking all the factors into consideration, there is no evidence for the indwelling presence of the Holy Spirit in believers in the tribulation. If believers are indwelt during the tribulation, however, it also would follow that they are sealed by the Spirit, the seal being His own presence in them.[9]

Since all of the Spirit's ministries to the believer today depend upon His indwelling presence, the absence of this prevents all the dependent ministries to the tribulation saints.

II. Salvation in the Tribulation

A field of investigation opened by the view that the Holy Spirit is the restrainer who is to be removed is the question of salvation during the tribulation period. One of the questions most frequently raised by those antagonistic to the dispensational premillennial position is that very question. Allis asks:

> If the Church consists only of those who have been redeemed in the interval between Pentecost and the rapture, and if the entire Church is to be raptured, then there will be no Christians on earth during the period between the rapture and the appearing. Yet during that period 144,000 in Israel and an innumerable multitude from the Gentiles (Rev. vii.) are to be saved. How is this to be brought about, if the Church has been raptured and the Holy Spirit removed from the earth?[10]

This author feels that he has dealt a death blow to dispensationalism in the very asking of such a question, for, to him, there could be no salvation apart from the presence and ministry of the church. He goes on to say:

---

[9] Walvoord, *op. cit.*, p. 230.
[10] Oswald T. Allis, *Prophecy and the Church*, p. 12.

> . . . the most serious objection to the claim of Dispensationalists, that the declaration that "the kingdom of heaven is at hand" meant that it could be set up "at any moment," was the fact that this involved the ignoring of the definite teaching of Jesus that the "Christ must suffer and enter into his glory." *It made the Cross unnecessary* by implying that the glorious kingdom of Messiah could be set up immediately. *It left no room for the Cross* since Messiah's kingdom was to be without end. It led to the conclusion that had Israel accepted Jesus as Messiah, the Old Testament ritual of sacrifice would have sufficed for sin. . . . *The only conclusion which can be drawn from such a statement is this, that the Church required the Cross while the kingdom did not,* that the gospel of the kingdom did not include the Cross, while the gospel of the grace of God did include it [italics mine].
>
> . . . it is the question . . . whether the "godly" Jewish remnant of the end-time will accept the Cross and preach the Cross or not.
>
> . . . .
>
> The "gospel of the kingdom" was preached before the Cross, before the Church age during which the gospel of the Cross is to be preached; and its preaching is to be resumed, apparently without change or addition, after the Church age. *The natural inference is that, if it did not involve the Cross when it was preached at the first advent, it will not include it when it is preached after the rapture.* Such a conclusion is all the more necessary, if it is to be preached by a Jewish remnant. . . . [italics mine].[11]

With this position the posttribulation rapturist is in full agreement.[12] It is necessary, in view of such accusations, to set forth the teaching of Scripture on the question of salvation in the tribulation.

A. *The nature of salvation in the Old Testament.* There are two separate and distinct aspects of salvation as that doctrine is presented in the Old Testament: individual and national.

1. The first aspect of salvation offered in the Old Testament was *individual* salvation. Concerning this aspect of salvation as offered in the Old Testament, Chafer writes:

> The Old Testament saints were in right and acceptable relation to God. . . . As for the estate of the Jew in the old dispensation it may be observed: (a) They were born into covenant relations

---

11 *Ibid.*, pp. 230-33.
12 Cf. Reese, *op. cit.*, pp. 112-14.

with God wherein there were no limitations imposed upon their faith in Him or upon their fellowship with Him. . . . (b) In case of failure to meet the moral and spiritual obligations resting upon them because of their covenant position, the sacrifices were provided as a righteous basis of restoration to their covenant privileges . . . (c) The individual Jew might so fail in his conduct and so neglect the sacrifices as, in the end, to be disowned of God and cast out . . . (d) The national salvation and forgiveness of Israel is yet a future expectation and is promised to occur when the Deliverer comes out of Sion (Rom. 11:26-27). . . . A very clear and comprehensive body of Scripture bears on eternal life as related to Judaism. However, it is there contemplated as an *inheritance.* (a) Isaiah 55:3 . . . (b) Daniel 12:2 . . . (c) Matthew 7:13-14 . . . (d) Luke 10:25-29 . . . (e) Luke 18:18-27 . . . (f) Matthew 18:8-9 . . . The receiving of eternal life will be for Israelites, as it is in the case of the Christian, a feature of salvation itself; and salvation for Israel is, in Romans 11:26-32, declared to be after the present age-purpose of the fulness of the Gentiles which is not accompanied by Israel's blindness (verse 25), and at the time when "there shall come out of Sion the Deliverer," who shall "turn away ungodliness from Jacob."[13]

It is thus evident that the salvation offered in the Old Testament was an individual salvation, accepted by faith, based on blood sacrifice, which sacrifices were the foreshadows of the true sacrifice to come. This salvation was presented as an inheritance, to be received at a future time, rather than as a present possession. The individual Israelite who believed God was truly saved, but awaited a future experience of the fulness of that salvation. Chafer says:

By the presentation of a sacrifice and by the placing of the hand upon the head of the victim, the offender acknowledged his sin before God and entered intelligently into an arrangement in which a substitute died in the sinner's place. Though, as stated in Hebrews 10:4—"it is not possible that the blood of bulls and goats should take away sins"—God did, nevertheless, provide a release for the offender, but with the expectation on His own part that a righteous ground for such release would eventually be secured by the one sacrificial death of His Son, which death the animal-slaying typified. . . . In Romans 3:25 the divine objective in the death of Christ is declared to be, "for the remission of sins that are past, through the forbearance of God."[14]

---

[13] Chafer, *op. cit.*, IV, 24-26.
[14] *Ibid.*, III, 103-4.

Thus was the individual offered salvation.

2. A second aspect of the salvation offered in the Old Testament was the *national* aspect. Of this Chafer writes:

> The Scriptures bear testimony to the fact that Israel as a nation is to be saved from her sin and delivered from her enemies by the Messiah when He shall return to the earth. . . . It is obvious that Israel as a nation is not now saved, nor are any of the features of Jehovah's eternal covenants with that people now in evidence. . . . The nation, but for certain rebels who are to be "purged out" (Ezek. 20:37-38), will be saved, and that by their own Messiah when He comes out of Zion (cf. Isa. 59:20-21; Matt. 23:37-39; Acts 15:16). "All Israel" of Romans 11:26 is evidently that separated and accepted Israel that will have stood the divine judgments which are yet to fall upon that nation (cf. Matt. 24:37-25:13). The Apostle distinguishes clearly between Israel the nation and a spiritual Israel (cf. Rom. 9:6; 11:1-36).
>
> . . . Jehovah will, in connection with the second advent of Christ and as a part of Israel's salvation, "take away their sins." This, Jehovah declares, is His covenant with them (Rom. 11:27). It has been observed that, in the age that is past, Jehovah's dealing with Israel's sins . . . was only a temporary covering of those sins, and that Christ in His death bore the judgment of those sins which Jehovah had before passed over; but the final application of the value of Christ's death in behalf of Israel awaits the moment of her national conversion. . . . It is then that, according to His covenant, Jehovah will "take away" their sins. In Hebrews 10:4 it is stated that it is impossible that the blood of bulls and goats should "take away" sin, and in Romans 11:27 it is promised that Israel's sins will yet be taken away. . . . The induction to be drawn from these and other portions of Scripture is that Jehovah will yet in the future, in the briefest portion of time, and as a part of Israel's salvation, take away their sins. . . . We conclude, therefore, that the nation Israel will yet be saved and her sins removed forever through the blood of Christ.[15]

It is thus to be observed that, while the individual Israelite who believed God was himself saved, that salvation was assured to him on the basis of a future work which God was going to do for the entire nation at the second advent, at which time the Messiah would make a final dealing with the sins of the people. A saved individual in Israel might rejoice in his own

---

[15] *Ibid.*, III, 105-7.

salvation and at the same time await the national salvation. To confess that his nation had not yet been saved was not to deny his own salvation as an individual.

It is at this very point that the criticisms aimed at our position, as previously cited, are unfounded. The individuals who will be saved in the tribulation will know the experience of salvation, but will yet look forward in anticipation of the completion of the national salvation at the appearance of the Deliverer. Having experienced the blessing of individual salvation, with new joy they will anticipate the coming Deliverer and His deliverance to complete that which was begun in their experience.

B. *Specific Old Testament promises of salvation.* There are numerous Old Testament passages which promise salvation to Israel. It should be borne in mind that, while the emphasis is placed on the national salvation, that national salvation must be preceded by individual salvation. Paul himself (Rom. 9:6) restricts the "all Israel" of Romans 11:26 to the saved individuals. Thus, in the Old Testament any promise of salvation must include both aspects.

> Alas! for that day is great, so that none is like it: it is even the time of Jacob's trouble, but he shall be saved out of it [Jer. 30:7].
>
> And I will cause you to pass under the rod, and I will bring you into the bond of the covenant:
>
> And I will purge from among you the rebels, and them that transgress against me . . . [Ezek. 20:37-38].
>
> . . . and at that time thy people shall be delivered, every one that shall be found written in the book [Dan. 12:1].
>
> The sun shall be turned into darkness, and the moon into blood, before the great and the terrible day of the Lord come.
>
> And it shall come to pass, that whosoever shall call on the name of the Lord shall be delivered: for in mount Zion and in Jerusalem shall be deliverance, as the Lord hath said, and in the remnant whom the Lord shall call [Joel 2:31-32].
>
> In that day there shall be a fountain opened to the house of David and to the inhabitants of Jerusalem for sin and for uncleanness.

> And it shall come to pass, that in all the land, saith the Lord, two parts therein shall be cut off and die; but the third shall be left therein.
>
> And I will bring the third part through the fire, and will refine them as silver is refined, and will try them as gold is tried: they shall call on my name, and I will hear them: I will say, It is my people: and they shall say, The Lord is my God [Zech. 13:1, 8-9].

The Old Testament specifically promises a salvation for Israel, which is associated with "that day," or the Day of the Lord. Since this salvation has not been experienced by Israel, it must be experienced by that nation during the time when God is dealing with them as a nation again in the tribulation period. Thus the unfulfilled Old Testament promises lead us to expect salvation to be experienced during the tribulation.

Not only does the Old Testament predict the salvation of Israelites before the coming of the Lord, but a host of Gentiles as well.

> And it shall come to pass in the last days, that the mountain of the Lord's house shall be established in the top of the mountains, and shall be exalted above the hills; and all nations shall flow unto it.
>
> And he shall judge among the nations, and shall rebuke many people . . . [Isa. 2:2, 4].
>
> And the Gentiles shall come to thy light, and kings to the brightness of thy rising.
>
> Then thou shalt see, and flow together, and thine heart shall fear, and be enlarged; because the abundance of the sea shall be converted unto thee, the forces of the Gentiles shall come unto thee [Isa. 60:3, 5].
>
> And the Gentiles shall see thy righteousness, and all kings thy glory . . . [Isa. 62:2].

The Lord, during His earthly ministry, reiterated the same promises in such passages as Matthew 13:47-50; Matthew 24:13; and John 3:1-21. The promises were not nullified.

C. *The fulfillment of the promised salvation.* The seventh chapter of Revelation gives to us a remarkable record of the fulfillment of the line of promise concerning individual salvation as promised in the Old Testament.

1. The promise concerning *individual Israelites* is fulfilled.

The first eight verses of the chapter are devoted to a description of the 144,000 sealed servants of God. In this passage the circumstances of their salvation are only implied. The fact that they are said to "have the seal of the living God" implies their salvation, for the seal is the designation of ownership. Again, their salvation is implied in that they are called "the servants of our God." Such a designation could only be ascribed to saved individuals. In chapter fourteen these 144,000 are specifically said to be "redeemed from among men" (v. 4), and are "the firstfruits unto God." The fact that they are associated with the four living creatures and the twenty-four elders in the worship of God assures us of their salvation. Thus the promise concerning individual salvation is seen to be fulfilled in the 144,000, even though these are only a portion of Israelites saved during that period.

2. The promise concerning *Gentiles* is fulfilled. Verses nine through seventeen give us the fulfillment of the promises of the Old Testament concerning the salvation of Gentiles, for here we have described a multitude that defies enumeration who experience salvation. The fact that they "have washed their robes and made them white in the blood of the Lamb" certifies their salvation.

3. The promise of *national salvation* is fulfilled. Revelation 19:11—20:6 gives the picture of the fulfillment of the second aspect of the promised Old Testament salvation. In this portion the Lord is seen to return as "KING OF KINGS, AND LORD OF LORDS." All hostile Gentile powers are destroyed and their leaders cast in the lake of fire. Satan is bound. The promised kingdom, in which all the promises and covenants are fulfilled, is inaugurated by the personal presence and reign of the King. Thus John depicts the fulfillment of the national salvation.

D. *The basis of salvation in the tribulation.* In considering the important question of the basis or method of salvation during the tribulation period, certain affirmations may be made.

1. Salvation in the tribulation will certainly be on *the faith principle.* Hebrews 11:1-40 makes it clear that the only individual who was ever accepted by God was the individual who believed God. The principle of verse six, "without faith it is

impossible to please him," is not a principle limited to this age, but is true in every age. The faith of Abraham is made the example of the method of approach to God (Rom. 4:2) and it will be the method of approach in the tribulation.

2. The descriptions of the saved of the tribulation make it very plain that they were saved *by the blood* of the Lamb. Of the saved Jews it was said that "These were redeemed from among men" (Rev. 14:4) and Israel never knew of a redemption apart from blood. Of the saved Gentiles it is said that they have "washed their robes, and made them white in the blood of the Lamb" (Rev. 7:14). Concerning the phrase "in the blood" Bullinger, a careful Greek student, says:

> Not "in the blood"; nothing under the Law was ever washed "in blood," nothing can be made white "washed in" blood. It is through a forced literal meaning of the proposition... (*en*) which has led to this false notion. This proposition constantly means *by*, or *through*: and is translated "by" 142 times and "through" 37 times. (See Matt. ix. 34; v. 34, 35; Gal. iii. 11; 2 Tim. ii. 10). In this very book (v. 9) it is rendered "by." So here and in 1. 5 this must be the meaning.[16]

In Revelation 12 we find Satan attacking the remnant of Israel, for such is the meaning of "the woman" in this chapter. This believing remnant is referred to in verse ten as "our brethren." The means of victory of the "brethren" is given to us in verse eleven, "they overcame him by the blood of the Lamb." So once again the believers are saved and delivered by "the blood of the Lamb."

Revelation 12:17 gives the reason for the special animosity of Satan: they "have the testimony of Jesus Christ." It is because of the message that this believing remnant proclaims that Satan is said to be "wroth." This is just one more indication of the message proclaimed in the tribulation period.

3. Salvation will be *by the work of the Holy Spirit.* With the identification of the Holy Spirit as the restrainer of 2 Thessalonians 2:7 comes the persistent allegation by the opponents of this view that says the Holy Spirit must cease to operate in the world in the tribulation because He is no longer indwelling

[16] E. W. Bullinger, *The Apocalypse*, pp. 290-1.

the body of Christ as His temple. Nothing could be further from the truth. It must be noted that the Holy Spirit did not undertake an indwelling ministry to every believer in the Old Testament, yet the Lord, addressing one under that economy indicates clearly that salvation was by the operation of the Holy Spirit (John 3:5-6). Apart from this indwelling ministry Old Testament saints were said to be saved by the Holy Spirit, even though He did not indwell that believer as a temple. So, in the tribulation period, the Holy Spirit, who is omnipresent, will do the work of regeneration as he did when God was previously dealing with Israel, but without an indwelling ministry. The present-day indwelling is related to empowerment, to union of believer with believer because of their relation to the Temple of God, but the indwelling is entirely distinct and separate from the work of the Spirit in regeneration. Thus, it should be clearly seen that even though the Spirit is not indwelling in the tribulation, He may still be operative in regeneration. Joel 2:28-32 relates the salvation of Israel to the ministry of the Holy Spirit before the second advent. Commenting on John 3, Walvoord says: "The discourse of Christ with Nicodemus (John 3:1-21) may be understood to confirm that there will be salvation during the tribulation, and that it will be a work of the Holy Spirit."[17] Kelly adds: "I wish, therefore, explicitly to state my own conviction . . . that the salvation of all the saved at all times depends on the work of Christ, and that the Spirit is the only efficacious applier of it to any soul."[18] It may be asserted with confidence, then, that the salvation offered through the blood of the Lamb, to be received by faith, will be made effectual through the working of the Holy Spirit.

E. *The relation of this gospel to the gospel of the kingdom.* The critics of this position have charged that since the gospel of the kingdom is being preached during the tribulation there can be no preaching of the cross. The tribulation will witness the preaching of the gospel of the kingdom. Matthew 24:14 makes this very clear. However, the preaching of the cross and the preaching of the gospel of the kingdom are not mutually exclusive.

---

[17] Walvoord, *op. cit.*, p. 229.

[18] William Kelly, *Lectures on the Revelation*, p. 164, footnote.

It must be recognized that the term *gospel* in its literal usage means simply "good news." The gospel of the kingdom was the good news that the promised King was soon to appear on the scene to offer the promised kingdom. In such usage the gospel of the kingdom was not primarily soteriological but eschatological in concept. The gospel of the kingdom did not offer a way of salvation, but rather offered the hope of the fulfillment of Israel's eschatological promises, which contained within them the fulfillment of the soteriological hopes, as has previously been seen in contemplating the two aspects of Old Testament salvation.

There were two phases to John's preaching of the gospel of the kingdom: "Repent ye, for the kingdom of heaven is at hand" (Matt. 3:2) and "Behold the Lamb of God that taketh away the sin of the world" (John 1:29). The one was just as much a part of John's message as the other. In these two declarations it may be stated that John proclaimed a cross as well as a kingdom. So it will be in the tribulation period.

The soteriological aspect of John's message is not in the words "the kingdom of heaven is at hand" but rather in the words "Repent ye." God, in dealing with a covenant people who had been brought into that relation by God Himself, required the erring one to offer a sacrifice and to receive cleansing, which would reinstate him in the blessing of the covenant. Such offerings and subsequent cleansing were inextricably tied in with repentance in the Old Testament sense of the word. John, as one in the Levitical line, could minister such sacrifices and administer such cleansing by water as the gospels record. We must then conclude that when John preached there were these two parts of his message. The promise of the king brought conviction of personal unworthiness, which brought the individual to seek cleansing. So it will be in the tribulation period. The announcement of the good news that the King is coming will bring about conviction of unworthiness. Such conviction will bring with it the good news of cleansing; not through the sacrifices and ceremonial applications of water, which typified the coming Lamb of God, but through the method of cleansing, "once and for all offered," the blood of the Lamb. As John announced the King and offered the cleansing in type, so the believing remnant will announce the King and offer cleansing, complete and final, through Him of whom John spake. The fact of the good news of the kingdom does not eliminate the good news of salvation from its message.

F. *The results of salvation.* The passages dealing with salvation in the tribulation indicate that there are several results to be anticipated.

1. There will be personal cleansing. Such passages as Revelation 7:9, 14; 14:4 indicate clearly that the individual who is saved is made acceptable to God. On no other basis could the individual be "before the throne of God." This must be seen to be the result of the fulfillment of the individual offers of salvation in the Old Testament.

2. There will be national salvation. The preparation of such a nation (Ezek. 20:37-38; Zech. 13:1, 8-9) will result in the salvation of the nation as promised in Romans 11:27 at the second advent. The national promises can be fulfilled because God, by the Holy Spirit, has redeemed a remnant in Israel to whom and through whom the covenants may be fulfilled.

3. There will be millennial blessings. Revelation 7:15-17; 20:1-6 make it plain that the salvation offered during this period will find its fulfillment in the millennial earth. All the blessings and privileges of service, position, and access to God are seen to be millennial in scope. It is thus that the national promises are realized through individual salvation during the tribulation to be enjoyed in the millennial earth.

The Old Testament promises have offered a salvation to the individual Israelite, to be received as an inheritance, and to be realized at the time of the national salvation at the second advent of the Messiah. Since these promises of individual and national salvation have not yet been fully accomplished they will be at a future time. When God again deals with the nation Israel, salvation will be offered on the basis of the blood of Christ, to be received by faith, and applied by the Holy Spirit. This is in perfect keeping with the preaching of the gospel of the kingdom, which was both soteriological and eschatological. This salvation offered in the tribulation will be received by multitudes of Jews and Gentiles who will receive individual salvation, to culminate in national salvation for Israel, and the full millennial blessing for all saved. The interpretation suggested would give a centrality to the cross, the death of Christ, the eternal purpose of redemption, which would render our position impervious to the attacks of our adversaries who charge, as does Allis:

> It cannot be too strongly emphasized that if the dispensational doctrine regarding the *nature* of the promised kingdom and the *meaning* of the words "at hand" is accepted, it leads logically to the view that the Cross, as an atoning sacrifice for sin, concerns the Church age and the Church saints only. As preached at the first advent it did not include or involve the Cross; as preached at the second advent it will not include or presuppose the Cross.[19]

Such charges are found to be unwarranted and untrue.

[19] Allis, *op. cit.*, p. 234.

Chapter XVIII

ISRAEL IN THE TRIBULATION

One of the Divine purposes to be accomplished in the tribulation is the preparation of the nation Israel for the kingdom to be instituted at the return of the Messiah in fulfillment of Israel's covenants.

I. The Olivet Discourse

A detailed chronology of predicted events in relation to the nation Israel is given to us in the important prophecy of the Lord in Matthew 24:1—25:46.

A. *The setting of the discourse.* This discourse, spoken two days before the Lord's death (Matt. 26:1-2), follows the announcement of woes upon the Pharisees (Matt. 23:13-36) and the announcement of judicial blindness upon the nation Israel (Matt. 23:37-39). On Matthew 23:37-39 Chafer writes:

> The address is to Jerusalem's children, which, in this instance is a representation of the nation Israel. . . . the entire discourse from Matthew 24:4 on, . . . immediately spoken to His disciples who are still classed as Jews and represented a people who will pass through the experiences described in this address, is directed toward the entire nation and especially to those who will endure the trials depicted therein. The phrase, "I would have gathered thy children together," not only discloses that He speaks to Israel, but refers to the fulfillment of much prophecy respecting the final regathering of Israel into their own land. . . . "Your house" is a reference to the house of Israel which became centered in the kingly line of David. . . . The term "desolate" is one of several words used to describe Israel's situation in the world throughout this age. . . . "Ye shall not see me" is an assertion which anticipates His total absence, respecting His peculiar relation to Israel "till" He returns, at which time "every eye shall see him" (Rev. 1:7), "and they shall see the Son

> of man coming in the clouds of heaven with power and great glory" (Matt. 24:30).[1]

Thus the discourse is set against the background of the rejection of the Messiah and the imposition of judicial blindness upon that nation.

B. *The questions of the disciples.* In Matthew 23 the Lord has announced judgment on the Pharisees and blindness on the nation. Now in chapter 24 He announces the overthrow of Jerusalem (Matt. 24:1-2). In the minds of the disciples they had eschatological significance, for their fulfillment was associated with Messiah's coming and the terminus of the age. They asked: "When shall these things be? and what shall be the sign of thy coming, and of the end of the world [age]?" (Matt. 24:3). Probably the promise of His return (Matt. 23:39) had given the disciples this eschatological association.

The answer to the first question is not recorded by Matthew, but is given in Luke 21:20-24. This portion of the discourse had to do with the destruction of Jerusalem under Titus in 70 A.D.[2]

Concerning the next two questions Gaebelein writes:

> Turning to the next two questions, "What is the sign of Thy coming and the completion of the age?" it is to be said that undoubtedly in the minds of the disciples this question was one, He had repeatedly spoken about His return. As true Jews they expected, and that with perfect right, the establishment of the messianic kingdom by the Messiah. They had seen how He . . . had been rejected. . . . they take heart and ask Him about the sign of His coming, the coming He had mentioned before. . . . This coming is His visible and glorious return to the earth. . . . Then they asked about the completion or consummation of the age . . . it is the ending of the Jewish age, which is still future.[3]

The entire passage in Matthew 24 and 25 was written to answer this question concerning the signs of Messiah's coming, which would terminate the age. The Lord is giving the course of the end of the age prior to the establishment of the Kingdom as it relates to Israel and Israel's program. This program is develop-

---

[1] Lewis Sperry Chafer, *Systematic Theology,* V, 116-17.
[2] Cf. *ibid.*, V, 118-19.
[3] Arno C. Gaebelein, *The Gospel According to Matthew,* II, 175-76.

ed in strict chronological order. Chafer observes, "Few portions of the New Testament place recorded events in a more complete chronological order than this address."[4]

C. *The interpretation of the discourse.* No question is of greater importance in the understanding of this passage than the method of interpretation. Gaebelein outlines three major methods of interpretation.

> The most widespread interpretation of this part of the discourse is that it all was fulfilled in the past. The great tribulation is a thing of the past and the Lord Jesus Christ came again in the destruction of Jerusalem. This is the foolish, spiritualizing method, which does such violence to the Word of God. . . .
>
> Another mode of explaining these first predictions of the Olivet discourse is to apply them to this Christian age in which we live. . . . They tell us that the Lord describes this entire Christian age and especially the closing of it, the end. Then they maintain that the church is to remain on the earth in this end of the age and to pass through the great tribulation, and therefore the exhortations contained in this chapter are meant for Christian believers living in the end of the age. . . .
>
> There remains the third way of interpreting these words of our Lord: it is to look upon these predictions about the end of the Jewish age as being still future. This is the right and only key to understand these verses. . . . the Olivet discourse of our Lord is a prediction of how the Jewish age will end.[5]

The first would be the view of the amillennialist, the second that of the posttribulation raputrist, and the third that of the pretribulation rapturist.

D. *The tribulation period.* The first event in Israel's program for the end of the age is the tribulation period, described in Matthew 24:4-26. There is a divergence of opinion among pretribulation rapturists as to the chronology of this section.

1. The first view is that of Chafer[6] who holds that Matthew 24:4-8 describes events of the present church age, which take place prior to the beginning of the seventieth week and are

[4] Chafer, *op. cit.*, V, 114.
[5] Gaebelein, op. cit., II. 167-70.
[6] Chafer, *op. cit.*, V, 120-25.

called "the beginning of sorrows," and verses 9-26 describe the tribulation period. He says of verses 4-8:

> These events . . . do not constitute a sign of the end of the Jewish age . . . though they are the characteristics of the unforeseen intervening or intercalary age. . . .
>
> This extended Scripture [Matthew 24:9-26] presents Christ's own message to Israel regarding the great tribulation.[7]

2. A second view is that of Scofield who holds that the passage has a double interpretation, partly applicable to the church age and partly to the tribulation. He says:

> Verses 4 to 14 have a double interpretation: They give (1) the character of the age—wars, international conflicts, famines, pestilences, persecutions, and false Christs (cf. Dan. 9:26). . . . (2) But the same answer (vs. 4-14) applies in a specific way to the *end* of the age, viz. Daniel's seventieth week. . . . All that has characterized the *age* gathers into awful intensity at the *end.*[8]

3. A third view is that of English, who says:

> In Matthew 24, verses four to fourteen refer to the first half of that week, the beginning of the end; and verses fifteen to twenty-six relate to the latter half, the Great Tribulation, and then shall the end come.[9]

4. A fourth view suggests that verses 4-8 outline the first half of the tribulation and verses 9-26 describe the second half of the week.

Consistency of interpretation would seem to eliminate any application of this portion of Scripture to the church or the church age, inasmuch as the Lord is dealing with the prophetic program for Israel. Further, the difference between interpretation and application would seem to eliminate the view that sees a double application of the passage. There seems to be evidence to support the view that the first half of the week is described in verses 4-8. The parallelism between verses 4-8 and Revelation 6 seems to indicate that the first half of the tribulation is here described. Gaebelein observes:

---

[7] *Ibid.*, V, 120-21.
[8] C. I. Scofield, *Reference Bible*, p. 1033.
[9] Schuyler English, *Studies in the Gospel According to Matthew*, p. 173.

> If this is the correct interpretation . . . then there must be a perfect harmony between that part of the Olivet discourse contained in Matthew xxiv and the part of Revelation beginning with the sixth chapter. *And such is indeed the case.*[10]

This parallelism is observed by English, who writes:

> The *first* seal was opened revealing a man on a white horse, who had a bow, who went forth to conquer. The Lord Jesus shall come on a white horse, but this is not He, but a false Christ, who establishes a temporary peace. What is the *first* prediction of Matthew twenty-four. "Many shall come in My name, saying, I am Christ" (vs. 5). The *second* seal was opened revealing a man on a red horse, who should take peace from the earth. The *second* prediction of Matthew twenty-four is found in verses six and seven: "Wars and rumours of wars . . . nation shall rise against nation." The *third* seal was opened revealing a man on a black horse, who had balances in his hand; and "a voice in the midst of the four beasts" indicated famine. The *third* prediction of Matthew twenty-four is: "There shall be famines" (vs. 7). The *fourth* seal was opened revealing one on a pale horse, whose name was Death, and the *fourth* prophecy of Matthew twenty-four tells of pestilences and earthquakes. The *fifth* seal has to do with those who were slain for the Word of God, who, under the altar, cry, "How long, O Lord, holy and true, dost Thou not judge and avenge our blood on them that dwell on the earth?" What is the fifth prophecy of Matthew twenty-four? "Then shall they deliver you up to be afflicted, and shall kill you" (vs. 9).[11]

There are indications that verses 9-26 describe the events of the last half of the week. The abomination of desolation (24:15) is clearly stated by Daniel (9:27) to appear in the middle of the week and continue to the end of the period. The word "then" in verse 9 seems to introduce the great persecutions against Israel that were promised them and were described in Revelation 12:12-17, where John reveals that this persecution will last for the last half of the tribulation period (Rev. 12:14).

The Lord's outline of the events of the tribulation period can thus be determined. In the first half of the week Israel will experience the chastisements of the events of verses 4-8 (the seals of Rev. 6), although they will dwell in relative safety under the false covenant (Dan. 9:27). In the middle of the week great

---

[10] Gaebelein, *op. cit.*, II, 182.
[11] English, *op. cit.*, pp. 173-74.

persecution will break out (v. 9; Rev. 12:12-17) because of the Desolator (v. 15; 2 Thess. 2; Rev. 13:1-10), who will cause Israel to flee from the land (vs. 16-20). Unbelieving Israel will be deceived by the false prophet (v. 11; Rev. 13:11-18) and go into apostasy (v. 12; 2 Thess. 2:11). Believing Israel will be a witnessing people, carrying the good news that these events herald the approach of the Messiah (v. 14). This period will be terminated by the second advent of the Messiah (v. 27). Such seems to be the Lord's summary of the chronology of the tribulation period.

E. *The second advent of the Messiah.* Following the description of the tribulation period the Lord carries the chronology of events a step further by describing the second advent (Matt. 24:30-37). Concerning this coming several things are mentioned. (1) It will take place "immediately after the tribulation of those days" (v. 29). The events of the tribulation age continue until the second advent of Messiah, whose coming terminates it. (2) It will be preceded by signs (v. 30). What these signs are is not revealed. Many signs have preceded this one, as described in verses 4-26, but this is a unique sign which will herald Messiah's advent. (3) This coming will be sudden (v. 27), and (4) it will be evident (v. 30), at which time His power and glory will be manifested throughout the earth.

F. *The regathering of Israel.* Verse 31 suggests that the event to follow the second advent will be the regathering of Israel. They had been scattered because of the anger of Satan (Rev. 12:12) and the desolation of the Beast (Matt. 24:15), but, according to promise, they will be regathered to the land (Deut. 30:3-4; Ezek. 20:37-38; 37:1-14). This regathering is through special angelic ministries. The "elect" of verse 31 must have reference to the saints of that program with which God is then dealing, that is, Israel (Dan. 7:18, 22, 27).

G. *The illustrative parables.* The chronology of the events of the end of the age is briefly interrupted in order to give practical exhortation to those who will be witnessing these events. These instructions are contained in verses 32-51. The parable of the fig tree (vs. 32-36) is spoken to show the certainty of the coming. Chafer writes:

> It is doubtless true that the fig tree represents in other Scriptures the nation Israel (cf. Matt. 21:18-20), but there is no occasion for this meaning to be sought in the present use of that symbol. When the things of which Christ had just spoken, including even the beginnings of travail, begin to come to pass, it may be accepted as certain that He is nigh, even at the doors.[12]

The fulfillment of the signs that were given in the preceding verses would herald the coming of Messiah as certainly as the new shoots on the fig tree heralded the approach of summer.

There has been a difference of opinion over the interpretation of "generation" in Matthew 24:34. Some have held that it applied to the present generation to which Christ spoke, so all this prophecy would have been fulfilled with the destruction of Jerusalem in 70 A.D. Others hold that the word has reference to the future, so that Christ is saying that those who witness the signs stated earlier in the chapter will see the coming of the Son of man within that generation. It hardly seems necessary to state this fact, inasmuch as it was known that only seven years would intervene between the beginning of this period and the coming of the Messiah, or three and a half years from the appearance of the Desolator to Messiah's advent. However, such may be the interpretation. Still others hold that the word generation is to be taken in its basic usage of "race, kindred, family, stock, breed,"[13] so that the Lord is here promising that the nation Israel shall be preserved until the consummation of her program at the second advent in spite of the work of the Desolator to destroy her. This seems to be the best explanation.

The parable showing the certainty of His coming is followed by exhortations to watchfulness because of the uncertainty of the time (vs. 36-51). The reference to the days of Noe (vs. 37-39) does not emphasize the licentiousness of the people of Noah's day, but rather the unpreparedness for the event that brought judgment. The unexpectedness of the Lord's coming is emphasized in the reference to the two who were in the field and the two at the mill (vs. 40-41), as well as in the illustration from the faithful and faithless servants (vs. 45-50). In each

---

12 Chafer, *op. cit.*, V, 127.
13 Scofield, *op. cit.*, p. 1034.

of the three illustrations that show the unexpectedness of the event the individuals concerned were occupied with the usual round of life without any thought of Messiah's return. The lesson to be drawn is in the words "watch" (v. 42), "be ye also ready" (v. 44) and "in such an hour as ye think not the Son of man cometh" (v. 44, also 50).

H. *The judgment on Israel.* The chronology of prophesied events is resumed after the illustrative instructions by the word "then" of Matthew 25:1. In the parable of the ten virgins the Lord is indicating that, following the regathering of Israel (Matt. 24:31), the next event will be the judging of living Israel on the earth to determine who will go into the kingdom. This has been anticipated in Matthew 24:28, where unbelieving Israel is likened unto a lifeless corpse which is consigned to the vultures, a picture of judgment.

1. There are two main views as to the identity of the virgins in this parable among men of our general viewpoint. The first is the view that the Lord has been dealing exclusively with Israel in Matthew 24:4-44, but that from 24:45—25:46 He is dealing with this present age and its conclusion so that the church is in view here. Gaebelein, who holds this view, says:

> The Lord still speaks to His disciples, but let us understand now while they are viewed in the first part as Jewish disciples and typical of the remnant of Israel in the end of the Jewish age, here the Lord looks upon them as soon to be in connection with something new, that is, Christianity.[14]

And further:

> . . . these parables have nothing more to do with the Jewish age and the remnant of His earthly people, which stands out so prominently in the first part of this discourse.[15]

This view is based on the fact that oil, which the wise virgins possessed, represents the Holy Spirit, who would have been taken away before the tribulation period. Further, it is based on the observation that the Jewish believers of the tribulation

---

[14] Gaebelein, *op. cit.*, II, 220.
[15] *Ibid.*, II, 225.

would not be slumbering because the signs would indicate the nearness of the Messiah's return.[16]

There seem to be several reasons for rejecting the view that the virgins represent the church during this present age. (1) The time indicated by the word "then" (Matt. 25:1) would not be a reference to the church age, but would continue the chronology of Israel's events as the Lord continues to reply to the original question which chronology was interrupted by the "now" in 24:32. (2) Since the Lord is returning to the earth to the marriage feast as a Bridegroom, He must be accompanied by the bride. Therefore those waiting on the earth could not be the bride. (3) Although oil is a type of the Holy Spirit, it is not used so exclusively in the church age. Since there will be a relation of the Holy Spirit to the saints of the tribulation, especially to those who are witnesses for Him, the reference to the Holy Spirit would be proper. (4) In the parable not only the wise but the unwise, who were appointed unto wrath, went to meet the Bridegroom. This could not picture the rapture, for no unsaved go out to meet Him at that time. (5) The term "weeping and gnashing of teeth" (Matt. 25:30) is used in every other occurrence in the gospels in reference to Israel (Matt. 8:12; 13:42, 50; 22:13; Luke 13:28) and it would seem to refer also to Israel here. (6) In Revelation 19:7-16 the wedding supper follows the wedding itself. Luke 12:35-36 seems to suggest that while the marriage is in heaven the marriage feast is on earth. This parable then would describe the coming of the Bridegroom and the bride to the earth for the marriage feast to which the five wise virgins will be admitted and the foolish excluded. 2. The second view sees the virgins as representing the nation Israel. It would seem best to conclude with English:

> The ten virgins represent the remnant of Israel after the church has been taken. The five wise virgins are the believing remnant, the foolish virgins the unbelieving, who only profess to be looking for Messiah's coming in power.[17]

The major consideration in this parable seems to be in verse 10: "they that were ready went in with him to the

[16] Cf. English, *op. cit.*, p. 183.
[17] *Ibid.*, p. 185.

marriage [feast]." Thus the Lord is teaching that following the second advent and the regathering of Israel there will be a judgment on the earth for living Israel to determine who will go into the kingdom, called in the parable "the marriage feast," and who will be excluded from it. Those with light will be admitted and those without it are excluded. Those with life are received and those without life are rejected.

The parable of the talents further illustrates this same truth that Israel will be judged at the second advent to determine who will go into the millennium and who will be excluded. English says:

> When the Lord Jesus comes again in power, He will reckon with the remnant of Israel (Ezek. 20) to determine who shall receive the Kingdom blessing. The "enter thou into the joy of thy Lord" is the entrance into the land for the Kingdom blessing (Ezek. 20:40-42), while the fate of the unprofitable servant who was cast into outer darkness is the "they shall not enter into the land of Israel" of Ezekiel 20:37, 38.[18]

I. *The judgment on the Gentile nations.* The chronology of events dealing with the course of the end of the age closes with a description of the judgment of God that will fall on all Israel's enemies subsequent to the second advent. This judgment will be examined in detail later. For the present consideration it is sufficient to observe that this judgment is a judgment to determine who among the Gentile peoples will be permitted to "inherit the kingdom prepared for you from the foundation of the world" (Matt. 25:34). It is to be observed that this is a judgment on the living individual Gentiles after the second advent and has no relationship to the judgment on the *dead* who are raised to appear at the great white throne (Rev. 20:11-15). This judgment has been preceded by a time in which the gospel of the kingdom has been preached by the 144,000 and the believing remnant. This judgment determines the response of the individual to this preaching. Concerning this judgment of the Gentiles, Kelly writes:

> . . . here [the judgment] is a simple and sole issue, which applies only to that living generation of all nations: how did

---

[18] *Ibid.*, pp. 187-88.

> you treat the King's messengers when they preached this gospel of the kingdom before the end came? The end was now evidently come. The test was an open undeniable fact; but it proved whether they had, or had not, faith in the coming King. Those who honoured the heralds of the kingdom showed their faith by their works; and so did those who despised them manifest their unbelief. The test was not only just but gracious, and "the King" pronounced accordingly.[19]

Thus, in this Olivet discourse, the Lord has given a chronology of the events of the seventieth week. His chronology is an accurate guide in interpreting the sequence of events of that period.

II. The Identity of the "Woman" in Revelation 12

One point of prophetic revelation that it is essential to clarify in dealing with Israel in the tribulation is the identity of the "woman" in Revelation 12. The major emphasis in Revelation 11:19—20:15 is the attack of Satan against the people with whom God is dealing at that time. This attack comes in chapter thirteen through the beasts, who offer a false Messiah and a false fulfillment of the Abrahamic covenant. It comes in chapters seventeen and eighteen through an apostate religious system, which falsely claims to be the Kingdom of God. It comes in chapter nineteen through the alliance of nations which is formed against this people and their King, which the Lord destroys at His coming. Since the major movement in this portion of Revelation is against the one called in chapter twelve *the woman*, it is important to identify this individual who occupies so important a place in the book.

Revelation 12 centers around three personages. It will help us in the identification of the woman to identify the other two. Fortunately their identification is made easy by the context itself.

A. *A great red dragon.* Verse nine makes the identification of this individual certain. It is none other than Satan. Chapter 20, verse 2, confirms this identification. Satan is clearly revealed as the author and instigator of the attacks against the people of God hereafter described in the book. Scott well observes:

---

[19] William Kelly, *The Lord's Prophecy on Olivet in Matthew xxiv., xxv.*, p. 68.

Why is the dragon used as a symbol of Satan? Pharaoh, king of Egypt, in his cruelty to God's people, and in proud and haughty independence of God, is termed "the great dragon" (Ezek. 29:3, 4). Nebuchadnezzar is similarly spoken of in respect to his violence and cruelty (Jer. 51:34). Gathering up the numerous scripture references in the Book of Psalms, and in the first three of the greater prophets, to the crocodile, the sovereign of the seas, who is identified with the dragon, insatiable cruelty seems the main feature. The Egyptians regarded the crocodile or dragon, according to their hieroglyphics, as the source and author of all evil, worshipped under the name of Typho. The color of the dragon, red, denotes his murderous, bloodthirsty character. This is the first time in Scripture that Satan is directly spoken of as a dragon. The heathen monarchs, Pharaoh and Nebuchadnezzar, enslaved and oppressed the people of God, and, thus far acting in satanic power, merited the appellation of dragon. But at the time treated of in our chapter, Satan is the prince of the world—its virtual ruler. The Roman power is the instrument through which he acts. Hence the title "great red dragon" can now for the first time be used of him.[20]

The dragon is seen to have seven heads and ten horns and seven crowns upon his heads (Rev. 12:3), which are the same as the beast possesses in chapters thirteen and seventeen. It is plainly stated in 13:2 that this individual derives his authority from Satan. This shows us that Satan is seeking a governmental authority over the woman's "remnant" (12:7), which authority rightly belongs to Christ Himself.

B. *A man child.* The quotation from Psalm 2, which all would agree is a Messianic Psalm, identifies the man child here as none other than Jesus Christ. The fact of the birth, the fact of the destiny of this child, for He is "to rule all nations with a rod of iron," and the fact of the ascension, since He is "caught up unto God, and to His throne," all cause the identification to point to one person, the Lord Jesus Christ, for of none other could all three statements be made.

C. *A woman clothed with the sun.* While there has been general agreement among commentators of all types concerning the identity of the two aforementioned individuals, there is a great diversity of interpretation concerning the key individual in this passage.

---

[20] Walter Scott, *Exposition of the Revelation of Jesus Christ*, pp. 249-50.

1. There have been many false interpretations of the identity of this woman. Some have held that it was Mary. However, the only feature to make this possible would be the fact of motherhood, for Mary was never persecuted, never fled into the wilderness, was never cared for for 1260 days.[21] Others have held that this woman is the church that is travailing to bring Christ to the nations.[22] This, however, is built on the allegorizing principle of interpretation and must be rejected. The church did not produce Christ, but Christ the church. Since the church is not seen on earth in chapters four through nineteen of Revelation, the church can not be represented by this woman. Still others have identified the woman as the leader of some particular sect. But only by the wildest vagaries of the imagination could some present day individual be pressed into the interpretation here.

2. It has been the interpretation of dispensational premillennialists that the woman in this passage represents the nation Israel. There are a number of considerations which support this interpretation.

a. The whole context in which this passage is set reveals that John is dealing with the nation Israel. Gaebelein writes:

> Revelation, chapters eleven to fourteen, leads us prophetically to Israel, Israel's land and Israel's final tribulation, the time of Jacob's trouble and the salvation of the godly remnant. The scene of the eleventh chapter is "the great city, which spiritually is called Sodom and Egypt, where also our Lord was crucified." That city is not Rome but Jerusalem. The twelfth chapter begins a connected prophecy, ending with the fourteenth.[23]

Grant says of Revelation 11:19, "The ark, then, seen in the temple in heaven is the sign of God's unforgotten grace toward Israel. . . ."[24] Thus, the context in which this passage is set shows that God is dealing with Israel again.[25]

b. Frequently in the Old Testament the sun, moon, and stars

---

21 Cf. F. C. Jennings, *Studies in Revelation*, pp. 310-11.
22 Cf. Ford C. Ottman, *The Unfolding of the Ages*, p. 280.
23 Gaebelein, *loc. cit.*
24 F. W. Grant, *The Revelation of Christ*, p. 126.
25 Cf. Ottman, *op. cit.*, pp. 278-79.

are used in reference to Israel.[26] They are so employed in Genesis 37:9, where the sons of Jacob are clearly understood. Compare Jeremiah 31:35-36; Joshua 10:12-14; Judges 5:20 and Psalm 89:35-37 where heavenly bodies are associated with Israel's history.

c. The significance of the number twelve. The number twelve not only represents the twelve tribes of Israel, but is used in Scripture as the governmental number.[27] Darby says:

> . . . after the question of personal salvation or relationship to God, two great subjects present themselves to us in scripture: the Church, that sovereign grace which gives us a place along with Christ Himself in glory and blessing; and God's government of the world, of which Israel forms the centre and the immediate sphere.[28]

Inasmuch then as the woman represents that which is to display divine government in the earth, and Israel is God's appointed instrument to that end, this woman must be identified as Israel.

d. The use of the term *woman.* Eight times the term *woman* is used in this chapter, and eight additional times the pronoun *she* or *her* is used in reference to the woman. We find this term used frequently in the Old Testament to refer to the nation Israel. It is so used in Isaiah 47:7-9; 54:5-6; Jeremiah 4:31; Micah 4:9-10; 5:3; Isaiah 66:7-8. While the church is called a *bride,* or a *chaste virgin,* we never find the church referred to as a *woman.*

e. The name of the adversary. The name *dragon* is used throughout the Old Testament to describe some particular adversary of the nation Israel. Inasmuch as this name is applied to Satan in this chapter, it must be because all those persecutors, who bore the name dragon, were only foreshadows of this great persecution that is to come through the instrumentality of Satan. The use of the name *dragon* in reference to the persecutor would identify the persecuted one as Israel from its past usages in the Word of God.

f. The use of the term *wilderness.* The wilderness is said

---

26 Cf. *ibid.*, p. 282.

27 Cf. Jennings, *op. cit.*, p. 312.

28 William Kelly, editor, *The Collected Writings of J. N. Darby,* Prophetical, XI, p. 190.

to be the place of refuge afforded the woman in her flight (Rev. 12:14). It can not be gainsaid that the wilderness has peculiar reference to Israel in her national history. Israel was taken into "the wilderness of the land of Egypt" (Ezek. 20:36). Israel, since she refused to follow God into the promised land, was turned back into the wilderness for forty years. Israel's unbelief caused Ezekiel to declare God's purpose: "I will bring you into the wilderness of the people, and there will I plead with you face to face" (Ezek. 20:35). Hosea reveals that in the long period Israel would spend "in the wilderness" God would be gracious to them (Hos. 2:14-23).[29]

g. The man child. The parallelism between Revelation 12 and Micah 5 helps to identify the woman as Israel. In Micah 5:2 is recorded the birth of the ruler. The rejection of this ruler results in the setting aside of the nation ("therefore will he give them up," Mic. 5:3). The nation will be in travail "until the time that she which travaileth hath brought forth" (Mic. 5:3), that is, until the accomplishment of God's purpose. The same program is outlined in Revelation 12. Kelly writes that this prophecy must be understood

> . . . in conjunction with the accomplishment of the purpose of God respecting Israel . . . Christ was born (Micah v. 2): then comes His rejection . . . the prophecy passes by all that has to do with the church and takes up Christ's birth figuratively, connecting it with the unfolding of the divine purpose, which is itself symbolized by a birth. . . . Here it is put figuratively, as Zion travailing till the birth of this great purpose of God touching Israel. . . . when God's earthly purpose begins to take effect in the latter day, the remnant of that time will form part of Israel and will resume their ancient Jewish place. The natural branches shall be grafted into their own olive-tree.[30]

h. The specific statement of Scripture. In Romans 9:4-5 Paul writes concerning the Israelites, "of whom as concerning the flesh Christ came" (Rom. 9:5). Since the "man child" may be identified with certainty, and since the one bearing the man child is said to be Israel, the woman must be identified as Israel.[31]

---

[29] Cf. W. C. Stevens, *Revelation, Crown-Jewel of Prophecy,* II, 212-13.
[30] William Kelly, *Lectures on the Revelation,* pp. 254-57.
[31] Cf. Ottman, *loc. cit.*

i. The thousand two hundred and threescore days. Twice in this passage reference is made to the period of three and a half years (Rev. 12:6, 14). This has reference to the last half of the week of Daniel's seventieth week prophecy (Dan. 9:24-27). This prophecy is specifically addressed to "thy people and thy holy city" (Dan. 9:24). Inasmuch as this is addressed to Daniel it could only refer to Israel and Jerusalem. Each time this period is mentioned in Scripture, whether as a thousand two hundred and threescore days, or forty-two months, or three and a half years, or time, times, and half a time, it always refers to Israel and a period in which God is dealing with that nation.

j. The reference to Michael. In Daniel 12:1 the angel Michael is called "the great prince which standeth for the children of thy people." Michael is united with the destiny of the nation Israel by this word of the Lord to Daniel. In Revelation 12:7 Michael appears again in reference to the warfare in heaven. The fact that Michael appears on the scene here indicates that God is again dealing with the nation Israel, and Michael is an actor here because the destiny of Israel is involved.

In the light of the above, the conclusion of Moorehead is justified. He writes:

> In xi:19 we read: "And the temple (sanctuary) of God was opened in heaven, and there was seen in his temple the ark of the covenant." This is strictly Jewish ground; the temple, the ark, the covenant belong to Israel, represent Hebrew relations with God and Hebrew privileges. The Spirit now takes up Jewish things, Jewish standing, covenant, hopes, dangers, tribulations and triumph.[32]

The woman can be none other than Israel, with whom God has His covenants, and to whom those covenants will be fulfilled.

III. The Remnant of the Tribulation Period

Until the present eschatological controversy, prophetic writers were in general agreement on the existence, the nature, the mission and the preservation of a remnant of Israel during the tribulation period.[33] At the present time the doctrine of

---

[32] William G. Moorehead, *Studies in the Book of Revelation*, p. 90.

[33] Cf. Kelly, editor, *Collected Writings of J. N. Darby*, Prophetical XI, 182-204.

the remnant is being attacked by the amillennialist,[34] who can not admit the existence of the remnant, since he affirms the church is fulfilling the covenants and no further fulfillment is possible. It is also being attacked by the posttribulation rapturist,[35] who can not admit the existence of the remnant, for he affirms that the church is going through the tribulation so it will be the witnessing remnant. Although for different reasons, the amillennialist and the posttribulation rapturist join hands in attacking this doctrine.

A. *The necessity of a remnant.* The existence of a remnant in the last days is inextricably tied in with the covenants which God made with the nation Israel. Since these covenants were unconditional, their very nature demands the existence of a remnant to whom and through whom these covenants can be fulfilled.

1. The Abrahamic covenant. This covenant made by God with Abraham is basic to the whole prophetic question. Stated and confirmed unconditionally by God (Gen. 12:1-3; 13:14-17; 15:4-21; 17:1-8; 22:17-18), promises are made by Him to give to Abraham a land, a seed, and a blessing, which would be universal and eternal. This covenant, then, necessitates a remnant to be that promised seed, who can occupy the land given that seed and through whom the promised blessing may come.

2. The Palestinic covenant. This covenant established by God (Deut. 30:1-9; Jer. 32:36-44; Ezek. 11:16-21; 36:21-38) gives the basis on which Israel will occupy the land which was first given Abraham's seed in the Abrahamic covenant. This covenant makes the existence of a remnant imperative to receive the promised inheritance of the land.

3. The Davidic covenant. This covenant, likewise unconditionally affirmed by God (2 Sam. 7:10-16; Jer. 33:20-21; Ps. 89), promises a king, a kingdom, and a throne to the seed of Abraham. This covenant promises an everlasting earthly kingdom over which David's son should reign. This covenant, like-

---

34 Oswald T. Allis, *Prophecy and The Church.* Cf. Index, Jewish Remnant, where ten passages are cited where this doctrine is attacked.

35 Alexander Reese, *The Approaching Advent of Christ.* Cf. Index, Jews, the Remnant, where eleven passages are devoted to the attack on this doctrine.

wise, makes necessary a remnant to whom the promises of the Davidic covenant can be fulfilled.

4. The new covenant. The fourth covenant, unconditionally affirmed by God with Israel (Jer. 31:31-34; Ezek. 16:60; Isa. 59:20-21; Hos. 2:14-23), promises Israel's restoration as a nation, the forgiveness of her sins, the cleansing of her heart, and the implantation of a new heart on the basis of regeneration. In order for these promises to be fulfilled, which are necessary before the fulfillment of the promises contained in the other covenants can be fully fulfilled, there must be a remnant of the nation continuing with whom God can fulfill His word.

5. The character of God. Since God has made these solemn promises to the nation Israel the very character of God is at stake in their fulfillment. God would be proved a liar if that which He promised is not fulfilled as promised. The integrity of God, then, makes the existence of a remnant necessary.

B. *The remnant in Israel's history.* Even a casual survey of Israel's recorded history will establish the principle that God dealt with a believing remnant within the nation. Caleb and Joshua (Num. 13—14), Deborah and Barak (Judges 4), Gideon (Judges 7), Samson (Judges 13—17), Samuel (1 Sam. 2), the Levites in Jeroboam's day (2 Chron. 11:14-16), Asa (2 Chron. 15:9), the seven thousand faithful ones in the days of Elijah (1 Kings 19:18) all illustrate this point. Concerning the existence of the remnant during Israel's early history Gaebelein well states:

> The Lord had a remnant, faithful remnant, among His people even at the time of their great apostasy. This is the thought and argument here. The *apostasy of Israel is never a complete* apostasy. The Lord has always a remnant faithful to Him and the covenants among them.[36]

God preserved for Himself a faithful, believing, witnessing remnant in times of apostasy, persecution, and indifference.

C. *The remnant in the prophets.* It would be impossible to cite all the references to the remnant in the prophetic books. A few passages will be cited to show that such a subject is a

[36] Arno C. Gaebelein, *Hath God Cast Away His People?* pp. 21-22.

main line of prophetic revelation. Isaiah speaks of it in 1:9; 4:3-4; 6:12-13; 10:21; 26:20; 49:6; 51:1; 65:13-14. Entire chapters, such as twenty-six, thirty-three, thirty-five, and sixty-five, are devoted to it. Jeremiah follows the same theme in passages such as Jeremiah 15:11; 33:25-26, and 44:28. The entire passage in chapters thirty through thirty-three is based upon the existence of the remnant. Ezekiel takes up the theme in such references as 14:22; 20:34-38; 37:21-22. It appears again in the other prophets: Hosea 3:5; Amos 9:11-15; Zechariah 13:8-9; Malachi 3:16-17. These references justify the conclusion of Darby, who says:

> I have gone through these prophecies that the reader may clearly see that the doctrine of a Jewish remnant . . . a remnant, pious, and waiting on Jehovah before His appearing to deliver them, and whose piety and confidence are owned by Him—is not a matter of speculation, or of the interpretation of some difficult or obscure text; but the clear, consistent, impressive, and prominent testimony of the Spirit of God.[37]

D. *The remnant in the New Testament.* In the New Testament there is a believing and expecting nucleus to whom the promises of the Old Testament are reaffirmed. Such were Zacharias and Elizabeth (Luke 1:6), John the Baptist (Luke 3), Mary and Joseph (Luke 1 and Matt. 1—2), Simeon (Luke 2:25), and the Disciples. These constitute a remnant within the remnant of Israel, a believing group within the spared nation. The Lord's earthly ministry, from the time of His presentation by John until His rejection by the nation, was confirmed to that nation alone. The kingdom offered by John, by Christ, by the twelve, and by the seventy witnesses sent out by Him was to Israel only. The principle must be observed that God was dealing throughout Christ's earthly life with the remnant that existed then.

From the time of Christ's rejection by Israel until the time when God deals specifically with Israel again in the seventieth week it is not possible to refer to a remnant of the nation Israel. In the body of Christ all national distinctions disappear. All Jews who are saved are not saved into a national relation-

---

[37] Kelly, editor, *op. cit.*, p. 204. The reader should consult pp. 179-204 for an extended treatment of the prophecies of Isaiah dealing with the remnant.

ship, but into a relationship to Christ in that body of believers. Therefore there is no continuing remnant of Israel with whom God is particularly dealing today.

Some have argued on the basis of Romans 11:5, "Even so then at this present time also there is a remnant according to the election of grace," that the church becomes the remnant and will be the witness in and through whom the promises of God are fulfilled to a "spiritual" Israel. The contrasts between the church and Israel, the concept of the church as a mystery, the distinctive relationship of the church to Christ, and the specified purpose for the church all make such an interpretation impossible. The New Testament expectation, then, is that:

> . . . there is yet to be a Jewish remnant, a strong and mighty witness that God hath not cast away His people. This future remnant of believing Hebrews will be called as soon as the church is complete and removed from the earth. This remnant to be called through Grace corresponds to the remnant at the beginning of this age.[38]

E. *The remnant in Revelation.* Paul declares clearly in Romans 11:25 that the blindness of Israel is a temporary blindness. Because that nation is now blinded, God can not have a remnant within the nation with whom the covenants will be fulfilled. In Romans 11:26-27 it is stated:

> And so all Israel shall be saved: as it is written, There shall come out of Sion the Deliverer, and shall turn away ungodliness from Jacob:
>
> For this is my covenant unto them, when I shall take away their sins.

Paul has previously declared (Rom. 9:6) that God is not numbering all the physical seed of Abraham as descendants, but that the promises are to those who are in faith. Thus we understand the "all Israel" in Romans 11:26 to refer to this believing remnant, the believing Jews at the second advent of Christ. The prophetic book of the New Testament presents a development and conclusion to the line of teaching concerning the remnant.

---

[38] Gaebelein, *op. cit.*, p. 28.

1. The *existence* of the remnant. When Satan is cast out of heaven (Rev. 12:13) and desires to pour out vengeance on that group with whom God is particularly dealing, since the church is not on earth, he attacks the nation Israel. It becomes necessary for this nation, regathered in unbelief back to the land (Ezek. 37:8), to flee for preservation from the Satanic attack (Rev. 12:13-17). Thus, we see that such a remnant does exist in the tribulation period. It is this remnant that God is preparing for the fulfillment of all Israel's covenants and promises.

2. The *status* of this remnant. When the nation Israel is brought back into her land after the rapture by the covenant enacted by the head of the Revived Roman Empire (Dan. 9:27) Israel is still in unbelief. God, however, is very definitely dealing with that nation to bring it to salvation. The whole seventieth week of Daniel is a period of preparation for the coming of the King. The gospel of the kingdom, which necessitates repentance, is being preached. There is a reception of this message. God uses many different means to bring "all Israel" to salvation during the seventieth week. The Word of God is available and may be used so that those Jews who are hungering and thirsting may search that Word for a knowledge of Christ. The Holy Spirit, while not indwelling a temple as He did in this age, is nevertheless operative and will do a work of convicting and enlightening. Signs will be given to point Israel to a knowledge of Jehovah. Such a sign is the destruction of the king of the north (Ezek. 39:21-29). There will be the ministry of the 144,000 sealed of Israel (Rev. 7) and the ministry of the two witnesses (Rev. 11), all with the intent of bringing the nation to repentance and salvation. The outpouring of the wrath of God is seen to be for the purpose of bringing men to repentance (Rev. 16:9-10). While the majority will not repent, some may be turned to Jehovah by these signs.

It would be concluded, then, that the nation, unsaved at the beginning of the tribulation, receives a multitude of witnesses of various kinds so that the individuals are experiencing salvation through the period and the nation will be saved finally at the second advent (Rom. 11:26-27). The fact that the brethren, referred to in Revelation 12:10-11, overcome by the blood of the Lamb and by the word of their testimony indicates that many will be saved during the tribulation period.

3. *The means of salvation* of the remnant. Allis asks the question:

> The difficult question raised by this Dispensational doctrine is obviously this, How does this great body . . . of redeemed ones come into being? According to Darby and Scofield the entire church has then been raptured, the Holy Spirit, whom they hold to be the one "that restraineth" (2 Thess. ii. 6), has been taken away. How then will the saints of the tribulation period be saved?[39]

This question has been considered in detail previously. Suffice it to say here that it is concluded that the restrainer is the Holy Spirit and that He will be taken away, yet it must be recognized that the Spirit is omnipresent. He will cease His particular ministry of indwelling the body of Christ, but that does not mean He will be inoperative. Before Pentecost the Lord told Nicodemus that a man must be born again by the Spirit (John 3:5-6). If a person could experience a new birth before the Holy Spirit began to indwell the body, certainly one could after He ceases that particular ministry. It should be noted that the indwelling ministry is related to the enablement of believers in their Christian walk, not to the method or means of salvation.

Matthew 24:14 makes it clear that the gospel being preached will be the "gospel of the kingdom." What is often ignored is the fact that in John's proclamation of the "gospel of the kingdom" there were two distinct facets of his message: "Repent ye, for the kingdom of heaven is at hand" (Matt. 3:2), and "Behold the Lamb of God that taketh away the sin of the world" (John 1:29). Revelation makes it clear that the salvation is through the blood of the lamb.

> And they overcame him by the blood of the Lamb, and by the word of their testimony: and they loved not their lives unto death [Rev. 12:11].

> These are they which came out of great tribulation, and have washed their robes, and made them white in the blood of the Lamb [Rev. 7:14].

---

[39] Allis, *op. cit.*, p. 224.

It may be that the word of Paul in 1 Corinthians 15:8 gives an indication of the sovereignty of God in the salvation of the remnant during the tribulation period. Evans writes:

> The conversion of Saul may be suggestive of much that will take place after the rapture of the saints when the Lord Jesus comes for His own who are in this world. The blindness and hatred which Saul held for the church of God, which was evidenced by his persecution of it, came to an end after the Lord had returned to heaven. The conversion of Saul resulted in his going forth as a flaming evangelist with the gospel seeking to reach all whom he could reach with the gospel. . . . Such will be the position taken by the apostles of the gospel of the seventieth week of Daniel.[40]

Thus, as God sovereignly called the Apostle Paul by a divine revelation, so may he call those who will be His witnesses for that period.

4. The *ministry* of the remnant. It is obvious from Revelation 12:11, 17 that this believing remnant holds the position of a witnessing body during the tribulation period. The particular animosity of Satan is due to the fact that they "have the testimony of Jesus Christ" (Rev. 12:17). The Old Testament pictures Israel as the witness for God to the nations of the earth. Israel was unfaithful to this ministry. God will raise up a faithful witness during the tribulation to fulfill this original purpose for this nation.

5. The *relation* of the 144,000 to the remnant. In considering the Old Testament prophecies it was noted that God has a remnant within the remnant of the nation. It is believed that the 144,000 of Revelation 7 and 14 constitute a special part of the remnant of Israel, set apart by a sovereign act of God, to be special witness during the tribulation period. Several considerations are important here. The first is as to whether the 144,000 are literal or figurative. Some have held that this was a representative number to symbolize an innumerable host of Israel saved during the tribulation. Darby says: "The number . . . is symbolical; it is the perfect number of those who escape of the

[40] J. Ellwood Evans, "New Testament Contribution to Israel's Eschatology," p. 184.

remnant in Israel. God alone can know the number of those He seals."[41] Scott takes the same view when he writes: "The number of the sealed is of course symbolic, and simply denotes that God has appropriated a certain, complete, yet limited number of Israel for Himself."[42] This would make the 144,000 identical to the saved of Israel of the tribulation period. Now it is made clear that many of the saints of Israel are slain during the tribulation (Rev. 13:7; 20:4) whereas these 144,000 are sealed, evidently with a view to their preservation through the period. Thus the remnant of the nation, which is subject to death, can not be the same as the 144,000 who are not subject to death. These must be viewed as a separate company. It would seem to be better to conclude, with Ottman, "To lose sight of a *literal* Israel here is to throw a pall of darkness over the whole subject,"[43] and again, "In this sealed company from the twelve tribes *Israel* is, whatever may be said to the contrary, plainly and literally before us."[44] And since Israel is literal here and the tribes are literal, it would seem best to take the numbers literally also. If these 144,000 are seen to be only a part of the total remnant, the comparative smallness of the number, when compared with the number of saved Gentiles (Rev. 7:9), creates no problem. And, if God is setting these apart as sovereignly appointed witnesses, why should there not be a specific number appointed?

It is to be noted that the remnant of Romans 11:26 is not converted until the second advent of Christ and the 144,000 are ministering as sealed witnesses immediately after the church has been raptured. It would thus seem that the 144,000 are a part of the remnant of Israel, but not the entire remnant itself. It may be that Paul was likening himself to one of these witnesses when he speaks of himself as "one born out of due time" (1 Cor. 15:8). Scofield remarks:

> Gr. *to ektromati,* "before the due time." Paul thinks of himself here as an Israelite whose time to be born again had not come, nationally (cf. Mt. 23:39), so that his conversion by the

41 Kelly, editor, *op. cit.,* II, 37.
42 Scott, *op. cit.,* p. 166
43 Ottman, *op. cit.,* p. 165.
44 *Ibid.,* p. 180.

> appearing of the Lord in glory (Acts 9:3-6) was an illustration, or instance before the time, of the future national conversion of Israel. See Ezek. 20:35-38; Hos. 2:14-17; Zech. 12:10—13:6; Rom. 11:25-27.[45]

They are the set-apart witnesses of whom Paul was the prototype. And as there were specifically numbered groups who were sent out as witnesses during the Lord's ministry (the twelve and the seventy), there will be a specifically designated group appointed here also.

The question arises as to whether the 144,000 of Revelation seven and fourteen are the same group. There are some commentators that hold that they are different. Kelly says of the group in chapter fourteen:

> . . . a remnant, not merely sealed as the servants of God (like a similar band out of the twelve tribes of Israel in chapter vii.), but brought into association with the Lamb in Zion, that is, with God's royal purpose in grace. These seem to be sufferers of Judah, who pass through unequalled tribulation, which it is not said that the other remnant do.[46]

His inference is that since these stand on Mt. Zion they must be from the tribe of Judah. He further holds that these in chapter fourteen have been through the tribulation and those in chapter seven have not. It is commonly held that those in chapter seven are on earth and these in heaven, making Mt. Zion the heavenly city New Jerusalem. Those in chapter fourteen are said to be identified with the Lamb and those in chapter seven are not. Those in chapter seven are "sealed" but those in chapter fourteen have "the Father's name written in their foreheads." The time of the appearance of the two, it is argued, is different. However, there is nothing decisive in any of these arguments. There is no proof given that those in chapter fourteen are from Judah. Since Mt. Zion is best taken as literal Zion these need not be from Judah. Further, those in chapter fourteen need not be placed in heaven. The "Father's name" in chapter fourteen may be simply a further explanation of what the seal of chapter seven was. The fact that the group in chapter fourteen is mentioned without an article, which is used by some as an

---

[45] Scofield, *op. cit.*, p. 1226.
[46] Kelly, *Lectures on the Book of Revelation*, p. 318.

argument as to their diversity, is not a determining factor, for as Seiss says: "The insertion of the article is needless where the identification is otherwise so clear."[47] Inasmuch as it is necessary to spiritualize certain things in the two chapters to make them two separate groups, and a literal interpretation would make them identical, it seems best to view them as being the same.

In chapter seven the 144,000 are sealed by God, set apart to a special ministry, before the great tribulation begins. They seem to be sealed at the very outset of the tribulation period. In all probability the multitude of Gentiles, described in the passage that follows (Rev. 7:9-17), has come to a knowledge of salvation through the ministry of this group. In chapter fourteen the same group is pictured at the termination of the tribulation, when the kingdom is established. The returning King is on Mt. Zion, as was predicted of Him (Zech. 14:4). At His return the faithful witnesses gather unto Him, having been redeemed (Rev. 14:4) and having faithfully witnessed in the midst of apostasy (Rev. 14:4-5). They are called "the first-fruits unto God and to the Lamb" (Rev. 14:4), that is, they are the first of the harvest of the tribulation period that will come into the millennium to populate the millennial earth. As the judgments are about to be poured out upon Babylon (Rev. 14:8), upon the Beast (Rev. 14:9-12), upon the Gentiles (Rev. 14:14-17), and upon unbelieving Israel (Rev. 14:18-20), these 144,000 are viewed as being preserved through all that the earth experiences so that they may be the firstfruits of that period. Stevens well summarizes:

> It seems both natural and reasonable to find in this company of one hundred and forty-four thousand—now come off more than conquerors and standing, translated and glorified . . . the company of the same number introduced in chapter 7, a selected company from all the tribes of Israel, sealed in their foreheads with the "seal of the living God" and as His "servants." It was as special standard-bearers of the faith beginning with the era of the seventh seal that these Israelites were seen to be commissioned. Now, in the fourteenth chapter, this company, it would seem, is presented again in the enjoyment of the reward and commenda-

[47] Joseph Seiss, *The Apocalypse*, III, 19.

tions which will be theirs after their course has been finished. It is noteworthy that not one of the number is seen to have failed.[48]

6. The *destiny* of the remnant. Speaking of those brought to the Lord through the ministry of the 144,000 in Revelation 7:15-16, John writes:

> Therefore are they before the throne of God, and serve him day and night in his temple: and he that sitteth on the throne shall dwell among them.
>
> They shall hunger no more, neither thirst any more; neither shall the sun light on them, nor any heat.
>
> For the Lamb which is in the midst of the throne shall feed them, and shall lead them unto living fountains of waters: and God shall wipe away all tears from their eyes.

They are seen "before the throne" (Rev. 14:3). Thus the destiny of this remnant is the kingdom over which Christ will rule from the "throne of David." These promises are not heavenly, but earthly, and will be fulfilled in the millennium.

IV. The Removal of Israel's Blindness

It is the teaching of the New Testament that the nation Israel is a blinded nation. Not only are they spiritually blind because they willfully rejected their Messiah, but a divine judgment has come upon them so that the nation is judicially blinded. Isaiah anticipated this very condition when he wrote:

> And he said, Go, and tell this people, Hear ye indeed, but understand not; and see ye, indeed, but perceive not. Make the heart of this people fat, and make their ears heavy, and shut their eyes: lest they see with their eyes, and hear with their ears, and understand with their heart, and convert, and be healed [Isa. 6:9-10].

This passage is quoted in the New Testament (Matt. 13:14-15; Mark 4:12; Luke 8:10; John 12:40; Acts 28:26-27) to show that Israel's attitude toward Christ brought about the fulfillment of that prophecy. John explains the unbelief of the nation (John 12:37) on the basis that "they could not believe, because that Esaias said again, He hath blinded their eyes, and hardened

---

[48] Stevens, *op. cit.*, II, 240.

their heart" (John 12:39-40). Paul makes it clear that that which was judicially pronounced on the nation (Matt. 23:38) was the continuing state of the people, for he says:

> But their minds were blinded: for until this day remaineth the same vail untaken away in the reading of the old testament; which vail is done away in Christ. But even unto this day, when Moses is read, the vail is upon their heart [2 Cor. 3:14-15].

However even here it is anticipated that this condition shall change, for Paul says, "Nevertheless when it [the heart] shall turn to the Lord, the vail shall be taken away" (2 Cor. 3:16).

The longest passage dealing with the subject is found in Romans 11. Paul shows (vs. 17-27) that Israel has been set aside from the place of blessing so that the Gentiles might be brought into the place of blessing, from which Israel was cut off and to which they will be returned. Paul's teaching is in the words:

> For I would not, brethren, that ye should be ignorant of this mystery, lest ye should be wise in your own conceits; that blindness in part is happened to Israel, until the fulness of the Gentiles be come in [Rom. 11:25].

The passage reveals several important factors concerning Israel's blindness. (1) This particular blindness is *a mystery.* A mystery, in the Scriptural use of the word, as has previously been seen, refers to some divine program that could not and would not have been known unless it had been revealed to men by God. The fact that this blindness is a mystery shows that it is a kind of blindness hitherto unrevealed. Therefore it must be distinguished from both the spiritual blindness, which was the experience of Israel as children of Adam and therefore under the curse of sin, and from wilful blindness, which was Israel's experience in sinning against revealed light. This is a new form of blindness, not hitherto experienced by men. It was the divine visitation of Israel by God because of the national sin of rejecting the Messiah (Matt. 27:25). (2) The *nature* of this blindness is revealed. The word *pōrōsis* (blindness) literally means "the covering with a callus" and comes from the verb which means "to cover with a thick skin, to harden by covering with a callus."[49] It suggests that the thick impenetrable covering has come because of repeated rejection of the revelation that was given, which now has become the settled condition. (3) Paul says that this blindness is *"in part."* This reveals the fact that the blindness is not universal so that no Jew can believe today. The possibility of an individual's salvation exists, although the nation has been judicially blinded. (4) It is to be noted that there is a definite time when *the blindness will be removed* from the nation. Paul says that "blindness in part is happened to Israel, *until* . . ." Robertson calls this clause a "temporal clause" which means "until which time."[50] This anticipates the removal of the blindness at some appointed time. (5) Finally, the *time of the removal* of this blindness is stated in the phrase, "until the fullness of the Gentiles be come in." It thus becomes necessary to identify the term "the fulness of the Gentiles." On this Walvoord writes:

> . . . a problem remains regarding the termination of the period of Gentile blessing. In Luke 21:24, Christ referred to the "times of the Gentiles" as continuing as long as Jerusalem is "trodden down of the Gentiles." The reference in Luke is to the political domination of Jerusalem by Gentiles which began with the fall of Jerusalem at the time of the captivity and has continued to the present day. While the terminology is not significant in itself from the context of the two passages involved, it seems clear that the expression "times of the Gentiles" has reference to political domination of Gentiles, while the expression "fulness of the Gentiles" has reference to Gentile blessing and opportunity in this present age. If this analysis is correct, the times of the Gentiles and the fulness of the Gentiles are two entirely different ideas. The times of the Gentiles began long before Christ and will continue until Christ returns to establish His kingdom. The fulness of the Gentiles began at Pentecost and will continue only as long as the present age of grace. From the standpoint of eschatology, the important point is that the fulness of the Gentiles will come to its close before the times of the Gentiles are run out. . . . it seems clear that the fulness of the Gentiles will come abruptly to its close when the church is caught up to heaven.[51]

Thus, Paul is signifying that this blindness will be taken away

---

[49] Joseph Henry Thayer, *Greek-English Lexicon of the New Testament*, p. 559.
[50] A. T. Robertson, *Word Pictures in the New Testament*, IV, 398.
[51] John F. Walvoord, "Israel's Blindness," *Bibliotheca Sacra* 102:287-88, July, 1945.

at the rapture of the church when the time of Gentile privilege gives way to the time when Israel will be restored to the place of blessing.

It should be noted that the removal of this blindness does not mean the clear revelation of spiritual truth to the individual. He still is possessed of the blindness of his sin nature. But it does mean that God has restored Israel to a place alongside the Gentiles in the place of blessing again. God is then dealing with the nation with whom He has not dealt since their rejection of their Messiah. It should be further noted that the final removal of blindness, that is the spiritual blindness to which they are yet heir, will not be accomplished until the second advent of Christ (Rom. 11:26-27). The removal of the judicial blindness permits Israel to hear the good news of the kingdom (Matt. 24:14) that is proclaimed in that day in order that they might be saved, both individually and nationally. It will be observed that the removal of this blindness makes possible the setting aside of the 144,000, the calling out of the believing remnant, and Israel's ministry to the nations during the tribulation period.

V. The Two Witnesses

An important consideration relative to Israel's position in the tribulation is given in Revelation 11:3-12, where the ministry of the two witnesses is described. There is a wide divergence of opinion in the interpretation of this passage.

A. *The symbolic interpretation.* There are two principal views that result from a symbolic interpretation of the two witnesses. (1) The first is the view that these *two witnesses represent the church,* which will be raptured in the middle of the tribulation period. This rapture, according to this view, occurs in verse 12. Such is the position of the midtribulation rapturist, which has been examined previously. (2) The second is the view that the two witnesses represent the *entire remnant* of the tribulation period.[52] This view is based on the observation that the number two is the number of witnesses and, since the 144,000 are witnesses during the period, they must be symboli-

[52] Cf. Harry A. Ironside, *What's the Answer?* p. 124; Scott, *op. cit.,* p. 213.

cally represented here. Both of these views depend on a non-literal method of interpretation.

There are several objections to these views. (1) While it is recognized that Revelation does employ symbols, it seems a mistake to take all that is revealed there as symbolic. The word "signify" in Revelation 1:1: does not primarily mean "to make known by symbols" but rather refers to an historical fact that has some spiritual significance to it. The seven "signs" in John's Gospel were not mere symbols, but actual historical events to which spiritual significance was attached. The use of "signify" would not give warrant for a non-literal interpretation here. Consistency to the literal method demands that that which is revealed be understood literally unless the text clearly indicates otherwise as it does, for instance, in Revelation 12:3, 9. (2) Since the other numbers in this passage are taken literally, this number two must be taken literally also. The forty and two months (11:2), the thousand two hundred and threescore days (11:3), are taken in a literal manner so as to be understood to describe one-half of the seventieth week period. There seems to be no reason not to take the three and one-half (11:9, 11) literally. Thus, since the other numbers are not spiritualized the number two should not be either. (3) The witnesses all perish at one point of time (11:7) so that their testimony ceases. We know that the believing remnant, although decimated by the activities of the Beast, will continue throughout the period unto the coming of the Lord. The continuing witness seems to argue against identifying them with the remnant. (4) As long as a portion of the remnant continues there would be no cause for rejoicing (11:10). The rejoicing comes because this particular witness has terminated. Thus the conclusion is that this does not refer to the believing witnessing remnant, but rather to two literal individuals, who have been specially set apart by God, called "my two witnesses" (11:3). As the two olive trees of Zechariah had reference to Zerubbabel and Joshua, so the two olive trees (11:4) denote two literal individuals. Their miracles, their ministry, their ascension all seem to identfy them as individual men.

B. *The literal interpretation.* Literalists are divided into two classes in their interpretation. There are those who hold that these men are two men who lived previously and have been restored to the earth for this ministry. There are also those who believe they are literal men but they can not be identified.

Those who hold the view that these will be men who lived previously hold that one of the two witnesses will be *Elijah.* There are several bases on which this view rests. (1) It is predicted in Malachi 3:1-3; 4:5-6 that Elijah would come before the second advent to prepare the way for the Messiah. (2) Elijah did not experience physical death (2 Kings 2:9-11) and thus could return and experience death as the witnesses do. (3) The witnesses have the same sign as was given to Elijah in regard to the rain (1 Kings 17:1; Rev. 11:6). (4) The period of drouth in Elijah's day (1 Kings 17:1) was of the same duration as the time of the ministry of the witnesses (Rev. 11:3). (5) Elijah was one of the two who appeared at the transfiguration (Matt. 17:3) and discussed that to which all witness would point, "his decease."

Many of those who identify one of the witnesses as Elijah identify the second witness as *Moses.* Several reasons are given to support this interpretation. (1) Moses appeared with Elijah at the transfiguration (Matt. 17:3) when the death of Christ was discussed. (2) The ministry of Moses in turning waters into blood (Ex. 7:19-20) is the same as that of the witnesses (Rev. 11:6). (3) Deuteronomy 18:15-19 requires the reappearance of Moses. (4) The body of Moses was preserved by God so that He might be restored (Deut. 34:5-6; Jude 9). Thus the law (Moses) and the prophets (Elijah) would be joining in witness unto Christ during the announcement of the coming of the King.

There are several difficulties in identifying Moses as one of the witnesses. (1) The phrase "like unto me" in Deuteronomy 18:15 seems to preclude any possibility that Moses himself will be one of the witnesses, for the prophet was not Moses, but one like Moses. (2) The similarity of the miracles does not signify identification. The miracles Moses wrought were signs to Israel. The signs of the witnesses will likewise be signs to that nation. It would be a striking thing to those to whom the signs came if God should reduplicate those signs which had been the great signs to Israel in past days. (3) While the transfiguration is identified with the millennial age (2 Pet. 1:16-19) it is nowhere identified with the tribulation period or the ministry of the witnesses. Because they appeared at the transfiguration, signifying they would be related to the Lord at His coming for His kingdom, it does not mean they must be the witnesses. (4) Moses' body at the transfiguration was not his resurrection body, since Christ is the firstfruits of the resurrection (1 Cor. 15:20, 23), nor an immortal body, so it can not be argued on the basis of Jude 9 that Moses' body was preserved so he might return to die.

Others, who identify one of the witnesses as Elijah, identify the second as *Enoch.* Several reasons are given to support this. (1) Enoch was translated without seeing death (Gen. 5:24). (2) Both Elijah and Enoch would have put on immortality (1 Cor. 15:53) at the time of their translation, but Christ is the only one who now has immortality (1 Tim. 6:16). Therefore these two were preserved without experiencing immortality that they might return to die. (3) Enoch was a prophet of judgment, as was Elijah (Jude 14-15) and this corresponds to the ministry of the two witnesses, for they prophesy in the sign of judgment—sackcloth (Rev. 11:3). (4) In Revelation 11:4 the word "standing" suggests that they were already there in John's day, and must be two people who have already been translated. Thus, it is held, only Elijah and Enoch could meet this requirement.

There seem to be several arguments against identifying one of these witnesses as Enoch (1) It is the stated purpose that Enoch was translated "in order that he might not see death" (Heb. 11:5). In view of this it could hardly be stated that he will be returned to die. (2) It would seem that the antediluvian prophet would not be sent into a time when God is dealing with Israel. (3) The position of Enoch and Elijah in translation does not differ from all the Old Testament saints who are before the Lord through physical death. Their means of entrance differed, but not their position upon entrance. Thus the fact that they were raptured does not necessitate a difference of state, nor make it necessary that they should return to die. (4) The witnesses have mortal bodies and are subject to death. Elijah and Moses on the mount of transfiguration evidently did not have mortal bodies, for they "appeared in glory." It is hardly likely that they would be given mortal bodies again.

English draws a conclusion concerning these views, when he says:

> If it could be said of a surety that the two witnesses are to be identified as characters who appeared on the earth in Old Testament times, then we should have to conclude, I think, that they will be Elijah and Moses, the former because he is named as to come again, and the latter because of his association with Elijah on the Mount of Transfiguration, because of the nature of his witness, and because he symbolizes the law as Elijah represents the Prophets, both bearing witness to the coming Lord of Glory.[53]

There are those who hold, because of the difficulties involved and the silence of Scripture on the identification, that *the two can not be identified.* English is representative of this group when he writes:

> . . . these two witnesses cannot be identified, but . . . they will simply appear in the spirit and power of Elijah. . . . The two witnesses are to have mortal bodies, and, though it is possible for God, to whom "all things" are possible, to send back to earth those who have long since gone to be with the Lord, we have no Scriptural precedent or word for such a re-advent of men. Yes, Lazarus, and the son of the widow of Zarephath, and others had mortal bodies when raised from the dead, but their demise was only a temporary experience, and allowed in order that God might be glorified through the miraculous power of His son (or, His prophet) by their resurrection. Our Lord's reappearance after He was raised from among the dead was in His glorified body, and as we have already pointed out, Moses and Elias, on the Mount of Transfiguration "appeared in glory" (Luke 9:31), that is, in bodies glorified for that occasion. . . . From this we conclude that the two witnesses cannot be identified, but rather that they will fulfill in a future day a destiny that John the Baptist would have fulfilled had Israel's heart been receptive.[54]

It would seem best to conclude that the identity of these men is uncertain. They, in all probability, are not men who lived before and have been restored, but are two men raised up as a special witness, to whom sign-working power is given. Their ministry is one of judgment, as their sackcloth clothing indicates.

---

[53] Schuyler English, "The Two Witnesses," *Our Hope,* 47:665, April, 1941.
[54] *Ibid.,* pp. 669-70.

They are slain by the beast (Rev. 13:1-10). Concerning the time of their death the same author says:

> Mental arithmetic will quickly reveal that the period of prophecy entrusted to the two witnesses, twelve hundred and sixty days, is three and one-half years in duration. In which half of the Tribulation, then, will these witnesses prophesy? Or will their witness not be limited by either half of the seven years, but run from one half into the other? I do not think we can be dogmatic about it. There is thought-provoking logic in the argument that their testimony will be given during the first half of Daniel's prophetic week, and that their martyrdom will be the first persecuting act of the Beast, after he breaks his covenant with the Jews (Dan. 9:27). Their ministry will be attended with power over their enemies, whereas, according to Daniel 7:21, the "little horn" (who is this Beast) will make war with the saints and prevail against them, and this will be in the last half of the week. On the other hand, in Revelation 11:2 the "forty and two months" undoubtedly refers to the second half of the Tribulation, and the period of the testimony of the two witnesses seems to be synchronous with this. Further, their witness is recorded just prior to the blowing of the Seventh Trumpet, and this event takes us right on into the Millennial Kingdom. But the exact period when the testimony will take place is unimportant to believers of this age—it will be in God's time, that we know, and that will be the proper time.[55]

VI. Will Elijah Come Again?

A question which is united to the previous discussion is the question concerning Elijah, whether he has come, whether he will come again literally, or whether one will come in the spirit and power of Elijah although not the prophet himself. This is important in itself and in its bearing on the identity of the witnesses.

A. *Elijah will not come again.* There is an interpretation of the questions which say that John the Baptist fully fulfilled all that was predicted of the forerunner and Elijah will not come again.[56] There are several essential arguments on which this position rests. (1) The established gap principle in Scripture is cited as proof. According to this view Malachi saw two widely

---

[55] *Ibid.*, p. 671.

[56] Cf. Carl Armerding, "Will There Be Another Elijah?" *Bibliotheca Sacra*, 100:89-97, January, 1943.

separated events in his prophecy (4:5-6), but treated them as one. Thus John could fulfill the first portion at the first advent of Christ although the remainder must await Christ's second advent for its fulfillment. (2) It was said that Elijah would come "before the coming of the great and dreadful day of the Lord" (Mal. 4:5). Thus, it must be said that John was Elijah or else Elijah must come before the tribulation period, which would destroy the doctrine of imminence. (3) Matthew twenty-four and twenty-five, which outline the program for Israel in the tribulation period, do not refer to the ministry of Elijah in that time. (4) The ministry of the two witnesses is a ministry of judgment, while that of Elijah is the ministry to "turn the hearts," so that the chronology of Revelation four through nineteen has no mention of a ministry like Elijah's. (5) Christ clearly states in Matthew 11:14 and 17:12 that John was the Elijah of the prophecy.

In reply to these arguments it may be stated: (1) The gap principle is clearly recognized, but, while a gap may be there, one is not necessarily there. This is an accommodation to support the position. (2) It is true that Elijah will come "*before* the coming of the great and dreadful day of the Lord" (Mal. 4:5). It should, however, be noted that the Day of the Lord may refer either to the entire period encompassed by that phrase, that is, from the beginning of the seventieth week of Daniel through the millennial age or it may refer to any of the events of that period under that name. Thus it is not necessary to hold that Elijah will appear during the church age because he will come "before" the Day of the Lord. This could have reference to his appearance before the awful judgments descend just prior to and in connection with the second advent, which is an event of the Day of the Lord. In fact, the descriptive adjectives, great and dreadful, seem to relate this prophecy to that very experience. (3) It must be noted that many important events are omitted from the chronology in Matthew, which must be filled in from other portions of Scripture, and, therefore, the omission does not make such a ministry impossible. (4) As thorough as the Revelation is, there are Old Testament events which are not included there and this ministry need not be denied because of its omission. The fact that the witnesses announce judgment does not eliminate the possibility of coupling with it a message of grace. (5) The Lord's statement that John was Elijah was a statement based on contingency. John was Elijah "if ye will receive it" (Matt. 11:14). The Lord indicated that if they received the offered kingdom John would be the one to do the work of Elijah. But they rejected this offer (Matt. 17:12) and therefore John is precluded from being the one to fulfill the prophecy.

B. *Elijah will come personally and minister again.* The second major view is the interpretation that John does not fulfill the prophecy and the Lord anticipates a future ministry of Elijah (Matt. 17:11). Therefore Elijah must come and minister again. This view has several arguments presented in its support. (1) In Luke 1:17 John is not identified as Elijah, but as one to "go before him in the spirit and power of Elias," showing that John was not a literal Elijah and literal Elijah therefore must yet come. (2) John denied that he was Elijah (John 1:21). (3) In Matthew 17:11 the word "come" is present, but since coupled with the word "shall restore," which is future, it must be interpreted as a futuristic present, so that the Lord is indicating a future ministry of Elijah. (4) The similarities in the ministries of the witnesses in Revelation 11 with those of Elijah argue for a future return of Elijah. (5) The historical argument is sometimes used that devout Jews are still looking for Elijah in fulfillment of the prophecy. (6) Since John did not restore all things one must come who will.

On the basis of the literal method of interpretation of the Scriptures these arguments seem to have weight and establish the fact that Elijah must come again. There seems to be one consideration that militates against it however. It is stated in Luke 1:17 that John is one who came "in *the spirit and power of Elias.*" When the Lord said: "And if ye will receive it, this is Elias, which was for to come" (Matt. 11:14), and "That Elias is come already, and they knew him not, but have done unto him whatsoever they listed" (Matt. 17:12) he was pointing to one who came, not a literal Elijah, but one who came in the spirit and power of Elijah and in this way satisfied the prophecy. The disciples clearly understood that the Lord was singling out

John in this identification (Matt. 17:13). It is stated by Christ that John became Elijah only upon the reception of the Messiah and His kingdom by Israel (Matt. 11:14) and whether John became the prophesied Elijah was based on contingency. It is true that whether John was the one to fulfill the prophecy or not depended upon whether Israel received or rejected the kingdom being offered, but the attitude toward the kingdom did not change the person of John. He was not and could not be literal Elijah under any circumstances and receiving the kingdom could not make him so. He was one who could have fulfilled the prophecy because the prophecy is interpreted by the Lord as being fulfilled, not in literal Elijah, but in one who comes in Elijah's spirit and power. If literal Elijah must appear Christ could not be making a *bona fide* offer of the kingdom, inasmuch as literal Elijah had to come and John could not have fulfilled that requirement. But if one coming in Elijah's spirit and power fulfills the requirements, then a genuine offer of the kingdom could be made. On the basis of the Lord's words it is concluded that Elijah personally need not appear, although one will come to fulfill this ministry (Matt. 17:12).

C. *One will come in the spirit and power of Elijah.* The third major view is that the prophecies have not been fulfilled in John and await a future fulfillment; but, since Elijah personally is not required to fulfill them, one will come in his spirit and power to fulfill that which is predicted (Mal. 4:5-6; Matt. 17:10-11). On this question English writes:

> . . . after the Transfiguration the disciples asked the Lord a question about His coming in power and glory: "Why then say the scribes that Elias (Elijah) must first come?" To this our Lord replied: "Elias truly shall first come, and restore all things" (Matt. 17:10-11). If there were no other references concerning the coming of Elijah we should be obligated to conclude that he must be one of the two witnesses of Revelation 11. But let us see. Some time before the Transfiguration, John the Baptist, who was in prison, sent two of his disciples to ask the Lord Jesus whether He was the Messiah or whether they were to look for another. Our Lord sent a message back to John drawing attention to His miraculous ministry as sufficient testimony that He was the One foretold by the prophets, and then He told the multitudes of John's greatness, and that the Baptist was indeed the Messenger of whom Malachi spoke (Mal. 3:1). And then the Lord added: "For all the

> prophets and the law prophesied until John. And if ye will receive it, this is Elias, which was for to come" (Matt. 11:12, 14). What did He mean? He was telling them this: that if Israel had been ready and willing to receive Him then, He would have established the Kingdom which He offered them, and that in that event, John's ministry would have been the fulfilment of the prophetic Elijah. It seems, therefore, that the prophecy of Malachi refers to one coming *in the spirit and with the power of Elijah* (as Luke 1:17), and that he will not need to be Elijah himself, literally. Our Lord gave us another indication of this in the conversation with His disciples to which we have already referred, which took place after the Transfiguration, for when He had assured them that Elijah must truly come, He added: "But I say unto you, that Elias *is come already*, and they knew him not," and we read: "Then the disciples understood that He spake unto them of John the Baptist" (Matt. 17:12, 13). It would seem that the Word of God clearly indicates that the one who comes will be a virtual rather than a literal Elijah.[57]

As this relates to the problem of the two witnesses English concludes:

> . . . if John the Baptist could have been Elijah, had Israel been willing to receive it (Matt. 11:13, 14), then those who will witness in that future day, coming in the spirit and power of Elijah, can assuredly fulfil the prophecies of Malachi and of our Lord (Mal. 4:5; Matt. 17:10, 11).[58]

Inasmuch as John could not have fulfilled the prophecies because Israel rejected the offered kingdom, it does not seem possible to assert that the prophecy of Malachi 4:5-6 has been fulfilled. The fact that John could have fulfilled it, even though he was not personally Elijah, seems to indicate that Elijah need not come personally to fulfill the prophecies. During the period preceding the second advent, and prior to the outpouring of judgments upon the earth, there will be a ministry by one in the spirit and power of Elijah, which will fulfill this prophecy.

---

[57] English, *op. cit.*, p. 666.
[58] *Ibid.*, p. 670.

CHAPTER XIX

THE GENTILES IN THE TRIBULATION

There is a divine program for the Gentile nations that is to come to fulfillment in the tribulation period. A great body of prophecy is devoted to this subject, which must be developed in order to have a clear picture of the events of the tribulation.

I. THE TRIBULATION AND THE "TIMES OF THE GENTILES"

The time period that is called by the Lord the "times of the Gentiles" in Luke 21:24, where He says: "Jerusalem shall be trodden down of the Gentiles, until the times of the Gentiles be fulfilled," is one of the important time periods in prophetic Scriptures.[1] The relation of Israel to the tribulation has been studied. Consideration is now given to the events related to the Gentiles as attention is directed to the "times of the Gentiles."

A. *The program with the Gentiles.* God has a program with the Gentile nations, leading to their salvation and blessing in the millennium. The program has been outlined as follows:

> 1. *The First Gentile Prediction.* A far-reaching prophecy was given by Noah with reference to the character that would be exhibited by each of his three sons as progenitors of the races to re-people the earth (Gen. 9:25-27) ....
>
> 2. *The Judgments upon Nations Adjacent to Israel.* . . . These predictions are set forth in various portions of the Old Testament, e. g.: Babylon and Chaldea (Isa. 13:1-22; 14:18-27; Jer. 50:1—51:64), Moab (Isa. 15:1-9; 16:1-14; Jer. 48:1-47), Damascus (Isa. 17:1-14; Jer. 49:23-27), Egypt (Isa. 19:1-25; Jer. 46:2-28), Philistia and Tyre (Isa. 23:1-18; Jer. 47:1-7), Edom (Jer. 49:7-22), Ammon (Jer. 49:1-6), Elam (Jer. 49:34-39).
>
> 3. *The Times of the Gentiles.* In contrast to times and seasons, which term refers to the divine dealing with Israel (cf. Acts 1:7; I Thess. 5:1), is the phrase *the times of the Gentiles,* which relates

[1] Cf. Lewis Sperry Chafer, *Systematic Theology,* VII, 170.

to divine dealings with the Gentiles. The latter term....measures the period in which Jerusalem will be under the overlordship of Gentiles....Gentile times are measured out to continue approximately 560 years....This period, however, is interrupted by the intercalary age of the Church, which age, being undefined with respect to duration, serves to introduce an element of indefiniteness into the period when Gentile times will end. Nevertheless, it is clear that Gentile times are now accomplished but for the seven years which will be experienced immediately upon the removal of the Church, which event closes this intercalary age.

4. *The Succession of Monarchies.* . . . Four world powers were foreseen by Daniel—Babylon, Medo-Persia, Greece and Rome. These, as foreseen by the prophet, were to dominate Gentile times and be terminated by the glorious coming of Christ, when the Messianic kingdom will supersede all human rule and authority....

5. *The Judgment of Gentile Nations.* . . . this stupendous event....is fully anticipated in the Old Testament (cf. Ps. 2:1-10; Isa. 63:1-6; Joel 3:2-16; Zeph. 3:8; Zech. 14:1-3).

6. *Gentile Nations and the Lake of Fire.* The destruction of opposing Gentile nations is also anticipated in the Old Testament but Christ himself—their Judge—has declared their actual destiny (Matt. 25:41).

7. *Gentile Nations and the Kingdom.* . . . prophecy foresees the share Gentiles will have in Israel's kingdom (cf. Isa. 11:10; 42:1, 6; 49:6, 22; chapters 60, 62, and 63)....Later revelation (Matt. 25:31-40) asserts the entrance of Gentiles into the kingdom by the authority of the King and as predetermined by the Father from the foundation of the world.[2]

B. *The duration of the "times of the Gentiles."* The "times of the Gentiles" has been defined by the Lord as that period of time in which Jerusalem was under the dominion of Gentile authority (Luke 21:24). This period began with the Babylonian captivity when Jerusalem fell into the hands of Gentiles. It has continued unto the present time and will continue through the tribulation period, in which era the Gentile powers will be judged. The dominion of the Gentiles ends at the second advent of Messiah to the earth. Scofield defines the time limits thus:

The Times of the Gentiles is that long period beginning with the Babylonian captivity of Judah, under Nebuchadnezzar, and

---

[2] *Ibid.*, IV, 379-81.

to be brought to an end by the destruction of Gentile world-power by the "stone cut out without hands" (Dan. 2:34, 35, 44), i. e. the coming of the Lord in glory (Rev. 19:11, 21), until which time Jerusalem is politically subject to Gentile rule (Luke 21:24).[3]

C. *The course of the "times of the Gentiles."* The fullest description of the period is given to us in the prophet Daniel. Dennett writes:

> What we have in Daniel is.... the course and character of Gentile powers, from the destruction of Jerusalem on to the appearing of Christ, together with the position of the remnant, and the sufferings of the Jewish people, while the Gentiles possess the dominion, until at last God, in His faithfulness in pursuance of His purposes, interposes, and, for His own glory, works for the rescue and blessing of His elect earthly people.[4]

1. The first prophetic outline of the course of this period is given in *Daniel 2,* where, through the medium of the great image, the successive empires that would exercise dominion over Jerusalem are outlined. Of this Chafer writes:

> Five world-dominions in their succession are foreseen—four of these are represented by the portions of the image and the fifth as that which will arise upon the wreckage of the four when the judgments of God fall. The fifth is distinctive as that which is to be set up by the God of heaven, and it is eternal in its duration. The first, Babylon as the head of gold, was already at the zenith of its power when Daniel gave his interpretation. The second was Media-Persia, in which kingdom also Daniel lived to share. The third dominion was Greece under Alexander, and the fourth was Rome, which was in its fullest development in the day that Christ was here on earth. It is this iron kingdom which merges in its final form into feet of iron and clay. It is in the time of the feet and clay that the Smiting Stone strikes.[5]

2. The second prophetic outline of the course of this period is given in *Daniel* 7. Whereas in Daniel 2 the course of world empire is viewed from man's perspective, in Daniel 7 the same course of empire is viewed from the Divine viewpoint, where the empires are seen, not as an attractive glorious image, but as four wild voracious beasts, which devour and destroy all

---

[3] C. I. Scofield, *Reference Bible,* p. 1345.
[4] Edward Dennett, *Daniel the Prophet,* p. 9.
[5] Chafer, *op. cit.,* IV, 333.

before them and, consequently, are worthy of judgment. Gaebelein explains this passage as he writes:

> The gold in the dream image and the first beast represent the Babylonian empire. In the beginning it was a lion with wings, but they were plucked out; it lost its strength and though it had a man's heart it was a beast still....
>
> The bear stands for the Medo-Persian empire, the empire seen as of silver, the chest and arms. One paw is lifted up, because the Persian element was stronger than that of the Medes. The bear had three ribs in its mouth, because Susiana, Lydia and Asia Minor had been conquered by this power....
>
> The leopard, with four wings and four heads, is the picture of the Graeco-Macedonian empire, corresponding to the thighs of brass in the image of Nebuchadnezzar. The four wings denote its swiftness, the four heads the partition of this empire into the kingdoms of Syria, Egypt, Macedonia and Asia Minor . . . . we call attention to the fact that in the selection of beasts to represent these world powers who domineer the times of the Gentiles, God tells us that their moral character is beastly. The lion devours, the bear crushes, the leopard springs upon its prey.
>
> . . . then we have the fourth world empire, the iron one, Rome. It is described in a way as none of the others are. It is dreadful, terrible, exceeding strong; it has great iron teeth. It devours, breaks in pieces and stamps down. It has ten horns and in their midst rises up a little horn with eyes like the eyes of man, and a mouth speaking great things.[6]

Thus the Scripture reveals that from the time of Daniel until the time when Jerusalem shall be given freedom from Gentile dominion at the second advent of Christ there will be four great empires which will rise and fall.

3. The last seven years of "the times and the seasons" appointed for Israel will also be the last seven years of the times of the Gentiles, for the termini of the two are identical according to the prophecy of Daniel 9:24-27. The period of tribulation must, therefore, be the final epoch in the development of the program within the times of the Gentiles. Thus the program outlined for the Gentiles will have an important bearing on the eschatological program.

From the chapters in Daniel just referred to the following

---

[6] Arno C. Gaebelein, *The Prophet Daniel,* pp. 73-76.

events will transpire: (1) There must be a realignment of nations to constitute the final form of the fourth world empire. This empire will be the one smitten by the "stone" (Dan. 2:35); will be made up of ten different parts (Dan. 2:33; 7:7); will have one head, who had overthrown three of the existing heads of state in his ascendancy (Dan. 7:8). (2) The head of this empire will be a blasphemer (Dan. 7:8, 25), a persecutor of the saints (Dan. 7:25), who will continue for three and a half years (Dan. 7:25) as the special enemy of God and God's program with Israel. (3) This head of the empire will make a covenant with Israel to restore their sovereignty (Dan. 9:27), which will be broken (Dan. 9:27). (4) This leader will invade Palestine (Dan. 11:41) and set up headquarters there (Dan. 11:45). (5) He will be judged at the return of the Lord (Dan. 7:11, 26). (6) The destruction of this leader and his hosts will redeem Jerusalem from Gentile dominion (Dan. 7:18, 22, 27). (7) This deliverance takes place at the second advent of Messiah (Dan. 7:13; 2:35).

II. The Final Form of Gentile World Power

There are several important passages of Scripture which have an important bearing on the question of the final form of Gentile world power.

A. *Daniel 2.* In the description of the times of the Gentiles given in Daniel 2 the prophet deals in a general way with the four successive empires that hold dominion over Palestine, but when dealing with the end of that Gentile world power he becomes very specific. He writes:

> And the fourth kingdom shall be strong as iron: forasmuch as iron breaketh in pieces and subdueth all things: and as iron that breaketh all these, shall it break in pieces and bruise. And whereas thou sawest the feet and toes, part of potters' clay and part of iron, the kingdom shall be divided; but there shall be in it of the strength of the iron, forasmuch as thou sawest the iron mixed with miry clay. And as the toes of the feet were part of iron, and part of clay, so shall the kingdom be partly strong, and partly broken. And whereas thou sawest iron mixed with miry clay, they shall mingle themselves with the seed of men: but they shall not cleave one to another, even as iron is not mixed with clay. And in the days of these kings shall the God of

> heaven set up a kingdom, which shall never be destroyed . . . . [Dan. 2:40-44].[7]

In these verses several important features concerning the final form of Gentile power are to be observed. (1) The final form of Gentile power is an outgrowth from and final development of the fourth great empire, the Roman. This final form is represented by the feet and ten toes (Dan. 2:41-42). (2) The final form of this power is marked by division (Dan. 2:41). Such is the signification of the emphasis on the ten toes and the clay and the iron. Tregelles writes:

> Thus we see this fourth empire especially brought before us at a time when in a divided condition, and when thus debased. The number of the toes of the feet appears to imply a tenfold division: this may be taken as a hint given to us here, although the more specific statement of the fact is not told us till farther on in this book. This kingdom is then divided into parts, which we shall see from other portions of the Scripture (especially chap. vii) to be exactly ten.[8]

(3) The final form of the Gentile power is marked by a federation of that which is weak and that which is strong, autocracy and democracy, the iron and the clay (Dan. 2:42). Kelly observes:

> There will be, before the age closes, the most remarkable union of two apparently contradictory conditions—a universal head of empire, and separate independent kingdoms besides, each of which will have its own king; but that one man will be the emperor over all these kings. Till that time comes, every effort to unite the different kingdoms under one head will be a total failure. Even then it will be not by fusing them together into one kingdom, but each independent kingdom will have its own king, though all subject to one head. God has said they shall be divided. This then is what is shown us here. "They shall not cleave one to another, even as iron is not mixed with clay." And if ever there was a portion of the world that has represented this incoherent system of kingdoms, it is modern Europe. As long as the iron predominated, there was one empire; but then came in the clay, or foreign material. In virtue of the iron there will be a universal monarchy, while in virtue of the clay there will be separate kingdoms.[9]

---

7 Cf. Robert Anderson, *The Coming Prince.*
8 S. P. Tregelles, *The Book of Daniel*, p. 19.
9 William Kelly, *Notes on Daniel*, p. 50.

Since the mixture of the iron and the clay is an unnatural one, it would seem to suggest that the federation is not brought about by force, else this condition would not continue. But it is brought about by mutual consent, so that each member in the alliance retains its own identity. This is in harmony with Revelation 17:13. (4). This final divided condition is not now historical but is yet prophetic. "These kings" (Dan. 2:44) do not come into existence until the time when the "stone . . . cut out of the mountain without hands" (Dan. 2:45) appears. Ironside says:

> The commentators generally tell us that the ten-toed condition of the empire was reached in the fifth and sixth centuries, when the barbarians from the North overran the Roman empire, and it was divided into something like ten different kingdoms. A number of different lists have been made, of ten kingdoms each; but few writers agree as to the actual divisions. One thing they all seem to have overlooked: the ten kingdoms are to exist *at one time,* not through a period of several centuries, and all are to form one confederation. There is nothing in the past history of the kingdoms of Europe that answers to this. They were generally warring enemies, each seeking the destruction of others. We reject utterly this interpretation, therefore, of the ten toes.[10]

It would seem best to view this Roman empire as a continuous development from its form at the time of the first coming of Christ until its final form at the second coming of Christ.

> It may seem a hard saying, but it is one which the facts fully bear out, that hardly one student in ten of mediaeval history really grasps *that one key* to the whole subject without which mediaeval history is simply an unintelligible chaos. The key is no other than *the continued existence of the Roman Empire.* As long as people are taught that the Empire came to an end in the year 476, a true understanding of the next thousand years becomes utterly impossible. No man can understand either the politics or the literature of that whole period, unless he constantly bears in mind that, in the ideas of the men of those days, the Roman Empire, the Empire of Augustus, Constantine, and Justinian, was not a thing of the past, but a thing of the present.[11]

It would seem, then, the problem is not so much the revival

---

[10] Harry A. Ironside, *Lectures on Daniel, The Prophet,* pp. 37-38.
[11] G. H. N. Peters, *Theocratic Kingdom,* II, 643.

of the empire, as the recasting of the continuing sphere of power into its final ten-toed form.

B. *Daniel* 7. The second great passage dealing with the last form of Gentile world power is found in Daniel 7, where the course of that power is revealed through the four voracious beasts. Concerning the end of the Gentile world power, Daniel reveals several things in this prophecy. (1) As in the former prophecy, it is revealed that the final form of Gentile power is to exist in a union of ten kings and their kingdoms (Dan. 7:7). The singular thing about this fourth beast was not its strength, nor its ferocity, nor the fact that it destroyed all the other beasts that preceded, but that it had ten horns. (2) These horns would be the final form of the empire. Kelly says:

> . . . the peculiarity of the Roman is the possession of "ten horns." Yet we are not to look for the actual development of history in this vision. Had this been the case, it is clear that the ten horns would not have been seen in the Roman beast, when it first met the eyes of the prophet. In fact, it was not until hundreds of years after Rome had existed as an empire, that it had more than one ruler. The Spirit of God clearly brings into the very first view the features that would be found at the close, and not at the beginning.[12]

It is clear from Daniel 7:24 that these ten kings are the heads of ten kingdoms which come out of the fourth great world kingdom. The fact that the ten rise "out of" the fourth kingdom seems to suggest that the fourth is not viewed as having passed out of existence, to be resurrected again, but rather, to have continued in some form until the ten horn condition merges. Young states it thus:

> The ten horns appear *on* the beast which is alive. . . . The beast does not die and come to life again in its ten horns. Rather, these horns grow out of the *live* beast. They must, therefore, represent a second phase in its history, and not a revived form of the beast's existence.[13]

(3) From among those ten kingdoms there will arise one individual who will have control over the whole dominion of the

[12] Kelly, *op. cit.*, pp. 125-26.

[13] Edward J. Young, *The Prophecy of Daniel*, p. 160. While exception is taken to this author's interpretation of the book, his observation is justified here.

ten kings (Dan. 7:8, 24; Rev. 13:1-10; 17:13). In gaining his authority three of the ten kings are overthrown. (4) This final authority over the empire is wielded by one who is marked by blasphemy, hatred of God's people, disregard for established law and order, who will continue for three and one-half years (Dan. 7:26). (5) This final form of world power will have world-wide influence (Dan. 7:23).

C. *Revelation 13:1-3.* In this passage John continues the line of revelation concerning the final form of Gentile power. There are several observations to be made. (1) As has been revealed earlier, the final form of power is the successor to all preceding forms, for the beast that arises is a composite beast, partaking of the features of the leopard, the bear, and the lion (Rev. 13:2). (2) This form of world power is marked by ten horns (Rev. 13:1), which are explained in Revelation 17:12 as "kings" over which the Beast rules. (3) There is the restoration of a former method of government that ceased to exist in relation to the whole kingdom. John notes that this beast had seven heads (Rev. 13:1) and the present head had been wounded to death (Rev. 13:3) but the wound had been healed. These heads, according to Revelation 17:10, are kings or forms of government under which Rome existed. They are usually viewed as: kings, consuls, dictators, decemvirs, military tribunes and emperors. Scofield comments on the deadly wound that was healed (Rev. 13:3):

> Fragments of the ancient Roman empire have never ceased to exist as separate kingdoms. It was the imperial form of government which ceased; the one head wounded to death. What we have prophetically in Rev. 13:3 is the restoration of the imperial form as such, though over a federated empire of ten kingdoms; the "head" is "healed," i.e. restored; there is an emperor again—the Beast.[14]

This would suggest that the thing that caused the world to wonder was the rise to power of an absolute monarch over the ten kingdom federation who wielded absolute power. (4) This whole development is attributed to satanic power (Rev. 13:4). As the Roman empire had been the agency through which Satan attacked Christ at His first advent, that empire in its final

[14] Scofield, *op. cit.,* p. 1342.

form will be the agency through which Satan works against the Messiah at His second advent.

D. *Revelation 17:8-14.* Another important passage which deals with the final form of Gentile world power presents several important considerations. (1) John seems to be giving the seat of authority in the end time (Rev. 17:9) since Rome is the "seven-hilled city." (2) The final form of Gentile power resides in an individual called an "eighth" king, who comes into authority over that kingdom ruled by the previous seven (Rev. 17:10-11). This eighth is variously interpreted. There is the view of Scott, who writes:

> The seven heads on the Beast represent seven successive forms of government from the rise of the fourth universal empire on through its history till its end.
>
> "Five have fallen." These are Kings, Consuls, Dictators, Decemvirs, and Military Tribunes."
>
> "One is." This is the sixth, or imperial form of government set up by Julius Caesar, and under which John was banished to Patmos under Domitian. The previous forms of authority had ceased. . . .
>
> "The other has not yet come." Thus between the dissolution of the empire and its future diabolic reappearance, many centuries have elapsed. . . . This is the seventh head. It is the rise of the fallen empire under new conditions as presented in chap. xiii. 1. . . .
>
> "And the beast that was and is not, he also is an eighth, and is of the seven." The gigantic confederation of Rome is here regarded in its essential features as ever the same. He is an "eighth."[15]

Thus the different forms of government are here in view. A second view is the view that these seven are seven historical Roman emperors, five of whom have already died, one under whom John lived, and one that shall come, in whose line the eighth, the Beast, will come.[16] A third view is the view that these eight represent the eight empires that have had dealings with Israel, all of whom will come to culmination in the Beast. Aldrich writes:

> . . . seven great kingdoms are meant. The belief is that John

[15] Walter Scott, *Exposition of the Revelation of Jesus Christ*, pp. 351-52.
[16] William R. Newell, *The Revelation*, p. 271.

> here goes back farther than the prophecy of Daniel and includes all the great empires that have stood as enemies of God's people. The five kingdoms which have fallen would be Egypt, Assyria, Babylon, Persia, and Greece. The sixth was the empire in authority when John wrote. . . . The sixth kingdom in Revelation is the Roman Empire and that means that the seventh (with its related eighth head) is just another form or stage of that empire.[17]

Whichever of these views is adopted, it will be evident that the final ruler is the heir to all Gentile authority that previously existed. Gentile world power reaches its final peak in him. (3) There will be a federation of ten separate kings, which will bring their kingdoms under the authority of the head of the empire (Rev. 17:12). (4) The empire is not built by force, but by mutual consent (Rev. 17:13). (5) The course of this fourth world empire is given in Revelation 17:8. "The Beast which thou sawest was, and is not; and shall ascend out of the bottomless pit, and go into perdition." "Was" describes the empire in the period of its impotency. "Shall ascend out of the abyss" shows the coming form of the empire. "Goes into perdition" depicts its future destruction. (6) The one particular object of the hatred of the last form of Gentile world power is Jesus Christ. "These shall make war with the Lamb" (Rev. 17:14). The godlessness of the world powers, who seek world dominion, manifests itself in animosity against the One to whom all dominion has been given (Phil 2:9-10; Rev. 19:16).

III. The Boundaries of the Last Form of the Roman Empire

It has commonly been held that the last stages of the Roman Empire, geographically, will coincide exactly with the boundaries of the Roman Empire in its former state. This is based on the view that the Roman Empire came into its ten-toed, tenhorn stage at the time of the fall of Rome in 476 A.D. Thus, according to this view, the revived form of the empire will be identical to the former dimensions. There seem to be good reasons for holding the view that the final future boundaries of the last Gentile world power need not coincide with the former boundaries, but, in fact, may exceed them greatly.

---

[17] Roy L. Aldrich, "Facts and Theories of Prophecy," pp. 120-21.

(1) As has already been suggested, the ten kingdom federation was not fulfilled in the fall of Rome, but awaits the last days before it reaches this state. Since this ten kingdom federation is yet future, and has never existed historically, it would not be possible for the future ten kingdoms to conform to any historical boundaries. These ten kingdoms are only the outgrowth from the former stage of development, not the revival of that exact former condition. (2) Scripture seems to indicate an empire of even greater dimensions than Rome has held up to the present. ". . . power was given him over all kindreds, and tongues, and nations" (Rev. 13:7). In addition, in Revelation 13:2 this beast is seen to be the successor to the three preceding empires. This may suggest not only the idea of power, but also geographical extent, so that this final form of Gentile power may encompass all the territory held by all the predecessors. (3) The relationship existing between the Beast and the Woman (Rev. 17) suggests the scope of the empire. Jennings presents this when he writes:

> . . . the Scriptures tell us unequivocally that the World-Empire that Rome once possessed will again be restored to her, and my purpose . . . is to gather such light as it has pleased the God of all grace to give in His word, as to the extent and limitations of that revived imperial world power . . . the future Empire was assumed to have precisely the same geographical boundaries . . . as at that time. . . . This I take to have been a fundamental mistake, for it ignores completely the introduction of another, and that a basic and characteristic element, into the earth. Mere geographic boundaries are but little in accord with the peculiarly *spiritual* character of this era; the introduction of a distinct *spiritual* element, demands even for earthly boundaries, a *spiritual* measurement. . . .
>
> Turning then to the seventeenth chapter of the book of the Revelation, we see the whole stage filled with two personalities only: a "Beast" and a "Woman" . . . these two . . . picture . . . the future prophetic earth . . . there can be no argument or discussion as to this speaking of both the Civil and Ecclesiastical conditions that will rule and characterize that part of the earth that is within the limits or boundaries of Prophecy. The whole of it will be filled with what shall answer to this "Beast" and this "Woman." The two are thus indissolubly co-related, and tell us to what end all . . . are trending; and that is that there will eventually be one World-Empire and one World-Church, and these will cover the whole of what is now called Christendom; the one

> Empire supporting the one Church, and the "Beast" in the Scripture supports the "Woman," and the "Woman" is supported by the "Beast." [Rev. 17:3]. So that wherever one of those may be, there will inevitably the other be, too, and the boundaries of the one inevitably mark the boundaries of the other. . . .
>
> . . . we are compelled to see that the boundaries of the Empire will be the boundaries of the professed, but utterly apostate Christianity; and *vice-versa* the boundaries of the apostate Church will be exactly co-terminous with those of the Empire. But that being assured and clear, it follows beyond all question, that the revived Roman Empire will include . . . every country everywhere in which there is any claim to apostate Christianity at all, and so, will include North and South America.[18]

IV. The Powers Aligned Against the Roman Empire in the Last Days

As each of the four successive powers had enemies who contested their right to rule, so, at the time of the end of Gentile world power, there will be kingdoms and federations of nations who contest the authority of the Roman Empire.

A. *The northern confederacy.* The first power arrayed against the authority of the Beast and his armies, the Roman empire, is the great northern confederacy. This confederacy is described in Ezekiel 38:1—39:25 (cf. 38:15; 39:2); Daniel 11:40; Joel 2:1-27 (cf. 2:20); Isaiah 10:12; 30:31-33; 31:8-9.

The principal passage describing this confederacy is found in Ezekiel 38:2-6. The problem here is to identify Gog and Magog, together with those nations allied with them. The problem is somewhat clarified by the corrected reading of the Revised Version, "Son of man, set thy face toward Gog, the land of Magog, the prince of Rosh, Meshech, and Tubal." Concerning the "chief prince" or the "prince of Rosh" (R.V.), Kelly says:

> It is true that . . . [Rosh], when the context requires it to be a common appellative, means "head" or "chief"; but it is this sense which in the present instance brings in confusion. There can be no doubt therefore that it must be taken as a proper name, and here not of a man as in Genesis xxvi. 2, if the common reading stand, but of a race. This at once furnishes a suitable sense, which is strengthened by the term which precedes it,

---

[18] F. C. Jennings, "The Boundaries of the Revived Roman Empire," *Our Hope*, xlvii: 387-89, December, 1940.

> as well as by those that follow. . . . Meshech and Tubal fix . . . [Rosh] as meaning a Gentilic name [Rosh].[19]

The Prince of Rosh is called Gog in Ezekiel 38:3. It is to be understood that Gog is the name given to the leader of this confederacy and his land is called Magog, which is composed of three parts: Rosh, Meshech and Tubal. Concerning these names Gaebelein says:

> We know from Genesis x:2 that Magog was the second son of Japheth. Gomer, Tubal and Meshech were also sons of Japheth; Togarmah was a grandson of Japheth, being the third son of Gomer. Magog's land was located in, what is called today, the Caucasus and the adjoining steppes. And the three Rosh, Meshech and Tubal were called by the ancients Scythians. They roamed as nomads in the country around and north of the Black and the Caspian Seas, and were known as the wildest barbarians . . . . Careful research has established the fact that . . . Rosh is Russia. . . . The prince of Rosh, means, therefore, the prince or king of the Russian empire.[20]

Bauman traces the identification more in detail. He writes:

> Magog was the second son of Japheth (Gen. 10: 1, 2), one of the three sons of Noah. Before the dawn of secular history his descendants seem to have inhabited exclusively the region of the Caucasus and of northern Armenia. . . . It is interesting to note that the very word "Caucasus" means "Gog's fort." . . .
>
> Josephus . . . said: "Magog founded those that from him were named Magogites, but who by the Greeks were called Scythians." . . . The Scythians themselves have a tradition that their ancestors originally came forth from Araxes, in Armenia. This concurs with the divine record which places the immediate descendants of Noah in Armenia. Historically speaking the Scythians (Magogites) must have emigrated northward in very early times. Historians agree that the Magogites were divided into two distinct races, one Japhetic, or European, the other Turanian, or Asiatic.
>
> The Japhetic race comprised those whom the Greeks and Romans called Sarmatians, but who, in modern times, are called Slavs or Russians. The Sarmatians were a mixture of Medes and Scythians who coalesced and emigrated in small bands into the region of the Black Sea and extending from the Baltic to the Ural mountains.

---

19 William Kelly, *Notes on Ezekiel*, pp. 192-93.
20 Arno C. Gaebelein, *The Prophet Ezekiel*, pp. 257-58.

> The Turanian race comprised those Asiatic Magogites (Scythians) who dwelt upon the great plateau of Central Asia. . . . Today their descendants are known as Tartars, Cossacks, Finns, Kalmuks, and Mongols.
>
> . . . If modern lexicographers are consulted as to what nation now represents "Rosh," nearly all of them, together with most expositors, say Russia.
>
> . . . Gesenius, whose Hebrew Lexicon has never been superseded, says that "Gog" is "undoubtedly the Russians." He declared that "Rosh" was a designation for the tribes then north of the Taurus mountains, dwelling in the neighborhood of the Volga, and he held that in this name and tribe we have the first trace in history of the "Russ" or Russian nation. Gesenius also identified "Meshech" as Moscow, the capital of modern Russia in Europe. "Tubal" he identified as Tobolsk, the earliest province of Asiatic Russia to be colonized, and, also, the name of the city wherein Peter the Great built the old fortress after the pattern of the Kremlin at Moscow. *Moscow* bespeaks *Russia in Europe,* and *Tobolsk* bespeaks *Russia in Asia.*
>
> . . . the *Biblical and Theological Dictionary.* Therein do we read: "Magog signifies the country or people, and Gog the king of that country; the general name of the northern nations of Europe and Asia, or the districts north of the Caucasus of Mount Taurus" (Pg. 417).
>
> *The New Schaff-Herzog Encyclopedia of Religious Knowledge* has this to say: "A stricter geographical location would place Magog's dwelling between Armenia and Media, perhaps on the shores of the Araxes. But the people seem to have extended farther north across the Caucasus, filling there the extreme northern horizon of the Hebrews (Ezek. xxxviii. 15, xxxix. 2). This is the way Meshech and Tubal are often mentioned in the Assyrian inscriptions (*Mushku* and *Tabal,* Gk. *Moschoi* and *Tibarenoi*)" (Vo. V. Pg. 14).[21]

Thus the identification of Rosh as modern Russia would seem to be well authenticated and generally accepted.

It was predicted that allied with Magog there would be "many peoples with thee" (Ezek. 38:15). The marginal reading adopted by the revisers in Ezekiel 38:7, "Be thou a commander unto them" indicates the place of prominence which will be Russia's in that day. The first nation federated with Russia will be *Persia* (Ezek. 38:5). This has reference to the

---

21 Louis Bauman, *Russian Events in the Light of Bible Prophecy,* pp. 23-25.

ancient domain of Persia, now known as Iran. The second ally is called *Ethiopia.* This name is used in Scripture nine times, according to Young's concordance, to refer to the area in Africa, and eleven times to refer to the land of Cush, a portion of Arabia. The *New Schaff-Herzog Encyclopedia of Religious Knowledge* defines "Cush" as follows:

> A tribal and place name appearing frequently in the Old Testament, in the versions generally rendered "Ethiopia," and until recently supposed always to refer to a region south of Egypt. Since the decipherment of the cuneiform inscriptions, and a more thorough examination of the historical inscriptions of Assyria, Babylonia, and Arabia, it has been discovered that the form may represent two other regions and peoples: (1) the inhabitants of a region east of central Babylonia, who were known as Kasshites or Kosshites (Gr. Kossaioi) and ruled Babylonia between the seventeenth and twelfth centuries B. C. . . . (2) a land and people in northern Arabia.[22]

The conclusion of Bauman is:

> Since Ezekiel says of Gog: *"Thou shalt come from thy place out of the uttermost parts of the north,* thou, and many people with thee" (38:15); and since "Cush" is one of the "many peoples" named as coming with Gog from out of "the uttermost parts of the north," it is quite evident that the "Cush" in Ezekiel's prophecy was not the "Ethiopia" of Africa but a country that was somewhere contiguous to Persia."[23]

The third mentioned ally is Libya or *Put.* Although this is usually identified with the Libya in Africa, Bauman observes:

> . . . if the Libya of Africa . . . is in view here, then to join the forces of Gog the army of Libya would have to march directly through the lands where all the forces hostile to Gog will be marshalled—a mighty and an innumerable host. The army would have to march eastward through Egypt, up through Arabia, on through Palestine into the land of Gog, and then turn around and march back again with Gog into the land of Palestine to battle with the mighty enemies Gog must meet! . . .
>
> If John D. Davis, in his *Dictionary of the Bible,* is right, and "Put" lay south or southeast of "Cush," and the "Cush" of the prophecy is adjacent to Persia, may we not look for the people of "Put," . . . to sally forth from that same part of the earth out

---

[22] Samuel Macauley Jackson, ed., *New Schaff-Hertzog Encyclopedia of Religious Knowledge,* III, 328.

[23] Bauman, *op. cit.,* p. 31.

> of which will come all the rest of the nations who may be joined together in the great "North-Eastern Confederacy"?[24]

Thus Put may be located as adjacent to Persia or Iran.

The fourth ally mentioned is *Gomer.* There seems to be evidence to support the view that this refers to modern Germany. Gaebelein says:

> Valuable information is given in the Talmud; Gomer is there stated to be the Germani, the Germans. That the descendants of Gomer moved northward and established themselves in parts of Germany seems to be an established fact.[25]

This identification is supported by most all commentators and historians.[26]

The fifth ally of Russia is said to be *Togarmah.* This is generally identified as Turkey or Armenia, although it is extended by some to include central Asia. Of this people Rimmer writes:

> Geographically, Togarmah has always been the land which we now call Armenia. It is so named in the records of Assyria. I feel sure that no informed person would be inclined to dispute this particular identification, as the Assyrian chronicles are amply aided by such ancient writers as Tacitus. Indeed, all Armenian literature refers to the land and its people as "The House of Togarmah," and they hold an unbroken tradition which antedates their literature by centuries, linking them to the grandson of Japheth.[27]

Bauman adds:

> Togarmah, probably the Turkoman tribes of Central Asia, together with Siberia, the Turks and the Armenias.
>
> Togarmah and all his hordes . . . can scarcely be other than the great Siberian tribes that stretch along the north of Asia to the Pacific Ocean.[28]

How far this people extends beyond Turkey or Armenia can not be positively determined, but it could include Asiatic peoples federated with Russia.

---

[24] *Ibid.*, p. 32.
[25] Gaebelein, *op. cit.*, p. 259.
[26] Cf. Bauman, *op. cit.*, pp. 34-36.
[27] Harry Rimmer, *The Coming War and the Rise of Russia*, p. 62.
[28] Bauman, *op. cit.*, p. 38.

From the prophecy in Ezekiel it is learned that there will be a great confederacy, known as the northern confederacy under the leadership of one who arises in the land of Magog—Russia. Allied with Russia will be Iran (Persia) certain Arab states (Put or Ethiopia), Germany, and some Asiatic peoples known as Togarmah, which may include an extensive coalition of Asiatic powers. That this is not an exhaustive list is seen from Ezekiel 38:6, "and many people with thee." This prophecy anticipates an extensive alliance of powers along with Russia that will resist Israel and the Roman empire in the last days.

B. *The Kings of the East.* According to Revelation 16:12, Palestine, which will have become the center of the activity of the Roman leader and his armies, will be invaded by a great army coming from beyond the Euphrates known as the forces of "the kings of the east." This represents a second great alliance of powers that challenges the authority of the Beast. Concerning the passage in Revelation Scott writes:

> The Euphrates formed the limit in the east of Roman conquest, and the eastern boundary of enlarged Palestine in the future. It has ever stood as a geographical barrier—a natural separating bulwark between the west and the east. . . . The barrier is removed by this act of judgment, so that the eastern nations can more readily pour their armies into Canaan.
>
> . . . the reason of divine judgment on the river is "*that* the way of the kings *from* (not "*of*" as in the A.V.) the rising of the sun might be prepared . . . it is not the king *of* the east, but *from* the east—peoples on the eastern side of the Euphrates—that are in question.[29]

It can thus be concluded that the second great opposing Gentile force will be that composed of the coalition of nations in Asia, who unite against the threat of world-wide dominion by the head of the Roman empire.

C. *The King of the South.* A third power in conflict with the Roman empire is the King of the South, mentioned in Daniel 11:40. This power advances on Palestine and sets off a movement of nations that brings about its destruction. Evidently this King of the South is allied with the King of the North, for

[29] Scott, *op. cit.*, pp. 331-32.

they simultaneously invade Palestine (Dan. 11:40). There is general agreement among interpreters that the King of the South has reference to Egypt, inasmuch as Egypt is frequently referred to as the land to the south in Scripture.

In studying the alignments of Gentile nations at the time of the tribulation period we find there will be: (1) a ten kingdom federation of nations that has become the final form of the fourth kingdom or the Roman empire under the leadership of the Beast (Rev. 13:1-10); (2) a northern confederacy, Russia and her allies; (3) an eastern or Asiatic confederacy; and (4) a north African power. The movements of these four allied powers against Palestine in the tribulation period are clearly stated in Scripture and constitute one of the major themes of prophecy.

V. The Person and Ministry of the Beast, the Head of the Empire

Scripture has a great deal to say concerning the individual who will appear in the end time as the head of the Gentile powers in their ten kingdom federation. His person and work are presented in Ezekiel 28:1-10; Daniel 7:7-8, 20-26; 8:23-25; 9:26-27; 11:36-45; 2 Thessalonians 2:3-10; Revelation 13:1-10; 17:8-14. A synthesis of the truths in these passages will reveal the following facts concerning his activities: (1) He will appear on the scene in the "latter times" of Israel's history (Dan. 8:23). (2) He will not appear until the Day of the Lord has begun (2 Thess. 2:2). (3) His manifestation is being hindered by the Restrainer (2 Thess. 2:6-7). (4) This appearance will be preceded by a departure (2 Thess. 2:3), which may be interpreted either as a departure from the faith or a departure of the saints to be with the Lord (2 Thess. 2:1). (5) He is a Gentile. Since he arises from the sea (Rev. 13:1) and since the sea depicts the Gentile nations (Rev. 17:15), he must be of Gentile origin. (6) He rises from the Roman empire, since he is a ruler of the people who destroyed Jerusalem (Dan. 9:26). (7) He is the head of the last form of Gentile world dominion, for he is like a leopard, a bear, and a lion (Rev. 13:1). (Cf. Dan. 7:7-8, 20,24; Rev. 17:9-11.) As such he is a political leader. The seven heads and ten horns (Rev. 13:1; 17:12) are federated under his authority. (8) His influence is world wide, for he rules over all nations (Rev. 13:8). This influence comes through the alliance which he makes with other nations (Dan. 8:24; Rev. 17:12). (9) He has eliminated three rulers in his rise to power (Dan 7:8, 24). One of the kingdoms over which he has authority has been revived, for one of the heads, representing a kingdom or king (Rev. 17:10), has been healed (Rev. 13:3). (10) His rise comes through his peace program (Dan. 8:25). (11) He personally is marked by his intelligence and persuasiveness (Dan. 7:8, 20; 8:23) and also by his subtlety and craft (Ezek. 28:6), so that his position over the nations is by their own consent (Rev. 17:13). (12) He rules over the nations in his federation with absolute authority (Dan. 11:36), where he is depicted as doing his own will. This authority is manifested through the change in laws and customs (Dan. 7:25). (13) His chief interest is in might and power (Dan. 11:38). (14) As the head of the federated empire he makes a seven year covenant with Israel (Dan. 9:27), which is broken after three and one-half years (Dan. 9:27). (15) He introduces an idolatrous worship (Dan. 9:27) in which he sets himself up as god (Dan. 11: 36-37; 2 Thess. 2:4; Rev. 13:5). (16) He bears the characterization of a blasphemer because of the assumption of deity (Ezek. 28:2; Dan. 7:25; Rev. 13:1, 5-6). (17) This one is energized by Satan (Ezek. 28: 9-12; Rev. 13:4), receives his authority from him, and is controlled by the pride of the devil (Ezek. 28:2; Dan. 8:25). (18) He is the head of Satan's lawless system (2 Thess. 2:3) and his claim to power and to deity is proved by signs wrought through satanic power (2 Thess. 2:9-19). (19) He is received as God and as ruler because of the blindness of the people (2 Thess. 2:11). (20) This ruler becomes the great adversary of Israel (Dan. 7:21, 25; 8:24; Rev. 13:7). (21) There will come an alliance against him (Ezek. 28:7; Dan. 11:40, 42) which will contest his authority. (22) In the ensuing conflict he will gain control over Palestine and adjacent territory (Dan. 11:42) and will make his headquarters in Jerusalem (Dan. 11:45). (23) This ruler, at the time of his rise to power, is elevated through the instrumentality of the harlot, the corrupt religious system, which consequently seeks to dominate him (Rev. 17:3). (24) This system is destroyed by the ruler so that he may rule unhindered (Rev. 17:16-17). (25) He becomes the special adversary of the Prince of Princes (Dan. 8:25), His program (2 Thess. 2:4; Rev. 17:14), and His people (Dan. 7:21, 25; 8:24; Rev. 13:7). (26) While he continues in power for seven years (Dan. 9:27), his satanic activity is confined to the last half of the tribulation period (Dan. 7:25; 9:27; 11:36; Rev. 13:5). (27) His rule will be terminated by a direct judgment from God (Ezek. 28:6; Dan. 7:22, 26; 8:25; 9:27; 11:45; Rev. 19:19-20). This judgment will take place as he is engaged in a military campaign in Palestine (Ezek. 28:8-9; Rev. 19:19), and he will be cast into the lake of fire (Rev. 19:20; Ezek. 28:10). (28) This judgment will take place at the second advent of Christ (2 Thess. 2:8; Dan. 7:22) and will constitute a manifestation of His Messianic authority (Rev. 11:15). (29) The kingdom over which he ruled will pass to the authority of the Messiah and will become the kingdom of the saints (Dan. 7:27).

Many names and titles are given to this individual in the Scriptures. Arthur W. Pink gives a list of names that are applicable to him:[30] The Bloody and Deceitful Man (Ps. 5:6), the Wicked One (Ps. 10:2-4), the Man of the Earth (Ps. 10:18), the Mighty Man (Ps. 52:1), the Enemy (Ps. 55:3), the Adversary Ps. 74:8-10), the Head of Many Countries (Ps. 111:6), the Violent Man (Ps. 140:1), the Assyrian (Isa. 10:5-12), the King of Babylon (Isa. 14:2), the Sun of the Morning (Isa. 14:12), the Spoiler (Isa. 16:4-5; Jer. 6:26), the Nail (Isa. 22:25), the Branch of the Terrible Ones (Isa. 25:5), the Profane Wicked Prince of Israel (Ezek. 21:25-27), the Little Horn (Dan. 7:8), the Prince that shall come (Dan. 9:26), the Vile Person (Dan. 11:21), the Wilful King (Dan. 11:36), the Idol Shepherd (Zech. 11:16-17), the Man of Sin (2 Thess. 2:3), the Son of Perdition (2 Thess. 2:3), the Lawless one (2 Thess. 2:8), the Antichrist (1 John 2:22), the Angel of the Bottomless Pit (Rev. 9:11), the Beast (Rev. 11:7; 13:1). To these could be added: the One Coming in His Own Name (John 5:43), the King of Fierce Countenance (Dan. 8:23), the Abomination of Desolation (Matt. 24:15), the Desolator (Dan. 9:27). It is thus possible to see how extensive the revelation concerning this individual is. It is not surprising, since

---

[30] Arthur W. Pink, *The Antichrist*, pp. 59-75.

this one is Satan's great masterpiece in the imitation of the program of God.

A. *Will the Beast be a resurrected individual?* On the basis of Revelation 13:3 and 17:8 many expositors have held that the Beast who will rule will gain a tremendous following because he has experienced death and resurrection at the hands of Satan. Some have held that the Beast will be the reincarnation of Nero. Others have insisted that he will be Judas restored to life.[31] Some have insisted that this will be a resurrected individual without attempting to identify him.[32] The question arises then as to whether this is a resurrected individual in whom the miracle of Christ's death and resurrection is imitated. Even though it is said that this one comes to power by satanic activity (Rev. 13:2), and is said to have a deadly wound that was healed (Rev. 13:3), and comes out of the abyss (Rev. 17:8) it seems best not to understand this as death and resurrection for several reasons. (1) In Revelation 13:3 and 17:8 the beast is explained as the composite kingdom. The reference to the healing seems to be the resurgence of power in the Gentile kingdom that had been dead for so long. (2) Satan is called the "angel of the bottomless pit" or the "abyss" in Revelation 9:11, so that Revelation 17:8 does not teach that the head of the empire arose out of the abyss, but rather that the empire itself was brought about "from the abyss" or by Satan. (3) The Scriptures reveal that men are brought out of the grave by the voice of the Son of God.

> Marvel not at this: for the hour is coming, in the which all that are in the graves shall hear his voice, And shall come forth; they that have done good, unto the resurrection of life; and they that have done evil, unto the resurrection of damnation [John 5:28-29].

Satan does not have the power to give life. Since Christ alone has the power of resurrection, Satan could not bring one back to life. (4) The wicked are not resurrected until the Great White Throne (Rev. 20:11-15). If a wicked one were resurrected at this point it would set aside God's divinely ordained program of resurrection. (5) Since all the references to this

---

31 Pink, *op. cit.*, pp. 50-55.

32 Newell, *op. cit.*, p. 186; Joseph Seiss, *The Apocalypse*, II, 397-400.

individual present him as a man, not as a supernatural being, it seems impossible to hold that he is a resurrected individual. It would be concluded that the Beast will not be a resurrected individual.

B. *The doom of the Beast.* It is strange that almost every passage that makes reference to the activities of the Beast also includes a notice of his final doom. It must occupy a large place in the program of God. His end is seen in Ezekiel 21:25-27; 28:7-10; Daniel 7:11, 27; 8:25; 9:27; 2 Thessalonians 2:8; Revelation 17:11; 19:20; 20:10. While the movements leading to his overthrow will be seen later, it is to be observed at this point that God is going to overthrow this satanic masterpiece of delusion and imitation violently. Pink writes:

> Scripture has solemnly recorded the end of various august evil personages. Some were overwhelmed by waters; some devoured by flames; some engulfed in the jaws of the earth; some stricken by a loathsome disease; some ignominiously slaughtered; some hanged; some eaten up of dogs; some consumed by worms. But to no sinful dweller on earth, save the Man of Sin, "the Wicked One," has been appointed the terrible distinction of being consumed by the brightness of the personal appearing of the Lord Jesus Himself. Such shall be his unprecedented doom, an end that shall fittingly climax his ignoble origin, his amazing career, and his unparalleled wickedness.[33]

VI. The Person and Ministry of the False Prophet, the Religious Leader

In close association with the Beast, the head of the federated empire, is another individual known as the "False Prophet" (Rev. 19:20; 20:10), called "the second beast" in Revelation 13:11-17, where his fullest description is given. In that passage of Scripture there are some important factors concerning him to be observed: (1) This individual is evidently a Jew, since he arises out of the earth, or land, that is Palestine (13:11); (2) he is influential in religious affairs (13:11, "two horns like a lamb"); (3) he is motivated by Satan as the first beast is (13:11); (4) he has a delegated authority (13:12, "the power of the first beast"); (5) he promotes the worship of the first beast

[33] Pink, *op. cit.*, pp. 119-20.

and compels the earth to worship the first beast as God (13:12); (6) his ministry is authenticated by the signs and miracles which he does, evidently proving that he is Elijah that was to come (13:13-14); (7) he is successful in deceiving the unbelieving world (13:14); (8) the worship promoted is an idolatrous worship (13:14-15); (9) he has the power of death to compel men to worship the beast (13:15); (10) he has authority in the economic realm to control all commerce (13:16-17); (11) he has a mark that will establish his identity for those who live in that day (13:18).

It will be observed that the Revelation, in relating the second beast to the first, presents him as subservient to the first. He is called "the false prophet" (Rev. 16:13; 19:20; 20:10), who ministers in connection with the first beast as his prophet or spokesman. We are presented, then, with a Satanic trinity, the unholy trinity, or the trinity of hell: the Dragon, the Beast, and the False Prophet (Rev. 16:13). That place occupied by God in His program is assumed by Satan, that place of Christ is assumed by the first Beast, that ministry of the Holy Spirit is discharged by the False Prophet.

VII. The Relation of Antichrist to the Two Beasts

The word *antichrist* appears only in the Epistles of John. It is used in 1 John 2:18, 22; 4:3 and 2 John 7. A study of these references will reveal that John is principally concerned with an immediate doctrinal error—the denial of the person of Christ. The emphasis is not on a future revelation of an individual, but rather on the present manifestation of false doctrine. To John antichrist was already present. The question arises then as to the relation between the "antichrist" of John's epistles and the beasts of Revelation.

The prefix *anti* may be used either in the sense of "instead of" or "against." Aldrich correctly observes:

> The solution of the problem of the identification of Antichrist would seem to depend upon whether light can be thrown on the question of whether he is primarily the great enemy of Christ or whether he is a false Christ.[34]

---

[34] Aldrich, *op. cit.*, p. 39.

That these possibilities exist is substantiated by Thayer, who says that the preposition has two primary usages: first, *over against or opposite to;* and second indicating an exchange, *instead of or in place of.*[35] A study of the five usages of antichrist in John's epistles seems clearly to indicate the idea of opposition rather than exchange. Trench observes:

> To me St. John's words seem decisive that resistance to Christ, and defiance of Him, this, and not any treacherous assumption of his character and offices, is the essential mark of the Anti-Christ; is that which, therefore, we should expect to find embodied in his name . . . and in this sense, if not all, yet many of the Fathers have understood the word.[36]

The word *antichrist* seems to be contrasted with "false Christ" in Scripture. This word is used in Matthew 24:24 and Mark 13:22. On the contrast between the words the same author says:

> The [*Pseudochristos,* false Christ] does not deny the being of a Christ; on the contrary, he builds on the world's expectations of such a person; only he appropriates these to himself, blasphemously affirms that he is the foretold One, in whom God's promises and men's expectations are fulfilled. . . .
>
> The distinction, then, is plain . . .[*antichristos,* antichrist] denies that there is a Christ; . . . [*Pseudochristos,* false Christ] affirms himself to be Christ.[37]

It would seem that John has the idea of opposition in mind rather than the idea of exchange. This idea of direct opposition to Christ seems to be the particular characterization of the first Beast, for he sets his kingdom against the kingdom of the Son of God. If antichrist must be identified with one of the two Beasts it would seem to be identified with the first.[38] It may be, however, that John is not referring to either of the two Beasts, but rather to the lawless system that will characterize them (2 Thess. 2:7). Since he is emphasizing the danger of a present doctrinal defection, he is reminding them that such teaching is the teaching of the antichrist philosophy of Satan that Paul held was already working (2 Thess. 2:7). Without

---

[35] Joseph Henry Thayer, *Greek-English Lexicon of the New Testament,* p. 49.
[36] Richard C. Trench, *Synonyms of the New Testament,* p. 107.
[37] *Ibid.,* p. 108.
[38] Cf. Newell, *op. cit.,* pp. 195-201 for arguments to support this view.

doubt this antichrist philosophy of Satan, referred to by John, will culminate in the Beasts in their corporate ministries, where the first Beast will be in direct opposition to Christ as one who falsely fulfills the covenant to give Israel their land and the second Beast will assume the place of leadership in the religious realm which rightly belongs to Christ. But John is not trying to identify either of these Beasts as antichrist, but to warn any who would deny the person of Christ that they are walking in that system which eventually would culminate in the manifestation of the lawless system in the activities of both Beasts. They, in their corporate unity, culminate lawlessness.

CHAPTER XX

THE CAMPAIGN OF ARMAGEDDON

The "kings of the earth and of the whole world" are to be gathered together through the activity of the trinity from hell to what is called "the battle of that great day of God Almighty" (Rev. 16:14). This confluence of the nations of the earth is in a place called Armageddon (Rev. 16:16). There God deals in judgment with the nations because of their persecution of Israel (Joel 3:2), because of their sinfulness (Rev. 19:15), and because of their godlessness (Rev. 16:9).

It has been held commonly that the battle of Armageddon is an isolated event transpiring just prior to the second advent of Christ to the earth. The extent of this great movement in which God deals with "the kings of the earth and of the whole world" (Rev. 16:14) will not be seen unless it is realized that the "battle of that great day of God Almighty" (Rev. 16:14) is not an isolated battle, but rather a campaign that extends over the last half of the tribulation period. The Greek word *polemos,* translated "battle" in Revelation 16:14, signifies a war or campaign, while *machē* signifies a battle, and sometimes even single combat. This distinction is observed by Trench,[1] and is followed by Thayer[2] and Vincent.[3] The use of the word *polemos* (campaign) in Revelation 16:14 would signify that the events that culminate in the gathering at Armageddon at the second advent are viewed by God as one connected campaign.

A. *The location of the campaign.* The hill of Megiddo, located west of the Jordan River in north central Palestine, some ten miles south of Nazareth and fifteen miles inland from the Mediterranean seacoast, was an extended plain on which many

---

1 Richard C. Trench, *New Testament Synonyms,* pp. 301-2.

2 Joseph Henry Thayer, *Greek-English Lexicon of the New Testament,* p. 528.

3 Marvin R. Vincent, *Word Studies in the New Testament,* II, 541.

of Israel's battles had been fought. There Deborah and Barak defeated the Canaanites (Judges 4 and 5). There Gideon triumphed over the Midianites (Judges 7). There Saul was slain in the battle with the Philistines (1 Sam. 31:8). There Ahaziah was slain by Jehu (2 Kings 9:27). And there Josiah was slain in the invasion by the Egyptians (2 Kings 23:29-30; 2 Chron. 35:22). Vincent says:

> Megiddo was in the plain of Esdraelon, "which has been a chosen place for encampment in every contest carried on in Palestine from the Days of Nabuchodonozor, king of Assyria, unto the disastrous march of Napoleon Bonaparte from Egypt into Syria. Jews, Gentiles, Saracens, Christian crusaders, and anti-Christian Frenchmen; Egyptians, Persians, Druses, Turks, and Arabs, warriors of every nation that is under heaven, have pitched their tents on the plains of Esdraelon, and have beheld the banners of their nation wet with the dews of Tabor and Hermon."[4]

There are several other geographical locations involved in this campaign. (1) Joel 3:2, 13 speaks of events taking place in "the valley of Jehoshaphat," which seems to be an extended area east of Jerusalem. Ezekiel 39:11 speaks of the "valley of the passengers," which may refer to the same area as the valley of Jehoshaphat inasmuch as that area was the travelled route going away from Jerusalem. (2) Isaiah 34 and 63 picture the Lord coming from Edom or Idumea, south of Jerusalem, when He returns from the judgment. (3) Jerusalem itself is seen to be the center of conflict (Zech. 12:2-11; 14:2). Thus the campaign is pictured as extending from the plains of Esdraelon on the north, down through Jerusalem, extending out to the valley of Jehoshaphat on the east and to Edom on the south. This wide area would cover the entire land of Palestine and this campaign, with all its parts, would confirm what Ezekiel pictures when he says the invaders will "cover the land" (Ezek. 38:9, 16). This area would conform to the extent pictured by John in Revelation 14:20. The conclusion of Sims is well taken:

> . . . it appears from Scripture that this last great battle of that great day of God Almighty will reach far beyond Armaged-

---

[4] *Ibid.*, II, 542-43.

> don, or the Valley of Megiddo. Armageddon appears to be mainly the place where the troops will gather together from the four corners of the earth, and from Armageddon the battle will spread out over the entire land of Palestine. Joel speaks of the last battle being fought in the Valley of Jehoshaphat, which is close by Jerusalem, and Isaiah shows Christ coming with blood-stained garments "from Edom," and Edom is south of Palestine. So the battle of Armageddon, it seems, will stretch from the Valley of Megiddo in the north of Palestine, through the Valley of Jehoshaphat, near Jerusalem, and on down to Edom at the extreme southern part of Palestine. And to this agree the words of the prophet Ezekiel that the armies of this great battle will "cover the land." The Book of Revelation also says the blood will flow to the bits of the horse bridles for 1,600 furlongs, and it has been pointed out that 1,600 furlongs covers the entire length of Palestine. But Jerusalem will no doubt be the center of interest during the battle of Armageddon, for God's Word says: "I will gather all nations against Jerusalem to battle."[5]

B. *The participants in the campaign.* The alignment of nations during the tribulation period has already been discussed. It was seen that there will be four great world powers: (1) the ten kingdom federation of nations under the Beast that constitutes the final form of the fourth great world empire; (2) the northern federation, Russia and her allies; (3) the Kings of the East, the Asiatic peoples from beyond the Euphrates; and (4) the King of the South, a north African power or powers. Another great power must be added, because of His active participation in the campaign; (5) the Lord and His armies from heaven. While the animosity of the first four is vented against each other and against Israel (Zech. 12:2-3; 14:2), it is particularly against the God of Israel that they fight (Ps. 2:2; Isa. 34:2; Zech. 14:3; Rev. 16:14; 17:14; 19:11, 14-15, 19, 21).

I. The Invasion by the Northern Confederacy

According to Daniel 9:26-27 the prince of the Roman empire will make a covenant with Israel for a seven year period. This covenant evidently restores Israel to a place among the nations of the world and the integrity of Israel is guaranteed by the Roman powers. This is not only an attempt to settle the long standing dispute among the nations as to Israel's claim to Pal-

---

[5] A. Sims, *The Coming War and the Rise of Russia*, p. 7.

estine, but is also a satanic imitation of the fulfillment of the Abrahamic covenant which gave Israel title deed to the land. This action is pictured by John (Rev. 6:2) as a rider going forth to conquer, to whom sovereignty is given by peaceful negotiations. This condition exists for three and one-half years, after which the covenant is broken by the Roman authorities and the period known as the great tribulation (Matt. 24:21) begins. This tribulation on the earth is evidently caused by Satan, who has been cast out of heaven into the earth at the middle of the tribulation period (Rev. 12:9). He goes forth in great wrath (Rev. 12:12) to attack the remnant of Israel and the saints of God (Rev. 12:17). The Satanic activity that moves nations in those days is clearly depicted by John when he says:

> And I saw three unclean spirits like frogs come out of the mouth of the dragon, and out of the mouth of the beast, and out of the mouth of the false prophet. For they are the spirits of devils, working miracles, which go forth unto the kings of the earth and of the whole world, to gather them to the battle of that great day of God Almighty [Rev. 16:13-14].

This is not to infer that this period is not the period of God's wrath upon sinful men, but it does show that God, to pour out His wrath, permits Satan to execute a program in his wrath against the whole world.

There are a number of theories as to the events in the campaign of Armageddon: (1) Armageddon will be a conflict between the Roman empire and the northern confederacy;[6] (2) it will be a conflict between the Roman empire and the kings of the east, or the Asiatic powers;[7] (3) Armageddon will be a conflict between all nations and God;[8] (4) it will be a conflict between four great world powers;[9] (5) it will be a conflict between the Roman empire, Russia, and the Asiatic powers;[10] (6) it will exclude Russia, but will take place between the Roman, eastern, and northern powers which will exclude Rus-

---

6 Cf. L. Sale-Harrison, *The Resurrection of the Old Roman Empire*, pp. 108-10.

7 Harry A. Ironside, *Lectures on Daniel the Prophet*, pp. 215-16.

8 William Pettingill, *God's Prophecies for Plain People*, pp. 109-10.

9 Alva J. McClain, *The Four Great Powers of the End Time*, p. 3.

10 Milton B. Lindberg, *Gog All Agog*, p. 31.

sia,[11] based on the theory that Ezekiel 38 and 39 takes place in the millennium; (7) Russia is the only aggressor at Armageddon,[12] based on the theory that there will be no revived form of the Roman empire. One can see what a wide divergence of opinion there is as to the chronology of events in this campaign.

The great movements of armies in the conflict of Armageddon begin with an invasion of Palestine by the King of the North and the King of the South (Dan. 11:40). The head of the Roman empire and the head of the Israeli state are so federated by the covenant (Dan. 9:27) that an attack against the one is an attack against the other. With this invasion the events of the campaign, which will shake the whole world, begin. This initial movement is described in Ezekiel 38:1—39:24.

The powers represented in this chapter have already been identified as Russia and her satellites. Therefore only the events need to be summarized. There is general agreement among Bible students concerning the outline of events. Russia is seen to make an alliance with Persia, Ethiopia, Libya, Germany and Turkey (vv. 2, 5, 6). Because Israel seems like easy prey (v. 11) this confederation decides to invade the land for a spoil (v. 12). A protest is made to this invasion (v. 13), but it is unheeded. The extent of this invasion must be learned from parallel passages, for Ezekiel omits the progress of the invasion, but, rather, describes the destruction of the invader on the mountains of Israel (39:2-4) as the result of divine intervention through a convulsion of nature (38:20-22). Seven months is consumed in disposing of the dead (39:12) and seven years in disposing of the debris (39:9-10). The scene of this destruction is said to be on the mountains of Israel (39:2-4) and the time is in "the latter years" (38:8) and "the latter days" (38:16). This destruction is a sign to the nations (38:23) and to Israel (39:21-24).

There are a number of considerations that make it clear that this invasion by Gog (Ezek. 38) is not the same as the battle of Armageddon (Rev. 16:16). (1) In the battle of Gog definite allies are mentioned, while in Armageddon all nations are

[11] W. W. Fereday, "Armageddon" *Our Hope,* xlvii:397-401. December, 1940.
[12] Harry Rimmer, *The Coming War and the Rise of Russia,* p. 27.

engaged (Joel 3:2; Zeph. 3:8; Zech. 12:3; 14:4). (2) Gog comes from the north (Ezek. 38:6, 15; 39:2), while at Armageddon the armies come from the whole earth. (3) Gog comes to take spoil (Ezek. 38:11-12), while at Armageddon the nations assemble to destroy the people of God. (4) There is protest against Gog's invasion (Ezek. 38:13), but at Armageddon there is no protest for all nations are joined against Jerusalem. (5) Gog is the head of the armies in his invasion (38:7 R.V.), but at Armageddon the Beast is the head of the invasion (Rev. 19:19). (6) Gog is overthrown by convulsions of nature (38:22), but the armies at Armageddon are destroyed by the sword that goes out of Christ's mouth (Rev. 19:15). (7) Gog's armies are arrayed in the open field (Ezek. 39:5), while at Armageddon they are seen in the city of Jerusalem (Zech. 14:2-4). (8) The Lord calls for assistance in executing judgment on Gog (Ezek. 38:21), while at Armageddon He is viewed as treading the winepress alone (Isa. 63:3-6).[13] Two diverse movements must then be acknowledged.

A. *Identification of the time in general.* The first problem to be settled is the problem of the time of this invasion.

1. This does not refer to a past event in Israel's history. It is obvious from the details given to us in the chapters before us that no invasion experienced in Israel's history is sufficient to be the fulfillment of this prophecy. There have been invasions in the past, which wrought hardship on the land and the people, but none that answer to the details presented here.

2. This can only refer to some future event in Israel's experience. There are a number of considerations which support this view.

a. The context in the book. Chapter thirty-seven deals with the restoration of the nation Israel to her land. This is pictured as a gradual process, for the prophet sees the process of bone being joined to bone, tied together with sinews, clothed with skin. It is a regathering in unbelief, for the prophet observes that there was no life in the assembled carcass (v. 8). Chapter forty carries us on to the millennial age. Thus the movements

[13] Cf. Louis Bauman, *Russian Events in the Light of Scripture*, pp. 180-84.

of Gog and Magog are seen, from the context, to transpire between the time of the beginning of the restoration of Israel to the land and the millennial age.

b. The specific statements in the passage. Twice a reference is made in chapter thirty-eight to a time element. It is said to take place "in the latter years" (v. 8) and "in the latter days" (v. 16). This has specific reference to the latter years and days of God's dealing with the nation Israel, which, since it is before the millennial age (ch. 40), must place it during God's dealing with Israel in the seventieth week of Daniel's prophecy.

c. It will be after the beginning of the restoration, for Israel is seen to be inhabiting their own land (38:11). This would indicate that it takes place after the covenant made by the "prince that shall come" of Daniel 9:27.

d. It will be connected with Israel's conversion, which is obviously future, for the destruction of the invader is a sign to that nation which opens their eyes to the Lord (39:22). Since the final removal of the blindness does not come to that nation until the second advent, this prophecy must have a definite relation to that event.

e. The indication that the land will be reforested (39:10) confirms this conclusion, for Israel has always been dependent on other sources of supply for her lumber.[14]

It is our conclusion, then, from the passage itself, that the events herein described must take place in the future, at a time when God is again dealing with Israel as a nation.

B. *The time in relation to specific events.* The invasion described by Ezekiel has been related to nearly every major prophetic event as to its time. Some of these positions must be examined in order to determine as carefully as possible just when this event will transpire.

1. Some hold, first of all, the invasion takes place prior to the rapture of the church. Such is the position taken by David L. Cooper, who says:

---

[14] I Kings 5:1-10.

> . . . it is utterly impossible for one to locate the fulfillment of this prediction after the Millennial Age. It cannot be placed in the beginning of the Millennium, nor at the end of the tribulation. It must, therefore, be located before the tribulation because there is no other place for it to occur since the three other suggested dates are impossible.
>
> . . . there will be a time between now and the beginning of the tribulation when the Jews will be dwelling in the Land in unwalled cities and will be at rest.[15]

This seems to be an impossible thesis from several considerations. (1) The New Testament teaching of the imminence of the rapture makes it impossible that an event such as this must first be fulfilled. (2) The context of the prophecy itself states that this will take place "in the latter years" (v. 8) and "in the latter days" (v. 16). Since this prophecy is addressed to Israel it must be their years and days being referred to in the prophecy. Since Israel and the church are two distinct groups with which God is dealing, it is impossible to make Israel's latter years apply to the latter years of the church as it would do if this is fulfilled prior to the rapture. (3) As far as can be determined Israel will not gain any title to the land, nor have the right to return to it, until the "prince that shall come" makes a covenant with her (Dan. 9:27). Israel is said to be out of the land and Jerusalem trodden down until the time of the Gentiles be fulfilled (Luke 21:24). It would be necessary, according to this theory, to maintain either that the covenant which gives Israel a false peace was made prior to the rapture, or that the times of the Gentiles ends at the rapture. Such is not the presentation of the Word.

2. Others teach, secondly, that the invasion takes place at the end of the tribulation. There are many Bible students who adopt this interpretation of the time element.[16] However there seem to be difficulties in this position which make it impossible to accept it. (1) The passage in Ezekiel does not mention a battle. The destruction there is at the hand of the Lord through the convulsion of nature (38:20-23). Even though the sword of verse 21 should be proven to be a nation, yet the Lord is seen

---

15 David L. Cooper, *When Gog's Armies Meet the Almighty*, pp. 80-81.
16 Cf. Bauman, *op. cit.*, pp. 174-75.

to be the agent in this destruction rather than a destruction through a war. In the conflagration of Armageddon there is a great battle fought between the Lord and His hosts and the assembled nations, in which the King of Kings emerges as the victor. (2) In Ezekiel the invasion is by the king of the north with his allies, which are limited in number. In Zechariah 14 and Revelation 19 all the nations of the earth are seen to be gathered together for the conflagration. (3) In Ezekiel the destruction takes place on the mountains of Israel (39:2-4). The events of Armageddon are said to take place at Jerusalem (Zech. 12:2; 14:2), at the valley of Jehoshaphat (Joel 3:12) and Edom (Isa. 63:1). (4) In Ezekiel Israel is said to be dwelling in her land in peace and safey (38:11). We know from Revelation 12:14-17 that Israel is not going to dwell in the land in peace and safety during the latter half of the seventieth week, but will be the special target of Satan's attack.

Thus it is concluded that the invasion can not be identified as the events of Zechariah 14 and Revelation 19 at the end of the tribulation.

3. Still others hold that the invasion takes place at the beginning of the millennium. This view is presented by Arno C. Gaebelein, who says:

> At what time does this invasion take place? We find the answer in the text. The statement is made in verse eight that Gog and Magog and the other nations with them invade the land "that is brought back from the sword, and is gathered out of many people"; they come "against the mountains of Israel . . ." In verse eleven the evil purpose of the invader is made known. . . . From all this we learn that the invasion takes place at the time when the Lord has brought back His people and resumed His relationship with the remnant of Israel.
>
> The invasion will happen some time after the beastly empire with its beasthead . . . and the false prophet, the personal Anti-christ . . . have been dealt with in judgment.
>
> . . . Micah tells us: "And this man (Christ) shall be the peace when the Assyrian shall come into the land" (verse 5). All this confirms the story of Ezekiel xxxviii.[17]

While the Scriptures cited may seem to prove the thesis stated above, there are arguments which prove this is an im-

[17] Arno C. Gaebelein, *The Prophet Ezekiel*, pp. 252-55.

possible explanation. (1) Ezekiel tells us that the land will be defiled by reason of the dead bodies for seven months (39:12). Such a picture seems impossible in view of the cleansing to be effected by the return of the Messiah. (2) In Jeremiah 25:32-33 it is stated that the Lord will destroy all the wicked of the earth at His return. This is further amplified in Revelation 19:15-18. It seems impossible to think of such a horde as described in Ezekiel escaping the destruction at His coming to rise up against Him shortly. (3) In Matthew 25:31-46 all Gentiles are brought before the Judge to determine who will enter the millennium. Since no unsaved person, whether Jew or Gentile, will enter that kingdom, it is impossible to think of such an apostasy of saved persons who would fulfill the prophecy of Ezekiel. (4) Isaiah 9:4-5 predicts the destruction of all weapons of war after the millennium begins. Where would the armies of the King of the North secure their armament in the light of this prediction? (5) Isaiah 2:1-4 states that wars will cease with the advent of Christ and the institution of the millennium. (6) According to Revelation 20:1-3 Satan will be bound at the beginning of the millennium and thus would not be operative to generate such a movement against Israel. (7) God is beginning to deal with the nation Israel at the beginning of the seventieth week after the translation of the church. That nation is being brought back into her land (Ezek. 38:11; 37:1-28), although in unbelief, to prepare that nation, through discipline, for the coming Messiah. Thus Micah may rightly say that "this man (Christ) shall be the peace, when the Assyrian shall come into our land" (5:5), even though these events take place before the second advent of Christ. Micah's prophecy does not make the visible presence of Christ necessary, but does promise His protection.

4. Still others teach that the invasion takes place at the end of the millennium. Those who hold to this position contend that the Gog and Magog of Ezekiel and that of Revelation 20:8 are the same. This seems to be an impossibility from the following considerations: (1) Ezekiel mentions only a northern coalition as being engaged in the invasion. In Revelation all the nations of the earth are gathered together. (2) In Ezekiel there is no specific mention made of the instrumentality of Sa-

tan, nor of his being bound for a thousand years prior to this invasion, while both things are emphasized in the Revelation account. (3) The context in Ezekiel shows that this invasion is before the institution of the millennium. In Revelation the millennium has been in existence for a thousand years. (4) In Ezekiel the bodies of the slain require the labor of seven months to dispose of the dead (39:12). In Revelation 20:9 the slain are said to be "devoured" by fire so that no disposal is necessary. (5) In Ezekiel the invasion is seen to be followed by the millennium (ch. 40-48). In Revelation this movement is followed by the new heaven and the new earth. Certainly the new earth could not conceivably be corrupted by unburied corpses for seven months.

Thus, these considerations make it impossible to accept this theory as to the time of the invasion.

5. Finally, it is suggested the invasion takes place at the middle of the seventieth week. There seem to be several considerations that may indicate that it is the invasion of the land of Palestine by the king of the North in the middle of the week that sets off the satanic attack against the people with whom God is dealing, the nation Israel, as recorded in Revelation 12:14-17.

a. The invasion takes place at a time when Israel is dwelling in their own land (Ezek. 38:8). There is no indication that Israel will be entitled to occupy their own land until the time of the covenant by the "prince that shall come" of Daniel 9:27. Evidently that one, because of the authority invested in him as the head of the revived Roman Empire, seeks to settle the Arab-Israeli dispute by giving Israel the right to occupy the land. The invasion will come some time after this covenant is confirmed.

b. The invasion takes place when Israel is dwelling in peace in the land (Ezekiel 38:11). Those who believe that this invasion takes place at the beginning of the millennium interpret this peace as the peace promised by the Messiah. There is nothing in the text here to indicate that this is the true Messianic peace. It rather seems to be the false peace that has been guaranteed Israel by the covenant, which is called "your agreement with hell" in Isaiah 28:18. Israel, as yet, is in unbelief, for the nation will not be a believing nation until after the second advent of Christ. This regathering is described in Ezekiel 37 and the lifeless condition of the nation is clearly indicated in verse eight. Israel could not be said to be at peace at the end of the tribulation period, for the land has been destroyed by invasion (Zech. 14:1-3) and the people scattered (Zech. 13:8-9). Yet, the nation could be dwelling in relative peace in the land in the first half of the week. Cooper says: "It is altogether possible that the first judgments of the tribulation may not affect Palestine so as to destroy the beauty and prosperity of the land."[18]

c. Ezekiel uses two expressions in chapter thirty-eight which may give an indication as to the time of this invasion. In verse eight there appears the expression "latter years" and in verse sixteen is the "latter days" of Israel's history. This, of course, can have no reference to the "latter days" of the church age, for God is dealing with Israel in His divine economy at this time.

There are several similar expressions used which may need clarification at this point. The term *last day* is an expression which is related to the resurrection and judgment program (John 6:39-40, 44, 54; 11:24; 12:48). The term *last days* is related to the time of Israel's glorification, salvation, and blessing in the kingdom age (Isa. 2:2-4; Micah 4:1-7). The term *latter days* or *latter years* is related to the time prior to the *last days* or the millennial age, which would be the tribulation period. In Deuteronomy 4:27 Moses predicts a scattering because of unfaithfulness but promises a restoration. In verse 30 he says: "When thou art in tribulation, and all these things are come upon thee, even in the latter days. . . ." Here the "latter days" are linked with tribulation. In Daniel 2:28 the prophet reveals "what shall be in the latter days" and then carries the kingdom down to the final form of Gentile world power in the 70th week. Again in Daniel 8:19, 23 in discussing the "indignation" the prophet speaks of the "latter time of their kingdom." Again in Daniel 10:14 the term "latter days" is used in reference to the events preceding the millennial age.

---

[18] Cooper, *op. cit.*, p. 84.

The conclusion, then, since Ezekiel uses these expressions, is that the events described by that prophet must take place within the 70th week. Daniel 11:40 seems to have reference to the same period, for the prophet places these events "at the time of the end." This expression seems to separate the event from "the end" itself.

d. Many commentators interpret Daniel 11:41 with reference to the occupation of the land of Palestine by the Beast. The event that causes the Beast to move in is the invasion of Palestine from the north by the King of the North (Dan. 11:40). The covenant made by the Beast (Dan. 9:27) has evidently guaranteed Israel an inviolate right to the land. Some event must be necessary to cause the Beast to abrogate his covenant. Since the covenant is said to be broken in the middle of the week (Dan. 9:27) and the invasion from the north is seen to be the cause of the breaking of the covenant (Dan. 11:41) it may be concluded that this invasion takes place in the middle of the week.

e. It is recognized that the events of the last half of the week are occasioned by the casting of Satan out of heaven (Rev. 12:7-13). Evidently Satan's first act in opposition to Israel is to move the King of the North to this invasion. This is the beginning of a great campaign which begins in the middle of the week and is continued until the destruction of Gentile powers at the return of the Lord. It has been noted that the word translated "battle" in Revelation 16:14, according to Thayer's lexicon, would better be translated "campaign," for this signifies the movements of armies and is in contrast to an isolated battle. The observation, then, is that God views all these movements of the armies as one great campaign, which will be terminated by their destruction at the return of Christ. The campaign, if this interpretation be correct, will be waged over a three and one-half year period.

f. In Isaiah 30:31-33; 31:8-9, and Micah 5:5 this invader from the north is called "the Assyrian." As Assyria was a rod in the hand of the Lord previously to punish Israel for their iniquity, so the Lord will take up a rod again for the same purpose. This coming scourge will bear the same name because of the identity of his mission, to chasten Israel. Isaiah 28:18 speaks of the "covenant with death" and the "agreement with hell" for which God will punish Israel. This must refer to the covenant of Daniel 9:27, when Israel seeks peace from the hands of men rather than from the hand of the Lord. For this covenant, Isaiah says, they will be punished "when the overflowing scourge shall pass through, then ye shall be trodden down by it." This scourge could hardly be the occupation by the Beast, for he was a party to the covenant, but must refer to the invasion by the "Assyrian" who will be used by the Lord to chasten Israel. The destruction of the Assyrian in the passages referred to seems to parallel the destruction of the armies of Gog in Ezekiel 38—39, and thus, are considered parallel references. God could not punish Israel for this false covenant until after the covenant had been made. This seems to give further cause to believe that the invasion takes place sometime in the middle of the week.

g. In Revelation 7:4-17 there is a description of a multitude of Jews and of Gentiles who are saved during the tribulation period. One wonders, in the face of the intense persecution against any believer, how any come to a knowledge of God in that time. In Ezekiel 38:23 it is revealed that the destruction of the armies of Gog is used as a sign to the nations and in 39:21 reference is made to this same fact again. In 39:22 the same event is a great sign to Israel. Since the book of Revelation pictures many people saved during the tribulation, and not just at the end of it, and since this event of Ezekiel's prophecy is used as a sign to bring many to the Lord, this event must have taken place before the end of the tribulation and at some time within that period. This destruction, so obviously by the hand of the Lord, is an event used by the Lord to remove some of the blindness to bring many to a knowledge of the Lord.

h. In Revelation 13:7 the Beast is pictured as having a world-wide power. This is true at the time of his manifestation as a world ruler in the middle of the tribulation. The question arises: "How could the Beast have world-wide power if the power of the northern confederation has not been broken?" The fact that the Beast is in authority over the earth at the middle of the week lends support to the thesis that the King of the North has been destroyed. This destruction would produce a chaos in the world conditions, which would bring the nations together as is seen in Psalm 2, at which time the government would be formed over which the Beast is the head. Since there could be no unity of nations as long as the King of the North is operative, this unity must be brought about after his destruction.

i. In Revelation 19:20 we are told that the Lord will deal specifically with the Beast and the False Prophet at His coming. All through the Old Testament and continuing through the New there appear three personages who will play a part in the final drama of the "times of the Gentiles," namely, the Beast, the False Prophet, and the King of the North or the Assyrian. Each of these must be dealt with before the Lord can manifest His world-wide authority. There must be a reason why Revelation 19:20 records only the destruction of the two mentioned. It can not be, as previously shown, that the third continues until after the millennium begins. It can not be that the third escapes judgment. It must be that he and his armies have already been dealt with on a previous occasion.

j. The chronology of several important passages dealing with these events seems to support the thesis. In Isaiah 30 and 31 there is a description of the destruction of the King of the North. This is followed in Isaiah 33 and 34 with the destruction of all the nations, and then follows a description of the millennium in Isaiah 35. In the book of Joel we find the same chronology. In Joel 2 there is the description of the invasion by the northern army (v. 20), followed by a description of the destruction of the nations in Joel 3 and then the millennium is described in 3:17-21. In both of these passages the chronology is the same. The armies of the north are destroyed at a separate time, in a distinct movement, prior to the destruction of the armies of the nations, which will be followed by the millennium. To place the events in the middle of the week is the only position consistent with the chronology of these extended passages. Such a view would lead us to this chronology of events: (1) Israel makes a false covenant with the Beast and occupies her land in a false security (Dan. 9:27; Ezek. 38:8, 11). (2) Because of a desire for spoil at the expense of an easy prey, the King of the

North, satanically motivated, invades Palestine (Ezek. 38:11; Joel 2:1-21; Isaiah 10:12, 30:31-33; 31:8-9). (3) The Beast breaks his covenant with Israel and moves into the land (Dan. 11:41-45). (4) The King of the North is destroyed on the mountains of Israel (Ezek. 39:1-4). (5) The land of Palestine is occupied by the armies of the Beast (Dan. 11:45). (6) At this time the great coalition of nations takes place that forms one government under the Beast (Ps. 2:1-3; Rev. 13:7). (7) The Kings of the East are brought in against the armies of the Beast (Rev. 16:12), evidently as a result of the dissolution of the government of Gog. (8) When the nations of the earth are gathered together around Jerusalem (Zech. 14:1-3) and the valley of Jehoshaphat (Joel 3:2), the Lord returns to destroy all Gentile world powers so that He might rule the nations Himself. This is further described in Zechariah 12:1-9; 14:1-4; Isaiah 33:1—34:17; 63:1-6; 66:15-16; Jeremiah 25:27-33; Revelation 20:7-10.

II. The Invasion by the Armies of the Beast

The invasion of Palestine by the northern confederacy will bring the Beast and his armies to the defense of Israel as her protector. This invasion is described by Daniel:

> . . . and he shall enter into the countries, and shall overflow and pass over. He shall enter also into the glorious land, and many countries shall be overthrown: but these shall escape out of his hand, even Edom, and Moab, and the chief of the children of Ammon. He shall stretch forth his hand also upon the countries: and the land of Egypt shall not escape. But he shall have power over the treasures of gold and of silver, and over all the precious things of Egypt: and the Libyans and the Ethiopians shall be at his steps. But tidings out of the east and out of the north shall trouble him: therefore he shall go forth with great fury to destroy, and utterly to make away many. And he shall plant the tabernacles of his palace between the seas in the glorious holy mountain; yet he shall come to his end, and none shall help him [Dan. 11:40b-45].

It is difficult to determine the activities of the nations involved in this chapter. Many have felt that the above invasion records that of the King of the North and of the South. However, in verse 36 the "wilful king," previously identified as the Beast, is introduced to us and his activities seem to be outlined in what follows. Verses 40-45 can hardly describe the activities of the combined forces of the Kings of the North and the South, for the pronoun "they" would have been used. Since "he" is used, the passage must describe further the activities of the Wilful King. On this Peters writes:

> "And he shall enter into the countries"—this is perhaps the clause which has caused the greatest difficulty to critics, owing to the sudden transition from one person to another. If we were to confine ourselves to this prophecy, it would be impossible from the language to decide *what king* this was that is to enter into the countries; whether the King of the North, or of the South, or of the Roman Empire, but we are not left *to conjecture* upon this point. The king who is thus victorious at the time of the end we find in Dan. 2 and 7 and Rev. 17 to be indentified *with the fourth beast, the Roman power*. Taking other prophecies as interpreters, it refers to the Roman power under its last head, who shall invade other countries, thus implying that the King of the South and the King of the North have been unsuccessful against him.[19]

From this passage several features concerning the movement of this invasion are to be seen. (1) The movement of the campaign begins when the King of the South moves against the Beast-False Prophet coalition (11:40), which, takes place "at the time of the end." (2) The King of the South is joined by the northern confederacy, who attacks the Wilful King by a great force over land and sea (11:40). Jerusalem is destroyed as a result of this attack (Zech. 12:2), and, in turn, the armies of the northern confederacy are destroyed (Ezek. 39; Zech. 12:4). (3) The full armies of the Beast move into Palestine (11:41) and shall conquer all that territory (11:41-42). Edom, Moab, and Ammon alone escape. It is evidently at this time that the coalition of Revelation 17:13 is formed. (4) While he is extending his dominion into Egypt, a report that causes alarm is brought to the Beast (11:44). It may be the report of the approach of the Kings of the East (Rev. 16:12), who have assembled because of the destruction of the northern confederacy to challenge the authority of the beast. (5) The Beast moves his headquarters into the land of Palestine and assembles his armies there (11:45). (6) It is there that his destruction will come (11:45).

---

[19] G. N. H. Peters, *Theocratic Kingdom*, II, 654.

III. The Invasion by the Armies of the East

Revelation 16:12 reveals that some supernatural event brings about the removal of that which kept the Asiatic powers from coming into the region of Palestine to challenge the authority of the Beast. Walvoord writes:

> The drying-up of the Euphrates is a prelude to the final act of the drama, not the act itself. We must conclude, then, that the most probable interpretation of the drying-up of the Euphrates is that by an act of God its flow will be interrupted even as were the waters of the Red Sea and of Jordan. This time the way will open not for Israel but for those who are referred to as the Kings of the East. . . . The evidence points, then, to a literal interpretation of Revelation 16:12 in relation to the Euphrates.[20]

Just who these forces will be, represented as the Kings of the East, can not be determined. But their coming brings us to the final stage of the campaign of Armageddon. They are brought toward the plains of Esdraelon for the purpose of meeting the armies of the Beast in conflict.

IV. The Invasion by the Lord and His Armies

With the King of the South defeated by the armies of the Beast and the northern confederacy defeated by the Lord upon the mountains of Israel, we find two opposing forces drawn up in battle array—the armies of the Beast and the armies of the Kings of the East. Before this battle can be joined there appears a sign in the heavens, the sign of the Son of man (Matt. 24:30). What this sign is is not revealed, but its effect is. It causes the armies to turn from their hostility toward each other to unite to fight against the Lord Himself. John says: "And I saw the beast, and the kings of the earth, and their armies, gathered together to make war against him that sat on the horse, and against his army" (Rev. 19:19). Such is the picture of the closing hostilities given in Zechariah 14:3; Revelation 16:14; 17:14; 19:11-21. It is at this point that the armies of the Beast and the east are destroyed by the Lord (Rev. 19:21).

---

[20] John F. Walvoord, "The Way of the Kings of the East," *Light for the World's Darkness*, p. 164.

As we survey the whole campaign of Armageddon we observe a number of results: (1) The armies of the South are destroyed in campaign; (2) the armies of the northern confederacy are smitten by the Lord; (3) the armies of the Beast and the east are slain by the Lord at the second advent; (4) the Beast and the False Prophet are cast into the lake of fire (Rev. 19:20); (5) unbelievers have been purged out of Israel (Zech. 13:8); (6) believers have been purged as the result of these invasions (Zech. 13:9); (7) Satan is bound (Rev. 20:2). Thus the Lord destroys every hostile force that would challenge His right to rule as Messiah over the earth.

CHAPTER XXI

THE JUDGMENTS OF THE TRIBULATION

It has been demonstrated previously that this entire tribulation period is a period characterized by judgments from the hand of the Lord. A number of distinct judgment programs are to be seen. Concerning the judgments in the Revelation, Scott writes:

> Now in the interval [between the rapture and the second advent] the septenary series of judgment under the Seals, the Trumpets, and the Vials run their course. These divine chastisements increase in severity as we pass from one series to another. The judgments are not contemporaneous but successive. The Trumpets succeed the Seals, and the Vials follow the Trumpets. Strict chronological sequence is observed. . . . The Seals were opened in order that the successive parts of God's revelation of the future might be disclosed, but to faith only—the mass would regard the judgments as merely providential. Such things had happened before. But the Trumpets' loud blast by angels intimates a public dealing with men of an intensely judicial character. These mystic Trumpets sound an alarm throughout the length and breadth of apostate Christendom. The public intervention of God in the guilty and apostate scene is thus intimated. Then in the third general symbol, that of the vials or bowls poured out, the concentrated wrath of God overwhelms the whole prophetic scene under heaven. Chapter 16 reveals a series of judgments hitherto unsurpassed in range and severity.[1]

I. THE SEALS

The picture of the opening of the sealed scroll by the Son of God is given in Revelation 6. Here is the beginning of the unfolding of the judgment program of God. Angels are mentioned throughout the book in connection with the execution of the judgment program. Ottman says:

---

[1] Walter Scott, *Exposition of the Revelation of Jesus Christ*, p. 176.

> When the first seal is broken a voice from the cherubim is heard, saying, "Come." . . . It is the voice of one of the cherubim calling forth the instrument of divine judgment. The cherubim are still in executive connection with the government of God. That government has respect to the earth upon which judgment is now to be executed. The successional calamities, coming forth as the seals are broken, are thus under the order and control of the divine administration. No instrument of judgment appears until summoned by the call of the cherubim.[2]

Darby calls the seals "the providential preparation of the divine government for the coming of Jesus.[3]" God is dealing in wrath (Rev. 6:16-17), through human agency, to pour out judgment upon the earth.

There is general agreement among commentators as to the interpretation of the seals. The first (6:2) is generally agreed to represent the peace movements on the part of men as they seek to establish peace on the earth. It may be associated with the covenant made by the Beast to establish peace on the earth. The second (6:3-4) represents the removal of peace from the earth and the wars that engulf the earth. The third (6:5-6) represents famine that results from the desolation of war. The fourth (6:7-8) prefigures the death that follows in the wake of the failure of men to establish peace. The fifth (6:9-11) reveals the fact of death among the saints of God because of their faith and their impassioned plea for vengeance. The sixth (6:12-17) speaks of the great convulsions that will shake the whole earth. This may signify the condition in which every authority and power loses its control over men and anarchy reigns. Kelly says: "The persecuting powers and those subject to them will be visited judicially, and there will ensue a complete disruption of authority on the earth."[4] These seals, then, are the beginning of God's judgments upon the earth. They are successive unfoldings of the judgment program, although they may continue throughout the period when once unfolded. They are mainly divine judgments through human

---

[2] Ford C. Ottman, *The Unfolding of the Ages*, p. 153.
[3] William Kelly, editor, *The Collected Writings of J. N. Darby*, Prophetic V, 30.
[4] William Kelly, *The Revelation Expounded*, p. 104.

agencies. They fall upon the earth in the first portion of the tribulation, and they will continue on through the period.

II. The Trumpets

A second portion of the judgment program is that revealed through the blowing of the seven trumpets (Rev. 8:2—11:15). Concerning the use of trumpets, Newell writes:

> The trumpets were appointed in Israel by God for calling of the princes, and the congregation, and for the journeying of the camps, as an alarm, or public notification (Numbers 10:1-6).
>
> The trumpets were to be blown also in the days of Israel's "gladness," "set feasts," and over their sacrifice in the beginning of their months—"for a memorial before your God." Jehovah also loved them (Numbers 10:10).
>
> But we find an especial use of the trumpet, in arousing to war the hosts of Jehovah against their enemies (Numbers 10:9). Compare Ezekiel 33:1-7, where the watchman's trumpet blown faithfully could deliver all who would "take warning." . . .
>
> So with the seven angels. They blow the very trumpets of heaven against an earth become "as it was in the days of Noah . . . as the days of Sodom," as Joshua and Israel blew the trumpets against Jericho.[5]

There is a wide divergence of opinion among the commentators concerning the interpretation of these trumpet judgments. Some interpret them with strict literalness, while others interpret them symbolically and the range in symbolical interpretation is wide indeed. It will be observed that the first four are separated from the last three judgments, in that these last three are specifically called "woe" judgments. The first trumpet (8:7) presents a judgment that falls upon the earth, in which a third of the inhabitants are slain. The second trumpet (8:8-9) presents a judgment that falls upon the sea and, again, a third part of the inhabitants are slain. It is suggested that the earth here may represent the land of Palestine, as it often does in this book, and the sea represents the nations. Thus these two depict judgments from God of unimaginable extent upon all the inhabitants of the earth. The third trumpet (8:10-11) presents a judgment that falls upon the rivers and

[5] William R. Newell, *The Revelation*, p. 119.

fountains of waters. Such are used in Scripture as the source of life, even spiritual life, and this may depict judgment upon those from whom living water is taken away because they believed the lie (2 Thess. 2:11). The fourth trumpet (8:12-13) is a judgment coming on the sun, moon, and stars. These represent governmental powers and may present the judgment of God upon world rulers. The fifth trumpet judgment, which is the first woe (9:1-12), pictures an individual energized by hell who can let torment of unprecedented dimension loose on the earth. It is generally accepted that these are not literal locusts in that they do not feed on that which is natural to the locust. The sixth trumpet judgment, which is the second woe (9:13-19), is seen to be a great army turned loose to march with destructive force across the face of the earth. Concerning these two woe judgments Kelly writes:

> First of all a tormenting Woe falls on the land, but not on those sealed out of the twelve tribes of Israel. Next the Euphratean horsemen are let loose on the western powers, overwhelming all Christendom, and in particular that west as the special object of the judgment of God. The former is emphatically torment from Satan on the reprobate Jews; as the latter is a most scathing infliction of man's aggressive energy, though not this only, from the east on the corrupt and idolatrous western world. The killing of the third of men represents, not the merely physical end, but the destruction even of all confession of relationship with the only true God.[6]

This suggests that the two woes will be great marching armies, one against Israel and one against Gentiles, which will destroy a third of the earth's population. Since Satan's weapon against Israel is the northern confederacy, it may be depicted by the fifth trumpet and Gentile warfare depicted by the sixth. The seventh trumpet and the third woe judgment (11:15) brings about the return of Christ to the earth and the subsequent destruction of all hostile powers at the conclusion of the Armageddon program.

It would seem as though there might be a parallelism in the seven trumpet judgments and the program of the seventieth week as outlined previously. The middle of the week begins

---

[6] Kelly, *op. cit.*, pp. 123-24.

with the rise of great military powers that are aligning themselves. Such would correspond to the first trumpet. Former kingdoms are overthrown, which brings death, as in the second trumpet. A great leader will arise, the Beast, in the third trumpet. His rise will bring about the overthrow of governments and authorities as in the fourth trumpet. There will be great military movements in the period. The armies of the northern confederacy will invade the land, as in the fifth trumpet, and Gentile powers will jockey for position, which causes great destruction, as in the sixth. These will all be climaxed by the second advent of Christ, as seen in the seventh trumpet.

III. The Vials or Bowls

The third series of judgments, which complete the outpouring of divine wrath, are the vials (Rev. 16:1-21). Although four of these vials are poured out on the same areas as the trumpets, they do not seem to be the same judgments. The trumpets begin in the middle of the tribulation and depict events during the entire second half of the week. The vials seem to cover a very brief period at the end of the tribulation just prior to the second advent of Christ. These bowls seem to have particular reference to unbelievers, as they undergo the special wrath of God (16:9, 11), and have special reference to the Beast and his followers (16:2).

The first bowl (16:2) is poured out upon the earth, as in the first trumpet. In this judgment God is pouring out wrath on all Beast-worshippers. The second bowl (16:3), as in the second trumpet, is poured out upon the sea. The result of this judgment is spiritual death. The sea here is seen to become lifeless, "as the blood of a dead man." The third bowl (16:4-7), like the third trumpet, is poured out upon the rivers and fountains of waters and they lose their power to nourish or satisfy or sustain life. It seems to have reference to removing the possibility of finding life from those who followed the Beast. The fourth bowl (16:8-9), like the fourth trumpet, falls upon the sun. That an individual is envisioned is seen in that the sun is referred to as "him." This may have reference to the judgment of God that imposes blindness upon the Beast's followers. The fifth bowl (16:10-11) has to do with the imposition of darkness on the center of the Beast's power, anticipating the destruction of the empire that claims to be the kingdom of the Messiah. The sixth bowl (16:12) prepares the way for an invasion of kings from the east, that they, with the Beast's armies, might come to judgment at Armageddon. The seventh bowl (16:17-21) has to do with a great convulsion that completely overthrows the ordered affairs of men as they experience the "fierceness of his wrath" (16:19).

IV. The Judgment on Babylon

Revelation 17 outlines the judgment on the great harlot, the apostate religious system, that exists in the tribulation period. The unbelieving professing church went into the tribulation period (Rev. 2:22; 3:10) and a great religious system, under the domination of the great harlot, arose.

A. *The description of the harlot.* John has given many details that furnish a description of this system. (1) The system bears the characterization of a harlot (Rev. 17:1-2, 15-16). It claimed to be Christ's bride, but had fallen from its pure position and become a harlot. (2) The system is a leader in ecclesiastical affairs (Rev. 17:2, 5). Spiritual fornication in the Scripture has reference to adherence to a false system. (3) The system is a leader in political affairs (Rev. 17:3). It is seen to be controlling the Beast upon which it sits. (4) The system has become very rich and influential (Rev. 17:4). (5) The system represents a phase of the development of Christendom that was hitherto unrevealed (Rev. 17:5) in that it is called a "mystery." (6) The system has been the great persecutor of the saints (Rev. 17:6). (7) The system is an organized system of worldwide scope (Rev. 17:15). (8) The system will be destroyed by the Beast, the head of the Roman coalition, so that his supremacy may not be threatened (Rev. 17:16-17).[7]

B. *The identity of the harlot.* Hislop, in his carefully documented book, *The Two Babylons,* has traced the relationship existing between ancient Babylon and the doctrine and practice

---

[7] Cf. Ottman, *op. cit.,* pp. 278-81.

of the harlot system, called Mystery Babylon. Ironside has traced the same development as he writes:

> The woman is a religious system, who dominates the civil power, at least for a time. The name upon her forehead should easily enable us to identify her. But in order to do that we will do well to go back to our Old Testament, and see what is there revealed concerning literal Babylon, for the one will surely throw light upon the other. . . .
>
> . . . we learn that the founder of Bab-el, or Babylon, was Nimrod, of whose unholy achievements we read in the 10th chapter of Genesis. He was the arch-apostate of the partriarchal age. . . . he persuaded his associates and followers to join together in "building a city and a tower which should reach unto heaven." . . . to be recognized as a temple or rallying centre for those who did not walk in obedience to the word of the Lord. . . . they called their city and tower Bab-El, the gate of God; but it was soon changed by divine judgment into Babel, Confusion. It bore the stamp of unreality from the first, for we are told "they had brick for stone, and slime had they for mortar." An imitation of that which is real and true has ever since characterized Babylon, in all ages.
>
> Nimrod, or Nimroud-bar-Cush . . . was a grandson of Ham, the unworthy son of Noah . . . Noah had brought through the flood the revelation of the true God . . . Ham on the other hand seems to have been all too readily affected by the apostasy that brought the flood, for he shows no evidence of self-judgment . . . His name . . . means "swarthy," "darkened," or more literally, "the sunburnt." And the name indicates the state of the man's soul . . . darkened by light from heaven. . . . [Ham] begat a son named Cush, "the black one," and he became the father of Nimrod, the apostate leader of his generation.
>
> Ancient lore now comes to our assistance, and tells us that the wife of Nimroud-bar-Cush was the infamous Semiramis the First. She is reputed to have been the foundress of the Babylonian mysteries and the first high-priestess of idolatry. Thus Babylon became the fountainhead of idolatry, and the mother of every heathen and pagan system in the world. The mystery-religion that was there originated spread in various forms throughout the whole earth . . . and is with us today . . . and shall have its fullest development when the Holy Spirit has departed and the Babylon of the Apocalypse holds sway.
>
> Building on the primeval promise of the woman's Seed who was to come, Semiramis bore a son whom she declared was miraculously conceived! and when she presented him to the people, he was hailed as the promised deliverer. This was Tam-

muz, whose worship Ezekiel protested against in the days of the captivity. Thus was introduced the mystery of the mother and the child, a form of idolatry that is older than any other known to man. The rites of this worship were secret. Only the initiated were permitted to know its mysteries. It was Satan's effort to delude mankind with an imitation so like the truth of God that they would not know the true Seed of the woman when He came in the fullness of time. . . .

From Babylon this mystery-religion spread to all the surrounding nations. . . . Everywhere the symbols were the same, and everywhere the cult of the mother and the child became the popular system; their worship was celebrated with the most disgusting and immoral practices. The image of the queen of heaven with the babe in her arms was seen everywhere, though the names might differ as languages differed. It became the mystery-religion of Phoenicia, and by the Phoenicians was carried to the ends of the earth. Astoreth and Tammuz, the mother and child of these hardy adventurers, became Isis and Horus in Egypt, Aphrodite and Eros in Greece, Venus and Cupid in Italy, and bore many other names in more distant places. Within 1000 years Babylonianism had become the religion of the world, which had rejected the Divine revelation.

Linked with this central mystery were countless lesser mysteries. . . . Among these were the doctrines of purgatorial purification after death, salvation by countless sacraments such as priestly absolution, sprinkling with holy water, the offering of round cakes to the queen of heaven as mentioned in the book of Jeremiah, dedication of virgins to the gods, which was literally sanctified prostitution, weeping for Tammuz for a period of 40 days, prior to the great festival of Istar, who was said to have received her son back from the dead; for it was taught that Tammuz was slain by a wild boar and afterwards brought back to life. To him the egg was sacred, as depicting the mystery of his resurrection, even as the evergreen was his chosen symbol and was set up in honor of his birth at the winter solstice, when a boar's head was eaten in memory of his conflict and a yule-log burned with many mysterious observances. The sign of the cross was sacred to Tammuz, as symbolizing the life-giving principle and as the first letter of his name. It is represented upon vast numbers of the most ancient altars and temples, and did not, as many have supposed, originate with Christianity.

From this mystery-religion, the patriarch Abraham was separated by divine call; and with this same evil cult the nation that sprang from him was in constant conflict, until under Jezebel, a Phoenician princess, it was grafted onto what was left of the religion of Israel in the northern kingdom in the day of Ahab, and was the cause of their captivity at last. Judah was polluted by it, for Baal-worship was but the Canaanitish form of the Babylonian mysteries, and only by being sent into captivity to Babylon itself did Judah become cured of her fondness for idolatry. Baal was the Sun-God, the Life-giving One, identical with Tammuz.

. . . though Babylon as a city had long been but a memory, her mysteries had not died with her. When the city and temples were destroyed, the high-priest fled with a company of initiates and their sacred vessels and images to Pergamos, where the symbol of the serpent was set up as the emblem of the hidden wisdom. From there, they afterwards crossed the sea and emigrated to Italy. . . . There the ancient cult was propagated under the name of the Etruscan Mysteries, and eventually Rome became the headquarters of Babylonianism. The chief priests wore mitres shaped like the head of a fish, in honor of Dagon, the fish-god, the Lord of life—another form of the Tammuz mystery, as developed among Israel's old enemies, the Philistines. The chief priest when established in Rome took the title Pontifex Maximus, and this was imprinted on his mitre. When Julius Caesar (who, like all young Romans of good family, was an initiate) had become the head of the State, he was elected Pontifex Maximum, and this title was held henceforth by all the Roman emperors down to Constantine the Great, who was, at one and the same time, head of the church and high priest of the heathen! The title was afterwards conferred upon the bishops of Rome, and is borne by the pope today, who is thus declared to be, not the successor of the fisherman-apostle Peter, but the direct successor of the high priest of the Babylonian mysteries, and the servant of the fish-god Dagon, for whom he wears, like his idolatrous predecessors, the fisherman's ring.

During the early centuries of the church's history, the mystery of iniquity had wrought with such astounding effect, and Babylonian practices and teachings had been so largely absorbed by that which bore the name of the church of Christ, that the truth of the Holy Scriptures on many points had been wholly obscured, while idolatrous practices had been foisted upon the people as Christian sacraments, and heathen philosophies took the place of gospel instruction. Thus was developed that amazing system which for a thousand years dominated Europe and trafficked in the bodies and souls of men, until the great Reformation of the 16th century brought in a measure of deliverance.[8]

It is not too much to say that the false doctrines and practices found within Romanism are directly attributable to the union of

[8] Harry A. Ironside, *Lectures on the Revelation*, pp. 287-95.

this paganism with Christianity when Constantine declared Rome to be a Christian empire. It is thus concluded that the harlot represents all professing Christendom united in a single system under one head.

C. *The judgment on the harlot.* John clearly depicts the judgment upon this corrupt system when he says:

> And the ten horns which thou sawest upon the beast, these shall hate the whore, and shall make her desolate and naked, and shall eat her flesh, and burn her with fire. For God hath put in their hearts to fulfil his will, and to agree, and give their kingdom unto the beast, until the words of God shall be fulfilled [Rev. 17:16-17].

The Beast, who was dominated by the harlot system (Rev. 17:3), rises against her and destroys her and her system completely. Without doubt the harlot system was in competition with the religious worship of the Beast, promoted by the False Prophet, and her destruction is brought about so that the Beast may be the sole object of false worship as he claims to be God.

V. The Judgment on the Beast and His Empire

In tracing the campaign of Armageddon it has been seen how God judges the Gentile world powers and brings about their downfall. The northern confederacy was judged by God upon the mountains of Israel in the middle of the tribulation period. The Kings of the East and their forces and the armies of the Beast were seen to be destroyed at the second advent of Christ to the earth. A fuller description of this judgment upon the Beast and his citadel is given in Revelation 18. There the political empire is seen to have been so closely united with the false religious empire that both are called by the same name, even though two different entities are in view in these two chapters. Scofield succinctly states:

> Two "Babylons" are to be distinguished in the Revelation: ecclesiastical Babylon, which is apostate Christendom, headed up under the Papacy; and political Babylon, which is the Beast's confederated empire, the last form of Gentile world-dominion. Ecclesiastical Babylon is "the great whore" (Rev. 17:1), and is destroyed by political Babylon (Rev. 17:15-18), that the beast may be the alone object of worship (2 Thess. 2:3, 4; Rev. 13:15). The power of political Babylon is destroyed by the return of the Lord in glory. . . . The notion of a literal Babylon to be rebuilt

> on the site of ancient Babylon is in conflict with Isaiah 13:19-22. But the language of Rev. 18 (e.g. vs. 10, 16, 18) seems beyond all question to identify "Babylon," the "city" of luxury and traffic, with Babylon the ecclesiastical centre, viz. Rome. The very kings who hated ecclesiastical Babylon deplore the destruction of commercial Babylon.[9]

The destruction of the seat of the Beast's power is accomplished by a divine visitation of judgment by fire (Rev. 18:8).

As the major lines of prophetic revelation concerning the tribulation period have been surveyed it becomes obvious that the revelation of God's program for this period constitutes one of the major sections of prophetic study. The program for Israel, for the Gentiles, for the program of Satan all reach a climax in that time immediately preceding the second advent of Christ.

---

[9] C. I. Scofield, *Reference Bible*, pp. 1346-47.

SECTION FIVE

PROPHECIES RELATED TO THE SECOND ADVENT

CHAPTER XXII

THE HISTORY OF THE DOCTRINE OF THE SECOND ADVENT

That to which all Scripture looks forward and to which all history presses is the second advent of the Lord Jesus Christ to the earth. At that time God's purposes, for which the Son came into the world, will be realized. Redemption will have been accomplished and sovereignty will have been manifested on earth. A great body of prophecy is related to this coming and the events associated with it.

Biblical interpreters are divided into a number of different schools on the question of the doctrines of chiliasm. The chiliastic question, so long considered unimportant in the realm of Biblical studies and interpretation, has come to be considered one of the major doctrines because of its determinative effect on the whole realm of theology.

> *Chiliasm,* so named from . . . . [*chilioi*]—meaning "one thousand"—refers in a general sense to the doctrine of the millennium, or kingdom age that is yet to be, and as stated in the *Encyclopedia Britannica* (14th ed., *s.v.*) is "the belief that Christ will return to reign for a thousand years. . . ." The distinctive feature of this doctrine is that He will return *before* the thousand years and therefore will characterize those years by His personal presence and by the exercise of His rightful authority, securing and sustaining all the blessings on the earth which are ascribed to that period. The term *chiliasm* has been superseded by the designation *premillennialism;* and . . . more is implied in the term than a mere reference to a thousand years. It is a thousand years which is said to intervene between the first and second of humanity's resurrections. . . . In this thou-

> sand years . . . every earthly covenant with Israel will be fulfilled. . . . The entire Old Testament expectation is involved, with its earthly kingdom, the glory of Israel, and the promised Messiah seated on David's throne in Jerusalem.[1]

I. Views of the Second Advent

Historically, there have been four major views concerning the second advent of Christ.

A. *The non-literal or spiritualized view.* The non-literal view denies that there will be a literal, bodily, personal, return of Christ to the earth. Walvoord summarizes this view:

> A common modern view of the Lord's return is the so-called spiritual view which identifies the coming of Christ as a perpetual advance of Christ in the Church that includes many particular events. William Newton Clarke, for instance, held that the promises of the second coming are fulfilled by "his spiritual presence with his people," which is introduced by the coming of the Holy Spirit at Pentecost, accompanied by the overthrow of Jerusalem, and ultimately fulfilled by continual spiritual advance in the church. In other words it is not an event, but it includes all the events of the Christian era which are the work of Christ. [This view is] . . . held by many liberals of our day.[2]

This view sees the second advent as being fulfilled in the destruction of Jerusalem, or the day of Pentecost, or the death of the saint, or the conversion of the individual, or any crisis in history or the individual's experience. Their controversy is as to whether there will be a literal second advent or not. Needless to say such a view is based on disbelief in the Word of God or the spiritualizing method of interpretation.

B. *The postmillennial view.* The postmillennial view, popular among covenant theologians of the post-Reformation period, holds, according to Walvoord:

> . . . that through preaching the Gospel the whole world will be Christianized and brought to submission to the Gospel *before* the return of Christ. The name is derived from the fact that in this theory Christ returns after the millennium (hence, *post* millennium).[3]

---

1 Lewis Sperry Chafer, *Systematic Theology*, IV, 264-65.

2 John F. Walvoord, "The Millennial Issue in Modern Theology," *Bibliotheca Sacra*, 106:44, January, 1948.

3 *Ibid.*, 106:45.

The followers of this view hold to a literal second advent and believe in a literal millennium, generally following the Old Testament teaching on the nature of that kingdom. Their controversy is over such questions as who institutes the millennium, the relation of Christ to the millennium, and the time of Christ's coming in relation to that millennium.

C. *The amillennial view.* The amillennial view holds that there will be no literal millennium on the earth following the second advent. All the prophecies concerning the kingdom are being fulfilled in the inter-advent period spiritually by the church. Concerning this view it has been stated:

> Its most general character is that of denial of a literal reign of Christ upon the earth. Satan is conceived as bound at the first coming of Christ. The present age between the first and second comings is the fulfillment of the millennium. Its adherents differ as to whether the millennium is being fulfilled on the earth (Augustine) or whether it is being fulfilled by the saints in heaven (Warfield). It may be summed up in the idea that there will be no more millennium than there is now, and that the eternal state immediately follows the second coming of Christ. It is similar to postmillennialism in that Christ comes after what they regard as the millennium.[4]

Their controversy is over the question as to whether there will be a literal millennium for Israel or whether the promises concerning the millennium are now being fulfilled in the church, either on earth or in heaven.

D. *The premillennial view.* The premillennial view is the view that holds that Christ will return to earth, literally and bodily, before the millennial age begins and that, by His presence, a kingdom will be instituted over which He will reign. In this kingdom all of Israel's covenants will be literally fulfilled. It will continue for a thousand years, after which the kingdom will be given by the Son to the Father when it will merge with His eternal kingdom. The central issue in this position is whether the Scriptures are to be fulfilled literally or symbolically. In fact this is the essential heart of the entire question. Allis, an ardent amillennialist, admits: ". . . Old Testament prophecies if literally interpreted cannot be regard-

[4] *Ibid.*, 106:45-46.

ed as having been yet fulfilled or as being capable of fulfilment in this present age."[5] It is not too much to say that the issues dividing these four views can be solved only by settling the question concerning the method of interpretation to be employed.

II. The Doctrine of the Second Advent in the Early Church

It is generally agreed that the view of the church for the centuries immediately following the Apostolic era was the premillennial view of the return of Christ. Allis, an amillenarian, says:

> [Premillennialism] was extensively held in the Early Church, how extensively is not definitely known. But the stress which many of its advocates placed on earthly rewards and carnal delights aroused widespread opposition to it; and it was largely replaced by the "spiritual" view of Augustine. It reappeared in extravagant forms at the time of the Reformation, notably among the Anabaptists. Bengel and Mede were among the first modern scholars of distinction to advocate it. But it was not until early in the last century that it became at all widely influential in modern times. Since then it has become increasingly popular; and the claim is frequently made that most of the leaders in the Church today, who are evangelical, are Premillennialists.[6]

Whitby, generally held to be the founder of postmillennialism, writes:

> The doctrine of the Millennium, or the reign of saints on earth for a thousand years, is now rejected by all Roman Catholics, and by the greatest part of Protestants; and yet it passed among the best Christians, for two hundred and fifty years, for a tradition apostolical; and, as such, is delivered by many Fathers of the second and third century, who speak of it as the tradition of our Lord and His apostles, and of all the ancients who lived before them; who tell us the very words in which it was delivered, the Scriptures which were then so interpreted; and say that it was held by all Christians that were exactly orthodox. It was received not only in the Eastern parts of the Church, by Papias (in Phrygia), Justin (in Palestine), but by Irenaeus (in Gaul), Nepos (in Egypt), Apollinaris, Methodius (in the West and South), Cyprian, Victorinus (in Germany), by Tertul-

---

[5] Oswald T. Allis, *Prophecy and the Church,* p. 238.
[6] *Ibid.,* p. 7.

lian (in Africa), Lactantius (in Italy), and Severus, and by the Council of Nice (about A.D. 323).[7]

That such concessions should be made by anti-premillenarians is only because history records the fact that such a premillennial belief was the *universal* belief of the church for two hundred and fifty years after the death of Christ.[8] Schaff writes:

> The most striking point in the eschatology of the ante-Nicene age is the prominent chiliasm, or millenarianism, that is the belief of a visible reign of Christ in glory on earth with the risen saints for a thousand years, before the general resurrection and judgment. It was indeed not the doctrine of the church embodied in any creed or form of devotion, but a widely current opinion of distinguished teachers.[9]

Harnack says:

> This doctrine of Christ's second advent, and the kingdom, appears so early that it might be questioned whether it ought not to be regarded as an essential part of the Christian religion.[10]

A. *Exponents of premillennialism.* Perhaps the most extensive compilation of premillennial advocates of the first centuries is that made by Peters. He lists as follows:

> 1. *Pre-Mill. Advocates of the 1st Century*
>
> a (1) *Andrew,* (2) *Peter,* (3) *Philip,* (4) *Thomas,* (5) *James,* (6) *John,* (7) *Matthew,* (8) *Aristio,* (9) *John the Presbyter*—all these are cited by Papias, who, according to Irenaeus, was one of John's hearers, and intimate with Polycarp. . . . Now this reference to the apostles *agrees* with the facts that we *have proven:* (a) that the disciples of Jesus did hold the Jewish views of the Messianic reign in the first part of this century, and (b) that, instead of discarding them, they linked them with the Sec. Advent. Next (10) *Clement of Rome* (Phil. 4:3), who existed about A.D. 40-100. . . . (11) *Barnabas,* about A.D. 40-100. . . . (12) *Hermas,* from A.D. 40 to 140. . . . (13) *Ignatius,* Bh. of Antioch, died under Trajan, about A.D. 50-115. . . . (14) *Polycarp,* Bh. of Smyrna, a disciple of the Apostle John, who lived about A.D. 70-167. . . . (15) *Papias,* Bh. of Hierapolis, lived between A.D. 80-163. . . .
>
> b Now on the other side, not a single name can be presented, which (1) can be quoted as positively against us, or (2)

[7] Cited by G. N. H. Peters, *Theocratic Kingdom,* I, 482-83.
[8] Cf. *ibid.,* for a list of historians who concede the fact.
[9] Philip Schaff, *History of the Christian Church,* II, 614.
[10] Cited by Chafer, *op. cit.,* IV, 277.

which can be cited as teaching, in any shape or sense, the doctrine of our opponents.

2. *Pre-Mill. Advocates of the 2nd Cent.*

a (1) *Pothinus*, a martyr. . . . A.D. 87-177. . . .(2) *Justyn Martyr*, about A.D. 100-168. . . . (3) *Melito*, Bh. of Sardis, about A.D. 100-170. . . . (4) *Hegisippus*, between A.D. 130-190. . . . (5) *Tatian*, between A.D. 130-190. . . . (6) *Irenaeus*, a martyr . . . about A.D. 140-202. (7) *The Churches of Vienne and Lyons*. . . . (8) *Tertullian*, about A.D. 150-220. . . . (9) *Hippolytus*, between A.D. 160-240.

b Now on the other side, *not a single writer* can be presented, not even a single name can be mentioned of any one cited, who opposed chiliasm in this century. . . . Now let the student reflect: here are *two centuries* . . . in which positively no direct opposition whatever arises against our doctrine, but it is held by *the very men*, leading and most eminent, *through whom we trace the Church*. What must we conclude? (1) That the common faith of the Church was Chiliastic, and (2) that such a generality and unity of belief could only have been introduced . . . by the founders of the Ch. Church and the Elders appointed by them.

3. *Pre-Mill. Advocates of the 3rd Cent.*

a (1) *Cyprian*, about A.D. 200-258. . . . (2) *Commodian*, between A.D. 200-270. . . . (3) *Nepos*, Bh. of Arsinoe, about A.D. 230-280. . . (4) *Coracion*, about A.D. 230-280. . . .(5) *Victorinus*, about A.D. 240-303. . . . (6) *Methodius*, Bh. of Olympus, about A.D. 250-311. . . . (7) *Lactantius* . . . between A.D. 240-330. . . .[11]

While the testimony of all the above men is not always equally clear, certain of them spoke unequivocally for the premillennial position. Clement of Rome wrote:

Of a truth, soon and suddenly shall His will be accomplished as the Scriptures also bear witness, saying, "Speedily will He come, and will not tarry:" and "The Lord shall suddenly come to His temple, even the Holy One, for whom ye look."[12]

Justin Martyr, in his Dialogue with Trypho, wrote:

But I and whoever are on all points right-minded Christians know that there will be resurrection of the dead and a thousand years in Jerusalem, which will then be built, adorned, and en-

---

[11] Peters, *op. cit.*, I, 494-96.
[12] Cited by Charles C. Ryrie, *The Basis of the Premillennial Faith*, p. 20.

larged as the prophets Ezekiel and Isaiah and the other declare. . . .

And, further, a certain man with us, named John, one of the Apostles of Christ, predicted by a revelation that was made to him that those who believed in our Christ would spend a thousand years in Jerusalem, and thereafter the general, or to speak briefly, the eternal resurrection and judgment of all men would likewise take place.[13]

Irenaeus, bishop of Lyons, gives a well developed Eschatology when he writes:

But when this Antichrist shall have devastated all things in this world, he will reign for three years and six months, and sit in the temple at Jerusalem; and then the Lord will come from heaven in the clouds, in the glory of the Father, sending this man and those who follow him into the lake of fire; but bringing in for the righteous the times of the kingdom, that is, the rest, the hallowed seventh day; and restoring to Abraham the promised inheritance, in which kingdom the Lord declared, that "many coming from the east and from the west should sit down with Abraham, Isaac, and Jacob. . . ."

The predicted blessing, therefore, belongs unquestionably to the times of the kingdom, when the righteous shall bear rule upon their rising from the dead.[14]

Tertullian adds his testimony when he says:

But we do confess that a kingdom is promised to us upon the earth, although before heaven, only in another state of existence; inasmuch as it will be after their resurrection for a thousand years in the divinely-built city of Jerusalem.[15]

According to Justin and Irenaeus there were

. . . three classes of men: (1) The Heretics, denying the resurrection of the flesh and the Millennium. (2) The exactly orthodox, asserting both the resurrection and the Kingdom of Christ on the earth. (3) The believers, who consented with the just, and yet endeavored to allegorize and turn into a metaphor all those Scriptures produced for a proper reign of Christ, and who had sentiments rather agreeing with those heretics who

---

[13] *Ibid.*, p. 22.
[14] *Ibid.*, p. 22-23.
[15] *Ibid.*, p. 23.

denied, than those exactly orthodox who maintained, this reign of Christ on earth.[16]

Justin evidently recognized premillennialism as "the criterion of a perfect orthodoxy." In his Dialogue with Trypho, where he writes: "some who are called Christians but are godless, impious heretics, teach doctrines that are in every way blasphemous, atheistical, and foolish,"[17] he shows he would include any who denied premillennialism in this category, since he included in it those that denied the resurrection, a companion teaching.

It would seem safe to conclude with Peters:

> When surveying the historical ground . . . we are forced to the conclusion that those writers . . . who insist upon the great extent of Chiliasm in the Apostolic and Primitive Church are most certainly correct. We, therefore, cordially indorse those who express themselves as Muncher (Ch. His., vol. 2, p. 415), that "it (Chiliasm) was universally received by almost all teachers," and (pp. 450, 452) refers it, with Justin, to "the whole orthodox community. . . ."[18]

B. *Antagonists against the premillennial position.* The third century gives rise to the first antagonism to the premillennial position that can be cited positively. Peters summarizes:

> In this century we for the first time . . . . come to opposers of our doctrine. Every writer, from the earliest period down to the present, who has entered the lists against us, has been able only to find these antagonists, and we present them in their chronological order, when they revealed themselves as adversaries. They number four, but three of them were powerful for mischief, and speedily gained adherents. . . . The first in order is (1) *Caius* (or *Gaius*), . . . in the beginning of the 3rd cent. . . . (2) *Clemens Alexandrinus,* . . . preceptor in the Catechetical School of Alexandria, and exerted a powerful influence (on Origen and others) as a teacher from A.D. 193-220. . . . (3) *Origen,* about A.D. 185-254. . . . (4) *Dionysius,* about A.D. 190-265. . . . these are the *champions* mentioned as directly hostile to Chiliasm.[19]

1. According to Allis this opposition arose because of "the stress which many of its advocates placed on earthly rewards

---

[16] Daniel Whitby, *Treatise on the Millennium,* cited by Peters, *op. cit.,* I, 483.
[17] Cited by D. H. Kromminga, *The Millennium in the Church,* p. 45.
[18] Peters, *op. cit.,* I, 498.
[19] *Ibid.,* I, 497.

and carnal delights [which] . . . aroused wide-spread opposition to it."[20] It would seem to be more correct to affirm that this opposition arose, first, because of the basic tenets of the Alexandrian School, of which Origen became the chief exponent, that had such a wide effect on the theological world. Origen's spiritualizing method of interpretation brought about the termination of the literal method of interpretation on which premillennialism rested. Mosheim has been cited in support of this influence of Origen.

> Mosheim, after declaring: "that the Saviour is to reign a thousand years among men, before the end of the world, had been believed by many in the preceding century, without offence to any," adds, "in this century the Millenarian doctrine fell into disrepute, through the influence especially of Origen, who strenuously opposed it, because it contravened some of his opinions." . . . "down to the times of Origen, all the teachers who were so disposed openly professed and taught it. . . . But Origen assailed it fiercely; for it was repugnant to his philosophy; and by the system of biblical interpretation which he discovered, he gave a different turn to those texts of Scripture on which the patrons of this doctrine relied." . . . In the third century the reputation of this doctrine declined; and the first in Egypt, through the influence especially of Origen. . . . And yet it could not be exterminated in a moment: it still had respectable advocates." Mosheim proceeds in various places to show how, by a philosophizing, most violent, system of interpretation, which began "most wretchedly to pervert and twist every part of those Divine oracles which opposed itself to their philosophical tenets or notions," the literal interpretation was finally crushed. He thus contrasts the interpretation adopted by the two systems: "He (Origen) wished to have the literal and obvious sense of the words disregarded, and an arcane sense, lying concealed in the envelope of the words, to be sought for. But the advocates of an earthly Kingdom of Christ rested their cause solely on the natural and proper sense of certain expressions of the Bible."[21]

2. The opposition came because of the rise of false doctrines which changed theological thinking.

> Gnosticism . . . was early prevailing, and whilst nearly all the doctrines of Christianity suffered, more or less, under its moulding influence, that of the Kingdom especially became, un-

[20] Allis, *loc. cit.*
[21] Peters, *op. cit.*, I, 500.

> der its plastic manipulations, one widely different from the Scriptural and early church doctrine. . . . it struck a heavy blow at the promised kingship of the Son of Man as David's Son. . . . Asceticism, the belief in the inherent corruption of matter . . . was antagonistic to it. . . . Docetism . . . denying, as it did the reality of the human body of Jesus, the Christ, effectually closed all access to an understanding of the Kingdom, spiritualizing not only the body, but everything else relating to Him as Messiah. . . . To reconcile these opposite tendencies, another and succeeding party arose, who assumed that reason occupied the position of umpire, and from the deductions of reason instituted a medium between the two, retaining something from both Gnosticism and Chiliasm, so far as interpretation was concerned, but also spiritualizing the Kingdom, applying it to the Church . . .[22]

3. The continuing Judaism, which began in the Apostolic period, gained strength, so that there was a rising enmity between Jewish and Gentile Christians. This antagonism ultimately led to the rejection of the millennium because it was "Jewish."

> . . . the Gentile Christians in their animosity to Judaism, which sought to impose its legality and ritualism, finally were carried to such an extreme that . . . . everything that savored in their estimation of Judaism was cast aside, including of course the long-entertained Jewish notion of a Kingdom.[23]

4. The union of church and state under Constantine brought about the death of the millennial hope. Smith, after stating that "the interval between the apostolic age and that of Constantine had been called the Chiliastic period of Apocalyptic interpretation," says:

> Immediately after the triumph of Constantine, the Christians, emancipated from oppression and persecution, and dominant and prosperous in their turn, began to lose their vivid expectation of our Lord's speedy Advent and their spiritual conception of His Kingdom, and to look upon the temporal supremacy of Christianity as a fulfilment of the promised reign of Christ on earth. The Roman Empire, become Christian, was regarded no longer an object of prophetic denunciation, but as the scene of a Millennial development. This view, however, was soon met by the figura-

[22] *Ibid.*, I, 501.
[23] *Ibid.*, I, 504.

tive interpretation of the Millennium, as the reign of Christ in the hearts of all true believers.[24]

5. The suppression of the writings of the church fathers by those antagonistic to their position to minimize their continuing influence de-emphasized this central teaching and tended to obliterate the place that the imminent hope had in their life and writings.

6. The influence of Augustine, who contributed more to theological thinking than any other individual between Paul and the Reformation, through whom amillennialism was systematized and the Roman system got its Ecclesiology, was a vital factor in the cessation of premillennialism.

7. The rise of the power of the Roman church, which taught that it was the kingdom of God on earth and its head the vicar of Christ on earth, was a major factor.

It is of extreme interest to note the methods used by the opponents of the premillennial view to counteract this teaching.

> (1) Gaius and Dionysius first cast doubt upon the genuineness and inspiration of the Apocalypse, it evidently being supposed that the appeals made to it . . . could not otherwise be set aside. (2) By rejecting the literal sense, and substituting a figurative or allegorical; this effectually modified covenant and prophecy. (3) Such portions of the Old Test. as literally taught the doctrine, had their prophetic inspiration discredited . . . (4) Accepting all the prophetical portions, and what could not be conveniently allegorized and applied to the church, was attributed to heaven for fulfillment . . . (5) Making promises directly given to the Jewish nation as such, either conditional in their nature or else merely typical of the blessings accruing to Gentiles.[25]

It must thus be observed that the opposition to premillennialism arose from those who were marked by their unbelief, whose doctrines in general were condemned by believing men down through the ages of church history, who opposed premillennialism, not because it was unscriptural, but because it contradicted their own philosophies and methods of interpretation.

---

[24] Cited by Peters, *op. cit.*, I, 505.
[25] *Ibid.*, I, 502.

III. The Rise of Amillennialism

With the contribution of Augustine to theological thinking amillennialism came into prominence. While Origen laid the foundation in establishing the non-literal method of interpretation, it was Augustine who systematized the non-literal view of the millennium into what is now known as amillennialism.

A. *The importance of Augustine.* The relationship of Augustine to the whole doctrine has been stated by Walvoord:

> Not only did his thinking crystalize the theology which preceded him, but to a large extent he laid the foundations for both Catholic and Protestant doctrine. B. B. Warfield, quoting Harnack, refers to Augustine as "incomparably the greatest man whom, 'between Paul the Apostle and Luther the Reformer, the Christian Church has possessed.'" While the contribution of Augustine is principally noted in the areas of the doctrine of the church, hamartiology, the doctrine of grace, and predestination, he is also the greatest landmark in the early history of amillennialism.
>
> The importance of Augustine to the history of amillennialism is derived from two reasons. First, there are no acceptable exponents of amillennialism before Augustine. . . . Prior to Augustine, amillennialism was associated with the heresies produced by the allegorizing and spiritualizing school of theology at Alexandria, which not only opposed premillennialism but subverted any literal exegesis of Scripture whatever. . . .
>
> The second reason for the importance of Augustinian amillennialism is that his viewpoint became the prevailing doctrine of the Roman Church, and it was adopted with variations by most of the Protestant Reformers along with many other teachings of Augustine. The writings of Augustine, in fact, occasioned the shelving of premillennialism by most of the organized church.[26]

B. *Augustine's view on the chiliastic question.* In his famous work, *The City of God,* Augustine set forth the idea that the church visible was the Kingdom of God on earth. Of the importance of this work Peters says:

> Probably no work has appeared that had such a powerful influence in overwhelming the more ancient doctrine, as Augustine's leading one, *The City of God.* This was specially designed

[26] Walvoord, *op. cit.,* 106:420-21.

> to teach *the existence of the Kingdom of God in the Church* beside or contemporaneous with the earthly or human Kingdom.[27]

Out of this basic Ecclesiology, which interpreted the church as being the kingdom, Augustine developed his doctrine of the millennium, which is summarized by Allis as follows:

> He taught that the millennium is to be interpreted spiritually as fulfilled in the Christian Church. He held that the binding of Satan took place during the earthly ministry of our Lord (Lk. x. 18), that the first resurrection is the new birth of the believer (Jn. v. 25), and that the millennium must correspond, therefore, to the inter-adventual period or Church age. This involved the interpreting of Rev. xx. 1-6 as a "recapitulation" of the preceding chapters instead of as describing a new age following chronologically on the events set forth in chap. xix. Living in the first half of the first millennium of the Church's history, Augustine naturally took the 1000 years of Rev. xx. literally, and he expected the second advent to take place at the end of that period. But since he somewhat inconsistently identified the millennium with what then remained of the sixth chiliad of human history he believed that this period might end about A.D. 650 with a great outburst of evil, the revolt of Gog, which would be followed by the coming of Christ in judgment.[28]

Thus Augustine made several important assertions which molded eschatological thinking: (1) He denied that the millennium would follow the second advent, (2) he held that the millennium would fall in the inter-advent period, and (3) he taught that the church is the kingdom and there would be no literal fulfillment of the promises made to Israel. These interpretations formed the central core of the eschatological system that dominated theological thinking for centuries. The fact that history has proved that Satan was not bound, that we are not in the millennium, experiencing all that was promised to those who enter it, and that Christ did not come in A.D. 650, has not been sufficient to dissuade the adherents of this system. In spite of its obvious failure it is still held widely.

IV. The Eclipse of Premillennialism

With the rise of Romanism, committed to the idea that their

---

[27] Peters, *ibid.*, I, 508.
[28] Allis, *op. cit.*, p. 3.

institution was the kingdom of God, premillennialism declined rapidly. Auberlen says:

> Chiliasm disappeared in proportion as Roman Papal Catholicism advanced. The Papacy took to itself, as a robbery, that glory which is an object of hope, and can only be reached by obedience and humility of the cross. When the Church became a harlot, she ceased to be a bride who goes out to meet her bridegroom; and thus Chiliasm disappeared. This is the deep truth that lies at the bottom of the Protestant, anti-papistic interpretation of the Apocalypse.[29]

Peters observes:

> It may then be briefly stated as a self-evident fact, that the entire spirit and aim of the Papacy is antagonistic to the early church view, being based on coveted ecclesiastical and secular power, on extended jurisdiction lodged in the hands of a Primate. . . . when a system was founded which decided that the reign of the saints had already begun—that the Bishop of Rome ruled on earth in Christ's place; that the deliverance from the curse would only be effected in the third heaven; that in the church, as a Kingdom, there was "an aristocracy" to which unhesitating obedience must be rendered; that the prophetical announcements respecting Messiah's Kingdom were fulfilling in Romish predominance, splendor, and wealth; that the rewarding and elevation of saints was not dependent upon the Sec. Advent, but upon the power lodged in the existing Kingdom, etc., etc.,—then it was that Chiliasm, so distasteful and obnoxious to these claims and doctrines, fell beneath the powerful and world-pervading influence exerted against it.[30]

In spite of the ascendancy of Roman amillenarianism there did continue a small remnant that held to the premillennial position. Ryrie cites the Waldensians and the Paulicians, together with the Cathari, who held the Apostolic belief.[31] Peters cites, in addition, the Albigenses, Lollard, Wickliffites, and the Bohemian Protestants who espoused the premillennial cause.[32]

V. Chiliasm Since the Reformation

In the Reformation period itself the Reformers' interest was centered upon the great doctrines of Soteriology and little,

---

29 Cited by Peters, *op. cit.*, I, 499.
30 *Ibid.*, I, 516-17.
31 Ryrie, *op. cit.* pp. 27-28.
32 Peters, *op. cit.*, I, 521.

if any, attention was given to the doctrines of Eschatology. The Reformers themselves continued, for the most part, in the Augustinian position, principally because that area of doctrine was not under discussion. However, certain bases were laid that opened the way for the rise of premillennialism. Peters writes:

> . . . each [of the Reformers] recorded their belief, in the duty of every believer to be constantly looking for the Advent, in a speedy Advent, in there being no future Millennial glory before the coming of Jesus, in the church remaining a mixed state to the end, in the design of the present dispensation, in the principle of interpretation adopted, in unbelief again extending and widening before the Advent, in the renewal of this earth, etc.—doctrines in unison with Chiliasm. The simple truth in reference to them is this: that they were not Chiliasts, although teaching several points that materially aid in sustaining Chiliasm.[33]

The return to the literal method of interpretation, upon which the Reformation movement was based, laid again the foundation for the resurgence of the premillennial faith.

A. *The rise of postmillennialism.* In the post-Reformation period there arose the interpretation known as postmillennialism, which came to supplant, for the most part, the Augustinian amillennialism in the Protestant church. The failure of amillennialism, as interpreted by Augustine, to meet the facts of history gave rise to a re-examination of his doctrine. The first exponent of the position that Christ would return after the millennium and bring in the final state with a general judgment and resurrection, according to Kromminga,[34] was Joachim of Floris, a twelfth century Roman Catholic writer. Walvoord says of him:

> His view of the millennium is that it begins and continues as a rule of the Holy Spirit. He had in view three dispensations, the first from Adam to John the Baptist; the second began with John; and the third with St. Benedict (480-543), founder of his monastaries. The three dispensations were respectively of the Father, of the Son, and of the Spirit. Joachim predicted that about 1260 the final development would take place and righteousness would triumph.[35]

During the sixteenth and seventeenth centuries many men in

---

33 *Ibid.*, I, 527.
34 Kromminga, *op. cit.*, p. 20.
35 Walvoord, *op. cit.*, 106:152.

the Netherlands held the view that the millennium was future. Coccejus, Alting, the two Kitringas, d'Outrein, Witsius, Hoornbeek, Koelman, and Brakel are cited by Berkhof as being postmillennial.[36] However, postmillennialism as a system is usually attributed to Daniel Whitby (1638-1726).[37] Concerning Whitby, Walvoord writes:

> Whitby himself was a Unitarian. His writings particulary as bearing on the Godhead were publicly burned and he was denounced as a heretic. He was a liberal and a freethinker, untrammelled by traditions or previous conceptions of the church. His views on the millennium would probably have never been perpetuated if they had not been so well keyed to the thinking of the times. The rising tide of intellectual freedom, science, and philosophy, coupled with humanism, had enlarged the concept of human progress and painted a bright picture of the future. Whitby's views of a coming golden age for the church was just what people wanted to hear. It fitted the thinking of the times. It is not strange that theologians scrambling for readjustment in a changing world should find in Whitby just the key they needed. It was attractive to all kinds of theology. It provided for the conservative a seemingly more workable principle of interpreting Scripture. After all, the prophets of the Old Testament knew what they were talking about when they predicted an age of peace and righteousness. Man's increasing knowledge of the world and scientific improvements which were coming could fit into this picture. On the other hand, the concept was pleasing to the liberal and skeptic. If they did not believe the prophets, at least they believed that man was now able to improve himself and his environment. They too believed a golden age was ahead.[38]

These two groups to which postmillennialism appealed—the liberal and the conservative—soon developed two different types of teaching.

> (1) A Biblical type of postmillennialism, finding its material in the Scriptures and its power in God; (2) the evolutionary or liberal theological type which bases its proof on confidence in man to achieve progress through natural means. These two widely separated systems of belief have one thing in common, the idea of ultimate progress and solution of present difficulties.[39]

---

[36] Louis Berkhof, *Systematic Theology*, p. 716.
[37] A. H. Strong, *Systematic Theology*, p. 1013.
[38] Walvoord, *op. cit.*, 106:154.
[39] *Ibid.*

Postmillennialism became the eschatological position of the theologians who dominated theological thinking for the last several centuries. The general features of the system may be summarized thus:

> Postmillennialism is based on the figurative interpretation of prophecy which permits wide freedom in finding the meaning of difficult passages—a latitude which is reflected in the lack of uniformity in postmillennial exegesis. The prophecies of the Old Testament relative to a righteous kingdom on earth are to be fulfilled in the kingdom of God in the interadvent period. The kingdom is spiritual and unseen rather than material and political. The divine power of the kingdom is the Holy Spirit. The throne which Christ is predicted to occupy is the Father's throne in heaven. The kingdom of God in the world will grow rapidly but with times of crisis. All means are used in advancing the kingdom of God—it is the center of God's providence. In particular the preaching of the Gospel and spread of Christian principles signal its progress. The coming of the Lord is regarded as a series of events. Any providential dealing of God in the human situation is a coming of the Lord. The final coming of the Lord is climactic and is in the very remote future. There is no hope of the Lord's return in the foreseeable future, certainly not within this generation. Postmillennialism like amillennialism believes that all the final judgments of men and angels are essentially one event and will occur after a general resurrection of all men and before the eternal state. Postmillennialism is distinguished from premillennialism which regards the millennium as future and after the second advent. Postmillennialism is distinguished from amillennialism by its optimism, assurance of the ultimate triumph of the kingdom of God in the world, and its relative fulfillment of the millennial idea on the earth. Theologians like Hodge find rather literal fulfillment, including the conversion and restoration of Israel as a nation. Others like Snowden regard the millennium of which Revelation 20 speaks as referring to heaven.[40]

Postmillennialism is no longer an issue in theology. World War II brought about the demise of this system. Its collapse may be attributed to (1) the inherent weakness of postmillennialism in that, based on the spiritualizing principle of interpretation, there was no coherence in it; (2) the trend toward liberalism, which postmillennialism could not meet, because of its spiritualizing principle of interpretation; (3) its failure to fit

[40] *Ibid.*, p. 165.

the facts of history; (4) the new trend toward realism in theology and philosophy, seen in neo-orthodoxy, which admits man is a sinner, and can not bring about the new age anticipated by postmillennialism; and (5) a new trend toward amillennialism, growing out of a return to Reformation theology as a basis of doctrine.[41] Postmillennialism finds no defenders or advocates in the present chiliastic discussions within the theological world.

B. *The recent rise of amillennialism.* Amillennialism has had a great rise in popularity in the last several decades, largely because of the collapse of the postmillennial position, of which the majority of theologians were followers. Since amillennialism depends on the same spiritualizing principle of interpretation as postmillennialism and viewed the millennium as an interadvent era preceding the second advent, as did postmillennialism, it was a relatively simple matter for the postmillennialist to shift to the amillennial view.

Amillennialism today is divided into two camps. (1) The first, of which Allis and Berkhof are adherents, holds essentially to the Augustinian amillennialism, although admitting the need for certain refinements. This of course is also the view of the Roman Church. It finds the fulfillment of all the Old Testament promises concerning a kingdom and kingdom blessings in Christ's reign from the Father's throne over the church, which is on earth. (2) The second is the view advocated by Duesterdieck and Kliefoth and promoted in this country by Warfield, which attacked the Augustinian position that the kingdom is earthly and viewed the kingdom as God's reign over the saints which are in heaven, thus making it a heavenly kingdom. Walvoord summarizes this view by saying:

> A new type of amillennialism has arisen, however, of which Warfield can be taken as an example which is actually a totally new type of amillennialism. Allis traces this view to Duesterdieck (1859) and Kliefoth (1874) and analyzes it as a reversal of the fundamental Augustinian theory that Revelation 20 was a recapitulation of the church age. The new view instead follows the line of teaching that the millennium is distinct from the church age though it precedes the second advent. To solve the problem of correlation of this interpretation with the hard facts of a world

---

[41] Cf. *ibid,* 106:165-68.

of unbelief and sin, they interpreted the millennium as a picture not of a time-period but of a state of blessedness of the saints in heaven. Warfield, with the acknowledged help of Kliefoth, defines the millennium in these words: "The vision, in one word, is a vision of the peace of those who have died in the Lord; and its message to us is embodied in the words of XIV. 13: 'Blessed are the dead which die in the Lord, from henceforth'—of which passage the present is indeed only an expansion. The picture that is brought before us here is, in fine, the picture of the 'intermediate state'—of the saints of God gathered in heaven away from the confused noise and garments bathed in blood that characterize the war upon earth, in order that they may securely await their end."

Among amillennialists who are classified as conservative, there are, then, two principal viewpoints: (1) which finds fulfillment in the present age on earth in the church; (2) which finds fulfillment in heaven in the saints. The second more than the first requires spiritualization not only of Revelation 20 but of all the many Old Testament passages dealing with a golden age of a righteous kingdom on earth.[42]

A number of reasons may be given for the current popularity of the amillennial system. (1) It is an inclusive system, which can include all strata of theological thought; liberal Protestant, conservative Protestant, and Roman Catholic. (2) With the exception of premillennialism, it is the oldest chiliastic theory and therefore has the patina of antiquity upon it. (3) It has the stamp of orthodoxy, in that it was the system adopted by the Reformers and became the foundation for many of the creedal statements. (4) It conforms to modern ecclesiasticism, which places great emphasis on the visible church that, to the amillennialist, is the center of God's whole program. (5) It presents a simple eschatological system, with only one resurrection, one judgment, and very little in a prophetic program for the future. (6) It readily conforms to the theological presuppositions of so-called "covenant theology." (7) It appeals to many as a "spiritual" interpretation of Scripture rather than a literal interpretation, which is referred to as a "carnal concept" of the millennium.

Seven dangers of the amillennial method of interpretation can be pointed out.

---

[42] *Ibid.*, 106:430.

> (1) . . . when they use the method of spiritualization of Scripture they are interpreting Scripture by a method which would be utterly destructive to Christian doctrine, if not limited largely to eschatology. (2) They do not follow the spiritualizing method of interpretation in relation to prophecy in general, but only where it is necessary to deny premillennialism. (3) They justify the spiritualizing method as a means of eliminating problems of fulfillment of prophecy—it is born of a supposed necessity rather than a natural product of exegesis. (4) They do not hesitate to use spiritualization in areas other than prophecy if it is necessary to sustain their system of doctrine. (5) As illustrated in current modernism which is almost entirely amillennial, the principle of spiritualization has been proved by history to spread easily into all basic areas of theological truth. . . . (6) The amillennial method does not provide a solid basis for a consistent system of theology. The hermeneutical method of amillennialism has justified conservative Calvinism, liberal modernism, and Roman theology alike. . . . (7) Amillennialism has not arisen historically from study of prophetic Scripture, but rather through its neglect.[43]

The effect of the amillennial system of interpretation is most keenly felt in three major fields of doctrine. (1) In the field of Soteriology amillennialism is guilty of the reductive error common to covenant theology, in which a minor point is made the major point in a program, and views the entire program of God as a redemptive program, so that all ages are variations in the progressive revelation of the covenant of redemption. (2) In the field of Ecclesiology they view all saints of all ages as members of the church. This loses sight of all the distinctions between God's program for Israel and that for the church and necessitates the denial of the teaching of Scripture that the church is a mystery, unrevealed until the present age. It sees the fulfillment of the entire kingdom program in the church in this interadvent period or else in the saints now in heaven. They have no concept of the church as the distinctive body of Christ, but view it only as an organization. This whole concept is one of the basic differences between premillennialism and amillennialism. (3) In the field of Eschatology, while there is universal rejection of the premillennial interpretations, there is little agreement among the branches of amillennialism. Liberal amillennialism denies such doctrines

[43] *Ibid.*, 107:49-50.

as resurrection, judgment, the second advent, eternal punishment, and related subjects. Roman amillennialism evolved the system of purgatory, limbo, and such non-Biblical doctrines, which have become a part of their system. Conservative amillennialism still holds to literal doctrines of resurrection, judgment, eternal punishment, and related themes. It is therefore difficult to systematize amillennial Eschatology. Yet it is in this field that the widest divergence from the premillennial and Scriptural position is felt.

C. *The resurgence of premillennialism.* While the Reformers did not adopt the premillennial interpretation of the Scriptures, without exception they did return to the literal method of interpreting the Scriptures, which is the essential basis on which premillennialism rests. The logical application of this method of interpretation soon led many of the post-Reformation writers to this position. Peters says:

> . . . we are chiefly indebted to a few leading minds for bringing forth a return to the old Patristic faith in all its essential forms. Prominently among these are the following: the profound Biblical scholar Joseph Mede (born 1586, died 1638), in his still celebrated *Clavis Apocalyptica* (translated into English) and *Exposition on Peter;* Th. Brightman (1644), *Exposition of Daniel and Apoc.;* J. A. Bengel (a learned divine, born 1687, died 1752), *Exposition of the Apocalypse* and *Addresses* on the same; also the writings of Th. Goodwin (1679); Ch. Daubuz (1730); Piscator (1646); M. F. Roos (1770); Alstedius (1643 and earlier); Cressener (1689); Farmer (1660); Fleming (1708); Hartley (1764); J. J. Hess (1774); Homes (1654); Jurieu (1686); Maton (1642); Peterson (1692); Sherwin (1665); and others (such as Conrade, Gallus, Brahe, Kett, Broughton, Marten, Sir I. Newton, Whiston, etc.) . . .[44]

From the influence of these men there emerged a stream of exegetes and expositors that brought premillennialism back to a place of prominence in Biblical interpretation.[45] Among them will be found the greatest exegetes and expositors that the church has known, such as Bengel, Steir, Alford, Lange, Meyer,

---

[44] Peters, *op. cit.*, I, 538.

[45] *Ibid.*, I, 542-46. Peters lists some 360 adherents of this position among the leaders of eleven denominations in this country, and some 470 writers and ministers of Europe who espoused the premillennial cause.

Fausset, Keach, Bonar, Ryle, Lillie, MacIntosh, Newton, Tregelles, Ellicott, Lightfoot, Westcott, Darby, to mention only a few. The statement of Alford, in speaking of the interpreters of the Apocalypse since the French Revolution, is pertinent: "The majority, *both in number, learning, and research,* adopt the Premillennial Advent, following the plain and undeniable sense of the sacred text."[46]

Without doubt Allis is correct when he says:

> The Dispensational teaching of today, as represented, for example, by the *Scofield Reference Bible,* can be traced back directly to the Brethren Movement which arose in England and Ireland about the year 1830. Its adherents are often known as Plymouth Brethren, because Plymouth was the strongest of the early centres of Brethrenism. It is also called Darbyism, after John Nelson Darby (1800-82), its most conspicuous representative.[47]

The Biblical studies promoted by Darby and his followers popularized the premillennial interpretation of Scriptures. It has been disseminated through the growing Bible conference movement, the Bible Institute movement, many periodicals devoted to Bible study, and is closely associated with the whole conservative theological movement in our country today.

Thus the historical survey reveals that the premillennial interpretation, which was held with unanimity by the early church, was supplanted through the influence of Origen's allegorizing method by Augustinian amillennialism, which became the viewpoint of the Roman church and continued to dominate until the Protestant Reformation, at which time the return to the literal method of interpretation again gave rise to the premillennial interpretation. This interpretation was challenged by the rise of postmillennialism, which came into ascendancy after the time of Whitby and continued until its rapid decline at the time of the World War. This decline brought about the rise of amillennialism, which now competes with premillennialism as the method of interpreting the chiliastic question.

---

[46] Henry Alford, *Greek Testament,* II, 350.
[47] Allis, *op. cit.,* p. 9.

VI. Resultant Observations

Too great importance cannot be attached to the doctrine of the second advent of the Lord Jesus Christ. Chafer says:

> The general theme concerning the return of Christ has the unique distinction of being the first prophecy uttered by man (Jude 1:14-15) and the last message from the ascended Christ as well as being the last word of the Bible (Rev. 22:20-21). Likewise, the theme of the second coming of Christ is unique because of the fact that it occupies a larger part of the text of the Scriptures than any other doctrine, and it is the outstanding theme of prophecy in both the Old and New Testaments. In fact, all other prophecy largely contributes to the one great end of the complete setting forth of this crowning event—the second coming of Christ.[48]

Concerning the second advent certain facts may be observed.

A. *The second advent is premillennial.* The literal method of interpreting the Scriptures, as previously set forth, makes necessary a premillennial coming of the Lord.

B. *The second advent is a literal advent.* In order to fulfill the promises made in the Word concerning His coming (Acts 1:11), His advent must be literal. This necessitates the bodily return of Christ to the earth.

C. *The second advent is necessary.* The large body of unfulfilled prophecy makes the second advent absolutely essential.[49] It has been promised that He shall come Himself (Act 1:11); that the dead will hear His voice (John 5:28); that He will minister unto His watching servants (Luke 12:37); that He will come to earth again (Acts 1:11), to the same Mount Olivet from which He ascended (Zech. 14:4), in flaming fire (2 Thess. 1:8), in the clouds of heaven with power and great glory (Matt. 24:30; 1 Pet. 1:7; 4:13), and stand upon the earth (Job 19:25); that His saints (the church) shall come with Him (1 Thess. 3:13; Jude 14); that every eye shall see Him (Rev. 1:7); that He shall destroy Antichrist (2 Thess. 2:8); that He shall sit on His throne (Matt. 25:-31; Rev. 5:13); that all nations will be gathered before Him and He will judge them (Matt. 25:32); that He shall have the throne

---

[48] Chafer, *op. cit.*, IV, 306.

[49] Cf. W. E. Blackstone, *Jesus Is Coming*, pp. 24-25.

of David (Isa. 9:6-7; Luke 1:32; Ezek. 21:25-27); that it will be upon the earth (Jer. 23:5-6); that He shall have a kingdom (Dan. 7:13-14); and rule over it with His saints (Dan. 7:18-27; Rev. 5:10); that all kings and nations shall serve Him (Ps. 72:11; Isa. 49:6-7; Rev. 15:4); that the kingdoms of this world shall become His kingdom (Zech. 9:10; Rev. 11:15); that the people shall gather unto Him (Gen. 49:10); that every knee shall bow to Him (Isa. 45:23); that they shall come and worship the King (Zech. 14:16; Ps. 86:9); that He shall build up Zion (Ps. 102:16); that His throne shall be in Jerusalem (Jer. 3:17; Isa. 33:20-21); that the Apostles shall sit upon twelve thrones, judging the twelve tribes of Israel (Matt. 19:28; Luke 22:28-30); that He shall rule all nations (Ps. 2:8-9; Rev. 2:27); that He shall rule with judgment and justice (Ps. 9:7); that the temple in Jerusalem will be rebuilt (Ezek. 40—48), and the glory of the Lord will come into it (Ezek. 43:2-5; 44:4); that the glory of the Lord will be revealed (Isa. 40:5); that the wilderness shall be a fruitful field (Isa. 32:15); that the desert will blossom as the rose (Isa. 35:1-2); and His rest shall be glorious (Isa. 11:10). The entire covenant program with Israel, which has not yet been fulfilled, necessitates the second advent of Messiah to the earth. The principle of literal fulfillment makes it essential that Christ return.

D. *The second advent will be visible.* Repeated references in the Scriptures establish the fact that the second advent will be a full and visible manifestation of the Son of God to the earth (Acts 1:11; Rev. 1:7; Matt. 24:30). As the Son was publicly repudiated and rejected, He shall be publicly presented by God at the second advent. This advent will be associated with the visible manifestation of glory (Matt. 16:27; 25:31), for in the completion of judgment and the manifestation of sovereignty God is glorified (Rev. 14:7; 18:1; 19:1).

E. *Practical exhortations arising from the second advent.* Extensive use is made of the doctrine of the second advent of Christ in the Scriptures as a basis of exhortation. It is used as an exhortation to watchfulness (Matt. 24:42-44; 25:13; Mark 13:32-37; Luke 12:35-38; Rev. 16:15); to sobriety (1 Thess. 5:2-6; 1 Pet. 1:13; 4:7; 5:8); to repentance (Acts 3:19-21; Rev. 3:3); to fidelity (Matt. 25:19-21; Luke 12:42-44; 19:12-13); to be unashamed of Christ (Mark 8:38); against worldliness (Matt. 16:26-27); to moderation (Phil. 4:5); to patience (Heb. 10:36-37; James 5:7-8); to mortification of the flesh (Col. 3:3-5); to sincerity (Phil. 1:9-10); to practical sanctification (1 Thess. 5:23); to ministerial faithfulness (2 Tim. 4:1-2); to incite obedience to the Apostle's injunctions (1 Tim. 6:13-14); to pastoral diligence and purity (1 Pet. 5:2-4); to purity (1 John 3:2-3); to abide in Christ (1 John 2:28); to endure manifold temptations and the severest trials of faith (1 Pet. 1:7); to bear persecution for the Lord (1 Pet. 4:13); to holiness and godliness (2 Pet. 3:11-13); to brotherly love (1 Thess. 3:12-13); to keep in mind our heavenly citizenship (Phil. 3:20-21); to love the second coming (2 Tim. 4:7-8); to look for Him (Heb. 9:27-28); to have confidence that Christ will finish the work (Phil. 1:6); to hold fast the hope firm unto the end (Rev. 2:25; 3:11); to separation from worldly lusts and to live godly (Titus 2:11-13); to watchfulness because of its suddenness (Luke 17:24-30); to guard against hasty judgment (1 Cor. 4:5); to the hope of a rich reward (Matt. 19:27-28); to assure the disciples of a time of rejoicing (2 Cor. 1:14; Phil. 2:16; 1 Thess 2:19); to comfort the apostles in view of Christ's departure (John 14:3; Acts 1:11); it is the principal event for which the believer awaits (1 Thess. 1:9-10); it is a crowning grace and assurance of blamelessness in the day of the Lord (1 Cor. 1:4-8); it is the time of reckoning with the servants (Matt. 25:19); it is the time of the judgment of the living Gentiles (Matt. 25:31-46); it is the time of the completion of the resurrection program for the saved (1 Cor. 15:23); it is the time of the manifestation of the saints (2 Cor. 5:10; Col. 3:4); it is a source of consolation (1 Thess. 4:14-18); it is associated with tribulation and judgment for the unsaved (2 Thess. 1:7-9); it is proclaimed at the Lord's table (1 Cor. 11:26).[50]

[50] *Ibid.*, pp. 180-81.

Chapter XXIII

THE RESURRECTIONS ASSOCIATED WITH THE SECOND ADVENT

The Old Testament associated the hope of resurrection with the Messianic hope of the Day of the Lord. In Daniel the resurrection (12:2) is seen to be an event subsequent to the time of trouble under the Desolator (12:1). In Isaiah the resurrection (26:19) is spoken of in reference to "the indignation" (26:20-21). In John's Gospel the resurrection is stated as a hope associated with the "last day," or the day of the Lord (11:24). Since this is true, it is necessary to consider the second advent in its relation to the resurrection program. It is not possible in this connection to consider the whole doctrine of resurrection, but confine the study to the eschatological or prophetic aspects of that doctrine.

It will readily be observed that the doctrine of resurrection is a cardinal doctrine of the Word of God. In the ministry of the apostles after Christ's resurrection the theme of the resurrection of Christ dominated their preaching, almost to the exclusion of His death. In more than forty New Testament references to resurrection, with the possible exception of Luke 2:34, it is always used of a literal resurrection, never in a spiritual or non-literal sense, and has to do with the raising up of the physical body. This is assumed and not debated at this point.

I. The Kinds of Resurrection

In Scripture two different kinds of resurrection are anticipated in God's resurrection program: the resurrection to life and the resurrection to judgment.

A. *The resurrection to life.* There are a number of passages which teach this distinctive part of the resurrection program.

> But when thou makest a feast, call the poor, the maimed, the lame, the blind: And thou shalt be blessed; for they cannot

> recompense thee: for thou shalt be recompensed *at the resurrection of the just* [Luke 14:13-14].
>
> That I may know him, and the power of his resurrection, and the fellowship of his sufferings, being made conformable unto his death; if by any means I might attain unto the resurrection of the dead (literally, *the resurrection, the one out from the dead*) [Phil. 3:10-14].
>
> Women received their dead raised to life again: and others were tortured not accepting deliverance; that they might obtain *a better resurrection* [Heb. 11:35].
>
> Marvel not at this: for the hour is coming, in the which all that are in the graves shall hear his voice, and shall come forth; they that have done good, unto *the resurrection of life;* and they that have done evil, unto the resurrection of damnation [John 5:28-29].
>
> Blessed and holy is he that hath part in *the first resurrection:* on such the second death hath no power, but they shall be priests of God and of Christ, and shall reign with him a thousand years [Rev. 20:6].

These references show that there is a part of the resurrection program that is called "the resurrection of the just," the "out-resurrection from the dead," "a better resurrection," "the resurrection of life," and "the first resurrection." These phrases suggest a separation; a resurrection of a portion of those who are dead, which resurrection leaves some dead unchanged while these resurrected undergo a complete transformation. Blackstone says:

> Now if Christ is coming to raise the righteous a thousand years before the ungodly, it would be natural and imperative that the former should be called a resurrection *from,* or *out of the dead,* the rest of the dead being left. . . . this is just what is most carefully done in the Word. . . . It consists in the use made, *in the Greek text* of the words . . . [*ek nekron*].
>
> These words signify "from the dead" or, out of the dead, implying that the other dead are left.
>
> The resurrection . . .[*nekron* or *ek nekron*] (. . . of the dead) is applied to both classes because all will be raised. But the resurrection . . . (ek nekron—out of the dead) is not once applied to the ungodly. The latter phrase is used altogether 49 times, to-wit: 34 times, to express Christ's resurrection, whom we know was thus raised *out of the dead.* 3 times, to express John's supposed resurrection, who, as Herod thought, had been

thus raised *out of the dead.* 3 times to express the resurrection of Lazarus, who was also raised *out of the dead.* 3 times, it is used figuratively, to express spiritual life out of the deadness of sin (Rom. 6:13; 11:15; Eph. 5:14). It is used in Luke 16:31 . . . "Though one rose *from the dead.*" And in Heb. 11:19, Abraham's faith that God could raise Isaac *from the dead.*

And the remaining 4 times it is used to express a future resurrection *out of the dead,* namely, in Mark 12:25 . . . "they rise *from the dead* . . . Luke 20:35-36 . . ." the *resurrection which is from among the dead* . . . Acts 4:1-2 *"the resurrection which is from among (the) dead"* . . .

And in Phil. 3:11 . . . the literal translation is *the out resurrection from among the dead,* which peculiar construction of language gives a special emphasis to the idea that this is a resurrection *out from among the dead.*

These passages clearly show, that there is yet to be a resurrection out of the dead; that is, that part of the dead will be raised, before all are raised. Olshausen declares that the "phrase would be inexplicable if it were not derived from the idea that out of the masses of the dead some would rise first."[1]

This resurrection, usually called *the first resurrection,* but which might be called *the resurrection unto life* (John 5:29) with greater clarity inasmuch as this resurrection is made up of a number of component parts, is that part of the resurrection program in which the individuals are raised to eternal life. It includes within it all who, at any time, are raised to eternal life. The destiny, not the time, determines to which part of the resurrection program any event is to be assigned.

B. *The resurrection to damnation.* Scripture anticipates another part of the resurrection program that deals with the unsaved. It is the second resurrection, or the resurrection to damnation.

. . . they that have done evil *unto the resurrection of damnation* [John 5:29].

But *the rest of the dead* lived not again until the thousand years were finished [Rev. 20:5].

And I saw a great white throne, and him that sat on it, from whose face the earth and the heaven fled away; and there was found no place for them. And I saw *the dead,* small and great,

---

[1] W. E. Blackstone, *Jesus Is Coming,* pp. 59-61.

> stand before God. . . . And the sea gave up the *dead* which were in it, and death and hell delivered up *the dead* which were in them . . . [Rev. 20:11-13].

Inasmuch as the first resurrection was completed before the thousand year reign began (Rev. 20:5), "the dead" referred to in Revelation 20:11-12 can only be those who were left behind at the out-resurrection from among the dead ones and who constitute those that are raised unto damnation. The second resurrection, better termed the resurrection of damnation, includes all who are raised to eternal condemnation. It is not chronology that determines who is in the second resurrection, but rather the destiny of the one raised.

II. The Time of the Resurrections

The introduction of a distinction in the time element in the different parts of the resurrection program brought consternation to the disciples. In connection with the transfiguration of the Lord, we read:

> And as they came down from the mountain, he charged them that they should tell no man what things they had seen, till the Son of man were risen from the dead. And they kept that saying with themselves, questioning one with another what the rising from the dead [*ek nekron,* out from among the dead] should mean [Mark 9:9-10].

Blackstone well observes:

> . . . we see . . . why the three favored disciples were "questioning one with another what the rising *from* the dead should mean." They understood perfectly, what the resurrection *of* the dead meant, for this was a common accepted doctrine of the Jews [Heb. 6:2]. But the resurrection *from* the dead was a new revelation to them.[2]

The Old Testament clearly taught the fact of the resurrection (Heb. 11:17-18; Job 14:1-13; 19:25-26; Ps. 16:10; 49:15; Hosea 5:15-6:2; 13:14, Isa. 25:8; 26:19; Dan. 12:2; John 5:28-29; 11:24), but no revelation was made concerning the time element involved. In fact, one might have concluded, were it not for the revelation contained in the New Testament, that there would be

---

[2] *Ibid.,* p. 62.

a general resurrection, in which the saved and unsaved are raised together to be separated to their final destiny as taught by the amillennialist. However, the New Testament contains clear revelation to the contrary.

There are several passages generally used to teach the false doctrine of a general resurrection. The first of these is Daniel 12:2-3, where the prophet writes:

> And many of them that sleep in the dust of the earth shall awake, some to everlasting life, and some to shame and everlasting contempt. And they that be wise shall shine as the brightness of the firmament; and they that turn many to righteousness as the stars for ever and ever.

No distinction in time seems to be made here and therefore it is concluded that a general resurrection is taught. Tregelles ably comments on this passage:

> I do not doubt that the right translation of this verse is . . . "And many from among the sleepers of the dust of the earth shall awake; these shall be unto everlasting life; but those [the rest of the sleepers, those who do not awake at this time] shall be unto shame and everlasting contempt." The word which in our Authorized version is twice rendered "some," is never repeated in any other passage in the Hebrew Bible, in the sense of taking up distributively any general class which has been previously mentioned; this is enough, I believe, to warrant our applying its first occurrence here to the whole of the many who awake, and the second to the mass of the sleepers, those who do not awake at this time. It is clearly not a general resurrection; it is "many *from among*"; and it is only by taking the words in this sense, that we gain any information as to what becomes of those who continue to sleep in the dust of the earth.
>
> This passage has been understood by the Jewish commentators in the sense that I have stated. Of course these men with the vail on their hearts are no guides as to the use of the Old Testament; but they are helps as to the grammatical and lexicographical value of sentences and words. Two of the Rabbis who commented on this prophet were, Saadiah Haggaon (in the tenth century of our era), and Aben Ezra (in the twelfth); the latter of these was a writer of peculiar abilities and accuracy of mind. He explains the verse in the following manner:
>
> . . . its interpretation is, *those who shall awake shall be unto*

> *everlasting life, and those who shall not awake shall be unto shame unto everlasting contempt. . .*[3]

It must be concluded that the prophet is affirming the fact of resurrection and the universality of the resurrection without affirming the specific time at which the parts of the resurrection take place.

A second passage often used to support the idea of a general resurrection is John 5:28-29. The Lord says:

> Marvel not at this: for the hour is coming, in the which all that are in the graves shall hear his voice, And shall come forth; they that have done good, unto the resurrection of life and they that have done evil, unto the resurrection of damnation.

It is affirmed that the Lord's use of the word "hour" necessitates a general resurrection of both saved and unsaved. However, this word need not imply such a general resurrection program. Harrison writes:

> It must be granted, however, that the language does not demand coincidence in the resurrections. John's use of the word . . . (*hora*) in 5:25 allows for its extension over a long period. The same is true of 4:21, 23. Jesus is speaking in the fashion of the Old Testament prophets, who grouped together without differentiation in time the events which they glimpsed upon the far horizon of history. The same feature is found in the eschatological discourses of Jesus in the Synoptic Gospels, wherein the impending fall of Jerusalem with its attendant woes can hardly be disentangled from the description of the far-off event that is associated with the Great Tribulation. Somewhat parallel, though in a different category, is the inclusive manner in which Jesus speaks of spiritual and physical quickening in one statement. An example is John 5:21[4].

The Lord, in this passage, is teaching the universality of the resurrection program and the distinctions within that program, but is not teaching the time at which the various resurrections will take place. To make the passage so teach is to pervert its original intent.

It is made very clear in Revelation 20 that the two parts of

---

[3] S. P. Tregelles, *Remarks on the Prophetic Visions in The Book of Daniel*, pp. 165-66.

[4] Everett F. Harrison, "The Christian Doctrine of Resurrection," p. 46.

the resurrection program are separated by an interval of a thousand years. John wrote:

> And I saw thrones, and they sat upon them, and judgment was given unto them: and I saw the souls of them that were beheaded for the witness of Jesus, and for the word of God, and which had not worshipped the beast, neither his image, neither had received his mark upon their foreheads, or in their hands; and they lived and reigned with Christ a thousand years. . . . This is the first resurrection. Blessed and holy is he that hath part in the first resurrection: on such the second death hath no power, but they shall be priests of God and of Christ, and shall reign with him a thousand years [Rev. 20:4-6].

It will be observed that the first part of verse five, "But the rest of the dead lived not again until the thousand years were finished," is a parenthetical statement that explains what happens to those who are left in the realm of death when the first resurrection is completed at the second advent of Christ. This passage teaches that one thousand years will intervene between the first resurrection, or the resurrection unto life, and the resurrection of the rest of the dead, which, according to Revelation 20:11-13, is the resurrection unto damnation. The only way that the obvious teaching of this passage can be obviated is to spiritualize it so that the passage is not speaking of physical resurrection, but rather of the blessedness of the souls who are in the presence of the Lord. Of this interpretation, Alford writes:

> . . . I cannot consent to distort its words from their plain sense and chronological place in the prophecy, on account of any considerations of difficulty, or any risk of abuses which the doctrine of the Millennium may bring with it. Those who lived next to the Apostles, and the whole Church for three hundred years, understood them in the plain literal sense; and it is a strange sight in these days to see expositors who are among the first in reverence of antiquity, complacently casting aside the most cogent instance of unanimity which primitive antiquity presents. As regards the text itself, no legitimate treatment of it will extort what is known as the spiritual interpretation now in fashion. If, in a passage where *two resurrections* are mentioned, where certain *souls lived* at the first, and the rest of the *dead lived* only at the end of a specified period after the first, if in such a passage, the first resurrection may be understood to mean *spiritual* rising with Christ, while the second means literal rising from the grave; then

> there is an end of all significance in language, and Scripture is wiped out as a definite testimony to anything. If the first resurrection is spiritual, then so is the second, which I suppose no one will be hardy enough to maintain. But if the second is literal, then so is the first, which in common with the whole primitive church and many of the best modern expositors, I do maintain and receive as an article of faith and hope.[5]

It must be concluded that, although there is no clear revelation in the Old Testament concerning the time relationship of the two parts of the resurrection program, the New makes it clear that the resurrection unto life and the resurrection unto judgment are separated by a span of one thousand years.

III. The Program of Resurrection

The Apostle Paul gives us an outline of the events in the resurrection program in 1 Corinthians 15.

> For as in Adam all die, even so in Christ shall all be made alive. But every man in his own order: Christ the firstfruits; afterward they that are Christ's at his coming. Then cometh the end, when he shall have delivered up the kingdom to God, even the Father; when he shall have put down all rule and all authority and power [1 Cor. 15:20-24].

That there will be a division in the resurrection program is suggested by the phrase, "but every man in his own order" (v. 23). The word *order* (*tagma*), according to Robertson and Plummer "is a military metaphor; 'company,' 'troop,' 'band,' or 'rank.' We are to think of each 'corps' or body of troops coming on in its proper position and order . . ."[6] The parts of the resurrection are viewed as the marching battalions in a well-organized parade of triumph. Yet the military concept of the word can not be overly stressed. Harrison says:

> . . . it is very doubtful if the military force of the world is to be insisted on in this connection, for the reason that the figure with which the section begins is that of "first fruits," and, as we have seen, that calls for a harvest similar in nature to the first-fruits. This idea must be regarded as more certainly regulative of the sense than the force of . . . [*tagma*]. Doubtless all that Paul

[5] Henry Alford, *Greek Testament*, IV, 730-31.

[6] Archibald Robertson and Alfred Plummer, *First Epistle to the Corinthians*, p. 354.

> intends to convey by the use of . . . [*tagma*] is the thought of sequence.[7]

In this sequence of resurrection parade Christ is admittedly the battalion leader or the "first fruits" of the harvest that promises a great abundance of like fruits to follow at the appointed time of harvest. This phase of the resurrection program was accomplished at the time of Christ's resurrection on the third day and marks the beginning of this whole resurrection program.

A second group is introduced by the word "afterward." This word (*epeita*) signifies a lapse of time of undesignated duration. Edwards comments, "He does not say that the one event follows the other immediately, nor does he say how soon it will follow."[8] There is latitude here to cover the span of time between the resurrection of Christ and the resurrection of "they that are Christ's at his coming."

There has been a difference of opinion as to who is envisioned in the second group. Some take the term *they that are Christ's* (*hoi tou Christou*) and make it synonymous with those "in Christ" (*en tō Christo*) of verse twenty-two. This would be the technical expression that states the relation of saints to Christ in this present age. Therefore, it is concluded, this is the resurrection of the church mentioned in 1 Thessalonians 4:16. This view is supported by a reference to the word *coming* (*parousia*), which is often applied to the rapture. Paul would thus be stating that the second great group in the parade of resurrection would be those resurrected from this present age at the rapture of the church. It would be further stated by those holding this view that Paul is not mentioning here the resurrection of the tribulation saints nor Old Testament saints in the program. However, since Paul is outlining the great program of resurrection, it would seem strange if those important groups were omitted. It may be better to take the alternative view that the expression *they that are Christ's* is a non-technical reference to all the redeemed, both of the church, of the Old Testament period, and the tribulation period, all of whom will be raised at the "coming" of Christ. The word *coming,* then, would be taken in its widest

[7] Harrison, *op. cit.*, p. 192.
[8] T. C. Edwards, *The First Epistle to the Corinthians*, p. 414.

sense as applying to the second advent and its program and not to the rapture only. Thus Paul would be saying that the second great group would be the saints of all ages who are raised because they belong to Christ and this will have been accomplished by the second advent.

There is vigorous debate among the expositors as to the meaning of the phrase, "then cometh the end" (v. 24). Some feel that the word resurrection should be supplied (then cometh the end *of the resurrection*), so that Paul is speaking of the termination of the resurrection program with the resurrection of the unsaved dead at the end of the thousand years. Others feel that the unsaved are not in view, but that Paul teaches that the resurrection will be followed by the end of this present age (then cometh the end *of the age*), as in Matthew 24:6, 14; Luke 21:9. The issue is decided by the interpretation of the relationship between the two uses of "all" in verse 22. Are they co-extensive or not?

The first view on the question holds that the "all" who die in Adam are not the same as the "all" who are made alive in Christ. The advocates of this position would interpret the verse as teaching that, while all who are in Adam die, the resurrection here outlined includes only those saved who are "in Christ," and "the end" must therefore refer to the end of the age. Harrison summarizes the arguments on this position when he writes:

> The interpretation of vs. 22 that is usually called in to sustain this construction finds the second . . . [*pantes,* all] coextensive with the first. The "all" is universal in both cases. It is right at this point that difficulties begin to beset the viewpoint outlined. As we have noted in another connection, the word . . . [*zoopoiethesontai*] is too strong a term, too spiritually complexioned, to be used of all men. The natural term for resurrection of an all-inclusive sort would be . . . [*egeiresthai*]. The words "in Christ" cannot have any lower significance than they bear elsewhere. This phase speaks of the most intimate and potent soteriological connection with Christ. Unbelievers do not qualify. Meyer and Godet are on the wrong track in supposing that . . . [*en christo*] has a diluted sense here which permits of application to unbelievers. Such an application would call for . . . [*dia christou*] rather than . . . [*en christo*]. A second diffi-

> culty is the fact that the whole discussion throughout the chapter has in view believers only. At least, nothing is said definitely of any others. In the third place, the immediate context is not favorable. Paul centers the attention of his readers upon Christ as the first-fruits of the Christian dead. Both the word . . . [*aparche*] (first-fruits) and the verb . . . [*koimao*] (sleep) fit only believers. Christ is not the first-fruits of others, since they must necessarily be utterly dissimilar to Him in their resurrection. Then, too, the non-Christian dead do not "sleep." They die. A fourth difficulty presents itself in the unnatural, unprecedented use of . . . [*telos*] which this construction calls for. The word means "end" in the absolute sense of termination or close. Occasionally it is used in the sense of purpose or aim. But its use as the equivalent of an adjective (end-resurrection) is unexampled. This difficulty may be met by taking it in its usual noun force, and supplying the words "of the resurrection," in which case the whole clause would be rendered, "then cometh the end of the resurrection." But a theory which necessitates the supplying of words which are crucial to its integrity must rest under a measure of suspicion.[9]

This same view is supported by Vine, who says:

> . . . as Adam is the head of the natural race, and, in virtue of this natural relation with him, death is the common lot of men, so by reason of the fact that Christ is the Head of the spiritual, all who possess spiritual relation with Him will be made alive. There is no idea of the universalism of the human race in the comparison of the second statement with the first. That unbelievers are "in Christ" is utterly contrary to the teaching of Scripture . . . therefore only those who become new creatures and possess spiritual life, and so are "in Christ" in their experience in this present life, are included in the "all" in the second statement, who will be "made alive."[10]

Thus, according to this view Paul is viewing two great stages in the first resurrection program: the resurrection of Christ, and the resurrection of all those who are Christ's, which would include church saints, tribulation saints, and Old Testament saints, who are raised by the time of the second advent, which resurrection would be followed by the end of the age.

There are those, however, who interpret the passage to understand that Paul is including the end of the resurrection

---

[9] Harrison, *op. cit.*, pp. 191-92.
[10] W. E. Vine, *First Corinthians*, p. 210.

program in his teaching. Accordingly the phrase "in Christ," would be understood as instrumental, by Christ. Robertson and Plummer say:

> Perhaps St. Paul is thinking of a third . . . [*tagma,* order], those who are not Christ's Own, to be raised from the dead some time before the End. But throughout the passage, the unbelievers and the wicked are quite in the background, if they are thought of at all.[11]

Feinberg writes:

> The context is one that speaks of resurrection, and the end-resurrection is here in view, according to a number of commentators. With the latter we agree. The apostle has shown that there are to be definite stages in the resurrection of the dead. First, Christ is the first-fruits; second, those who are Christ's at His coming; third, the end-resurrection of all unbelievers.[12]

Pridham states the order thus:

> . . . the apostle has distributed the great work of resurrection, as a manifestation of divine power, into three definite and widely sundered acts:—1. The raising of the Lord Jesus. 2. The awakening of His own at His coming; and 3. The final emptying of every grave at the close of the Son's administration of the kingdom when the dead not included in the first resurrection shall stand, both small and great, for judgment before God.[13]

Inasmuch as the word "end" (*telos*) in its basic usage refers to the end of an act or a state and has to do with the termination of a program,[14] it may be preferable to understand that Paul is including the final or end resurrection in the marching groups here depicted.

Once again it must be observed Paul is anticipating an interval of time between the resurrection of those that are Christ's and the end, whether it be the end of the age or the end of the resurrection program. Vine says:

---

[11] Robertson and Plummer, *loc. cit.*

[12] Charles Feinberg, *Premillennialism or Amillennialism,* p. 233.

[13] Arthur Pridham, *Notes and Reflections on the First Epistle to the Corinthians,* p. 392.

[14] Joseph Henry Thayer, *Greek-English Lexicon of the New Testament,* pp. 619-20.

> . . . the word rendered "then" is not *tote,* then immediately, but *eita,* indicating sequence in time, "then" after an interval e.g., Mark 4:17, 28, and verses 5 and 7 of the present chapter. The interval implied here in verse 24 is that during which the Lord will reign in His Millennial Kingdom of righteousness and peace.[15]

IV. The Resurrection of Israel

In order to outline properly the events of the resurrection program it is necessary to establish the time of Israel's resurrection so that the proper sequence may be observed. It has commonly been taught among dispensationalists that the resurrection of 1 Thessalonians 4:16 included the Old Testament saints as well as the church saints. Ignoring the essential differences in God's program with the two groups, their resurrections are said to be simultaneous on several grounds: (1) the redemption of Israel depends on the work of Christ, as does the redemption of the church, and so they may be said to be "in Christ" and be raised together; (2) the "voice of the archangel" in 1 Thessalonians 4 has particular significance to Israel, as "the trump of God" has for the church, and so both are included; (3) the twenty-four elders in Revelation include Old Testament as well as New Testament saints and therefore both must have been resurrected; (4) Daniel 12:2-3 does not speak of literal resurrection, but of national restoration, so the passage does not indicate the time of Israel's resurrection but rather the time of her restoration.[16]

In reply certain observations may be made. Concerning (1), even though Israel is redeemed by the blood of Christ, Israel never experienced the baptism of the Holy Spirit which placed them "in Christ," so this phrase can only describe those saints of the present age who are thus related to Christ. Concerning (2), the idea that the mention of an "archangel" must necessarily include Israel because of the special ministries of angels to that nation (cf. Dan. 12:1), it is to be noted that such an assertion overlooks the fact that in the book of Revelation angelic ministries are mentioned in connection with the pro-

---

[15] Vine, *op. cit.,* p. 211.

[16] Cf. William Kelly, *Lectures on the Book of Daniel,* p. 255.

gram of the judgments preceding the second advent and in connection with the advent itself, not only when the event is related to Israel, but when related to others as well. Concerning (3), that the nation Israel is included because of the twenty-four elders, it has previously been shown that these represent the church alone and Israel need not be included there. Finally, concerning (4), Daniel 12:2-3 can not be treated figuratively without doing violence to the whole principle of literal interpretation. The comment of Tregelles has been noted before. West adds:

> The true rendering of Dan. xii. 2-3, in connection with the context, is "and (at that time) *Many* (of thy people) shall awake (or be separated) *out from among* the sleepers in the earth dust. *These* (who awake) shall be unto life everlasting but *those* (who do not wake at that time) shall be unto shame and contempt everlasting." So the most renowned Hebrew Doctors render it, and the best Christian exegetes; and it is one of the defects of the *Revised Version* that . . . it has allowed the wrong impression King James' version gives to remain.[17]

Gaebelein, commenting on this passage. says:

> Physical resurrection is not taught in the second verse of this chapter, if it were the passage would be in clash with the revelation concerning resurrection in the New Testament. There is no general resurrection, but there will be the first resurrection in which only the righteous participate and the second resurrection, which means the raising of the wicked dead for their eternal and conscious punishment. . . .
>
> We repeat the message has nothing to do with physical resurrection. Physical resurrection is however used as a figure of the national revival of Israel in that day.[18]

This interpretation seems to be based on the preconceived idea that the church and Israel are to be raised together and also on the false interpretation that, literally interpreted, Daniel 12:2 must teach a general resurrection and therefore it was felt necessary to spiritualize the passage. It must be noted that this spiritualization arises, not out of the interpretation of the passage, but out of an attempt to alleviate certain discrepancies,

---

[17] Nathaniel West, *The Thousand Years in Both Testaments*, p. 266.
[18] Arno C. Gaebelein, *The Prophet Daniel*, p. 200.

which, it has been shown, do not exist. It seems far better to understand this passage as teaching literal physical resurrection.

In another parallel passage, which deals with Israel's resurrection, Isaiah 26:19, Kelly again spiritualizes the resurrection so as to make it teach restoration. He says:

> But in chapter xxvi. the allusion to resurrection is employed as a figure, because the context proves that it can not refer to that literal fact; for if it did, it would be to deny that the unrighteous are to rise.[19]

However, the question of the resurrection of the unsaved is not in view here. Harrison says:

> While it might appear that vs. 14 teaches no resurrection for the lords who have exercised dominion over Israel, hence no resurrection for the unrighteous, proof is wanting that the verse refers to them. The two terms, "dead" and "shades" ("deceased" in the R.V.) lack the definite article. Apparently all that is included here is an observation that, so far as experience goes, death continues to hold sway over those who have come under its power. Then in vs. 19 comes a great exception. It seems that we have no allusion in the context to a non-resurrection of the unrighteous.[20]

Therefore the passages must be interpreted as referring to the literal resurrection of Israel.

In this connection a word is necessary concerning Ezekiel 37, the vision of the valley of dry bones. It is held by some that the mention of "graves" in Ezekiel 37:13-14 would seem to show that resurrection is in view here, for it does not seem to mean "a place among the nations," but rather "a place of burial." However, the bones are not seen in a grave, but scattered over the valley. Ezekiel must be using the figure of burial and resurrection here to teach restoration.

> Then he said unto me, Son of man, these bones are the whole house of Israel: behold, they say, Our bones are dried, and our hope is lost; we are cut off from our parts. Therefore prophesy and say unto them, Thus saith the Lord God; Behold, O my people, I will open your graves, and cause you to come up out of your graves, and bring you into the land of Israel.

---

[19] William Kelly, *Exposition of Isaiah*, p. 265.
[20] Harrison, *op. cit.*, p. 30.

> And ye shall know that I am the Lord, when I have opened your graves, O my people, and brought you up out of your graves, and shall put my spirit in you, and ye shall live, and I shall place you in your own land. . . . Thus saith the Lord God; Behold, I will take the children of Israel from among the heathen, whither they be gone, and will gather them on every side, and bring them into their own land: And I will make them one nation in the land upon the mountains of Israel [Ezekiel 37:11-14, 21-22].

In the explanation of the vision (vv. 21-22) Ezekiel clearly explains that restoration is in view. It would be concluded here that Ezekiel is speaking of restoration and not resurrection. Gaebelein says:

> In this vision of the dry bones physical resurrection is used as a type of the national restoration of Israel. . . . When we read here in Ezekiel of graves it must not be taken to mean literal graves, but the graves are symbolical of the nation as being buried among the Gentiles. If these dry bones meant the physical dead of the nation, how could it be explained that they speak and say, "Our bones are dried up, and our hope is lost?"[21]

Therefore it is to be concluded that the resurrection of Israel does not take place at the time of the rapture because that resurrection includes only those who are "in Christ" (1 Thess. 4:16) and Israel does not have that position. Further, the point is substantiated because the church is a mystery and God will complete the program for the church before resuming His program with Israel. Resurrection is viewed as a terminating event and Israel's resurrection could not come until her program were terminated. Finally, the impossibility of spiritualizing Daniel 12:2 and Isaiah 26:19 into restoration makes it imperative that the resurrection of the church and Israel take place at two different times.

The Old Testament references already cited indicate that Israel's resurrection takes place at the second advent of Christ. In Daniel 12:1-2 the resurrection is said to take place "at that time," which must be the time previously described, or at the time of the closing events of the seventieth week, when the end comes to the Beast. "At that time" there will be both a de-

---

[21] Arno C. Gaebelein, *The Prophet Ezekiel*, p. 246.

liverance (v. 1) and a resurrection (v. 2). This passage seems to indicate that the resurrection is associated with the act of deliverance from the Beast at the second advent. In like manner Isaiah 26:19 shows us that the promised deliverance of resurrection does not come until "the indignation be overpast" (v. 20). This indignation is none other than the tribulation period and the resurrection of Israel is said to take place at the termination of that period. It seems to be an error to affirm that the church and Israel are both resurrected at the rapture. Scripture shows that Israel will be resurrected at the close of the tribulation period, while the church will be resurrected prior to it.

The order of events in the resurrection program would be: (1) the resurrection of Christ as the beginning of the resurrection program (1 Cor. 15:23); (2) the resurrection of the church age saints at the rapture (1 Thess. 4:16); (3) the resurrection of the tribulation period saints (Rev. 20:3-5), together with (4) the resurrection of Old Testament saints (Dan. 12:2; Isa. 26:19) at the second advent of Christ to the earth; and finally (5) the final resurrection of the unsaved dead (Rev. 20:5, 11-14) at the end of the millennial age. The first four stages would all be included in the first resurrection or resurrection to life, inasmuch as all receive eternal life and the last would be the second resurrection, or the resurrection unto damnation, inasmuch as all receive eternal judgment at that time.

CHAPTER XXIV

THE JUDGMENTS ASSOCIATED WITH THE SECOND ADVENT

The Scriptures anticipate a coming judgment by God on all men. Such was the expectation of the Psalmist as he wrote:

> . . . for he cometh, for he cometh to judge the earth: he shall judge the world with righteousness, and the people with his truth [Ps. 96:13].

Paul verifies the same truth by saying:

> Because he hath appointed a day in the which he will judge the world in righteousness by that man whom he hath ordained; whereof he hath given assurance unto all men, in that he hath raised him from the dead [Acts 17:31].

The subject of judgment is a large one in the Word of God and encompasses such judgments as the judgment of the cross (John 5:24; Rom. 5:9; 8:1; 2 Cor. 5:21; Gal. 3:13; Heb. 9:26-28; 10:10, 14-17), the judgment on the believer in chastening (1 Cor. 11:31-32; Heb. 12:5-11), the self judgment of the believer (1 John 1:9; 1 Cor. 11:31; Ps. 32; 51), the judgment of the believer's works at the judgment seat of Christ (Rom. 14:10; 1 Cor. 3:11-15; 4:5; 2 Cor. 5:10). With the exception of the last mentioned judgment, which has already been considered, these judgments are not related with the eschatological program of God. It is necessary to consider four judgments that have eschatological implications: the judgment on the nation Israel (Ezek. 20:37-38; Zech. 13:8-9), the judgment of the nations (Matt. 25:31-46; Isa. 34:1-2; Joel 3:11-16), the judgment on fallen angels (Jude 6) and the judgment of the great white throne (Rev. 20:11-15).

I. The Judgment on the Nation Israel

The Scriptures teach that the future judgment program will begin with a judgment upon the nation Israel. To them was promised, through the covenants, a kingdom over which the Messiah, David's son, should reign. Before this kingdom can be instituted at His personal return to the earth, there must be a judgment on Israel to determine those that will enter into this kingdom, for it is clearly revealed that "they are not all Israel which are of Israel" (Rom. 9:6).

A. *The time of the judgment.* The clearest indication of the time of Israel's judgment is given to us in the chronology of prophesied events by the Lord in Matthew 24 and 25. As previously outlined, these chapters give us the chronology as follows: (1) the tribulation period (24:4-26), (2) the second advent of Messiah to the earth (24:27-30), (3) the regathering of Israel (24:31), (4) the judgment on Israel (25:1-30), (5) the judgment on Gentiles (25:31-46), (6) the kingdom to follow. In this carefully developed chronology of events, the judgment on Israel follows the second advent of Christ to the earth and the consequent regathering of Israel as a nation.

B. *The place of the judgment.* Since Israel is an earthly people, this judgment must take place on the earth after the Lord's physical return to the earth (Zech. 14:4). It can not be spiritualized so as to teach a judgment of souls at death or some such thing. Since the Lord is on the earth judgment must be where He is. Ezekiel says:

> And I will bring you out from the people, and will gather you out of the countries wherein ye are scattered, with a mighty hand, and with a stretched out arm, and with fury poured out. And I will bring you into the wilderness of the people, and there will I plead with you face to face. Like as I pleaded with your fathers in the wilderness of the land of Egypt, so will I plead with you, saith the Lord God. And I will cause you to pass under the rod, and I will bring you into the bond of the covenant: And I will purge out from among you the rebels, and them that transgress against me: I will bring them forth out of the country where they sojourn, and they shall not enter into the land of Israel: and ye shall know that I am the Lord [Ezek. 20:34-38].

It would seem from this reference that the judgment would take place at the borders of the land, as divine judgment fell on the Israelites at Kadesh-Barnea, at which time rebels were not permitted to enter into the land. So here, this judgment will prevent any rebels from entering into the land in that day.

C. *The ones judged.* It is evident from the passage just cited in Ezekiel, as well as the numerous passages dealing with Israel's restoration, that this judgment will be upon all living Israel, all of whom are to be regathered and judged. Matthew 25:1-30 envisions a judgment on the entire nation. Resurrected Israel must be examined for rewards and this doubtless will be done in connection with Israel's resurrection at the second advent. However, resurrected Israel is not in view in this judgment.

D. *The basis of the judgment.* It has already been shown, from the study of Matthew 25:1-30, that God is judging to separate the saved from the unsaved in Israel. The individual's works will be brought into judgment. Ezekiel makes this clear:

> And I will cause you to pass under the rod, and I will bring you into the bond of the covenant: And I will purge out from among you the rebels, and them that transgress against me [Ezek. 20:37-38].

This is further described by Malachi:

> But who may abide the day of his coming? and who shall stand when he appeareth? for he is like a refiner's fire, and like a fuller's soap; And he shall sit as a refiner and purifier of silver: and he shall purify the sons of Levi, and purge them as gold and silver, that they may offer unto the Lord an offering in righteousness.
>
> And I will come near to you to judgment; and I will be a swift witness against the sorcerers, and against the adulterers, and against false swearers, and against those that oppress the hireling in his wages, the widow, and the fatherless, and that turn aside the stranger from his right, and fear not me, saith the Lord of Hosts [Mal. 3:2-3,5].

One's actions will reveal clearly the spiritual condition of the heart in this judgment, which is to divide saved from unsaved.

E. *The result of the judgment.* There is a twofold result of this judgment. (1) First of all, the unsaved are cut off from the land. ". . . they shall not enter into the land of Israel" (Ezek. 20:37); "And cast ye the unprofitable servant into outer darkness: there shall be weeping and gnashing of teeth" (Matt. 25:30). Thus, the unsaved are destroyed before the millennial age begins. (2) In the second place, the saved are taken into millennial blessing.

> . . . I will bring you into the bond of the covenant [Ezek. 20:37].

> And so all Israel shall be saved: as it is written, There shall come out of Sion the Deliverer, and shall turn away ungodliness from Jacob: For this is my covenant unto them, when I shall take away their sins [Rom. 11:26-27].

Thus, God is going to regather the nation Israel at the second advent and divide the saved from the unsaved. The unsaved will be cut off and the saved living Israel will be taken into the millennium which He will institute to fulfill their covenants.

II. The Judgment on the Gentiles

A. *The time of the judgment.* In the chronology of Matthew 24 and 25 the judgment of the Gentiles (Matt. 25:31-46) is seen to follow the judgment upon Israel. This judgment takes place following the second advent of Christ to the earth. Joel says:

> For, behold, in those days, and in that time, when I shall bring again the captivity of Judah and Jerusalem, I will also gather all nations, and will bring them down into the valley of Jehoshaphat, and will plead with them there for my people and for my heritage Israel, whom they have scattered among the nations, and parted my land [Joel 3:1-2].

The prophet reveals that this judgment on the Gentiles will take place at the same time that the Lord restores the nation Israel to their land, which is at the second advent. Therefore this judgment must fall at the time of the second advent after the regathering and judgment on Israel. It must precede the institution of the millennium, for those accepted in this judgment are taken into that kingdom (Matt. 25:34).

B. *The place of the judgment.* Inasmuch as this judgment follows the second advent, it must be an event that takes place on the earth. It can not be said to take place in the eternal state. Peters says:

> As there is no statement that any of these nations arose from the dead, so there is none that any part of them descended from heaven to be judged; the language, provided no previous theory is made to influence it, simply describing nations *here on the earth*, in some way, gathered together at the Second Advent.[1]

Joel 3:2 states that this judgment will take place in the "valley of Jehoshaphat." This location is not easy to determine. Some hold that it is synonymous with the "valley of Berachah" (2 Chron. 20:26) where Jehoshaphat defeated the Moabites and Ammonites, which victory gave the place a new name. Bewer, however, says:

> It is certain that our author did not have in mind the valley of Berakhah which was connected with Jehoshaphat's victory over the Moabites, Ammonites, and Meunites, 2 Chr. 20:20-28. Not only its name, but also the distance is against it. That there was a valley near Jerusalem named after King Jehoshaphat in ancient times is unknown.[2]

Others hold that it is the valley of Kidron which is outside of Jerusalem. However,

> It is well known that there is a deep ravine now bearing this name just outside Jerusalem, separating the holy city from the mount of Olives. But it is likely that the name was given it only in view of this prophecy—not that it was so called when Joel spoke, nor yet for centuries afterward, as we have to come down to the fourth century of the Christian era before it was thus designated.[3]

Perhaps the solution as to the place involved is given in Zechariah 14:4 where we are told that at the Lord's return to the mount of Olives a great valley shall be opened.

> And his feet shall stand in that day upon the mount of Olives, which is before Jerusalem on the east, and the mount of Olives shall cleave in the midst thereof toward the east and

---

[1] G. N. H. Peters, *Theocratic Kingdom*, II, 375.

[2] J. A. Bewer, *International Critical Commentary*, "Obadiah and Joel," p. 128.

[3] Harry A. Ironside, *Notes on the Minor Prophets*, p. 129.

> toward the west, and there shall be a very great valley; and half of the mountain shall remove toward the north, and half of it toward the south [Zech. 14:4].

A valley which is not in existence today shall come into being at the time of the second advent. Since the name Jehoshaphat means "Jehovah judges," it may be that the newly opened valley outside Jerusalem will bear that name because of the momentous event to transpire there.

C. *The subjects of the judgment.* It is to be observed that those brought into this judgment are living individuals, not the dead that have been resurrected and brought to judgment. Peters says:

> The question before us is this: Does the "all nations" include *"the dead,"* or only *living* nations? In deciding this point we have the following: (1) Nothing is said of "the dead." To say that they are denoted is inferred from the fact that this passage is made—wrongfully—to synchronize with Rev. 20:11-15. (2) The word translated "nations" is *never,* according to the uniform testimony of critics and scholars, used to designate *"the dead,"* unless this be a solitary exception. . . . (3) The word is employed to denote living, existing nations, and almost exclusively "Gentile" nations. (4) The Spirit gives us abundant testimony that precisely *such a gathering of living nations* shall take place *just before* the Mill. age commences, and that there shall be *both* an Advent and judging. . . . (6) National judgments are only poured out upon living, existing nations, and not upon the dead who are devoid of any organization belonging to the idea of nation or state. . . . (7) As there is no statement that any of these nations arose from the dead, so there is none that any part of them descended from heaven to be judged. . . .[4]

According to Strong's Concordance the word *nation* (*ethnos*) is translated as "people" twice, "heathen" five times, "nation" sixty-four times, and "Gentiles" ninety-three times. This then must be seen to be a judgment on living Gentiles at the second advent of Christ.

D. *The basis of the judgment.* The basis on which judgment is meted out at this judgment is the treatment received by a group called "my brethren."

---

[4] Peters, *op. cit.,* II, 374-75.

> And the King shall answer and say unto them, Verily I say unto you, Inasmuch as ye have done it unto one of the least of these my brethren, ye have done it unto me.
>
> Then shall he answer them, saying, Verily I say unto you, Inasmuch as ye did it not to one of the least of these, ye did it not to me [Matt. 25:40, 45].

It is to be observed from Joel 3:2 that Israel is the very center of the whole judgment program: "I will also gather all nations . . . and will plead with them there for my people and for my heritage Israel, whom they have scattered among the nations, and parted my land."

The prophecy of Isaiah would seem to narrow this reference to Israel down to the believing witnesses, mentioning the ministry of a specific group, for he writes:

> And I will set a sign among them, and I will send those that escape of them unto the nations, to Tarshish, Pul, and Lud, that draw the bow, to Tubal, and Javan, to the isles afar off, that have not heard my fame, neither have seen my glory; and they shall declare my glory among the Gentiles. And they shall bring all your brethren for an offering unto the Lord out of all nations upon horses, and in chariots, and in litters, and upon mules, and upon swift beasts, to my holy mountain Jerusalem, saith the Lord, as the children of Israel bring an offering in a clean vessel into the house of the Lord [Isa. 66:19-20].

According to the Book of Revelation God will seal a believing remnant, the 144,000, at the beginning of the tribulation period. They will be a witnessing remnant for that entire period and the fruits of their ministry are described in Revelation 7:9-17, where a great multitude is seen to have been redeemed. The "brethren" are evidently these same believing witnesses of the tribulation period.

This judgment must be a judgment to determine the spiritual condition of those being judged. It is to determine whether the one judged is saved or unsaved. A casual glance at the passage seems to show that this is a judgment based on works, with the outcome depending on the works of the one judged. A closer observation will not support this conclusion. (1) First of all, it is the accepted principle in Scripture that a man is never saved by works, for nowhere is salvation offered on a works basis. In Matthew 25:46 it says, "And these shall go away into everlasting punishment, but the righteous into life eternal." We thus see that the eternal destiny of the people appearing before the judgment was being decided. It could not be a judgment of works, for eternal destiny is never decided on that basis, but on the basis of the acceptance or rejection of Christ's work for us. (2) Further, those that had fed, given to drink, clothed, and visited the "brethren" were called righteous. If this is a judgment of works, they must have been constituted as righteous on the basis of what they had done. Such would be contrary to the teaching of Scripture.

During the period of the ministry of the brethren, "this gospel of the kingdom shall be preached in all the world for a witness unto all nations" (Matt. 24:14). It has been demonstrated, previously, that this gospel of the kingdom entails the preaching of the death of Christ and the blood of Christ as the way of salvation. Such a gospel these brethren were proclaiming. The Gentiles at this judgment were received or rejected on the basis of their reception or rejection of the gospel that was preached by the brethren. Those who accepted their gospel accepted the messenger and those who rejected their gospel rejected the messenger. The Lord had said, "Except ye be converted, and become as little children, ye shall not enter into the kingdom of heaven" (Matt. 18:3). This gospel of the kingdom required personal faith and the new birth. Such faith and new birth were best evidenced by the works which they produced. Peters says:

> The Saviour, therefore, *in accord* with *the general analogy* of the Scripture on the subject, declares that when He comes with His saints in glory to set up His kingdom, out of the nations, those who exhibited *a living faith by active deeds of sympathy and assistance* shall—with those that preceded them, inherit (i.e. be kings in) a Kingdom.[5]

Gaebelein similarly writes:

> Some of the nations will receive their testimony. They believe the Gospel of the Kingdom, this last great witness.

[5] *Ibid.*, II, 376.

> They manifest the genuineness of their faith by works. The preachers who are going about are prosecuted and hated by others, suffering, hungry, and some cast into prison. These nations who believe their testimony show their faith by giving them to eat, clothing them, visiting them in prison, and by showing love to them. The case of Rahab may be looked at as a typical foreshadowing. She believed. It was at a time when the judgment was gathering over Jericho (the type of the world). "By faith the harlot Rahab perished not with them that believed not, when she had received the spies with peace." And again it is written of her, "Likewise also was not Rahab the harlot justified by works, when she had received the messengers, and had sent them out another way?" She had faith and manifested it by works. And so these nations believe the messengers and treat them in kindness. Grace thus covers them because they believed.[6]

Thus it is concluded that these Gentiles are judged on the basis of their works to determine whether they are saved or lost as they have received or rejected the preaching of the gospel by the remnant during the tribulation period.

A question related to this whole consideration is whether the nations are here being judged on a *national basis* or on an *individual basis*. There is a wide divergence of opinion on this question. However, several considerations seem to support the view that those being judged here are judged, not in their national units, but rather as individuals. (1) The nations will be judged on the basis of a reception or rejection of the message of the gospel of the kingdom. Any message given is given expecting a personal response. Since this message required faith and a resultant new birth, those being judged as to their response to the message must be judged on a personal basis as to their individual response. Revelation 7:9-17 reveals that a great multitude have come out of the tribulation who "washed their robes, and made them white in the blood of the Lamb." They could be saved only as individuals. (2) If this judgment is on a national basis whole nations must be permitted to enter the millennium. Thus, since no nation is made up of all saved people, unsaved would enter the millennium. Scripture teaches that no unsaved person will enter the millennium (John 3:3; Matt. 18:3; Jer. 31:33-34; Ezek. 20: 37-38; Zech. 13:9; Matt. 25:30, 46).

---

[6] Arno C. Gaebelein, *The Gospel According to Matthew*, II, 247.

Thus this must be an individual judgment to determine the fact of salvation. (3) If this is a national judgment, it must be on a works basis, since nations can not believe. This would introduce into the Scripture a new method of salvation on the basis of works. Since it can not be shown anywhere in Scripture that a person is given eternal life on a works basis, this must be an individual judgment. (4) All the other judgments in God's judgment program are individual judgments. No other part of this program is ever interpreted other than individually and thus this interpretation would be in harmony with the whole program. (5) Other parallel references to the judgment at the end of the age in connection with the second advent seem to be individual judgments:

> Let both grow together until the harvest: and in the time of harvest I will say to the reapers, Gather ye together first the tares, and bind them in bundles to burn them: but gather the wheat into my barn [Matt. 13:30].
>
> Again, the kingdom of heaven is like unto a net, that was cast into the sea, and gathered of every kind: Which, when it was full, they drew to shore, and sat down, and gathered the good into vessels, but cast the bad away. So shall it be at the end of the world [age]: the angels shall come forth and sever the wicked from among the just, and shall cast them into the furnace of fire: there shall be wailing and gnashing of teeth [Matt. 13:47-50].
>
> . . . Behold, the Lord cometh with ten thousand of his saints, To execute judgment upon all, and to convince all that are ungodly among them of all their ungodly deeds which they have ungodly committed, and of all their hard speeches which ungodly sinners have spoken against him [Jude 14-15].

In each of these instances, which depict this same process of judgment in separating the unsaved from the saved prior to the millennium, it is an individual judgment. None interpret these passages nationally. It must be concluded that Matthew 25 similarly depicts this same individual judgment.

It might be questioned whether the term *the nations* could properly be used of individuals. The word is used in relation to individuals in Matthew 6:31-32; 12:21; 20:19; 28:19; Acts 11:18; 15:3; 26:20. Therefore, since it is used of individuals in other passages, it may also do so in Matthew 25:31.

E. *The result of the judgment.* There will be a twofold result of the judgment on the living Gentiles. (1) To those who have been appointed to the King's right hand the invitation is extended, "Come, ye blessed of my Father, inherit the kingdom prepared for you from the foundation of the world" (Matt. 25:34). (2) To those consigned to the King's left the judgment is pronounced, "Depart from me, ye cursed, into everlasting fire, prepared for the devil and his angels" (Matt. 25:41). The one group is taken into the kingdom to become subjects of the King, while the other group is excluded from the kingdom and consigned to the lake of fire. This group of Gentiles taken into the kingdom fulfills the prophecies (Dan. 7:14; Isa. 55:5; Micah 4:2) that state that a great group of Gentiles will be brought under the King's reign, even though this is Israel's kingdom.

III. The Judgment of Fallen Angels

A. *The time of the judgment.* Jude reveals the fact that angels are to be brought into judgment.

> And the angels which kept not their first estate, but left their own habitation, he hath reserved in everlasting chains under darkness unto the judgment of the great day [Jude 6].

The time element is in the words "the great day." This must be the Day of the Lord, in which all judgment is to be fulfilled. These angels are evidently associated with Satan in his judgment, which is seen to precede the great white throne judgment (Rev. 20:10). It would be concluded that the fallen angels will be judged after the millennial age is over, but prior to the judgment of the great white throne.

B. *The place of the judgment.* Scripture is silent as to the place at which this judgment takes place. However, since it is a judgment of angelic beings, it would seem logical to suppose that it takes place in the angelic realm or sphere. Since the one who judges them is King in the very realm in which their activity was centered, the scene of their activity could become the scene of their judgment.

C. *The subjects of the judgment.* Peter makes it plain that all the fallen angels will be included in this judgment.

For if God spared not the angels that sinned, but cast them down to hell, and delivered them into chains of darkness, to be reserved unto judgment. . . . [2 Pet. 2:4].

D. *The basis of the judgment.* Judgment comes on the fallen angels for their one sin of following Satan in his rebellion against God (Isa. 14:12-17; Ezek. 28:12-19).

E. *The result of the judgment.* All those on whom this judgment is meted are consigned to the lake of fire forever.

And the devil that deceived them was cast into the lake of fire and brimstone, where the beast and the false prophet are, and shall be tormented day and night for ever and ever [Rev. 20:10].

IV. The Great White Throne Judgment

This great white throne judgment (Rev. 20:11-15) may rightly be called the "final judgment." It constitutes the termination of God's resurrection and judgment program.

A. *The time of the judgment.* It is clearly indicated that this judgment takes place after the expiration of the millennial reign of Christ.

But the rest of the dead lived not again until the thousand years were finished.

And I saw the dead, small and great, stand before God; and the books were opened: and another book was opened, which is the book of life: and the dead were judged out of those things which were written in the books, according to their works. And the sea gave up the dead which were in it; and death and hell delivered up the dead which were in them: and they were judged every man according to their works [Rev. 20:5, 12-13].

B. *The place of the judgment.* This judgment takes place, not in heaven, nor on earth, but somewhere in between the two.

And I saw a great white throne, and him that sat on it, from whose face the earth and the heaven fled away; and there was found no place for them [Rev. 20:11].

C. *The subjects of the judgment.* It is evident from the passage itself that this judgment is a judgment of those called "the dead." It has been demonstrated previously that the resurrection program of the saved was completed before the millennium began. The only ones left unresurrected were the unsaved dead. These must then be the subjects of the judgment. Peters says:

> The Judgment of Rev. 20:11-15, after the thousand years, is not one of living nations, but pre-eminently of "the dead." The dead only are mentioned, and whoever adds "living nations" to it (in order to make out a universal judgment) is most certainly adding to the prophecy. Precisely such a judgment is required to fill out in due proportions what otherwise would be lacking, the order of the Divine procedure in the administration of justice. For, if one had no such prophecy of the judgment of "the dead" at the end of the Mill. era, it would justly be regarded as a grave defect in our system of faith. With it, we have a consonant whole.[7]

D. *The basis of the judgment*. This judgment, contrary to popular misconception, is not to determine whether those who stand before this judgment bar are saved or not. All those that are to be saved have been saved and have entered into their eternal state. Those that are to be blessed eternally have entered into their blessing. This is rather a judgment on the evil works of the unsaved. The sentence of the "second death" is passed upon them.

> . . . and the books were opened: and another book was opened, which is the book of life: and the dead were judged out of those things which were written in the books, according to their works [Rev. 20:12].

As in the judgment of the Gentiles the works demonstrated faith or lack of faith, so here the works demonstrate the absence of life. That there will be degrees of punishment meted out to these unsaved is suggested from other Scripture (Luke 12:47-48). But the sentence of the second death will be passed on all. The first death was that spiritual death which was suffered in Adam. This second death is the confirmation and making eternal that separation from God which the first death entailed.

E. *The result of the judgment*. The result of this judgment is made very clear in Revelation 20:15, "And whosoever was not found written in the book of life was cast into the lake of fire."

---

[7] Peters, *op. cit.*, II, 382.

Eternal separation from God is the eternal destiny of the unsaved.

It would seem that even the casual observer could see that the Word of God can not be made to support the idea of a general judgment, when there are no less than eight different judgments mentioned in Scripture, each with a different time, place, subject, basis and result. Those who posit such a general judgment identify the judgment of the Gentiles (Matt. 25:31-46) with the judgment of the great white throne (Rev. 20:11-15). There are a number of distinctions between these two judgments which makes it impossible to make them the same judgment. In Matthew there is no resurrection before the judgment, but only a gathering of his elect (24:31), while in Revelation there is a resurrection of all the wicked. In Matthew the judgment is of living nations, but in Revelation it is of the dead. In Matthew the nations are judged, but in Revelation it could not be of national entities, for heaven and earth have fled away and, since nations are confined to the earth, the same event could not be described. In Matthew the judgment is on earth, but in Revelation heaven and earth have fled away. In Matthew there are no books brought forth to be consulted, while in Revelation the books were opened, the book of life was brought forth, and those not found in it were cast into hell. In Matthew the judgment occurs at the return of Christ to earth, but in Revelation it occurs after the expiration of a thousand years of Christ's presence on the earth. In Matthew two classes appear, the righteous and the wicked, but in Revelation only the wicked appear. In Matthew some went into the kingdom and some into punishment, but in Revelation none go into blessing, but all go into eternal punishment. In Matthew the judge is seated on the "throne of His glory" (25:31) but in Revelation He is seated on the "great white throne." In Matthew the basis of judgment is the treatment of the brethren, while in Revelation the judgment is based on their evil works. In Matthew the coming of Christ precedes, but in Revelation no coming is mentioned since Christ has been on earth for the millennium. In Matthew the Son of man, three classes of men (sheep, goats, brethren) and angels are mentioned, but in Revelation God and one class of men only are seen. In Matthew the sentence is pronounced and the separation is made before the cause of the judgment is known, but there is no judgment in Revelation until after a careful examination of the books. In Matthew there has been no millennial era preceding, for we find those who hungered, thirsted, were naked, strangers, sick, in prison, but in Revelation a millennial age preceded the event (Rev. 20:5). These considerations would seem to be sufficient to support the affirmation that these are not one and the same judgment, but two separate parts of the judgment program of God.

The second advent is a climactic event in the program of God. It is climactic in the program in dealing with evil in that Satan will be bound and righteousness will be manifested. It is climactic in the program of judgment in that every living enemy of God's program is judged. It is climactic for the program for the earth in that the earth can rejoice in the lifting of the curse. It is climactic in the program of resurrection in that all the righteous are raised to share His glory. It is climactic in the program to manifest sovereignty in that the Son is manifested in glory in His kingdom. Such an event can not be minimized nor deleted from its rightful place in God's program of the ages.

SECTION SIX

PROPHECIES OF THE MILLENNIUM

Chapter XXV

THE KINGDOM CONCEPT IN THE OLD TESTAMENT

God's kingdom program occupies a large body of Scripture. But, in spite of all that the Scripture has to say on this subject, one is faced with a great variety of interpretations and explanations as to the nature and purpose of the kingdom program of God. To some the kingdom of God is synonymous with the eternal state, or heaven into which one comes after death, so that it has no relationship to the earth whatsoever. To others it is a non-material or "spiritual" kingdom in which God rules over the hearts of men, so that, while it is related to the present age, it is unrelated to the earth. To still others the kingdom is purely earthly, without spiritual realities attached to it, so that it is a political and social structure to be achieved by the efforts of men and thus becomes the goal of a social and economic evolution to which men press. To others with the same general concept, it has to do with a nationalistic movement on the part of Israel that will reconstitute that nation as an independent nation in the political realm. Then there are those who view the kingdom as synonymous with the visible organized church, so that the church becomes the kingdom, thus making the kingdom both spiritual and political. In addition there are those who view the kingdom as the manifestation, in the earthly realm, of the universal sovereignty of God, in which He rules in the affairs of men, so that the kingdom is conceived as being both spiritual and material in its concept. Through this maze of interpretations it is almost impossible to make one's way. The truths related to the kingdom will not be derived by an examination of the writings of men, but rather only by an inductive study of the teaching of the Word of God on this great subject.

I. The Eternal Kingdom

Throughout the Scriptures there seems to be a contradiction in the line of revelation concerning the kingdom over which God rules. On the one hand the kingdom is viewed as eternal and on the other as temporal, with a definite historical beginning, progress, and termination. Again it is depicted as both universal and local. Further, it is seen to be the direct administration of the sovereignty of God as well as the indirect administration through appointed sovereigns. It thus becomes necessary to see that the kingdom over which God rules has two separate aspects, the eternal and the temporal, the universal and the local, the immediate and the mediated.

A. *The timeless aspect.* There are passages of Scripture which demonstrate the proposition that God has always possessed absolute sovereignty and rules as king.

> The Lord is King forever and ever . . . [Ps. 10:16].
>
> . . . the Lord sitteth King for ever [Ps. 29:10].
>
> For God is my King of old [Ps. 74:12].
>
> But the Lord is the true God, he is the living God, and an everlasting king . . . [Jer. 10:10].
>
> Thou, O Lord, remainest for ever; thy throne from generation to generation [Lam. 5:19].

God could not be rightly called a king without a recognized sovereignty and a realm in which that sovereignty is exercised.

B. *The universal aspect.* There is reference to the unlimited scope of God's sovereignty.

> Thine, O Lord, is the greatness, and the power and the glory, and the victory, and the majesty: for all that is in the heaven and in the earth is thine; thine is the kingdom, O Lord, and thou are exalted as head above all. Both riches and honour come of thee, and thou reignest over all . . . [1 Chron. 29:11-12].
>
> The Lord hath prepared his throne in the heavens; and his kingdom ruleth over all [Ps. 103:19].
>
> . . . the most High ruleth in the kingdom of men, and giveth it to whomsoever he will . . . [Dan. 4:17, 25, 32].

This sovereignty is seen to be exercised over both the heaven and the earth.

C. *The providential aspect.* It is presented in Scripture that, while God exercises absolute authority, this sovereignty may be exercised through individuals as secondary causes.

> The king's heart is in the hand of the Lord . . . [Prov. 21:1].
>
> O Assyrian, the rod of mine anger, and the staff in their hand is mine indignation. I will send him against an hypocritical nation, and against the people of my wrath will I give him a charge, to take the spoil . . . [Isa. 10:5-6].

This may be further illustrated in Jeremiah 25:8-12; 27:4-8; 51:11-24, 27; Isaiah 44:24-45:7 with Ezra 1:1. God deals sovereignly through men, some of whom recognize it, some of whom reject it, and some of whom are ignorant of it, yet God's will is executed. This not only is true in the realm of humanity, but nature as well. The Psalmist says: "Fire, and hail; snow, and vapours; stormy wind fulfilling his word" (Ps. 148:8).

D. *The miraculous aspect.* There are occasions when this sovereignty is manifested through the direct intervention of God in the affairs of men with a demonstration of sovereignty by miracles.

> And I will harden Pharaoh's heart, and multiply my signs and my wonders in the land of Egypt. But Pharaoh shall not hearken unto you, that I may lay my hand upon Egypt, and bring forth mine armies, and my people the children of Israel, out of the land of Egypt by great judgments. And the Egyptians shall know that I am the Lord . . . [Ex. 7:3-5].

The whole question of miracles is only the question as to whether an infinite Sovereign has the power and the right to intervene in a demonstration of that power within the sphere over which He rules.

E. *The use of the word* kingdom. Ladd well presents the use of this word, when he writes:

> The primary meaning of the New Testament word for kingdom, *basileia,* is "reign" rather than "realm" or "people." A great deal of attention in recent years has been devoted by critical scholars to this subject, and there is a practically unanimous agreement that "regal power, authority" is more basic to *basileia*

than "realm" or "people". "In the general linguistic usage, it is to be noted that the word *basileia,* which we usually translate by *realm, kingdom,* designates first of all the *existence,* the *character,* the *position* of the king. Since it concerns a king, we would best speak of his *majesty,* his *authority*" (Schmidt, *Theologisches Wörterbuch zum Neuen Testament,* I, p. 579).

. . . .

Several illustrations of this abstract meaning of *basileia* are found in the New Testament. When Jesus came to Jerusalem, the people thought that the kingdom of God was to appear immediately. Jesus told them a parable of a nobleman who went into a far country to receive a *basileia* and then to return. His subjects hated him and sent an embassy to declare that they did not want him to be their ruler. When the nobleman returned, having received his *basileia,* he at once exercised this new kingly authority which he had received over his subjects by rewarding the faithful and punishing the rebellious. Here the *basileia* is clearly neither the domain nor the subjects, but the authority to rule as king in the given domain over its people (Luke 19:11-27).

The same use is found in Revelation 17:12. "And the ten horns that thou sawest are ten kings, who have received no *basileia* as yet; but they receive *authority as kings,* with the beast for one hour." Clearly the *basileia* which has not yet been received is synonymous with the "authority as kings". In Revelation 5:10 the *basileia* is a redeemed people; but they constitute the *basileia* not because they are subjects of the king, but *because they share his regal power:* "and they reign upon the earth."[1]

According to this concept, this eternal kingdom must be God's kingly rule and sovereignty over "all intelligences in heaven or on earth who are willingly subject to God"[2] in His exercise of sovereignty.

F. *The universal kingdom challenged.* The original challenge to God's eternal sovereign right to rule is recorded in Ezekiel 28:11-19 and Isaiah 14:12-17, where, Chafer says:

. . . it is stated in this passage that Lucifer's sin consisted in five awful *I will's* against the will of God . . . These five "I will's" of Satan are evidently various aspects of one sin . . . Satan's five "I will's" are:

---

[1] George E. Ladd, *Crucial Questions about the Kingdom of God,* pp. 78-80.
[2] Lewis Sperry Chafer, *Systematic Theology,* VII, 223.

> 1. *"I Will Ascend into Heaven."* In this, the first aspect of Satan's sin, he apparently proposed to take up his *abode* in the third or highest heaven where God and the redeemed abide (2 Cor. 12:1-4) . . . Satan has no right either by position or redemption to claim that sphere as the place of his abode. His self-seeking intention as disclosed in this declaration is an outrage against the Creator's plan and purpose.
>
> 2. *"I Will Exalt My Throne above the Stars of God."* By this statement it is revealed that Satan, though appointed to the guardianship of the throne of God, aspired to the possession of a throne of his own and to rule over the "stars of God". The angelic beings . . . are obviously in view . . . The sinful character of Satan's purpose to secure a throne is apparent.
>
> 3. *"I Will Sit Also upon the Mount of the Congregation, in the Sides of the North."* . . . "the mount" is a phrase which evidently refers to the seat of divine government in the earth (Isa. 2:1-4), and the reference to "the congregation" is as clearly of Israel. Thus this specific assumption seems to aim at a share at least (note the word *also*) in the earthly Messianic rule . . .
>
> 4. *"I Will Ascend above the Heights of the Clouds."* . . . Of upwards of one hundred and fifty references in the Bible to clouds, fully one hundred are related to the divine presence and glory . . . Satan is evidently seeking to secure for himself some of the glory which belongs to God alone.
>
> 5. *"I Will be Like the Most High."* This . . . may be considered as a key to the understanding and tracing of his motives and methods. In spite of an almost universal impression that Satan's ideal for himself is to be *unlike* God, he is here revealed as being actuated with the purpose to be *like* God. However, this ambition is not to be like Jehovah, the self-existent One, which no created being could ever be; but to be like the Most High, which title signifies the "possessor of heaven and earth" (Gen. 14:19, 22). Satan's purpose, then, is to gain authority over heaven and earth.[3]

A careful study of these observations will lead to the conclusion that each phase of Satan's original sin was an act of rebellion against the constituted authority of God and was motivated by a covetous desire to appropriate that very sovereignty for himself. Because of this sin, which brought about the fall of Satan, a kingdom over which Satan rules was formed in opposition to the kingdom over which God ruled. Satan is pictured

---

[3] *Ibid.*, II, 47-49.

as the god of this age (2 Cor. 4:4), the prince of the powers of the air (Eph. 2:2), and the possessor of the kingdoms of the world, for we read:

> . . . the devil taketh him up into an exceeding high mountain, and sheweth him all the kingdoms of the world, and the glory of them; And saith unto him, All these things will I give thee, if thou wilt fall down and worship me [Matt. 4:8-9].

It is significant that Christ did not challenge Satan's right to make the offer to surrender these Kingdoms. He viewed them as in Satan's domain, so that Satan had the right to do with them as he willed.

In view of this overt act that challenged the right of God to rule in His kingdom, God instituted a program, prior to the foundation of the world, to manifest His sovereignty before all created intelligences. The Lord can say to those invited to partake of the blessings of the millennial reign: "Come, ye blessed of my Father, inherit the kingdom prepared for you from the foundation of the world" (Matt. 25:34). This kingdom, which issues into the eternal kingdom (1 Cor. 15:24), is seen to be a part of the eternal counsel of God. And the earth, which was the center of Satanic authority, and the scene of his kingdom, becomes the place God chooses to make this very demonstration. Miller says:

> While we are amazed beyond measure at the immensity of creation or the far reaches of the Kingdom of God, our amazement turns to wonder as we realize that the earth, one of the smallest of the heavenly bodies, is destined to be the theater to display the mighty works of God. It is here that He chooses to make known the riches of His grace to the utmost bounds of His universal kingdom.[4]

This program of God to demonstrate His sovereignty and manifest the universality of His kingdom may be called the theocratic kingdom program. Peters says: "The institution of the Theocracy with the claims annexed to it, and the laudation put upon it by God Himself, marks not only its desirableness, but that it is the settled purpose of God ultimately to establish its supremacy."[5]

---

[4] Earl Miller, *The Kingdom of God and the Kingdom of Heaven*, p. 14.
[5] G. N. H. Peters, *The Theocratic Kingdom*, I, 223.

II. The Theocratic Kingdom

From the outset of God's program to manifest His sovereignty by His rule in this earthly sphere until the consummation of that program, when universal sovereignty is acknowledged (1 Cor. 15:24), there has been one continuous, connected, progressive development of that program. While there might be various phases of the program and different media through which that sovereignty was exercised, it has been the development of one program. This whole program may be called the theocratic kingdom.

The word *theocracy* has been defined:

> The "Theocracy is a government of the State by the immediate direction of God; Jehovah condescended to reign over Israel in the same direct manner in which an earthly king reigns over his people." . . . "With wisdom worthy of Himself, He assumed not merely a religious, but a political, superiority, over the descendants of Abraham; He constituted Himself, in the strictest sense of the phrase, King of Israel, and the government of Israel became, in consequence, strictly and literally, a Theocracy."[6]

McClain defines this theocratic kingdom as:

> . . . the rule of God through a divinely chosen representative who speaks and acts for God; a rule which has especial reference to the human race, although it finally embraces the universe; and its mediatorial ruler is always a member of the human race.[7]

In this whole discussion the usual designation "the kingdom of God" and "the kingdom of heaven" have not been employed. Premillennialists are accustomed to designating the eternal kingdom as the kingdom of God and the earthly program as the kingdom of heaven. Such a categorical distinction does not seem to be supported by Scriptural usage. Both terms are used in respect to the eternal kingdom (Matt. 6:33 with 18:3-6; 7:21 and 19:14 with Mark 10:14). Both terms are used in reference to the future millennial kingdom (Matt. 4:17 and Mark 1:14-15; cf. Matt. 3:2; 5:3, 10; 6:10; Mark 9:1, 47; 14:25; Luke 19:11; 21:31). And both terms are used in reference to the present form of the

---

[6] Cf. *ibid.*, I, 216.

[7] Alva J. McClain, "The Greatness of the Kingdom," unpublished classroom notes, p. 2.

kingdom (Matt. 13:11; Mark 4:11; Luke 8:10). The differentiation does not lie in the terms, inherently, but in the usage in the context. Feinberg says:

> In the Gospel according to Matthew this kingdom is designated in the main as the kingdom of heaven, whereas the Kingdom of God is mentioned but a few times. The explanation of Dr. Vos is offered. Matthew was writing to the Jews who had a peculiar reverence for the name "God"—mark this, in spite of their most evident lack of perception of the true nature of the kingdom—and would easily understand the meaning of "the kingdom of heaven". Mark and Luke, on the other hand, are writing to Gentiles, so they use the phrase "kingdom of God" rather than the other. The kingdom is characterized as the kingdom of heaven because it is patterned after heaven and its perfection. Reference is also made in this name to the eternal and lasting value of this dominion. Furthermore, there is involved the thought of the heavenly origin and source of the kingdom, the God of heaven being He who will set it up. The name "kingdom of God" is employed because it points to the spiritual character of the reign and dominion. The glory of God is its chief and sole object. Christ's work in which He seeks only to glorify His Father is complete when God is glorified. This is the aim and purpose of the kingdom of God.[8]

Walvoord comments:

> While dispensationalists are apt to emphasize the term *kingdom of heaven* as relating to the future Messianic kingdom, the term also applies to the kingdom in the present age. . . . It is also true that the term *kingdom of God* is used both of the present age and of the future Messianic kingdom. In other words, neither the term *kingdom of God* nor *kingdom of heaven* is in itself a technical term applying to the Messianic kingdom. In the context of each reference it can be determined whether the reference is to the present form of the kingdom or the future Messianic kingdom.[9]

Since, then, the terms *kingdom of God* and *kingdom of heaven* are used interchangeably, even though two different phases of the kingdom are in view, it has been deemed advisable to refer to the eternal aspects as the eternal kingdom and the development of that kingdom in time as the theocratic kingdom. This

---

[8] Charles Feinberg, *Premillennialism and Amillennialism*, pp. 163-64.
[9] John F. Walvoord, *Bibliotheca Sacra*, 110:5-6, January, 1953.

whole theocratic kingdom program must be traced through the Scriptures.[10]

A. *The theocratic kingdom in Eden.* A true theocracy was established at the time of creation, when God was recognized as sovereign and the sovereignty that belonged to God was delegated unto man, who was to rule over the earth in an exercise of mediate authority. In this theocracy Adam was seen to derive his authority from God and therefore, since he was called upon to be in submission, the rulership was God's. Authority to rule in the theocracy must have belonged to Adam or else Christ in His reign could not be contrasted with Adam and the name "Last Adam" belong to Him (1 Cor. 15:22-24, 45). "Let them have dominion" (Gen. 1:26) established the theocratic relationship. The responsibility to "subdue" the earth was an exercise of theocratic authority. Submission to her husband was enjoined upon Eve in that Adam was the divinely appointed ruler in the theocracy. Feinberg states:

> The kingdom of God was actually realized in the Garden of Eden. There God ruled and reigned supreme, with all His subjects giving Him the proper obedience that is befitting a King. All the blessings that can flow from the kingdom of God on earth were there. Nevertheless, the highest ideal had not been reached. Eternal life depended upon the perfect obedience of man, and had this been forthcoming, the everlasting kingdom would have come into existence with all its glory. When sin entered, it meant nothing more or less than that man was ridding himself of the sovereign rule of God, his King. This disobedience was the occasion for the setting up in the world of another kingdom, that of Satan himself.[11]

With the repudiation of this authority of God by Adam's disobedience, God announced (Gen. 3:15) the inception of a program that would manifest that authority, which was repudiated, by bringing a new creation into existence through the "Seed of the woman" that would be willingly subject to Himself. The redemptive program now parallels the development of the kingdom program and is a necessary adjunct to it, but is not identical with it. The method of establishing God's authority is through

---

[10] Cf. Peters, *op. cit.,* I, 161.
[11] Feinberg, *op. cit.,* p. 160.

the medium of redemption, but the re-establishment of that authority remains God's primary purpose.

After the fall the theocratic kingdom seems to be administered through the godly line born to Eve. Her statement in Genesis 4:1, "I have gotten a man from the Lord," may be better rendered "I have gotten a man, the Lord,"[12] and may have in it a hint that the theocracy is to be administered through this line. After the death of Abel his place is assumed by Seth (Gen. 4:25), whose name means "appointed," perhaps with the idea of appointment within the theocracy. The period of history ends with the flood because of the sinfulness of the race (Gen. 6:6-7), which sinfulness itself was a rejection of God's right to rule over them.

B. *The theocratic kingdom under human government.* After the flood God instituted human government (Gen. 9:1-7) and this government became the medium through which the theocratic kingdom was administered. Fear of the person in whom this authority resides was inherent in the administration of the kingdom program (Gen. 9:2). It is made clear by Paul (Rom. 13:1-4) that the governor is "the minister of God." This administration of the kingdom program continued until the repudiation of this form of authority by the establishment of the kingdom of Nimrod at Babel, in which a new authority was recognized and a new system of worship instituted (Gen. 10:8-10; 11:1-9).

C. *The theocratic kingdom under the patriarchs.* With the call of Abraham God selected one man through whom He would establish His purpose upon earth and through whom all men should receive blessing. The purpose of God with Abraham centers in certain promises concerning a land, a seed, and a blessing which are made the matter of an eternal, unconditional covenant. This covenant has been studied in detail previously and need not be repeated here. The important observation here is to notice that the anticipated fulfillment of this whole program comes through one that is to be King (Gen. 49:10). Feinberg writes:

> Upon his deathbed the vision of a prophet is vouchsafed to the aged Jacob and he foretells the fortunes of his sons. The

[12] *Ibid.*, p. 54.

> blessing upon Judah and the prophecy concerning him are of special interest for our study. It narrows down the promised seed to the tribe of Judah and adds another and most important element of the kingdom—the king. The twelve sons of the patriarch are told that the sceptre, the emblem of regal authority, will not depart from Judah nor one who issues decrees, until Shiloh comes to whom the gathering of the people will be. Many believe Shiloh to have reference to Ezekiel 21:27 where the prophet exclaims: "I will overturn, overturn, overturn it: and it shall be no more, until he come whose right it is; and I will give it him." . . . Others feel that Shiloh refers to the man of peace and rest. . . . In either case the majority of orthodox and reverent students of the Word are of the opinion that direct mention is here made of the Messiah who is to come to the line of Judah. The scope of his sway is revealed: "unto him shall the gathering of the people (the nations) be." The peaceful character of His kingdom and the plenty that will be present in it are all alluded to. . . . Finally, the surpassing beauty of the King is also mentioned in highly figurative language.[13]

There is a further reference to the anticipated fulfillment of this theocratic program in Numbers 24:17-19, where it is promised that the "Sceptre shall rise out of Israel." This "Sceptre" is the One in whom the authority resides, who will destroy His enemies and raise up Israel to prominence.

During the period of the patriarchs this theocracy was administered through certain divinely appointed representatives. That is why God could say to Moses, concerning his relationship to Aaron, "thou shalt be to him instead of God" (Ex. 4:16), and concerning his relationship to Pharaoh, "I have made thee a god to Pharaoh" (Ex. 7:1). In the capacity of the appointed representative of the theocracy he could be called god. It was because of Moses' place in this theocratic kingdom that God could say of the coming Ruler: "I will raise them up a Prophet from among their brethren, like unto *thee*" (Deut. 18:18). And it was in this capacity that he led Israel through the wilderness. The enormity of Israel's repeated sin of murmuring is thus seen, for in murmuring against Moses they were murmuring against God's appointed representative in theocratic administration. The fiery serpents brought judgment for "the people spake against God, and against Moses" (Num. 21:5). Only their confession

---

[13] *Ibid.*, pp. 56-57.

that they had sinned, "for we have spoken against the Lord, and against thee" (Num. 21:7), brought alleviation. Joshua was the last in this period to lead the people as God's administrator (Josh. 1:2-9). Under his leadership the people were brought into subjection to the authority of God:

> Now therefore fear the Lord, and serve him in sincerity and in truth. . . . And if it seem evil unto you to serve the Lord, choose you this day whom ye will serve. . . . And the people answered and said, God forbid that we should forsake the Lord to serve other gods. For the Lord our God, he it is that brought us up and our fathers out of the land of Egypt . . . therefore will we also serve the Lord; for he is our God [Josh. 24:14-18].

D. *The theocratic kingdom under the judges.* When Israel accepted the overlordship of Jehovah, God moved to a new administration of the theocratic kingdom—administration through the judges (Judg. 2:16, 18; Acts 13:20). The statement of Gideon is clear:

> Then the men of Israel said unto Gideon, Rule thou over us, both thou, and thy son, and thy sons' son also: for thou hast delivered us from the hand of Midian, And Gideon said unto them, I will not rule over you, neither shall my son rule over you: the Lord shall rule over you [Judg. 8:22-23].

Gideon refused the place of absolute authority, for such was to belong to God. The experience of Samuel with the Lord (1 Sam. 3:1-18) reveals that God was actively administering the affairs in Israel through this human agency. The acceptance of Samuel by Israel (1 Sam. 3:19-4:1) is the recognition by the people that Samuel is the divinely appointed representative of the theocracy. Such administration continued until the close of Samuel's life, when:

> . . . all the elders of Israel gathered themselves together, and came to Samuel unto Ramah, And said unto him, Behold, thou art old, and thy sons walk not in thy ways: now make us a king to judge us like all the nations" [1 Sam. 8:4-5].

The spiritual declension of Israel is noted in the closing history of the period of the judges. "Every man did that which was right in his own eyes" (Judg. 21:25). This spiritual condition brought about the rejection of the form of the theocracy under which God had operated and brought about the request for the king like all the nations. God revealed to Samuel that such an action constituted a rejection of the theocracy, for "they have not rejected thee, but they have rejected me, that I should reign over them" (1 Sam. 8:7). God, therefore, passed to a new administration of the theocratic kingdom—the administration through the kings who ruled over Israel.

E. *The theocratic kingdom under the kings.* The monarchial form of government was God's ideal for the theocratic kingdom. Such a king had been promised to Abraham (Gen. 17:5-7) and to Jacob (Gen. 35:11). The authority of the kingdom was to reside in a king eventually (Gen. 49; Num. 24:17). At the induction of Saul into the kingly office the appointment was seen to be a divine appointment, for Samuel announced, "behold, the Lord hath set a king over you" (1 Sam. 12:13). And yet Samuel reminds Israel that they had sinned in repudiating the former form of the theocracy, saying, "ye have this day rejected your God" (1 Sam. 10:19), and adding, "your wickedness is great, which ye have done in the sight of the Lord, in asking you a king" (1 Sam. 12:17). Peters observes:

> No deeper insult could scarcely be offered to God than such a request indicated. This is seen by considering the Being who condescended to be their Ruler, the blessing that He promised, and the design He had in view in thus becoming, in a direct manner, King over the nation. The only extenuation for such "wickedness," as Samuel intimates, is found in their distressed circumstances, also brought upon them by unbelief.[14]

The institution of this kingdom form of theocratic administration carries the theocratic kingdom a step further toward its ultimate completion. Concerning the king himself, it is stated:

> The king was also in a way the *summus episcopus* in Israel. His very kingship was of an entirely religious character and implied a unity of the heavenly and earthly rule over Israel through him who as Jeh's substitute sat "upon the throne of the kingdom of Jeh over Israel" (I Ch. 17:14; 28:5; 29:23), who was "Jeh's anointed" (I Sam. 24:10; 26:9; 2 Sam. 1:14), and also bore the title of "son of Jeh" and "the firstborn." . . .[15]

---

[14] Peters, *op. cit.*, I, 226.

[15] S. D. Press, "Kingdom," *International Standard Bible Encyclopedia*, III, 1801.

It is a mistake to visualize this theocracy over Israel as merely typical of the future theocracy. Peters says:

> . . . Lange calls the Theocracy the Kingdom of God in its typical form. . . . What, perhaps, leads to such an error is the fact that typical rites and temporary observances were connected with the Theocracy. But while this is so, the Theocratic ordering or government, which for the time adopted these rites and observances, is never represented as a type. This is utterly opposed by covenant, and prophecy, and fact. The Theocracy did not adumbrate something else, but was itself the Kingdom of God in its initiatory form—a commencement of that rule of God's as earthly King, which, if the Jews had rendered the obedience required, would have extended and widened itself until all nations had been brought under its influence and subjection.[16]

That this was a continuing part of the theocratic kingdom program is observed from the fact that perfect obedience on the part of the kings was demanded by God.

> According to Samuel's statement God pardons the nation on the conditions that it still, with the king included, acknowledges him as *the continuous Supreme Monarch,* and that the king chosen shall enforce the laws given by his Superior in authority. In this entire transaction God's theocratic rule *is preserved intact.* The earthly king was under certain imposed restrictions, and was threatened, in case of disobedience, with the displeasure of, and punishment from, *the still recognized Civil Head* of the nation. This was felt and freely confessed by Saul (I Sam. 13:12, and 28:15), David (1 Sam. 6:20, and 7:23-26, etc.), Solomon (I Kings 3:8-9, and 6:12-14, also ch. 8, etc.), and others.[17]

Early in Saul's reign it was announced that God had rejected him (1 Sam. 13:11-14). The authority was transferred to David (1 Sam. 16:1-13) and his reign was particularly associated with the development of the theocratic kingdom. This is noted in two areas. (1) God identified His kingdom with the Davidic kingdom. Peters writes:

> [God] . . . received that throne and Kingdom and adopted the same as His own throne and Kingdom. The Theocracy and Davidic kingdom, in virtue of a special and peculiar covenant relationship between the two, were regarded as one, and in the

---

[16] Peters, *op. cit.,* I, 218.
[17] *Ibid.,* I, 228.

> future so identical in destiny that they are inseparably linked together. . . .
>
> This is evidenced by three things—(1) The Davidic throne and Kingdom is called the Lord's. Thus, e.g. in I Chron. 28:5, it is "the throne of the Kingdom of the Lord over Israel"; in 2 Chron. 13:8, "the Kingdom of the Lord"; and in 2 Chron. 9:8, the King is placed by God "on His throne to be King for the Lord thy God." (2) The King was expressly designated "the Lord's Anointed" (1 Sam. 24:6, 2 Sam. 19:21, etc.). (3) The Prophets, after the establishment of the Davidic throne and kingdom, invariably identify the glorious Kingdom of God, the blessed Theocratic rule, as manifested through the same, e.g. Jer. chs. 33 and 36, Amos 9 etc. The reason for this lies in the firm and perpetual union.[18]

(2) God entered into an eternal, unconditional covenant with David (2 Sam. 7:16) in which God guaranteed that the Davidic kingdom should be the kingdom in which the theocratic kingdom should come to full realization as one from David's line reigned forever. This covenant has been examined in detail previously and need not be enlarged upon here. Suffice it to say that God has now developed the theocratic kingdom to the point where it has assumed the form of a monarchy over which a God-appointed king reigned and Messiah will come to bring the program to completion in that form.

F. *The theocratic kingdom under the prophets.* With the decline of the nation under the kings who succeeded Solomon, the last divinely appointed ruler, we find the rise in importance in the prophetic office. The prophets were the divinely appointed spokesmen for God, who relayed God's message to the kings, who sometimes obeyed, but with greater frequency did not. Peters says, "King and priest were to yield to the authority of the Prophet, simply because the latter directly revealed the will of the Supreme King."[19]

The prophet Ezekiel traces the departure of the Shekinah Glory, which, in the Old Testament, was a symbol of the presence of God. With the departure of the Shekinah Glory from the temple (Ezek. 8:4; 9:3; 10:4; 10:18; 11:22, 23), God marks the close of the theocratic kingdom in Israel's past history and

---

18 *Ibid.*, I, 234.
19 *Ibid.*, I, 229.

the nation and the kings that were to have manifested that kingdom were scattered out of their land. The "times of the Gentiles" began, in which Israel is set aside until Messiah should come. The future theocratic kingdom now becomes the major theme of the prophets' message. That line of revelation, which began as a small stream, now becomes a great river, flooding the Word with knowledge concerning the kingdom to be established in its final form. It is referred to by nearly every Old Testament prophet: *Isaiah* 2:1-4; 4:2-6; 9:6-7; 11:1-13; 24:1-23; 32:1-5, 14-20; 33:17-24; 35:1-10; 40:1-11; 42:1-4; 52:7-10; 60:1-61:6; 65:17-25; 66:15-23; *Jeremiah* 23:1-8; 31:1-37; 33:14-26; *Ezekiel* 20:33-42; 34:20-31; 36:22-36; 37:1-28; 39:21-29; 43:1-7; *Daniel* 2:31-45; 7:1-28; 9:1-3, 20-27; 12:1-4; *Hosea* 3:4-5; *Joel* 2:28-3:2, 9-21; *Amos* 9:9-15; *Obadiah* 1:15-21; *Micah* 4:1-5:5; *Zephaniah* 3:8-20; *Haggai* 2:1-9; *Zechariah* 2:1-13; 6:11-13; 8:1-8, 20-23; 9:9-10; 12:1-10; 14:1-21; *Malachi* 3:1-5; 4:1-6. In addition it is referred to frequently in the *Psalms*: 2:1-12; 22:1-21, 27-31; 24:1-10; 45:1-17; 46:1-11; 48:1-14; 67:1-7; 72:1-17; 89:1-50; 96:1-13; 98:1-9; 110:1-7. While these and other prophecies will be studied in detail later to develop the full doctrine of the kingdom, certain facts concerning the prophetic anticipation of the theocratic kingdom may be observed here. Chafer summarizes the teaching, showing that the kingdom is:

> a. *To be theocratic.* The King will be "Emmanuel . . . God with us," for He is by human birth a rightful heir to David's throne and born of a virgin in Bethlehem. . . . Isaiah 7:14 . . . Matthew 1:22-23. . . . Isaiah 11:1-5 . . . Jeremiah 23:5 . . . Ezekiel 34:23; 37:24 . . . Hosea 3:4-5 . . . Micah 5:2.
>
> b. *To be heavenly in character.* . . . Isaiah 2:4 . . . Isaiah 11:4-5 . . . Jeremiah 33:14-17 . . . Hosea 2:18.
>
> c. *To be in Jerusalem and world-wide.* First, Emmanuel's kingdom will be in the earth . . . Psalm 2:8 . . . Isaiah 11:9 . . . Isaiah 42:4 . . . Jeremiah 23:5 . . . Zechariah 14:9. Second, Emmanuel's kingdom will be centered at Jerusalem . . . Isaiah 2:1-3 . . . Isaiah 62:1-7 . . . Zechariah 8:20-23. Third, Emmanuel's kingdom will be over regathered and converted Israel . . . Deuteronomy 30:3-6 . . . Isaiah 11:11-12 . . . Isaiah 14:1-2 . . . Jeremiah 23:6-8 . . . Jeremiah 32:37-38 . . . Jeremiah 33:7-9 . . . Ezekiel 37:21-25 . . . Micah 4:6-8. Fourth, Emmanuel's kingdom shall extend to the nations in earth . . . Psalm 72:11, 17 . . . Psalm 86:9

. . . Isaiah 55:5 . . . Daniel 7:13-14 . . . Micah 4:2 . . . Zechariah 8:22. . . .

d. *To be established by the returning king.* Deuteronomy 30:3 . . . Psalm 50:3-5 . . . Psalm 96:13 . . . Zechariah 2:10-13 . . . Malachi 3:1-4.

e. *To be spiritual.* The kingdom is not incorporeal or separate from that which is material, but still it is spiritual in that the will of God will be directly effective in all matters of government and conduct. The joy and blessedness of fellowship with God will be experienced by all. The universal, temporal kingdom will be conducted in perfect righteousness and true holiness. The kingdom of God will again be "in the midst" (Luke 17:21, R. V. marg.) in the person of the Messiah King and He will rule in the grace and power of the sevenfold Spirit (Isa. 11:2-5). . . .[20]

McClain summarizes the prophetic anticipation of the theocratic kingdom as follows:

First, as to its *literality,* the future kingdom will not be merely an ideal kingdom. . . . It will be as literal as the historical kingdom of Israel. . . . All prophecy from first to last asserts and implies such literality; in such details as location, nature, ruler, citizens, and the nations involved; in the fact that it will destroy and supplant literal kingdoms; in its direct connection as a restoration and continuation of the historical and Davidic kingdom.

Second, the *time of its establishment* often seems near to hand; it will come "in a little while". Yet other statements indicate that it is far in the future after "many days" and in the "latter days". . . .

Third, *the Ruler* of this future kingdom will be both human and divine. He is called "a Man", "a Son of Man", the Son of God, a Shoot of the stock of Jesse, a Righteous Branch of David, God, the Lord Jehovah, Wonderful-Counselor, the Mighty God, the Father of Eternity, the Prince of Peace. . . .

Fourth, the . . . kingdom set forth in Old Testament prophecy is *monarchial* in form. The ruler sits upon a "throne" and the government is "upon His shoulder". He receives his authority and holds it by divine grant. All the functions of government are centered in His Person: Isaiah sees Him and names Him as "Judge", "Lawgiver", and "King". . . .

Fifth, in its *external organization,* the prophets picture the Kingdom with the Mediator-King at its head; associated with Him

---

[20] Chafer, *op. cit.,* V, 334-40.

are "princes"; the "saints" possess the Kingdom; the nation of Israel is given the place of priority; and the subjects include all tribes and nations. . . .

Sixth, as to the *nature of this Kingdom* and its effect in the world the prophets all agree that its complete establishment will bring about such a sweeping change in every department of human life that the result is spoken of as "a new heaven and *a new earth.*" . . .

The Old Testament prophets describe the Mediatorial Kingdom as first of all a *spiritual* affair. It brings forgiveness of sin, spiritual cleansing, the provision of divine righteousness, a new heart and a new spirit, a direct knowledge of God, inward harmony with the laws of God, the outpouring of the Spirit upon all flesh, and the restoration of joy to human life [Jer. 31:34; 23:5-6; Ezek. 36:24-28; Zech. 8:20-23; Jer. 31:33; Joel 2:28; Isa. 35:10].

The Kingdom will also be *ethical* in its effects . . . a proper estimate of moral values . . . An adjustment of moral inequalities will sweep through every department of human relations . . . [Isa. 32:5; 40:4; Jer. 31:28-30].

The establishment of this Kingdom will also introduce great *social* and *economic* changes . . . war will be eliminated . . . arts and sciences will be turned to economic uses . . . world-wide peace is ushered in . . . social justice for all . . . [Zech. 9:10; Isa. 2:4; 9:7; 42:3; 65:21-22; Ps. 72:1-4; 12-14; Zeph. 3:9].

The more completely *physical aspects of life* will also feel the effects of this Mediatorial Kingdom. Disease will be abolished. Long life will be restored . . . death will be experienced only by those incorrigible and sturdy individualists who rebel against the laws of the Kingdom. The ordinary hazards of physical life will be under supernatural control. . . . The earth shall be under the direct control of One whose voice even the winds and the waves obey . . . geological changes . . . climatic changes . . . a great increase in the fertility and productivity of the soil . . . [Isa. 32:14; 35:5-6; 65:20-22; Zech. 14:3-4; Amos 9:13; Isa. 11:6-9; 32:15-16].

In what may be called the *political sphere*. . . . *A central* authority is set up for the settlements of international disputes . . . "Out of Sion shall go forth the Law, and the Word of Jehovah from Jerusalem" . . . [Isa. 2:4; 32:18; Amos 9:14-15; Ezek. 37:1 ff.; Isa. 60:1-4].

The Mediatorial Kingdom will also have an *ecclesiastical* aspect. The supreme Ruler combines in His Person the offices of both King and Priest. Church and State become one in aim and action . . . [Ps. 110:1-7; Ezek. 37:26-28; 43:1-7; Isa. 61:6; 66:23; Zech. 14:16-19].

> Such is the nature of the . . . Kingdom as presented in Old Testament prophecy. And I would like to suggest just here that it satisfies and reconciles all legitimate viewpoints. The Kingdom is spiritual, ethical, social, economic, physical, political and ecclesiastical. To single out any one of these aspects and deny the others is to narrow the breadth of the prophetic vision.[21]

It thus becomes quite evident that the departure of the presence of the Lord from Israel and the captivity and dispersion of the theocratic nation did not nullify the expectation of the establishment of the theocratic kingdom. Peters observes:

> The Prophets, with one voice, describe this one Kingdom, thus restored, in terms expressive of the most glorious additions. They predict, from the Psalmist down to Malachi, a restoration of the identical overthrown Kingdom, linked with the most astounding events which shall produce a blessedness and glory unexampled in the history of the world. . . . Since the overthrow of the Theocratic-Davidic Kingdom, these predicted events have not taken place as delineated, and therefore, the predicted, covenanted Kingdom has not yet appeared. . . . It is the same Kingdom overthrown that receives those additions, and not another Kingdom that obtains them; hence, no professed Kingdom, however loudly proclaimed and learnedly presented, should, lacking these, be accepted by us. . . . Those additions are so great in their nature, so striking in their characteristics, so manifesting the interference of the Supernatural, that no one can possibly mistake when this Kingdom is restored. . . . After the downfall of the Davidic Kingdom, the Prophets predict this Kingdom as future.[22]

---

[21] McClain, *op. cit.*, pp. 4-6.
[22] Peters, *op. cit.*, I, 248.

CHAPTER XXVI

THE KINGDOM PROGRAM IN THE NEW TESTAMENT

It is a well established fact that the Jews at the time of Christ were anticipating a literal fulfillment of the Old Testament theocratic kingdom promises. It has been stated:

> It has been universally admitted by writers of prominence (e.g. Neander, Hagenbach, Schaff, Kurtz, etc.) whatever their respective views concerning the Kingdom itself, that the Jews, including the pious, held to a personal coming of the Messiah, the literal restoration of the Davidic throne and kingdom, the personal reign of Messiah on David's throne, the resultant exaltation of Jerusalem and the Jewish nation, and the fulfilment of the Millennial descriptions of that reign. It is also acknowledged that the utterances of Luke 1:71; Acts 1:6; Luke 2:26, 30, etc., include the above belief, and that down, at least to the day of Pentecost, the Jews, the disciples, and even the apostles held to such a view. . . . they regarded the prophecies and covenanted promises as literal (i.e. in their naked grammatical sense); and, believing in the fulfilment, looked for such a restoration of the Davidic Kingdom under the Messiah, with an increased power and glory befitting the majesty of the predicted King; and also that the pious of former ages would be raised up from the dead to enjoy the same.[1]

I. THE THEOCRATIC KINGDOM OFFERED AT THE FIRST ADVENT OF CHRIST

There are different views currently held as to the kingdom that was announced at the first advent of Christ. The *liberal* view is that Jesus adopted the social and political aspirations of the people of His day and announced a kingdom in close conformity to that expected by Israel on the basis of the Old Testament prophecies. However, during the course of His life it became apparent that Israel would not receive His offered kingdom and

[1] G. N. H. Peters, *Theocratic Kingdom*, I, 183.

therefore He abandoned that expectation because of the opposition and subsequent discouragement. The *spiritualized* view is that Jesus adopted the spiritual elements of the Old Testament prophets, abandoning all the political and national aspects, and offered a spiritual kingdom to all who would believe. The *literal* view, supported by the study of the New Testament, is that the kingdom announced and offered by the Lord Jesus was the same theocratic kingdom foretold through the Old Testament prophets.

A. *The Old Testament theocracy was offered.* The kingdom offered to Israel was the same theocracy anticipated in the Old Testament. Bright says:

> But for all his repeated mention of the Kingdom of God, Jesus never once paused to define it. Nor did any hearer ever interrupt him to ask, "Master, what do these words, 'Kingdom of God', which you use so often, mean?" On the contrary, Jesus used the term as if assured it would be understood, and indeed it was. The Kingdom of God lay within the vocabulary of every Jew. It was something they understood and longed for desperately.[2]

The same observation is stated again:

> The New Testament begins the announcement of the kingdom in terms expressive of its being previously well known . . . The preaching of the kingdom, its simple announcement, without the least attempt *to explain* its meaning or nature, the very language in which it was conveyed to the Jews—all presupposed that it was a subject *familiar* to all. John the Baptist, Jesus, and the Seventy, all proclaimed the kingdom in a way, without definition or explanation, that indicated that their hearers *were acquainted* with its meaning.[3]

McClain points out that that kingdom offered in the Gospels was the same as that anticipated by the prophets. He writes:

> . . . in the works and teaching of Christ may be found every aspect of the prophetic Kingdom. It is basically *spiritual;* so much so that "Except a man be born anew" he cannot even see the Kingdom of God. Its *ethical* aspect is fully set forth in the Sermon on the Mount. . . . The correction of *social* evils appears in Christ's

[2] John Bright, *The Kingdom of God*, pp. 17-18.
[3] Peters, *op. cit.*, I, 181.

forecast of the establishment of His Kingdom when all such evils shall be sternly gathered out by supernatural agency. The *ecclesiastical* nature of His Kingdom is recognized when He whips the money-changers out of the temple. Why not simply ignore the temple if, as some say, that God is done with Israel and the theocratic idea? On the contrary . . . He lays claim to the Jewish temple, and quotes a prophecy of the Kingdom in defence of His action, "*My* house shall be called a house of prayer for *all nations.*" Even the *political* aspect of the prophetic kingdom is assigned an important place in Matthew 25 . . . which presents Christ's own description of Himself sitting upon a throne of glory judging between living nations on earth. . . . As to the *physical* aspects of His kingdom read the New Testament record of blind men that saw, lame that walked, deaf that heard, lepers that were cleansed; read the record of multitudes fed by supernatural power; read the records of deliverance from the hazards of wind and storm and violence.[4]

B. *The recognition of the Messiah.* Christ at His birth was recognized as Messiah. The angelic messenger, announcing His birth to Mary, made it clear concerning the work of Mary's Son:

> And, behold, thou shalt conceive in thy womb, and bring forth a son, and shall call his name JESUS. He shall be great, and shall be called the Son of the Highest: and the Lord God shall give unto him the throne of his father David: And he shall reign over the house of Jacob forever; and of his kingdom there shall be no end [Luke 1:31-33].

The hymn of thanksgiving voiced by Mary (Luke 1:46-55) makes it also clear that Mary so understood the angelic announcement. Elizabeth spoke prophetically of the advent of "my Lord" before His birth (Luke 1:43) as moved by the Holy Ghost (Luke 1:41). To Simeon, who was "waiting for the consolation of Israel" (Luke 2:25), the fact was revealed and the Person of Christ was clearly discerned, as we observe from his prophecy (Luke 2:29-35). Anna, the prophetess, who "looked for redemption in Jerusalem" (Luke 2:38), saw the fulfillment of her hopes in the Messiah who had appeared. The wise men came looking for the one "that is born King of the Jews" (Matt. 2:2) and were given divine attestation that they had found the One in whom their hopes could be realized. Matthew, writing to present Jesus as the Messiah to Is-

---

[4] Alva J. McClain, "The Greatness of the Kingdom," unpublished classroom notes, pp. 7-8.

rael, begins his record with the genealogy which traces the lineage, not, as might have been expected, to Abraham alone, in whose lineage He might come to redeem, but to David, in whose lineage He might come to reign. All the events associated with His birth attest His Messiahship.

C. *The Messiah announced by His herald.* Christ is preceded by the forerunner who announces the approach of the kingdom. The ministry of John the Baptist, according to the Lord's own words (Matt. 11:13-14; 17:10-13), was that ministry anticipated by Malachi (4:5-6) in which one would announce the arrival of the King of Israel. John's spoken word is significant: "Repent ye, for the kingdom of heaven is at hand" (Matt. 3:2). Without defining the concept of the kingdom in his mind, he simply announces the imminency of that theocracy. The baptism administered by John was the ritual of cleansing through the application of water, dependent upon the confession of sins, in anticipation of the coming of the Messiah, administered by one born in the priestly line. It was a confession of sinfulness, of need, and of anticipation of One coming who, according to the Old Testament expectation, would fully meet that need. It identified those who were, like John, anticipating the Messiah.

D. *The theocracy announced by Christ.* Jesus Christ, both in His own ministry and in that ministry committed to the disciples, announced the fact that the theocratic kingdom was at hand. After the termination of the ministry of the Herald (Matt. 4:12), the Lord began his public ministry with the announcement: "Repent: for the kingdom of heaven is at hand" (Matt. 4:17). In sending out the twelve, Jesus commissioned them to preach, saying, "The kingdom of heaven is at hand" (Matt. 10:7). The seventy are sent forth and the command is given: "say unto them, The kingdom of God is come nigh unto you." (Luke 10:9, 11). To these messengers the word is spoken:

> Blessed are the eyes which see the things that ye see: For I tell you, that many prophets and kings have desired to see those things which ye see, and have not seen them; and to hear those things which ye hear, and have not heard them [Luke 10:23-24].

By the term "at hand" the announcement is being made that the kingdom is to be expected imminently. It is not a guarantee that the kingdom will be instituted immediately, but rather that all impending events have been removed so that it is now imminent.

E. *The theocratic message limited to Israel.* The kingdom that was announced was announced only to Israel.

> These twelve Jesus sent forth, and commanded them, saying, Go not into the way of the Gentiles, and into any city of the Samaritans enter ye not: But go rather to the lost sheep of the house of Israel. And as ye go, preach, saying, The kingdom of heaven is at hand [Matt. 10:5-7].
>
> I am not sent but unto the lost sheep of the house of Israel [Matt. 15:24].

It is for this reason that Paul could say that "Jesus Christ was a minister of the circumcision for the truth of God, to confirm the promise made unto the fathers" (Rom. 15:8). There could be no universal blessings of the Abrahamic covenant applied to the Gentiles until Israel had experienced the realization of the theocratic kingdom, in which kingdom and in whose King the nations would be blessed.

F. *The theocratic message confirmed.* The authenticity of the kingdom offer was substantiated by signs and miracles. When John the Baptist asked Christ, "Art thou he that should come, or do we look for another?" (Matt. 11:3), doubtless because John felt the Messiah could not be received if the forerunner had been rejected, the Lord replied:

> Go and shew John again those things which ye do hear and see: The blind receive their sight, and the lame walk, the lepers are cleansed, and the deaf hear, the dead are raised up, and the poor have the gospel preached to them. And blessed is he, whosoever shall not be offended in me [Matt. 11:4-6].

The signs given by Christ were evidences of the power that would reside in the theocratic king and manifestations of the blessings that would exist in the kingdom. Peters well states:

> [The miracles of Christ] are so related to the kingdom that they cannot be separated from it without mutual defacement. Thus it is represented by Jesus Himself (Matt. 12:28), "But if I cast out devils by the Spirit of God, *then* the kingdom of God is come unto (or as some, upon) you". Here we have, 1. The relationship existing between the kingdom and miracles; that without

the latter the former cannot be revealed. 2. That miracles are a manifestation of possessed power, which Jesus will exert when He establishes His kingdom. 3. That the miraculous casting out of devils, or Satan, is an event connected with the kingdom, and its accomplishment through Jesus is thus verified as predicted, e.g., Rev. 20:1-6. 4. That the miraculous casting out of devils by Jesus is a premonition, anticipating, foreshowing, or foreshadowing . . . like the transfiguration, of the kingdom itself. The miracles then are *assurances* vouchsafed that the kingdom will come as it is predicted. The miracles of Jesus are so varied and significant in the light of the kingdom that it can be readily perceived *how* they give us the needed confidence in its several requirements and aspects. The resurrection of dead ones is connected with the kingdom; that the keys of death hang at Christ's girdle is shown in the miracles of [raising the dead]. . . . Sickness and death are banished from the inheritors of the kingdom; the numerous miracles of healing various sicknesses and of restoring the dying, establish the power existing that can perform it. The utmost perfection of body is to be enjoyed in the kingdom; this is foreshadowed by the removal of blindness, lameness, deafness, and dumbness. Hunger, thirst, famine, etc., give place to plenty in the kingdom; the miracles of feeding thousands attest to the predicted power that will accomplish it. The natural world is to be completely under the Messiah's control in that kingdom; the miracles of the draught of fishes, the tempest stilled, the ship at its destination, the walking on the sea, the fish bringing the tribute money, the barren fig tree destroyed, and the much-ridiculed one of water changed into wine, indicate that He who sets up this kingdom has indeed power over nature. The spiritual, unseen, invisible world is to be, as foretold, in contact and communication with this kingdom; and this Jesus verifies by the miracles of the transfiguration, the demoniac cured, the legion of devils cast out, passing unseen through the multitude, and by those of His own death, resurrection and ascension. Indeed there is scarcely a feature of this kingdom foretold which is to be formed by the special work of the Divine, that is not also confirmed to us by some glimpses of the Power that shall bring them forth. The kingdom—the end—is designed to remove the curse from man and nature, and to impart the most extraordinary blessings to renewed man and nature, but all this is to be done through One who, it is said, shall exert supernatural power to perform it. It is reasonable therefore to expect that *as part* of the developing of the plan itself, that when He first comes, through whom man and nature are to be regenerated, a manifestation of power—more abundant and superior to everything preceding—

> over man and nature should be exhibited, to confirm our faith in Him and His kingdom.[5]

Every miracle which the Lord performed, then, may be understood to be not only a demonstration of the theocratic power of the Messiah, but also that which depicts the conditions which will exist in the theocratic kingdom when it is established.

G. *The theocratic offer in relation to the Old Testament prophecies.* The authenticity of the kingdom offer was substantiated by an appeal to the Old Testament promise. On numerous occasions the Lord explains a course of action, about which question had been raised, by appealing to Old Testament Messianic promises to show that He fulfilled that which Mesisah would do at His coming. His right to possess the temple of God and cleanse it is justified by an appeal to a Psalm that was recognized as Messianic (John 2:17 with Ps. 69). His first public appearance in the synagogue brings forth a statement of Messiah's work (Luke 4:18-19 with Isa. 61:1). The question as to whether He has been preceded by the promised Herald is established from the Messianic Scriptures (Luke 7:27 with Mal. 3:1). The question as to whether He is qualified to be the Messiah, personally, brings forth an exposition of the Messianic promise (Luke 20:41-44). The final cleansing of the temple is justified again by an appeal to the Messianic promise (Matt. 21:13 with Isa. 56:7). In the resurrection ministry Christ clearly established the relationship between the Old Testament prophets and Himself (Luke 24:25-27). Such citations are sufficient to show that Christ constantly appealed to the theocratic kingdom promises to explain His course of action.

H. *The relation of Christ to the offer.* The kingdom was offered in the person of the king. The Lord's statement is: "behold, the kingdom of God is within you" (Luke 17:21). The Lord is not asserting that His kingdom was to be a spiritual kingdom in the hearts of men. Such is contrary to the entire tenor of the Word of God. He is asserting that the kingdom to which they were looking was already "at hand" in the person of the king. The rightful king was present and all that was required was repentance on the part of the nation and a reception of Christ as the theocratic Messiah.

---

[5] Peters, *op. cit.*, I, 89-90.

I. *The contingency of the offer.* The offer of the kingdom was a contingent offer. God knew full-well the response of the nation Israel to the offer of the kingdom, yet the establishment of the theocratic kingdom depended upon the repentance of the nation, the recognition of John the Baptist as the promised fore-runner, and the reception of Jesus Christ as the theocratic king. McClain says:

> More than one expositor has stumbled over the ultimatum of Christ, "I was not sent but unto the lost sheep of the house of Israel." The only adequate explanation is to see, what our Lord understood clearly, the contingent nature of His message of the Kingdom. To put the matter in a word: *the immediate and complete establishment of His Kingdom depended upon the attitude of the nation of Israel,* to whom pertained the divine promises and covenants. . . .
>
> That our Lord clearly understood the contingent nature of His Kingdom message is plain from His evaluation of John the Baptist and his meteoric career. Every intelligent Jew knew that the final word of the final Old Testament prophet predicted the appearance of Elijah as the precursor to the establishment of the Kingdom. And Jesus declares, in Matthew 11, concerning John, "*If* ye are willing to receive him, *this is Elijah,* that is to come." Still later, when historical events have demonstrated the certainty of His rejection and death at the hands of the Jewish nation, our Lord again refers to John, but now the die is cast, "Elijah indeed cometh, and shall restore all things," He assures the disciples; but He adds, "I say unto you that Elijah is come already, and they knew him not." I do not hesitate to say that you have here the key to one of the most puzzling problems of New Testament eschatology in relation to the Kingdom: The *immediate establishment of the Mediatorial Kingdom on earth was contingent upon the attitude of Israel.*[6]

Throughout both Testaments the blessings of the theocratic kingdom were made to depend upon the repentance of the individual and the reception of a new heart from the Messiah. Even in the theocratic administration of the Old Testament the unbeliever and the defiled were cut off from participation with the believing and prepared people. This is clearly presented by Peter in Acts when He calls upon the nation to repent (Acts 2:38; 3:19).

[6] McClain, *op. cit.*, pp. 8-9.

J. *The bona fide offer*. This offer of the kingdom was, nevertheless, a bona fide offer. It would be a mockery for God to present the theocratic kingdom if it were not a genuine offer. Peters says:

> This Kingdom was offered to the nation in good faith, *i.e.* it would have been bestowed *provided* the nation had repented. The foreknown result made no difference in the tender of it, so far as the free agency of the nation is concerned; that result flowed from *a voluntary choice*. The national unbelief did not change God's faithfulness, Rom. 3:3. It would be derogatory to the mission of Christ to take any other view of it, and *the sincerity and desire* of Jesus that the nation might accept, is witnessed in His tears over Jerusalem, in His address to it, in His unceasing labors, in sending out the twelve and the seventy, and in His works of mercy and love. It follows, then, that the Jews had *the privilege* accorded to them of accepting the Kingdom, and if the condition annexed to it had been complied with, *then* the Kingdom of David would have been most gloriously re-established under the the Messiah.[7]

There are many who argue that the bona fide offer of a kingdom at the first advent minimizes the cross and leaves no place for the accomplishment of the redemptive program of God.[8] In reply to this contention it may be said that the offer and the rejection of the theocratic kingdom was the design of God by which His eternal purpose was actually accomplished. That which accomplished the divine purpose of salvation through Christ's death was the rejection of a kingdom offered to Israel. Peters well observes:

> The question, How, then, would the atonement have been made by the shedding of blood? has nothing whatever to do with the sincerity of this offer, for "the manifold wisdom of God" would have been equal to the emergency, either by antedating to some other period, or by providing for it previously; or in some other, to us unknown, way. As it was, God's purposes, His determinate counsel, are shaped by what was *a foreseen voluntary choice* of the nation. God's mercy was willing to bestow, but the nation's depravity prevented the gift. That the Kingdom would have been established had the nation believed, is evident from Deut., ch. 32; 2 Chron. 7:12-22; Isa. 48:18; Ps. 81:8-16, etc.

---

[7] Peters, *op. cit.*, I, 377.
[8] Cf. Oswald T. Allis, *Prophecy and the Church*, pp. 74-75.

> . . . Paul's argument in Romans proceeds on the supposition that the nation had the power of choice, that it wilfully chose the evil, and that God in mercy overruled its fall for the salvation of the Gentiles. They stumbled and fell, not through necessity, and not because God's Purpose required it, but solely through their own unbelief; and God's plan, as the Omniscient, embraced the same as a foreknown result, and made provision accordingly.[9]

The principle that God makes a genuine offer even though it is foreknown that it will not be accepted is recognized in Scripture. Chafer points out:

> This first offer of the kingdom had been typified by the events at Kadesh-Barnea. There this same nation, which had already tasted the discomforts of the desert, were given an opportunity to immediately enter their promised land. Thus left to choose, they failed to enter, and returned to forty years more of wilderness wandering and added judgments. They might have entered the land in blessing. God knew they would not; still it was through their own choice that the blessing was postponed. Later they were brought again to the land after their judgments and afflictions in the wilderness. This time, however, it was without reference to their own choice.[10]

There are some who hold that the offer could not have been a genuine offer because the Old Testament predicted His sufferings first then His glory to follow.[11] It is contended that the order makes the death necessarily come first and therefore there could have been no genuine offer of the kingdom. It is sufficient to point out that the prophets saw the events in the light of the rejection, in the actual order in which it took place, not in its contingent order. This order does not violate the genuineness of the offer, but does show that the rejection of the offer was the appointed means of accomplishing God's desired end.

Some contend that neither the Lord nor John ever offered Israel an earthly kingdom, but only a spiritual kingdom.[12] Such a view entirely fails to comprehend the nature of "the kingdom" preached by John, the Lord, and His disciples. The fact has been shown that they preached the same kingdom the Old Testament

---

[9] Peters, *op. cit.*, I, 378.
[10] Lewis Sperry Chafer, *The Kingdom in History and Prophecy*, p. 56.
[11] Cf. Allis, *op. cit.*, p. 75.
[12] Philip Mauro, *God's Present Kingdom*, pp. 172-73.

promised and Israel expected without change of concept whatsoever.

II. The Presentation and Rejection of the Theocratic Kingdom Recorded by Matthew

The purpose of the writing of the Gospel of Matthew was to record the presentation of Jesus Christ as Messiah, to trace the opposition to Him and His offered kingdom by the nation, and to record the official and final rejection of that King and kingdom by Israel. An analysis of the theme of Matthew will be undertaken to trace this argument because of its crucial relationship to the whole kingdom concept and program.

There are three major movements in the Gospel of Matthew: (1) the presentation and authentication of the king (1:1-11:1); (2) the opposition to the King (11:2-16:12); and (3) the final rejection of the King (16:13-28:20).

A. *The presentation and authentication of the King.* Matthew devotes the first division of his gospel to the presentation and authentication of Jesus as the Messiah to Israel (1:1-11:1).

1. In this division the first section is the presentation of the King of Israel (1:1-4:11). Within it Matthew presents His arrival (1:1-2:23), describing His ancestry (1:1-17) to show His right to the throne, and His advent (1:18-2:23) to show through the virgin birth that He possessed the legal right to the throne. The name given to Him at His birth (1:24-25) links Him to Joshua, who led the people into the land and life of peace and rest. In His infancy (2:1-23) there is portrayed the homage of the Gentiles (2:1-12) and the rejection by the Jews (2:13-15). Matthew further presents the ambassador of the King (3:1-12) to show that the prophetic Scriptures were fulfilled. This presentation is followed by the approval of the King (3:13-4:11), in which division Matthew records the witness in His baptism (3:13-17), where God's approval is placed upon the Messiah, and also the witness of His victory over Satan (4:1-11), where His moral right to rule is established.

2. In the second section of this division Matthew records the proclamations of the King (4:12-7:29), where His judicial right

to rule is established. Regal authority is demonstrated in His being able to bring men to obedience (4:12-22). The credentials of the King are presented by Him (4:23-25). The pronouncements of the King (5:1-7:29) demonstrate regal authority. It has been announced by Jesus and John that the kingdom is near. The miracles have proved the validity of that announcement. The multitudes desire to know what the requirements for entrance into that announced kingdom are. The Sermon on the Mount was spoken to expound more fully the requirements for entrance into this anticipated kingdom. The subjects of the kingdom are described (5:1-16), the relation of the King to the law is established (5:17-20), the false interpretations of the Pharisees of the requirements of the law are exposed (5:21-48), and the false practices of the Pharisees are revealed (6:1-7:6). Instructions are given to those who would enter the kingdom concerning prayer (7:7-11), true righteousness (7:12), the way of access into the kingdom (7:13-14), false teachers (7:15-23), and concerning the two foundations (7:24-29).

3. The third section of this division of the gospel is a presentation of the power of the King (8:11-11:1) to authenticate His claim to the Messianic office. Messiah's authority is proved in the realm of disease as He heals the leper (8:1-4), the paralytic (8:5-13), and the one held by fever (8:14-15). His authority is demonstrated in the demonic realm (8:16-17), the realm of men (8:18-22; 9:9), in the realm of nature (8:23-27), in the realm of sin (9:1-8), in the realm of tradition (9:10-17), in the realm of death (9:18-26), and in the realm of darkness (9:27-34). All these demonstrations of authority were to demonstrate His right to Messianic office (9:35). The final demonstration of this authority is seen in that He can delegate this authority to others (9:35-11:1). This delegation of authority becomes the climactic evidence of His Messianic prerogatives, for only one possessing authority could delegate that authority to others. In this portion of the gospel the Messiah is motivated by compassion (9:35-38), issues a call to the disciples (10:1-4), and gives them a commission (10:5-11:1). The message entrusted to them (10:5-15) is seen to be a message to Israel exclusively (10:4-5) because of their lost condition (10:6) and revolves about the same message John and Christ proclaimed (10:7) and was to be substantiated by the same

signs that authenticated Jesus as the Messiah (10:8). This ministry is but an extension of His ministry to Israel and an announcement of the same message He brought to them. The reception of the message of the kingdom is to be the same as the reception afforded John's proclamation of it. They will be persecuted and rejected because of their announcement (10:16-23). However, they are to be comforted in that they are the special objects of the Father's care (10:24-33). Even though there be divisions because of this ministry (10:34-39), there will be a reward to them for their preaching and for those who receive it from them (10:40-42). Matthew thus far in the gospel has carefully presented a Person to the nation. His legal right, moral right, judicial right, and prophetical right to the Messianic throne were proved. Full authentication to support this contention has been presented.

B. *The opposition and rejection of the King.* The second division of the Gospel of Matthew is devoted to the opposition and rejection of the King by the nation Israel (11:2-16:12).

1. First, Matthew traces the commencement of the rejection (11:2-27), which begins with opposition to the forerunner, John (11:2-15), and continues in the critical (11:16-19) and culminates with the opposition of the careless (11:20-24). The adverb of time in Matthew 11:20 shows a change in the emphasis in the ministry of Christ stemming from this attitude toward Him. In spite of the opposition there is an invitation extended to the childlike (11:25-30).

2. Matthew next traces the controversies with the authorities. The first controversy is about the Sabbath question (12:1-8), the second likewise over the Sabbath question (12:9-21), the third over the healing of a demoniac (12:22-37). Because of this miracle, Messiah is accused of ministering in Satanic power and authority. This charge is refuted by Christ by showing that division within the kingdom of Satan is impossible (12:25-26), the exorcists are not accused of Satanic power (12:27), and this must be interpreted as a demonstration of Messianic authority (12:28). This whole controversy is followed by a severe warning (12:31-37) as to the gravity of the sin of rejecting the testimony of the Holy Spirit to the person of Christ. The fourth controversy (12:38-42) centers around a request for further evidence of His

Messiahship. The conclusion of this controversy is given in Matthew 12:43-50 where Christ repudiates natural relationships, such as Israel sustained to Him, and anticipates a new relationship based upon faith, which is to be established. It is to be noted in all this controversy that there is just one essential question before the nation, "Is not this the son of David?" (12:23).

3. Matthew traces the consequences of rejection (13:1-52). In the parables of this chapter Messiah outlines the development of the kingdom program in the light of the rejection of the Messiah by Israel, and outlines the time period from Israel's rejection of the Messiah unto Israel's future reception of Messiah at the second advent.

4. Matthew presents the culmination of the rejection by the nation (13:53-16:12). There is rejection in Nazareth (13:53-58), rejection by Herod (14:1-36), rejection by the Scribes and Pharisees (15:1-39) in spite of the sign of the healing of the daughter of the Syrophenician woman (15:21-28), the sign of the healing of many (15:29-31), and the feeding of the four thousand (15:32-39). The final rejection is by the Pharisees and Sadducees (16:1-12), which results in the withdrawal of any further signs to Israel but the sign of Jonah, that is, the coming sign of Messiah's death and resurrection. Thus this whole division of Matthew (11:2-16:12) is a record of progressive opposition to the Messiah. It manifested itself first in opposition to His forerunner and then to the Messiah Himself. The opposition took the form of open conflict between Messiah and the leaders of the nation. As a result of this opposition and anticipated rejection, the Messiah outlines His kingdom program from His rejection until His reception. The opposition develops into open rejection by the various parties in the nation until it is evident that there is no possibility that the nation will receive Him as their Messiah and His death is an eventuality.

C. *The final rejection of the King.* The third division of the gospel describes the final rejection of the Messiah by Israel (16:13-28:20).

1. Within this division Matthew presents the preparation of the disciples by the Messiah in view of this rejection (16:13-20:

34). A revelation is given to the disciples of His person in view of His coming death (16:13-16). This is followed by a revelation of His program for the church (16:17-20), the program for His death (16:21-26), and the program for the kingdom (16:26-17:21). The transfiguration was a revelation of the coming of the Son of man in glory (16:27), and must be understood to be a miniature and premature picture of the second coming of the Messiah in His glory to establish His kingdom (2 Pet. 1:16-18). Matthew presents the instructions of the Messiah in view of His death (17:22-20:34). In this section there are instructions concerning persecution (17:22-23), the privileges of sons (17:24-27), humility (18:1-5), offences (18:6-14), discipline (18:15-20), forgiveness (18:21-35), divorce (19:1-12), receiving children (19:13-15), wealth (19:16-26), service (19:27-20:16), His death (20:17-19), ambition (20:20-28), and Messianic authority (20:29-34).

2. In the second place in this division, Matthew records the formal presentation and rejection of the King (21:1-27:66). Within this section is given the formal presentation of the King in His triumphal entry (21:1-17), which conformed to the time of Messiah's coming announced in Daniel 9:24-27. The cleansing of the temple (21:12-13) is a further part of His formal presentation, as Messiah is seen to be acting in the name of His Father to possess His Father's temple. The healing of the sick (21:14) is yet further formal presentation, as His authority is demonstrated. The final act in His formal presentation of Himself as Messiah is the acceptance of praise from the populace (21:15-17). Following this formal presentation Messiah withdrew from Jerusalem (21:17). This is a significant act because of the rejection of Him by the nation. This is followed by the curse upon the fig tree by Messiah (21:18-22). Inasmuch as the fig tree is used to represent the nation Israel in Scripture, this act will be seem to be the setting aside of the nation by the Messiah because of their rejection of Him.

3. The third movement within this division is the final conflict with the nation (21:23-22:46). There is a conflict with the priests and elders (21:23) over the question of His authority. Three parables illustrate this tragic conflict: the parable of the two sons (21:28-32), showing their attitude toward the ministry

of John; the parable of the householder (21:33-46), showing the attitude toward Himself; and the parable of the marriage feast (22:1-14), showing their attitude toward God's invitation to enter the kingdom. There is a conflict with the Herodians (22:15-22) over the question of taxes. There is a conflict with the Sadducees (22:23-33) over the question of resurrection. There is a conflict with the Pharisees (22:34-46) over the question of the interpretation of the law.

4. The fourth movement brings us to the rejection of the nation Israel by Christ because of their rejection of Him and His kingdom (23:1-39). The chapter records the woes pronounced upon the Pharisees, which culminates in an announcement of judgment (23:33) and a final pronouncement of desolation (23:38).

5. This rejection brings the predictions of the King (24:1-25:46), in which section the chronology of events for the nation Israel is developed. In response to the questions of the disciples concerning the future for the city and nation He describes the tribulation period (24:4-26), the second advent (24:27-30), and the regathering of Israel (24:31). The chronological development is interrupted to give parabolic instructions to watchfulness (24:32-51). The chronology of events is resumed with a revelation concerning judgment on Israel (25:1-13 and 25:14-30) and judgment on Gentiles (25:31-46) to show that only saved will enter the millennium, which is to follow the second advent of the Messiah.

6. The sixth movement in the division is the portrayal of the passion of the King (26:1-27:66). The events preceding His death are described (26:1-27:32): the announcement of the time of the death (26:1-2); the conspiracy (26:3-5); the anointing (26:6-13); the betrayal (26:14-16); the observance of the Passover and the institution of the Lord's Supper (26:17-30); the prediction of the denial by Peter (26:31-35); the experience in the garden (26:36-46); the arrest and trial of the Messiah (26:47-27:32), where the one question before the judicatory was the question as to whether Jesus was the Messiah, the Son of God (26:63). The events of His death and burial are outlined (27:33-66). There are a number of incidences in the crucifixion itself that bear evi-

dence that it was the Messiah the Jews were putting to death. The mockery of the soldiers who cried, "Hail, King of the Jews" bears witness to this. The parting of the garments (27:35) is seen to be the fulfillment of the Messianic Psalm, and thus relates this event to the Messiah Himself. The superscription over the cross (27:37) is further witness. The taunts thrown to Him (27:40) were because He claimed Messianic powers. The jeers of the priests (27:42-43) were over the fact that He had offered a salvation that only Messiah could present to the people. The supernatural darkness (27:45) and the cry from His lips (27:46) as well as the offer of vinegar (27:46) are all in fulfillment of what the Psalmist predicted of the Messiah's death. The miracles which accompany His death (27:45, 51, 52) are all to be seen as evidences that He was truly God's Messiah. His very entombment (27:57-60) is in fulfillment of the very central Messianic portion of the Old Testament, Isaiah 53. There is a subtle hint in the request for a seal for the tomb (27:62-66) that the leaders knew He was the Messiah and were afraid that their judgment would be proven false by an empty tomb and thus they sought to make it as secure as possible. Even the death and burial of Christ, a seeming defeat of His purpose to fulfill the covenants with Israel, abounds in Messianic testimony.

7. The final movement in this division of the gospel is a record of the proof of the Messianic right of the King—the resurrection of the Messiah (28:1-20). The empty tomb (28:1-8) and the appearances after the resurrection (28:9-10) are sufficient evidence of His Messiahship to call forth a fabricated tale to explain the empty tomb (28:11-15). Israel has been given her great sign concerning the person of Christ. The final commission to the disciples (28:16-20) is the last demonstration of the Messianic authority of Christ.

The Gospel of Matthew was written to present the Messiah to Israel and to record the attitude of the nation to Him. The first movement of the book has to do with His presentation and authentication, as He is shown to have the legal, moral, judicial, and prophetical rights to the throne, which rights are fully authenticated by the King in His miracles. The second movement observed is the opposition and rejection of the Messiah by the nation

Israel. The opposition grows into the open rejection by the nation. As a result of this rejection a mystery program for a new age is revealed. The third great movement has to do with the culmination of the rejection in the death of the Messiah. It was the King of the Jews that was crucified. The resurrection of the Crucified One is a divine approval of all His claims and His authentication as Messiah. Because Israel rejected the Messiah, they bear their sin until He comes to redeem the nation and to reign in glory, acclaimed as Messiah by all.

III. The Theocratic Kingdom Offer Withdrawn and Postponed after the Rejection by Israel

It has been shown in tracing the theme of the Gospel of Matthew that the pivotal point in the Lord's ministry to Israel was reached in the twelfth chapter, where the rejection of Israel by Christ, because of their announced rejection of Him, and the withdrawal of the offer of the kingdom is recorded. Gaebelein, speaking of the events in chapters eleven and twelve, says: "It is the great turning point in this Gospel and with it the offer of our Lord to Israel as their King, as well as the offer of the Kingdom ceases."[13] Barnhouse notes the importance of the event recorded in Matthew 12:14-15:

> The hatred in the hearts of the religious leaders had come to the point where they held a council against Him, how that they might destroy Him (Mt. 12:14). It was then that there occurred an act, so dramatic and so significant that we must not fail to see it. We read that "when Jesus knew it"—knew that they were holding a council against Him—"He withdrew Himself from thence" (v. 15). It was a sad day for Israel. When the Messiah of Israel withdrew Himself from His people, there could be nothing but bitterness left in their cup.[14]

Because the nation has rejected Him, the Lord announces the severance of every natural tie by which He was bound to the nation (Matt. 12:46-50).

From this announcement of the Lord concerning the rejection of the nation a definite movement may be traced in the with-

---

[13] Arno C. Gaebelein, *The Gospel of Matthew*, I, 234.
[14] Donald Grey Barnhouse, *His Own Received Him Not, But . . .*, pp. 114-15.

drawal of the offer of the kingdom. In the parables (Matt. 13:1-50) the Lord outlines the program in the development of the theocratic kingdom during the period of the King's absence, and announces the inception of an entirely new, unheralded, and unexpected program—the church (Matt. 16:13-20). He prepares the disciples for a long delay in the kingdom program as it relates to Israel (Luke 19:11-27). He promises the second advent, at which time the kingdom program with Israel will be resumed (Matt. 24:27-31), and gives the nation signs that will herald His second advent (Matt. 24:4-26). He prepares the disciples for their ministry in the new age (John 14-16), but promises them participation in the kingdom, despite its delay (Matt. 19:28-30; Luke 22:28-30). The Lord even gives to the disciples a miniature and premature picture of the second coming of Christ to establish His kingdom (Matt. 16:27-17:8). Thus we see the Lord is preparing the disciples for the withdrawal of the offer of the kingdom and the institution of a new program and age before the kingdom program is consummated.

In the Lord's public ministry there is a progression of announcements that assert the withdrawal of the offer of the kingdom. The announcement of the woes upon the leaders of the nation (Matt. 23) signifies that they have no expectation but that of judgment. The statement of the Lord is final:

> O Jerusalem, Jerusalem, thou that killest the prophets, and stonest them which are sent unto thee, how often would I have gathered thy children together, even as a hen gathereth her chickens under her wings, and ye would not! Behold, your house is left unto you desolate. For I say unto you, Ye shall not see me henceforth, till ye shall say, Blessed is he that cometh in the name of the Lord [Matt. 23:37-39].

> If thou hadst known, even thou, at least in this thy day, the things which belong unto thy peace! but now they are hid from thine eyes. For the days shall come upon thee, that thine enemies shall cast a trench about thee, and compass thee round, and keep thee in on every side, And shall lay thee even with the ground, and thy children within thee; and they shall not leave in thee one stone upon another; because thou knewest not the time of thy visitation [Luke 19:42-44].

> . . . Jerusalem shall be trodden down of the Gentiles, until the times of the Gentiles be fulfilled [Luke 21:24].

> The stone which the builders rejected, the same is become the head of the corner: this is the Lord's doing, and it is marvellous in our eyes? Therefore say I unto you, The kingdom of God shall be taken from you, and given to a nation bringing forth the fruits thereof [Matt. 21:42-43].

There are two explanations of the "nation" to whom the kingdom of God was now to be given. (1) The first explanation understands the word *nation* as "generation" and would interpret the passage thus: the kingdom of God, which is being offered to this generation, will no longer be offered to this generation of Israel, but will be offered to that generation of Israel living in a future day before the advent of Christ, which manifests belief in the coming of Messiah by their works. This is to say that the kingdom, then being offered, will again be offered to Israel prior to the second advent. This is in keeping with the promise that the gospel of the kingdom will be preached again and accepted by a remnant in Israel (Matt 24:14). (2) The second explanation interprets the word *nation* in reference to the Gentiles, to whom the good news would go after the death of Christ and through whom the kingdom program would be developed (the mystery program of Matt. 13) until its final realization at the second advent. Peters states this view when he writes:

> This Kingdom of God, offered to the Jewish nation, lest the purpose of God fail, is to be given to others who are adopted.
>
> This Kingdom is incorporated by covenant promise with the seed of Abraham; that seed is chosen, but refusing the Kingdom on the condition annexed to it, now, that the Divine Purpose revealed in the covenants may *not fail* in its accomplishment through the unbelief and depravity of the nation, another seed must be raised up *unto* Abraham, to whom the Kingdom, in a peculiar sense . . . is to be given.[15]

And again:

> The Kingdom which by promise exclusively belonged to the Jewish nation, the rightful seed of Abraham, was not to be given to an engrafted people.
>
> . . . as the promises of God are sure . . . this people, this very nation, *must be engrafted or incorporated* with this elected seed of Abraham . . . Rather than have so precious a word to fail, God is able, . . . to raise up children unto Abraham, even,

[15] Peters, *op. cit.*, I, 386.

> if necessary, from the stones (Matt. 3:9); but instead of resorting to miraculous intervention to produce such a result, God raises up a seed unto Abraham *out of* the Gentiles by engrafting them through faith in Christ, and *accounting them* as the children of Abraham by virtue of their Abrahamic justifying faith.[16]

Whichever of these two views be adopted, the Lord's word still constitutes the announcement of the withdrawal of the offer of the kingdom to Israel at that time because of their rejection of Him as Messiah. Peters observes:

> Jesus, toward the close of His ministry, preached that the Kingdom was not nigh.
>
> . . . Just so soon as the representatives of the nation met in council and conspired to put Jesus to death, then, released from the first part of His mission, His style of preaching also changed. Instead of proclaiming that the Kingdom was nigh to the nation, He now directly intimates and declares that it was not nigh. Matt. 21:43, "The kingdom of God shall be taken from you and given to a nation bringing forth the fruits thereof", is already conclusive. . . .
>
> But we have more explicit announcements. Thus, Luke 19:41-44 . . . instead of a Kingdom, is presented a direful threatening of fearful incoming evils. Again: in Matt. 23:37, 38 . . . instead of a Kingdom coming then to them, dispersion and the destruction of the city is determined, owing to their unrepentant state . . . In Luke 21:31 . . . since His death was actually contemplated by the representatives of the nation, the offer is withdrawn, and the postponement of the Kingdom, its not being nigh to them, is directly stated by an enumeration of certain events which are previously to take place before it is nigh again . . . none of them took place between their utterance and the day of Pentecost; hence the Kingdom was not established. . . . Luke 19:11-27 forcibly demonstrates our Proposition. Jesus uttered this parable "because they thought that the Kingdom of God should immediately appear" . . . the parable is given to . . . indicate that it would not soon appear, but only after an undefined period of time had elapsed. . . . Christ only openly predicted His sufferings and death toward the close of His ministry, Matt. 20:17-20, John 12:32-34, etc. This was designedly done. . . . When He was rejected, and efforts were made to destroy Him, then He was free to unfold what God had further purposed in view of, and to overrule, this rejection.[17]

---

16 *Ibid.*, I, 396.
17 *Ibid.*, I, 379-83.

CHAPTER XXVII

THE KINGDOM PROGRAM IN THE PRESENT AGE

That God is continuing the development of His over-all theocratic kingdom program has been presented previously in the study of the parables in Matthew 13. It was entirely unknown in the Old Testament that a great interval of time would intervene between the offer of the kingdom by Messiah at His coming to the earth and the reception of that offer. The parables of Matthew 13 reveal the whole course of the development of the theocratic kingdom from the rejection of the King by Israel during His first advent until His reception as Messiah by Israel at His second advent. In commenting on Luke 19:11-27, Peters develops the whole program. He writes:

> Jesus uttered this parable "because they thought that the Kingdom of God should immediately appear." In His reply there is no intimation . . . that the Jews were mistaken in their idea of the kingdom, and that, if modern notions are correct, the Kingdom had already come and was established. If this had been so, then the answer of Jesus would be cruelly irrelevant; but with the proper conception of the Kingdom it is finely consistent and forcibly expressed. For there is (as there could not be) no declaration that they were wrong in believing that the Kingdom which they expected, the Messianic, was still in the future. They were only mistaken in the opinion, carefully announced, "that the Kingdom of God should immediately appear." Now the parable is given to correct this belief in the immediate setting up of the Kingdom, but only after an undefined period of time had elapsed. For He represents Himself as a nobleman, who, having a right to the Kingdom, goes "into a far country to receive" (to have His title confirmed) "for Himself a Kingdom, and to return." During His absence His servants "occupy till I come." Then after an interval of time, not definitely stated, the period having come to enter upon His reign, having received the Kingdom, He returns, judgment follows, and those who rejected Him (saying, "we will not have this man to reign over us") are destroyed. Here we have: (1) the Jews thought that

> the Kingdom would now appear; (2) but it was not nigh, for (a) He would leave, (b) they had refused His proffered reign, (c) those, however, who were devoted to Him should "occupy" until He returned, (d) during His absence there was no Kingdom, being gone to receive the power to reign; (3) He would return and then manifest His acquired power . . . in the establishment of His Kingdom. Thus we have the absence, and then "the appearing and Kingdom" of Christ.[1]

The relation of the theocratic kingdom to this present age may be seen in the relation of the theocratic kingdom people, Israel, to the present program. This is traced in Romans 11. Paul makes certain statements there in tracing God's dealing. God has not cast Israel away (vv. 1-2), for God has always maintained a remnant for Himself (vv. 3-4) and there is a continuing remnant according to the election of grace (v. 5). National Israel has been blinded, judicially (v.7), which blindness was anticipated in the Old Testament (vv. 8-10). Through this blinding of Israel God instituted a program with the Gentiles (vv. 11-12), in which, after the natural branches have been taken out of the place of blessing (vv. 13-16), wild branches, that is, Gentiles, have been grafted into the place of blessing (17-24). However, after the fulness of the Gentiles has come in, that is, after the completion of the program with the Gentiles, God will bring Israel back into the place of blessing again (vv. 25-29) and will bring salvation to the nation (v. 26) because such was his irrevocable covenant (vv. 27-29). This salvation (v. 26) is the salvation that was promised Israel in the Old Testament, which was to be realized when the Messiah instituted the millennial reign. Therefore Paul is showing us that after the rejection of Israel, because of the rejection of the offered kingdom, God brought the Gentiles into the place of blessing, which program continues throughout the present age. When that program is ended, God will inaugurate the theocratic kingdom at the return of the Messiah and fulfill all the covenanted blessings. Thus, throughout the New Testament the kingdom is not preached as having been established, but is still anticipated. In Acts 1:6 the Lord did not rebuke the disciples because their expectation of a yet future kingdom was in error, but only stated that the time of that kingdom, although future, was not to be known by them.

---

[1] G. N. H. Peters, *Theocratic Kingdom*, I, 382.

There are many who hold that the theocratic kingdom program was offered to Israel after the institution of the church at Pentecost, and the inauguration of the age of grace. Scofield says in commenting on Acts 3:19-21:

> The appeal here is national to the Jewish people as such, not individual as in Peter's first sermon (Acts 2:38, 39). There those who were pricked in heart were exhorted to save themselves from (among) the untoward nation; here the whole people is addressed, and the promise to *national* repentance is *national* deliverance: "and he shall send Jesus Christ" to bring in the times which the prophets had foretold. . . . The official answer was the imprisonment of the apostles, and the inhibition to preach, so fulfilling Lk. 19:14.[2]

Pettingill says: "Did Christ give the Jewish nation another chance in the first few chapters of The Acts to have the Kingdom set up? Yes. In Acts 3:17-21 the offer is found."[3]

While this view is shared by many excellent students of the Word, there seem to be reasons to hold to the view that after the rejection of Christ there was and could be no reoffer of the kingdom until the gospel of the kingdom is preached prior to the second advent. (1) All the signs mentioned by Christ in Matthew 24 and Luke 21, which were to precede the setting up of the kingdom, had not been fulfilled, thus preventing a reoffer of the kingdom in Acts. (2) Peter established the divine principle that Christ could not reinstitute the kingdom then, for he says of Him, "Whom the heaven must receive until the times of restitution of all things" (Acts 3:21). This age with its program would transpire during His absence. (3) The institution of the church on the day of Pentecost, with all that that program entailed, precluded any offer of the kingdom at that time. (4) The new command of Christ, "Ye shall be witnesses unto me both in Jerusalem, and in all Judea, and in Samaria, and unto the uttermost part of the earth" (Acts 1:8) does not coincide with the gospel of the kingdom which must precede the institution of the kingdom. (5) No offer of the kingdom could be rightly made apart from the pres-

---

[2] C. I. Scofield, *Reference Bible*, p. 1153.
[3] William Pettingill, *Bible Questions Answered*, p. 114.

ence of the King. Since, at His ascension, He had entered into a work on behalf of the church, which He must continue until the termination of that program, the kingdom, which necessitated His presence, could not be offered. (6) The baptism enjoined by Peter (Acts 2:38) could not be related to the offer of the kingdom as another example of the baptism of John, inasmuch as this baptism is "in the name of Jesus Christ." This has to do with the new age, not the old.

Some have insisted that Peter is reoffering the kingdom to Israel in chapter two of Acts since he quotes the passage from Joel that promises the fulness of the Spirit in the millennial age. However, it seems better to understand that Peter is not citing the experience before them as the fulfillment of Joel's prophecy, so that they must be considered to be in the kingdom, but rather Peter is citing Joel's prophecy to substantiate the fact, which Israel knew through her Scriptures, that such an experience as filling by the Spirit was possible. The climax of the quotation from Joel is reached in the words "whosoever shall call on the name of the Lord shall be saved" (Acts 2:21). It is this salvation Peter is proclaiming through the risen Christ. Because "Jesus, whom ye have crucified" has been made "both Lord and Christ" (Acts 2:36), Peter calls upon them to repent and be baptized. Ironside comments:

> So Peter says, "Change your attitude." . . . He calls on them to do something that will separate them visibly from this nation that is under condemnation: "Be baptized, every one of you, in the name of the Lord Jesus Christ, for the remission of sins."[4]

The baptism was that act which took them out of the community of Israel and identified them with the Christian community. A complete change of mind in regard to their attitude toward Christ was necessary before this step could be taken.

Another passage used to prove the reoffer of the kingdom in Acts is the passage of Peter in Acts 3:19-21. In this passage, because of the impact of the healing of the lame man, Peter is privileged to make another declaration concerning

[4] Harry A. Ironside, *Lectures on the Book of Acts*, p. 68.

Jesus Christ to Israel. Because God "hath glorified his Son Jesus" (Acts 3:13) Peter calls upon the nation to change her mind toward Him, that is, to repent "so that the times of refreshing may come from the presence of the Lord" [literally translated]. The "times of refreshing" must be related to the realization of the reign of Messiah because of the emphasis on the second advent in Acts 3:20. It was an established Old Testament principle, which is equally true in the New, that the millennial blessings can not come apart from the return of Christ and that event will be accompanied by the salvation and repentance of the nation Israel. On such a basis Peter's appeal is made here. Peter's preaching does not constitute a reoffer of the kingdom, but does stress the nation's responsibility to change the mind in relation to Christ, whom they crucified. Ironside adds:

> . . . if Israel will turn to the Lord it will hasten the time when the Lord Jesus will come back again and bring with Him refreshing for all the world. That is still true. The final blessing of the poor world is wrapped up in Israel's repentance. When the people of Israel repent and turn to God they will become the means of blessing to the whole earth.[5]

Thus Peter calls on them individually to do what the nation was always required to do before receiving blessing in any form—turn to God.

During this present age, then, while the King is absent, the theocratic kingdom is in abeyance in the sense of its actual establishment on the earth. Yet it remains as the determinative purpose of God. Paul declared this purpose when he was "preaching the kingdom of God" (Acts 20:25). Believers have been brought into "the kingdom of his dear Son" (Col. 1:13) through the new birth. Unbelievers are warned they will not have part in that kingdom (1 Cor. 6:9-10; Gal. 5:21; Eph. 5:5). Others were seen to have labored with Paul "unto the kingdom of God" (Col. 4:11). Believers were enjoined to suffer to "be counted worthy of the kingdom of God" (2 Thess. 1:5). It was Paul's expectation to be preserved "unto his heavenly kingdom" (2 Tim. 4:18). Such references, undoubtedly, are related to the eternal kingdom and emphasize the believer's part in it.

---

[5] *Ibid.*, p. 93.

They can not be made to support the theory that the church is that earthly kingdom that fulfills all the prophecies of the Word.

I. The Theocratic Kingdom Reoffered to Israel

The "gospel of the kingdom" as announced by John (Matt. 3:3), by the disciples who were specially commissioned (Matt. 10:7), by the seventy (Luke 10:9), and by the Lord (Matt. 4:17) proclaimed the good news that the promised kingdom was "at hand." The Lord indicates this same good news will be announced again. "And this gospel of the kingdom shall be preached in all the world for a witness unto all nations" (Matt. 24:14). Although the news at the first advent was restricted to Israel, prior to the second advent it will be announced not only to Israel but to the whole world. This preaching through the believing remnant during the tribulation period (Rev. 7), as well as through the two witnesses (Rev. 11) and through Elijah (Matt. 17:11), marks the beginning of the final step in the realization of the theocratic kingdom program.

II. The Theocratic Kingdom Instituted at the Second Advent

The angelic announcement heralds the establishment of the theocratic kingdom in the words:

> The kingdom of the world of our Lord and of his Christ has begun, and he shall reign unto the ages of the ages. And the twenty-four elders, who sit upon their thrones before God, fell on their faces and worshipped God, saying, We give thanks to thee, Lord God Almighty, who is and who was, because thou hast taken thy great power and hast reigned [Rev. 11:15-17, literal tr.].

Another angel, who has "the everlasting Gospel to preach unto them that dwell on the earth, and to every nation, and kindred, and tongue, and people" (Rev. 14:6) says:

> Fear God, and give glory to him; for the hour of his judgment is come: and worship him that made heaven, and earth, and the sea, and the fountains of water [Rev. 14:7].

The "everlasting gospel" is the announcement that God's eternal purpose is now being accomplished. The everlasting gospel is substantially the same as the gospel of the kingdom. It is the good news that the king is at hand to establish the kingdom which was God's eternal purpose. Kelly, speaking of the eternal gospel, says:

> It is called by Matthew the "gospel of the kingdom." The "gospel of the kingdom" and the "everlasting gospel" are substantially like. In the Revelation it is thus described, because it was always in the purpose of God, through the bruised Seed of the woman, to crush the foe and to bless man himself here below. This Matthew, in accordance with his design, calls rather the "gospel of the kingdom," because Christ is going to be King of a kingdom prepared from the foundation of the world.[6]

The world is brought into subjection to the authority of the King and worship is given to God. The unprayed prayer of the rightful King has been offered and answered (Ps. 2:8) and dominion has been given to Him who possesses the earth in God's name.

A number of reasons may be given why this theocratic kingdom is an absolute necessity. (1) It is necessary in order to preserve the integrity of the character of God. Peters writes:

> If such a Theocratic Kingdom, as God Himself instituted, is not permanently and gloriously re-established here upon earth, then it follows that God's efforts at the establishment of government and the interest which He manifests in it are fruitless of abiding results. Or, in other words, His own Kingdom has proven a failure. . . . God's honor, majesty, etc., are immediately concerned in its restoration, or otherwise it will be said that the Almighty undertook a work which, owing to man, He could not accomplish.[7]

(2) It is necessary to accomplish God's purpose of demonstrating His perfect government over the earth.

> This is a Theocracy in deed and in truth, for in this reorganized Kingdom we find the Theocratic idea—God's idea of a perfect government—fully consummated. The Rulership is safely and powerfully lodged in one Person, who in Himself unites the human and the Divine, who becomes, according to "the everlasting covenant" and "the sure mercies of David" (Isa. 55:3, 4, Alexander's version), "the Chief and Commander of nations."[8]

---

[6] William Kelly, *The Revelation Expounded*, p. 173.
[7] Peters, *op. cit.*, II, 125-26.
[8] *Ibid.*, II, 123.

(3) It is necessary to restore the original harmony between God and His creation, between the supernatural and the natural.

> Now the kingdom being designed to restore and manifest the original concord once existing between the natural and supernatural, the Bible closes with that kingdom in such accordance. Without the supernatural the kingdom cannot be produced, for it requires, as predicted a supernatural king, who has been provided in a supernatural manner, and rulers who have experienced a supernatural transforming power. Even in its conception and the preparatory measures, as well as in its final manifestation, is it indissolubly bound with the Divine. . . . The kingdom and the supernatural cannot possibly be dissevered. . . . When Jesus, of supernatural origin and glorified by supernatural power, shall come the second time unto salvation, His supernatural might shall be exerted in behalf of this kingdom in the most astounding manner.[9]

(4) It is necessary in order to redeem the earth from the curse imposed upon it.

> The prophets with one voice proclaim that this kingdom is to be established in order that in it man may find complete, perfect deliverance from sin and evil. The kingdom is to be set up, so that man and nature may be happily rescued from the curse entailed by sin under which both labor and groan.[10]

(5) It is necessary in order to fulfill all God's eternal covenants made with Israel. Apart from the earthly theocratic kingdom there would be no fulfillment of the Abrahamic covenant, which promised Israel possession of the land, perpetuity as a nation, and universal blesings through that nation. Apart from the kingdom the Davidic covenant could not be fulfilled, which had promised Israel a king in David's line, a throne or recognized seat of authority from which that king would rule, and a people or kingdom over which the king reigned. Apart from that kingdom the Palestinian covenant, which promised Israel possession of the land, and blessings in the possession of it, would not be fulfilled. Apart from that theocratic kingdom the new covenant, which promised Israel a conversion, a new heart, and the fulness of God's blessings, would not be fulfilled.

---

[9] *Ibid.*, I, 80-81.
[10] *Ibid.*, I, 102.

(6) It is necessary in order to provide a final test of fallen humanity. Man will be placed under the most ideal circumstances. With all outward source of temptation removed, in that Satan is bound, and every want supplied, so that there is nothing to covet, it will be demonstrated through those who are born in the millennium with a fallen, sinful nature that man is corrupt and worthy of judgment. In spite of the visible presence of the King and all the blessings that come from Him, by rebellion at the termination of the millennium (Rev. 20:7-9), men will prove that the heart is corrupt.

(7) It is necessary to make a full manifestation of the glory of Christ in the kingdom over which He rules.

> In every aspect that we view the subject, it seems suitable and necessary to have such a Theocracy as predicted. Besides the reasons adduced derived from covenant, the faithfulness of God, the redemption of the earth, etc., it does appear eminently proper that the theatre of King Jesus' humiliation, sufferings, and death should witness also His exaltation and glory. The Bible, in addition to the pleas presented to us, points to the time coming when Christ shall be openly and visibly recognized as the glorious One, who, as the Second Adam, having substituted Himself through love, is the efficacious Head of Humanity in its newly begun destiny; who, as Redeemer, having offered expiation to and honored the justice of God, now practically manifests the fruits of salvation; who, as Prophet, having taught restitution, now exhibits Himself as the Truth evidenced by the work performed before Him; who, as Priest, having made an acceptable sacrifice, now presents before the world the fruit resulting from it; who, as King, in virtue even of His Divine union and showing it by guidance, supporting, etc., now manifests it in the special ordained manner as Sovereign Ruler. In brief, this Theocracy is the restoration of a God again dwelling with man, accessible, and constituting in Jesus an infallible Head, just such as the world needs, just such as man for ages has longed for, and just such as will place David's Son in honor and glory in a world where He suffered and died. The past treatment and brief stay of the Son of God and David's Son insures a triumphant return, and a sojourn in power among men whom He will save, verifying the name Immanuel, God with us, in the Theocratical sense.[11]

[11] *Ibid.*, II, 129.

Chapter XXVIII

THE SCRIPTURAL DOCTRINE OF THE MILLENNIUM

A larger body of prophetic Scripture is devoted to the subject of the millennium, developing its character and conditions, than any other one subject. This millennial age, in which the purposes of God are fully realized on the earth, demands considerable attention. An attempt will be made to deduce from the Scriptures themselves the essential facts and features of this theocratic kingdom. While much has been written on the subject of the millennium, that which is clearly revealed in the Word can be our only true guide as to the nature and character of that period.

I. The Millennium and Israel's Covenants

Much has been said previously to show that this age will see the complete fulfillment of all the covenants that God made with Israel. It is sufficient here to show from the Scriptures that the kingdom on earth is viewed as the complete fulfillment of those covenants, and that the millennial age is instituted out of necessity in order to fulfill the covenants.

A. *The Abrahamic covenant.* The promises in the Abrahamic covenant concerning the land and the seed are fulfilled in the millennial age (Isa. 10:21-22; 19:25; 43:1; 65:8-9; Jer. 30:22; 32:38; Ezek. 34:24, 30-31; Mic. 7:19-20; Zech. 13:9; Mal. 3:16-18). Israel's perpetuity, their possession of the land, and their inheritance of blessings are directly related to the fulfillment of this covenant.

B. *The Davidic covenant.* The promises in the Davidic covenant concerning the king, the throne, and the royal house are fulfilled by Messiah in the millennial age (Isa. 11:1-2; 55:3, 11; Jer. 23:5-8; 33:20-26; Ezek. 34:23-25; 37:23-24; Hos. 3:5; Mic. 4:7-8). The fact that Israel has a kingdom, over which David's Son reigns as King, is based on this Davidic covenant.

C. *The Palestinic covenant.* The promises in the Palestinic covenant concerning the possession of the land are fulfilled by Israel in the millennial age (Isa. 11:11-12; 65:9; Ezek. 16:60-63; 36:28-29; 39:28; Hos. 1:10-2:1; Mic. 2:12; Zech. 10:6). These references to the possession of the land promise fulfillment of the Palestinic covenant.

D. *The new covenant.* The promises of the new covenant of a new heart, the forgiveness of sin, the filling of the Spirit are fulfilled in the converted nation in the millennial age (Jer. 31:31-34; 32:35-39; Ezek. 11:18-20; 16:60-63; 37:26; Rom. 11:26-29). All the spiritual blessings Israel receives are fulfillment of this covenant.

It will thus be observed that the millennial age finds the complete fulfillment of all that God promised to the nation Israel.

II. The Relation of Satan to the Millennium

Immediately following the second advent Satan is bound for a thousand years. John writes:

> And I saw an angel come down from heaven, having the key to the bottomless pit and a great chain in his hand. And he laid hold on the dragon, that old serpent, which is the Devil, and Satan, and bound him a thousand years, And cast him into the bottomless pit, and shut him up, and set a seal upon him, that he should deceive the nations no more, till the thousand years should be fulfilled . . . [Rev. 20:1-3].

Satan, as the god of this age (2 Cor. 4:4), has carried on his work to defeat the purpose and program of God. The millennial age is to be the age in which divine righteousness is to be displayed (Isa. 11:5; 32:1; Jer. 23:6; Dan. 9:24). It is also to be God's final test of fallen humanity under the most ideal circumstances. All outward sources of temptation must be removed so that man will demonstrate what he is apart from Satanic influence. So that there can be the full manifestation of righteousness and a test of humanity apart from external temptation, Satan must be removed from the sphere. Therefore, at the second advent he will be bound and removed from the scene for the entirety of that millennial period.

III. The Relation of Christ to the Millennium

It is evident that there can and will be no earthly theocratic kingdom apart from the personal manifested presence of the Lord Jesus Christ. This whole age depends upon His return to the earth as promised. All that exists in the millennium has its origin in the King who is revealed.

> How can the curse be repealed; how can death be overcome, how can all the fearful evils pertaining to man and nature be removed; how can the unspeakably great blessings be obtained; all of which are to be realized in this Kingdom under Messiah's reign without a mighty display of Supernatural power beyond anything that the world has ever witnessed, and beyond the understanding of weak and mortal man with his limited powers. If there is a truth conspicuously displayed in Holy Writ, it is, that this Kingdom, the tabernacle of David now in ruins but then gloriously rebuilt under David's Son, cannot be manifested without the most wonderful display of Almighty energy.[1]

The millennium could not be apart from the manifestation of Christ, upon whom the entire age depends.

A. *The names and titles applied to Christ in the millennium.* Something of the manifold relationship which Christ sustains to the millennium is to be observed in the many names and titles given to Him during that period, each suggesting some facts of His person and work in that day.

The Branch (Isa. 4:2; 11:1; Jer. 23:5; 33:15; Zech. 3:8-9; 6:12-13). Scofield comments:

> A name of Christ, used in a fourfold way: (1) "The Branch of Jehovah" (Isa. 4:2), that is, the "Immanuel" character of Christ (Isa. 7:14) to be fully manifested to restored and converted Israel after His return in divine glory (Mt. 25:31); (2) the "Branch of David" (Isa. 11:1; Jer. 23:5; 33:15), that is, the Messiah, "of the seed of David according to the flesh" (Rom. 1:3), revealed in His earthly glory as King of kings, and Lord of lords; (3) Jehovah's "Servant, the Branch" (Zech. 3:8), Messiah's humiliation and obedience unto death according to Isa. 52:13-15; 53:1-12; Phil. 2:5-8; (4) The "man whose name is the Branch" (Zech. 6:12, 13), that is, His character as Son of

[1] G. N. H. Peters, *Theocratic Kingdom*, III, 220-21.

> man, the "last Adam," the "second Man" (I Cor. 15:45-47), reigning, as Priest-King, over the earth in the dominion given to and lost by the first Adam.[2]

The Lord of Hosts (Isa. 24:23; 44:6), *thy God* (Isa. 52:7), *the Lord our righteousness* (Jer. 23:6; 33:16), *the Ancient of Days* (Dan. 7:13), *the Lord* (Mic. 4:7; Zech. 14:9), *the Most High* (Dan. 7:22-24), *the Son of God* (Isa. 9:6; Dan. 3:25; Hos. 11:1), *Jehovah* (Isa. 2:2-4; 7:14; 9:6; 12:6; 25:7-10; 33:20-22; 40:9-11; Jer. 3:17; 23:5-6; Ezek. 43:5-7; 44:1-2; Joel 3:21; Mic. 4:1-3, 7; Zech. 14:9, 16-17) are all names which show that the One ruling is truly God, so that the reign may rightly be called a theocracy.

The rod of Jesse (Isa. 11:1, 11), *the Son of man* (Dan. 7:13), *the servant* (Isa. 42:1-6; 49:1-7; 53:11), *the Tender Plant* (Isa. 53:2; Ezek. 17:22-24) are used of the Messiah to emphasize His humanity, and His right to rule over men because of His relation with them.

The regal authority of the Messiah is designated in such names as: *the King* (Isa. 33:17, 22; 44:6; 2:2-4; 9:3-7; 11:1-10; 16:5; 24:21-26:15; 31:4-32:2; 42:1-6; 42:13; 49:1-9; 51:4-5; 60:12; Dan. 2:44; 7:15-28; Obad. 17-21; Mic. 4:1-8; 5:2-5, 15; Zeph. 3:9-10; 3:18-19; Zech. 9:10-15; 14:16-17), *the Judge* (Isa. 11:3-4; 16:5; 33:22; 51:4-5; Ezek. 34:17, 20; Joel 3:1-2; Mic. 4:2-3), *the Lawgiver* (Isa. 33:22), *Messiah the Prince* (Dan. 9:25-26), the *Prince of princes,* (Dan. 8:25), in which His right to the throne and the royal powers associated with the throne are attributed to Him.

The work of the King as Redeemer in bringing salvation to the people is emphasized in names such as: *the Redeemer* (Isa. 59:20), *the Sun of Righteousness* (Mal. 4:2), *the Wall Breaker* (Mic. 2:13), *the Shepherd* (Isa. 40:10-11; Jer. 23:1, 3; Ezek. 34:11-31; 37:24; Mic. 4:5; 7:14), *the Lord our righteousness* (Jer. 23:6; 33:16), *the Stone* (Isa. 28:16; Zech. 3:9), *the Light* (Isa. 60:1-3). Thus the Messiah, through His names, is presented as the Son of God and Son of man who redeems and reigns throughout the kingdom age.

---

[2] C. I. Scofield, *Reference Bible,* pp. 716-17.

B. *The manifestation of Christ in the millennium.* The prophetic Scriptures state a number of ministries and manifestations associated with the Messiah at His second advent. The fact of the second advent is clearly established (Isa. 60:2; 61:2; Ezek. 21:27; Dan. 7:22; Hab. 2:3; Hag. 2:7; Zech. 2:8; Mal. 3:1). His coming will see Him manifested as the *son of Abraham* (Gen. 17:8; Matt. 1:1; Gal. 3:16), in which He will possess the land of Palestine in God's name, and institute the kingdom with Abraham's seed. He will be manifested as the *son of David* (Luke 1:32-33; Matt. 1:1; Isa. 9:7), in which He will, as rightful heir to the throne, assume the throne and reign. He will be manifested as *the Son of man* (Acts 1:11; John 5:27), and as such will execute judgment at the inception of the kingdom and throughout that age. He will be manifested as God's theocratic *King,* so that He will be a King of Righteousness (Isa. 32:1), a King over Israel (John 12:13), He will be the King of Kings (Rev. 19:16), and King over all the earth (Zech. 14:9; Phil. 2:10). He will be manifested as *God the Son* (Isa. 9:6; Ps. 134:3; Heb. 1:8-10), so that it can be said "the tabernacle of God is with men" (Rev. 21:3). In these manifestations He will do the work of *Redeemer* (Isa. 59:20-21; 62:11; Mal. 4:2), *Judge* (Isa. 61:2; 62:11; 63:1; Dan. 2:44-45; Dan. 7:9-10), *Rewarder of the Saints* (Isa. 62:12), *Teacher* (Isa. 2:3; Zech. 8:22), *King* (Isa. 33:17-22; 40:9-11; 52:7; Dan. 2:45; 7:25-27; Mic. 5:2-5; Zeph. 3:15), *Prophet* (Deut. 18:15, 18), *Lawgiver* (Isa. 33:22; Gen. 49:10), *Shepherd* (Isa. 40:10-11; Jer. 23:1, 3; Mic. 4:5; 7:14).

The millennium will be the period of the full manifestation of the glory of the Lord Jesus Christ.[8] There will be the manifestation of glory associated with the *humanity* of Christ. There will be the glory of a glorious *dominion,* in which Christ, by virtue of his obedience unto death, is given universal dominion to replace that dominion which Adam lost. There will be the glory of a glorious *government,* in which Christ, as David's son, is given absolute power to govern (Isa. 9:6; Ps. 45:4; Isa. 11:4; Ps. 72:4; Ps. 2:9). There will be the glory of a glorious *inheritance,* in which the land and the seed promised to Abraham are realized through Christ (Gen. 17:8; 15:7; Dan. 11:16, 41; 8:9).

---

[8] Chester Woodring, "The Millennial Glory of Christ," pp. 62-134.

There will be the glory of a glorious *judiciary,* in which Christ, as the spokesman for God, announces God's will and law throughout the age (Deut. 18:18, 19; Isa. 33:21-22; Acts 3:22; Isa. 2:3-4; 42:4). There will be the glory of a glorious *house and throne,* in which Christ, as David's son, shall fulfill that promised to David (2 Sam. 7:12-16) in His reign (Isa. 9:6-7; Luke 1:31-33; Matt. 25:21). There will be the glory of a glorious kingdom over which Christ reigns (Ps. 72; Isa. 11:10; Jer. 23:6; Zech. 3:10; Isa. 9:7).

There will also be the manifestation of the glory associated with the *deity* of the Lord Jesus Christ. His *omniscience* is recognized (Isa. 66:15-18). His *omnipotence* is that which sustains throughout the age (Isa. 41:10, 17-18; Ps. 46:1, 5). He *receives worship* as God (Ps. 45:6; Isa. 66:23; Ps. 86:9; Zech. 14:16-19). *Righteousness* will be fully manifested (Ps. 45:4, 7; 98:2; Dan. 9:24; Isa. 1:27; 10:22; 28:17; 60:21; 63:1; Mal. 4:2). There will be a full display of divine *mercy* (Isa. 63:7-19; 54:7-10; 40:10-13; Hos. 2:23; Ps. 89:3). Divine *goodness* will also be displayed through Him (Jer. 33:9, 15; Zech. 9:17; Isa. 52:7). The *will of God* will be fully revealed through the Messiah (Matt. 6:10) and will be accomplished on the earth. The *holiness* of God will be manifested through Messiah (Isa. 6:1-3; Rev. 15:4; Ezek. 36:20-23; Isa. 4:3, 4; 35:8-10; Ezek. 45:1-5; Joel 3:17; Zech. 2:12). There will be a glorious manifestation of divine *truth* through the King (Micah 7:20; Isa. 25:1; 61:8). Thus, through the King, there will be a full display of the divine attributes, so that Christ might be glorified as God.

IV. The Spiritual Character of the Millennium

The amillennialist extols his view of the kingdom as a highly "spiritual" view and minimizes the premillennial concept because it demands the literal and material fulfillment of the earthly blessings. One says:

> What was the nature of the kingdom which they announced? . . . it is the claim of all Dispensationalists that the kingdom offered the Jews by John and by Jesus was an earthly kingdom similar to that of David the son of Jesse. . . .
>
> The kingdom announced by John and by Jesus was primarily and essentially a moral and spiritual kingdom. . . . He

> declared to Pilate, "My kingdom is not of this world" (Jn. xviii. 36). Had Jesus come to set up such a kingdom as Dispensationalists describe He could not have made this reply to Pilate. Or, at least, His words would have to be taken as meaning, "My kingdom is not *now* of this world," for according to the Dispensational view it was a worldly kingdom, a kingdom which would involve the forcible overthrow of Rome that Jesus had offered the Jews, and would have given them . . . had they been willing to receive it.[4]

It is thus argued that the amillennialist envisions the kingdom as a "spiritual" kingdom and the premillennialist sees it as "carnal" or "material" only. Such a presentation fails to distinguish between the spiritualized view of the millennium and the spiritual realities in the millennium, or between a spiritual kingdom and a spiritualized view of the kingdom. Although emphasizing the multitude of material blessings offered in the millennium, the theocratic kingdom is essentially a spiritual kingdom even though it exists in the realm of the earth. Peters states:

> This Kingdom, although visible with a world dominion, is also necessarily spiritual.
>
> This Proposition is the more needed since we are charged with gross carnality, etc., because we insist upon retaining the plain grammatical meaning assigned to the Kingdom in the Holy Scriptures. While a purely material, naturalistic Kingdom, without spirituality, is unscriptural, so likewise an entire spiritual Kingdom, without the sanctified union of the material or natural, is utterly opposed to the Word of God.[5]

A. *The kingdom characterized by righteousness.* Woodring writes:

> . . . only the "righteous" are admitted to the kingdom; "then shall *the righteous answer*" (Matt. 25:37). Of Israel likewise it is written, "Thy people also shall be righteous: they shall inherit the land forever" (Isa. 60:21). The gates of Zion are opened "that the righteous nation which keepeth the truth may enter in" (Isa. 26:2). . . .
>
> In the millennium, righteousness becomes an appelative synonymous with the Messiah. Unto those that fear His name "shall the Sun of righteousness rise with healing in his wings" (Mal. 4:2). At the second coming of the Messiah, He says, "I bring near my righteousness; it shall not be far off" (Isa. 46:

---

[4] Oswald T. Allis, *Prophecy and the Church*, pp. 69-71.
[5] Peters, *op. cit.*, III, 460.

13; 51:5). As a priest after the order of Melchizedek, He is the mediatorial king of righteousness (Psa. 110:4; Heb. 7:2). . . .

The key words of Christ's millennial reign are *righteousness* and *peace,* the former being the root of which the latter is the fruit. . . . Messiah's people "shall dwell in a peaceable habitation, and in sure dwellings, and in quiet resting places (Isa. 32:18). Zion's officers shall be peace, her exactors righteousness (Isa. 60:17). For "In his days shall the righteous flourish; and abundance of peace so long as the moon endureth" (Ps. 72:7). Then shall be fulfilled in truth the prophecy, "Mercy and truth are met together; righteousness and peace have kissed each other" (Ps. 85:10).

Because of the presence of Messiah, Jerusalem shall be the source from which all millennial righteousness will emanate in dazzling glory. Her righteousness shall "go forth as a brightness, and the salvation thereof as a lamp that burneth. And Gentiles shall see thy righteousness, and all kings thy glory" (Isa. 62:1c-2a). Zion shall be called "the city of righteousness" (Isa. 1:26) and shall be filled with judgment and righteousness (Isa. 33:5).

Righteousness will be the descriptive term characterizing the rule of the Messiah as a whole. Christ will be a king reigning in righteousness (Isa. 32:1). Righteousness shall be the girdle of His loins (Isa. 11:5). With righteousness shall He judge the poor (Isa. 11:4; *Cf.* Ps. 72:104). and in judging and seeking judgment He shall be swift to bring about righteousness (Isa. 16:5). It will be proclaimed among the Gentiles, "Jehovah reigneth! He shall judge the people righteously" (Psa. 96:10).

Under the beneficent sway of Christ, those who hunger and thirst after righteousness shall be filled (Matt. 5:6) and shall receive righteousness from the God of their salvation (Isa. 24:5). They shall be granted discernment between the righteous and the wicked (Mal. 3:18). Israel will offer an offering of righteousness (Mal. 3:3); then Jehovah will be pleased with "sacrifices of righteousness, with burnt offerings, and whole burnt offerings" (Psa. 51:19). The changed character of Israel will be a spontaneous response arising from Jehovah's inwrought righteousness, a far cry from the false legalism of bygone days (*Cf.* Matt. 5:20). As the earth bringeth forth her bud, "the Lord God will cause righteousness and praise to spring forth before all nations" (Isa. 61:11) so that the people shall be called trees of righteousness, the planting of the Lord, that He might be glorified (Isa. 61:3).[6]

---

[6] Woodring, *op. cit.,* pp. 113-16.

B. *The kingdom characterized by obedience.* One essential purpose of the original creation was to establish a kingdom in which there was a complete and willing obedience on the part of the subject to God. The tree was placed in the garden as a test of this obedience (Gen. 2:16-17). Disobedience soon followed. God did not surrender His purpose of bringing all things into subjection to Himself. Paul states this continuing purpose:

> Having made known unto us the mystery of his will, according to his good pleasure which he hath purposed in himself: That in the dispensation of the fulness of times he might gather together in one all things in Christ, both which are in heaven, and which are on earth, even in him [Eph.1:9-10].

God will bring all things into subjection to the One who said, "I come to do thy will, O God," (Heb. 10:9a).

> The doing of the will of God in the millennium will be greatly facilitated for a number of reasons: (1) Through fulfillment of the new covenant, Israel will experience a renewed heart and mind that they may have God's law in their inward parts (Jer. 31:33). (2) The Holy Spirit will be poured out upon all flesh to indwell, fill, and teach (Jer. 31:33, 34; *cf.* Joel 2:28-32; Ezek. 36:25-31). (3) Satan will be bound, evil doers will be cut off (Psa. 37:9-10; Jer. 31:29-30), and the wicked social, religious, economic, and political systems of the Satanic cosmos will be liquidated. (4) Instead of disunity in Israel, unanimity will be such that they will see eye to eye again in Zion (Isa. 52:8). (5) Universal knowledge of the Lord will eliminate the inadvertent opposition to God's will through ignorance. (6) There will be a wide-spread Gentile submission to the authority of Christ (Psa. 22:27-28; Mal. 1:11).[7]

This perfect obedience will be another manifestation of the spiritual character of the millennium.

C. *The kingdom characterized by holiness.* Adam, by creation, was given an untried innocence. This would have become holiness, without doubt, by obedience to the Lord. This innocence was lost by his act of disobedience. It is God's purpose to manifest holiness in His creatures in the kingdom.

> The various aspects of millennial holiness are so extensive it is not possible to give more than a brief catalogue at this

[7] *Ibid.*, p. 129.

> point. Above all, holiness will be the great distinguishing characteristic of the Jewish people in all categories of their national life, a "holiness" not their own but imparted to them by Messiah who is in their midst, and possessed by them through a life of faith. The following is offered in the way of brief recapitulation: The Lord will make bare His holy arm (revelation of Messiah) and gain the victory over His enemies (Psa. 98:1; Isa. 52:10). The holy seed shall be the nucleus of the restored Jewish nation (Isa. 6:13). All those remaining in Zion shall be called holy, having had their filth washed away (Isa. 4:3-4). A way of holiness will be raised up to allow the rest of the ransomed of the Lord to return to Zion (Isa. 35:8-10). God will speak in holiness, allotting the land to His people (Psa. 60:6). The Lord will inherit Judah his portion in the land now rightly called holy (Zech. 2:12), and Jerusalem shall be holy (Joel 3:17). A holy oblation dedicated to the Lord will be especially reserved for the sanctuary and its ministers (Ezek. 45:1-5). The Lord will exalt His holy mountain (Psa. 48:1; Jer. 31:23; Isa. 27:13) and establish His holy house, the law of which shall be holiness (Ezek. 43:12). It shall be His dwelling and the place of the soles of His feet so that Israel shall no more defile His holy name forever (Ezek. 43:7), and all nations shall know that the Lord, the Holy One is in Israel (Ezek. 39:7). Christ will reign over the nations of the earth from the throne of His holiness (Psa. 47:8-9), according to the holy oath that sealed the Davidic covenant (Psa. 89:35-36). The priests will teach the people the difference between the holy and profane (Ezek. 44:23), and they shall appear before the Messiah in holy array (Psa. 110:3). In that day upon the bells of the horses will be inscribed "HOLINESS UNTO THE LORD," and all the pots in Jerusalem and Judah shall be just as holy as the sacred vessels in the Lord's house (Zech. 14:20-21).[8]

D. *The kingdom characterized by truth.* It is a cause of judgment that men "changed the truth of God into a lie" (Rom. 1: 25). Through the Messiah, who could say, "I am the way, the truth, and the life" (John 14:6), there will be the full manifestation of truth in the millennium, which establishes further the essential spiritual character of that kingdom.

> The following is offered as a brief summation of millennial truth: The impious little horn, who has cast truth to the earth (Dan. 8:12), will be vanquished by Christ in His triumphant ride on behalf of truth, meekness and righteousness (Ps.

[8] *Ibid.*, pp. 132-34.

45:4). Peters says, "Truth, indeed, will ultimately triumph, but not through man. Jesus, the truth, will come Himself and vindicate it" [Peters *op. cit.* III, 258]. Instead of their misguided confidence in the man of sin, the escaped remnant "shall stay upon the Lord, the Holy One of Israel, in truth" (Isa. 10:20), and He will be their God in truth and righteousness (Zech. 8:8; cf. Isa. 65:16). Jehovah will betroth Israel to Him in faithfulness, and they shall acknowledge Him (Hos. 2:20). Christ, Jehovah's servant, will bring forth judgment unto truth (Isa. 42:3) and reveal unto Israel abundance of peace and truth (Jer. 33:6). Truth shall be met together with mercy and spring out of the earth (Psa. 85:10-11). Then shall Israel say, "He hath remembered his mercy and truth toward the house of Israel; all ends of the earth have seen the salvation of our God" (Psa. 98:3). The throne shall be established and Christ shall sit upon it in truth in the tabernacle of David (Isa. 16:5). Faithfulness will be the girdle of His reins (Isa. 11:5), and He will judge the peoples of the world with His truth (Psa. 96:10). The faithfulness of Jehovah will insure that in the presence of the once despised one, Kings shall see and arise and princes shall worship (Isa. 49:7). Jerusalem shall be called the faithful city (Isa. 1:26), for "Thus saith the Lord; I am returned to Zion, and will dwell in the midst of Jerusalem: and Jerusalem shall be called a city of truth" (Zech. 8:3).[9]

E. *The kingdom characterized by the fulness of the Holy Spirit.* At the institution of the theocratic kingdom the prophecy of Joel will be fulfilled:

> And it shall come to pass afterward, that I will pour out my spirit upon all flesh; and your sons and your daughters shall prophesy, and your old men shall dream dreams, your young men shall see visions: And also upon the servants and upon the handmaids in those days will I pour out my spirit [Joel 2:28-29].

Concerning this experience Walvoord writes:

> The prophecies picturing the millennium . . . unite in their testimony that the work of the Holy Spirit in believers will be more abundant and have greater manifestation in the millennium than in any previous dispensation. It is evident from the Scriptures that all believers will be indwelt by the Holy Spirit in the millennium even as they are in the present age (Ezek. 36:27; 37:14; cf. Jer. 31:33).
>
> The fact of the indwelling presence of the Holy Spirit is

---

[9] *Ibid.*, pp. 138-40.

> revealed as part of the glorious restoration of Israel depicted in Ezekiel 36:24 ff. . . . In Ezekiel 37:14, it is stated, "And I will put my Spirit in you, and ye shall live, and I will place you in your own land. . . ."
>
> The filling of the Holy Spirit will be common in the millennium, in contrast to the infrequency of it in other ages, and it will be manifested in worship and praise of the Lord and in willing obedience to Him as well as in spiritual power and inner transformation (Isa. 32:15; 44:3; Ezek. 39:29; Joel 2:28-29). In contrast to present-day spiritual apathy, coldness, and worldliness, there will be spiritual fervor, love of God, holy joy, universal understanding of spiritual truth, and a wonderful fellowship of the saints. . . . The emphasis will be on righteousness in life and on joy of spirit.[10]

Peters correctly observes the relation of the fullness of the Spirit to the spiritual character of the age. He writes:

> The *remarkable, astounding outpouring of the Holy Spirit* as presented in the Millennial descriptions . . . so powerful in its transforming, glorifying, and imparting miraculous gifts to the saints; so pervading in and over the Jewish nation that all shall be righteous from the least to the greatest; so widereaching over the Gentiles that they shall rejoice in the light bestowed; and so extended in its operation that the whole earth shall ultimately be covered with glory—this, with the magnificent portrayals of the Millennial and succeeding ages, is so sublime with the indwelling, abiding, communicated Divine, that no one can contemplate it, without being profoundly moved at the display of spirituality.[11]

It must, thus, be observed that the outstanding characterization of the millennium is its spiritual nature. An earthly kingdom, to be sure, but spiritual as to its character.

V. Conditions Existing Within the Millennium

Much Scripture is devoted to stating the untold blessing and glory poured out upon earth through the beneficence of the Lord Jesus Christ in the kingdom. Many of these have been alluded to previously, but an outline of the conditions on the earth will show the "greatness of the kingdom" (Dan. 7:27).

A. *Peace.* The cessation of war through the unification of

---

[10] John F. Walvoord, *The Holy Spirit*, pp. 233-34.
[11] Peters, *op. cit.*, III, 465.

the kingdoms of the world under the reign of Christ, together with the resultant economic prosperity, since nations need not devote vast proportions of their expenditure on munitions, is a major theme of the prophets. National and individual peace is the fruit of Messiah's reign (Isa. 2:4; 9:4-7; 11:6-9; 32:17-18; 33:5-6; 54:13; 55:12; 60:18; 65:25; 66:12; Ezek. 28:26; 34:25, 28; Hos. 2:18; Mic. 4:2-3; Zech. 9:10).

B. *Joy.* The fulness of joy will be a distinctive mark of the age (Isa. 9:3-4; 12:3-6; 14:7-8; 25:8-9; 30:29; 42:1, 10-12; 52:9; 60:15; 61:7, 10; 65:18-19; 66:10-14; Jer. 30:18-19; 31:13-14; Zeph. 3:14-17; Zech. 8:18-19; 10:6-7).

C. *Holiness.* The theocratic kingdom will be a holy kingdom, in which holiness is manifested through the King and the King's subjects. The land will be holy, the city holy, the temple holy, and the subjects holy unto the Lord (Isa. 1:26-27; 4:3-4; 29:18-23; 31:6-7; 35:8-9; 52:1; 60:21; 61:10; Jer. 31:23; Ezek. 36:24-31; 37:23-24; 43:7-12; 45:1; Joel 3:21; Zeph. 3:11, 13; Zech. 8:3; 13:1-2; 14:20-21).

D. *Glory.* The kingdom will be a glorious kingdom, in which the glory of God will find full manifestation (Isa. 24:23; 4:2; 35:2; 40:5; 60:1-9).

E. *Comfort.* The King will personally minister to every need, so that there will be the fulness of comfort in that day (Isa. 12:1-2; 29:22-23; 30:26; 40:1-2; 49:13; 51:3; 61:3-7; 66:13-14; Jer. 31:23-25; Zeph. 3:18-20; Zech. 9:11-12; Rev. 21:4).

F. *Justice.* There will be the administration of perfect justice to every individual (Isa. 9:7; 11:5; 32:16; 42:1-4; 65:21-23; Jer. 23:5; 31:23; 31:29-30).

G. *Full knowledge.* The ministry of the King will bring the subjects of His kingdom into full knowledge. Doubtless there will be an unparalleled teaching ministry of the Holy Spirit. (Isa. 11:1-2, 9; 41:19-20; 54:13; Hab. 2:14).

H. *Instruction.* This knowledge will come about through the instruction that issues from the King (Isa. 2:2-3; 12:3-6; 25:9; 29:17-24; 30:20-21; 32:3-4; 49:10; 52:8; Jer. 3:14-15; 23:1-4; Mic. 4:2).

I. *The removal of the curse.* The original curse placed upon creation (Gen. 3:17-19) will be removed, so that there will be abundant productivity to the earth. Animal creation will be changed so as to lose its venom and ferocity. (Isa. 11:6-9; 35:9; 65:25).

J. *Sickness removed.* The ministry of the King as a healer will be seen throughout the age, so that sickness and even death, except as a penal measure in dealing with overt sin, will be removed (Isa. 33:24; Jer. 30:17; Ezek. 34:16).

K. *Healing of the deformed.* Accompanying this ministry will be the healing of all deformity at the inception of the millennium (Isa. 29:17-19; 35:3-6; 61:1-2; Jer. 31:8; Mic. 4:6-7; Zeph. 3:19).

L. *Protection.* There will be a supernatural work of preservation of life in the millennial age through the King (Isa. 41: 8-14; 62:8-9; Jer. 32:27; 23:6; Ezek. 34:27; Joel 3:16-17; Amos 9:15; Zech. 8:14-15; 9:8; 14:10-11).

M. *Freedom from oppression.* There will be no social, political or religious oppression in that day (Isa. 14:3-6; 42:6-7; 49:8-9; Zech. 9:11-12).

N. *No immaturity.* The suggestion seems to be that there will not be the tragedies of feeble-mindedness nor of dwarfed bodies in that day (Isa. 65:20). Longevity will be restored.

O. *Reproduction by the living peoples.* The living saints who go into the millennium in their natural bodies will beget children throughout the age. The earth's population will soar. These born in the age will not be born without a sin nature, so salvation will be required (Jer. 30:20; 31:29; Ezek. 47:22; Zech. 10:8).

P. *Labor.* The period will not be characterized by idleness, but there will be a perfect economic system, in which the needs of men are abundantly provided for by labor in that system, under the guidance of the King. There will be a fully developed industrialized society, providing for the needs of the King's subjects (Isa 62:8-9; 65:21-23; Jer. 31:5; Ezek. 48:18-19). Agriculture as well as manufacturing will provide employment.

Q. *Economic prosperity.* The perfect labor situation will produce economic abundance, so that there will be no want (Isa. 4:1; 35:1-2, 7; 30:23-25; 62:8-9; 65:21-23; Jer. 31:5, 12; Ezek. 34:26; Mic. 4:1, 4; Zech. 8:11-12; 9:16-17; Ezek. 36:29-30; Joel 2:21-27; Amos 9:13-14).

R. *Increase of light.* There will be an increase of solar and lunar light in the age. This increased light probably is a major cause in the increased productivity of the earth (Isa. 4:5; 30:26; 60:19-20; Zech. 2:5).

S. *Unified language.* The language barriers will be removed so that there can be free social intercourse (Zeph. 3:9).

T. *Unified Worship.* All the world will unite in the worship of God and God's Messiah (Isa. 45:23; 52:1, 7-10; 66:17-23; Zech. 13:2; 14:16; 8:23; 9:7; Zeph. 3:9; Mal. 1:11; Rev. 5:9-14).

U. *The manifest presence of God.* God's presence will be fully recognized and fellowship with God will be experienced to an unprecedented degree (Ezek. 37:27-28; Zech. 2:2, 10-13; Rev. 21:3).

V. *The fulness of the Spirit.* Divine presence and enablement will be the experience of all who are in subjection to the authority of the King (Isa. 32:13-15; 41:1; 44:3; 59:19, 21; 61:1; Ezek. 36:26-27; 37:14; 39:29; Joel 2:28-29; Ezek. 11:19-20).

W. *The perpetuity of the millennial state.* That which characterizes the millennial age is not viewed as temporary, but eternal (Joel 3:20; Amos 9:15; Ezek. 37:26-28; Isa. 51:6-8; 55:3, 13; 56:5; 60:19-20; 61:8; Jer. 32:40; Ezek. 16:60; 43:7-9; Dan. 9:24; Hos. 2:19-23).

The wide diversity of the realms in which the blessings of the King's presence is felt is thus clearly seen.

VI. The Duration of the Millennium

It is taught in Scripture that the kingdom over which Christ is to rule between the first and the second resurrection is of one thousand years duration.

> And I saw an angel come down from heaven, having the key of the bottomless pit and a great chain in his hand. And he laid hold on the dragon, that old serpent, which is the Devil,

> and Satan, and bound him a thousand years, And cast him into the bottomless pit, and shut him up, and set a seal upon him, that he should deceive the nations no more, till the thousand years should be fulfilled: and after that he must be loosed a little season. And I saw thrones, and they sat upon them, and judgment was given unto them: and I saw the souls of them that were beheaded for the witness of Jesus, and for the word of God, and which had not worshipped the beast, neither his image, neither had received his mark upon their foreheads, or in their hands; and they lived and reigned with Christ a thousand years. But the rest of the dead lived not again until the thousand years were finished. This is the first resurrection. Blessed and holy is he that hath part in the first resurrection: on such the second death hath no power, but they shall be priests of God and of Christ, and shall reign with him a thousand years [Rev. 20:1-6].

It is generally held, even by those denying the literalness of the thousand year period, that the angel, heaven, the pit, Satan, the nations, the resurrections mentioned in this chapter are literal. It would be folly to accept the literalness of those and deny the literalness of the time element. Alford says:

> Those who lived next to the Apostles, and the whole Church for 300 years, understood them in the plain literal sense; and it is a strange sight in these days to see expositors who are among the first in reverence of antiquity, complacently casting aside the most cogent instance of consensus which primitive antiquity presents. As regards the text itself, no legitimate treatment of it will extort what is known as the spiritual interpretation now in fashion.[12]

Six times in this passage it is stated that Christ's millennial kingdom will continue for a thousand years.

A question has been raised concerning the premillennial position in that the Scriptures teach that Christ will reign over an endless kingdom. This is affirmed in 2 Samuel 7:16, 28-29; Psalms 89:3-4, 34-37; 45:6; 72:5, 17; Isaiah 9:6-7; 51:6, 8; 55:3, 13; 56:5; 60:19-20; 61:8; Jeremiah 32:40; 33:14-17, 20-21; 37:24-28; Ezekiel 16:60; 43:7-9; Daniel 7:13-14, 27; 9:24; Hosea 2:19; Joel 3:20; Amos 9:15; Luke 1:30-33; 1 Timothy 1:17; Revelation 11:15. The amillennialist sees a conflict here and insists that the eternality of Christ's kingdom does not permit any place for a thousand year reign on earth. Calvin's reason for rejecting the

---

[12] Henry Alford, *The Greek Testament*, IV, 732.

premillennial view was his concept that the thousand year reign nullified the eternal reign of Christ.[13] Did the premillennialist limit the reign of Christ to a thousand years, his contention that "their fiction is too puerile to require or deserve refutation"[14] would be true. However such is not the case.

An important Scripture bearing on the discussion is 1 Corinthians 15:24-28.

> Then cometh the end, when he shall have delivered up the kingdom to God, even the Father; when he shall have put down all rule and authority and power. For he must reign, till he hath put all enemies under his feet. The last enemy that shall be destroyed is death. For he hath put all things under his feet. But when he saith all things are put under him, it is manifest that he is excepted, which did put all things under him. And when all things shall be subdued unto him, then shall the Son also himself be subject unto him that put all things under him, that God may be all in all.

In these words the Apostle is stating the ultimate purpose of the theocratic kingdom: "that God may be all in all." This envisions the absolute accomplishment of the original purpose in the establishment of the theocratic kingdom, "prepared . . . before the foundation of the world" (Matt. 25:34). A paraphrase of the verses above will make Paul's progressive thought clearer: "The Father has put all things under Christ's feet. (But when the Father saith all things are put under Christ's feet, it is evident that the Father Himself is excepted from this subjection, inasmuch as the Father did the subjecting.) And when all things are ultimately subjected unto Christ, then shall the Son also himself be subject unto the Father, who put all things under Christ, that God may be all in all." The means by which all things are brought under subjection to God, so that He becomes all in all, is that Christ unites the authority that is His as King with the Father's after He has "put down all rule and all authority and power" (1 Cor. 15:24). God's original purpose was to manifest His absolute authority and this purpose is realized when Christ unites the earthly theocracy with the eternal kingdom of God. Thus, while Christ's earthly theocratic rule is limited to one thousand years, which is sufficient time to manifest

---

[13] John Calvin, *Institutes of the Christian Religion*, II, 250-51.
[14] *Ibid.*

God's perfect theocracy on the earth, His reign is eternal. This line of thought is stated by Peters, who says:

> There is only one passage in Scripture which is supposed to teach the yielding up or ending of the distinctive Messianic Kingdom, viz., 1 Cor. 15:27, 28. Whatever view is engrafted upon or derived from these verses, nearly all . . . admit, whatever delivering up is intended, that Jesus Christ still reigns, either as God, the humanity being subordinate, or as God-man. . . . In the language of Van Falkenburg . . . "As the Father was excepted when all things were put under the son, so also shall He be excepted when all things are subdued unto Him. It appears, then, that this passage does not even intimate that there will ever be a termination of Christ's kingdom, or that He will ever deliver up His Kingdom to the Father. The dominion shall indeed be rescued from His enemies, and restored to the Godhead, but not in any such sense, but that His dominion is an everlasting dominion, and that of His Kingdom there shall be no end." Storr . . . takes the ground that "the government which, it is said, verse 24, He shall restore to God, even the Father, must not be supposed to mean Christ's government, but that of every opposing power, which is evidently declared to be destroyed, that the power may be restored to God"— adding truly and most forcibly . . . "the government is restored to God when it is restored to Christ." Thus the passage is made by them to be in accord with Rev. 11:15, "The Kingdoms (or Sovereignty) of our Lord and His Christ," and when this is done, Father and Son united in this Theocratic ordering and Personage, "He shall reign forever and ever." . . . The honor of both the Father and Son are identified with the perpetuity of this Theocratic Kingdom, for it is just as much the Father's Kingdom as it is the Son's—the most perfect union existing between them constituting a Oneness in rule and dominion.[15]

Concerning the question of the surrender of authority by the Son to the Father, Chafer writes:

> The delivery to God of a now unmarred kingdom does not imply the release of authority on the part of the Son. The truth asserted [in 1 Cor. 15:27, 28] is that at last the kingdom is fully restored—the kingdom of God to God. The distinction to be noted lies between the presentation to the Father of a restored authority and the supposed abrogation of a throne on the part of the Son. The latter is neither required in the text nor even intimated. The picture presented in Revelation 22:3 is of the New Jerusalem in the eternal state, and it is declared

---

[15] Peters, *op. cit.*, II, 634-36.

> that "the throne of God and of the Lamb shall be in it." The translation in the Authorized version of 1 Corinthians 15:28 is not clear. It reads: "And when all things shall be subdued unto him, then shall the Son also himself be subject unto him that put all things under him, that God may be all in all." The statement is meant to signify that, when all is subdued and divine authority is restored in full, the Son, who has ruled by the authority of the Father throughout the thousand years and has put down all enemies, will go on ruling under that same authority of the Father's as subject as ever to the First Person. This more clarified meaning of the text removes the suggestion of conflict between an everlasting reign and a supposed limited reign of Christ, He will, as so fully assured elsewhere, reign on the throne of David forever.[16]

McClain outlines the consummation of the program as follows:

> 1. When the last enemy of God is put down by our Lord, as the Mediatorial King, the purpose of the Mediatorial Kingdom will have been fulfilled (1 Cor. 15:25-26).
>
> 2. At this time Christ will hand over the Mediatorial Kingdom to God, to be merged into the eternal Kingdom, so that the Mediatorial Kingdom is perpetuated forever, but no longer having a separate identity (1 Cor. 15:24, 28).
>
> 3. This does not mean the end of our Lord's rule. He only ceases to rule as a Mediatorial King. But as the eternal Son, second person the one true God, He shares the throne with the Father in the final Kingdom (Rev. 22:3-5; cf. 3:21).[17]

By the establishment of the theocracy on earth for a thousand years, under the Messianic theocratic King, God has accomplished His purpose of demonstrating His rule in the sphere in which that authority was first challenged. By merging this earthly theocracy with the eternal kingdom God's eternal sovereignty is established. Such was the purpose of God in planning the theocratic kingdom and developing it through successive stages throughout history until it reaches the climax of the program in the theocracy under the enthroned Christ in the millennium. That authority, which Satan first challenged, Christ has now demonstrated belongs solely to God. God's right to rule is eternally vindicated.

---

16 Lewis Sperry Chafer, *Systematic Theology,* V, 373-74.

17 Alva J. McClain "The Greatness of the Kingdom," unpublished classroom notes, p. 31.

Chapter XXIX

THE GOVERNMENT AND THE GOVERNED IN THE MILLENNIUM

I. The Government in the Millennium

Scripture has a great deal to say concerning the government of the theocracy, inasmuch as the government administered by the King is the very manifestation of the authority that God seeks to re-establish.

A. *The government will be a theocracy.* It is hardly necessary to reaffirm the fact that the government will be a theocracy after all that has been presented previously. Peters, writing on this form of government, says:

> . . . some writers . . . endeavor to make the Theocracy a Republic, but the Theocracy, in the nature of the case, is not a republic. While it is not a monarchy in the sense adverted to by Samuel, viz.: of a purely human origin, yet it is a monarchy in the highest sense. It is not a Republic, for the legislative, executive, and judicial power is not potentially lodged in the people, but in God the King; and yet it embraces in itself the elements both of a Monarchy and of a Republic;—a Monarchy in that the absolute Sovereignty is lodged in the person of the One great King, to which all the rest are subordinated, but Republican in this, that it embraces a Republican element in preserving the rights of every individual, from the lowest to the highest. . . . In other words, by a happy combination, Monarchy under divine direction, hence infallible, brings in the blessings that would result from a well-directed ideally Republican form of government, but which the latter can never fully, of itself, realize, owing to the depravity and diversity of man.[1]

This theocracy is to be viewed, not as a convenience, but as an absolute necessity. This is shown conclusively:

> The relation that man and this earth sustains to the most High God requires that the honor and majesty of God should

[1] G. N. H. Peters, *Theocratic Kingdom*, I, 221.

> demand the establishment of a Theocracy here on the earth, by which the race is brought under a government honorable alike to God and man. . . . (1) At the creation God had determined upon this form of government; . . . (2) man by disobedience forfeited a dominion which God through him was to exercise over the earth . . . ; (3) God has resolved to restore that dominion in the Person of Jesus, the Second Adam . . . ; (4) God—to indicate in what form of government this dominion should be incorporated when restored, to test man's present capacity for it, and to make certain indispensable provisions for the future—erected a Theocracy . . . ; (5) man, owing to sinfulness, was unfitted for a Theocratic ordering, and, therefore, it was withdrawn . . . ; (6) God promised at some future time to restore it . . . ; (7) this Theocracy is God's own preference for a form of government, and if not restored makes His proposed government a failure . . . ; (8) God has sent His Son to make provision for Salvation . . . ; (9) this Salvation in its ultimate realization is invariably linked with this still future Coming Kingdom . . . ; (10) God, to insure the future permanent establishment of the Theocracy, is preparing a body of rulers for the same to be associated with "the Christ" . . . ; (11) that until this Theocracy is set up the race is not brought into subjection to God . . . ; (12) however glorious in design this dispensation may be, there is still an incompleteness in Redemption and which will continue until "the Messiah" comes to restore the Theocracy . . . ; (13) when this Theocracy is re-established, then under the rulership of Christ and His saints the race itself is brought into subjection to God—a revolted province is brought back to its pristine allegiance and blessedness . . . ; (14) the Theocracy is the form of government most admirably adapted to secure this result . . . ; (15) a theocracy being in its nature a visible government, such a sovereignty and redemption completed must be visibly shown in the sight of the world, so that—as rightly belongs to God and is done in heaven itself—it be publicly recognized . . . ; (16) the personal relationship of God to Adam in Paradise, to the Theocracy once established in the past, to man in and through Jesus at the First Advent, insures a future special and continued personal relationship in a restored throne and kingdom . . . as exhibiting His Supremacy in the most tangible and satisfactory manner, and that the recovery of a rebellious people and race, as well as the manifestation of God's will being done on earth as in heaven, includes such a personal relationship in the Person of Him who is "the Son of Man. . . .[2]

B. *Messiah is the King in the millennium.* Scripture makes it clear that the government of the millennium is under the

---

[2] *Ibid.*, III, 583-84.

Messiah, the Lord Jesus Christ (Isa. 2:2-4; 9:3-7; 11:1-10; 16:5; 24:21-23; 31:4-32:2; 42:1-7, 13; 49:1-7; 51:4-5; 60:12; Dan. 2:44; 7:15-28; Obad. 17-21; Mic. 4:1-8; 5:2-5, 15; Zeph. 3:9-10, 18-19; Zech. 9:10-15; 14:16-17). His regal authority is universal. This position is by Divine appointment. The Psalmist gives the word of Jehovah, "Yet have I set my king upon my holy hill of Zion" (Ps. 2:6).

> This bestowal of the Kingdom to the Son of Man by the Father, is clearly and explicitly taught in the covenant. Hence in agreement with it, we have the language of Dan. 7:13, 14; Isa. 49: Luke 22: 29 and 1:32, etc. The Divine Sovereignty insures it unto Him.
>
> Daniel (7:14) says that "there was given unto Him (the Son of Man) dominion, and glory, and a Kingdom, that all people," etc. Luke (1:32) "the Lord God shall give unto Him the throne of His father David," etc. . . . The Saviour Himself seems to refer to this fact in the Parable of the Ten pounds (Luke 19:15), "that when he was returned, having received the kingdom," etc. . . .
>
> This giving of the Kingdom by the Father to the Son of Man, shows . . . that this Kingdom is something very different from the general Divine Sovereignty exercised by God. The Kingdom is an outgrowth from it, and the Divine Sovereignty will be exhibited through it, being constituted in the Theocratic form, which in its initiatory form was separated in its Rulership by two persons (i.e. God and David) but is now happily conjoined—making it thus efficacious, irresistible, and ever-enduring—in one, i.e., "the Christ."[3]

The New Testament record firmly establishes Christ's right to assume the Davidic throne. Girdlestone writes:

> 1. The genealogies contained in Matt. 1 and Luke 3 sufficiently establish, and on independent grounds, that Joseph was the lineal descendant of David; and they make it probable, if not certain, that if the throne of David were to be re-established Joseph would be the person on whose head the crown would be placed. Accordingly he is called the Son of David both in Matt. 1.20 and in Luke 1.27.
>
> 2. It is equally clear from Matt. 1 and Luke 1 that Joseph was not literally the father of Jesus, though Mary was literally His mother. Joseph, however, acted the part of father to him.

[3] *Ibid.*, I, 577.

The child was born under Joseph's protection, and grew up under his guardianship . . . Joseph adopted Jesus as his son. He is called in Luke 3.23 the reputed father. . . .

3. To what tribe Mary belonged is not absolutely certain; but her kinship with Elizabeth does not preclude her from being a Judean, intermarriage between the tribes of Judah and Levi being traceable back to the time of Aaron. The words in Luke 1.32, "the Lord shall give unto Him the throne of His father David," seem hardly consistent with any other view than that Mary was of the lineage of David, and no difficulty on this score seems to have occurred to her mind. . . .

4. The Evangelists, however, never discuss the genealogy of Mary. They consider it enough to establish the claim of Joseph. (Cf. Acts 2:30; 13:22, 23, 33; Heb. 7:14; Rom. 1:3; Rev. 5:5; 22:16).

5. We are thus led to the conclusion that our Lord's position as Son of David was established, humanly speaking, by the action of Joseph in adopting Him, rather than by the fact that Mary was in all probability of David's descent.

Succession in the kingly line was not altogether by birth, but by appointment.[4]

C. *David is regent in the millennium.* There are a number of references which establish the regency of David in the millennium (Isa. 55:3-4; Jer. 30:9; 33:15, 17, 20-21; Ezek. 34:23-24; 37:24-25; Hos. 3:5; Amos 9:11). There is no question but that the Lord Jesus Christ will reign in the theocratic kingdom on earth by virtue of the fact that He was born in David's line and possesses the royal and legal rights to the throne (Matt. 1:1; Luke 1:32-33). The question involved in the passages cited is whether the Lord Jesus Christ will exercise the government over Palestine directly or indirectly through a regent. There are several answers given to this question, which is important in developing the government of the millennium.

1. The first answer is that the term *David* is used *typically,* and refers to Christ. Ironside presents this view when he says:

I do not understand this to mean that David himself will be raised and caused to dwell on the earth as king . . . the implication is that He who was David's Son, the Lord Jesus Christ Him-

[4] R. B. Girdlestone, *The Grammar of Prophecy,* pp. 73-75.

> self is to be the King, and thus David's throne will be re-established.[5]

This view is based on the fact that (1) many prophetic Scriptures predict that Christ will sit on David's throne and any reference to rulership is assumed to apply to Christ, and (2) Christ's name is closely associated with David's in the Word, so that He is called the Son of David and is said to sit on David's throne.

The objections to this view arise (1) from the fact that Christ is never called David in the Scriptures. He is called the Branch unto David (Jer. 23:5), Son of David (15 times), Seed of David (John 7:42; Rom. 1:3; 2 Tim. 2:8), Root of David (Rev. 5:5), and Root and Offspring of David (Rev. 22:16), but never David. (2) The appellation "my servant, David" is used repeatedly for the historical David. (3) In Hosea 3:5; Ezekiel 37:21-25; 34:24; Jeremiah 30:9 and Isaiah 55:4 Jehovah is clearly distinguished from David. If in these passages David typically referred to Christ, no distinction could be made, nor would one need be so carefully drawn. (4) There are statements concerning this prince which preclude the application of the title to Christ. In Ezekiel 45:22 the prince is said to offer a sin offering for himself. Even if these are memorial sacrifices, as shall be shown, Christ could not offer a memorial sacrifice for His own sin, since He was sinless. In Ezekiel 46:2 the prince is engaged in acts of worship. Christ receives worship in the millennium, but does not engage in acts of worship. In Ezekiel 46:16 the prince has sons and divides an inheritance with them. Such could not be done by Christ. For these reasons it seems that the prince referred to as David could not be Christ.

2. The second answer is that David refers to *a literal son of David* who will sit on the Davidic throne. This view recognizes that Christ can not do all that is stated concerning this prince and holds that it will be fulfilled by a lineal descendant of David.

> It would seem, too, from a careful comparison of this passage with the latter part of Ezekiel's prophecy, that a lineal descendent of David's line (called "the prince") shall exercise regency on earth over the restored nation, under the authority of

---

[5] Harry A. Ironside, *Ezekiel the Prophet*, p. 262.

> Him whose capitol city will be the new and heavenly Jerusalem.[6]

The references in Jeremiah 33:15, 17, 20-21 would seem to indicate that a son is anticipated who will fulfill this office.

There are several objections to this view. (1) No Jew is able to trace his family lineage after the destruction of Jerusalem. Ottman writes:

> Whatever may be the traditional belief of a Jew as to his family and his tribe, no man can bring legal documentary proof that he is of the tribe of Judah and lineage of David and rightful heir to David's throne. Therefore, the *only living man* who today can bring forward an unbroken genealogy, directly and incontrovertibly from David, is Jesus of Nazareth, born King of the Jews, crucified King of the Jews, and to come again King of the Jews.[7]

(2) If another must come after Christ, it is to say that Christ was not, Himself, the complete fulfillment of the Davidic promises. (3) Literal interpretation would demand that David mean what the word implies under normal usage.

3. A third interpretation is the literal interpretation, which holds that David means *the historical David,* who comes into regency by resurrection at the second advent of Christ. Newell represents this view when he says:

> We must not confuse in our minds this situation. We must believe the plain words of God. David is not the Son of David. Christ, as Son of David, will be King; and David, His father after the flesh, will be *prince,* during the Millennium.[8]

There are several considerations which support this interpretation. (1) It is most consistent with the literal principle of interpretation. (2) David alone could sit as regent in the millennium without violating the prophecies concerning David's reign. (3). Resurrected saints are to have positions of responsibility in the millennium as a reward (Matt. 19:28; Luke 19:12-27). David might well be appointed to this responsibility since he was "a man after God's own heart." It would be concluded

---

[6] Harry A. Ironside, *Notes on the Minor Prophets,* p. 33.
[7] Ford C. Ottman, *God's Oath,* p. 74.
[8] William R. Newell, *The Revelation,* p. 323.

that in the government of the millennium David will be appointed a regent over Palestine and will rule over that land as prince, ministering under the authority of Jesus Christ, the King. The prince thus might lead in worship, offer memorial sacrifices, divide the land allotted to him among his faithful seed without violating his position by resurrection.

D. *Nobles and governors will reign under David.* In the millennial age Jesus Christ will be "King of kings, and Lord of lords" (Rev. 19:16). As such He is sovereign over a number of subordinate rulers. Under David the land of Palestine will be ruled through these individuals.

> And their nobles shall be of themselves, and their governor shall proceed from the midst of them . . . [Jer. 30:21].
>
> Behold, a king shall reign in righteousness, and princes shall rule in judgment [Isa. 32:1].
>
> . . . my princes shall no more oppress my people; and the rest of the land shall they give to the house of Israel according to their tribes. Thus saith the Lord God; Let it suffice you, O princes of Israel: remove violence and spoil, and execute judgment and justice, take away your exactions from my people, saith the Lord God [Ezek. 45:8-9].

In the New Testament it is revealed that authority over the twelve tribes of Israel will be vested in the hands of the twelve disciples.

> . . . ye which have followed me, in the regeneration when the Son of man shall sit in the throne of his glory, ye also shall sit upon twelve thrones, judging the twelve tribes of Israel [Matt. 19:28].

This would indicate that under David there will be many subordinate rulers, who exercise theocratic power and administer the government of the millennium.

E. *Many lesser authorities will rule.* There will be yet a smaller subdivision of authority in the administration of the government. The parable in Luke 19:12-28 indicates that authority will be appointed to individuals over ten cities and five cities in the kingdom. They evidently are responsible to the head of the tribe, who, in turn will be responsible to David, who is responsible to the King Himself. Such positions of authority are appointed as a reward for faithfulness. The Old Testament anticipated this very thing:

> Behold, the Lord God will come with strong hand, and his arm shall rule for him: behold, his reward is with him, and his work before him [Isa. 40:10].
>
> Thus saith the Lord of hosts; If thou wilt walk in my ways, and if thou wilt keep my charge, then thou shalt also judge my house, and shalt also keep my courts, and I will give thee places to walk among those that stand by [Zech. 3:7].

Those that are brought into the millennium are said to "reign with him a thousand years." It is anticipated that positions of authority will be given as a reward.

F. *Judges will be raised up.* As the judges of the Old Testament were of divine appointment and were representatives through whom the theocratic kingdom was administered, so those who rule in the millennium will have the same characterization as judges, so that it may be evident that their authority is a demonstration of theocratic power.

> . . . thou shalt also judge my house . . . [Zech. 3:7].
>
> And I will restore thy judges as at the first, and thy counsellors as at the beginning . . . [Isa. 1:26].

G. *The nature of the reign.* A number of characteristics of this reign are mentioned in Scripture. (1) It will be a *universal* reign. The subdivided authority from Christ through David to the twelve and on down to the rulers over the cities, as outlined above, relates to Palestine. Since Christ will be "King of kings, and Lord of lords" this same subdivided authority will obtain in other portions of the earth as well. There will be no part of the earth that will not own the authority of the King (Dan. 2:35; 7:14, 27; Mic. 4:1-2; Zech. 9:10).

> And there was given him dominion, and glory, and a kingdom, that all people, nations, and languages, should serve him: his dominion is an everlasting dominion, which shall not pass away, and his kingdom that which shall not be destroyed.
>
> And the kingdom and dominion, and the greatness of the kingdom under the whole heaven, shall be given to the people of the saints of the most High, whose kingdom is an everlasting kingdom and all dominions shall serve and obey him [Dan. 7:14, 27].

(2) The reign will be one of *inflexible righteousness and justice* (Isa. 11:3-5; 25:2-5; 29:17-21; 30:29-32; 42:13; 49:25-26; 66:14; Dan. 2:44; Mic. 5:5-6, 10-15; Zech. 9:3-8).

> . . . he shall not judge after the sight of his eyes, neither reprove after the hearing of his ears: But with righteousness shall he judge the poor, and reprove with equity for the meek of the earth: and he shall smite the earth with the rod of his mouth, and with the breath of his lips shall he slay the wicked. And righteousness shall be the girdle of his loins, and faithfulness the girdle of his reins [Isa. 11:3-5].

(3) The reign will be one exercised *in the fulness of the Spirit.*

> And the Spirit of the Lord shall rest upon him, the spirit of wisdom and understanding, the spirit of counsel and might, the spirit of knowledge and of the fear of the Lord; And shall make him of quick understanding in the fear of the Lord [Isa. 11:2-3].

(4) The government will be a *unified government.* No longer will Israel and Judah be divided, nor will the nations be divided the one against the other. The "world government" coveted by men as the answer to international strife will have been realized (Ezek. 37:13-28).

> Then shall the children of Judah and the children of Israel be gathered together, and appoint themselves one head [Hosea 1:11].

(5) The government will *deal summarily with any outbreak of sin* (Ps. 2:9; 72:1-4; Isa. 29:20-21; 65:20; 66:24; Zech. 14:16-21; Jer. 31:29-30). "He shall smite the earth with the rod of his mouth, and with the breath of his lips shall he slay the wicked" (Isa. 11:4). Any overt act against the authority of the King will be punished with physical death. It seems as though sufficient enablement is given to the saints through the fulness of the Spirit, the universality of the knowledge of the Lord, the removal of Satan, and the manifestation of the King's presence to restrain them from any sin. (6) It will be an *eternal* reign (Dan. 7:14, 27).

II. The Subjects in the Millennium

The earthly theocratic kingdom, instituted by the Lord Jesus Christ at His second advent, will include all the saved of Israel and the saved of the Gentiles, who are living at the time of His return. Scripture makes it very clear that all sinners will be cut off before the institution of the Kingdom (Isa. 1:19-31; 65:11-16; 66:15-18; Jer. 25:27-33; 30:23-24; Ezek. 11:21; 20:33-44; Mic. 5:9-15; Zech. 13:9; Mal. 3:2-6; 3:18; 4:3). In the record of the judgment of the nations (Matt. 25:35) it is revealed that only the saved enter the kingdom. In the parable of the wheat and tares (Matt. 13:30-31) and in the parable of the good and bad fish (Matt. 13:49-50) it is shown that only the saved go into the kingdom. Daniel makes it clear that the kingdom is given to the saints:

> But the saints of the most High shall take the kingdom, and possess the kingdom for ever, even for ever and ever.
>
> . . . and judgment was given to the saints of the most High; and the time came that the saints possessed the kingdom.
>
> And the kingdom and dominion, and the greatness of the kingdom, under the whole heaven, shall be given to the people of the saints of the most High, whose kingdom is an everlasting kingdom, and all dominions shall serve and obey him [Dan. 7:18, 22, 27].

A. *Israel in the Millennium.*

1. *Israel's restoration.* A great body of Old Testament prophecy is concerned with the restoration of the nation to the land since the covenants could not be fulfilled apart from this regathering. That this regathering is associated with the second advent is observed from the words of the Lord:

> And then shall appear the sign of the Son of man in heaven: and then shall all the tribes of the earth mourn, and they shall see the Son of man coming in the clouds of heaven with power and great glory. And he shall send his angels with a great sound of a trumpet, and they shall gather together his elect from the four winds, from one end of heaven to the other [Matt. 24:30-31].

This regathering is a major subject of the prophetic message as the following passages will show.

> . . . ye shall be gathered one by one [Isa. 27:12].
>
> . . . I will bring thy seed from the east, and gather thee from the west; I will say to the north, Give up; and to the south, Keep not back: bring my sons from far, and my daughters from the

ends of the earth; even every one that is called by my name [Isa. 43:5-7].

And it shall come to pass, after I have plucked them out I will return, and have compassion on them, and will bring them again, every man to his heritage, and every man to his land [Jer. 12:15].

. . . I will bring them again to this land [Jer. 24:6].

And ye shall know that I am the Lord, when I shall bring you into the land of Israel, into the country for the which I lifted up mine hand to give it to your fathers [Ezek. 20:42].

When I shall have gathered the house of Israel from the people among whom they are scattered . . . then shall they dwell in their land that I have given to my servant Jacob. And they shall dwell safely therein . . . [Ezek. 28:25-26].

And I that am the Lord thy God from the land of Egypt will yet make thee to dwell in tabernacles, as in the days of the solemn feast [Hosea 12:9].

For behold, in those days, and in that time, when I shall bring again the captivity of Judah and Jerusalem [Joel 3:1].

And I will bring again the captivity of my people Israel, and they shall build the waste cities, and inhabit them; and they shall plant vineyards, and drink the wine thereof; they shall also make gardens, and eat the fruit of them. And I will plant them upon their land, and they shall no more be pulled up out of their land which I have given them, saith the Lord thy God [Amos 9:14-15].

In that day, saith the Lord, will I assemble her that halteth, and I will gather her that is driven out, and her that I have afflicted [Micah 4:6].

At that time will I bring you again, even in the time that I gather you; for I will make you a name and a praise among all people of the earth, when I turn back your captivity before your eyes, saith the Lord [Zeph. 3:20].

I will bring them again also out of the land of Egypt, and gather them out of Assyria; and I will bring them into the land of Gilead and Lebanon; and place shall not be found for them [Zech. 10:10].

Thus, this hope, which is a dominant theme throughout the prophetic Scriptures, will come to fulfillment at the second advent of Christ.

2. *Israel's regeneration.* The nation Israel is to experience a conversion, which will prepare them to meet the Messiah and

to be in His millennial kingdom. Paul establishes the fact that this conversion is effected at the second advent, for he writes:

> And so all Israel shall be saved: as it is written, There shall come out of Sion the Deliverer, and shall turn away ungodliness from Jacob: For this is my covenant unto them, when I shall take away their sins [Rom. 11:26-27].

Once again we find that this is a major theme of the prophetic writings. A few references will suffice.

> Zion shall be redeemed with judgment, and her converts with righteousness [Isa. 1:27].
>
> . . . he that remaineth in Jerusalem, shall be called holy. . . . When the Lord shall have washed away the filth of the daughter of Zion, and shall have purged the blood of Jerusalem . . . [Isa. 4:3-4].
>
> In his days Judah shall be saved, and Israel shall dwell safely: and this is his name whereby he shall be called, THE LORD OUR RIGHTEOUSNESS [Jer. 23:6].
>
> And I will give them an heart to know me, that I am the Lord: and they shall be my people, and I will be their God: for they shall return unto me with their whole hearts [Jer. 24:7].
>
> I will put my law in their inward parts, and write it in their hearts; and will be their God, and they shall be my people. And they shall teach no more every man his neighbour, and every man his brother, saying, Know the Lord: for they shall all know me, from the least of them unto the greatest of them, saith the Lord: for I will forgive their iniquity, and I will remember their sin no more [Jer. 31:33-34].
>
> And I will give them one heart, and I will put a new spirit within you; and I will take the stony heart out of their flesh, and will give them an heart of flesh [Ezek. 11:19].
>
> Then will I sprinkle water upon you, and ye shall be clean; from all your filthiness, and from all your idols, will I cleanse you. A new heart also will I give you, and a new spirit will I put within you [Ezek. 36:25-26].
>
> And it shall come to pass, that whosoever shall call on the name of the Lord shall be delivered: for in mount Zion and in Jerusalem shall be deliverance . . . [Joel 2:32].
>
> Who is a God like unto thee, that pardoneth iniquity, and passeth by the transgression of the remnant of his heritage? he retaineth not his anger for ever, because he delighteth in mercy. He will turn again, he will have compassion upon us; he will

> subdue our iniquities; and thou wilt cast all their sins into the depths of the sea [Mic. 7:18-19].
>
> I will also leave in the midst of thee an afflicted and poor people, and they shall trust in the name of the Lord. The remnant of Israel shall not do iniquity, nor speak lies; neither shall a deceitful tongue be found in their mouth: for they shall feed and lie down, and none shall make them afraid [Zeph. 3:12-13].
>
> In that day there shall be a fountain opened to the house of David and to the inhabitants of Jerusalem for sin and for uncleanness [Zech. 13:1].
>
> And I will bring the third part through the fire, and will refine them as silver is refined, and will try them as gold is tried: they shall call on my name, and I will hear them: I will say, It is my people: and they shall say, The Lord is my God [Zech. 13:9].

Since no unsaved person is to enter the millennium, Israel anticipated a conversion that would prepare them for this promised kingdom. The second advent will witness this conversion of the nation, that is, all true Israel, so the covenants given to them may find fulfillment during the age of the Messiah's reign.

3. *Israel as Messiah's subjects in the millennium.* Israel will become the subjects of the King's reign (Isa. 9:6-7; 33:17, 22; 44:6; Jer. 23:5; Mic. 2:13; 4:7; Dan. 4:3; 7:14, 22, 27). In order to be the subjects (1) Israel will have been converted and restored to the land, as has already been shown. (2) Israel will be reunited as a nation (Jer. 3:18; 33:14; Ezek. 20:40; 37:15-22; 39:25; Hos. 1:11). (3) The nation will again be related to Jehovah by marriage (Isa. 54:1-17; 62:2-5; Hos. 2:14-23). (4) She will be exalted above the Gentiles (Isa. 14:1-2; 49:22-23; 60:14-17; 61:6-7). (5) Israel will be made righteous (Isa. 1:25; 2:4; 44:22-24; 45:17-25; 48:17; 55:7; 57:18-19; 63:16; Jer. 31:11; 33:8; 50:20, 34; Ezek. 36:25-26; Hos. 14:4; Joel 3:21; Mic. 7:18-19; Zech. 13:9; Mal. 3:2-3). (6) The nation will become God's witnesses during the millennium (Isa. 44:8, 21; 61:6; 66:21; Jer. 16:19-21; Mic. 5:7; Zeph. 3:20; Zech. 4:1-7; 4:11-14; 8:23). (7) Israel will be beautified to bring glory to Jehovah (Isa. 62:3; Jer. 32:41; Hos. 14:5-6; Zeph. 3:16-17; Zech. 9:16-17).

B. *The Gentiles in the Millennium*

The universal aspects of the Abrahamic covenant, which promised universal blessing, will be realized in that age. The

Gentiles will be brought into relationship with the King. (1) The fact of the Gentiles' participation in the millennium is promised in the prophetic Scriptures (Isa. 2:4; 11:12; 16:1-5; 18:1-7; 19:16-25; 23:18; 42:1; 45:14; 49:6, 22; 59:16-18; 60:1-14; 61:8-9; 62:2; 66:18-19; Jer. 3:17; 16:19-21; 49:6; 49:39; Ezek. 38:23; Amos 9:12; Mic. 7:16-17; Zeph. 2:11; 3:9; Zech. 8:20-22; 9:10; 10:11-12; 14:16-19). Such admission is essential so that Messiah's dominion will be a universal dominion. (2) The Gentiles will be Israel's servants during that age (Isa. 14:1-2; 49:22-23; 60:14; 61:5; Zech. 8:22-23). The nations which usurped authority over Israel in past ages find that downtrodden people exalted and themselves in subjection in their kingdom. (3) The Gentiles that are in the millennium will have experienced conversion prior to admission (Isa. 16:5; 18:7; 19:19-21, 25; 23:18; 55:5-6; 56:6-8; 60:3-5; 61:8-9; Jer. 3:17; 16:19-21; Amos 9:12; Obad. 17-21). (4) They will be subject to the Messiah (Isa. 42:1; 49:6; 60:3-5; Obad. 21; Zech. 8:22-23). These Gentiles are those to whom the invitation is given: "Come, ye blessed of my Father, inherit the kingdom prepared for you from the foundation of the world" (Matt. 25:34).

III. Jerusalem and Palestine in the Millennium

Because the covenants made with Israel guaranteed them the possession of the land, which is fully realized in the millennial age, Palestine and Jerusalem figure largely in the prophetic Scriptures.

A. *Jerusalem in the millennium.* A number of facts are made clear from a study of the prophecies concerning the place of Jerusalem in that age. (1) Jerusalem will become the center of the millennial earth (Isa. 2:2-4; Jer. 31:6; Mic. 4:1; Zech 2:10-11). Because the world is under the dominion of Israel's King, the center of Palestine becomes the center of the entire earth. (2) Jerusalem will be the center of the kingdom rule (Jer. 3:17; 30:16-17; 31:6, 23; Ezek. 43:5-6; Joel 3:17; Mic. 4:7; Zech. 8:2-3). The city that was the center of David's government will become the center of the government of David's greater Son. (3) The city will become a glorious city, bringing honor unto Jehovah (Isa. 52:1-12; 60:14-21; 61:3; 62:1-12; 66:10-14; Jer. 30:18; 33:16; Joel 3:17; Zech. 2:1-13). So closely is the King associated with Jerusalem that the city will partake of His glory. (4) The city will be protected by the power of the King (Isa. 14:32; 25:4; 26:1-4; 33:20-24) so that it never again need fear for its safety. (5) The city will be greatly enlarged over its former area (Jer. 31:38-40; Ezek. 48:30-35; Zech. 14:10). (6) It will be accessible to all in that day (Isa. 35:8-9) so that all who seek the King will find audience within its walls. (7) Jerusalem will become the center of the worship of the age (Jer. 30:16-21; 31:6, 23; Joel 3:17; Zech. 8:8, 20-23). (8) The city will endure forever (Isa. 9:7; 33:20-21; 60:15; Joel 3:19-21; Zech. 8:4).

B. *Palestine in the millennium.* A number of essential facts concerning the land itself are presented in the prophecies. (1) Palestine will become the particular inheritance of Israel (Ezek. 36:8, 12; 47:22-23; Zech. 8:12). This is essential to fulfill Israel's covenants. (2) The land will be greatly enlarged in comparison to its former area (Isa. 26:15; 33:17; Obad. 17-21; Mic. 7:14). For the first time Israel will possess all the land promised to Abraham (Gen. 15:18-21). (3) The topography of the land will be altered (Isa. 33:10-11; Ezek. 47:1-12; Joel 3:18; Zech. 4:7; 14:4, 8, 10). Instead of the mountainous terrain which characterizes Palestine today, a great fertile plain will come into existence at the second advent of Messiah (Zech. 14:4) so that Palestine will truly be "beautiful for situation" (Ps. 48:2). This changed topography will permit the river to flow out from the city of Jerusalem and divide to the seas to water the land (Ezek. 47:1-12). (4) There will be renewed fertility and productivity in the land (Isa. 29:17; 32:15; 35:1-7; 51:3; 55:13; 62:8-9; Jer. 31:27-28; Ezek. 34:27; 36:29-35; Joel 3:18; Amos 9:13). Then the plowman will overtake the reaper because of the productivity of the land. (5) There will be an abundance of rainfall (Isa. 30:23-25; 35:6-7; 41:17-18; 49:10; Ezek. 34:26; Zech. 10:1; Joel 2:23-24). Throughout the Old Testament the rain was a sign of God's blessing and approval and the absence of rain a sign of God's disapproval and judgment. The abundance of rain on the earth will be a sign of God's blessing in that day. (6) The land will be reconstructed after being ravaged during the tribulation period (Isa. 32:16-18; 49:19; 61:4-5; Ezek. 36:33-38; 39:9; Amos 9:14-15). The remnants of destruction will be removed that the earth may be clean again. (7) Palestine will be redistributed among the twelve tribes of Israel. In Ezekiel 48:1-29 this redistribution is outlined. In that chapter the land is seen to be divided into three portions. In the northern portion land is apportioned to the tribes of Dan, Asher, Naphtali, Manasseh, Ephraim, Reuben and Judah (Ezek. 48:1-7). The land seems to be divided by a line running from east to west all across the enlarged dimensions of Palestine. In like manner in the southern portion land is allotted to Benjamin, Simeon, Issachar, Zebulun and Gad (Ezek. 48:23-27). Between the northern and southern divisions is an area known as the "holy oblation" (Ezek. 48:8-20), that is, that portion of the land which is set apart for the Lord. This is to be an area twenty-five thousand reeds long and wide (Ezek. 48:8, 20), to be divided into one area 25,000 by 10,000 reeds for the Levites (Ezek. 45:5; 48:13-14), one the same area for the temple and the priests (Ezek. 45:4; 48:10-12), and one 25,000 by 5,000 reeds for the city (Ezek. 45:6; 48:15-19). Unger writes:

> But how long is a reed? This is given as being "six cubits," "of a cubit and a handbreadth each" (40:5). "The cubit is a cubit and a handbreadth" (43:13). So the real problem is, How long is the cubit specified by Ezekiel?
>
> Archeological research has established the fact that three cubits were employed in ancient Babylonia. . . . The smallest of 10.8 inches or three palms (handbreadths) was used in gold work. The second of four palms or 14.4 inches was applied to buildings, and the third of five handbreadths or 18 inches was utilized in land spaces. The shortest cubit of three handbreadths, or palms (a palm is 3.6 inches), equalling 10.8 inches is the basic fundamental unit. . . . As the prophet is very specific in stating that the unit of measurement in his vision is a "cubit and a handbreadth" (40:5; 43:13), he, no doubt, means the smallest cubit of three handbreadths as the basic measure, plus one handbreadth or what is equivalent to the middle cubit of 14.4 inches. Upon this calculation the reed would be 7.2 feet. The holy oblation would be a spacious square, thirty-four miles each way, containing about 1160 square miles. This area would be the centre of all the interests of the divine government and worship as set up in the millennial earth.[9]

---

[9] Merrill F. Unger, "The Temple Vision of Ezekiel," *Bibliotheca Sacra*, 105:427-28, October, 1948.

If the larger cubit were employed it would enlarge the holy oblation to about fifty miles each way. This could only be possible in view of the enlarged area included within the boundaries of Palestine in the millennium.[10]

[10] Cf. Arno C. Gaebelein, *The Prophet Ezekiel*, p. 339.

Chapter XXX

WORSHIP IN THE MILLENNIUM

The restored theocracy is marked by the adoration given to the Lord Jesus Christ (Isa. 12:1-6; 25:1—26:19; 56:7; 61:10-11; 66:23; Jer. 33:11, 18, 21-22; Ezek. 20:40-41; 40:1—46:24; Zech. 6:12-15; 8:20-23; 14:16-21). "And it shall come to pass . . . shall all flesh come to worship before me, saith the Lord" (Isa. 66:23).

I. The Temple in the Millennium

A large portion of the prophecy of Ezekiel (40:1—46:24) is devoted to the temple; its structure, its priesthood, its ritual, and its ministry. Various views have been presented concerning this important prophecy. Gray outlines these views:

> There are five interpretations of these chapters:
>
> (1) Some think they describe the temple at Jerusalem prior to the Babylonian captivity, and are designed to preserve a memorial of it. But the objection is that such a memorial is unnecessary because of the records in Kings and Chronicles; while the description is untrue because in many particulars it does not agree with that in the books named.
>
> (2) Some think these chapters describe the temple in Jerusalem after the return from the seventy years in Babylon, but this can not be, because there are more marks of contrast than likeness between the temple here described and that.
>
> (3) Some think they describe the ideal temple which the Jews should have built after the seventy years' return, and which they never realized. But this lowers the character of the divine Word. Why should this prophecy in Ezekiel have been given if it was never to be fulfilled?
>
> (4) Some think this temple in Ezekiel symbolizes the spiritual blesssings of the church in the present age. But this appears unlikely, because even those who hold the theory can not explain the symbolism of which they speak. Moreover, even as

> symbolism it leaves out several important features of Christianity, such as the atonement and intercession of the high priest.
>
> (5) The last view is that in the preceding comments, that we have here a prediction of the temple that shall be built in the millennial age. This appears a fitting and intelligent sequel to the preceding prophecies.[1]

While the views of Gray stated above contain their own refutation, Gaebelein more fully answers the anti-literal views. Concerning the view that sees these chapters in Ezekiel's prophecy fulfilled by the return of the remnant from Babylon, he writes:

> The temple which the remnant built does in no way whatever correspond with the magnificent structure which Ezekiel beheld in his vision. The fact is, if this temple is a literal building (as it assuredly is) it has never yet been erected. Furthermore, it is distinctly stated that the glory of the Lord returned to the temple and made His dwelling place there, the same glory which Ezekiel had seen departing from the temple and from Jerusalem. But the glory did not return to the second temple. No glory cloud filled that house. And furthermore no high priest is mentioned in the worship of the temple Ezekiel describes, but the Jews after their return from Babylon had high priests again. Nor can the stream of healing waters flowing from the temple as seen by Ezekiel be in any way applied to the restoration from the Babylonian captivity.[2]

The same author dismisses as unworthy the explanation that the vision is the result of the prophet's own imagination and refutes the idea that the passage from the prophet is to be applied symbolically to the church by saying:

> This is the weakest of all and yet the most accepted. But his theory gives no exposition of the text, is vague and abounds in fanciful applications, while the greater part of this vision is left unexplained even in its allegorical meaning, for it evidently has no such meaning at all.[3]

His conclusion as to the method of interpretation is in these words:

> The true interpretation is the literal one which looks upon these chapters as a prophecy yet unfulfilled and to be fulfilled

---

[1] James M. Gray, *Christian Worker's Commentary*, pp. 265-66.
[2] Arno C. Gaebelein, *The Prophet Ezekiel*, p. 272.
[3] *Ibid.*, pp. 272-73.

when Israel has been restored by the Shepherd and when His glory is once more manifested in the midst of His people. The great building seen in his prophetic vision will then come into existence and all will be accomplished.[4]

Unger likewise concludes: "Ezekiel's temple is a literal future sanctuary to be constructed in Palestine as outlined during the Millennium."[5]

The location of the temple in the land is clearly presented in Scripture.

The temple itself would be located in the middle of this square [the holy oblation] (and not in the city of Jerusalem), upon a very high mountain, which will be miraculously made ready for that purpose when the temple is to be erected. This shall be "the mountain of Jehovah's house," established upon the "top of the mountain" and "exalted above the hills," into which all nations shall flow (Isa. 2:4; Mic. 4:1-4; Ez. 37:26). Ezekiel gives the picture in chapter 37, verse 27: "My tabernacle also shall be with ["over" or "above"] them . . ." The prophet sees the magnificent structure on a grand elevation commanding a superb view of all the surrounding country.[6]

A. *The details of the temple.* Through the prophet Ezekiel numerous details are given to us concerning this temple that becomes the center of the millennial earth.[7] The gates and courts surrounding the temple are first described (Ezek. 40:5-47). The entire area is enclosed by a wall (40:5) which is to separate that which would defile. The outer courtyard is described (40:6-27) where the people gather. This is entered by three gates, one of which, built like all the rest, is the east gate (40:6-16), a structure 25 by 50 cubits (40:21), through which the Shekinah glory enters the temple (43:1-6), which is kept closed (44:2-3). There is a gate on the northern side (40:20-23), and on the southern side (40:24-27), each of which is entered by seven steps (40:26), but none on the west (40:24). In connection with each gate there were six small chambers, three on each side (40:7-10). Around the outer court were thirty cham-

---

4 *Ibid.*, p. 273.

5 Merrill F. Unger, "The Temple Vision of Ezekiel," *Bibliotheca Sacra*, 105:423. October, 1948.

6 *Ibid.*, 105:428-29.

7 Cf. *ibid.*, 106:48-57.

bers, five on each side of each of the gates, arranged around the northern, eastern, and southern walls (40:17-19). Before these chambers is a pavement (40:17-18) that extends around three sides of the area.

The prophet next describes the inner court (40:28-47), an area 100 cubits on each side (40:47), where the priests minister. There are three gates, each directly opposite the gates in the outer wall and 100 cubits within that outer wall, through which access is gained to the inner court; one on the south (40:28-31), east, and north (40:32-37). This inner court area is reached by eight steps (40:37), so that it is elevated above the outer court. Adjacent to the north gate in this area there were eight tables for preparing sacrifices (40:40-43). And within the outer court, but without the inner court, were chambers for the ministering priests (40:44-46). The center of this area is occupied by an altar (40:47; 43:13-17) where sacrifices are offered.

Ezekiel then describes the temple itself (40:48—41:4). He describes first the porch or vestibule of the temple (40:48-49), which is 20 cubits by 11 cubits. The porch has two large pillars on it (40:49), and is reached by steps (40:49), so that this area is elevated above the rest. This porch leads into the "temple" which would be the holy place, an area forty cubits by twenty cubits (41:2), in which is a wooden table (41:22). Beyond this is the inner part of the temple, or most holy place, a chamber twenty cubits by twenty cubits (41:3-4). Surrounding the wall of the house were chambers, three stories high, thirty to a story (41:5-11), concerning whose use the prophet does not speak. The temple is surrounded by an area 20 cubits by 100 cubits, called the separate place (41:12-14), which surrounds the temple on all sides except the east side, where the porch is located. The interior of the temple is described (41:15-26). It was paneled with wood (41:16) and ornamented with palm trees and cherubim (41:18). There were two doors into the sanctuary (41:23-26). It is noteworthy that in all the description there is no mention of an ark, or mercy seat, or veil, or cherubim above the mercy seat, or tables of stone. The only article of furniture described is the table or altar of wood (41:22) that answers to the table of shewbread, that which bespeaks communion with God. Included also in the temple area was a separate building, located on the west side of the enclosure (41:12), areas where the sacrifices were prepared (46:19-20), and areas at the four corners where there was a court in which sacrifices for the people were prepared (46:21-24).

An extensive description of the throne is given in the prophecy (43:7-12), which is seen to be the very seat of authority. The altar description is detailed (43:12-18), followed by a recounting of the offerings which will be made (43:19-27). The priests' ministry is outlined (44:9-31) and the entire worship ritual described (45:13—46:18). The vision climaxes in the description of the river that flows out of the sanctuary (47:1-12; cf. Isa. 33:20-21; Joel 3:18; Zech. 14:8). This river flows from the temple south through the city of Jerusalem and then divides to flow into the Dead Sea and the Mediterranean Sea, furnishing life along its banks.

B. *The purpose of the temple.* Unger gives five purposes to be realized in this temple. He says it is erected:

> (1) *To Demonstrate God's Holiness.*
>
> . . . [the] infinite holiness of Jehovah's nature and government . . . had been outraged and called into question by the idolatry and rebellion of His professed people. . . .
>
> This has necessitated the fullest exposure, arraignment and judgment of sinful Israel . . . along with the pronouncement of judgment upon the wicked surrounding nations. . . . This is followed by the display of divine grace in restoring the prodigal nation to Himself. . . .
>
> (2) *To Provide a Dwelling-Place for the Divine Glory.*
>
> . . . "This is the place of my throne, and the place of the soles of my feet, where I will dwell in the midst of the children of Israel forever" (43:7). . . .
>
> (3) *To Perpetuate the Memorial of Sacrifice.*
>
> It is not sacrifice, of course, rendered with a view of obtaining salvation, but sacrifice commemorative of an accomplished salvation maintained in the presence of the revealed glory of Jehovah. . . .
>
> (4) *To Provide the Centre for the Divine Government.*
>
> When the divine Glory takes up its residence in the temple, the announcement is not only that the temple is God's dwelling-place and the seat of worship, but also that it is the radiating centre of the divine government. "This is the place of my throne . . ." (43:7). . . .

(5) *To Provide Victory over the Curse* (*47:1-12*).

From under the threshold of the temple house the prophet sees a marvelous stream issuing and flowing eastward in ever increasing volumes of refreshment until it enters in copious fulness into the Dead Sea, whose poisonous waters are healed. . . . Traversing the course of this wondrous life-giving water, the seer finds both banks clothed with luxuriant growth of trees of fadeless leaf and never-failing fruit, furnishing both medicine and food.[8]

II. Will There Be Literal Sacrifices in the Millennium?

One of the problems accompanying the literal interpretation of the Old Testament presentation of the millennium is the problem surrounding the interpretation of such passages as Ezekiel 43:18—46:24; Zechariah 14:16; Isaiah 56:6-8; 66:21; Jeremiah 33:15-18 and Ezekiel 20:40-41, all of which teach the restoration of a priesthood and the reinstitution of a bloody sacrificial system during that age. An alleged inconsistency between this interpretation and the teaching of the New Testament concerning the finished work of Christ, which brought about the abolition of the Old Testament sacrificial system, has been used by the amillennialists to reduce the premillennial system to an absurdity and to affirm the fallacy of the literal method of interpretation. Allis feels that he has presented an insurmountable obstacle to premillennialism,[9] by saying:

> . . . Its literalistic and Old Testament emphasis leads almost inevitably, if not inevitably, to a doctrine of the millennium which makes it definitely Jewish and represents a turning back from the glory of the gospel to those typical rites and ceremonies which prepared the way for it, and having served that necessary purpose have lost for ever their validity and propriety.[10]

That which confronts the premillennialists, then, is the necessity of reconciling the teaching of the Old Testament that bloody sacrifices will be offered in the millennium with the New Testament doctrine of the abolition of the sacrifices of the Old Testament order because of the sacrifice of Christ. If a consistent literalism leads to the adoption of literal sacrifices

---

[8] *Ibid.*, 106:57-64.

[9] Oswald T. Allis, *Prophecy and the Church*, p. 245.

[10] *Ibid.*, p. 248.

during the millennium, it becomes necessary to give reason why such a system should be reinstituted.

A. *Is the Mosaic order re-established?* A question which faces the advocate of animal sacrifices during the millennial age is that of the relationship existing between the former Mosaic system and the system operative in the millennium. Allis says:

> The crux of the whole question is undoubtedly the restoration of the Levitical ritual of sacrifice. This is referred to or implied a number of times. In Ezek. xlvi. burnt offerings and sin offerings are mentioned. The bullock, the he-goat, the ram are to be offered. The blood is to be sprinkled on the altar. The priests, who are Levites of the seed of Zadok, are to officiate. Literally interpreted, this means the restoration of the Aaronic priesthood and of the Mosaic ritual of sacrifices essentially unchanged.[11]

He states further:

> Since the pictures of the millennium are found by Dispensationalists in the Old Testament kingdom prophecies and are, consequently, markedly Jewish in character, it follows that the question of the re-establishment of the Mosaic economy, its institutions and ordinances, must be faced by them.[12]

There is one grave error in his observation and conclusion. The kingdom expectation is based on the Abrahamic covenant, the Davidic covenant, and the Palestinic covenant, but is in no way based on the Mosaic covenant. It is insisted that the covenants will be fulfilled in the kingdom age. This does not, however, link the Mosaic covenant with the kingdom necessarily. It is therefore fallacious to reason that because one believes in the fulfillment of the determinative covenants he must also believe in the restoration of the Mosaic order, which was a conditional covenant, non-determinative and non-eschatological in intent, but given rather to govern the life of the people in their relation to God in the old economy. One great stumbling block that hinders the acceptance of literal sacrifices in the millennium is removed by observing that, while there are many similarities between the Aaronic and millennial systems, there

---

11 *Ibid.*, p. 246.
12 *Ibid.*, p. 245.

are also many differences between them that make it impossible that they should be equated.

1. There are certain *similarities* between the Aaronic and millennial systems. In the millennial system we find the worship centers in an altar (Ezekiel 43:13-17) on which blood is sprinkled (43:18) and on which are offered burnt offerings, sin offerings, and trespass offerings (40:39). There is the re-institution of a Levitical order in that the sons of Zadok are set aside for a priestly ministry (43:19). The meal offering is incorporated in the ritual (42:13). There are prescribed rituals of cleansing for the altar (43:20-27), for the Levites who minister (44:25-27), and for the sanctuary (45:18). There will be the observance of new moon and sabbath days (46:1). Morning sacrifices will be offered daily (46:13). Perpetual inheritances will be recognized (46:16-18). The Passover feast will be observed again (45:21-25) and the feast of Tabernacles becomes an annual event (45:25). The year of jubilee is observed (46:17). There is a similarity in the regulations given to govern the manner of life, the dress, and the sustenance of the priestly order (44:15-31). This temple, in which this ministry is executed, becomes again the place from which is manifested the glory of Jehovah (43:4-5). It can thus be seen that the form of worship in the millennium will bear a strong similarity to the old Aaronic order.

The very fact that God has instituted an order strangely like the old Aaronic order is one of the best arguments that the millennium is not being fulfilled in the church, composed of Gentile and Jew, in the present age. That this worship was particularly planned for a redeemed Israel is well observed by Kelly, who writes:

> Israel shall yet return to the land, and be converted indeed, and blessed, under Jehovah their God, but as Israel, not as *Christians,* which all believers do become meanwhile, whether Jews or Gentiles. They belong to Christ in heaven, where such differences are unknown, and therefore one of the great characteristics of Christianity is that such distinctions disappear while Christ is head on high, and His body is being formed on earth by the Holy Ghost sent down from heaven. When Ezekiel's visions shall be accomplished, it will be the reign of Jehovah-Jesus on earth, and the distinction of Israel from the Gentiles

> will again be resumed, though for blessing under the new covenant, not as of old for curse under the law. . . . The heavenly people rest upon one sacrifice, and draw near into the holiest of all, where Christ is at the right hand of God. But the earthly people will have a sanctuary as well as land suited to them, and such are all the ordinances of their worship.[13]

It is the argument of the book of Hebrews that Israel sought access to God in the old economy through the order or arrangement of the Aaronic priesthood, but that we are brought to God through Christ as He ministered in a new order or arrangement, the Melchisedec priesthood. It is particularly emphasized in Hebrews 7:15 that Christ came to minister in a new order of the priesthood. The requirements or rituals of the two orders need not vary appreciably for them to be two different orders. Since both these orders point to Christ, it would be expected that similarities should exist.

2. There are many basic *differences* between the Aaronic and millennial systems. The significance is not in the similarities but rather in the marked differences between the two systems. The millennial system is marked by omissions from the Aaronic order that make the two systems so different.

a. First of all, there are *changes* in the millennial order. West notes this emphasis on change when he says:

> There are *Changes* in the dimensions of the Temple so that it is neither the temple of Solomon, nor that of Zerubbabel, nor that of Herod; changes in the measures of the outer court, the gates, the walls, the grounds, and the locality of the temple itself, raised on a high mountain, and even separate from the city. The Holy Places have hardly anything like the furniture that stood in the Tabernacle of Moses or the Temple of Solomon.[14]

This change in the physical temple and its environs is so marked that it is necessary for Ezekiel to give detailed descriptions of it.

One of the major changes to be observed is in the relation of the Levites to this order. In a number of passages the existence of a Levitical order is affirmed (Ezekiel 40:46; 43:19; 44:15-31). Yet it is to be noted that the priests who serve are not

---

13 William Kelly, *Notes on Ezekiel*, pp. 236-37.
14 Nathaniel West, *The Thousand Years in Both Testaments*, pp. 429-30.

taken from the whole Levitical line, for the line as a whole was set aside because of their apostasy, but are taken from the sons of Zadok. The Levites are restricted in their ministry to that of guarding and maintaining the temple and are excluded from the priestly ministry, with the exception of the sons of Zadok. Concerning the line of Zadok Grant writes:

> Zadok fills a prominent place in the history of Israel, being high priest in David's and Solomon's reigns. He remained faithful to David during Absalom's rebellion, and with Nathan the prophet espoused the cause of Solomon when Adonijah sought to secure the throne. David being of one mind with them instructed Zadok to anoint Bathsheba's son (1 Kings i. 26, 32-45). Zadok thus stands as representative of the priesthood in association with the king of God's choice, and with the kingdom as established by Him in David's seed—type of Christ.[15]

It is thus to be observed that God has set aside the whole Levitical line because of their apostasy, has singled out the line of Zadok from within the Levitical line, and appointed to his seed the important priestly ministry of the millennial age. If it should be argued that tribal lines have vanished and no genealogy exists by which the line of Zadok should be established, let it be observed that the God who, in infinite wisdom, can call twelve thousand from each of the tribes of Israel (Rev. 7) can preserve and identify the line of Zadok.

b. The millennial system is marked by the *deletion* of much that had the highest place in the Aaronic system. West has keenly observed:

> There is no Ark of the Covenant, no Pot of Manna, no Aaron's rod to bud, no Tables of the Law, no Cherubim, no Mercy-Seat, no Golden Candlestick, no Shew-bread, no Veil, no unapproachable Holy of Holies where the High-Priest alone might enter, nor is there any High-Priest to offer atonement to take away sin, or to make intercession for the people. None of this. The Levites have passed away as a sacred order. The priesthood is confined to the sons of Zadok, and only for a special purpose. There is no evening sacrifice. The measures of the Altar of Burnt-Offering differ from those of the Mosaic altar, and the offerings themselves are barely named. The preparation for the Singers is different from what it was. The social,

[15] F. W. Grant, *The Numerical Bible*, IV., 270.

> moral, and civil prescriptions enforced by Moses with such emphasis, are all wanting.[16]

While there is mention made of the five great offerings in force under the Aaronic order, yet, in the millennial age, these offerings are given a different emphasis. The complete system is not restored. In like manner, while there is emphasis on the Passover in Ezekiel and a mention is made of the feast of Tabernacles (Ezek. 45:25), there is an omission of any reference to the feast of Pentecost. While portions of the Aaronic system are seen in the millennial system, yet it is marked by incompleteness and deletion of much that was observed formerly. The very center of the whole Levitical system revolved around the day of Atonement, with its ritual of sprinkling of the blood of atonement by the High Priest on the mercy seat. It is significant that all the necessary parts of this important ritual—the High Priest, the ark and mercy seat, and even the day itself—are all omitted from the record. The absence of that which was most vital to the Levitical system shows that the millennial age will not see the re-establishment of Judaism.

c. There are *additions* to the Levitical system to be observed in the millennial age. To quote West again:

> The entrance of the "Glory" into Ezekiel's temple to dwell there, forever; the Living Waters that flow, enlarging from beneath the Altar; the Suburbs, the wonderful trees of healing, the new distribution of the land according to the 12 tribes, their equal portion therein, the re-adjustment of the tribes themselves, the Prince's portion and, the City's new name, *"Jehovah-Shammah,"* all go to prove that New Israel restored is a converted people, worshiping God "in Spirit and in Truth."[17]

As established by God, the Levitical order of the old economy was unaltered and fixed so that Israel might be confronted with a picture of the unchangeable holiness of God. The change in the order for the millennial age bespeaks an entirely new order.

One of the greatest changes to be observed in the coming millennial order is the person and ministry of "the prince," who not only has royal prerogatives but priestly ones as well.

---

[16] West, *loc. cit.*
[17] *Ibid.*

Ezekiel describes one who is a king-priest in the office of high priest. Concerning this one Grant writes:

> . . . we have "the Prince," who has a unique and highly favored position. It is his privilege to occupy the eastern gate at which the glory of Jehovah entered. To him the offerings of the people are given, and by him administered in providing for the ritual of sacrifice. It does not appear that the people bring sacrifices of themselves, but that it is the Prince who gives all for the prescribed ritual, including the daily burnt offering (xlv. 17). The people are spoken of as simply worshipping at the times of offering by the Prince, but the act of offering is his, the priests and Levites acting in their respective capacities. He thus fills a representative position on behalf of the people in the matter of specific offerings, while in all of these the people may be considered as having their part, since, in the first instance, they present their offerings to the Prince (xlv. 13-17), and join in worship when he offers. It would seem also that he occupies a representative position for God toward the people, since he is privileged to commune with Jehovah at the East Gate.[18]

Concerning the person and the work of this prince the same author writes in another place:

> This important personage, the Prince, is apparently one of the nation, not Christ Himself; his sons are spoken of (xlvi. 16) and he offers a sin-offering for himself (xlv. 22). It seems clear that he occupies a representative position, yet neither the same as that of the high priest, of whom Ezekiel does not speak, nor that of the king as formerly known in Israel. He is not accorded the privileges nor the power of either. He seems to occupy an intermediary place between the people and the priesthood, since he is found among the former in their seasons of worship (xlvi. 10), not among the priests, nor privileged to enter the inner court, yet drawing nearer than the people themselves, since he may worship in the inner east gate which opens upon the inner court, while the people worship in the outer court as gathered at the door of this gate (xlvi. 2). But he is responsible to supply the various offerings at the feasts, the new moons, the sabbaths, in all the solemnities of the house of Israel, and he is therefore the recipient and holder of what the people offer for those occasions; and thus too the priesthood would look to him for the provision needed to carry on the national worship (xlv. 13-22). Then he is given his own special

[18] Grant, *op. cit.*, IV, 239.

> portion in the land, and he is enjoined not to take any of the people's inheritance. . . .[19]

It must be obvious that such a person, with such an important ministry, is unique to the millennial age and has no counterpart in the Levitical order and thus represents a major change in that coming age. In all probability this personage will be an earthly representative of the king-priest ministry of Christ after the order of Melchizedek, perhaps resurrected David, as previously suggested.

The system to be inaugurated in the millennial age will be a new order that will replace the Levitical order, for there are too many changes, deletions, and additions to the old order to sustain the contention that, literally interpreted, Ezekiel teaches the institution of the Levitical order again. The whole concept of the new covenant of Jeremiah 31 envisions an entirely new order after the passing of the old.

B. *The purpose of the sacrifices.* Several factors are observed concerning the millennial sacrifices which make them entirely legitimate.

1. It is to be observed, in the first place, that the millennial sacrifices *will have no relation to the question of expiation.* They will not be expiatory for it is nowhere stated that they are offered with a view to salvation from sin. Allis writes:

> They must be expiatory in exactly the same sense as the sacrifices described in Leviticus were expiatory. To take any other view of them is to surrender that principle of literal interpretation of prophecy which is fundamental to Dispensationalism and to admit that the Old Testament kingdom prophecies do not enter the New Testament "absolutely unchanged." It is true that they are only "weak and beggarly elements" when viewed in the light of the Cross from which they derive their entire efficacy. But they were not memorial but efficacious in the days of Moses and of David; and in the millennium they must be equally efficacious if the Dispensational system of interpretation is a true one. And this they cannot be unless the teaching of the Epistle to the Hebrews is completely disregarded.[20]

There is error in several points of this argument that these sacrifices, logically, must be interpreted by the dispensationalist

---

[19] *Ibid.*, IV., 273.
[20] Allis, *op. cit.*, p. 247.

as expiatory. (1) The insistence on the literal fulfillment of the Davidic covenant does not carry as a necessary corollary the re-establishment of the Mosaic order, for they were unrelated to each other. The Davidic covenant was eternal and unconditional, governing God's future dealing with the nation, while the Mosaic was temporal and conditional, governing man's relation to God. The fulfillment of the one does not necessitate the fulfillment of the other, inasmuch as the Mosaic was viewed as temporary. (2) It is an error in the doctrine of Soteriology to teach that the sacrifices ever could or did take away sin. That is in contradiction of the clear teaching of Hebrews 10:4, "For it is not possible that the blood of bulls and of goats should take away sins," which Allis himself quotes. The only way it can be held that the sacrifices will be efficacious in the millennium is to hold that they were so in the Old Testament and this is a clear contradiction of the whole New Testament. What folly to argue that a rite could accomplish in the future what it never could, or did, or was ever intended to do, in the past.

2. In the second place, the sacrifices *will be memorial* in character. There is general agreement among premillennialists as to the purpose of the sacrificial system as inaugurated in the millennial age. Interpreted in the light of the New Testament, with its teaching on the value of the death of Christ, they must be memorials of that death. Grant states it clearly:

> [This is] the permanent memorial of *sacrifice*, maintained in the presence of the revealed glory. It is not sacrifice rendered with a view of obtaining salvation, but sacrifices in view of accomplished salvation. . . .[21]

Gaebelein takes the same view of the memorial character of the sacrifices when he writes:

> While the sacrifices Israel brought once had a prospective meaning, the sacrifices brought in the millennial temple have a retrospective meaning. When during this age God's people worship in the appointed way at His table, with the bread and wine as the memorial of His love, it is a retrospect. We look back to the Cross. We show forth His death. It is "till He comes." Then this memorial feast ends forever. Never again will the Lord's Supper be kept after the Saints of God have left the earth to be

[21] Grant, *op. cit.*, IV, 238.

with the Lord in glory. The resumed sacrifices will be the memorial of the Cross and the whole wonderful story of the redemption for Israel and the nations of the earth, during the kingdom reign of Christ. And what a memorial it will be! What a meaning those sacrifices will have! They will bring to a living remembrance everything of the past. The retrospect will produce the greatest scene of worship, of praise and adoration this earth has ever seen. All the Cross meant and the Cross has accomplished will be recalled and a mighty "Hallelujah Chorus" will fill the earth and the heavens. The sacrifices will constantly remind the people of the earth of Him who died for Israel, who paid the redemption price for all creation and whose glory now covers the earth as the waters cover the deep.[22]

Adolph Saphir has given us a word concerning the parallelism existing between the Lord's Supper in its relation to the death of Christ and the memorial sacrifices in relation to that death:

. . . may we not suppose that what was typical before the first coming of Christ, pointing to the great salvation which was to come, may in the kingdom be commemorative of the redemption accomplished?

In the Lord's Supper we commemorate Christ's death; we altogether repudiate the Popish doctrine of a repetition of the offering of Christ; we do not believe in any such renewal of the sacrifice, but we gratefully obey the command of Christ to commemorate His death in such a way that both an external memorial is presented to the world, and an outward and visible sign and seal given to the believing partaker. May not a similar plan succeed the Lord's Supper, which we know shall cease at Christ's coming? It is also possible that both the glorified saints in heaven and the nations on the earth will contemplate during the millennium the full and minute harmony between type and reality. Even the Church has as yet only a superficial knowledge of the treasures of wisdom in the Levitical institutions and its symbols.[23]

Wale has stated the proposition succinctly in the words:

. . . the bread and wine of the Lord's supper are, to the believer, physical and material symbols and memorials of a redemption already accomplished on his behalf. And this will be the case with the reinstituted sacrifices at Jerusalem, they will be *commemorative,* as the sacrifices of old were anticipative. And

---

[22] Gaebelein, *op. cit.,* pp. 312-13.
[23] Adolph Saphir, *Christ and Israel,* p. 182.

> why should they not be? Was there any virtue in the legal sacrifices which prefigured the sacrifice of Christ? None whatever. Their only value and meaning was derived from the fact that they pointed to Him. And such will be the value and meaning of those future sacrifices which God has declared shall yet be offered in that future temple. Whatever the difficulty the reader may imagine in the way of the accomplishment of the prediction, it is sufficient for us that GOD HAS SAID IT.[24]

It is concluded, then, that these sacrifices are not expiatory, for no sacrifice ever accomplished the complete removal of sin, but are memorials of the perfect sacrifice of the One typified by all sacrifice, the Lamb of God that taketh away the sin of the world.

C. *Some objections considered.* There are certain objections to this view which must be considered. 1. Some insist that sacrifices reinstituted would contradict Hebrews. It is emphasized in such passages as Hebrews 9:26; 7:27 and 9:12 that Christ once and for all offered an acceptable sacrifice to God, which needs not be repeated. Such an alleged contradiction can only arise when one fails to see the distinction, dispensationally, between God's program for the church and his program for Israel. Unger has well stated the necessary distinction to be observed:

> Regarding the imagined clash between the teaching of the Epistle to the Hebrews and Ezekiel's prophecy, it may be said the whole conflict vanishes when the ground and position of the one are seen to be entirely different from the ground and position of the other. One has in view members of the Body of Christ, the Church, since their redemption while Christ is on high. The other is concerned with earthly Israel, and embraces the Glory of Jehovah once more dwelling in the land of Canaan. One concerns Christianity where there is neither Jew nor Gentile, but all are one in Christ. The other deals with restored Judaism, where Israel is blessed directly, and the Gentiles only mediately or subordinately to the Jews—a state of things in diametrical contrast with Christianity.
>
> . . . .
>
> The particular difficulty in accepting the literal-futuristic view is Christendom's conceit (Rom. 11:15-26) in presuming that the fall of the Jew is final, and that the Gentile has supplanted him forever. When the truth of Israel's recall to blessing is com-

[24] Burlington B. Wale, *The Closing Days of Christendom*, p. 485.

> prehended, a literal-futuristic interpretation of Ezekiel's prophecy is the normal explanation of the vision.[25]

In reference to the church, Christ stands as One who has offered a completed eternal sacrifice. She looks to Him alone. Such is the teaching of Hebrews. Yet, in dealing with Israel in their future relation to Christ, in Hebrews 8:8-13 and 10:16 there is the anticipation of the enactment of a new covenant. The new covenant of Jeremiah 31 served notice that the old (Mosaic) order was to be supplanted, because of its insufficiency, by a new order. Ezekiel's temple vision gives detail concerning the new priestly order to be inaugurated by God after the fulfillment of the new covenant with Israel. Such an interpretation is in perfect harmony with the teaching of Hebrews.

2. Some would argue that sacrifices reinstituted must be expiatory. This subject has been dealt with previously, and in this connection only the words of Wale, previously quoted need be mentioned. He says: "Was there any virtue in the legal sacrifices which prefigured the sacrifice of Christ? None whatever. Their only value and meaning were derived from the fact that they pointed to Him."[26] Such an objection can only arise from a false Soteriology.

3. Some affirm that such a view denies Ephesians 2:14-16. Objection is sometimes raised that God has forever broken down the barrier that separates Jew and Gentile and makes them one. This view arises from a failure to realize that this is God's purpose for the present age, but has no reference to God's program in the millennial age. As to the relation between the two, Saphir well observes:

> "The Apostle Paul teaches that in Christ Jesus there is neither Jew nor Gentile; but you are building up again the wall of separation which has been abolished!" It is true that in the Church of Christ Jew and Gentile are one; it is true that in the kingdom also Jew and Gentile shall have one way of access to God, one fountain of pardon and renewal, one Spirit to enlighten, guide, and strengthen. But it by no means follows that the position of Jew and Gentile must be the same, or that

---

[25] Unger, *op. cit.*, 106:170-71.
[26] Wale, *loc. cit.*

> their *distinctive positions* in the kingdom militate against their oneness in the Lord Jesus Christ. In Christ there is neither male nor female, yet man and woman continue to hold different positions, and even in the Church, though equal in privilege, a woman is not allowed to speak.[27]

Scripture is unintelligible until one can distinguish clearly between God's program for his earthly people Israel and that for the church.

4. Some state that it is geographically impossible to reinstitute such a worship. It has been argued that it is necessary to spiritualize Ezekiel's prophecy, for the temple and its environs is far in excess of the dimensions of the ancient temple area and thus could not possibly be understood literally. Such a view overlooks the important geographical and topographical changes anticipated in Zechariah:

> And his feet shall stand in that day upon the mount of Olives, which is before Jerusalem on the east, and the mount of Olives shall cleave in the midst thereof toward the east and toward the west, and there shall be a very great valley; and half of the mountain shall remove toward the north, and half of it toward the south [Zech. 14:4].

Such predicted changes in the topography of Palestine make full allowance for the temple site so that it is not necessary to interpret the prophecy of Ezekiel non-literally.

5. There are some who hold that the existence of the prince of Ezekiel is inconsistent with the reign of Christ. If it be argued that the literal fulfillment of the Davidic covenant demands the reign of Christ on the throne of David and this is contradicted by Ezekiel's prophecy concerning the person and ministry of the "prince," let it be noted that one is said to be reigning when exercising the authority of the throne, regardless of his relationship to the physical throne, which is the emblem of authority. Christ may fulfill the promise in the Davidic covenant without being seated on a literal throne on earth. Concerning the prince and his relation to Christ, Gaebelein says:

> . . . the prince is not identical with the Lord. Who is he then? He is the viceregent of the King, a future prince of the house of David, who will represent the Lord on earth. David's

[27] Saphir, *op. cit.* p., 183.

> throne will be established at Jerusalem. The Lord Jesus Christ will reign supreme over all; His throne is above the earth in the New Jerusalem. He will visit the earth and manifest His glory as King of kings and Lord of lords. This probably will be during the great celebrations of the feast of Tabernacles, when the nations send their representatives to Jerusalem to worship the King, the Lord of Hosts (Zech. xiv. 16). Upon David's throne will sit this prince of David as viceregent.[28]

Since Scripture reveals that the government of the millennium will be under the authority of Christ, but exercised under Him by appointed men (Matt. 19:28; Matt. 25:21 and Luke 19:17), there is no conflict in seeing the prince as a vice-regent under Christ.

6. Finally, many reject this interpretation saying such a system is a retrogression. If it be argued that the institution of such a system is a retrogression, let it be noted that Ezekiel sees this system (43:1-6) as the greatest manifestation of the glory of God that the earth has seen, apart from the glory of God in the face of Jesus Christ. If the system be planned by God as a memorial of Jesus Christ, it can no more be said to be a retrogression to the "weak and beggarly elements" than the bread and wine can be said to be weak and beggarly memorials of the broken body and shed blood of Christ.

This whole discussion raises the question of salvation in the millennial age. Such a view as presented is counted by some to minimize the cross and to restrict the value of the cross to this present age.[29] Such an allegation can not rightly be made. The new covenant (Jer. 31:31) guarantees to all who enter this millennium and to all who are born in the millennium and who thus need salvation (1) a new heart (Jer. 31:33), (2) the forgiveness of sins (Jer. 31:34), and (3) the fullness of the Spirit (Joel 2:28-29). The New Testament makes it very clear that the new covenant is based on the blood of the Lord Jesus Christ (Heb. 8:6; 10:12-18; Matt. 26:28). It may, therefore, be affirmed that salvation in the millennium will be based on the value of the death of Christ and will be appropriated by faith (Heb. 11:6) even as Abraham appropriated God's promise and was justified

---

28 Gaebelein, *op. cit.*, pp. 314-15.
29 Allis, *op. cit.*, p. 249.

(Rom. 4:3). The expression of that saving faith will differ from the expressions that are required in this present day, but the sacrifices must be viewed as mere expressions of faith and not the means of salvation.

The glorious vision of Ezekiel reveals that it is impossible to locate its fulfillment in any past temple or system which Israel has known, but it must await a future fulfillment after the second advent of Christ when the millennium is instituted. The sacrificial system is not a reinstituted Judaism, but the establishment of a new order that has as its purpose the remembrance of the work of Christ on which all salvation rests. The literal fulfillment of Ezekiel's prophecy will be the means of God's glorification and man's blessing in the millennium.

Chapter XXXI

THE RELATION BETWEEN LIVING AND RESURRECTED SAINTS IN THE MILLENNIUM

There has been general confusion, even among premillennialists, concerning the relationship that would exist during the millennial age between the resurrected and translated saints of the church age, the resurrected saints of the Old Testament, and the living saints from among both Jews and Gentiles, all of whom would bear some relationship to that period. There has been no specific delineation as to the positions these various groups would occupy, their spheres of activity, their relation to the rule of the King, their relation to the earth, nor their relationship to each other. It has been recognized that the church would reign as a bride with Christ. The Old Testament saints, it is agreed, are to be resurrected and rewarded in that age. The saved Jews, who are found to be righteous at the judgment on Israel, together with the saved Gentiles, who are declared righteous at the judgment on the Gentiles at the time of the second advent, are to be the subjects of the King in the millennium. But there has been little said concerning their specific relationship to that period. One writer ridicules the whole premillennial position by saying:

> Another question . . . emerges from the assertion that during the supposed millennium, resurrected and raptured saints will mingle freely and do business with those still in their mortal bodies. It is presumed that the resurrected saints shall rule the earth and enforce the laws of Christ during the millennium. Here again premillennialism makes no provision for the reconciliation of such irreconciliables as resurrected saints and mortal sinners in the same society. . . . Premillennialism blends together the two classes without regard to the fact that one has gone through the process of death and resurrection, and the other has not, and that, therefore, their organisms are adapted to two different modes of existence—one material, and the other spiritual. In

> fact, premillennialism suggests a perfectly normal society made up of these differing elements during the millennium, and also anticipates that during this period the earth's population will greatly increase. This is bewildering when we remember that, according to premillennialism, the earth's millennial population will consist of vast numbers of resurrected saints, and that Jesus Christ plainly stated that there is no marrying or sex life in the resurrection. . . . If the resurrected saints are like angels, how can it be imagined, much less asserted, that for one thousand years they shall mingle freely with men and women still in their carnal and mortal bodies, and live together under identical conditions? Premillennialism does not solve this question. The Bible does not solve it either, for the simple reason that the Bible does not propound it. It did not originate with the Bible.[1]

In the light of such accusations, the problem at hand is to attempt to draw a clear distinction as to the relationship which each group, the Old Testament saints who have been resurrected, the church saints who have been resurrected and translated, and the living saints from among the Jews and Gentiles who are brought into the millennium, bears to the King and His kingdom. The task is somewhat difficult, for the problem is not that of reconciling differing views held by premillennialists, but that of establishing the teaching of Scripture on a subject on which premillennialists are generally silent. It does not seem sufficient to dismiss the question as though no problem existed by pointing out that since our Lord mingled freely with the disciples in a resurrection body after the resurrection with no difficulty, so, in the millennium, the resurrected may mingle freely with the unresurrected with no difficulty.

I. The Nature of the Old Testament Hope

The Old Testament Scriptures abound with descriptions of the glory and blessing that wait the "heirs of promise." A glorious expectation was clearly presented as the hope of the saints. In order to present the relation between the Old Testament and New Testament saint, between the resurrected and unresurrected individual in the millennial age, it is necessary to distinguish certain aspects of the promises given in the Old Testament as the hope of the saint.

---

[1] George L. Murray, *Millennial Studies*, pp. 91-92.

A. *National promises.* The Old Testament made certain promises to the nation Israel. The vast majority of the promises of future blessing and glory were given, not to individuals to buoy their hope, but were given to the nation as the basis of their confidence and expectation. These promises rest on the eternal and unconditional covenants which God made with the nation and which find their fulfillment by the nation itself. The Abrahamic covenant, as originally stated in Genesis 12:1-3, and reiterated in Genesis 13:14-17; 15:1-21 and 17:1-18, while it included certain individual promises to Abraham, concerned itself with a posterity in the line of Abraham and their possession of the land given to Abraham by promise. All subsequent covenant promises are reiterations, enlargements, and clarifications of parts of this original covenant made through Abraham with the nation and establish certain national promises and hopes.

The Davidic covenant, stated in 2 Samuel 7:4-17, and reiterated in Psalm 89, takes the promises concerning the seed in the original Abrahamic covenant and makes that seed the subject of an enlarged promise, as a kingdom, a house, and a throne is promised to the seed. While this promise is made to David and includes certain individual blessings to him, yet the fulfillment of this promise is found in the nation itself, not in individuals from that nation.

The Palestinic covenant, first stated in Deuteronomy 30:1-10, takes the promises in the Abrahamic covenant which are concerned with the land and enlarges on that portion of the covenant. This is a promise of possession of and blessing in the land that was given to the nation as a whole. Deuteronomy 30:6, which says "The Lord thy God will circumcise thine heart, and the heart of thy seed," shows clearly that the promises stated therein were national.

The new covenant, stated in Jeremiah 31:31-34, takes the promises of blessing found in the original Abrahamic covenant and makes those promises the subject of enlargement. The New Testament makes it clear that this promise is to be fulfilled only by the conversion of the nation at the second advent of Christ.

> And so all Israel shall be saved: as it is written, There shall come out of Sion the Deliverer, and shall turn away ungodliness

> from Jacob: For this is my covenant unto them, when I shall take away their sins [Rom. 11:26-27].

Thus it will be observed that all Israel's hopes were based on the four determinative covenants which God made with them, that these covenants confirmed certain national hopes and blessings and necessitate the preservation, continuity, and restoration of the nation if they are to be fulfilled literally.

Chafer observes:

> The kingdom Scriptures of the Old Testament are occupied largely with the character and glory of Messiah's reign, the promises to Israel of restoration and earthly glory, the universal blessings to Gentiles, and the deliverance of creation itself. There is little revealed in the Old Testament Scripture concerning the responsibility of the individual in the kingdom; it is rather a message to the nation as a whole. Evidently the details concerning individual responsibility were, in the mind of the Spirit, reserved for the personal teaching of the King, at the time when the kingdom would be "at hand."[2]

Thus we see that the Old Testament was occupied with national promises and programs and not primarily individual expectation.

B. *Individual promises.* It is true, however, that certain individual hopes were indicated in the old economy. Israelites were given the hope of a resurrection. Isaiah 26:19-20; Daniel 12:2-3, 13; Hosea 13:14 and Job 19:25-27 indicate this. Israelites were given the expectation of individual judgment and reward, as witnessed by such passages as Isaiah 40:10; Ezekiel 11:21; 20:33-44; 22:17-22; Daniel 12:3; Zechariah 3:7; 13:9, and Malachi 3:16-18; 4:1. Israelites were promised blessings in the new heaven and new earth in Isaiah 65:17-18; 66:22.

There is no question in the mind of the literal interpreter of the Scriptures but that Israel's national promises will be fulfilled by the nation itself in the millennial age, which follows the advent of Messiah. All the covenanted national promises are earthly in content and will be fulfilled in the time of the earthly reign of Messiah. Concerning the individual promises, there is no such clear statement as to the sphere in which they will be fulfilled. In the passages teaching individual resurrec-

2 Lewis Sperry Chafer, *Systematic Theology,* IV, 170.

tion and individual judgment and reward, these provisions are said to be fulfilled at the advent of the Messiah, but the Old Testament does not make clear the sphere of the individual's expectation. Commenting on Revelation 21:1-8 Ottman writes:

> The new heavens and a new earth, wherein dwelleth righteousness, succeed the dissolution of the old, and they are, without question, the subject of the present apocalyptic vision. . . .
>
> Referring to this vision Grant says: "This is manifestly a reference to Isaiah's word: 'Behold, I create new heavens and a new earth, and the former things shall not be remembered nor come to mind.' It is but a glance, for the prophets of the Old Testament, apart from this, never seem to go beyond that kingdom which we, indeed, have learned to call 'millennial,' as having its limits defined for us in this way. For Israel, there was no such necessary limitation; there was a bright scene before them upon which their eyes should rest, assured that whatever might be beyond could only be additional blessing. . . ."[8]

It is not until the New Testament that a more specific delineation of the individual Israelite's hope is given to us. The writer to the Hebrews says:

> For he looked for a city which hath foundations, whose builder and maker is God [Heb. 11:10].
>
> But ye are come unto mount Sion, and unto the city of the living God, the heavenly Jerusalem, and to an innumerable company of angels, To the general assembly and church of the firstborn, which are written in heaven, and to God the Judge of all, and to the spirits of just men made perfect [Heb. 12:22-23].

It would thus seem that while the national promises were to be fulfilled both *at the time of* and *in* the millennium, the individual promises were to be fulfilled *at the time of* the millennium, but not necessarily *in* the millennial earth. The passages teaching resurrection indicate that Israel's resurrection will be completed at the time of the second advent of Christ, but do not say that the individuals will be resurrected to the millennial earth. The passages that teach individual judgment and reward indicate, likewise, that the judgment and reward will coincide with the second advent, but do not state that the rewards will be enjoyed in the millennium, but rather at the time of the millennium.

---

[8] Ford C. Ottman, *The Unfolding of the Ages*, pp. 443-44.

It is concluded, then, from the consideration of the promises given in the Old Testament, that the national promises will be fulfilled on the earth in the millennial age, but that the individual promises of resurrection will be fulfilled at the time of the millennium, but not necessarily by placing the individual in the millennium itself.

II. The Nature of the Millennium

In order to understand the relation of the resurrected saints of both the Old and New Testaments to the millennial age it is necessary to have a clear concept of the teaching of Scripture as to the nature and purpose of the millennium. Newell has given a good summary:

> I. What the Thousand Years' Reign Is
>
> The thousand year's reign is the direct administration of divine government on earth for one thousand years by our Lord and His saints. Its earthly center will be Jerusalem and the nation Israel, though Christ and His saints will rule in heavenly resurrection bodies in the New Jerusalem and will take the place now occupied by angels (Hebrews 2:5-8). . . .
>
> II. Object of the Thousand Years' Reign
>
> 1. *Looked at from God the Father's side:*
>
> *a.* It will be the public earthly honoring of His Son just where men dishonored Him on this earth. . . .
>
> *b.* It will be the carrying out of God's promises to His Son, and the prophecies concerning Him, to "give unto him the throne *of his father David.*" . . .
>
> *c.* It is the final divine trial of sinful man on this earth before the earth is destroyed. . . .
>
> *d.* It will be God's answer (so far as is possible before the *new* earth) of the prayer of His saints: "Thy kingdom come, thy will be done on earth as it is in heaven."
>
> 2. *Looked at from Christ's side:*
>
> *a.* He receives, after long patience, the kingdom of this world which He has been constantly "expecting," there at God's right hand. . . . And He will reign in that righteousness. . . .
>
> *b.* At last He will be able to confer upon the meek of the earth the place and inheritance He ever loved to promise them!
>
> *c.* He will share . . . all His kingly honors with His saints!

> 3. *Looked at from the saints' side:*
>
> *a.* The Millennium brings the three classes of saints . . . and also earthly Israel, into a state of indescribable blessedness! . . .
>
> *b.* The very physical changes made in the earth . . . reveal a little of the loving care God will have taken for the comforts and joys of His earthly saints. . . .
>
> 4. *Looked at from the side of the nations, the peoples of the earth:*
>
> *a.* It will be a thousand years under the *iron-rod scepter.* . . .
>
> *b.* Yet there will be *peace* at last among the nations—enforced certainly, but real. . . .
>
> *c.* All nations will be compelled to go up from year to year to worship the King, Jehovah of Hosts, and to keep the feast of tabernacles. . . .
>
> 5. *Looked at from the side of "creation":*
>
> *a.* . . . "the creation itself also shall be delivered from the bondage of corruption into the liberty of the glory of the children of God" (*Romans 8:20-22*).
>
> *b.* At the "revealing of the sons of God," at Christ's coming back to earth, this deliverance will be effected. . . .[4]

It should be evident that the millenium is the time of the fulfillment of Israel's national covenanted blessings, during which time God will make a divine display of the absolute authority of divine government through the rule of the Messiah, during which time living men are being subjected to and tested by the authority of the King. The millennial age is designed by God to be the final test of fallen humanity under the most ideal circumstances, surrounded by every enablement to obey the rule of the king, from whom the outward sources of temptation have been removed, so that man may be found and proved to be a failure in even this last testing of fallen humanity. In such a period, when such a program is being executed, it is obvious that resurrected individuals, who need no testing because they are righteous already and who need not be brought into subjection to the authority of the King because they are completely subjected to Him, can have no rightful place on the earth at that time. Those who would place resurrected individuals on the earth to undergo the rigors of the King's reign miss the purpose of God in the millennial age.

---

[4] William R. Newell, *The Book of the Revelation*, pp. 318-22.

The essential character of and purpose in the millennium leads to the conclusion that resurrected individuals, although having a part in the millennium, are not on the earth to be subjects of the King's reign.

III. The Occupants of the Heavenly Jerusalem

Of Abraham it was said that his hope centered in the realization of life in a city, "For he looked for a city which hath foundations, whose builder and maker is God" (Heb. 11:10). That this was the expectation, not only of Abraham, but also of other Old Testament saints is seen in Hebrews 11:16, where it is stated: "But now they desire a better country, that is, an heavenly: wherefore God is not ashamed to be called their God: for he hath prepared for them a city." It is observed that the hope of these heroes of faith, according to this verse, was a heavenly city. This same heavenly city is further described in Hebrews 12:22-24, where it is called the heavenly Jerusalem. In Galatians 4:26, where it is called "Jerusalem which is above," Revelation 3:12, where it is called "The city of my [Christ's] God," and "new Jerusalem," Revelation 21:2, where it is called "the holy city, new Jerusalem," and Revelation 21:10, where it is called "that great city, the holy Jerusalem," it is clearly seen to be the place of the realization of all the hopes of the church saints. Without doubt this is the "place" our Lord promised He would go to prepare and to which He would come and take us in John 14:2. It is no real problem, then, to identify the "church of the first born" who occupy this heavenly Jerusalem according to Hebrews 12:23. Kelly writes:

> . . . the Christian Hebrews are said to have come "to the assembly of firstborns enrolled in heaven." There need be no hesitation in identifying this heavenly company. It is the church of God, of which we hear so much and of the deepest interest in the Acts of the Apostles and the other Epistles, as the Lord when here below spoke of it as about to be founded (Matt. xvi. 18), so that Hades' gates should not prevail against it. The day of Pentecost (that followed His death, resurrection, and ascension) first saw the new sight. It is described here according to the divine design of the Epistle. This accounts for putting forward the aggregate of those who compose it, firstborn ones, rather than the else-

where familiar figures of the body of Christ, and of the temple of God—His habitation by the Spirit.[5]

There can be no doubt that this heavenly city will be composed, in part, of the church, the body of Christ, from this present age.

Saphir gives us a word that leads us to expect other redeemed men to be in that heavenly city in addition to the saints of this age. He writes: "The term general assembly . . . [*panēguris*] implies not merely a great, but the *full* number. And this circumstance, that *all* the members are collected, gives the assembly a character of solemn and joyous festivity."[6] The question is: "Who joins with the unfallen angels and the church saints to make up the full complement of the inhabitants of that heavenly city?" The answer is in the phrase "the spirits of just men made perfect." Kelly says:

> . . . These are the O. T. saints. They had had to do with God before grace reigned through righteousness unto eternal life by Jesus Christ as we know it in the gospel. When faith rested on promise, they looked for the coming One; and they will have a blessed part in His kingdom (Rev. xx), when they too shall judge the world (I Cor. vi. 2). The like distinction from "we" may be seen at the end in the closing verses 39, 40 of Heb. xi.; and it is remarkable, as this instance proves, that they are shown, not as they will be but as they are, "to the spirits of just men made perfect." They will not be in the separate state when "that day" is come; they will be raised from among the dead at the presence of Christ.[7]

Ottman asks:

> Shall Abraham, and these others of like faith, fail to find the city they looked for? No, they shall not fail. "These all died in faith, not having received the promises, but having seen them afar off, and were persuaded of them, and embraced them, and confessed that they were strangers and pilgrims on the earth. For they that say such things declare plainly that they seek a country. And truly, if they had been mindful of that country, from whence they came out, they might have had opportunity to have returned. But now they desire a better country, that is, an heavenly: wherefore God is not ashamed to be called their God:

---

[5] William Kelly, *Exposition of the Epistle to the Hebrews*, p. 250.
[6] Adolph Saphir, *The Epistle to the Hebrews*, II, 849-50.
[7] Kelly, *op. cit.*, pp. 250-51.

for he hath prepared for them a city" (Heb. 11:13-16). Again, at the close of this remarkable chapter, it says: "These all, having obtained a good report through faith, received not the promise: God having provided some better thing for us, that they without us should not be made perfect" (Heb. 11:39-40). Without *us* they cannot be made perfect.[8]

It would seem, then, that the writer to the Hebrews is giving us a picture of the heavenly city, in which place there will be gathered together with Christ the unfallen angels, the resurrected and translated saints of the church age, and all resurrected Old Testament and tribulation saints.

This interpretation finds support in Revelation 21:12-14, where the walls of the "holy Jerusalem" are described. Here the same three-fold occupancy is indicated, for in verse 12 there is reference to the angels and the twelve tribes of the children of Israel and in verse 14 reference to the names of the twelve apostles of the Lamb. Thus the angels, saints of Israel and the Old Testament, and the saints of the church are included within the wall.

In referring to the dwelling place of the redeemed as a "city," the word of Grant is pertinent here. He writes:

> The city is the expression of human need, and the provision for it. In the midst of strife and insecurity, men gather together for protection; but that is only a small part of what is implied in it. There are other needs more universal than this, as that of cooperation, the division of labor, the result of that inequality of aptitudes by which God has made us mutually dependent. Our social nature is thus met, and there are formed and strengthened the ties by which the world is bound together; while the intercourse of mind with mind, of heart with heart, stimulates and developes every latent faculty. . . .
>
> The eternal city implies for us association, fellowship, intercourse, the fulness of what was intimated in the primal saying, "It is not good for man to be alone," but which in respect of the bride city, which this is, has still a deeper meaning. Here, the relationship of the saints to Christ, who as the Lamp of divine glory enlightens it, alone adequately explains all. "Alone" can we nevermore be. "With Him" our whole manhood shall find its complete answer, satisfaction, and rest.[9]

---

[8] Ottman, *op. cit.*, p. 446.
[9] F. W. Grant, *The Revelation of Christ*, pp. 224-25.

The city, thus, would have as much relevancy for the Old Testament saints as for the New Testament believers.

It would thus be concluded that it is the consistent teaching of Scripture that the Lord will gather unto Himself in the eternal city the unfallen angels, the Old Testament saints, and the New Testament believers, where they, in resurrected glorified bodies, will share in the literal city and its glory, into which place they can only enter by resurrection. It should be noted that this heavenly Jerusalem is not the sphere of the living saved who go into the millennium, for they will look to the rebuilt earthly Jerusalem as their capital city, but is rather the dwelling place of the resurrected saints during the millennium. The living will realize the fulfillment of the national promises of the Old Testament in the millennium, while the resurrected will realize the fulfillment of the expectation of a "city which hath foundations" during the millennial age.

IV. A Consideration of Related Passages

There are certain passages which seem to indicate that there will not be a great gulf between the saved of Israel and the saved of the church age, but that they will bear a direct relation the one to the other in their final state.

> Other sheep I have, which are not of this fold: them also I must bring, and they shall hear my voice; and there shall be one fold, and one shepherd [John 10:16].

This passage would seem to indicate that there will be a relation of all saved to one another because they are related to the same shepherd. All the redeemed seem to be viewed as united into one flock under one shepherd.

> Then answered Peter and said unto him, Behold, we have forsaken all, and followed thee; what shall we have therefore? And Jesus said unto them, Verily I say unto you, that ye which have followed me, in the regeneration when the Son of man shall sit in the throne of his glory, ye also shall sit upon twelve thrones, judging the twelve tribes of Israel [Matt. 19:27-28].
>
> Do ye not know that the saints shall judge the world [1 Cor. 6:2]?

This portion indicates that the saints who are included in the church are not to be entirely dissociated from the millennial age. If the saints were separated entirely from it, the only way the Twelve could exercise the privilege promised to them would be to lose their position in the body of Christ. This indicates that there will be a relation sustained between the living saints on the earth and the resurrected saints in the heavenly Jerusalem. The saints will exercise the ministry now committed to angels (Heb. 2:5-6).

> And had a wall great and high, and had twelve gates, and at the gates twelve angels, and names written thereon, which are the names of the twelve tribes of the children of Israel.
>
> And the wall of the city had twelve foundations, and in them the names of the twelve apostles of the Lamb [Rev. 21:12, 14].

It would seem to be clear that the occupants of this city are from the Old Testament age, the New Testament age, as well as unfallen angels.

> Blessed and holy is he that hath part in the first resurrection; on such the second death hath no power, but they shall be priests of God and of Christ, and shall reign with him a thousand years [Rev. 20:6].

The first resurrection is composed, not of church age saints alone, but of all individuals, of whatever age, who are raised to eternal life. While this resurrection takes place at different times in reference to different groups, the result is the same in each case —the resurrection to eternal life. These resurrected ones are said to be priests and to reign with Him. This first resurrection in Revelation 20:6 can not be made to apply only to the church saints, for those here resurrected are those that have gone through the great tribulation and thus would not be included in the body of Christ, since the resurrection of the church has preceded this. And yet they are in the first resurrection and will reign with Christ. This must mean that all those who partake in the first resurrection have a common destiny, the New Jerusalem, from which they will be associated with Christ in His reign, whether they be Old or New Testament saint.

> His lord said unto him, Well done, thou good and faithful servant: thou hast been faithful over a few things, I will make thee ruler over many things: enter thou into the joy of thy lord [Matt. 25:21].

In this passage, which teaches the fact of Israel's judgment and reward, it is significant to notice that, while the rewards are said to be positions of privilege and responsibility in the millennium, the individual is not said to be placed in the millennium itself, but rather that he exercises his authority during the millennium.

> And I heard a great voice out of heaven saying, Behold, the tabernacle of God is with men, and he will dwell with them, and they shall be his people, and God himself shall be with them, and be their God [Rev. 21:3].

A comparison of the statement here with that in Ezekiel 37:27, where it was promised to Israel that God would tabernacle with men, and with such passages of Scripture as Isaiah 65:19 or Isaiah 25:8, where God promised release from sorrow, crying, and death, will show that what is promised here is the fulfillment of that which is the expectation of the Old Testament saint. While it may be argued that the church has similar promises, and Revelation 21:3 may refer to the fulfillment of these rather than those of Israel, yet the parallelism seems too significant to affirm that Israel is not included in this blessing. One would not say that there will not be the realization of these promises to Israel on the earth in the millennial age, yet it is suggested that resurrected Israel may experience those promises in the heavenly Jerusalem together with the church saints. It is to be noted that the word translated "people" is plural, "they shall be his peoples," indicating a plurality.

> And they that be wise shall shine as the brightness of the firmament; and they that turn many to righteousness as the stars forever and ever [Dan. 12:3].

A comparison of this verse with Revelation 21:11 and 18, in which context Israel is mentioned (v. 12), would show that the reflected glory of Christ, who is the source of all light, was the expectation of the Old Testament saint. This hope will be realized in the heavenly city in which the Old Testament saint will have a part and will experience the fulfillment of this promise.

> And these all, having obtained a good report through faith, received not the promise: God having provided some better thing for us, that they without us should not be made perfect [Heb. 11:39-40].

It seems to be indicated here that Israel can not be made perfect until the body of Christ has been perfected. This would have added meaning if the place of Israel's saints' perfection and the place of the perfecting of the believers of this age should be one and the same.

If it be argued that such a view would rob the church of her heavenly heritage by uniting her with resurrected Israel and bringing her into a relation to the earth during the millennial age and the new earth to follow, let us follow the observation of Ottman:

> The Church must be located somewhere in eternity, and if God has decreed to make the scene of her conflict the place of her eternal glory, who shall make His purpose void? Such a concrete conception as that of the Church being eternally connected with a literal city descending from heaven may be stigmatized as materialistic and sensuous, but it is better than the vague and misty fog that constitutes the idea of eternity entertained by so many. This city cannot be heaven, for it is said to descend from it. Heaven loses nothing by the loss of the city, nor does the Church lose her heavenly inheritance in her association with Him who has now come to fill the earth with His glory.[10]

If it be argued that such a view would empty heaven and take God from His dwelling place, one would conclude with Newell that

> Several considerations lead us toward the conclusion that the New Jerusalem is God's one eternal resting place.
>
> 1. Immediately we see the new heaven and new earth and the New Jerusalem descending to the new earth (21:1, 2), we are told "Behold, the tabernacle of God is with men" . . . The object of the new heaven and earth is to bring about this—*that God shall eternally have His home* in this capital city of the new creation!
>
> 2. No other eternal habitation of God is seen than this of the New Creation's capital. . . .
>
> 3. This heavenly city has the glory of God (21:11, 23; 22:5). . . .
>
> 4. It also has the *throne* of God, and the "service" of 22:3, properly called priestly service, or spiritual worship. . . .
>
> 5. They shall see his face. . . . This, therefore, must be the place of God's rest forever.

[10] Ottman, *op. cit.*, p. 447.

6. We need only to remember that the dwellers in the New Jerusalem "shall reign unto the ages of the ages" (22:5). This could not be written of others than the inhabitants of the capital of the new creation.[11]

The conclusion to this question would be that the Old Testament held forth a national hope, which will be realized fully in the millennial age. The individual Old Testament saint's hope of an eternal city will be realized through resurrection in the heavenly Jerusalem, where, without losing distinction or identity, Israel will join with the resurrected and translated of the church age to share in the glory of His reign forever. The nature of the millennium, as the period of the test of fallen humanity under the righteous reign of the King, precludes the participation by resurrected individuals in that testing. Thus the millennial age will be concerned only with men who have been saved but are living in their natural bodies. This heavenly city will be brought into a relation to the earth at the beginning of the millennium, and perhaps will be made visible above the earth. It is from this heavenly city that David's greater Son exerts His Messianic rule, in which the Bride reigns, and from which the rewarded Old Testament saints exercise their authority in government.

If such an interpretation be correct, there would be a solution to the perplexing problem that arises from placing resurrected saints on the earth to mingle freely with the unresurrected during the millennium. The fulfillment of Israel's national promises would be realized, not in resurrected individuals, but rather in natural saved Israel who are living at the second advent. The unity of God's redemptive purposes in Christ would be preserved by bringing the first resurrection group together into one place, where the Bride will share in His reign and His servants serve Him forever (Rev. 22:3). Such a view is in harmony with the Scriptures and solves some of the problems inherent in the premillennial system.

---

[11] Newell, *op. cit.*, pp. 353-54.

SECTION SEVEN

PROPHECIES OF THE ETERNAL STATE

Chapter XXXII

THE PREPARATION FOR THE ETERNAL KINGDOM

While the Word of God does not give a great mass of detail concerning the eternal kingdom, sufficient is given to give the child of God a full assurance of the glorious expectation that awaits him in his eternal relation to the Father and the Son. Between the termination of the earthly theocratic kingdom and the union of that kingdom with the eternal kingdom of God certain momentous events transpire, so that every vestige of rebellion shall be obliterated and God shall reign supreme. In this study consideration will not be given to the broad areas of the doctrines of the eternal state, but discussion will be restricted to the questions related to the prophecies of that time.

I. The Purging for the Eternal Kingdom

There are three events predicted in the Scripture that may be viewed as acts of purging the universe of the remnants of the curse so that the eternal kingdom may be fully manifested: (1) the release of Satan and the satanically led revolt, (2) the purging of the earth by fire, and (3) the judgment on sinners at the great white throne.

A. *The release of Satan and the satanically led revolt.* John depicts a scene on the earth at the termination of the millennial age that staggers the imagination.

> And he laid hold on the dragon, that old serpent, which is the Devil, and Satan, and bound him a thousand years, And cast him into the bottomless pit, and shut him up, and set a seal upon

> him, that he should deceive the nations no more, till the thousand years should be fulfilled: and after that he must be loosed a little season.
>
> And when the thousand years are expired, Satan shall be loosed out of his prison, And shall go out to deceive the nations which are in the four quarters of the earth, Gog and Magog, to gather them together to battle: the number of whom is as the sand of the sea. And they went up on the breadth of the earth, and compassed the camp of the saints about, and the beloved city: and fire came down from God out of heaven, and devoured them [Rev. 20:2-3, 7-9].

It has been the interpretation of amillennialists from Augustine to the present day that the "little season" (Rev. 20:3) refers to the present age.[1] According to this view Satan was bound during the earthly ministry of Christ (Luke 10:18), but was to be released at the end of this age. To many, the "little season" has been an extended period, perhaps even the entire age. However, Revelation 20 reveals that the binding of Satan does not take place until after the second advent of Christ and that he continues bound until the termination of the thousand years. The "little season" in which Satan is loosed is after the thousand year reign is completed, prior to the union of the theocratic kingdom with the eternal kingdom. Revelation 20:7 ("When the thousand years are expired, Satan shall be loosed out of his prison") sets the time of this release clearly.

The purpose for which Satan is released is readily discerned from his activity at the time of his loosing. He goes forth to deceive the nations, in order to lead a final revolt against the theocracy of God. There is yet one more attempt on the part of Satan to reach the goal of his first sin. The release of Satan is viewed in Scripture as the final test that demonstrates the corruption of the human heart. God has subjected fallen humanity to numerous tests in the development of His program of the kingdom and of redemption. Man has failed under every test. Scott says: "Alas! what is man? He has been tried and tested under every possible condition, in every possible way — under goodness, government, law, grace, and now under glory."[2] The purpose for which Satan was released, then, was to demonstrate

---

[1] O. T. Allis, *Prophecy and the Church*, p. 3.
[2] Walter Scott, *Exposition of the Revelation of Jesus Christ*, p. 407.

that, even when tested under the reign of the King and the revelation of His holiness, man is a failure. While those going into the millennium were saved, they were not perfected. The progeny born to them during the millennial age were born with the same fallen sin nature with which their parents were born and consequently needed regeneration. During the administration of the King, in which He ruled with a "rod of iron," outward conformity to His law was necessary. The binding of Satan, the removal of external sources of temptation, the fulness of knowledge, the bountiful provision from the King, caused many, whose hearts had not been regenerated, to give this required conformity to the law of the King. There must be a test to determine the true heart condition of the individuals in the age. Jennings writes:

> Has human nature changed, at least apart from sovereign grace? Is the carnal mind at last friendship with God? Have a thousand years of absolute power and absolute benevolence, both in unchecked activity, done away with all war forever and forever? These questions must be marked by a practical test. Let Satan be loosed once more from his prison. Let him range once more earth's smiling fields that he knew of old. He saw them last soaked with blood and flooded with tears, the evidence and accompaniments of his own reign, he sees them now "laughing with abundance." . . .
>
> But as he pursues his way further from Jerusalem, the center of this blessedness, these tokens become fainter; until, in the far-off "corner of the earth," they cease altogether, for he finds myriads who have instinctively shrunk from close contact with that holy center, and are not unprepared once more to be deceived.[3]

The results of this test are set forth by Ottman, who says:

> But even such a sovereignty over the earth does not change the heart of man. A righteous reign, together with all the blessings associated with it, and the full enjoyment of a world redeemed from the curse, does not avail to make man other than he is naturally and the testing and proving of this is accomplished by the loosing of Satan after the thousand years are finished. A thousand years in prison has wrought no moral change in the nature of this evil spirit. He comes up out of his dungeon with his heart filled with the smouldering fire of hate,

[3] F. C. Jennings, *Studies in Revelation*, p. 538.

which immediately flames forth and kindles a revolution among the nations that are in the four corners of the earth.[4]

The problems of the origin of the hosts called "Gog and Magog" (Rev. 20:8) thus finds a solution. To the amillennialist, who views the kingdom as entirely "spiritual," no such rebellion is conceivable. To him the fact of a rebellion proves that there could not have been a millennium such as the premillennialist teaches, else there would have been no rebellion on earth. Allis presents it thus:

> The question as to where Gog, whose armies according to Ezekiel were utterly destroyed before the kingdom age, is to raise up a multitude "the number of whom is as the sand of the sea," with which to attack "the camp of the saints and the beloved city," has been a stumbling-block to Premillennialists, as David Brown pointed out many years ago. Dispensationalists can answer it, as it would seem, only in one or another of three ways: by holding that a race of evil men will come into existence after the millennium, by restricting the extent of the millennial kingdom to a comparatively small part of the earth, or by concluding that the millennial age will to no small degree resemble the present dispensation as an age during which good and evil will both be present and contending for the mastery, so that evil both within the realm of Messiah and outside of it will be kept in subjection only by the rod-of-iron rule of the King who sits on David's throne.[5]

The first two of these explanations must be rejected. There is no Scriptural evidence for the creation of a race of evil men after the millennium. The kingdom of Christ on earth is presented as universal. The third view is in harmony with the Word of God, for Christ's reign is always presented as one of inflexible justice, in which the King does rule "with a rod of iron" (Ps. 2:9). But from among those unregenerated in that day will come the multitude known as "Gog and Magog," who come up against the "camp of the saints," which must be Palestine, and "the beloved city," which must be Jerusalem. It has been demonstrated before that this rebellion can not be identified with that invasion of Gog and Magog, described in Ezekiel 38 and 39, but bears the same name in that the purpose is identical

---

[4] Ford C. Ottman, *The Unfolding of the Ages*, p. 437.
[5] Allis, *op. cit.*, 239-40.

in these two satanically motivated movements: to destroy the seat of theocratic power and the subjects of the theocracy.

This whole program is admittedly difficult. Concerning it Chafer writes:

> It is difficult to understand how such an enterprise will be possible with Christ upon the throne and in immediate authority, as described in Isaiah 11:3-5. . . . There is no solution to this problem other than that of a divine permission in the consummation of evil in the universe. To the same end it may be inquired why with Him upon the throne of the universe He ever permitted the evil which He hates. When, in the light of heaven's understanding, the one problem is solved, the other will be solved also.[6]

Apart from some comprehension of the depth of depravity of the human heart there is no understanding how a multitude, "the number of whom is as the sand of the sea" (Rev. 20:8), could revolt against the Lord Jesus Christ, when they have lived under His beneficence all their lives. But in this rebellion it is demonstrated once again that God is just when He judges sin. And the judgment comes in the form of physical death, through the pouring out of fire, on all the rebels assembled under Satan's leadership (Rev. 20:9). In this manner God removes all unbelief from the theocratic kingdom in anticipation of its merger with the eternal kingdom of God.

B. *The purging of creation.* Because of Adam's sin in the garden a curse was placed upon the earth by God, as He said: "Cursed is the ground for thy sake; in sorrow shalt thou eat of it all the days of thy life; Thorns also and thistles shall it bring forth to thee" (Gen. 3:17-18). It thus becomes necessary to remove the last vestige of this curse from the earth before the manifestation of the eternal kingdom. This event is described by Peter:

> But the day of the Lord will come as a thief in the night; in the which the heavens shall pass away with a great noise, and the elements shall melt with fervent heat, the earth also and the works that are therein shall be burned up. Seeing then that all these things shall be dissolved, what manner of persons ought ye to be in all holy conversation and godliness, Looking for and

---

[6] Lewis Sperry Chafer, *Systematic Theology*, V, 361.

> hasting unto the coming of the day of God, wherein the heavens being on fire shall be dissolved, and the elements shall melt with fervent heat? Nevertheless we, according to his promise, look for new heavens and a new earth, wherein dwelleth righteousness [2 Pet. 3:10-13].[7]

This passing of the present earth is anticipated in a number of passages (Matt. 24:35; Heb. 1:10-12; Rev. 20:11).

It is held by some that this purging of the earth precedes the millennial age. According to this view this purgation will take place at the beginning of the millennium and will be the cause of the removal of the curse so that productivity may be restored to the earth during that time. There are several bases on which this view rests.

(1) They hold that the "day of the Lord" (2 Pet. 3:10), in which this event is said to take place, is a time of judgment and includes only the time from the rapture to the institution of the millennium, with its attendant judgments. (2) Because judgment by fire is said to be a means of the visitation of divine wrath at the second advent (Isa. 66:15, 17; Ezek. 39:6; Joel 2:1-11; 2 Thess. 1:7-10), and since this purging is by fire, it is argued that it must be the same event. (3) Isaiah 65:17 promises a new earth, and that in connection with the millennium, so the purging must take place after the second advent but prior to the millennium. In reply it may be pointed out, as it has been demonstrated previously, that (1) the Day of the Lord includes the whole program from the beginning of the tribulation period through to the new heaven and new earth after the millennium. (2) Further, fire may be a means of divine visitation without making every use of it necessarily come within the same event. Fire is used throughout Scripture as a symbol of judgment and since this event is judgment upon a cursed earth it is fitting to see the purgation by fire at the time the earth is to have every blot of the curse removed from it. (3) And again, since the millennial earth merges with the new heaven and new earth at the end of the age, Isaiah may well describe the millennial scene in view of its eternal dwelling place, the new heavens and new earth, without stating that the new heaven and new earth

---

7 Cf. G. N. H. Peters, *Theocratic Kingdom,* II, 506-23.

is realized at the beginning of the millennium, although anticipated from that point.

It is to be noted that Peter does not say that the Day of the Lord commences with the dissolution of the present earth, but that *within* the day of the Lord this dissolution will take place. His word is: "The day of the Lord will come as a thief in the night; *in the which* [italics mine] the heavens shall pass away with a great noise and the elements shall melt with fervent heat . . ." (2 Pet. 3:10). Further, Peter states: "But the heavens and the earth, which are now, by the same word are kept in store, reserved unto judgment and perdition of ungodly men" (2 Pet. 3:7). In this statement he seems to relate the dissolution of the present heaven and earth to the time of the judgment and perdition of ungodly men, which we know from Revelation 20:11-15, takes place at the great white throne judgment after the millennium. If it be held that this cannot refer to the same time since John says, "from whose face the earth and the heaven fled away" (Rev. 20:11) and Peter says, "reserved unto fire against the day of judgment" (2 Pet. 3:7), it is sufficient to say that John's statement gives the fact that the old heaven and earth have passed away without giving the means by which this is accomplished, while Peter gives the means through which the dissolution takes place. There is no contradiction here. It is thus concluded that the purging is the act of God at the end of the millennial age after the final revolt against His authority, in which the earth, the scene of rebellion, is judged because of its curse.

C. *The judgment on sinners.* Before the great white throne appear all "the dead" (Rev. 20:12). Those resurrected unto life have all been called out of the grave a thousand years earlier (Rev. 20:3-6). Those resurrected here are to be judged to be appointed unto the "second death" (Rev. 20:14), that is, eternal separation from the kingdom of God. This is the final act in the program that was enacted "that God may be all in all" (1 Cor. 15:28). Since this program has been developed previously it need not be repeated here. The summary of Kelly suffices:

> The dead were judged, but not out of the book of life which has nothing to do with judgment. "The dead were judged out of

> those things which were written in the books according to their works." Why then is the book of life mentioned? Not because any of their names were written therein, but in proof that they were not. The book of life will confirm what is gathered from the books. If the books proclaim the evil works of the dead that stand before the throne, the book of life offers no defense on the score of God's grace. Scripture records no name whatever as written there among those judged. There was the sad register of undeniable sins on the one side; there was no writing of the name on the other side. Thus, whether the books or the book be examined, all conspire to declare the justice, the solemn but most affecting righteousness, of God's final irrevocable sentence. They were judged, each one, according to their works. "And if any one was not found written in the book of life, he was cast into the lake of fire." Thus the only use that seems made of the book is negative and exclusive. Not that any of those judged (and the scene described is solely a resurrection of judgment) are said to be written there: we are shown rather that they were *not* found in the book.
>
> Neither the sea nor the unseen world could longer hide their prisoners. "'And the sea gave up the dead that [were] in it, and death and hades gave up the dead that [were] in them: and they were judged, each one, according to their works."
>
> Again, Death and Hades are said to come to their end, personified as enemies. "And death and hades were cast into the lake of fire. This is the second death, the lake of fire." Thus was concluded all dealing on the Lord's part with soul and body, and all that pertains to either. The race was now in the resurrection state either for good or for ill; and thus it must be forever. Death and Hades, which had so long been executioners in a world where sin reigned, and still did their occasional office when righteousness reigned, themselves disappear where all traces of sin are consigned for ever. God is "all in all."[8]

God's purpose in the judgments prior to the millennium was to "gather out of his kingdom all things that offend, and them which do iniquity; And shall cast them into a furnace of fire: there shall be wailing and gnashing of teeth" (Matt. 13:41-42). God's purpose in the judgments at the end of the millennium is to remove from the eternal kingdom "all things that offend, and them which do iniquity." By this judgment God's absolute sovereignty has now been manifested.

---

[8] William Kelly, *The Revelation Expounded*, pp. 243-44.

D. *The destiny of the lost.* The destiny of the lost is a place in the lake of fire (Rev. 19:20; 20:10, 14-15; 21:8). This lake of fire is described as everlasting fire (Matt. 25:41; 18:8) and as unquenchable fire (Mark 9:43-44, 46, 48), emphasizing the eternal character of the retribution of the lost. In this connection Chafer well observes:

> In attempting to write a comprehensive statement of the most solemn doctrine of the Bible, the term *retribution* is chosen in place of the more familiar word *punishment* since the latter implies discipline and amendment, which idea is wholly absent from the body of truth which discloses the final divine dealing with those who are eternally lost. It is recognized that, in its earlier and broader meaning, the term *retribute* was used for any reward, good or evil. The word is used . . . of the doctrine of hell only as reference is made to the eternal perdition of the *lost.*[9]

Concerning the retribution of the lost, it is important to observe that the lake of fire is *a place,* not just a state, although a state is involved.

> As heaven is a *place* and not a mere state of mind, in like manner those reprobated go to a place. This truth is indicated by the words *hades* (Matt. 11:23; 16:18; Luke 10:15; 16:23; Rev. 1.18; 20:13-14) and *gehenna* (Matt. 5:22, 29-30; 10:28; James 3:6) —a place of "torment" (Luke 16:28). That it is a condition of unspeakable misery is indicated by the figurative terms used to describe its sufferings—"everlasting fire" (Matt. 25:41); "Where their worm dieth not, and the fire is not quenched" (Mark 9:44); "the lake which burneth with fire and brimstone" (Rev. 21:8); "bottomless pit" (Rev. 9:2); "outer darkness," a place of "weeping and gnashing of teeth" (Matt. 8:12); "fire unquenchable" (Luke 3:17); "furnace of fire" (Matt. 13:42); "blackness of darkness" (Jude 1:13), and "the smoke of their torment ascendeth up for ever and ever: and they have no rest day nor night" (Rev. 14:11). In these instances a figure of speech is not a license to modify the thought which the figure expresses; it is rather to be recognized that a figure of speech, in these passages, is a feeble attempt to declare in language that which is beyond the power of words to describe. . . . It is well to observe, also, that nearly every one of these expressions fell from the lips of Christ. He alone has disclosed almost all that is revealed of this place of

[9] Chafer, *op. cit.*, IV, 429.

> retribution. It is as though no human author could be depended upon to speak forth *all* of this terrible truth.[10]

1. There are four different words used in the Scriptures to describe the place of the dead until the time of resurrection. In no instance do these words describe the eternal state, but rather the temporary place in which the dead await resurrection. The first is *Sheol,* which is used sixty-five times in the Old Testament, translated "hell" thirty-one times (cf. Deut. 32:22; Ps. 9:17; 18:5; Isa. 14:9), "grave" thirty-one times (cf. 1 Sam. 2:6; Job 7:9; 14:13), and "pit," three times (cf. Num. 16:30, 33; Job 17:16). This was the Old Testament word for the abode of the dead. It was presented, not just as a state of existence, but as a place of conscious existence (Deut. 18:11; 1 Sam. 28:11-15; Isa. 14:9). God was sovereign over it (Deut. 32:22; Job 26:6). It was regarded as temporary and the righteous anticipated the resurrection out of it into the millennial age (Job 14:13-14; 19:25, 27; Ps.16:9-11; 17:15; 49:15; 73:24). On this word *Sheol* it has been written:

> . . . a few facts stand out very clearly. (i.) It will be observed that in a majority of cases *Sheol* is rendered "the grave." . . . *The grave,* therefore, stands out on the face of the above list as the best and commonest rendering. (ii.) With regard to the word "pit," it will be observed that in each of the three cases where it occurs (Num. 16:30, 33; and Job 17:16), *the grave* is so evidently meant, that we may at once substitute that word, and banish "pit" from our consideration as a rendering of *Sheol.* (iii.) as to the rendering "hell," it does *not* represent *Sheol,* because both by Dictionary definition and by colloquial usage "hell" means the place of *further punishment, Sheol* has no such meaning, but denotes *the present state of death.* "The grave" is, therefore, a far more suitable translation, because it visibly suggests to us what is invisible to the mind, *viz.,* the state of death. It must, necessarily, be misleading to the English reader to see the former put to represent the latter. (iv.) The student will find that "THE grave," taken literally as well as figuratively, will meet all the requirements of the Hebrew *Sheol:* not that *Sheol* means so much specifically A grave, as generically THE grave. Holy Scripture is all-sufficient to explain the word *Sheol* to us. (v.) If we enquire of it in the above list of occurrences of the word *Sheol,* it will teach (a) That as to *direction* it is down. (b)

---

[10] *Ibid.,* IV, 430-31.

That as to *place* it is in the earth. (c) That as to *nature* it is put for the *state of death.* Not the *act* of dying, for which we have no English word, but the *state* or duration of death. The Germans are more fortunate, having the word *sterbend* for the act of dying. *Sheol* therefore means *the state of death;* or *the state of the dead,* of which *the grave* is a tangible evidence. It has to do only with the dead. It may sometimes be personified and represented by a coined word, "Grave-dom," as meaning the dominion or power of *the grave.* (d) As to *relation* it stands in contrast with the state of the living, see Deut. 30:15, 19, and I Sam. 2:6-8. It is never once connected with the living, except by contrast. (e) As to *association,* it is used in connection with mourning (Gen. 37:34-35), sorrow (Gen. 42:38; 2 Sam. 22:6; Ps. 18:5; 116:3), fright and terror (Num. 16:27-34); weeping (Isa. 38:3, 10, 15, 20), silence (Ps. 31:17; 6:5; Eccles. 9:10), no knowledge (Eccles. 9:5-6, 10), punishment (Num. 16:27-34; I Kings 2:6, 9; Job 24:19; Ps. 9:17, R. V., RE-turned, as before their resurrection). (f) And, finally, as to *duration,* the dominion of *Sheol* or the grave will continue until, and end only with, *resurrection,* which is the only exit from it (see Hos. 13:14, etc., and compare Ps. 16:10 with Acts 2:27, 31; 13:35).[11]

2. The second word to describe the place of the dead is *Hades.* In the New Testament this word is practically equivalent to Sheol, translated "hell" in every instance but one (1 Cor. 15:55, where it is translated "grave"). Generally this word has in view the unsaved dead, who are in misery, awaiting the resurrection unto the great white throne. On *Hades* it is observed:

If now the *eleven* occurrences of Hades in the New Testament be carefully examined, the following conclusions will be reached: (a) *Hades* is invariably connected with *death;* but *never with life:* always with *dead* people; but never with the *living.* All in *Hades* will "NOT LIVE AGAIN," until they are raised from the dead (Rev. 20:5). If they do not "live again" until after they are raised, it is perfectly clear that they cannot be *alive* now. Otherwise we do away with the doctrine of resurrection altogether. (b) That the English word "hell" by no means represents the Greek *Hades;* as we have seen that it does not give a correct idea of its Hebrew equivalent. *Sheol.* (c) That *Hades* can mean only and exactly what *Sheol* means, viz., the place

[11] E. W. Bullinger, *A Critical Lexicon and Concordance to the English and Greek New Testament,* pp. 368-69.

where "corruption" is seen (Acts 2:31; compare 13:34-37); and from which, *resurrection* is the only exit."[12]

Scofield is representative of many who distinguish between the abode of departed saved individuals before and after Christ's resurrection. He says:

(1) *Hades before the ascension of Christ.* The passage in which the word occurs make it clear that hades was formerly in two divisions, the abodes respectively of the saved and of the lost. The former was called "paradise" and "Abraham's bosom." Both designations were Talmudic, but adopted by Christ in Lk. 16:22; 23:43. The blessed dead were with Abraham, they were conscious and were "comforted" (Lk. 16:25). The believing malefactor was to be, that day, with Christ in "paradise." The lost were separated from the saved by a "great gulf fixed" (Lk. 16:26). The representative man of the lost who are now in hades is the rich man of Lk. 16:19-31. He was alive, conscious, in the full exercise of his faculties, memory, etc., and in torment.

(2) *Hades since the ascension of Christ.* So far as the unsaved dead are concerned, no change of their place or condition is revealed in Scripture. At the judgment of the great white throne, hades will give them up, they will be judged, and will pass into the lake of fire (Rev. 20:13-14). But a change has taken place which affects paradise. Paul was "caught up to the third heaven . . . into paradise" (2 Cor. 12:1-4). Paradise, therefore, is now in the immediate presence of God. It is believed that Eph. 4:8-10 indicates the time of the change. "When he ascended up on high he led a multitude of captives." It is immediately added that He had previously "descended first into the lower parts of the earth," i. e., the paradise division of hades. During the present church-age the saved who die are "absent from the body, at home with the Lord." The wicked dead in hades, and the righteous dead "at home with the Lord," alike await the resurrection (Job 19:25; I Cor. 15:52).[13]

3. The third word is *Tartaros* and is used only in 2 Peter 2:4 in reference to the judgment on the wicked angels. It seems to have specific reference to the eternal abode of the wicked angels.

Tartaros . . . is not *Sheol* or *Hades* . . . where all men go in death. Nor is it where the wicked are to be consumed and destroyed, which is Gehenna . . . Not the abode of men in any con-

---

[12] *Ibid.*, p. 369.
[13] C. I. Scofield, *Reference Bible*, pp. 1098-99.

> dition. It is used only here, and here only of "angels that sinned" (see Jude 6). It denotes the bounds or verge of this material world. The extremity of this lower air — of which Satan is "the prince" (Eph. 2:2) and of which Scripture speaks as having "the rulers of the darkness of this world" and "Wicked spirits in aerial regions." "*Tartaros* is not only the bounds of this material creation, but is so called from its coldness."[14]

4. The fourth word used of the abode of the dead is *Gehenna,* used twelve times in the New Testament (Matt. 5:22, 29-30; 10:28; 18:9; 23:15, 33; Mk. 9:43, 45, 47; Luke 12:5; Jas. 3:6). In each instance it is used as a geographical term and has the final state of the unsaved in view. Judgment is presupposed and this is the resultant place and state. Vos writes:

> In the NT . . . it designates the place of eternal punishment of the wicked, generally in connection with the final judgment. It is associated with fire as the source of torment. Both body and soul are cast into it. This is not to be explained on the principle that the NT speaks metaphorically of the state after death in terms of the body; it presupposes the resurrection. In AV and RV Gehenna is rendered by "hell" . . . That "the valley of Hinnom" became the technical designation for the place of final punishment was due to two causes. In the first place the valley had been the seat of the idolatrous worship of Molech, to whom children were immolated by fire (2 Ch. 28:3; 33:6). Secondly, on account of these practices the place was defiled by King Josiah (2 K. 23:10), and became in consequence associated in prophecy with the judgment to be visited upon the people (Jer. 7:32). The fact, also, that the city's offal was collected there may have helped to render the name synonymous with extreme defilement.[15]

Gehenna would then have in view the retribution in the lake of fire as the destiny of the wicked.

In Matthew 25:41 the Lord said to the wicked, "Depart from me, ye cursed, into everlasting fire, prepared for the devil and his angels." The word "prepared" literally is "having been prepared," suggesting that the lake of fire is already in existence and awaiting its occupants. It is the thesis of C. T. Schwarze, then of New York University, that such a place as a lake of fire is known to science today. He writes:

---

14 Bullinger, *op. cit.,* p. 370.

15 Geerhardus Vos, "Gehenna" *International Standard Bible Encyclopedia,* II, 1183.

The word *lake* must connote a body of matter having liquid form. Therefore, if Scripture is truth, this eternal fire must be in liquid form.

. . . .

. . . the very simple proof of the portions of Scripture we have been discussing *lies in the existence of the singular phenomena of the skies known as midget or white dwarf stars!* . . . a midget star is one which, because of some things which have happened to it (not quite clear at this time), should be roughly 5,000 or more *times* as big as it really is! Applying this idea for illustration to such a planet as the earth, you must conceive the earth as having shrunk to such an extent that its diameter would be about 400 miles . . . instead of being 8,000 miles in diameter as it really is.

. . . .

This enormous density . . . has a great deal to do with our subject. . . . Most people know the sun, our nearest star is rather hot . . . there is general agreement that the temperature at or near the center of stars is between 25 million and 30 million degrees Fahrenheit! . . . at such temperatures, much can happen, like the bursting of atoms, which helps to explain the phenomenon of the white dwarf. . . .

. . . .

. . . a temperature of 30,000,000 degrees Fahrenheit could explode atoms. . . .

It would cause the atoms to lose their electrons even though the attraction between nucleus and electrons is an octillion . . . times the attraction of gravity. The separated parts could then be better packed in, particularly under such great pressure. . . . With the constant activity of X-rays, atom walls could not be re-formed; therefore enormous densities, such as are found in the midgets, can be attained. Now, please note, at such high temperatures all matter would be in the form of gas . . . in a white dwarf the pressure is so great that gasses become compressed to the consistency of a liquid although they may still respond to the characteristics of a gas. . . .

. . . .

. . . Before such a star could cool off and gradually become dark it would have to expand to normal proportions. That is, it would have to get to be more than 5,000 times its present size. Here is the difficulty. Such expansion would cause enormous heat which, in turn, would absolutely keep the star compressed, so that, *insofar as astronomers and physicists know, the midget stars can never cool off!* . . . The white dwarf, to all intents, *can never burn out.*

> . . . may I summarize to show that the Bible, God's Word, is scientifically accurate? We find, first, an eternal fire which cannot burn out. Being of a liquid consistency it is, secondly, a lake of fire. In the third place, it cannot be quenched, for any quenching material, such as water, would immediately have its atoms stripped of electrons and be packed in with the rest. In the fourth place, since astronomers have been, and still are, studying this strange phenomenon, it is only too evident that the lake of fire *has been prepared* and is now ready. Although we cannot say that God will actually use these lakes of fire in fulfilling His Word, the answer to the skeptic is in the heavens where there *are* lakes of fire. . . .[16]

The resurrection body of the unsaved, evidently, will be of such character that it is indestructible even in the midst of such a lake of fire.

II. The Creation of the New Heaven and New Earth

After the dissolution of the present heaven and earth at the end of the millennium, God will create a new heaven and a new earth (Isa. 65:17; 66:22; 2 Pet. 3:13; Rev. 21:1). By a definite act of creation God calls into being a new heaven and a new earth. As God created the present heavens and earth to be the scene of His theocratic display, so God will create the new heavens and earth to be the scene of the eternal theocratic kingdom of God.

Israel's covenants guarantee that people the land, a national existence, a kingdom, a King, and spiritual blessings in perpetuity. Therefore there must be an eternal earth in which these blessings can be fulfilled. By a translation out of the old earth Israel will be brought into the new earth, there to enjoy forever all that God has promised to them. Then it shall be eternally true, "Behold, the tabernacle of God is with men, and he will dwell with them, and they shall be his people, and God himself shall be with them, and be their God" (Rev. 21:3). The creation of the new heavens and new earth is the final preparatory act anticipating the eternal kingdom of God. It is now true that God has a kingdom "wherein dwelleth righteousness" (2 Pet. 3:13).

---

[16] C. T. Schwarze, "The Bible and Science on the Everlasting Fire," *Bibliotheca Sacra*, 95:105-112, January, 1938.

In relation to the eternal destiny of the church saints, it is to be observed that their destiny primarily is related to a Person rather than a place. While the place looms with importance (John 14:3), the place is overshadowed by the Person into whose presence the believer is taken.

> And if I go and prepare a place for you, I will come again, and receive you *unto myself*, that where I am, there ye may be also [John 14:3].
>
> When Christ, who is our life, shall appear, then shall ye also appear *with him* in glory [Col. 3:4].
>
> For the Lord himself shall descend from heaven with a shout, with the voice of the archangel, and with the trump of God; and the dead in Christ shall rise first: Then we which are alive and remain shall be caught up together with them in the clouds, *to meet the Lord* in the air: and so shall we ever be *with the Lord* [1 Thess. 4:16-17].
>
> Beloved, now are we the sons of God, and it doth not yet appear what we shall be: but we know that, when he shall appear, we shall be like him; we shall *see him* as he is [1 John 3:2]. [Italics mine.]

It is the Person who is emphasized in all the passages dealing with the glorious expectation of the church rather than the place to which they are taken.

It has already been demonstrated from passages such as Revelation 21:3 that the Lord Jesus Christ will be dwelling with men on the new earth in the eternal kingdom. Since Scripture reveals that the church will be with Christ, it is concluded that the eternal abode of the church will likewise be in the new earth, in that heavenly city, New Jerusalem, that has been especially prepared by God for the saints. Such a relationship would be the answer to the Lord's prayer for those God had given Him: "Father, I will that they also, whom thou hast given me, be with me where I am; that they may behold my glory, which thou hast given me" (John 17:24). Since the eternal glory of Christ will be manifested in the eternal kingdom, in his eternal rule, it is natural that the church should be there to behold that glorification of Christ forever.

Chapter XXXIII

THE HEAVENLY CITY NEW JERUSALEM

There are few passages of Scripture on which there is such a wide divergence of opinion among dispensational premillennialists as Revelation 21:9 to 22:7. Some see this as descriptive of the eternal state while others see it as descriptive of the millennial age. Some interpret the city as referring to the church in relation to Christ and others as referring to Israel in her relation to Christ. Some take this as a literal city and others as a symbolical representation. Many and varied are the interpretations given to this passage of Scripture.

I. Where Does Revelation 21:9 to 22:7 Fit into the Prophetic Picture?

The main features of the major interpretations of this passage must be examined in an effort to establish a position which is in harmony with the whole revelation of the Word of God.

A. *Revelation 21:9 to 22:7 describes the millennium.*

The view held by Darby, Gaebelein, Grant, Ironside, Jennings, Kelly, Pettingill, Seiss, Scott, and others is the view that after describing the eternal state in Revelation 21:1-8 John gives a recapitulation of the millennial age, in order to describe more fully that period of time. There are a number of arguments presented by the advocates of this interpretation to support their view.

1. *The principle of retrospection in the book of Revelation.* Kelly, one of the foremost exponents of the view that this passage relates to the millennial age, writes:

> . . . it is the manner of God in this book to take a retrospect. I say this to shew that I am not at all arguing for something without precedent. . . . Take for instance, chapter xiv. There we had seen a regular sevenfold series of events, in the

> course of which the fall of Babylon occupies the third place . . . Babylon there has got its place assigned very clearly . . . But long after this in the prophecy, when the Spirit of God has given us the seven vials of God's wrath, we have Babylon again. . . . In this case the Holy Ghost has carried us down in chapter xiv. to events subsequent to Babylon's fall, and even to the Lord's coming in judgment; and then He returns to shew us details about Babylon and her connection with the beast, and the kings of the earth, in chapters xvii-xviii.
>
> Now it appears to me that this exactly answers to the order of the events in Chapter xxi.[1]

In reply to such a position, Ottman writes:

> This expanded vision of the new Jerusalem does not, for its interpretation, demand a return in thought to the conditions existing during the Millennium. The Millennium is the theme, indeed, of the prophecies in the Old Testament, and beyond the Millennium these prophecies rarely go. There are only two passages— and both of them in Isaiah—that give but a brief glance at what lies beyond the Millennial reign of Christ. . . . This is the general character of Old Testament prophecy, which does not contemplate anything beyond the earthly reign of the Messiah. Such a limitation, however, is found nowhere in the New Testament, and a return to the Millennial earth in this vision of John would be incongruous and perplexing.[2]

It could be further argued that the two passages referred to by Kelly are not parallel, for in the first retrospection we have a return from time to an event in time, but in the second it is a retrospection from eternity back into time. Thus the parallelism is destroyed.

2. *The ministry of the vial angel.* Many writers agree with Darby in identifying this passage as millennial because of the speaker who introduces the scenes in Revelation 17:1 and 21:9. Darby says:

> In comparing verse 9 with chapter xvii. 1, you will find this likeness, that it is one of the seven angels who have the seven vials that gives the description of Babylon, and that it is one of them also who describes the bride of the Lamb, the holy city, with the whole of the prophecy from verse 9. . . .

---

1 William Kelly, *Lectures on the Revelation*, pp. 460-61.
2 Ford C. Ottman, *The Unfolding of the Ages*, p. 458.

> What is found in chapters xxi. 9-27 and xxii. 1-5 does not form a continuation, either historical or prophetic, of what precedes. It is a description of the New Jerusalem, and there are many circumstances which precede what is in the beginning of the chapter. The angel, in the same manner, describes Babylon after having given her victory.[3]

To this it could be replied that there is no real parallelism between the revelation of the angel in these two passages. Babylon is introduced in Revelation 16:19 and the retrospection follows immediately in chapters 17 and 18. But in revealing the events at the close of chapter 20, with which 21:9—22:5 would be associated if it refers to the millennium, eternity intervenes between the statement and the retrospection and explanation. Thus the parallelism is destroyed.

3. *The use of dispensational names.* Kelly seeks to further substantiate his interpretation by observing:

> It will be observed also that in the portion relative to the millennium (that is, from verse 9 of chap. xxi.) we have dispensational names, such as the Lord God Almighty and the Lamb; not so in chapter xxi. 1-8, which discloses eternity, where God shall be all in all.[4]

In reply to this it could be stated that these names are not necessarily dispensational in their connotation. The title *Lamb,* as applied to Christ antedates time, for it is so used in 1 Peter 1:19. It is used by John in the age of law in John 1:29. It is employed in the age of grace in Acts 8:32. It is used in the tribulation period in Revelation 7:14. The name *Lamb* is an eternal name given to Christ in view of His completed sacrifice and eternal redemption and can not be confined to one age or people. The name *Almighty* is used more than thirty times in the prepatriarchal book of Job and thus can not be confined to one people or age. This name will take on new significance in that it has been demonstrated through the destruction of the last enemy that God is the Almighty.

4. *The healing of the nations.* It is argued that the necessity of healing, as taught in Revelation 22:2, requires that this pas-

[3] J. N. Darby, *Notes on the Apocalypse*, pp. 149-50.
[4] William Kelly, *The Revelation,* p. 460.

sage be viewed as millennial. Jennings says, "Healing is applicable to the inevitable consequences of that evil principle, sin, still in us, as then in the nations; compassion and grace can meet those consequences with healing.[5] And Kelly adds, ". . . in eternity nations will not exist as such; neither will any need healing then."[6] Scott notes the parallelism between this passage and Ezekiel 47:12, and says:

> The millennial nations are dependent on the city above, for light, for government, and for healing. All this has its counterpart in that remarkable chapter in Ezek. 47. "The fruit thereof shall be for meat, and the leaf thereof for medicine" (v. 12). Both the scene above (Rev. 22), and the scene below (Ezek. 47) are millennial, and both exist at the *same* time, but the blessing of the former infinitely transcends that of the latter. The tree of life sustains; the river of life gladdens.[7]

In reply to this reasoning Ottman says:

> But the two visions are not the same. The range of Ezekiel's prophecy does not extend beyond the Millennium, whereas John's is of Eternity. Ezekiel's, nevertheless, is typical of the one in Revelation. . . . We must remember that the Millennium represents Heaven only typically, and even though their descriptive terms seem to harmonize here, we are not to confuse the two. The healing of the nations here spoken of does not necessarily involve a return to Millennial conditions. The nations that are in existence at the close of the thousand years of Christ's reign need healing for the full and final blessing which is afterwards to be ushered in.[8]

It could further be observed that often times in the prophets healing is used in a spiritual sense rather than a literal sense. Thus a reference to some specific sin or infirmity which necessitates a millennial interpretation need not be inferred.

It could be noted further that a tree of life was in the garden to sustain life for Adam in his unfallen state. It did not there have reference to sin or disease and need not here.

5. *The existence of nations.* Kelly argues at length that

---

[5] F. C. Jennings, *Studies in Revelation*, p. 588.
[6] Kelly, *op. cit.*, p. 488.
[7] Walter Scott, *Exposition of the Revelation of Jesus Christ*, pp. 440-41.
[8] Ottman, *op. cit.*, p. 472.

the mention of nations in this passage necessitates its reference to the millennial age.

> In the eternal state God has to do with men. All time distinctions are at an end. There is no such thing then as kings and nations. . . . if we look at the latter part of the chapter, we have again to do with nations and earthly kings. . . . When eternity begins, God has done dealing with things according to the order of the world—kings and nations, and the like provisions of a temporal nature. All this implies government, as government supposes that there is evil which requires suppression. Consequently, in the latter part of our chapter it is not the eternal condition which we have, but a previous state. . . .[9]

In answer to this objection Ottman writes:

> Although the earth be dissolved by fire, Israel does not cease to be the object of God's love, but as a nation survives this judgment. This is perfectly evident from the passage in Isaiah that goes beyond the Millennial reign, and declares the continuance of Israel in connection with the new heavens and the new earth. (Is. 66:22). That none of the other Millennial nations should in like manner survive the dissolution of the earth is almost inconceivable. . . . Thus they also shall have their connection with the new earth, but distinct from the Church and Israel.[10]

Much of the argument seems to turn on the interpretation of the preposition *eis* in Revelation 21:26. Kelly, a careful Greek student, states, "Not *into,* but *unto,* for which in Greek there is but one word, *eis*."[11] He thus, by this translation, substantiates his view that this scene in Revelation 21:26 is millennial and the nations will approach *unto* the city. Ottman insists on the translation *into* and says:

> At the close of the Millennium, as during it, there shall be nations. In this conception there is no difficulty, nor is there any in the fact of their having access to the holy city, unto which they shall bring their glory and honor.
>
> Dean Alford says: . . . "If the kings of the earth, and the nations bring their glory and their treasures into her, and if none shall ever enter into her that is not written in the book of life, it follows, that these kings, and these nations, are written

---

[9] Kelly, *op. cit.*, pp. 459-60.
[10] Ottman, *op. cit.*, p. 470.
[11] Kelly, *op. cit.*, p. 481, footnote.

in the book of life. . . . There may be . . . those who have been saved by Christ without ever forming a part of His visible organized Church."[12]

6. *The ministry of angels.* Scott argues that this must be millennial because "We have had no angelic ministrations in the scene of eternity, here they are prominent."[13] Such a ministry, he feels, necessitates a millennial interpretation.

Against this it may be stated that the description given to us of the eternal state in Revelation 21:1-8 is very brief. It is an argument from silence to infer that there will be no angelic ministry in eternity. In Hebrews 12:22 angels are said to inhabit the heavenly Jerusalem, the city of the living God. It is not necessary to exclude them from eternity because of the silence in Revelation 21:1-8.

Such are the main arguments of the protagonists of this position and the refutations given by its antagonists. It is interesting to note the observation of Kelly, who, although holding strongly to the millennial position, states, "But there are certain features in it which are true everlastingly."[14]

B. *Revelation 21:9 to 22:7 describes the eternal state.*

The view held by Govett, Larkin, Newell, Ottman and others is the view that Revelation 21:1 through 22:7 refers to the eternal state. They offer a number of arguments to support their position.

1. *The adjective "new" as used in Revelation 21:1-2.* There are three new things mentioned in these verses: a new heaven, a new earth, and a new Jerusalem. It is argued that the new Jerusalem of verse 2 and the holy Jerusalem of verse 10 must be the same and since it is related to the new heaven and new earth, which represents eternity in the first instance, it must represent eternal positions in the second also.

To this argument it may be replied that the city of verse 10 is seen in the process of descent, not to the earth, but to be sus-

---

[12] Ottman, *op. cit.*, p. 469.
[13] Scott, *op. cit.*, p. 429.
[14] Kelly, *op. cit.*, p. 489.

pended over the earth. It is not until eternity (verse 2) that the final descent to the earth is described, at which time the new heaven, the new earth, and the new Jerusalem will be in relationship to each other.

2. *The position of the city in Revelation 21:10.* It is generally agreed by interpreters of both views that the city seen in Revelation 21:10 is suspended over the earth. On this basis it is argued that this could not be the millennial scene, for in the millennium the Lord returns to the earth and His feet stand on the mount of Olives (Zech. 14:4). The Lord, it is argued, will reign from earthly Jerusalem, not heavenly Jerusalem. Since this city is not on the earth it can not be millennial, for it obviously is the center of the habitation of the Lamb.

In reply it may be argued that Christ will return to the earth at the second advent and He will reign on David's throne. The center of that authority is recognized to be earthly Jerusalem. That does not necessitate the presence of Christ on that throne constantly. Christ may still reign on David's throne over David's Kingdom, but make the heavenly Jerusalem His place of residence with His Bride.

3. *The characteristics of the city are eternal, not millennial.* Advocates of the position that this passage refers to the eternal state point out a number of descriptions within it that are eternal in character. It has the "glory of God" within it. Unsaved could not stand that glory, but would be struck down as Paul was (Acts 9:3). It has no temple (v. 22), and it is clearly predicted in Ezekiel 40—48 that there will be a temple in the millennial earth. There is no night there (v. 25), and there will be day and night in the millennium (Isa. 30:26; 60:19-20). The throne of God is there (22:3). There is no more curse there (22:3), so the effects of the fall are removed. All who are there are saved (21:27) so this must be eternity, since unsaved will be born during the millennium. There is no more death (21:4) and since individuals will die during the millennium (Isa. 65:20) it must refer to the eternal state.

To these observations it could be replied that Matthew 25:31 indicates that Christ will assume the "throne of His glory" at the second advent and will certainly occupy that throne throughout the millennium. The absence of the temple is not a deciding argument for Ezekiel's temple is in the earthly Jerusalem and there would be no need of a temple in the heavenly Jerusalem for the Lamb Himself is there. In like manner, the absence of night is not decisive, for there will be night on the the millennial earth, but need not be in the heavenly city, since the Lamb is there to give light. The curse could refer to the lifting of the curse on the earth because of sin, so that productivity may return to original capacity and the venom of animal creation and the enmity between man and the animals may be removed (Isa. 11) and it need not refer to the final removal of the curse through the conflagration described in 2 Peter 3:10. Only saved could enter this city to dwell there, but unsaved might dwell on the earth during the millennium in its light. Such a line of argument could be used to show that these references are not necessarily confined to eternity.

4. *The length of the reign.* It is stated in Revelation 22:5 that the saints are to reign "forever and ever." When the reign of the saints who are in the millennium is referred to in Revelation 20:4 they are said to reign "with Christ for a thousand years." A thousand years is not forever. Since these reign forever it must refer to eternity and not the millennium.

In reply to this argument it could be pointed out that Christ's kingdom is not limited to a thousand years. He will reign forever. The millennial kingdom issues into the eternal kingdom so the saints may be said to reign for a thousand years although they will continue to reign on into eternity.

5. *The existence of nations in eternity.* Newell, in defending the position that this whole section describes eternity, writes at length on the interpretation of "the nations" in Revelation 21:24-26. He states:

> In chapter 21:3, where we read that the tabernacle of God is at last with men, we also read that "they shall be his peoples" (Greek *laoi*). It is amazing to find discerning men apparently almost wilfully translating the plural *laoi*, as if it were *laos*. . . . The Revised Version . . . translates truly and plainly, "They shall be his *peoples*," and thus prepares us to avoid the impos-

sible assumption that 21:9 to 22:5 is a passage that reverts to millennial scenes.

We know positively that at least *one* nation and *one* seed, ISRAEL, will belong upon the new earth . . . Isaiah 66:22 . . . God says Israel's "seed and name" shall *remain* in the heavens and earth, that is, in that new order, beginning in Revelation 21:1. . . .

Now, Israel is God's elect nation—elect not for the past, or even through the millennial age, but *forever*. Yet, if Israel be the elect nation, the existence of other nations is presupposed! . . .

But that *national* existence will not cease, is shown clearly by verse 20 [of Zeph. 3]: "At that time will I bring you (Israel) in, and at that time will I gather you; for I will make you a name and a praise among all the *peoples* (plural!) of the earth."

Finally, the language of the first 5 verses of chapter 22 of the Revelation, and especially of verses 4 and 5, is just as eternal in its character as anything at the beginning of chapter 21. "The throne of God and of the Lamb shall be therein: and his servants shall serve him; and they shall see his face; and his name *shall be* on their foreheads . . . and *they shall reign unto the ages of the ages.*" Why should such statements be connected with a passage that is meant merely to go back and describe millennial conditions? That would be incongruous. Furthermore, it is not in keeping, we feel, for the Scripture to go back after the *last judgment* has been held, and *the new creation* has come in, to times before that last judgment and new creation.[15]

To this argument from the eternal existence of Israel as a nation and the consequent continuance of other nations, Kelly writes:

. . . In Isaiah lxv. a new heaven and a new earth were announced: but how differently! There the language must be taken in a very qualified sense indeed. . . . it is said of the Lord, "He shall reign over the house of Jacob forever, and of his kingdom there shall be no end." This is an Old Testament hope, though said in the New, and it means of course that He shall reign over the house of Jacob as long as it exists as such upon the earth. When the earth disappears and Israel is no longer seen as a nation, they will be blessed, no doubt, in another and better way; but there will be no reign of Christ over them as an earthly people here below; so that this kingdom, while it has

---

[15] William R. Newell, *The Book of the Revelation*, pp. 343-45.

> no end as long as the earth subsists, must necessarily be limited by the earth's continuance. . . . The New Testament uses the phrase fully and absolutely, as an unending state; but in the Old Testament it is tied down to the earthly relations of which the Holy Ghost was then speaking.[16]

Further support for Newell's position would be seen in Matthew 25:34 where the saved Gentiles are to inherit a kingdom prepared for them from the foundation of the world. Since they are said to inherit life (Matt. 25:46), it must be eternal life. This would indicate that individuals will be saved and have eternal life and yet will be distinct from Israel.

Such are the main arguments used by those who seek to support the view that this passage represents eternal ages rather than the millennial age. It has been observed that strong men have presented strong arguments which, in turn have been refuted by equally strong men who hold a different view. In the light of this presentation of argument and rebuttal is there any solution to the problem? An examination of some of the statements made concerning the new Jerusalem may help us arrive at a solution.

C. *Revelation 21:9 to 22:7 describes the eternal habitation of the resurrected saints during the millennium.*

1. *The city is a literal city.* An important consideration at this point is whether the city described in Revelation 21 and 22 is a literal or a mystical city. Scott is representative of those who hold the city to be a mystical one when he writes:

> We beg the reader's careful attention to the distinction between the new Jerusalem of the Apocalypse, which is the glorified Church, and the *heavenly* Jerusalem spoken of by Paul (Heb. 12:22). This latter, unlike the former, does not refer to people, but *is* the city of the living God, an actual city, the location of *all* the heavenly saints. It is the same that is referred to in the previous chapter, for which saints and patriarchs looked (Heb. 11:10-16), a material city, built and prepared by God Himself, grand and vast beyond all telling. The city of Paul is a *material* one; the city of John is a *mystical* one.[17]

---

[16] Kelly, *op. cit.*, pp. 463-64.
[17] Scott, *op. cit.*, p. 421.

It is to be observed that Scott offers no proof of his distinction, but merely makes the affirmation. There is much evidence to show that this city of Revelation 21 and 22 is a literal city, as well as that of Hebrews 12. Peters gives a summary of the arguments to prove that this city is a literal city.

> 1. In the usage of the east when a king entered his capitol to rule therefrom, or a prince ascended the throne, it was represented under the figure of a marriage, i.e. he was wedded, intimately and permanently united to the city, or throne, or people. The use of the figure in the Scriptures shows that we are not to limit it unless specified to the church. . . . It designates the permanent union of a people with the land, as in Isa. 62 where in the Millennial description the land is called "Beulah," that is "married" . . . when the last time does come . . . there is no impropriety but rather eminent fitness that the union of the King of Kings with His metropolitan city should be designated under the same figure, implying the most intimate and permanent relationship. Thus the figure of marriage, which to many is the main objection to the idea of a literal city, serves rather to indicate it. 2. For, the figure itself is explained in the description of the city in so significant a manner, and in such contrast to the use made of it formerly in reference to the earthly Jerusalem, that it cannot possibly be applied to any other than a literal city. It is expressly declared that "the throne of God and the Lamb" is in this city. This affirms its Theocratic position, as the capitol of the Kingdom. . . . 3. The dwelling-place of God, the place where He tabernacled among men always, in former days (as in the tabernacle and temple) assumed a material form . . . looking forward to the period when a glorified humanity, unity to the divine . . . should dwell with men. . . . That dwelling-place which was once a tent, then a temple, now is exhibited as a city, but still designated "the tabernacle of God." . . . 4. In the portraiture of the city, the saints or inhabitants of it and the righteous are represented as separate and distinct from it. . . . 5. The declaration (Rev. 21:22) that the city had no temple (such as the earthly Jerusalem) . . . can only be predicated of a material city. 6. The distinction between the saints and the city . . . is evidenced by a large class of passages which speak of the ancient saints "looking for a city, " of all believers "seeking a continuing city," and of God "having prepared for them a city." 7. This corresponds with another class of passages which describe Jerusalem as putting on her beautiful garments . . . making herself a glorious city by reason of the number, holiness and happiness of her citizens, etc. . . . Isa. 54:11, 12 and Isa. 60:14-20 . . . 8. But that the saints are not de-

noted and that the reference is to a material city, is found in the fact that the saints are represented . . . when the marriage takes place as guests, the called or invited. . . . They cannot be, in this case, the guests and the Bride at the same time. . . . 9. Allow this Theocratic ordering . . . in view of the glorification, greatness, and majesty of this King, . . . a city commensurate with the august Personage should be provided.[18]

Speaking of the literalness of this city, Grant writes:

In Heb. xii. we have a still more definite testimony. For there the "Church of the first-born ones which are written in heaven," as well as "the spirits of just men made perfect"—in other words, both Christians and the saints of the Old Testament—are mentioned as distinct from "the city of the living God, the heavenly Jerusalem"; and this will not allow them to be the same thing, although, in another way, the identification of a city with its inhabitants is easy.[19]

Newell adds the thought that it is literal

Because of the literalness of its description. If gold does not mean gold, nor pearls—pearls, nor precious stones—stones, nor exact measurements—real dimensions, then the Bible gives nothing accurate or reliable.[20]

Thus, there seems ample evidence to support the view that this city is a literal city.

2. *The inhabitants of the city.* Newell presents the thesis that the new Jerusalem is "the eternal dwelling place, 'habitation,' of God—Father, Son and Holy Spirit."[21] He writes:

Several considerations lead us toward the conclusion that the New Jerusalem is God's one eternal resting place.

1. Immediately we see the new heaven and new earth and the New Jerusalem descending to the new earth (21:1, 2), we are told, "Behold, the tabernacle of God is with men" . . . The object of the new heaven and earth is to bring about this—*that God shall eternally have His home* in this capital city of the new creation!

2. No other eternal habitation of God is seen than this of the New Creation's capital. . . .

---

18 G. N. H. Peters, *Theocratic Kingdom*, III, 42-46.
19 F. W. Grant, *The Revelation of Christ*, p. 227.
20 Newell, *op. cit.*, p. 348.
21 *Ibid.*, p. 352.

> 3. This heavenly city has the glory of God (21:11, 23; 22:5). . . .
>
> 4. It also has the *throne* of God, and that "service" of 22:3, properly called priestly service, or spiritual worship. . . .
>
> 5. They shall see his face. . . . This, therefore, must be the place of God's rest forever.
>
> 6. We need only to remember that the dwellers in the New Jerusalem "shall reign unto the ages of the ages" (22:5). This could not be written of others than the inhabitants of the capital of the new creation.[22]

This city is not only the dwelling place of God, Father, Son and Holy Spirit, but is the dwelling place of the bride, the Lamb's wife (Rev. 21:9) as well. When the angel would reveal the glory and blessedness of the bride, that angel reveals the dwelling place of the bride, with which the bride is identified. This heavenly city is promised as the destiny of the church.

> But ye are come unto mount Sion, and unto the city of the living God, the heavenly Jerusalem, and to an innumerable company of angels, to the general assembly and church of the firstborn, which are written in heaven, and to God the Judge of all, and to the spirits of just men made perfect [Heb. 12:22-23].
>
> Him that overcometh will I make a pillar in the temple of my God, and he shall go no more out: and I will write upon him the name of my God, and the name of the city of my God, which is new Jerusalem, which cometh down out of heaven from my God: and I will write upon him my new name [Rev. 3:12].

Without doubt this is the same place the Lord had in mind when he said:

> In my Father's house are many mansions, if it were not so, I would have told you. I go to prepare a place for you.
>
> And if I go and prepare a place for you, I will come again and receive you unto myself, that where I am, there ye may be also [John 14:2-3].
>
> For we have now no continuing city, but we seek one to come [Heb. 13:14].

The relation of the church to this city is further signified in that John observes the name of the twelve Apostles of the Lamb therein (Rev. 21:14).

---

[22] *Ibid.*, pp. 353-54.

As the inhabitants of the city are contemplated it is observed that Scripture includes more than the church among the inhabitants. A *city* is seen to be the expectation of the Old Testament saints. Of Abraham it was said: "He looked for a city which hath foundations, whose builder and maker is God" (Heb. 11:10). In contrasting the earthly and heavenly Jerusalem in Galatians 4 Paul states that whereas the Jew in bondage longed for earthly Jerusalem, there is held out through the promise a greater city or dwelling place in the words, "But Jerusalem which is above is free, which is the mother of us all" (Gal. 4:26). Old Testament saints are pictured in the words, "Ye are come unto mount Sion, and unto the city of the living God, the heavenly Jerusalem . . . to the spirits of just men made perfect" (Heb. 12:22-23). It would appear then that the author includes not only the church, but the redeemed of the Old Testament as well as angels in the company of the inhabitants of the new Jerusalem. Jennings observes:

> But since thus all saints of the olden time, be they prior to any distinction, as Enoch; or Gentile, as Job; or Jewish, as Abraham, may have their place in this city, she must by no means be accounted as characteristically Jewish.[23]

And although the term *new Jerusalem* is not strictly Jewish in concept, we find that Israel has her part in that city, for John (Rev. 21:12) sees the names of the twelve tribes of Israel, indicating that the redeemed of Israel have their part there.

From this consideration, then, it may be stated that the city is to be inhabited by God, by the church, by the redeemed of Israel, and by the redeemed of all ages, together with the unfallen angels. However, this city seems to take her chief characterization from the bride who dwells there.

3. *Means of entrance into the city.* This whole question will be easier to solve if it be noted that the church can enter into that place He has gone to prepare for us only by rapture and resurrection. After the judgment seat of Christ and the marriage of the Lamb the bride will be settled into her permanent abode. Rapture and resurrection make entrance possible. Israel can enter this place prepared for her only by resurrection. Since

---

[23] Jennings, *op. cit.*, p. 566.

the resurrection of Israel takes place at the second advent, the saved of Israel could not enter the city until after the rapture and resurrection of the church and their own resurrection. Living Israel and living Gentiles on the earth at the second advent do not enter this city, but they enter the millennial reign of Christ. The saved Old Testament saints, who were looking for this city with foundations, enter this city by resurrection. Thus all the redeemed of the ages who enter this city do so by resurrection. The city thus becomes the abode of all the resurrected saints, who enter it at the time of their resurrection.

4. *The relation of this city to the millennial age.* When the church has been joined in marriage to the Bridegroom and is installed in her prepared place she will never be moved out of it again. The church enters into her eternal state at the rapture. When the Lord returns with His bride to reign, her dwelling place is not to be left unoccupied for a thousand years. Rather, the place of occupancy is transferred from heaven to a position over the earth. Thus John sees the "great city, the holy Jerusalem, descending out of heaven from God." This dwelling place remains in the air, to cast its light, which is the shining of the effulgence of the Son, onto the earth so that "the nations of them which are saved shall walk in the light of it: and the kings of the earth do bring their glory and honour unto it" (Rev. 21:24). At the second advent, the time of the descent of the city into the air over the earth, the church saints are joined by the Old Testament saints, who are resurrected and take up residence at that time.

Many writers see the city as the dwelling place of the church during the millennial reign. Jennings says:

> . . . we go back a thousand years, even from the borders of eternity to consider more carefully than we have yet done the Bride, the Lamb's wife, and her relation to the earth during the Millennium.[24]

Scott, in like vein, writes:

> After a passing allusion to the millennial reign of Christ and His heavenly saints (chap. 20:4-6), we are brought back from

[24] *Ibid.*, p. 565.

> the consideration of the eternal state to a lengthened description of the bride, the Lamb's wife in her millennial relation to Israel and to the world at large.[25]

Kelly writes:

> Thus, if we had the bride in relation to the Lamb in chapter xix. and as the holy city, New Jerusalem, in relation to the eternal state, verse 9 and the following verses of this chapter shew us that, during the interval between the marriage of the Lamb, and the new heaven and earth in the eternal state, she has a very blessed place in the eyes of God and man. It is the church's millennial display.[26]

Or again:

> All the account, from the 9th verse of chap. xxi. to verse 5, inclusively, of chap. xxii., presents the relation of the heavenly city to the earth during the millennium.[27]

It may thus be seen that even though the earth is not in its eternal state, and though it is necessary for the King to rule the earth with a rod of iron, and though there will be a rebellion against the authority of the King (and against what light they will sin!), yet, as far as the church is concerned, she is in her eternal state, enjoying her eternal fellowship, and the fruits of her salvation. From that heavenly city she will reign with Him, the one who bears the title of King of kings and Lord of lords. It is not eternity, but the church and the redeemed of the ages are in their eternal state. We believe Kelly summarizes well:

> Carefully bear this in mind, however, that if we look at the heavenly city itself, it is eternal. *It will make little difference to the city whether seen in the millennium, or in the eternal state that succeeds.* There are two descents of the city in chap. xxi, one at the beginning of the millennium, and the other at the commencement of the eternal state. The second verse of that chapter gives us its descent when the eternal state is come, and the tenth verse its descent for the millennium. The reason, I think, is that at the end of the millennium the old heaven and earth pass away; and naturally the city would disappear from the scene of the convulsion. Then, when the new

---

[25] Scott, *op. cit.*, p. 429.
[26] Kelly, *op. cit.*, p. 462.
[27] *Ibid.*, p. 489.

> earth dawns on our view, the heavenly city again comes down, and takes its place permanently in the new heavens and earth, wherein dwelleth righteousness. This is necessary to remark; because, *while at the end of the thousand years all will be changed, still the heavenly city will abide forever.* [Italics mine.][28]

If it be objected by some that resurrected Israel has no part with the church, but is destined to be on the earth and not in such an intimate relation to Christ and the church, let us make several observations. (1) The first resurrection will include not only those in Christ (1 Thess. 4:16), but "those that are Christ's (1 Cor. 15:23). (2) The destiny of the saved patriarchs, and the "just men made perfect" (Heb. 12:23) is said to be the New Jerusalem, which can only be entered by resurrection. (3) Old Testament saints are not to be subjected to the discipline of the King. (4) Old Testament saints are to reign in the millennium (Rev. 20:3) even as the church (Rev. 3:21) and they may reign from the heavenly city, inasmuch as it is seen to be in relation to the earth and in the sphere of the earth, even though not on the earth. There would be no restriction on them to keep them from coming and going at will.

It would thus be concluded that during the millennium the heavenly city will be brought into a relation to the earth, although not settled on the earth. The resurrected saints of all ages in that city will be in their eternal state and possessed of their eternal blessings, even though such is not true of things down on the earth itself.

5. *The relation of this city to eternity.* Note again the quotation from Kelly above to the effect that as far as the city itself is concerned, or the status of its occupants, there will be no change whatsoever when the Son surrenders the kingdom to His Father and eternity begins. The locale of the city may be changed but the inhabitants will undergo no change whatsoever. The city may be removed during the purgation of the earth (1 Pet. 3:10) and will return and take up its abode on the new earth (Rev. 21:2) but there will be no change within it whatsoever.

---

[28] *Ibid.*, p. 488. Scott says, [the church is seen] "before the reign (chap. 19:7), after the reign (chap. 21:2), during the reign (chap. 21:9)." *Op. cit.*, p. 420.

The survey of the arguments on the question as to whether Revelation 21:9 to 22:5 belongs in the millennium or in the eternal state has revealed a wide divergence of opinion, supported by sound arguments both for and against both positions. The study has led to the conclusion that the mistake lies in trying to establish an either-or proposition. A mediating view, that the eternal state of the resurrected during the millennium is seen in the passage, is suggested as a better view. When the occupants of the city are described it must be seen that they are in their eternal state, possessing their eternal inheritance, in eternal relationship with God who has tabernacled among them. There will be no change in their position or relation whatsoever. When the occupants of the earth are described they are seen in the millennial age. They have an established relationship to the heavenly city which is above them, in whose light they walk. Yet their position is not eternal nor unchangeable, but rather millennial.

The Lord promised to prepare a place for His own. At the rapture and resurrection of the church the saints of this age are, after judgment and marriage, installed in that prepared place. They are joined by the saints of the Old Testament at the time of their resurrection at the second advent. This dwelling place prepared for the bride, in which the Old Testament saints find their place as servants (Rev. 22:3), is moved down into the air to remain over the land of Palestine during the millennium, during which time the saints exercise their right to reign. These saints are in their eternal state and the city enjoys its eternal glory. At the expiration of the millennial age, during the renovation of the earth, the dwelling place is removed during the conflagration, to find its place after the recreation as the connecting link between the new heavens and the new earth.

II. Life in the Eternal City

Nowhere does Scripture give details of the life in the eternal kingdom of God. Occasionally the curtain is drawn back to give a slight glimpse of that life, of which our present experience with Him is only "a foretaste of glory divine."

A. *A life of fellowship with Him.*

For now we see through a glass, darkly; but then face to face [1 Cor. 13:12].

Beloved, now are we the sons of God, and it doth not yet appear what we shall be: but we know that, when he shall appear, we shall be like him; for we shall see him as he is [1 John 3:2].

I will come again, and receive you unto myself, that where I am, there ye may be also [John 14:3].

And they shall see his face [Rev. 22:4].

B. *A life of rest.*

And I heard a voice from heaven saying unto me, Write, Blessed are the dead which die in the Lord from henceforth: Yea, saith the Spirit, that they may rest from their labours; and their works do follow them [Rev. 14:13].

C. *A life of full knowledge.*

. . . now I know in part; but then shall I know even as also I am known [1 Cor. 13:12].

D. *A life of holiness.*

And there shall in no wise enter into it any thing that defileth, neither whatsoever worketh abomination, or maketh a lie: but they which are written in the Lamb's book of life [Rev. 21:27].

E. *A life of joy.*

And God shall wipe away all tears from their eyes; and there shall be no more death, neither sorrow, nor crying, neither shall there be any more pain: for the former things are passed away [Rev. 21:4].

F. *A life of service.*

And there shall be no more curse: but the throne of God and of the Lamb shall be in it; and his servants shall serve him [Rev. 22:3].

G. *A life of abundance.*

I will give unto him that is athirst of the fountain of the water of life freely [Rev. 21:6].

H. *A life of glory.*

For our light affliction, which is but for a moment, worketh for us a far more exceeding and eternal weight of glory [2 Cor. 4:17].

When Christ, who is our life, shall appear, then shall ye also appear with him in glory [Col. 3:4].

I. *A life of worship.*

> And after these things I heard a great voice of much people in heaven, saying Alleluia; Salvation, and glory, and honour, and power unto the Lord our God [Rev. 19:1].
>
> After this I beheld, and, lo, a great multitude, which no man could number, of all nations, and kindreds, and people, and tongues, stood before the throne, and before the Lamb, clothed with white robes, and palms in their hands; And cried with a loud voice, saying, Salvation to our God which sitteth upon the throne, and unto the Lamb. . . . Blessing and glory, and wisdom, and thanksgiving, and honour, and power, and might, be unto our God for ever and ever. Amen [Rev. 7:9-12].

No redeemed individual could ever fully understand the glory of the prospect set before him. John summarized the anticipated glory by saying, "we know that, when he shall appear, we shall be like him" (1 John 3:2). The glory of our expectation is that we shall be transformed into His likeness, being sinless, deathless, and experiencing the perfection of development.

> Oh, Christ! He is the fountain—
> The deep sweet well of love!
> The streams on earth I've tasted,
> More deep I'll drink above!
> There, to an ocean fullness,
> His mercy doth expand,
> And glory, glory dwelleth
> In Immanuel's land.

There is the danger that the redeemed one will become so occupied with the anticipation of his own experience of glory that the supreme glorification of the Godhead is lost. Our occupation in the eternal state will not be with our position or glory but with God, Himself. John writes: "We shall see Him as he is" (1 John 3:2). We shall be fully occupied with the One "that loved us, and washed us from our sins in his own blood, And hath made us kings and priests unto God and his Father" (Rev. 1:5-6), ascribing "Blessing, and honour, and glory, and power, . . . unto him that sitteth upon the throne, and unto the Lamb forever and ever" (Rev. 5:13), saying, "Blessing, and glory, and wisdom, and thanksgiving, and honour, and power, and might, be unto our God for ever and ever. Amen" (Rev. 7:12), for "Worthy is the Lamb that was slain to receive power, and riches, and wisdom, and strength, and honour, and glory and blessing" (Rev. 5:12).

> The bride eyes not her garment,
> But her dear bridegroom's face;
> I will not gaze at glory,
> But on my King of Grace—
> Not at the crown He giveth,
> But on His pierced hand:—
> The Lamb is all the glory
> Of Immanuel's land.

BIBLIOGRAPHY

A. Books

Abbott-Smith, G. *A Manual Greek Lexicon of the New Testament.* Edinburgh. T. & T. Clark, 1937. 512 pp.

Alford, Henry. *The New Testament.* New York: Harper and Brothers, 1859. IV vols.

Allis, Oswald T. *Prophecy and the Church.* Philadelphia: Presbyterian and Reformed Publishing Company, 1945. 339 pp.

Anderson, Robert. *The Coming Prince.* London: Hodder and Stoughton, 1909. 311 pp.

Andrews, Samuel J. *Christianity and Anti-Christianity in Their Final Conflict.* Chicago: The Bible Institute Colportage Association, 1898. 358 pp.

Angus, Joseph and Samuel G. Green. *The Bible Handbook.* New York: Fleming H. Revell Company, [n.d.]. 837 pp.

Armerding, Carl. *The Four and Twenty Elders.* New York: Loizeaux Brothers, [n.d.]. 11 pp.

Barnhouse, Donald Grey. *His Own Received Him Not, But. . . .* New York: Fleming H. Revell, 1933. 185 pp.

Baron, David. *Israel's Inalienable Possessions.* London: Morgan and Scott, [n.d.]. 93 pp.

Bauman, Louis. *Russian Events in the Light of Bible Prophecy.* Philadelphia: The Balkiston Co., 1942. 191 pp.

Berkhof, Louis. *The Kingdom of God.* Grand Rapids, Michigan: Wm. B. Eerdman's Publishing Company. 1951. 177 pp.

.... *Principles of Biblical Interpretation.* Grand Rapids, Michigan: Baker Book House, 1950. 169 pp.

.... *The Second Coming of Christ.* Grand Rapids, Michigan: Wm. B. Eerdman's Publishing Company, 1953. 102 pp.

.... *Systematic Theology.* Grand Rapids, Michigan: Wm. B. Eerdman's Publishing Company, 1941. 759 pp.

Bewer, J. A. "Obadiah and Joel," *International Critical Commentary.* Charles Augustus Briggs, Samuel Rolles Driver, and Alfred Plummer, editors; New York: Charles Scribner's Sons, 1912. 147 pp.

Blackstone, W. E. *Jesus Is Coming.* New York: Fleming H. Revell, 1932. 252 pp.

Boutflower, Charles. *In and Around the Book of Daniel.* London: Society for Promoting Christian Knowledge, 1923. 314 pp.

Briggs, Charles Augustus. *General Introduction to the Study of Holy Scripture.* New York: Charles Scribner's Sons, 1899. 688 pp.

Bright, John. *The Kingdom of God.* New York: Abingdon-Cokesbury Press, 1953. 288 pp.

Brock, A. Clutton. *What Is the Kingdom of Heaven?* New York: Charles Scribner's Sons, 1920. 152 pp.

Brooks, Keith L. *Prophetic Questions Answered.* Grand Rapids, Michigan: Zondervan Publishing House, 1941. 164 pp.

Brown, David. *Christ's Second Coming: Will It Be Pre-Millennial?* New York: Robert Carter and Brothers, 1851. 499 pp.

Bruce, Alexander Balmain. *The Kingdom of God.* Edinburgh: T. & T. Clark, 1904. 361 pp.

Bullinger, E. W. *A Critical Lexicon and Concordance to the English and Greek New Testament.* London: Longmans, Green, & Company, 1924. 999 pp.

.... *The Apocalypse.* London: Eyre & Spottiswoode, [n.d.]. 725 pp.

.... *How to Enjoy the Bible.* London: Eyre & Spottiswoode, 1907. 435 pp.

Burton, Alfred H. *Russia's Destiny in the Light of Prophecy.* New York: Gospel Publishing House, 1917. 64 pp.

Calvin, John. *Institutes of the Christian Religion.* Philadelphia: Presbyterian Board of Christian Education, [n.d.]. 2 vols.

Cameron, Robert. *Scriptural Truth About the Lord's Return.* New York: Fleming H. Revell, 1922. 176 pp.

Case, Shirley Jackson. *The Millennial Hope.* Chicago: The University of Chicago Press, 1918. 253 pp.

Chafer, Lewis Sperry. *The Kingdom in History and Prophecy.* Chicago: The Bible Institute Colportage Association, 1936. 167 pp.

.... *Must We Dismiss the Millennium?* Crescent City, Florida: Biblical Testimony League, 1921. 32 pp.

.... *Systematic Theology.* Dallas, Texas: Dallas Seminary Press, 1947. 8 vols.

Chafer, Rollin T. *The Science of Biblical Hermeneutics.* Dallas, Texas: Bibliotheca Sacra, 1939. 92 pp.

Chalmers, Thomas M. *Israel in Covenant and History.* New York: Author, 1926. 61 pp.

Cooper, David L. *The God of Israel.* Los Angeles: The Biblical Research Society, 1945. 164 pp.

.... *Preparing for the World-Wide Revival.* Los Angeles: The Biblical Research Society, 1938. 62 pp.

.... *When Gog's Armies Meet the Almighty.* Los Angeles: The Biblical Research Society, 1940. 112 pp.

.... *The World's Greatest Library Graphically Illustrated.* Los Angeles: The Biblical Research Society, 1942. 124 pp.

Darby, J. N. *Notes on the Apocalypse.* London: G. Morrish, [n.d.]. 165 pp.

.... *Synopsis of the Books of the Bible.* London: G. Morrish, [n.d.]. 5 vols.

.... *Will the Saints Be in the Tribulation?* New York: Loizeaux Brothers, [n.d.]. 16 pp.

Davidson, A.B. *Old Testament Prophecy.* Edinburgh: T. & T. Clark, 1903. 507 pp.

DeHaan, M. R. *The Jew and Palestine in Prophecy.* Grand Rapids, Michigan: Zondervan Publishing House, 1950. 183 pp.

Dennett, Edward. *Daniel the Prophet.* London: G. Morrish, 1919. 206 pp.

Edwards, Thomas Charles. *Commentary on the First Epistle to the Corinthians.* London: Hodder and Stoughton, 1897. 491 pp.

Elliott, Charles and W. J. Harsha. *Biblical Hermeneutics* (chiefly a translation of Manual d'Hermeneutique Biblique, by J. E. Cellerier). New York: Anson D. F. Randolph & Company, 1881. 282 pp.

English, E. Schuyler. *Re-Thinking the Rapture.* Travelers Rest, South Carolina: Southern Bible Book House, 1954. 123 pp.

.... *Studies in the Gospel According to Matthew.* New York: Our Hope, 1943. 516 pp.

Fairbairn, Patrick. *Hermeneutical Manual.* Edinburgh: T. & T. Clark, 1858. 480 pp.

.... *Prophecy Viewed in Respect to Its Distinctive Nature, Its Special Function, and Proper Interpretation.* Edinburgh: T. & T. Clark, 1956. 530 pp.

.... *The Typology of Scripture.* New York: Funk and Wagnalls Company, 1900. 2 vols.

Farrar, F. W. *History of Interpretation.* New York: E. P. Dutton and Company, 1886. 553 pp.

Feinberg, Charles. *Premillennialism or Amillennialism?* Grand Rapids, Michigan: Zondervan Publishing House, 1936. 250 pp.

Froom, LeRoy Edwin. *The Prophetic Faith of Our Fathers.* Washington, D. C.: Review and Herald, 1945. 4 vols.

Frost, Henry W. *The Second Coming of Christ.* Grand Rapids, Michigan: Wm. B. Eerdman's Publishing Co., 1934. 251 pp.

Gaebelein, Arno C. *The Annotated Bible.* Wheaton, Ill.: Van Kampen Press, 1913. 9 vols.

.... *As It Was—So Shall It Be.* New York: Our Hope, 1937. 190 pp.

.... *The Gospel According to Matthew.* Wheaton, Ill., Van Kampen Press, 1916. 2 vols. in one.

.... *Hath God Cast Away His People?* New York : Gospel Publishing House, 1905. 279 pp.

.... *The Prophet Daniel.* New York: Our Hope, 1911. 228 pp.

.... *The Prophet Ezekiel.* New York: Our Hope, 1918. 346 pp.

.... *Studies in Prophecy.* New York: Our Hope, 1918. 166 pp.

Gigot, Francis E. *General Introduction to the Study of the Holy Scriptures.* New York: Benziger Brothers, 1901. 606 pp.

Gilbert, George Holley. *Interpretation of the Bible.* New York: The Macmillan Company, 1908. 308 pp.

Girdlestone, R. B. *The Grammar of Prophecy.* London: Eyre and Spottiswoode, 1901. 192 pp.

Govett, R. *Entrance into the Kingdom.* London: Charles J. Thynne, 1922. 222 pp.

Grant, F. W. *The Numerical Bible.* New York: Loizeaux Brothers, 1891. 7 vols.

.... *The Revelation of Christ.* New York: Loizeaux Brothers, [n.d.]. 245 pp.

Gratton Guiness, H. *The Approaching End of the Age.* New York: A. C. Armstrong, 1884. 776 pp.

.... *Light for the Last Days.* London: Hodder and Stoughton, 1886. 673 pp.

Gray, James M. *Christian Worker's Commentary.* New York: Fleming H. Revell, 1915. 447 pp.

.... *Prophecy and the Lord's Return.* New York: Fleming H. Revell, 1917. 119 pp.

.... *A Text-Book on Prophecy.* New York: Fleming H. Revell, 1918. 215 pp.

Haldeman, I. M. *The History of the Doctrine of Our Lord's Return.* New York: First Baptist Church, [n.d.]. 40 pp.

Hamilton, Floyd. *The Basis of Millennial Faith.* Grand Rapids, Michigan: Wm. B. Eerdman's Publishing Company, 1942. 160 pp.

Hamilton, Gavin. *Will the Church Escape the Great Tribulation?* New York: Loizeaux Brothers, 1941. 79 pp.

Harrison, Norman B. *The End.* Minneappolis, Minnesota: Harrison Service, 1941. 239 pp.

Hendriksen, William. *And So All Israel Shall Be Saved.* Grand Rapids, Michigan: Baker's Book Store, 1945. 36 pp.

.... *Bible Survey.* Grand Rapids, Michigan: Baker Book House, 1953. 515 pp.

Hodge, Charles, *Commentary on Romans.* Philadelphia: H. B. Garner, 1883. 716 pp.

Hogg, C. F., and W. E. Vine. *The Church and the Tribulation.* London: Pickering and Inglis, [n.d.]. 63 pp.

.... *The Epistles of Paul the Apostle to the Thessalonians.* Glasgow: Pickering and Inglis, 1914. 307 pp.

Horne, Thomas Hartwell. *An Introduction to the Critical Study and Knowledge of the Holy Scriptures.* New York: Robert Carter and Brothers, 1859. 2 vols.

Hospers, Gerrit H. *The Principle of Spiritualization.* East Williamson, New York: Author, 1935. 53 pp.

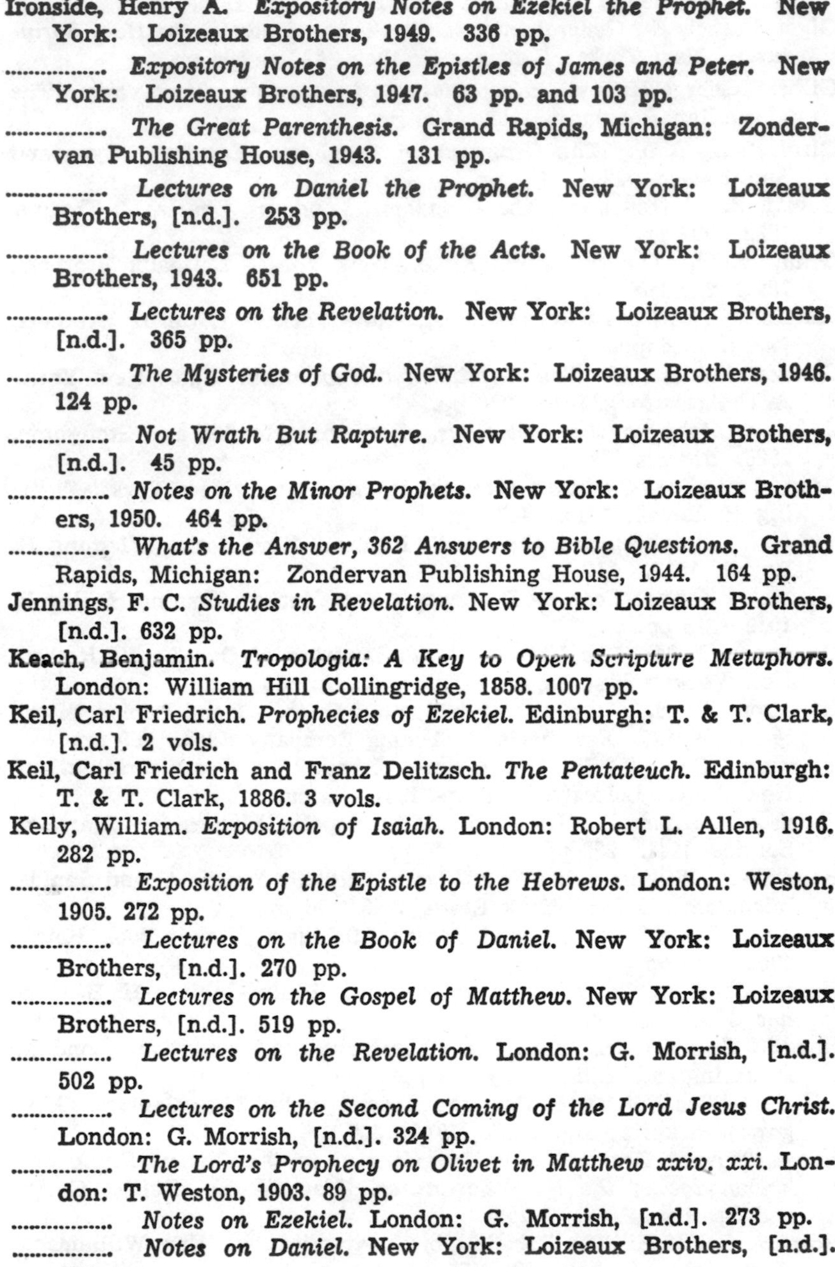

Ironside, Henry A. *Expository Notes on Ezekiel the Prophet.* New York: Loizeaux Brothers, 1949. 336 pp.

.... *Expository Notes on the Epistles of James and Peter.* New York: Loizeaux Brothers, 1947. 63 pp. and 103 pp.

.... *The Great Parenthesis.* Grand Rapids, Michigan: Zondervan Publishing House, 1943. 131 pp.

.... *Lectures on Daniel the Prophet.* New York: Loizeaux Brothers, [n.d.]. 253 pp.

.... *Lectures on the Book of the Acts.* New York: Loizeaux Brothers, 1943. 651 pp.

.... *Lectures on the Revelation.* New York: Loizeaux Brothers, [n.d.]. 365 pp.

.... *The Mysteries of God.* New York: Loizeaux Brothers, 1946. 124 pp.

.... *Not Wrath But Rapture.* New York: Loizeaux Brothers, [n.d.]. 45 pp.

.... *Notes on the Minor Prophets.* New York: Loizeaux Brothers, 1950. 464 pp.

.... *What's the Answer, 362 Answers to Bible Questions.* Grand Rapids, Michigan: Zondervan Publishing House, 1944. 164 pp.

Jennings, F. C. *Studies in Revelation.* New York: Loizeaux Brothers, [n.d.]. 632 pp.

Keach, Benjamin. *Tropologia: A Key to Open Scripture Metaphors.* London: William Hill Collingridge, 1858. 1007 pp.

Keil, Carl Friedrich. *Prophecies of Ezekiel.* Edinburgh: T. & T. Clark, [n.d.]. 2 vols.

Keil, Carl Friedrich and Franz Delitzsch. *The Pentateuch.* Edinburgh: T. & T. Clark, 1886. 3 vols.

Kelly, William. *Exposition of Isaiah.* London: Robert L. Allen, 1916. 282 pp.

.... *Exposition of the Epistle to the Hebrews.* London: Weston, 1905. 272 pp.

.... *Lectures on the Book of Daniel.* New York: Loizeaux Brothers, [n.d.]. 270 pp.

.... *Lectures on the Gospel of Matthew.* New York: Loizeaux Brothers, [n.d.]. 519 pp.

.... *Lectures on the Revelation.* London: G. Morrish, [n.d.]. 502 pp.

.... *Lectures on the Second Coming of the Lord Jesus Christ.* London: G. Morrish, [n.d.]. 324 pp.

.... *The Lord's Prophecy on Olivet in Matthew xxiv, xxi.* London: T. Weston, 1903. 89 pp.

.... *Notes on Ezekiel.* London: G. Morrish, [n.d.]. 273 pp.

.... *Notes on Daniel.* New York: Loizeaux Brothers, [n.d.]. 270 pp.

.... *The Revelation Expounded.* London: F. E. Race, [n.d.]. 264 pp.

.... Editor, *The Collected Writings of J. N. Darby.* London: G. Morrish, [n.d.]. "Prophetical" 4 vols.

Kromminga, D. H. *The Millennium.* Grand Rapids, Michigan: Wm. B. Eerdman's Publishing Company, 1948. 121 pp.

.... *The Millennium in the Church.* Grand Rapids, Michigan: Wm. B. Eerdman's Publishing Company, 1945. 360 pp.

Ladd, George E. *Crucial Questions About the Kingdom of God.* Grand Rapids, Michigan: Wm. B. Eerdman's Publishing Company, 1952. 193 pp.

.... *The Blessed Hope.* Grand Rapids, Michigan: Wm. B. Eerdman's Publishing Company, 1956. 167 pp.

Laidlaw, R. A. *Will the Church Go Through the Great Tribulation.* New York: Loizeaux Brothers, [n.d.]. 16 pp.

Lang, G. H. *The Revelation of Jesus Christ.* London: Oliphants, 1945. 420 pp.

Lange, John Peter. *A Commentary on the Holy Scriptures: Critical, Doctrinal and Homiletical.* Translated from the German, revised, enlarged, and edited by Phillip Schaff. New York: Scribner, Armstrong and Company, 1872. 10 vols. New Testament.

Larkin, Clarence. *Dispensational Truth or God's Plan and Purpose in the Ages.* Philadelphia: Author, 1920. 176 pp.

Leupold, H. C. *Exposition of Daniel.* Columbus, Ohio: Wartburg Press, 1949. 549 pp.

Lincoln, William. *Lectures on the Book of Revelation.* New York: Fleming H. Revell, [n.d.]. 254 pp.

Lindberg, Milton B. *Gog All Agog "in the Latter Days."* Findlay, Ohio: Fundamental Truth Publishers. 1939. 32 pp.

Lockhart, Clinton. *Principles of Interpretation.* Fort Worth, Texas: S. H. Taylor, 1915. 260 pp.

Marsh, F. E. *Will the Church or Any Part of It Go Through the* Great *Tribulation.* London: Pickering and Inglis, [n.d.]. 31 pp.

Masselink, W. *Why Thousand Years?* Grand Rapids, Michigan: Wm. B. Eerdman's Publishing Company, 1930. 222 pp.

Mauro, Philip. *God's Present Kingdom.* New York: Fleming H. Revell, 1919. 270 pp.

.... *The Gospel of the Kingdom.* Boston: Hamilton Brothers, 1928. 256 pp.

.... *The Seventy Weeks and the Great Tribulation.* Boston: Hamilton Brothers, 1923. 283 pp.

Mayor, Joseph B. *The Epistle of James.* London: Macmillan and Company, 1897. 256 pp.

McClain, Alva J. *Daniel's Prophecy of the Seventy Weeks.* Grand Rapids, Michigan: Zondervan Publishing Company, 1940. 62 pp.

McPherson, Norman Spurgeon. *Triumph Through Tribulation.* Otego, New York: Author, 1944. 78 pp.

Miller, Earl. *The Kingdom of God and the Kingdom of Heaven.* Meadville, Pennsylvania: The Author, 1950. 92 pp.

Moorhead, William G. *Studies in the Book of Revelation.* Pittsburgh, Pennsylvania: United Presbyterian Board of Publication, 1908. 153 pp.

Murray, George L. *Millennial Studies.* Grand Rapids, Michigan: Baker Book House, 1948. 207 pp.

Needham, Mrs. George C. *The Antichrist.* New York: Charles C. Cook, [n.d.]. 107 pp.

Newell, William R. *The Book of the Revelation.* Chicago: Moody Press, 1935. 405 pp.

.... *Hebrews Verse by Verse.* Chicago: Moody Press, 1947. 494 pp.

Oehler, Gustav Friedrich. *Theology of the Old Testament.* New York: Funk and Wagnalls, 1883. 593 pp.

Orr, James. *The Progress of Dogma.* Grand Rapids, Michigan: Wm. B. Eerdman's Publishing Company, 1952. 365 pp.

Ottman, Ford C. *God's Oath.* New York: Our Hope, 1911. 278 pp.

.... *Imperialism and Christ.* New York: Our Hope, 1912. 317 pp.

.... *The Unfolding of the Ages.* New York: Baker and Taylor, 1905. 511 pp.

Pember, G. H. *The Great Prophecies. London.* Hodder and Stoughton, 1881. 378 pp.

Pettingill, William. *Bible Questions Answered.* Wheaton, Illinois: Van Kampen Press, 1923. 559 pp.

.... *Israel—Jehovah's Covenant People.* Harrisburg, Pennsylvania: Fred Kelker, 1915. 70 pp.

.... *Simple Studies in the Revelation.* Wilmington, Delaware: Just A Word, Inc., [n.d.]. 132 pp.

Peters, George N. H. *The Theocratic Kingdom.* Grand Rapids, Michigan: Kregel Publications, 1952. 3 vols.

Pieters, Albertus. *The Seed of Abraham.* Grand Rapids, Michigan: Wm. B. Eerdman's, 1941. 161 pp.

Pink, Arthur W. *The Antichrist.* Swengel, Pennsylvania: Bible Truth Depot, 1923. 308 pp.

Plummer, Alfred. *A Critical and Exegetical Commentary on the Second Epistle of St. Paul to the Corinthians.* New York: Scribner's Sons, 1915. 404 pp.

Pridham, Arthur. *Notes and Reflection on the Epistle to the Hebrews.* London: Yapp, [n.d.]. 434 pp.

.... *Notes and Reflections on the Second Epistle to the Corinthians.* London: James Nisbet and Company, 1869. 375 pp.

Ramm, Bernard. *Protestant Biblical Interpretation.* Boston: W. A. Wilde Company, 1950. 197 pp.

Reese, Alexander. *The Approaching Advent of Christ.* London: Marshall, Morgan and Scott, [n.d.]. 328 pp.

Ridout, S. *The Person and Work of the Holy Spirit.* New York: Loizeaux Brothers, [n.d.]. 224 pp.

Rimmer, Harry. *The Coming War and the Rise of Russia.* Grand Rapids, Michigan: Wm. B. Eerdman's Publishing Company, 1940. 87 pp.

Roberts, Alexander and James Donaldson. *The Ante-Nicene Fathers.* New York: Charles Scribner's Sons, 1889. 10 vols.

Robertson, Archibald T. *Word Pictures in the New Testment.* New York: Harpers, 1930. 6 vols.

Robertson, Archibald T. and Alfred Plummer. *A Critical and Exegetical Commentary on the First Epistle of St. Paul to the Corinthians.* New York: Charles Scribner's Sons, 1911. 424 pp.

Rose, George L. *Tribulation Till Translation.* Glendale, California: Rose Publishing Company, 1943. 286 pp.

Rutgers, William H. *Premillennialism in America.* Goes, Holland: Oosterbaan & Le Cointre, 1930. 290 pp.

Ryrie, Charles C. *The Basis of the Premillennial Faith.* New York: Loizeaux Brothers, 1953. 160 pp.

Sale-Harrison L. *Judgment Seat of Christ.* New York: Hepzibah House, Sale-Harrison Publications, 1938. 97 pp.

.... *The Coming Great Northern Confederacy.* New York: Sale-Harrison Publications, 1918. 102 pp.

.... *The Remarkable Jew.* London: Pickering & Inglis, [n.d.]. 222 pp.

.... *The Resurrection of the Old Roman Empire.* Harrisburg, Pennsylvania: The Evangelical Press, [n.d.]. 40 pp.

Saphir, Adolph. *Christ and Israel.* London: Morgan & Scott, 1911. 227 pp.

.... *The Epistle to the Hebrews.* New York: Christian Alliance Publishing Company, [n.d.]. 2 vols.

Schaff, Phillip. *History of the Christian Church.* New York: Charles Scribner and Company, 1884. 7 vols.

Scofield, C. I. *Addresses on Prophecy.* New York: A. C. Gaebelein, [n.d.]. 134 pp.

.... *Will the Church Pass Through the Great Tribulation.* Philadelphia: Philadelphia School of the Bible, 1917. 36 pp.

.... Editor, *The Scofield Reference Bible.* New York: Oxford University Press, 1909. 1362 pp.

Scott, Walter. *At Hand.* London: Pickering and Inglis, [n.d.]. 213 pp.

.... *Exposition of the Revelation of Jesus Christ.* London: Pickering and Inglis, [n.d.]. 456 pp.

Scroggie, W. Graham. *A Guide to the Gospels.* London: Pickering and Inglis, 1948. 664 pp.

.... *The Lord's Return.* London: Pickering and Inglis, [n.d.]. 171 pp.

——— *Prophecy and History*. London: Marshall, Morgan & Scott, [n.d.]. 149 pp.

Seiss, Joseph. *The Apocalypse*. New York: Charles C. Cook, 1900. 3 vols.

——— *Voices from Babylon*. Philadelphia: Porter & Coates, 1879. 391 pp.

Shodde, George H. *Outlines of Biblical Hermeneutics*. Columbus, Ohio: Lutheran Book Concern, 1917. 235 pp.

Silver, Jesse Forrest. *The Lord's Return*. New York: Fleming H. Revell Company, 1914. 311 pp.

Sims, A. *The Coming War and the Rise of Russia*. Toronto: Author, 1932. 52 pp.

Smith, Wilbur. *World Crises and the Prophetic Scriptures*. Chicago: Moody Press, 1951. 384 pp.

Stanton, Gerald B., *Kept From The Hour*. Grand Rapids, Michigan: Zondervan Publishing House, 1956. 320 pp.

Steinmueller, John E. *A Companion to Scripture Studies*. New York: Joseph F. Wagner, 1941. 502 pp.

Stevens, W. C. *The Book of Daniel*. New York: Fleming R. Revell Company, 1918. 224 pp.

——— *Revelation, the Crown-Jewel of Prophecy*. New York: Christian Alliance Publishing Company, 1928. 2 vols.

Strombeck, J. F. *First the Rapture*. Moline, Illinois: Strombeck Agency, Inc., 1950. 197 pp.

Strong, Augustus Hopkins. *Systematic Theology*. Philadelphia: American Baptist Publication Society, 1907. 3 vols.

Terry, Milton S. *Biblical Hermeneutics*. New York: Phillips and Hunt, 1883. 781 pp.

Thayer, Joseph Henry. *A Greek-English Lexicon of the New Testament*. New York: American Book Company, 1889. 727 pp.

Thiessen, Henry C. *Will the Church Pass Through the Tribulation?* New York: Loizeaux Brothers, 1941. 63 pp.

Tregelles, S. P. *Remarks on the Prophetic Visions in the Book of Daniel*. London: Samuel Bagster and Sons, 1883. 302 pp.

Trench, Richard C. *Synonyms of the New Testament*. London: Kegan Paul, Trench, Trubner and Company, 1906. 384 pp.

Trotter, William. *Essays on Prophetic Interpretation*. Glasgow: R. L. Allan, [n.d.]. 141 pp.

Vincent, Marvin R. *Word Studies in the New Testament*. Grand Rapids, Michigan: Wm. B. Eerdman's Publishing Company, 1946. 4 vols.

Vine, W. E. *First Corinthians*. London: Oliphants, 1951. 237 pp.

Vos, Geerhardus. *The Pauline Eschatology*. Grand Rapids, Michigan: Wm. B Eerdman's Publishing Company, 1952. 365 pp.

Wale, Burlington B. *The Closing Days of Christendom*. London: Partridge, [n.d.]. 546 pp.

——— "The Way of the Kings of the East," *Light for the World's Darkness*. John W. Bradbury, editor; New York: Loizeaux Brothers, 1944. pp. 162-72.

Washington, Canon M. *The Period of Judgment and the Saved Remnant*. London: Thynne, 1919. 45 pp.

Waugh, Thomas. *When Jesus Comes*. London: Charles H. Kelly, 1901. 186 pp.

West, Nathaniel. *The Thousand Years in Both Testaments*. New York: Fleming H. Revell, 1880. 493 pp.

Westcott, Brooke Foss. *The Epistle to the Hebrews*. London: Macmillan, 1892. 504 pp.

Wilkinson, Samuel Hinds. *"Israel My Glory."* London: Mildmay Mission to the Jews Book Store, 1894. 310 pp.

Wyngaarden, Martin J. *The Future of the Kingdom in Prophecy and Fulfillment*. Grand Rapids, Michigan: Zondervan Publishing House, 1934. 211 pp.

Young, Edward J. *The Prophecy of Daniel*. Grand Rapids, Michigan: Wm. B. Eerdman's Publishing Company, 1949. 330 pp.

B. Encyclopaedia Articles

Harnack, Adolf. "Millennium," *The Encyclopaedia Britannica*, XV, 495-95.

Press, S. D. "Kingdom," *International Standard Bible Encyclopaedia*, III, 1799-1808.

Von Orelli, C. "Prophecy, Prophets," *International Standard Bible Encyclopaedia*, IV, 2459-66.

Vos, Geerhardus. "Gehenna," *International Standard Bible Encyclopaedia*, II, 1183.

C. Periodical Articles

Aldrich, Roy L. "An Apologetic For Dispensationalism," *Bibliotheca Sacra*, 112:46-54, January, 1955.

——— "Anglo-Israelism Refuted," *Bibliotheca Sacra*. 93:41-63, January, 1936.

Aldrich, Willard M. "The Interpretation of Acts 15:13-18," *Bibliotheca Sacra*, 111:317-23, October, 1954.

Anonymous. "The Angels of the Seven Churches," *Bibliotheca Sacra*, 91:433-41, October, 1934.

Armerding, Carl. "Will There Be Another Elijah?" *Bibliotheca Sacra*, 100:89-97, January, 1943.

Barnard, Edward R. "How To Study Prophecy," *Our Hope*, 60:77-85, August, 1953.

Bennetch, John H. "The Apologetic Argument From Fulfilled Prophecy," *Bibliotheca Sacra*, 93:348-54, July, 1936.

Campbell, Donald K. "The Interpretation of Types," *Bibliotheca Sacra*, 112:248-55, July, 1955.

Chafer, Lewis Sperry. "An Introduction to the Study of Prophecy," *Bibliotheca Sacra,* 100:98-133, January, 1943.

Chafer, Rollin Thomas. "The Boundaries of Greater Canaan," *Bibliotheca Sacra,* 95:231-36, April, 1938.

Ehlert, Arnold D. "A Bibliography of Dispensationalism," *Bibliotheca Sacra,* 102:95-101, January, 1944; 199-209, April, 1944; 319-28, July, 1944; 447-60, October, 1944; 103:84-92, January, 1945; 207-219, April, 1945; 322-34, July, 1945; 455-67, October, 1945; 104:57-67, January, 1946.

Elliott, Russell. "The Antichrist," *Our Hope,* 54:335-38, December, 1947.

.... "The Prophetic Scriptures and Their Interpretation," *Our Hope,* 55:161-66, September, 1948.

English, E. Schuyler. "The Judgment of the Nations," *Our Hope,* 51:561-65, February, 1945.

.... "The Judgment Seat of Christ," *Our Hope,* 51:416-22, December, 1944.

.... "The Two Witnesses," *Our Hope,* 47:665-75, April, 1941.

Evans, W. Glyn. "Will Babylon Be Restored?" *Our Hope,* 107:335-42, July, 1950; 481-87, October, 1950.

Fereday, W. W. "Armageddon," *Our Hope,* 47:397-401, December, 1940.

Ferrin, Howard W. "All Israel Shall Be Saved," *Bibliotheca Sacra,* 112:235-47, July, 1955.

Fritch, Charles T. "Biblical Typology," *Bibliotheca Sacra,* 104:87-100, January, 1946; 214-22, April, 1947.

Govett, R. "One Taken and One Left," *The Dawn,* 12:515-18, February 15, 1936.

Ironside, Harry A. "Setting the Stage for the Last Act of the Great World Drama," *Our Hope,* 55:589-97, April, 1949; 661-66, May, 1949; 722-29, June, 1949.

Jennings, F. C. "The Boundaries of the Revived Roman Empire," *Our Hope,* 47:386-90, December, 1940.

Johnson, S. Lewis, Jr. "The Out-Resurrection from the Dead," *Bibliotheca Sacra,* 110:139-46, April, 1953.

Kann, Herbert. "The History of Israel's Blindness: The Mystery of It," *Bibliotheca Sacra,* 94:442-57, October, 1937.

Kellogg, S. H. "Premillennialism: "Its Relation to Doctrine and Practice," *Bibliotheca Sacra,* 99:235-44, April, 1942; 364-72, July, 1942; 486-99, October, 1942; 100:301-8, April, 1943.

Kopecky, Donald W. "Salvation in the Tribulation," *Bibliotheca Sacra,* 109:266-70, July, 1952; 358-63, October, 1952.

Ladd, George E. "The Kingdom of God in the Jewish Apocryphal Literature," *Bibliotheca Sacra,* 109:55-62, January, 1952.

.... "The Kingdom of God in I Enoch," *Bibliotheca Sacra,* 110:32-49, January, 1953.

Mackenzie, Herbert. "The Destruction of Babylon," *Bibliotheca Sacra,* 92:226-32, April, 1935; 339-53, July, 1935.

MacRae, Allan A. "The Millennial Kingdom of Christ," *Our Hope,* 53:463-80, February, 1947.

McClain, Alva J. "The Greatness of the Kingdom," *Bibliotheca Sacra,* 112:11-27, January, 1955; 107-24, April, 1955; 209-24, July, 1955; 304-10, October, 1955.

Mitchell, John L. "The Question of Millennial Sacrifices," *Bibliotheca Sacra,* 110:248-67, July, 1953; 342-61, October, 1953.

Munro, John Ker. "The Signs of the Times," *Bibliotheca Sacra,* 96:224-42, April, 1939.

Murphy, Charles Henry. "God and the Gentiles," *Bibliotheca Sacra,* 109:364-73, October, 1952.

Panton, D. M. "Are We in the Great Tribulation?" *The Dawn,* 12:485-90, February 15, 1936.

Payne, Homer Lemuel. "Contemporary Amillennial Literature," *Bibliotheca Sacra,* 106:200-10, April, 1949; 342-51, July, 1949; 486-92, October, 1949; 107:103-8, January, 1950.

Pieters, Albertus. "Darbyism Vs. the Historic Christian Faith," *The Calvin Forum,* 2:225-28, May, 1936.

Rae, William. "The Rider on the White Horse," *Our Hope,* 54:734-38, June, 1948.

—————. "The Two Beasts of Revelation," *Our Hope,* 54:14-18, July, 1947.

Rand, James F. "Problems in a Literal Interpretation of the Sermon on the Mount," *Bibliotheca Sacra,* 112:28-38, January, 1955; 125-36, April, 1955.

Schwarze, C. T. "The Bible and Science on the Everlasting Fire," *Bibliotheca Sacra,* 95:105-12, January, 1938.

Scofield, C. I. "The Course and End of the Age," *Bibliotheca Sacra,* 108:105-16, January, 1951.

—————. "The Last World Empire and Armageddon," *Bibliotheca Sacra,* 108:355-62, July, 1951.

—————. "The Return of Christ in Relation to the Church," *Bibliotheca Sacra,* 109:77-89, January, 1952.

—————. "The Return of Christ in Relation to the Jews and the Earth," *Bibliotheca Sacra,* 108:477-87, October, 1951.

—————. "The Times of the Gentiles," *Biblotheca Sacra,* 107:343-55, July, 1950.

Smith, Wilbur M. "The Prophetic Literature of Colonial America," *Bibliotheca Sacra,* 100:67-82, January, 1943; 273-88, April, 1943.

Tenny, Merrill C. "The Importance and Exegesis of Revelation 20:1-8," *Bibliotheca Sacra,* 111:137-147, April, 1954.

Thiessen, Henry C. "The Place of Israel in the Scheme of Redemption As Set Forth in Romans 9-11," *Bibliotheca Sacra,* 98:78-91, January, 1941, 203-17, April, 1941.

Unger, Merrill F. "Ezekiel's Vision of Israel's Restoration," *Bibliotheca Sacra,* 106:312-24, July, 1949; 432-45, October, 1949; 107:51-70, January, 1950.

.... "The Temple Vision of Ezekiel," *Bibliotheca Sacra,* 105:418-42, October, 1948; 106:48-64, January, 1949; 169-77, April, 1949.

Walden, J. W. "The Kingdom of God—Its Millennial Dispensations," *Bibliotheca Sacra,* 102:433-41, October, 1945; 103:39-49, January, 1946.

Walvoord, John F. "Amillennialism," *Bibliotheca Sacra,* 106:291-302, July, 1949; 420-32, October, 1949; 107:42-50, January, 1950; 154-67, April, 1950; 281-90, July, 1950; 420-29, October, 1950; 108:7-14, January, 1951.

.... "The Fulfillment of the Abrahamic Covenant," *Bibliotheca Sacra,* 102:27-36, January, 1945.

.... "The Fulfillment of the Davidic Covenant," *Bibliotheca Sacra,* 102:153-66, April, 1945.

.... "Is Moral Progress Possible," *Bibliotheca Sacra,* 101:149-63, April, 1944.

.... "Is Satan Bound?" *Bibliotheca Sacra,* 100:497-512, October, 1943.

.... "Is the Church the Israel of God," *Bibliotheca Sacra,* 101:403-16, October, 1944.

.... "Is the Seventieth Week of Daniel Future?" *Bibliotheca Sacra,* 101:30-49, January, 1944.

.... "Israel's Blindness," *Bibliotheca Sacra,* 102:282-91, July, 1945.

.... "Israel's Restoration," *Bibliotheca Sacra,* 102: 405-16, October, 1945.

.... "The Kingdom Promised to David," *Bibliotheca Sacra,* 110:97-110, April, 1953.

.... "The Millennial Issue in Modern Theology," *Bibliotheca Sacra,* 106:34-47, January, 1949.

.... "The New Covenant With Israel," *Bibliotheca Sacra,* 103:16-27, January, 1946.

.... "The New Covenant With Israel," *Bibliotheca Sacra,* 110:193-205, July, 1953.

.... "New Testament Words for the Lord's Coming," *Bibliotheca Sacra,* 101:283-89, July, 1944.

.... "Postmillennialism," *Bibliotheca Sacra,* 106:149-68, April, 1949.

.... "Premillennialism," *Bibliotheca Sacra,* 108:153-66, April, 1951, 270-81, July, 1951; 414-22, October, 1951.

.... "Premillennialism and the Abrahamic Covenant," *Bibliotheca Sacra,* 109:37-46, January, 1952; 136-60, April, 1952; 217-25, July, 1952; 293-303, October, 1952.

.... "Premillennialism and the Abrahamic Covenant," *Bibliotheca Sacra,* 109:37-46, January, 1952; 136-60, April, 1952; 217-25, July, 1952; 293-303, October, 1952.

.... "Premillennialism and the Church," *Bibliotheca Sacra,* 110:289-98, October, 1953; 111:1-10, January, 1954; 97-104, April, 1954.

.... "Premillennialism and the Tribulation," *Bibliotheca Sacra,* 111:193-202, July, 1954; 289-301, October, 1954; 112:1-10, January, 1955; 97-106, April, 1955; 193-208, July, 1955; 289-303, October, 1955.

.... "A Review of 'Crucial Questions About the Kingdom of God,'" *Biblotheca Sacra,* 110:1-10, January, 1953.

Whiting, Arthur B. "The Rapture of the Church," *Bibliotheca Sacra,* 102:360-72, July, 1945; 490-99, October, 1945.

D. Unpublished Materials

Aldrich, Roy L. "Facts and Theories of Prophecy." Unpublished Doctor's dissertation, Dallas Theological Seminary, Dallas, Texas, 1942. 198 pp.

Evans, J. Elwood. "The New Testament Contribution to Israel's Eschatology." Unpublished Doctor's dissertation, Dallas Theological Seminary, Dallas, Texas, 1946. 223 pp.

Harrison, Everett F. "The Christian Doctrine of Resurrection." Unpublished Doctor's dissertation, Dallas Theological Seminary, Dallas, Texas, 1938. 216 pp.

Lincoln, Charles Fred. "The Covenants." Unpublished Doctor's dissertation, Dallas Theological Seminary, Dallas, Texas, 1942. 247 pp.

McClain, Alva J. "The Greatness of the Kingdom." Unpublished class notes, Grace Theological Seminary, Winona Lake, Indiana, [n.d.]. 31 pp.

McGahey, John F. "The Identity of the Twenty Four Elders." Unpublished Master's thesis, Dallas Theological Seminary, Dallas, Texas, 1954. 61 pp.

Prichard, Dewitt H. "The Last Days." Unpublished Master's thesis, Dallas Theological Seminary, Dallas, Texas, 1944. 67 pp.

Woodring, Chester. "The Millennial Glory of Christ." Unpublished Master's thesis, Dallas Theological Seminary, Dallas, Texas, 1950. 154 pp.

SUBJECT INDEX

(Page numbers refer to the beginning of the treatment of the subject.)

SCRIPTURE INDEX

LAMENTATIONS

EZEKIEL